S0-ABP-919

Dear NFT User:

Forget partisan politics—the real debates inside the nation's capital rage over whether Columbia Heights or H St. NE corridor housing will better appreciate, or if U Street has eclipsed Georgetown for shopping, or if Mt Pleasant is jumping the gentrification shark. The city's economic boom has transformed old notions of what's what and where's where. NFT is here to help.

We're on top of the changing dynamics all across the city and even in some of the suburbs. Since we're small enough to stuff in a backpack or tuck in a glove compartment, bring us along when you're searching for nourishment in Clarendon, tin-framed mirrors in Capitol Hill, or the easiest route to a Nats game. Our latest version can help the newcomer or the DC veteran or anyone who still thinks of Logan as the frontier.

Check out our 2007 updates, including **scales** on every map to help you navigate. New listings for **van & truck rentals** will come in handy when you find that one-of-kind chest at Good Wood and it won't fit on the Schwinn. And the new **self-storage** listings will be a must when your roommate points out that your new chest won't fit in your apartment either. The **DC Circulator** routes will give you a comfy option when the bus is jammed. We've got **WiFi** and **internet** listings all over the city and **restaurant closing hours**, so you know just how long you can keep that laptop fired up before they kick you out of Tryst. Plus new pages for the **C&O Canal** and **George Mason University**.

And, please, whenever you find a good nook we missed, let us know. Our stable of writers fanned out to make the book in your hands the best insider information available, but it's all about pooling tips and suggestions so that we're keeping up with all the changes. Talk to us at www.notfortourists.com.

Thanks for joining us—here's keeping Washington DC, and its neighborhoods, a true people's democracy.

Here's hoping you find what you need,

Jane, Rob & Janice

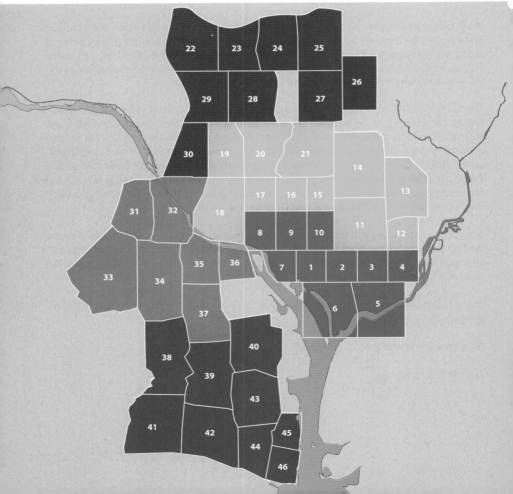

Map 1 · **National Mall**

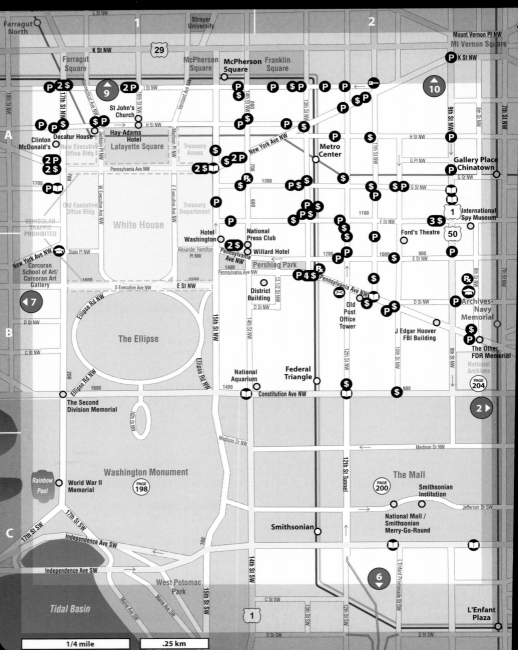

Here you'll find pretty much every reason DC is a top tourist destination—The White House, the Washington monument, the cherry blossoms, etc. If you didn't see them on a school trip, try to check them off on the weekdays. The Mall, on weekends, especially in warm weather, is a mob scene. Tip: When you've had enough of the white marble, photocopy this map and let it substitute as the tour guide when relatives arrive.

Banks

- **Bank of America** · 1001 Pennsylvania Ave NW
- **Bank of America** · 1501 Pennsylvania Ave NW
- **Bank of America** · 700 13th St NW
- **Bank of America** · 888 17th St NW
- **BB&T** · 601 13th St NW
- **BB&T** · 815 Connecticut Ave NW
- **Chevy Chase** · 1200 F St NW
- **Chevy Chase** · 1299 Pennsylvania Ave NW
- **Chevy Chase** · 1717 Pennsylvania Ave NW
- **Chevy Chase (ATM)** · 10th St NW & Constitution Ave NW
- **Chevy Chase (ATM)** · 1100 Pennsylvania Ave NW
- **Chevy Chase (ATM)** · 12th St NW & Constitution Ave NW
- **Chevy Chase (ATM)** · 1300 Pennsylvania Ave NW
- **Chevy Chase (ATM)** · 1400 I St NW
- **Chevy Chase (ATM)** · 607 13th St NW
- **Chevy Chase (ATM)** · 815 14th St NW
- **Citibank** · 1400 G St NW
- **Citibank** · 435 11th St NW
- **Independence Federal Savings** · 1006 E St NW
- **Industrial** · 1317 F St NW
- **M&T** · 555 12th St NW
- **Mercantile Potomac** · 1100 H St NW
- **PNC** · 1503 Pennsylvania Ave NW
- **PNC** · 800 17th St NW
- **PNC (ATM)** · 1101 New York Ave NW
- **PNC (ATM)** · 1300 New York Ave NW
- **PNC (ATM)** · 1455 Pennsylvania Ave NW
- **PNC (ATM)** · 900 F St NW
- **Sun Trust** · 1100 G St NW
- **Sun Trust** · 1445 New York Ave NW
- **Sun Trust** · 900 17th St NW
- **United** · 1001 G St NW
- **United** · 1275 Pennsylvania Ave NW
- **Wachovia** · 1300 I St NW
- **Wachovia** · 1301 Pennsylvania Ave NW
- **Wachovia** · 1310 G St NW
- **Wachovia** · 1700 Pennsylvania Ave NW
- **Wachovia** · 740 15th St NW
- **Wachovia** · 801 Pennsylvania Ave NW
- **Wachovia (ATM)** · 1201 G St NW
- **Wachovia (ATM)** · 529 14th St NW

Car Rental

- **Hertz** · 901 11th St NW · 202-628-6174

o Landmarks

- **The Clinton McDonald's** · 750 17th St NW
- **Decatur House** · 1610 H St NW
- **District Building** · 1350 Pennsylvania Ave NW
- **Ford's Theatre** · 511 10th St NW
- **Hay-Adams Hotel** · 16th St & H St NW
- **Hotel Washington** · 515 15th St NW
- **International Spy Museum** · 800 F St NW
- **J Edgar Hoover FBI Building** · 935 Pennsylvania Ave NW
- **National Aquarium** · 14th St NW & Constitution Ave NW

- **National Mall/Smithsonian Merry-Go-Round** · 1000 Jefferson Dr SW
- **National Press Club** · 529 14th St NW, 13th Fl
- **Old Post Office Tower** · 1100 Pennsylvania Ave NW
- **The Other FDR Memorial** · Pennsylvania Ave NW, b/w 7th St NW & 9th St NW
- **The Second Division Memorial** · 17th St NW & Constitution Ave NW
- **Smithsonian Institution** · 1000 Jefferson Dr SW
- **St John's Church** · 16th St NW & H St NW
- **Willard Hotel** · 1401 Pennsylvania Ave NW

Libraries

- **Dibner Library** · 12th St & Constitution Ave NW
- **Federal Aviation Administration Libraries** · 800 Independence Ave SW
- **Martin Luther King Jr Memorial Library** · 901 G St NW
- **National Endowment for the Humanities Library** · 1100 Pennsylvania Ave NW
- **Office of Thrift Supervision Library** · 1700 G St NW
- **Robert S Rankin Memorial Library** · 624 9th St NW, Rm 600
- **Treasury Library** · 1500 Pennsylvania Ave NW, Rm 1314
- **US Department of Commerce Library** · 1401 Constitution Ave NW
- **US Department of Energy Library** · 1000 Independence Ave SW, RM GA-138

Parking

Pharmacies

- **CVS** · 1275 Pennsylvania Ave NW
- **CVS** · 435 8th St NW
- **CVS** · 717 14th St NW

Post Offices

- **Benjamin Franklin** · 1200 Pennsylvania Ave NW

Schools

- **Corcoran College of Art & Design (Downtown Campus)** · 500 17th St NW
- **Marriott Hospitality Public Charter** · 410 8th St NW

Map 1 · **National Mall**

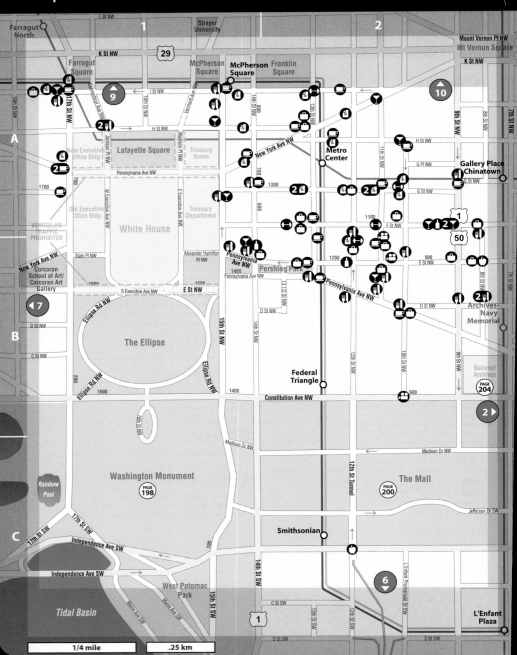

Galleries, Entertainment

This neighborhood caters mostly to tourists and office workers during the daylight. Au Bon Pain, Starbucks, and museum cafeterias are aplenty. After five, the mall clears out and action migrates to the northeast, where happy hours kick in at dozens of bars and restaurants—especially the new trendy places that seem to open weekly. Not hungry? Catch an indie flick at the Landmark E Street Cinema to build up an appetite.

Coffee

- **Caribou Coffee** •
  1701 Pennsylvania Ave NW
- **Caribou Coffee** • 601 13th St NW
- **Coffee Espress** • 1250 H St NW
- **Cosi** • 1001 Pennsylvania Ave NW
- **Cosi** • 1333 H St NW
- **Cosi** • 1700 Pennsylvania Ave NW
- **Cosi** • 700 11th St NW
- **Dean & Deluca Expresso** •
  1299 Pennsylvania Ave NW
- **Firehook Bakery & Coffee House** •
  555 13th St NW
- **Firehook Bakery & Coffee House** •
  912 17th St NW
- **ME Swing** • 1702 G St NW
- **Starbucks** • Grand Hyatt •
  1000 H St NW
- **Starbucks** •
  1301 Pennsylvania Ave NW
- **Starbucks** • 1401 New York Ave NW
- **Starbucks** • 555 11th St NW
- **Starbucks** • 700 14th St NW
- **Starbucks** • 701 9th St NW
- **Starbucks** • 901 15th St NW
- **Wally's World Coffee** • 1225 I St NW

Copy Shops

- **Ace Press** • 910 17th St NW
- **Advanced Printing** •
  1201 New York Ave NW
- **Alpha Graphics Printshop** •
  1325 G St NW
- **Ikon Office Solutions** •
  1120 G St NW
- **Metro Press** • 1444 I St NW
- **Minuteman Press** • 1308 G St NW
- **Penn Press II** • 750 17th St NW
- **Reliable Copy** • 555 12th St NW ⊛
- **Reprodoc** • 1300 I St NW
- **Sir Speedy Printing** • 1212 G St NW
- **Sir Speedy Printing** • 1429 H St NW
- **Staples** • 1250 H St NW
- **Superior Group** •
  1401 New York Ave NW ⊛
- **Whitmont Legal Copying** •
  1725 I St NW ⊛

Farmer's Markets

- **Freshfarm Market
  (May–Oct, Thurs 3 pm–7 pm)** •
  8th St NW & E St NW
- **US Dept of Agriculture
  Farmers Market (Jun–Oct,
  Fri 10 am–2 pm** • 12th St SW &
  Independence Ave SW

Gyms

- **Club Fitness at Washington
  Center** • 1001 G St NW
- **Downtown Boxing Club** •
  1101 F St NW
- **Fitness Center at Franklin
  Square** • 1300 I St NW
- **Fitness Co** • 555 12th St NW
- **Washington Sports Clubs** •
  1345 F St NW

Liquor Stores

- **Central Liquor Store** •
  917 F St NW
- **Press Liquors** • 527 14th St NW
- **Washington Wine & Liquor** •
  1200 E St NW

Movie Theaters

- **E Street Cinema** • 555 11th St NW
- **Johnson IMAX Theater** •
  Museum of Natural History •
  Constitution Ave NW & 10th St NW
- **Landmark E St Cinema** •
  555 11th St NW

Nightlife

- **Capitol City Brewing Company** •
  1100 New York Ave NW
- **Eyebar** • 1716 I St NW
- **Gordon Biersch Brewery** •
  900 F St NW
- **Grand Slam Sports Bar** •
  1000 H St NW
- **Harry's Saloon** • 436 11th St NW
- **Home** • 911 F St NW
- **Le Bar** • 806 15th St NW
- **Old Ebbitt Grill** • 675 15th St NW
- **Platinum** • 915 F St NW
- **Poste Brasserie Bar** •
  555 8th St NW
- **Round Robin Bar** •
  Intercontinental Hotel •
  1401 Pennsylvania Ave NW

Restaurants

- **Bistro D'Oc** • 518 10th St NW
- **Café Asia** • 1720 I St NW
- **Café Atlantico** • 405 8th St NW
- **Caucus Room** • 401 9th St NW
- **Ceiba** • 701 14th St NW
- **Chef Geoff's** •
  1301 Pennsylvania Ave NW
- **Equinox** • 818 Connecticut Ave NW

- **ESPN Zone** • 555 12th St NW
- **Gerard's Place** • 915 15th St NW
- **Harry's Restaurant and Saloon** •
  436 11th St NW
- **Les Halles** •
  1201 Pennsylvania Ave NW
- **Loeb's Perfect New York Deli** •
  832 15th St NW
- **Occidental** •
  1475 Pennsylvania Ave NW
- **Old Ebbitt Grill** • 675 15th St NW
- **Ollie's Trolley** • 432 11th St NW
- **Teaism** • 400 8th St NW
- **Teaism** • 800 Connecticut Ave NW
- **TenPenh** •
  1001 Pennsylvania Ave NW
- **Willard Room** • Willard
  InterContinental • 1401
  Pennsylvania Ave NW
- **Zaytinya** • 701 9th St NW
- **Zola** • 800 F St NW

Shopping

- **American Apparel** •
  555 11th St NW
- **Barnes & Noble** • 555 12th St NW
- **Blink** • 1776 I St NW
- **Café Mozart** • 1331 H St NW
- **Celadon Spa** • 1180 F St NW
- **Chapters Literary Bookstore** •
  445 11th St NW
- **Coup de Foudre Lingerie** •
  1001 Pennsylvania Ave NW
- **Fahrney's** • 1317 F St NW
- **Filene's Basement** •
  529 14th St NW
- **H&M** • 1025 F St NW
- **Hecht's** • 1201 G St NW
- **International Spy Museum
  Gift Shop** • 800 F St NW
- **Kemp Mill Music** • 1309 F St NW
- **Penn Camera** • 840 E St NW
- **Political Americana** •
  1331 Pennsylvania Ave NW
- **Utrecht Art & Drafting Supplies** •
  1250 I St NW

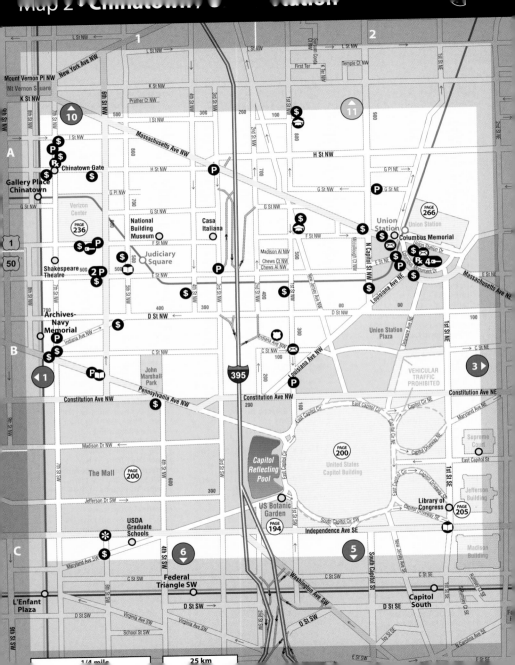

Well, more like Chinablock, but the real draw of DC's fastest growing neighborhood is 7th Street, which decided to swap its drug dealers for art dealers and now anchors the development of the most luxurious new apartment complexes in the city. Flanking the palatial Verizon Center, the yuppie-christened promenade even plays holiday music in December, uniting suburban revelers with a few pre-boom homeless, who are oddly appreciated for maintaining the neighborhood's urban authenticity.

$ Banks

- **Adams National** · 50 Massachusetts Ave NE
- **Adams National** · 802 7th St NW
- **BB&T** · 614 H St NW
- **BB&T (ATM)** · 707 7th St NW
- **Chevy Chase** · 650 F St NW
- **Chevy Chase** · 701 Pennsylvania Ave NW
- **Citibank (ATM)** · 440 1st St NW
- **Industrial (ATM)** · 441 4th St NW
- **Industrial (ATM)** · 500 Indiana Ave NW
- **Industrial (ATM)** · 515 5th St NW
- **PNC** · 301 7th St NW
- **PNC** · 833 7th St NW
- **PNC (ATM)** · 4th St NW & Constitution Ave NW
- **PNC (ATM)** · 600 New Jersey Ave NW
- **PNC (ATM)** · 601 E St NW
- **PNC (ATM)** · 820 1st St NE
- **Sun Trust** · 2 Massachusetts Ave NW
- **Sun Trust (ATM)** · 30 Massachusetts Ave NE
- **Wachovia** · 444 N Capitol St NW
- **Wachovia** · 600 Maryland Ave SW
- **Wachovia (ATM)** · 50 Massachusetts Ave NE

Car Rental

- **Alamo** · 50 Massachusetts Ave NE · 202-842-7454
- **Budget** · 50 Massachusetts Ave NE · 202-289-5373
- **Hertz** · 50 Massachusetts Ave NE · 202-842-0819
- **National** · 50 Massachusetts Ave NE · 202-842-7454
- **Thrifty** · 601 F St NW · 202-371-0485

Community Gardens

o Landmarks

- **Casa Italiana** · 595 1/2 3rd St NW
- **Chinatown Gate** · H St NW & 7th St NW
- **Columbus Memorial** · Massachusetts Ave & First St (near Union Station)
- **Library of Congress** · 1st St SE b/w Independence Ave SE & E Capitol St SE
- **National Building Museum** · 401 F St NW
- **Shakespeare Theatre** · 450 7th St NW
- **Supreme Court of the United States** · 1st St NE b/w E Capitol St SE & Maryland Ave NE
- **US Botanic Garden** · 100 Maryland Ave SW
- **USDA Graduate Schools** · 600 Maryland Ave SW

Libraries

- **Federal Trade Commission Library** · 600 Pennsylvania Ave NW
- **National Research Council Library** · 500 5th St NW, Room 304
- **US Library of Congress** · 101 Independence Ave SE
- **US Senate Library** · Russell Senate Office Bldg, B15

Parking

Pharmacies

- **CVS** · 801 7th St NW ◎
- **Tschiffely Pharmacy** · 50 Massachusetts Ave NE

Police

- **MPDC Headquarters** · 300 Indiana Ave NW

 Post Offices

- **National Capitol Station** · 2 Massachusetts Ave NE
- **Union Station** · 50 Massachusetts Ave NE

Schools

- **Georgetown University Law Center** · 600 New Jersey Ave NW
- **Gonzaga College High** · 19 I St NW

Map 2 · **Chinatown / Union Station**

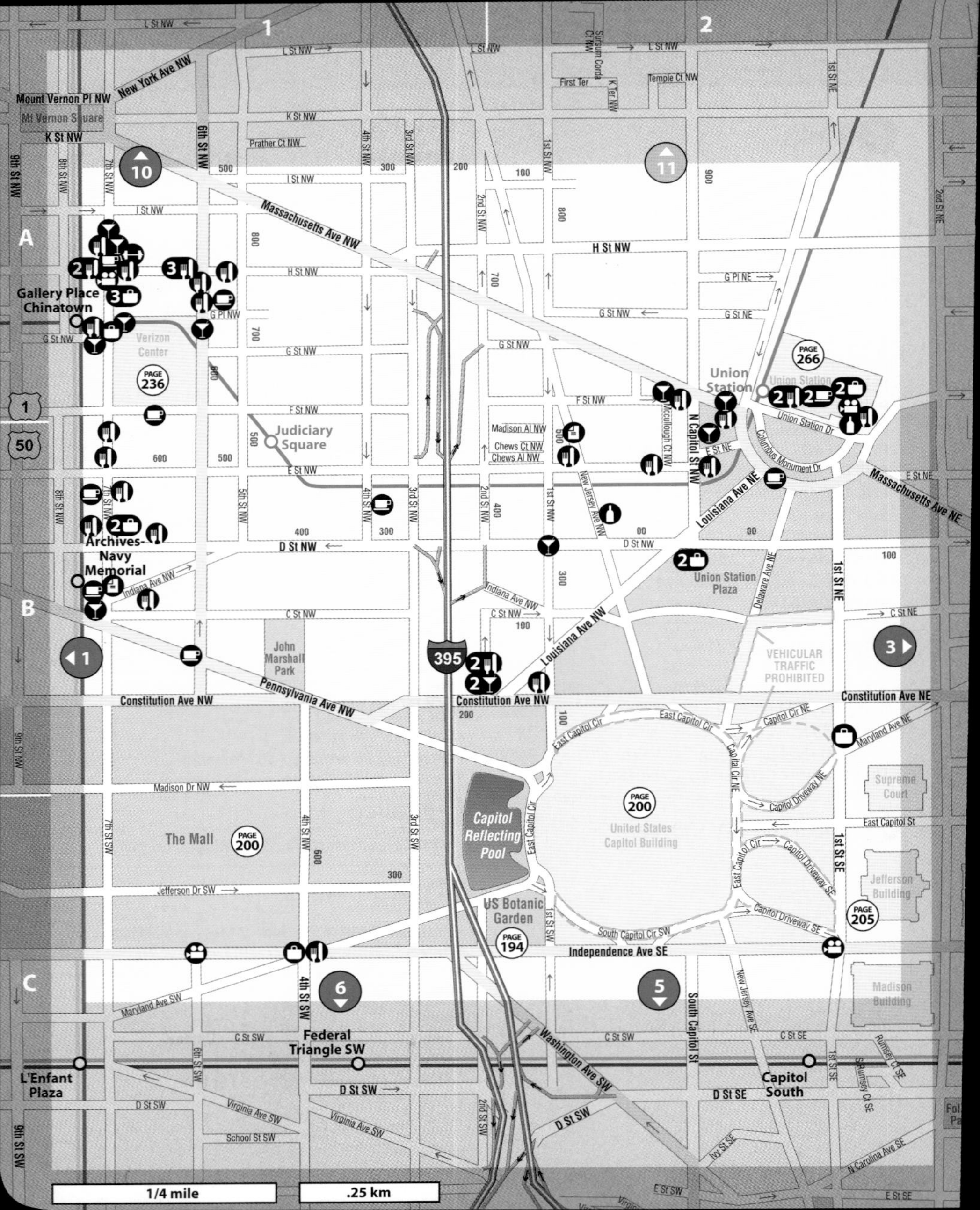

N

L St NW

New York Ave NW

Mount Vernon Pl NW

Mt Vernon Square

K St NW

6th St NW

L St NW

Prather Ct NW

K St NW

Massachusetts Ave NW

4th St NW

3rd St NW

First Ter

Temple Ct NW

L St NE

1st St NE

2

Sudan Cords

Ct NW

L St NW

10

I St NW

I St NW

800

H St NW

11

900

2nd St NE

A

Gallery Place Chinatown

2

3

3

G St NW

H St NW

G Pl NW

G St NW

700

700

G St NW

Verizon Center

PAGE 236

G St NW

F St NW

G Pl NE

G St NW

G St NE

Union Station

PAGE 266

Union Station

2

2

1

50

F St NW

F St NW

Madison Al NW

Chews Ct NW
Chews Al NW

500

Mcallough Ct NW

N Capitol St NW

Columbus Monument Dr

Union Station Dr

Massachusetts Ave NE

1st St NE

Judiciary Square

E St NW

600

500

E St NW

300

Louisiana Ave NW

Delaware Ave NE

Massachusetts Ave NE

100

B

8th St NW

Archives-Navy Memorial

2

400

D St NW

300

Indiana Ave NW

300

New Jersey Ave NW

D St NW

00

D St NW

00

2

Union Station Plaza

C St NE

3

John Marshall Park

Indiana Ave NW

C St NW

C St NW

100

Louisiana Ave NW

VEHICULAR TRAFFIC PROHIBITED

Constitution Ave NE

1

Pennsylvania Ave NW

Constitution Ave NW

395

2
2

Constitution Ave NW

200

East Capitol Cir

East Capitol Cir

Capitol Cir NE

Maryland Ave NE

Supreme Court

9th St SW

Madison Dr NW

7th St NW

4th St NW

600

3rd St SW

300

The Mall

PAGE 200

Capitol Reflecting Pool

PAGE 200

United States Capitol Building

Capitol Cir

Capitol Driveway NE

1st St SE

East Capitol St

Jefferson Building

PAGE 205

Jefferson Dr SW

US Botanic Garden

PAGE 194

Capitol Driveway SE

Independence Ave SE

Madison Building

C

Maryland Ave SW

4th St SW

6

Federal Triangle SW

C St SW

Washington Ave SW

5

South Capitol St

C St SW

New Jersey Ave SE

1st St SE

C St SE

1st St SE

S Rumsey Ct SE

L'Enfant Plaza

D St SW

Virginia Ave SW

School St SW

D St SW

2nd St SW

D St SW

South Capitol Cir SW

D St SW

Capitol South

D St SE

New Jersey Ave SE

N Carolina Ave SE

9th St SW

1/4 mile

.25 km

E St SW

Toto, we're not in Bejing anymore. Once defined by its ethic and culinary connections to China, the retail has exploded in the last few years to become an after-hours urban playground. There are still a few vestiges of the past—the Chinese characters, the elaborate gate, a string of Chinese restaurants along H Street. Otherwise, this is the place to find new trendy restaurants and all-American chains. Hmmm.

Coffee

- **Bucks County Coffee** · 50 Massachusetts Ave NE
- **Café Renee** · 50 Massachusetts Ave NE
- **Camiles Sidewalk Café of Washington** · 650 F St NW
- **Cosi** · 601 Pennsylvania Ave NW
- **Firehook Bakery & Coffee House** · 441 4th St NW
- **Starbucks** · 325 7th St NW
- **Starbucks** · 40 Massachusetts Ave NE
- **Starbucks** · 443-C 7th St NW
- **Starbucks** · 800 7th St NW

Copy Shops

- **FedEx Kinko's** · 325 7th St NW
- **Minuteman Press** · 555 New Jersey Ave NW

Gyms

- **Washington Sports Clubs** · 783 7th St NW

Liquor Stores

- **Kogod Liquors** · 441 New Jersey Ave NW
- **Union Wine & Liquors Store** · 50 Massachusetts Ave NE

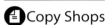Movie Theaters

- **AMC Union Station 9** · 50 Massachusetts Ave NE
- **Lockheed Martin IMAX Theater** · National Air and Space Museum · 601 Independence Ave SW
- **Mary Pickford Theater** · Library of Congress, James Madison Memorial Bldg, Independence Ave SE b/w 1st St SE & 2nd St SE
- **Regal Gallery Place Stadium** · 707 7th St NW

Nightlife

- **Bullfeather's** · 410 1st St SE
- **Capitol City Brewing Company** · 2 Massachusetts Ave NE
- **Coyote Ugly** · 717 6th St NW
- **The Dubliner** · 520 N Capitol St (entrance on F St)
- **Fadò Irish Pub** · 808 7th St NW
- **Flying Scotsman** · 233 2nd St NW
- **IndeBleu** · 707 G St NW
- **Kelly's Irish Times** · 14 F St NW
- **Lucky Strike Lanes** · 701 7th St NW
- **My Brother's Place** · 237 2nd St NW
- **RFD Washington** · 810 7th St NW

Restaurants

- **701** · 701 Pennsylvania Ave NW
- **America** · 50 Massachusetts Ave NE
- **Andale** · 401 7th St NW
- **B Smith's** · 50 Massachusetts Ave NE
- **Billy Goat Tavern & Grill** · 500 New Jersey Ave NW
- **Bistro Bis** · 15 E St NW
- **Burma** · 740 6th St NW
- **Capital Q** · 707 H St NW
- **Capitol City Brewing Company** · 2 Massachusetts Ave NE
- **Center Café at Union Station** · 50 Massachusetts Ave NE
- **Charlie Palmer** · 101 Constitution Ave NW
- **Chinatown Express** · 746 6th St NW
- **District Chophouse** · 509 7th St NW
- **The Dubliner Restaurant** · Phoenix Park Hotel · 520 N Capitol St NW
- **Fadò Irish Pub** · 808 7th St NW
- **Flying Scotsman** · 233 2nd St NW
- **Full Kee** · 509 H St NW
- **IndeBleu** · 707 G St NW
- **Jaleo** · 480 7th St NW
- **Kelly's Irish Times** · 14 F St NW
- **Le Paradou** · 678 Indiana Ave NW
- **Lei Garden** · 631 H St NW
- **Matchbox** · 713 H St NW
- **Mitsitam Native Foods Café** · National Museum of the American Indian · 4th St SW & Independence Ave SW
- **My Brother's Place** · 237 2nd St NW
- **Rasika** · 633 D St NW
- **Rosa Mexicano** · 575 7th St NW
- **Tony Cheng's Mongolian Restaurant** · 619 H St NW, downstairs
- **Tony Cheng's Seafood Restaurant** · 619 H St NW, upstairs
- **Zengo Restaurant** · 781 7th St NW

Shopping

- **Alamo Flags** · 50 Massachusetts Ave NE
- **Apartment Zero** · 406 7th St NW
- **Appalachian Spring** · 50 Massachusetts Ave NE
- **Aveda Institute** · 713 Seventh St NW
- **Bed, Bath and Beyond** · 709 7th St NW
- **Comfort One Shoes** · 50 Massachusetts Ave NE
- **Godiva Chocolatier** · 50 Massachusetts Ave NE
- **Marvelous Market** · 730 7th St NW
- **National Air and Space Museum Shop** · Independence Ave & 4th St SW
- **Olsson's Books** · 418 7th St NW
- **Urban Outfitters Downtown** · 737 7th St NW
- **Windows Café & Market** · 101 1st St NW

Map 3 · **The Hill**

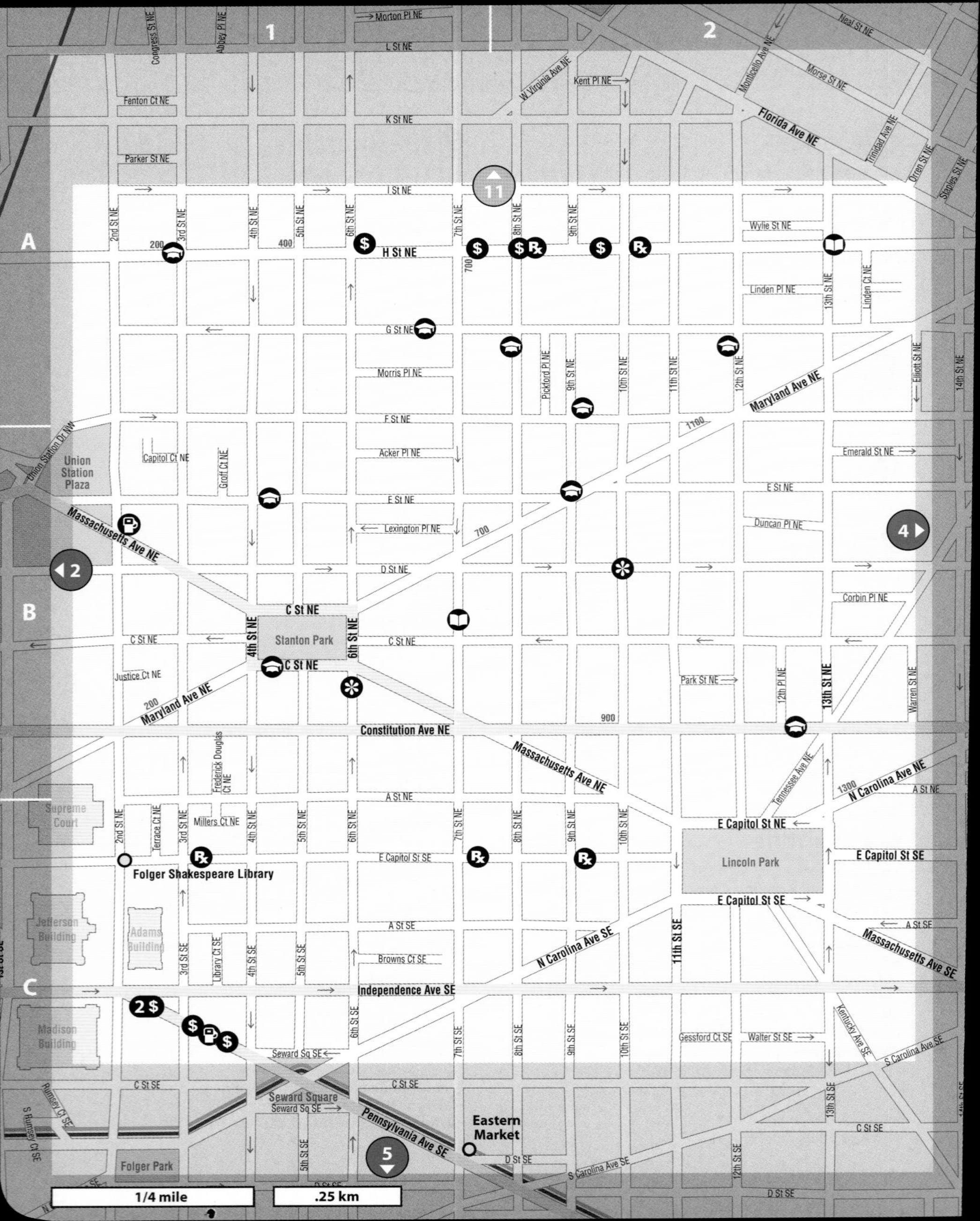

N

1

2

Morton Pl NE

Congress St NE

Abbey Pl NE

L St NE

Neal St NE

Morse St NE

Fenton Ct NE

Montello Ave NE

Kent Pl NE

N Virginia Ave NE

Florida Ave NE

Trinidad Ave NE

Oran St NE

K St NE

Staples St NE

Parker St NE

11

A

I St NE

2nd St NE

200

3rd St NE

4th St NE

5th St NE

6th St NE

$

H St NE

7th St NE

700

8th St NE

$

$ Rx

9th St NE

$

Rx

Wylie St NE

13th St NE

Linden Ct NE

Linden Pl NE

400

G St NE

Morris Pl NE

Pickford Pl NE

9th St NE

10th St NE

11th St NE

12th St NE

Maryland Ave NE

Elliott St NE

13th St NE

F St NE

Capitol Ct NE

Groff Ct NE

Acker Pl NE

1100

Emerald St NE

Union
Station
Plaza

Massachusetts Ave NE

E St NE

E St NE

Duncan Pl NE

◄2

Lexington Pl NE

700

D St NE

Corbin Pl NE

4►

B

C St NE

4th St NE

Stanton Park

6th St NE

C St NE

*

Park St NE

12th Pl NE

13th St NE

Warren St NE

C St NE

Justice Ct NE

200

Maryland Ave NE

C St NE

*

Constitution Ave NE

900

Massachusetts Ave NE

Tennessee Ave NE

1300

N Carolina Ave NE

A St NE

A St NE

Frederick Douglass Ct NE

A St NE

2nd St NE

Millers Ct NE

4th St NE

5th St NE

6th St NE

7th St NE

8th St NE

9th St NE

10th St NE

E Capitol St NE

E Capitol St NE

E Capitol St SE

Supreme
Court

Terrace Ct NE

Rx

Folger Shakespeare Library

E Capitol St SE

Rx

Rx

11th St SE

Lincoln Park

E Capitol St SE

E Capitol St SE

C

Jefferson
Building

Adams
Building

3rd St SE

Library Ct SE

4th St SE

5th St SE

A St SE

Browns Ct SE

N Carolina Ave SE

Massachusetts Ave SE

A St SE

Independence Ave SE

6th St SE

7th St SE

8th St SE

9th St SE

10th St SE

11th St SE

Gessford Ct SE

Walter St SE

Kentucky Ave SE

S Carolina Ave SE

Madison
Building

2 $

$ $

C St SE

Seward Sq SE

Seward Square

Seward Sq SE

C St SE

C St SE

13th St SE

C St SE

Folger Park

Pennsylvania Ave SE

5th St SE

Eastern
Market

5

D St SE

S Carolina Ave SE

D St SE

D St SE

1/4 mile	.25 km

With very little noticeable sloping, "The Hill" feels more like "The Plateau." Tucked in the shadow of the Capitol, the area is home to an eclectic collection of political hangers-on: international entrepreneurs, young professionals, rowdy interns and working stiffs. They may be of different political parties, but they all complain about the rising property taxes in this increasingly posh neighborhood.

Banks

- **Bank of America** · 201 Pennsylvania Ave SE
- **Bank of America** · 722 H St NE
- **Bank of America (ATM)** · 961 H St NE
- **Chevy Chase** · 336 Pennsylvania Ave SE
- **M&T (ATM)** · 610 H St NE
- **PNC** · 800 H St NE
- **Sun Trust** · 300 Pennsylvania Ave SE
- **Wachovia** · 215 Pennsylvania Ave SE

Community Gardens

Gas Stations

- **Exxon** · 200 Massachusetts Ave NE ⊚
- **Exxon** · 339 Pennsylvania Ave SE

oLandmarks

- **Folger Shakespeare Library** · 201 E Capitol St SE

Libraries

- **Northeast Library** · 330 7th St NE
- **RL Christian Community Library** · 1300 H St NE

Pharmacies

- **Grubb's CARE Pharmacy & Medical Supply** · 326 E Capitol St NE
- **Morton's CARE Pharmacy** · 724 E Capitol St NE
- **Rite Aid** · 801 H St NE
- **Robinson's Apothecary** · 922 E Capitol St NE
- **Super CARE Pharmacy** · 1019 H St NE

Schools

- **Cesar Chavez Public Charter** · 709 12th St SE
- **Cornerstone Community** · 907 Maryland Ave NE
- **Ludlow-Taylor Elementary** · 659 G St NE
- **Maury Elementary** · 1250 Constitution Ave NE
- **Options Middle** · 800 3rd St NE
- **Peabody Elementary** · 425 C St NE
- **Prospect Learning Center** · 920 F St NE
- **Sasha Bruce Middle** · 745 8th St SE
- **Stuart-Hobson Middle** · 410 E St NE

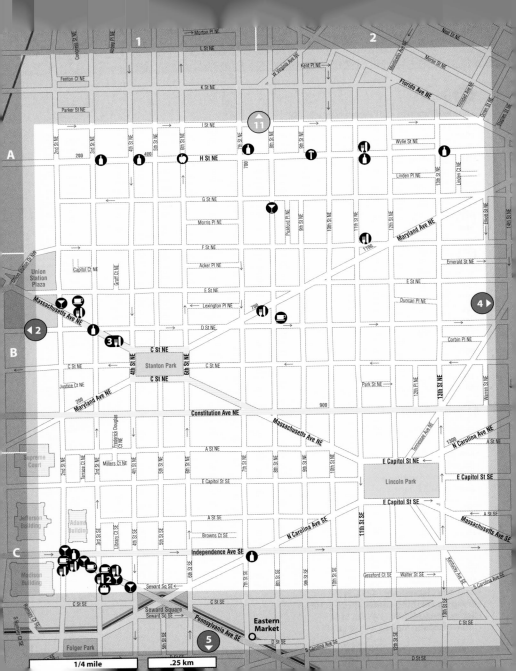

Map 3

With a startling per-capita share of dry cleaners, you'll be all dressed up with few places to go. The exception, however, are the haunts close to the Capitol and Union Station where weeknights staffers share bar space with...well, other staffers, mostly. These are the bars where being local means having been around since the last election. On the weekend, the clientele are generally those who can walk home from the bar.

Coffee

- **Cosi** · 301 Pennsylvania Ave SE
- **Firehook Bakery & Coffee House** · 215 Pennsylvania Ave SE
- **Jacobs Coffee House** · 401 8th St NE
- **Neb's Café** · 201 Massachusetts Ave NE
- **Starbucks** · 237 Pennsylvania Ave SE

Farmer's Markets

- **H Street Freshfarm Market (May–Oct, Sat 9 am–1 pm)** · 600 H St NE

Hardware Stores

- **Park's Hardware** · 920 H St NE

🍾Liquor Stores

- **Family Liquors** · 710 H St NE
- **Gandel's Liquors** · 211 Pennsylvania Ave SE
- **H Street Liquor Store** · 303 H St NE
- **Hayden's Liquor Store** · 700 North Carolina Ave SE
- **Jumbo Liquors** · 1122 H St NE
- **Kelly's Liquor Store** · 415 H St NE
- **Northeast Beverage** · 1344 H St NE
- **Schneider's of Capitol Hill** · 300 Massachusetts Ave NE

🍸Nightlife

- **Capitol Lounge** · 229 Pennsylvania Ave SE
- **Hawk and Dove** · 329 Pennsylvania Ave SE
- **Lounge 201** · 201 Massachusetts Ave NE
- **Sonoma** · 223 Pennsylvania Ave SE
- **Top of the Hill** · 319 Pennsylvania Ave SE
- **Tune Inn** · 331 1/2 Pennsylvania Ave SE

🍴Restaurants

- **Café Berlin** · 322 Massachusetts Ave NE
- **Four Sisters** · 1118 H St NE
- **Hawk and Dove** · 329 Pennsylvania Ave SE
- **Kenny's Smokehouse** · 732 Maryland Ave NE
- **La Loma Mexican Restaurant** · 316 Massachusetts Ave NE
- **Pete's Diner** · 212 2nd St SE
- **The Pour House** · 319 Pennsylvania Ave SE
- **Ristorante Tosca** · 1112 F St NW
- **Sonoma** · 223 Pennsylvania Ave SE
- **Two Quail** · 320 Massachusetts Ave NE
- **White Tiger** · 301 Massachusetts Ave NE

🛍Shopping

- **Pulp on the Hill** · 303 Pennsylvania Ave SE

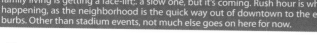

The area once better known for its booming crack economy than good, clean family living is getting a face-lift;. a slow one, but it's coming. Rush hour is when it's happening, as the neighborhood is the quick way out of downtown to the eastern burbs. Other than stadium events, not much else goes on here for now.

Banks

- **Bank of America (ATM)** · Mandarin Oriental Hotel · 1330 Maryland Ave NE
- **PNC (ATM)** · 2400 E Capitol St NE

Community Gardens

Gas Stations

- **Amoco** · 1396 Florida Ave NE
- **Amoco** · 1950 Benning Rd NE ⊘
- **Amoco** · 814 Bladensburg Rd NE
- **Exxon** · 2651 Benning Rd NE ⊘

Libraries

- **Langston Community Library** · 2600 Benning Rd NE

Pharmacies

- **Sterling CARE Pharmacy** · 1647 Benning Rd NE

Post Offices

- **Northeast Station** · 1563 Maryland Ave NE

Schools

- **The Academy for Ideal Education Upper** · 702 15th St NE
- **Browne Center Special Education** · 1830 Constitution Ave NE
- **Eastern High** · 1700 E Capitol St NE
- **Eliot Junior High** · 1830 Constitution Ave NE
- **Friendship Edison: Blow Pierce Campus** · 725 19th St NE
- **Gibbs Elementary** · 500 19th St NE
- **Holy Comforter-St Cyprian** · 1503 E Capitol St SE
- **Miner Elementary** · 601 15th St NE
- **Spingarn Center** · 2500 Benning Rd NE
- **St Benedict of the Moor** · 320 21st St NE
- **Two Rivers Elementary** · 1830 Constitution Ave NE
- **Village Learning Center Public Charter** · 702 15th St NE

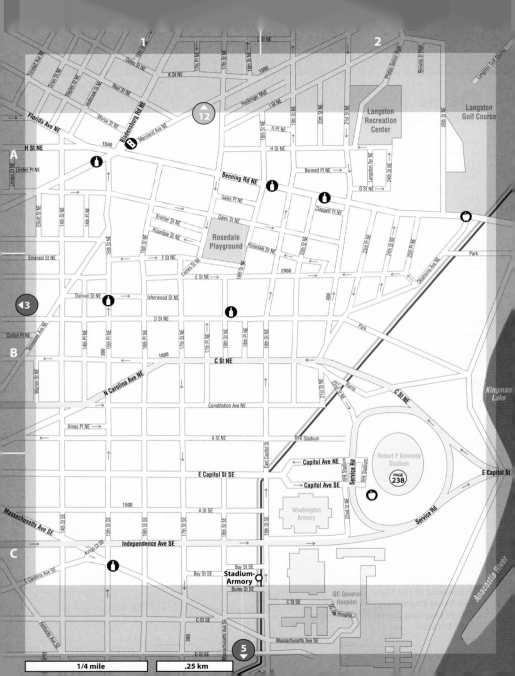

Sundries / Entertainment

Catch a baseball game while you still can; the Nats are soon to go the way of the Redskins. DC United soccer fans will finally have a stadium of their own, and you can join them during the season on weekends to practice your Spanish and percussion skills. The Metro conveniently has a stop here for those looking for something to do after a game.

Farmer's Markets

- **DC Open Air Farmers Market**
  (All year, Thurs & Sat, 7 am–5 pm;
  July–Nov, Tues, Thurs, & Sat from 7 am–5 pm) ·
  RFK Stadium parking lot 6, Independence Ave & 22nd St SE
- **Open Air Farmers Markets**
  (May–Dec, Tues, Thurs & Sat, 7 am–4 pm;
  Jan–Apr, Thurs & Sat 7 am–4 pm) ·
  Oklahoma Ave NE & Benning Rd NE

Liquor Stores

- **Madison Liquors** · 1806 D St NE
- **New York Liquor Store** · 1447 Maryland Ave NE
- **S&J Liquor Store** · 1500 Massachusetts Ave SE
- **Silverman's Liquor** · 2033 Benning Rd NE
- **Sylvia's Liquor Store** · 1818 Benning Rd NE
- **Viggy's Liquors** · 409 15th St NE

Video Rental

- **Blockbuster** · 1555 Maryland Ave NE

21

Map 5 • **Southeast / Anacostia**

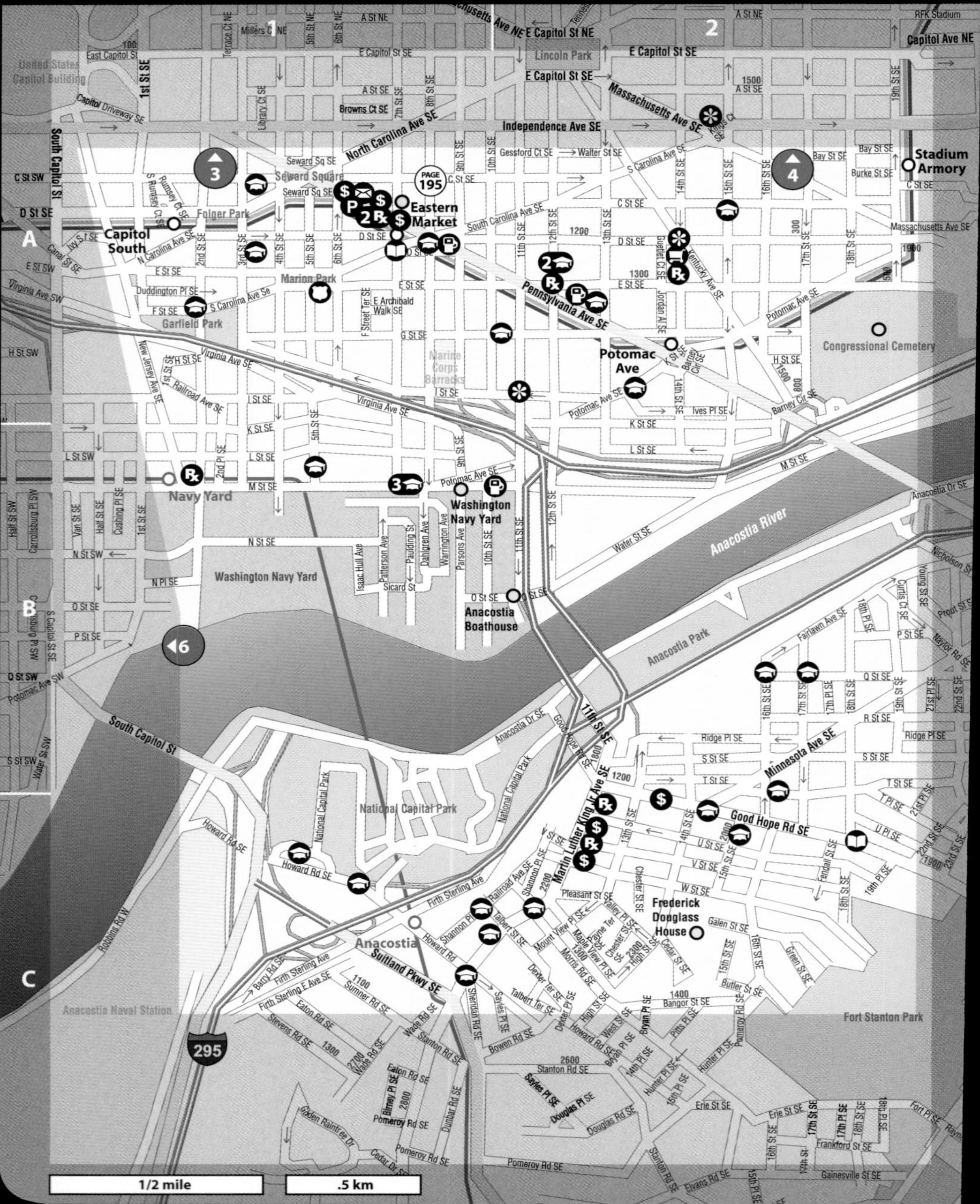

Ⓝ

United States
Capitol Building

3

Capitol
South

4

Stadium
Armory

RFK Stadium

Capitol Ave NE

2

Lincoln Park

Folger Park

Seward Square

Eastern
Market

PAGE
195

Marion Park

Congressional Cemetery

Garfield Park

Duddington Pl SE

2

Pennsylvania Ave SE

Potomac
Ave

Marine
Corps
Barracks

A

Navy Yard

3

Washington
Navy Yard

Anacostia
Boathouse

Anacostia River

Anacostia Park

B

6

Washington Navy Yard

South Capitol St

National Capital Park

National Capital Park

Anacostia Dr SE

Minnesota Ave SE

Ridge Pl SE

Good Hope Rd SE

Howard Rd SE

Frederick
Douglass
House

C

Anacostia
Suitland Pkwy SE

Anacostia Naval Station

Fort Stanton Park

295

1/2 mile   .5 km

A microcosm of America itself, here you'll find snapshots of life ranging from urban decay to disturbin' decadence, with a splash of semi-suburban simplicity a stone's skip away across the Anacostia. Congressional cemetery is a lesser-known jewel in a city crowned with famous landmarks, where you can visit the final resting places of multiple forgotten congressmen from previous centuries and enjoy views of the river.

Banks

- **Bank of America** · 2100 Martin Luther King Jr Ave SE
- **Chevy Chase (ATM)** · 701 Pennsylvania Ave SE
- **Citibank** · 600 Pennsylvania Ave SE
- **PNC** · 2000 Martin Luther King Jr Ave SE
- **PNC** · 650 Pennsylvania Ave SE
- **Sun Trust** · 1340 Good Hope Rd SE

 Community Gardens

Gas Stations

- **Amoco** · 823 Pennsylvania Ave SE
- **Exxon** · 1022 M St SE
- **Exxon** · 1201 Pennsylvania Ave SE
- **Sunoco** · 1248 Pennsylvania Ave SE

Landmarks

- **Anacostia Boathouse** · 1105 O St SE
- **Congressional Cemetery** · 1801 E St SE
- **Eastern Market** · 225 7th St SE
- **Frederick Douglass House** · 1411 W St SE
- **Washington Navy Yard** · 9th St SE & M St SE

Libraries

- **Anacostia Library** · 1800 Good Hope Rd SE
- **Southeast Library** · 403 7th St SE

Parking

Pharmacies

- **Capitol Hill CARE Pharmacy** ·
  650 Pennsylvania Ave SE
- **CVS** · 1100 New Jersey Ave SE
- **CVS** · 500 12th St SE
- **CVS** · 661 Pennsylvania Ave SE
- **Neighborhood CARE Pharmacy** ·
  1932 Martin Luther King Jr Ave SE
- **Safeway** · 415 14th St SE
- **State CARE Pharmacy** ·
  2041 Martin Luther King Jr Ave SE

Police

- **MPDC 1st District Substation** · 500 E St SE

Post Offices

- **Southeast Station** · 600 Pennsylvania Ave SE

Schools

- **Ambassador Baptist Church Christian Academy** ·
  1412 Minnesota Ave SE
- **Anacostia Bible Church Christian** · 1610 T St SE
- **Anacostia High** · 1601 16th St SE
- **Birney Elementary** ·
  2501 Martin Luther King Jr Ave SE
- **Brent Elementary** · 330 3rd St SE
- **Capitol Hill Day** · 210 S Carolina Ave SE
- **Clara Muhammad** · 2313 Martin Luther King Jr Ave SE
- **Eagle Academy** · 770 M St SE
- **Friendship Edison: Chamberlain Campus** ·
  1345 Potomac Ave SE
- **Hine Junior High** · 335 8th St SE
- **Holy Temple Christian Academy** · 439 12th St SE
- **Howard Road Academy** · 701 Howard Rd SE
- **Ketcham Elementary** · 1919 15th St SE
- **Kipp DC/Key Academy** · 770 M St SE
- **Kramer Middle** · 1700 Q St SE
- **Payne Elementary** · 305 15th St SE
- **Rose Elementary** · 821 Howard Rd SE
- **Savoy Elementary** · 2400 Shannon Pl SE
- **St Peters Interparish** · 422 3rd St SE
- **Thurgood Marshall Academy** ·
  2427 Martin Luther King Jr Ave SE
- **Tyler Elementary** · 1001 G St SE
- **Van Ness Elementary** · 1150 5th St SE
- **Washington Math Science Technology High** ·
  770 M St SE
- **Watkins Elementary** · 420 12th St SE

 Supermarkets

- **Safeway** · 415 14th St SE

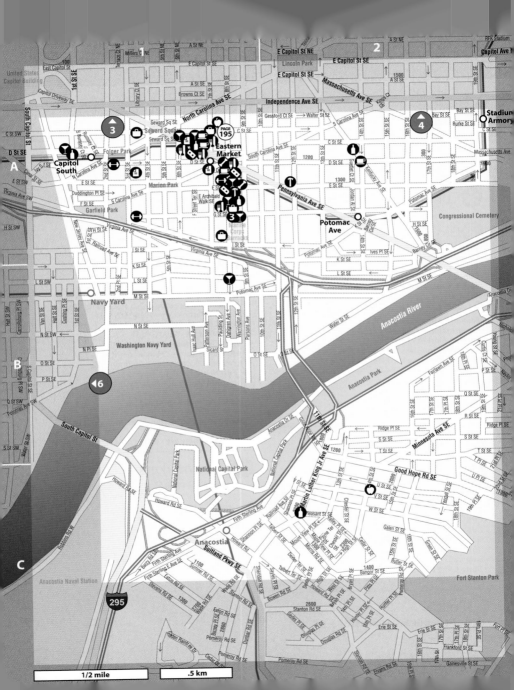

If you're looking for nightlife and have wandered farther east than Eighth Street, you are either an adventurous optimist or are researching for NFT 2008. Good luck and bring a book. Eighth Street itself is a nightlife epicenter that offers a variety of restaurants, bars, and a smattering of live music options. Check out Eastern Market on the weekends for arts and crafts outside and a mind-boggling selection of sausages inside.

 Map 5

☕ Coffee

- **Bread & Chocolate** · 666 Pennsylvania Ave SE
- **Murky Coffee** · 660 Pennsylvania Ave SE
- **Starbucks** · 401 8th St SE
- **Starbucks** · 415 14th St SE

🖨 Copy Shops

- **FedEx Kinko's** · 715 D St SE
- **UPS Store** · 611 Pennsylvania Ave SE

🍎 Farmer's Markets

- **Anacostia Farmers Market (Jun–Nov, Wed 3 pm–7 am)** · 14th St SE b/w U St SE & V St SE
- **Eastern Market Outdoor Farmers Market (Sat & Sun, 7 am–4 pm)** · 225 7th St SE

💪 Gyms

- **Curves (women only)** · 407 8th St SE
- **Results the Gym** · 315 G St SE
- **Washington Sports Clubs** · 214 D St SE

🔧 Hardware Stores

- **District Lock & Hardware** · 505 8th St SE
- **Frager's Hardware** · 1115 Pennsylvania Ave SE

🍷 Liquor Stores

- **Albert's Liquor Store** · 328 Kentucky Ave SE
- **Big K Liquors** · 2252 Martin Luther King Jr Ave SE
- **Chat's Liquors** · 503 8th St SE
- **Congressional Liquors** · 404 1st St SE
- **JJ Mutts Wine & Spirits** · 643 Pennsylvania Ave SE

🍸 Nightlife

- **Bachelor's Mill** · 1104 8th St SE
- **Ellington's on Eighth** · 424A 8th St SE
- **Finn macCool's** · 713 8th St SE
- **Marty's** · 527 8th St SE
- **Mr Henry's Capitol Hill** · 601 Pennsylvania Ave SE
- **Remington's** · 639 Pennsylvania Ave SE
- **Tapatinis** · 711 8th St SE
- **Tortilla Coast** · 400 1st St SE
- **Tunnicliff's Tavern** · 222 7th St SE
- **The Ugly Mug** · 723 8th St SE

🐾 Pet Shops

- **Chateau-Animaux** · 524 8th St SE
- **Pawticulars Gourmet Pet Boutique** · 407 8th St SE

🍴 Restaurants

- **Banana Café & Piano Bar** · 500 8th St SE
- **Bread & Chocolate** · 666 Pennsylvania Ave SE
- **Meyhane** · 633 Pennsylvania Ave SE
- **Montmartre** · 327 7th St SE
- **Starfish** · 539 8th St SE
- **Tortilla Coast** · 400 1st St SE

🛍 Shopping

- **Backstage** · 545 8th St SE
- **Capitol Hill Bikes** · 709 8th St SE
- **Capitol Hill Books** · 657 C St SE
- **Eastern Market** · 225 7th St SE
- **Woven History & Silk Road** · 311 7th St SE

🎞 Video Rental

- **Blockbuster** · 400 8th St SE
- **Capitol Video Sales** · 514 8th St SE
- **Penn Video** · 645 Pennsylvania Ave SE

The Waterfront's best offer is fresh seafood from the Maine Ave fish market, which complements the Waterfront's second best offer, its quiet for its homebody residents. The condos, apartments, and townhouses in this area were built in the early 1960s, and the Waterfront area hides some of DC's funkiest residential architecture.

Banks

- **Bank of America** · 401 M St SW
- **M&T** · 500 C St SW
- **M&T (ATM)** · 550 C St SW
- **PNC** · 935 L'Enfant Plz SW
- **Sun Trust** · 965 L'Enfant Plz SW

Car Rental

- **Enterprise** · 970 D St SW · 202-554-8100
- **Rent-A-Wreck** · 1252 Half St SE · 202-408-9828

Car Washes

- **Splash the Car Wash** · 10 I St SE

❋Community Gardens

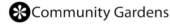Gas Stations

- **Amoco** · 1244 S Capitol St SE
- **Exxon** · 1001 S Capitol St SW ⊘
- **Exxon** · 950 S Capitol St SE ⊘
- **Sunoco** · 50 M St SE

○Landmarks

- **Arena Stage** · 1101 6th St SW
- **The Awakening Statue** ·
  Tip of Hains Point, East Potomac Park
- **Ft Lesley J McNair** · 4th St SW & P St SW
- **Gangplank Marina** · 6th St SW & Water St SW
- **Odyssey Cruises** · 6th St SW & Water St SW
- **Spirit of Washington** · 6th St SW & Water St SW
- **Thomas Law House** · 1252 6th St SW
- **Tiber Island** · 429 N St SW
- **USS Sequoia** · 6th St SW & Maine Ave SW

Libraries

- **DOT Law Library, Coast Guard Branch** ·
  2100 2nd St SW, Rm B726
- **International Trade Commission Library** ·
  500 E St SW
- **NASA Headquarters Library** · 300 E St SW
- **Southwest Library** · 900 Wesley Pl SW
- **US Housing & Urban Development Library** ·
  451 7th St SW

Parking

℞Pharmacies

- **CVS** · 401 M St SW
- **CVS** · 433 L'Enfant Plz SW

Police

- **MPDC 1st District Station** · 415 4th St SW

✉Post Offices

- **Fort McNair Station** · 300 A St SW
- **L'Enfant Plaza Station** · 437 L'Enfant Plz SW
- **Southwest Station** · 45 L St SW

Schools

- **Amidon Elementary** · 401 I St SW
- **Bowen Elementary** · 101 M St SW
- **Jefferson Junior High** · 801 7th St SW
- **National Defense University** · Ft Lesley J McNair
- **Southeastern University** · 501 I St SW

Supermarkets

- **Safeway** · 401 M St SW

Map 6 · **Waterfront**

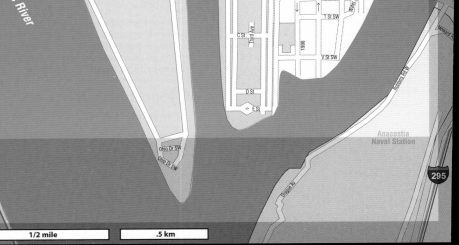

Map 6 · Waterfront

N

Madison Dr NW
Madison Dr NW
East Capitol St
Torrace CT NE

1
The Mall
Jefferson Dr SW
2
United States Capitol Bldg
Capitol Driveway SE

PAGE 200
Washington Monument
PAGE 198
Smithsonian
50
395
PAGE 194
PAGE 205

Independence Ave SW
1000
Independence Ave SE
South Capitol Cir SW
Capitol Driveway SE

Maryland Ave SW
Federal Center SW
Washington Ave
Capitol South

A
West Potomac Park
Tidal Basin

L'Enfant Plaza
C St SW
D St SW
Virginia Ave SW
School St SW
D St SE
E St SW
E St SE
Duddington Pl SE

15th St SW
14th St SW
13th St SW
12th St SW
11th St SW
L'Enfant Promenade St SW
7th St SW
9th St SW
10th St SW
Maryland Ave SW
Maine Ave SW

395

Frontage Rd SW
Virginia Ave SW
Garfield Park

Maiden La SW
Water St SW

D St SE
Folger Park

Jefferson Memorial
900

East Potomac Park

Southeastern University
Waterfront SEU

Randall Playground
Navy Yard

H St SW
G St SW
K St SW
L St SW
M St SW
N St SW
O St SW
P St SW

S Capitol St SE

Washington Channel

B
Potomac River

East Potomac Park Golf Course

Fort McNair

5

South Capitol St

295

C
Anacostia Naval Station

Ohio Dr SW

1/2 mile   .5 km

Map 6

This concrete tundra is where fun comes to die. Flanked by tourist's buses, the fortress-like restaurants along the Waterfront's main drag, Water Street, are as dull and inhospitable as they look. But there are destinations—Arena Stage is a world-class theater, Zanzibar can jam and there's always a beer waiting at the storied Market Inn's saloon.

Coffee

- **Olympic Espresso** · 945 L'Enfant Plz SW
- **Starbucks** · 409 3rd St SW
- **Starbucks** · 550 C St SW

Farmer's Markets

- **US Dept of Transportation Farmers Market (May–Nov, Tues 10 am–2 pm)** · 400 7th St SW

Gyms

- **Gold's Gym** · 409 3rd St SW
- **Metro Fitness** · 480 L'Enfant Plz SW
- **Waterside Fitness & Swim Club** · 901 6th St SW

Liquor Stores

- **Bernstein's Reliable Liquor Store** · 39 M St SW
- **Cap Liquors** · 1301 S Capitol St SW
- **Shulman's Southwest Liquor** · 1550 1st St SW

Nightlife

- **Cantina Marina** · 600 Water St SW
- **Edge** · 52 L St SE
- **H20** · 800 Water St SW
- **Zanzibar on the Waterfront** · 700 Water St SW

Restaurants

- **Cantina Marina** · 600 Water St SW
- **H2O at Hogate's** · 800 Water St SW
- **Jenny's Asian Fusion** · 1000 Water St SW
- **Market Inn** · 200 E St SW
- **Phillip's Flagship** · 900 Water St SW
- **Pier 7** · 650 Water St SW

Shopping

- **Maine Avenue Fish Market** · Maine Ave SW & Potomac River
- **Safeway** · 401 M St SW

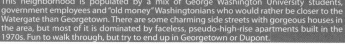

This neighborhood is populated by a mix of George Washington University students, government employees and "old money" Washingtonians who would rather be closer to the Watergate than Georgetown. There are some charming side streets with gorgeous houses in the area, but most of it is dominated by faceless, pseudo-high-rise apartments built in the 1970s. Fun to walk through, but try to end up in Georgetown or Dupont.

$ Banks

- **Bank of America** · 2001 Pennsylvania Ave NW
- **Bank of America (ATM)** · 1900 F St NW
- **Bank of America (ATM)** · 801 22nd St NW
- **Chevy Chase (ATM)** · 2000 Pennsylvania Ave NW
- **Chevy Chase (ATM)** · 2150 Pennsylvania Ave NW
- **Chevy Chase (ATM)** · 900 18th St NW
- **Citibank** · 1775 Pennsylvania Ave NW
- **PNC** · 1919 Pennsylvania Ave NW
- **PNC** · 2600 Virginia Ave NW
- **PNC (ATM)** · 2700 F St NW
- **PNC (ATM)** · 606 23rd St NW
- **PNC (ATM)** · 700 19th St NW
- **Sun Trust** · 1750 New York Ave NW
- **Sun Trust (ATM)** · GWU—Thurston Hall · 1900 F St NW
- **United** · 1875 I St NW
- **Wachovia** · 502 23rd St NW

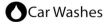 Car Washes

- **Nab Auto Appearance Salon** · 2211 H St NW

✚ Emergency Rooms

- **George Washington University Hospital** · 900 23rd St NW ⌖

Gas Stations

- **Chevron** · 2643 Virginia Ave NW
- **Exxon** · 2708 Virginia Ave NW

○ Landmarks

- **Einstein Statue** · Constitution Ave NW & 22nd St NW
- **Kennedy Center** · 2700 F St NW
- **The Octagon** · 1799 New York Ave NW
- **Watergate Hotel** · 2650 Virginia Ave NW

Libraries

- **Federal Reserve Board Research & Law Libraries** · 20th St NW & Constitution Ave NW
- **General Services Administration Library** · 1800 F St NW, RM 1033
- **Ralph J Bunch Library** · Dept of State · 2201 C St NW, Room 3239
- **US Department of the Interior Library** · 1849 C St NW

P Parking

℞ Pharmacies

- **CVS** · 1901 Pennsylvania Ave NW
- **CVS** · 2125 E St NW
- **CVS** · 2530 Virginia Ave NW
- **Foer's CARE Pharmacy** · 818 18th St NW

✉ Post Offices

- **McPherson Station** · 1750 Pennsylvania Ave NW
- **Watergate Station** · 2512 Virginia Ave NW

Schools

- **George Washington University** · 2121 I St NW
- **School Without Walls** · 2130 G St NW

Supermarkets

- **Safeway** · 2550 Virginia Ave NW

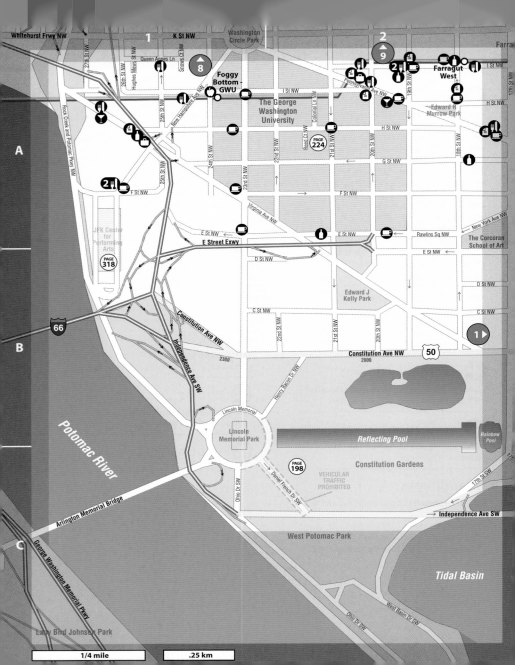

The mix of upscale and college dive is obvious. Aquarelle and Kinkead's are reserved for the power players and their hangers-on. If you forgot your jacket, duck into a gyro joint and then head for the nearest neon window to mingle with the co-ed crowd. Do check out the Watergate complex, however—its architecture will at least initiate a healthy debate.

Coffee

- **Casey's Coffee Inc** · 508 23rd St NW
- **Cup'a Cup'a** · 600 New Hampshire Ave NW
- **Dunkin Donuts** · 616 23rd St NW
- **Karma** · 1900 I St NW
- **Starbucks** · 1730 Pennsylvania Ave NW
- **Starbucks** · 1825 I St NW
- **Starbucks** · 1919 Pennsylvania Ave NW
- **Starbucks** · 1957 E St NW
- **Starbucks** · 2130 H St NW
- **Starbucks** · 800 21st St NW
- **Starbucks** · 801 18th St NW
- **Starbucks** · 900 23rd St NW

Copy Shops

- **B&B Duplicators** · 818 18th St NW
- **Discovery Copy** · 2001 Pennsylvania Ave NW
- **Fast Copying & Printing** ·
  1745 Pennsylvania Ave NW
- **U Nik Press** · 900 19th St NW
- **UPS Store** · 2000 Pennsylvania Ave NW
- **Watergate Photo & Copy** · 2560 Virginia Ave NW

Farmer's Markets

- **Foggy Bottom Freshfarm**
  (Apr–Nov, Wed, 3 pm–7 pm) ·
  I St NW & 24th St NW

Liquor Stores

- **McReynold's Liquors** · 1776 G St NW
- **Pan Mar Wine & Liquors** · 1926 I St NW
- **Riverside Liquors** · 2123 E St NW
- **S&R Liquors** · 1800 I St NW
- **Watergate Wine & Beverage** ·
  2544 Virginia Ave NW

Nightlife

- **Froggy Bottom Pub** · 2142 Pennsylvania Ave NW
- **Potomac Lounge** · Watergate Hotel ·
  2650 Virginia Ave NW

Restaurants

- **600 Restaurant at the Watergate** ·
  600 New Hampshire Ave NW
- **Aquarelle** · Watergate Hotel ·
  2650 Virginia Ave NW
- **Bread Line** · 1751 Pennsylvania Ave NW
- **Dish** · The River Inn · 924 25th St NW
- **Karma** · 1919 I St NW
- **Kaz Sushi Bistro** · World Bank · 1915 I St NW
- **Kinkead's** · 2000 Pennsylvania Ave NW
- **Notti Bianche** · 824 New Hampshire Ave NW
- **Primi Piatti** · 2013 I St NW
- **Roof Terrace Restaurant and Bar** · Kennedy Ctr ·
  2700 F St NW
- **Taberna Del Alabardero** · 1776 I St NW

Shopping

- **Saks Jandel** · 2522 Virginia Ave NW
- **Tower Records** · 2000 Pennsylvania Ave NW

Map 8 · **Georgetown**

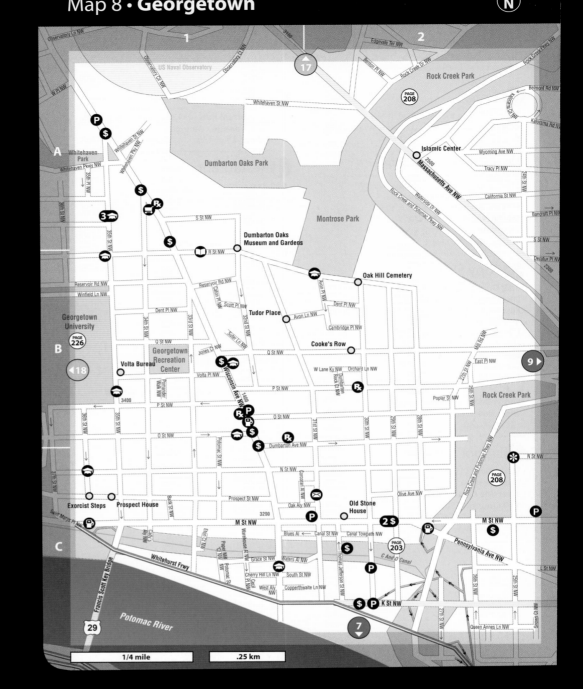

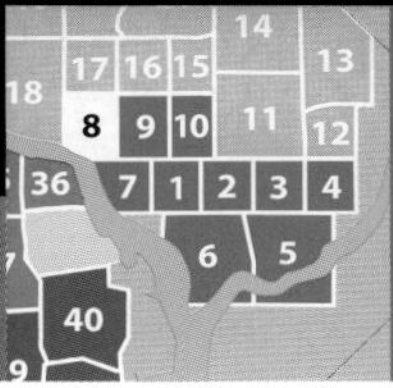

Essentials

18 17 16 15 14 13
8 9 10 11 12
36 7 1 2 3 4
6 5
40

Map 8

Precious townhouses and stately manses, cobblestone streets and garden tours—yes, darling, this is a beautiful neighborhood. Society matrons have good reason to cluck, though the main drags of K and Wisconsin are another matter altogether. Jammed by car and foot traffic day and night, no one worries that the upper-crust class on the side streets is rubbing off.

$ Banks

- **Adams National** · 1729 Wisconsin Ave NW
- **Bank of America** · 1339 Wisconsin Ave NW
- **BB&T** · 1365 Wisconsin Ave NW
- **Chevy Chase** · 1545 Wisconsin Ave NW
- **Chevy Chase (ATM)** · 3222 M St NW
- **Citibank** · 1901 Wisconsin Ave NW
- **PNC** · 1201 Wisconsin Ave NW
- **PNC** · 2550 M St NW
- **PNC (ATM)** · 2101 Wisconsin Ave NW
- **PNC (ATM)** · 3050 K St NW
- **Provident** · 1055 Thomas Jefferson St NW
- **Sun Trust** · 2929 M St NW
- **Wachovia** · 2901 M St NW

✳ Community Gardens

ⓟ Gas Stations

- **Amoco** · 2715 Pennsylvania Ave NW ⊙
- **Exxon** · 1601 Wisconsin Ave NW ⊙
- **Exxon** · 3607 M St NW ⊙

○ Landmarks

- **Cooke's Row** · 3009–3029 Q St NW
- **Dumbarton Oaks Museum and Gardens** · 1703 32nd St NW
- **Exorcist Steps** · 3600 Prospect St NW
- **Islamic Center** · 2551 Massachussetts Ave NW
- **Oak Hill Cemetery** · 30th St NW & R St NW
- **Old Stone House** · 3051 M St NW
- **Prospect House** · 3508 Prospect St NW
- **Tudor Place** · 1644 31st St NW
- **Volta Bureau** · 1537 35th St NW

📖 Libraries

- **Georgetown Library** · 3260 R St NW

Ⓟ Parking

℞ Pharmacies

- **CVS** · 1403 Wisconsin Ave NW ⊙
- **Dumbarton Pharmacy** · 3146 Dumbarton St NW
- **Morgan CARE Pharmacy** · 3001 P St NW
- **Safeway** · 1855 Wisconsin Ave NW

✉ Post Offices

- **Georgetown Station** · 1215 31st St NW

🎓 Schools

- **Corcoran School of Art & Design (Georgetown Campus)** · 1801 35th St NW
- **Devereux Children's Center of Washington, DC** · 3050 R St NW
- **Ellington School of the Arts** · 3500 R St NW
- **Fillmore Arts Center Elementary** · 1819 35th St NW
- **Georgetown Montessori** · 1041 Wisconsin Ave NW
- **Georgetown Visitation Preparatory** · 1524 35th St NW
- **Hardy Middle** · 1819 35th St NW
- **Holy Trinity** · 1325 36th St NW
- **Hyde Elementary** · 3219 O St NW
- **Montessori of Washington** · 1556 Wisconsin Ave NW

🛒 Supermarkets

- **Safeway** · 1855 Wisconsin Ave NW

35

Map 8 · **Georgetown**

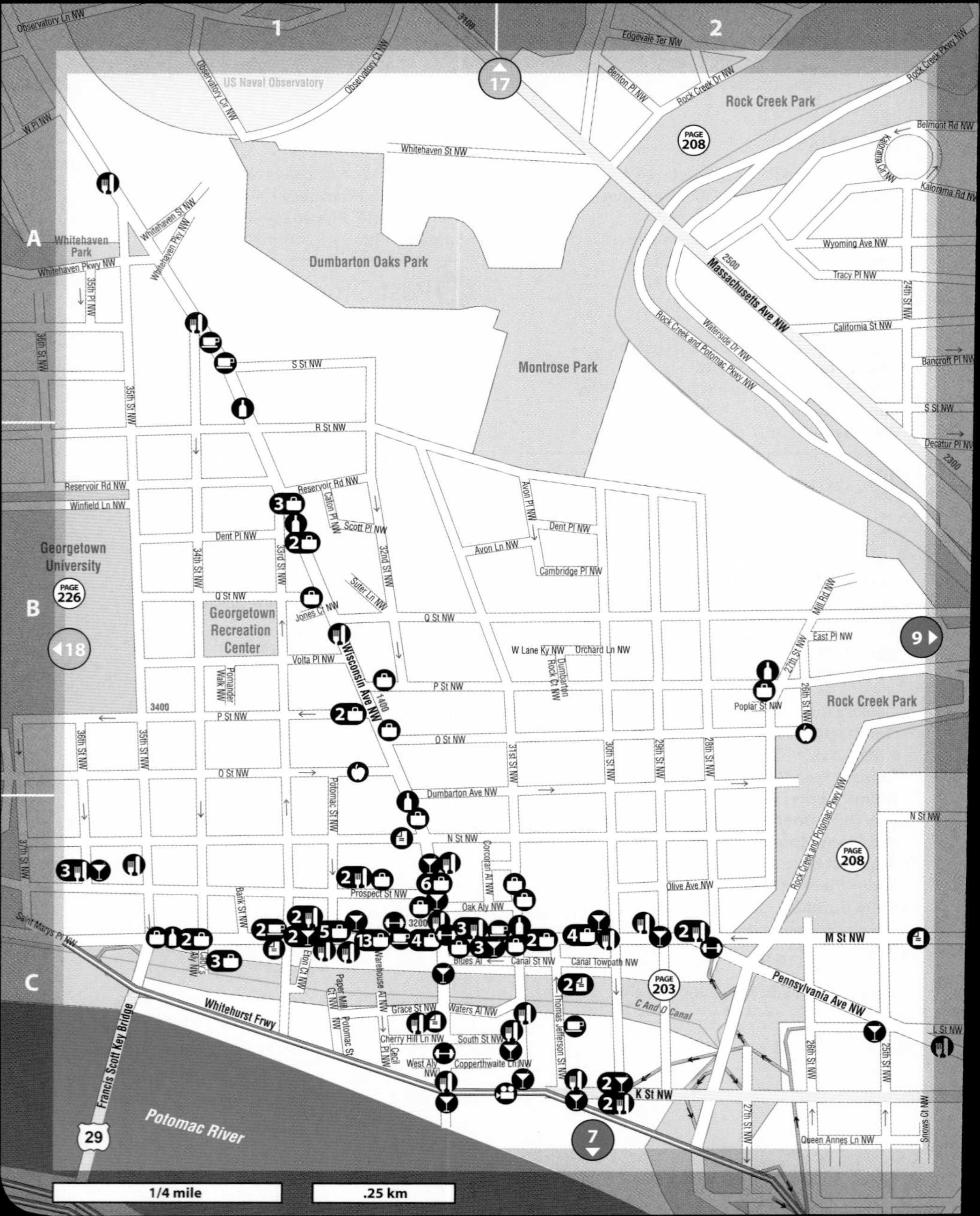

N

Observatory Ln NW

31st

Edgevale Ter NW

Belton Pl NW

Rock Creek Dr NW

Rock Creek Pkwy NW

US Naval Observatory

Rock Creek Park

17

Observatory Pl NW

Observatory Cr NW

PAGE
208

Whitehaven St NW

Belmont Rd NW

Kalorama Rd NW

W Pl NW

Massachusetts Ave NW

7500

Wyoming Ave NW

25th St NW

Whitehaven Pkwy NW

Whitehaven St NW

Tracy Pl NW

A

Whitehaven
Park

Dumbarton Oaks Park

California St NW

35th Pl NW

Whitehaven Pkwy NW

Montrose Park

Rock Creek and Potomac Pkwy NW

Waterside Pl NW

Bancroft Pl NW

35th St NW

S St NW

S St NW

Decatur Pl NW

23rd

R St NW

Reservoir Rd NW

Reservoir Rd NW

3

Avon Pl NW

Dent Pl NW

Winfield Ln NW

Dent Pl NW

2

Tolton Pl NW

Scott Pl NW

Avon Ln NW

B

Georgetown
University

PAGE
226

34th St NW

32nd St NW

Cambridge Pl NW

Mill Rd NW

East Pl NW

9

18

Q St NW

Jones Ct NW

Q St NW

W Lane Ky NW

Orchard Ln NW

Poplar St NW

Rock Creek Park

Georgetown
Recreation
Center

Wisconsin Ave NW

Volta Pl NW

P St NW

Dumbarton Rock St NW

3400

Potomac Walk NW

P St NW

O St NW

PAGE
208

36th St NW

35th St NW

O St NW

31st St NW

30th St NW

29th St NW

28th St NW

27th St NW

N St NW

Dumbarton Ave NW

Potomac St NW

N St NW

2

N St NW

Prospect St NW

6

3200

Oak Aly NW

Olive Ave NW

M St NW

C

3

Bank St NW

2 2 5 13 4 3

3 2

 Eno Ct NW

Blues Al NW

Canal St NW

Canal Towpath NW

4

PAGE
203

Pennsylvania Ave NW

L St NW

Saint Marys Pl NW

Whitehurst Frwy

Paper Mill Ct NW

Potomac St NW

Grace St NW

Waters Al NW

Thomas Jefferson St NW

C And O Canal

26th St NW

25th St NW

Cecil Pl NW

Cherry Hill Ln NW

South St NW

South St NW

West Al
NW

Copperthwaite Ln NW

K St NW

2
2

7

Francis Scott Key Bridge

29

Potomac River

Queen Annes Ln NW

Virginia Ave NW

| 1/4 mile | | .25 km |

Hands-down, the most comprehensive shopping strips in the city are here. Once the sun sets, the human traffic jams don't disperse as Georgetown plays host to a raging, predominately preppy, nightlife scene. The bars and restaurants roughly fall into three categories: The Tombs and the like for the college crowd, a few joints like Martin's for regular folks, and Café Milano and Fahrenheit for those annoying few who like to see themselves referred to in print as "glitterati."

Coffee

- **Baked & Wired** •
  1052 Thomas Jefferson St NW
- **Café Europa** • 3222 M St NW
- **Starbucks** • 1810 Wisconsin Ave NW
- **Starbucks** • 1855 Wisconsin Ave NW
- **Starbucks** • 3122 M St NW

Copy Shops

- **Copy General** •
  1055 Thomas Jefferson St NW
- **FedEx Kinko's** • 3329 M St NW
- **National Reprographics Inc** •
  3210 Grace St NW
- **UPS Store** • 3220 N St NW
- **Westend Press** • 2445 M St NW
- **Zap Copies & Communications** •
  1052 Thomas Jefferson St NW

Farmer's Markets

- **Georgetown Freshfarm Market**
  (Jun–Oct, Sat 9 am–1 pm) • 3219 O St NW
- **Georgetown Market in Rose Park**
  (Apr–Oct, Wed, 4 pm–7 pm) • 26th St NW
  & O St NW

Gyms

- **Fitness Co** • 1010 Wisconsin Ave NW
- **Four Seasons Fitness Club** •
  2800 Pennsylvania Ave NW
- **Washington Sports Clubs** •
  3222 M St NW, Ste 140

Liquor Stores

- **Bacchus Wine Cellar** •
  1635 Wisconsin Ave NW
- **Dixie Wine & Spirits** • 3429 M St NW
- **Georgetown Wine & Spirits** • 2701 P St NW
- **Potomac Wines and Spirits** • 3100 M St NW
- **Towne Wine & Liquors** •
  1326 Wisconsin Ave NW
- **Wagner's Liquor Shop** •
  1717 Wisconsin Ave NW

Movie Theaters

- **Loews Georgetown 14** • 3111 K St NW

Nightlife

- **51st State Tavern** • 2512 L St NW
- **Blues Alley** • 1073 Wisconsin Ave NW
- **Chadwick's** • 3205 K St NW
- **Clyde's** • 3236 M St NW
- **Degrees** • Ritz Carlton • 3100 S St NW
- **Garrett's** • 3003 M St NW
- **The Guards** • 2915 M St NW
- **Martin's Tavern** • 1264 Wisconsin Ave NW
- **Mate** • 3101 K St NW
- **Mie N Yu** • 3125 M St NW
- **Modern** • 3287 M St NW
- **Mr Smith's** • 3104 M St NW
- **Old Glory** • 3139 M St NW
- **Rhino Bar & Pumphouse** • 3295 M St NW
- **Riverside Grill** • 3050 K St NW
- **Sequoia** • 3000 K St NW
- **The Third Edition Bar** •
  1218 Wisconsin Ave NW
- **The Tombs** • 1226 36th St NW
- **Tony and Joe's** • 3000 K St NW

Restaurants

- **1789** • 1226 36th St NW
- **Aditi** • 3299 M St NW
- **Amma Vegetarian Kitchen** • 3291 M St NW
- **Café Bonaparte** • 1522 Wisconsin Ave NW
- **Café Divan** • 1834 Wisconsin Ave NW
- **Café LaRuche** • 1039 31st St NW
- **Café Milano** • 3251 Prospect St NW
- **Chadwick's** • 3205 K St NW
- **Citronelle** • Latham Hotel • 3000 M St NW
- **Clyde's** • 3236 M St NW
- **Fahrenheit & Degrees** • Ritz Carlton •
  3100 S St NW
- **Furin's** • 2805 M St NW
- **J Paul's** • 3218 M St NW
- **La Chaumiere** • 2813 M St NW
- **The Landmark** • Melrose Hotel •
  2430 Pennsylvania Ave NW
- **Martin's Tavern** • 1264 Wisconsin Ave NW
- **Mendocino** • 2917 M St NW
- **Morton's of Georgetown** •
  3251 Prospect St NW
- **Mr Smith's** • 3104 M St NW
- **Nathan's** • 3150 M St NW
- **Old Glory All-American BBQ** •
  3139 M St NW
- **Prince Café** • 1042 Wisconsin Ave NW
- **Riverside Grill** • 3050 K St NW
- **Romeo's Café and Pizzeria** •
  2132 Wisconsin Ave NW
- **Sequoia** • 3000 K St NW
- **The Third Edition** • 1218 Wisconsin Ave NW
- **The Tombs** • 1226 36th St NW
- **Tony And Joe's Seafood Place** •
  3000 K St NW
- **Wisemiller's** • 1236 36th St NW

Shopping

- **Abercrombie & Fitch** • 1208 Wisconsin Ave
- **Ann Sacks** • 3328 M St NW
- **Anthropologie** • 3222 M St NW
- **April Cornell** • 3278 M St NW
- **Banana Republic** • 3200 M St NW
- **BCBG** • 3210 M St NW
- **Betsey Johnson** • 1319 Wisconsin Ave NW
- **Blue Mercury** • 3059 M St NW
- **Bo Concepts** • 3342 M St NW
- **Commander Salamander** •
  1420 Wisconsin Ave NW
- **Dean & DeLuca** • 3276 M St NW
- **Design Within Reach** • 3307 Cady's Aly NW
- **Diesel** • 1249 Wisconsin Ave NW
- **Dolcezza** • 1560 Wisconsin Ave NW
- **Express** • 3276 M St NW
- **Georgetown Running Company** •
  3401 M St NW
- **Georgetown Tobacco** • 3144 M St NW
- **Georgetown Wine and Spirits** • 2701 P St NW
- **GIA & Co** • 3222 M St NW
- **H&M** • 3222 M St NW
- **The Hattery** • 3222 M St NW
- **Illuminations** • 3323 Cady's Aly NW
- **Intermix** • 3222 M St NW
- **J Crew** • 3222 M St NW
- **Jaryam** • 1631 Wisconsin Ave NW
- **Jinx Proof Tattoo** • 3289 M St NW
- **Kate Spade** • 3061 M St NW
- **Kenneth Cole** • 1259 Wisconsin Ave NW
- **Ligne Roset** • 3306 M St NW
- **lil' thingamajigs** • 3222 M St NW
- **Lush** • 3066 M St NW
- **MAC** • 3067 M St NW
- **Marvelous Market** • 3217 P St NW
- **Old Print Gallery** • 1220 31st St NW
- **Patisserie Poupon** • 1645 Wisconsin Ave NW
- **Pottery Barn** • 3077 M St NW
- **Proper Topper** • 3213 P St NW
- **Puma** • 1237 Wisconsin Ave NW
- **Ralph Lauren Polo Shop** •
  1245 Wisconsin Ave NW
- **Relish** • 3312 Cady's Aly NW
- **Restoration Hardware** •
  1222 Wisconsin Ave NW
- **Revolution Cycles** • 3411 M St NW
- **Sassanova** • 1641 Wisconsin Ave NW
- **Secret Garden** • 3230 M St NW
- **See** • 1261 Wisconsin Ave NW
- **Sephora** • 3065 M St NW
- **The Sharper Image** • 3222 M St NW
- **Sherman Pickey** • 1647 Wisconsin Ave NW
- **Smash** • 3285 1/2 M St NW
- **Smith & Hawken** • 1209 31st St NW
- **Sugar** • 1633 Wisconsin Ave NW
- **Talbots** • 3222 M St NW
- **Thomas Sweet Ice Cream** • 3214 P St NW
- **Toka Salon** • 3251 Prospect St NW
- **Up Against the Wall** • 3219 M St NW
- **Urban Outfitters** • 3111 M St NW
- **Victoria's Secret** • 3222 M St NW
- **White House/Black Market** •
  3222 M St NW
- **Zara** • 1234 Wisconsin Ave NW

Map 9 • Dupont Circle / Adams Morgan

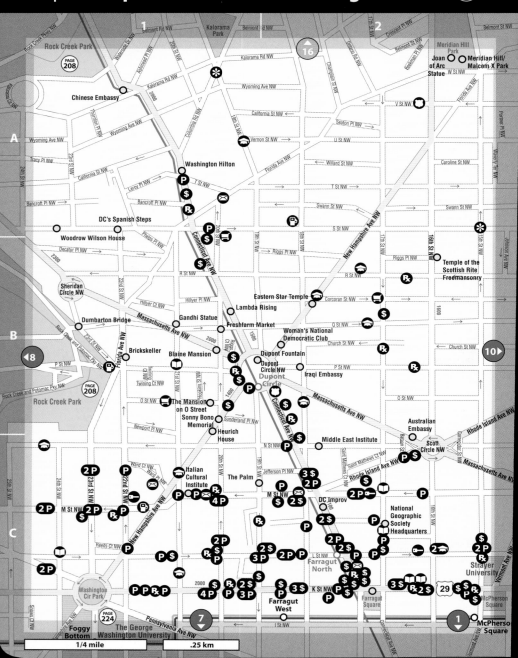

Neither tourist trap nor chain-store stuffed, boutique-y Dupont is a standard destination for locals. North and east of the circle, toward grittier Adams-Morgan and the trendy Logan Circle/U Street areas, is where the scene really is: shops, cafes, and great people-watching. Dupont is a little too settled to be considered bohemian or edgy any more, though. South of the Circle is just too corporate.

Map

$ Banks

- **Adams National** • 1130 Connecticut Ave NW
- **Adams National** • 1501 K St NW
- **Adams National** • 1604 17th St NW
- **Bank of America** • 1801 K St NW
- **Bank of America** • 2101 L St NW
- **Bank of America** • 3 Dupont Cir NW
- **Bank of America (ATM)** • 1612 K St NW
- **BB&T** • 1730 Rhode Island Ave NW
- **BB&T** • 1909 K St NW
- **Chevy Chase** • 1100 17th St NW
- **Chevy Chase** • 1700 K St NW
- **Chevy Chase** • 1800 M St NW
- **Chevy Chase** • 1850 K St NW
- **Chevy Chase (ATM)** • 1001 Connecticut Ave NW
- **Chevy Chase (ATM)** • 1050 Connecticut Ave NW
- **Chevy Chase (ATM)** • 1743 Connecticut Ave NW
- **Chevy Chase (ATM)** • 1800 K St NW
- **Citibank** • 1000 Connecticut Ave NW
- **Citibank** • 1225 Connecticut Ave NW
- **Commerce** • 1753 Connecticut Ave NW
- **Eagle** • 1228 Connecticut Ave NW
- **Eagle** • 2001 K St NW
- **HSBC** • 1130 Connecticut Ave NW
- **Independence Federal Savings** • 1020 19th St NW
- **Independence Federal Savings** • 1229 Connecticut Ave NW
- **M&T** • 1680 K St NW
- **M&T** • 1725 K St NW
- **M&T** • 1899 L St NW
- **Mercantile Potomac** • 1629 K St NW
- **PNC** • 1101 15th St NW
- **PNC** • 1800 M St NW
- **PNC** • 1875 Connecticut Ave NW
- **PNC** • 1913 Massachusetts Ave NW
- **PNC** • 1920 L St NW
- **PNC (ATM)** • 1333 New Hampshire Ave NW
- **PNC (ATM)** • 1600 Rhode Island Ave NW
- **Presidential Savings** • 1660 K St NW
- **Sun Trust** • 1111 Connecticut Ave NW
- **Sun Trust** • 1369 Connecticut Ave NW
- **Sun Trust** • 1925 K St NW
- **United** • 1667 K St NW
- **United** • 2301 M St NW
- **Wachovia** • 1100 Connecticut Ave NW
- **Wachovia** • 1300 Connecticut Ave NW
- **Wachovia** • 1510 K St NW
- **Wachovia** • 1800 K St NW
- **Wachovia** • 1850 M St NW
- **Wachovia** • 2001 L St NW
- **Washington First** • 1025 Connecticut Ave NW
- **Washington First** • 1500 K St NW

🔑 Car Rental

- **Avis** • 1722 M St NW • 202-467-6585
- **Budget** • 1620 L St NW • 202-466-4544
- **Enterprise** • 1221 22nd St NW • 202-872-5790

✳ Community Gardens

⛽ Gas Stations

- **BP/Amoco** • 1800 18th St NW
- **Exxon** • 2150 M St NW
- **Mobil** • 2200 P St NW ⊘

○ Landmarks

- **Australian Embassy** • 1601 Massachusetts Ave NW
- **Blaine Mansion** • 2000 Massachusetts Ave NW
- **The Brickskeller** • 1523 22nd St NW
- **Chinese Embassy** • 2300 Connecticut Ave NW
- **DC Improv** • 1140 Connecticut Ave NW
- **DC's Spanish Steps** • S St NW & 22nd St NW
- **Dumbarton Bridge** • 23rd St NW & Q St NW
- **Dupont Fountain** • Dupont Cir
- **Eastern Star Temple** • 1618 New Hampshire Ave NW
- **Farragut Square** • K St NW & 17th St NW
- **Freshfarm Market** • 20th St NW near Q St NW
- **Gandhi Statue** • Massachusetts Ave NW & 21st St NW
- **Heurich House** • 1307 New Hampshire Ave NW
- **Iraqi Embassy** • 1801 P St NW
- **Italian Cultural Institute** • 2025 M St NW
- **Joan of Arc Statue** • Meridian Hill Park
- **Lambda Rising** • 1625 Connecticut Ave NW
- **The Mansion on O Street** • 2020 O St NW
- **Meridian Hill/Malcolm X Park** • 16th St NW b/w W St NW & Euclid St NW
- **Middle East Institute** • 1761 N St NW
- **National Geographic Society Headquarters** • 1145 17th St NW
- **The Palm** • 1225 19th St NW
- **Sonny Bono Memorial** • 20th St NW & New Hampshire Ave NW
- **Temple of the Scottish Rite of Freemasonry** • 1733 16th St NW
- **Washington Hilton** • 1919 Connecticut Ave NW
- **Woman's National Democratic Club** • 1526 New Hampshire Ave NW
- **Woodrow Wilson House** • 2340 S St NW

📖 Libraries

- **Arthur R Ashe Jr Foreign Policy Library** • 1629 K St NW, Ste 1100
- **Foundation Center** • 1627 K St NW, 3rd Fl
- **National Geographic Society Library** • 1145 17th St NW
- **Polish Library in Washington** • 1503 21st St NW
- **US Institute of Peace** • 1200 17th St NW, Ste 200
- **West End Library** • 1101 24th St NW

Ⓟ Parking

℞ Pharmacies

- **Alpha Drugs** • 1642 R St Nw
- **CVS** • 1025 Connecticut Ave NW
- **CVS** • 1500 K St NW
- **CVS** • 1637 P St NW
- **CVS** • 1990 K St NW
- **CVS** • 2000 L St NW
- **CVS** • 2000 M St NW
- **CVS** • 2240 M St NW
- **CVS** • 6 Dupont Cir NW ⊘
- **Foer's CARE Pharmacy** • 2141 K St NW
- **Pharmacare** • 1517 17th St NW
- **Rite Aid** • 1034 15th St NW
- **Rite Aid** • 1815 Connecticut Ave NW ⊘
- **Tschiffely Pharmacy** • 1145 19th St NW
- **Tschiffely Pharmacy** • 1330 Connecticut Ave NW

👮 Police

- **MPD Gay & Lesbian Liaison Unit** • 1369 Connecticut Ave NW
- **MPDC 3rd District Station** • 1620 V St NW

✉ Post Offices

- **Farragut Station** • 1800 M St NW
- **Temple Heights Station** • 1921 Florida Ave NW
- **Twentieth St Station** • 2001 M St NW
- **Ward Place Station** • 2121 Ward Pl NW
- **Washington Square Station** • 1050 Connecticut Ave NW

🎓 Schools

- **Academy for learning Through the Arts** • 2100 New Hampshire Ave NW
- **Adams Elementary** • 2020 19th St NW
- **Emerson Preparatory** • 1324 18th St NW
- **Francis Junior High** • 2425 N St NW
- **Rock Creek International Upper** • 1621 New Hampshire Ave NW
- **Ross Elementary** • 1730 R St NW
- **School for Arts in Learning** • 1100 16th St NW
- **Stevens Elementary** • 1050 21st St NW
- **Strayer University (Washington Campus)** • 1133 15th St NW

🛒 Supermarkets

- **Safeway** • 1701 Corcoran St NW
- **Safeway** • 1800 20th St NW

39

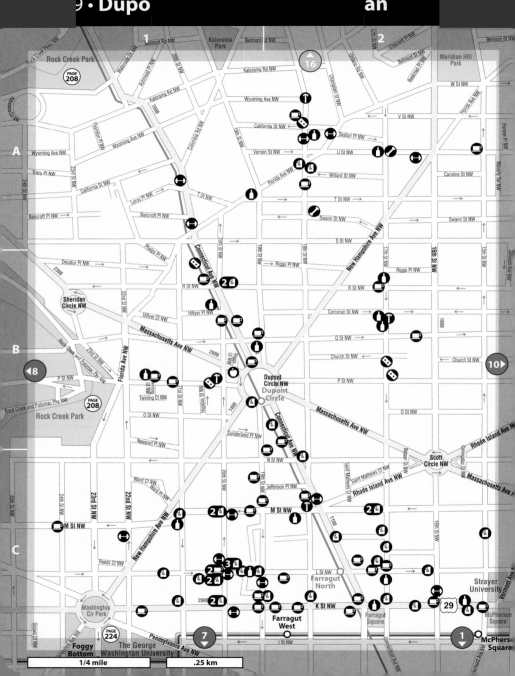

This is about as complete a neighborhood as you can find in DC and still be able to afford to live here…as a renter. Condos are passing half-a-million bucks but at least you can get a tofu wrap, ibus for the hangover, and a copy of the London *Daily Mirror* in the same block. Now if we could just get a *real* bagel.

Coffee

- **Azela Coffee Shop** · 2118 18th St NW
- **Caribou Coffee** · 1101 17th St NW
- **Caribou Coffee** · 1700 K St NW
- **Caribou Coffee** · 1800 M St NW
- **Casey's Coffee** · 2000 L St NW
- **Coffee Espress** · 2001 L St NW
- **Coffee Express** ·
  1101 Connecticut Ave NW
- **Coffee & the Works** ·
  1627 Connecticut Ave NW
- **Cosi** · 1350 Connecticut Ave NW
- **Cosi** · 1501 K St NW
- **Cosi** · 1647 20th St NW
- **Cosi** · 1875 K St NW
- **Cosi** · 1919 M St NW
- **Cozy Café** · 1828 L St NW
- **Dupont Coffee Shop** · 1234 19th St NW
- **Firehook Bakery & Coffee House** ·
  1909 Q St NW
- **Java Green** · 1020 19th St NW
- **Java House** · 1645 Q St NW
- **Jolt'n Bolt Coffee & Tea House** ·
  1918 18th St NW
- **Krispy Kreme** ·
  1350 Connecticut Ave NW
- **LA Café II** · 1850 K St NW
- **Love Café** · 1501 U St NW
- **Soho Tea & Coffee** · 2150 P St NW
- **Starbucks** · 1001 Connecticut Ave NW
- **Starbucks** · 1205 19th St NW
- **Starbucks** · 1301 Connecticut Ave NW
- **Starbucks** · 1501 Connecticut Ave NW
- **Starbucks** · 1600 K St NW
- **Starbucks** · 1600 U St NW
- **Starbucks** · 1700 Connecticut Ave NW
- **Starbucks** · 1734 L St NW
- **Starbucks** · 1900 K St NW
- **Starbucks** · 2101 P St NW
- **Starbucks** · 2175 K St NW
- **Starbucks** · 2400 M St NW
- **Steam Café** · 1700 17th St NW

Copy Shops

- **AAA Printing & Duplicating** ·
  1353 Connecticut Ave NW
- **ABC Imaging** · 1147 20th St NW
- **ABS Complete Printing** · 1150
  Connecticut Ave NW
- **Commercial Duplicating Service** ·
  1920 L St NW
- **Copy Cats** · 1140 17th St NW
- **Copy General** · 2000 L St NW
- **Deadline Press** · 1020 19th St NW
- **Document Technology** · 2000 M St NW
- **Dupont Circle Copy** · 11 Dupont Cir NW
- **Eagle Printing** · 1156 15th St NW
- **EZ Business Services** · 1929 18th St NW
- **FedEx Kinko's** · 1612 K St NW
- **FedEx Kinko's** · 2020 K St NW

- **Hot-Line Duplicating** · 1718 20th St NW
- **Huff Printing & Ad Specialties** ·
  1100 17th St NW
- **Ikon Office Solutions** · 1120 20th St NW
- **Imagenet** · 2000 M St NW ⊗
- **Impress Print & Copy** · 2001 L St NW
- **Minuteman Press** · 2000 K St NW
- **National Reprographics Inc** ·
  1705 Desales St NW
- **NRI** · 1705 Desales St NW
- **Omnidox** · 2101 L St NW ⊗
- **Park Press** · 1518 K St NW
- **Press Express Copy & Printing** ·
  1015 18th St NW
- **Print Time** · 1714 20th St NW
- **Printer** · 1803 Florida Ave NW
- **Reprographic Technologies** ·
  2000 L St NW
- **Sequential** · 1615 L St NW ⊗
- **Service Point USA** · 1129 20th St NW
- **Sir Speedy Printing** · 1025 17th St NW
- **Sir Speedy Printing** ·
  1300 Connecticut Ave NW
- **Sir Speedy Printing** · 2134 L St NW
- **Staples** · 1901 L St NW
- **UPS Store** · 1718 M St NW
- **UPS Store** · 2100 M St NW
- **US Printing & Copying** · 1725 M St NW

Farmer's Markets

- **Dupont Circle Freshfarm**
  (Mar–Jan, Sun 9 am–1 pm;
  Jan–Mar, Sun 10 am–1 pm) ·
  1913 Massachusetts Ave NW

Gyms

- **Bally Total Fitness** · 2000 L St NW
- **Capital City Club and Spa** · Hilton ·
  1001 16th St NW
- **Curves (women only)** ·
  1710 Rhode Island Ave NW
- **Fitness First** · 1075 19th St NW
- **Gold's Gym** · 1120 20th St NW
- **Mint** · 1724 California St NW
- **Results the Gym** · 1612 U St NW
- **Sports Club/LA** · 1170 22nd St NW
- **Third Power Fitness** · 2007 18th St NW ⊗
- **Washington Hilton Sport Club** ·
  1919 Connecticut Ave NW
- **Washington Sports Clubs** ·
  1211 Connecticut Ave NW
- **Washington Sports Clubs** ·
  1835 Connecticut Ave NW
- **Washington Sports Clubs** ·
  1990 K St NW
- **Washington Sports Clubs** ·
  1990 M St NW

Hardware Stores

- **Adams Morgan Hardware** ·
  2200 18th St NW
- **Candey Hardware** · 1210 18th St NW
- **District True Value Hardware** ·
  2003 P St NW
- **True Value on 17th** · 1623 17th St NW

Liquor Stores

- **Barmy Wine & Liquor** · 1912 L St NW
- **Bell Liquor & Wine Shoppe** ·
  1821 M St NW
- **Benmoll Liquors** · 1700 U St NW
- **Best Cellars (wine only)** ·
  1643 Connecticut Ave NW
- **Cairo Wine & Liquor Store** ·
  1618 17th St NW
- **Casa Pena Spanish Grocery Store** ·
  1636 17th St NW
- **Connecticut Avenue Liquors** ·
  1529 Connecticut Ave NW
- **DeVino's** · 2001 18th St NW
- **Downtown Spirits & Deli** · 1522 K St NW
- **Imperial Liquor** · 1050 17th St NW
- **La Salle Liquors** · 1719 K St NW
- **Martin's Wine & Spirits** ·
  1919 Florida Ave NW
- **Rosebud Liquors** · 1711 17th St NW
- **State Liquors** · 2159 P St NW
- **Wine Specialists** · 2115 M St NW

Pet Shops

- **Companions Pet Shop** · 1626 U St NW
- **Doggie Style** · 1825 18th St NW

Video Rental

- **Blockbuster** · 1639 P St NW
- **Capitol Video Sales** ·
  1729 Connecticut Ave NW
- **Capitol Video Sales** · 2028 P St NW
- **Video Americain** ·
  2104 18th St NW
- **The Video Rack** · 1511 17th St NW

Map 9 · **Dupont Circle / Adams Morgan**

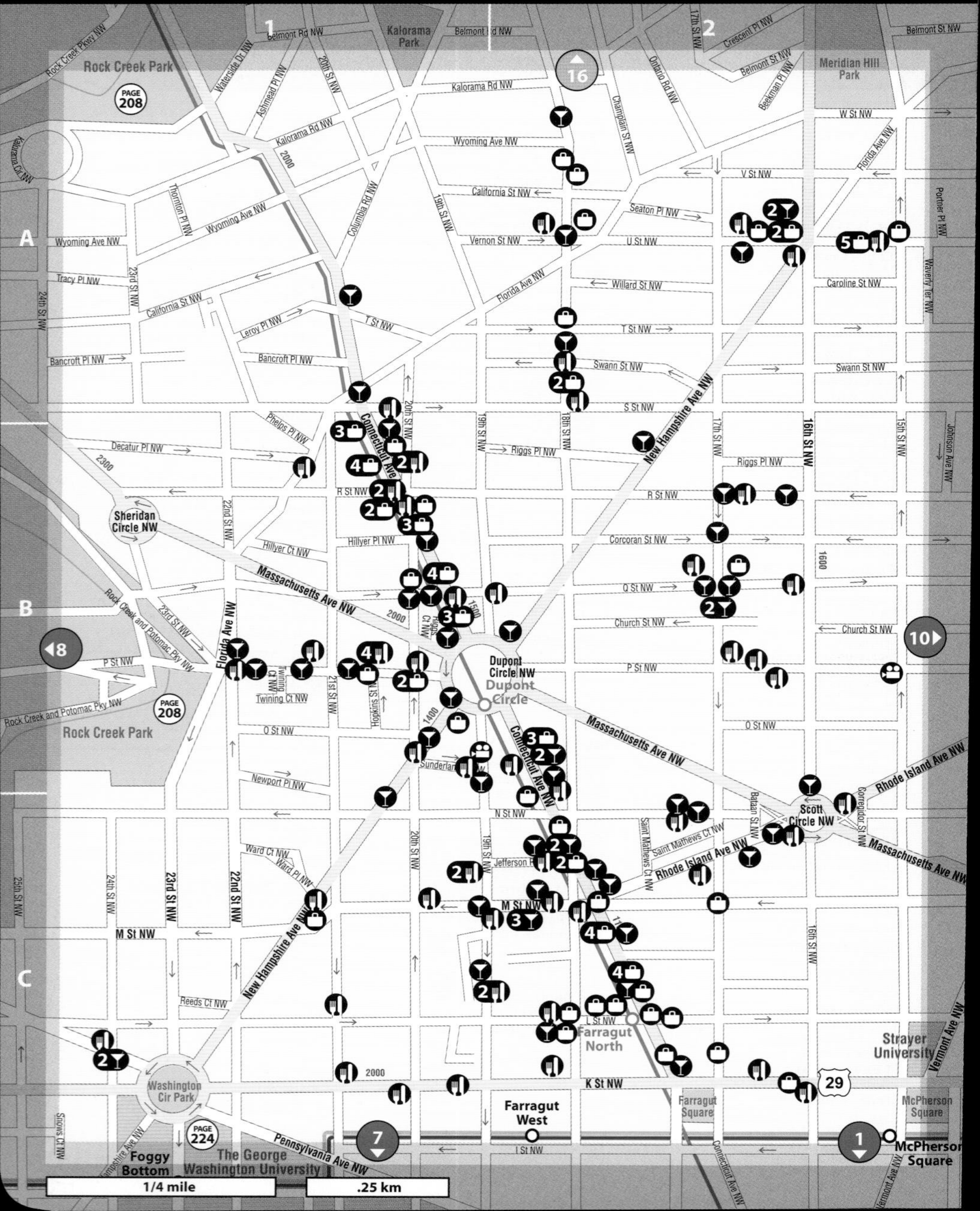

Ⓝ

Rock Creek Park

PAGE 208

Kalorama Park

Belmont Rd NW

Kalorama Rd NW

Meridian Hill Park

1

2

16

Wyoming Ave NW

California St NW

Seaton Pl NW

V St NW

W St NW

Vernon St NW

U St NW

2

5

Caroline St NW

A

Florida Ave NW

Willard St NW

T St NW

T St NW

Swann St NW

Swann St NW

2

S St NW

Riggs Pl NW

R St NW

R St NW

3

4

2

Corcoran St NW

2

Hillyer Pl NW

Q St NW

4

2

Church St NW

Church St NW

3

Sheridan Circle NW

Massachusetts Ave NW

P St NW

P St NW

B

8

PAGE 208

10

Dupont Circle NW

Dupont Circle

Rock Creek Park

Twining Ct NW

O St NW

O St NW

4

2

Newport Pl NW

3

N St NW

2

Scott Circle NW

Rhode Island Ave NW

Ward Ct NW

Ward Pl NW

2

Jefferson Pl

Saint Mathews Ct NW

Massachusetts Ave NW

C

M St NW

M St NW

3

2

Reeds Ct NW

4

2

4

Farragut North

2

Washington Cir Park

PAGE 224

Pennsylvania Ave NW

K St NW

Farragut Square

Strayer University

29

1

Foggy Bottom

The George Washington University

7

Farragut West

L St NW

Farragut North

McPherson Square

1/4 mile

.25 km

Dupont is where DC bubbles over with its nightlife options. From beer-soaked sports bars to clubs that are so painfully hip that their name is their address…in Roman numerals. It's still a vibrant singles 'hood, and the yuppies are gaining on the guppies (isn't that always the way?). But despite Bistrot du Coin, no one will ever mistake Connecticut Avenue for the Champs-Elysées.

Movie Theaters

- **Carnegie Institute** • 1530 P St NW
- **Loews Dupont Circle 5** • 1350 19th St NW

Nightlife

- **Aroma** • 2401 Pennsylvania Ave NW
- **Bar Rouge** • Rouge Hotel • 1315 16th St NW
- **Beacon Bar & Grill** • 1615 Rhode Island Ave NW
- **Biddy Mulligan's** • Jurys Washington Hotel • 1500 New Hampshire Ave NW
- **Big Hunt** • 1345 Connecticut Ave NW
- **Bravo Bravo** • 1001 Connecticut Ave NW
- **The Brickskeller** • 1523 22nd St NW
- **Buffalo Billiards** • 1330 19th St NW
- **Café Citron** • 1343 Connecticut Ave NW
- **Café Japone** • 2032 P St NW
- **Camelot** • 1823 M St NW
- **Chaos** • 1603 17th St NW
- **Chi-Cha Lounge** • 1624 U St NW
- **Childe Harold** • 1610 20th St NW
- **Cloud Dining Lounge** • 1 Dupont Cir NW
- **Cobalt/30 Degrees** • 1639 R St NW
- **Dragonfly** • 1215 Connecticut Ave NW
- **Eighteenth Street Lounge** • 1212 18th St NW
- **Firefly** • 1310 New Hampshire Ave NW
- **Fireplace** • 2161 P St NW
- **Fox and Hounds Lounge** • 1537 17th St NW
- **Front Page** • 1333 New Hampshire Ave NW
- **Gazuza** • 1629 Connecticut Ave NW
- **Improv** • 1140 Connecticut Ave NW
- **JR's** • 1519 17th St NW
- **Kramerbooks & Afterwords Café** • 1517 Connecticut Ave NW
- **La Frontera Cantina** • 1633 17th St NW
- **Lauriol Plaza** • 1835 18th St NW
- **Local 16** • 1602 U St NW
- **Lucky Bar** • 1221 Connecticut Ave NW
- **Madhatter** • 1831 M St NW
- **McClellan's** • Hilton • 1919 Connecticut Ave NW
- **MCCXXIII** • 1223 Connecticut Ave NW
- **McFadden's** • 2401 Pennsylvania Ave NW
- **Mercury Bar** • 1602 17th St NW
- **Omega DC** • 2122 P St NW
- **Ozio** • 1813 M St NW
- **Recessions** • 1823 L St NW
- **Rumors** • 1900 M St NW
- **Russia House Restaurant and Lounge** • 1800 Connecticut Ave NW
- **Science Club** • 1136 19th St NW
- **Sign of the Whale** • 1825 M St NW
- **Soussi** • 2228 18th St NW
- **Staccato** • 2006 18th St NW
- **Stetson's Famous Bar & Restaurant** • 1610 U St NW
- **Tabard Inn** • 1739 N St NW
- **Timberlake's** • 1726 Connecticut Ave NW
- **Topaz Bar** • Topaz Hotel • 1733 N St NW
- **The Town & Country** • Mayflower Hotel • 1127 Connecticut Ave NW
- **Townhouse Tavern** • 1637 R St NW
- **The Wave!** • 1731 New Hampshire Ave NW

Restaurants

- **15 Ria** • Washington Terrace Hotel • 1515 Rhode Island Ave NW
- **Al Tiramisu** • 2014 P St NW
- **Annie's Paramount** • 1609 17th St NW ☺
- **Bacchus Restaurant** • 1827 Jefferson Pl NW
- **Bistrot du Coin** • 1738 Connecticut Ave NW
- **The Brickskeller** • 1523 22nd St NW
- **Bua** • 1635 P St NW
- **Café Citron** • 1343 Connecticut Ave NW
- **Café L'Enfant** • 2000 18th St NW
- **Café Luna** • 1633 P St NW
- **Chi-Cha Lounge** • 1624 U St NW
- **Daily Grill** • 1200 18th St NW
- **Food Bar** • 1639 R St NW
- **Front Page Restaurant and Grill** • 1333 New Hampshire Ave NW
- **Galileo/Il Laboratorio del Galileo** • 1110 21st St NW
- **Hank's Oyster Bar** • 1624 Q St NW
- **I Ricchi** • 1220 19th St NW
- **Johnny's Half Shell** • 2002 P St NW
- **Kramerbooks & Afterwords Café** • 1517 Connecticut Ave NW
- **Lauriol Plaza** • 1835 18th St NW
- **Levante's** • 1320 19th St NW
- **Local 16** • 1602 U St NW
- **Love Café** • 1501 U St NW
- **Luna Grill & Diner** • 1301 Connecticut Ave NW
- **Mackey's Public House** • 1823 L St NW
- **Malaysia Kopitiam** • 1827 M St NW
- **Marcel's** • 2401 Pennsylvania Ave NW
- **McCormick and Schmick's** • 1652 K St NW
- **Meiwah** • 1200 New Hampshire Ave NW
- **Mimi's** • 2120 P St NW
- **Nage** • 1600 Rhode Island Ave NW
- **Nirvana** • 1810 K St NW
- **Nooshi** • 1120 19th St NW
- **Obelisk** • 2029 P St NW
- **Olives** • 1600 K St NW
- **The Palm** • 1225 19th St NW
- **Pesce** • 2016 P St NW
- **Pizzeria Paradiso** • 2029 P St NW
- **The Prime Rib** • 2020 K St NW
- **Raku** • 1900 Q St NW
- **Restaurant Nora** • 2132 Florida Ave NW
- **Rosemary's Thyme** • 1801 18th St NW
- **Sam and Harry's** • 1200 19th St NW
- **Sette Osteria** • 1666 Connecticut Ave NW
- **Smith and Wollensky** • 1112 19th St NW
- **Sushi Taro** • 1503 17th St NW
- **Tabard Inn** • 1739 N St NW
- **Teaism** • 2009 R St NW
- **Teatro Goldoni** • 1909 K St NW
- **Thai Chef** • 1712 Connecticut Ave NW
- **Thaiphoon** • 2011 S St NW
- **Timberlake's** • 1726 Connecticut Ave NW
- **Vidalia** • 1990 M St NW
- **Yee Hwa** • 1009 21st St NW

Shopping

- **Andre Chreky, the Salon Spa** • 1604 K St NW
- **Ann Taylor** • 1140 Connecticut Ave NW
- **Ann Taylor Loft** • 1611 Connecticut Ave NW
- **Bang Salon** • 1612 U St NW
- **Bedazzled** • 1507 Connecticut Ave NW
- **Best Cellars** • 1643 Connecticut Ave NW

- **Betsy Fisher** • 1224 Connecticut Ave NW
- **Blue Mercury** • 1619 Connecticut Ave NW
- **Books-A-Million** • 11 Dupont Cir NW
- **Borders** • 1800 L St NW
- **Brooks Brothers** • 1201 Connecticut Ave NW
- **Burberry** • 1155 Connecticut Ave NW
- **Cake Love** • 1506 U St NW
- **Chocolate Moose** • 1743 L St NW
- **Comfort One Shoes** • 1621 Connecticut Ave NW
- **Comfort One Shoes** • 1630 Connecticut Ave NW
- **Companions Pet Shop** • 1626 U St NW
- **Custom Shop Clothiers** • 1033 Connecticut Ave NW
- **Designer Consignor** • 1515 U St NW
- **DeVino's** • 2001 18th St NW
- **Doggie Style** • 1825 18th St NW
- **Downs Engravers & Stationers** • 1746 L St NW
- **Drilling Tennis & Golf** • 1040 17th St NW
- **Dupont Market** • 1807 18th St NW
- **Filene's Basement** • 1133 Connecticut Ave NW
- **The Gap** • 1120 Connecticut Ave NW
- **Ginza** • 1721 Connecticut Ave NW
- **Godiva Chocolatier** • 1143 Connecticut Ave NW
- **The Grooming Lounge** • 1745 L St NW
- **The Guitar Shop** • 1216 Connecticut Ave NW
- **Habitat Home Accents & Jewelry** • 1510 U St NW
- **Human Rights Campaign** • 1629 Connecticut Ave NW
- **J Press** • 1801 L St NW
- **Jos A Bank** • 1200 19th St NW
- **The Kid's Closet** • 1226 Connecticut Ave NW
- **Kramerbooks** • 1517 Connecticut Ave NW
- **Kulturas** • 1706 Connecticut Ave NW
- **Lambda Rising Bookstore** • 1625 Connecticut Ave NW
- **Leather Rack** • 1723 Connecticut Ave NW
- **Lucky Brand Dungarees** • 1739 Connecticut Ave NW
- **Marvelous Market** • 1511 Connecticut Ave NW
- **Meeps and Aunt Neensie's** • 1520 U St NW
- **Melody Records** • 1623 Connecticut Ave NW
- **Millennium Decorative Arts** • 1528 U St NW
- **Nana** • 1528 U St NW
- **National Geographic Shop** • 1145 17th St NW
- **Newsroom** • 1803 Connecticut Ave NW
- **Olsson's Books & Records** • 1307 19th St NW
- **Pasargad Antique and Fine Persian** • 1217 Connecticut Ave NW
- **Pleasure Place** • 1710 Connecticut Ave NW
- **Proper Topper** • 1350 Connecticut Ave NW
- **Rizik's** • 1100 Connecticut Ave NW
- **Salon Cielo** • 1741 Connecticut Ave NW
- **Second Story Books and Antiques** • 2000 P St NW
- **Secondi** • 1702 Connecticut Ave NW
- **Sisley** • 1606 Connecticut Ave NW
- **Skynear and Co** • 2122 18th St NW
- **Sticky Fingers Bakery** • 1904 18th St NW
- **Tabletop** • 1608 20th St NW
- **The Third Day** • 2001 P St NW
- **Thomas Pink** • 1127 Connecticut Ave NW
- **Tiny Jewel Box** • 1147 Connecticut Ave NW
- **United Colors of Benetton** • 1666 Connecticut Ave NW
- **Universal Gear** • 1601 17th St NW
- **Video Americain** • 2104 18th St NW
- **Wild Women Wear Red** • 1512 U St NW
- **Wine Specialists** • 2115 M St NW
- **The Written Word** • 1365 Connecticut Ave NW

Map 10 · **Logan Circle / U Street**

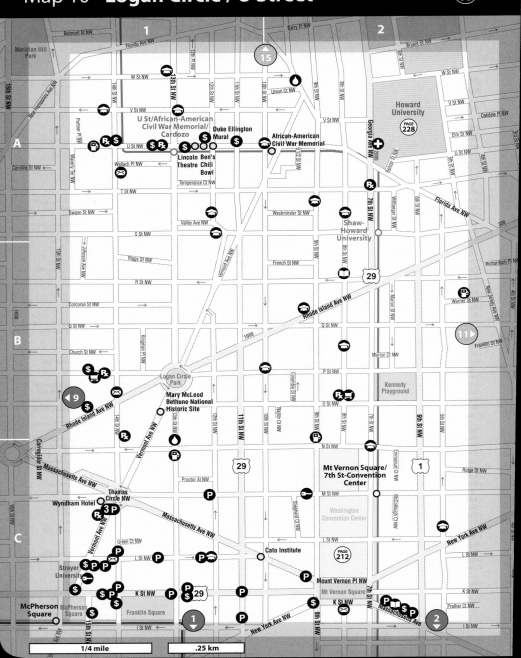

1

2

Belmont St NW

Meridian Hill Park

Florida Ave NW

Barry Pl NW

Bryant St NW

Florida Ave NW

W St NW

Howard University
PAGE 228

V St NW

Oakdale Pl NW

Elm St NW

A

U St/African-American Civil War Memorial/ Cardozo

Duke Ellington Mural

African-American Civil War Memorial

Lincoln Theatre

Ben's Chili Bowl

Temperance Ct NW

T St NW

Swann St NW

Valley Ave NW

Westminster St NW

Shaw-Howard University

Florida Ave NW

S St NW

Riggs St NW

French St NW

29

R St NW

Corcoran St NW

Richardson Pl NW

Q St NW

Rhode Island Ave NW

B

Church St NW

Marion Ct NW

Franklin St NW

11

9

Kennedy Playground

Rhode Island Ave NW

Mary McLeod Bethune National Historic Site

Logan Circle Park

O St NW

N St NW

Mt Vernon Square/ 7th St-Convention Center

1

Ridge St NW

29

Proctor Al NW

Thomas Circle NW

Washington Convention Center

PAGE 212

C

Wyndham Hotel

Massachusetts Ave NW

Cato Institute

New York Ave NW

Green Ct NW

Strayer University

Mount Vernon Pl NW

Mt Vernon Square

Prather Ct NW

K St NW

K St NW

29

McPherson Square

McPherson Square

Franklin Square

New York Ave NW

1

2

1/4 mile

.25 km

A better name would be Boom Town. Ribbons are cut on new restaurants and loft buildings all the time here, where the march of gentrification has slammed into a deep-rooted arts scene. Some of the most interesting shopping and eating is happening along the main thoroughfares of U Street and 14th Street.

Banks

- **Bank of America** · 1090 Vermont Ave NW
- **Bank of America** · 635 Massachusetts Ave NW
- **BB&T** · 1316 U St NW
- **Chevy Chase** · 901 New York Ave NW
- **Chevy Chase** · 925 15th St NW
- **Citibank** · 1000 Vermont Ave NW
- **Eagle** · 1425 K St NW
- **Industrial** · 2000 11th St NW
- **Industrial** · 2000 14th St NW
- **Industrial (ATM)** · 1213 U St NW
- **PNC** · 1400 K St NW
- **PNC (ATM)** · 1444 Rhode Island Ave NW
- **Sun Trust** · 1250 U St NW
- **Sun Trust** · 1275 K St NW
- **Wachovia** · 1447 P St NW

Car Rental

- **Enterprise** · 1029 Vermont Ave NW · 202-393-0900
- **Rent-A-Wreck** · 910 M St NW · 202-408-9828

Car Washes

- **Mr Wash** · 1311 13th St NW
- **Sparkle Car Wash** · 933 Florida Ave NW

Emergency Rooms

- **Howard University** · 2041 Georgia Ave NW ⓐ

Gas Stations

- **Amoco** · 1301 13th St NW
- **Amoco** · 1317 9th St NW
- **Chevron** · 4200 Burroughs Ave NE
- **Mobil** · 1442 U St NW ⓐ

oLandmarks

- **African-American Civil War Memorial** ·
  1000 U St NW
- **Ben's Chili Bowl** · 1213 U St NW
- **Cato Institute** · 1000 Massachusetts Ave NW
- **Duke Ellington Mural** · 1200 U St NW
- **Lincoln Theatre** · 1215 U St NW
- **Mary McLeod Bethune National Historic Site** ·
  1318 Vermont Ave NW
- **Wyndham Hotel** · 1400 M St NW

Libraries

- **Bureau of Alcohol & Tobacco Library** ·
  650 Massachusetts Ave NW
- **Watha T Daniel Branch Library** · 1701 8th St NW

Parking

Pharmacies

- **CVS** · 1199 Vermont Ave NW ⓐ
- **CVS** · 1418 P St NW
- **CVS** · 1900 7th St NW
- **Giant Food Pharmacy** · 1414 8th St NW
- **Municipal Drug Store** · 2000 14th St NW
- **Rite Aid** · 1306 U St NW
- **Stat Script Pharmacy** · 1325 14th St NW

Post Offices

- **Martin Luther King Jr Station** · 1400 L St NW
- **T Street** · 1915 14th St NW
- **Techworld Station** · 800 K St NW

Schools

- **Children's Studio** · 1301 V St NW
- **Cleveland Elementary** · 1825 8th St NW
- **FLOC Learning Center** · 1816 12th St NW
- **Garnet-Patterson Middle** · 2001 10th St NW
- **Garrison Elementary** · 1200 S St NW
- **Immaculate Conception** · 711 N St NW
- **Maya Angelou Public Charter** · 1851 9th St NW
- **Potomac Lighthouse Public Charter** ·
  1325 W St NW
- **Seaton Elementary** · 1503 10th St NW
- **Shaw Junior High** · 925 Rhode Island Ave NW
- **St Augustine** · 1419 V St NW
- **Sunrise Academy** · 1130 6th St NW
- **Thomson Elementary** · 1200 L St NW
- **Ujima Ya Ujamaa** · 1554 8th St NW

Supermarkets

- **Giant Food** · 1414 8th St NW
- **Whole Foods Market** · 1440 P St NW

Map 10 · **Logan Circle / U Street**

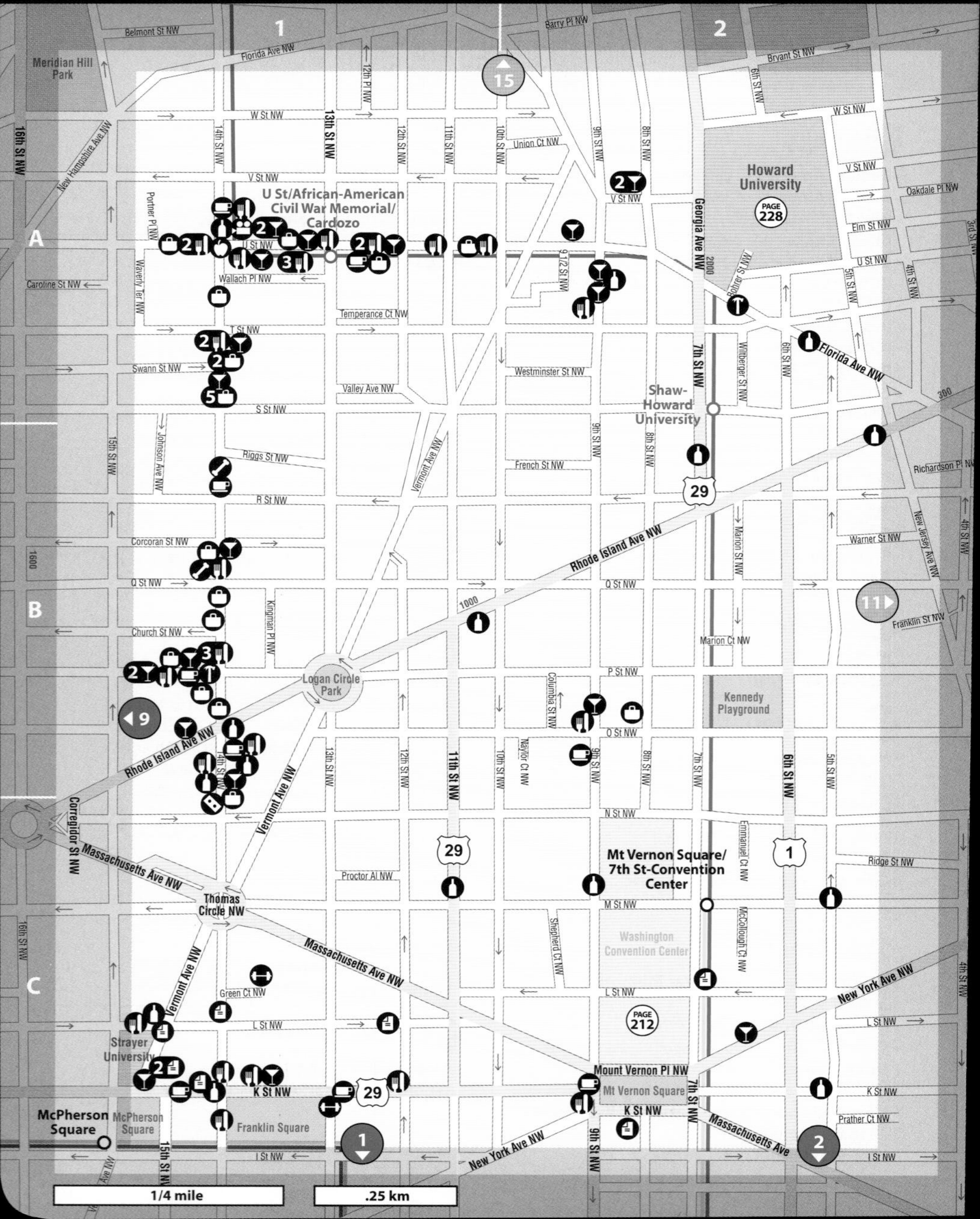

N

1

2

Belmont St NW

Florida Ave NW

Barry Pl NW

Bryant St NW

Meridian Hill
Park

W St NW

15

12th Pl NW

13th St NW

12th St NW

11th St NW

10th St NW

Union Ct NW

8th St NW

9th St NW

6th St NW

W St NW

Oakdale Pl NW

Howard
University

PAGE
228

Elm St NW

16th St NW

New Hampshire Ave NW

14th St NW

A

Caroline St NW

V St NW

U St/African-American
Civil War Memorial/
Cardozo

U St NW

V St NW

7th St NW

5th St NW

Georgia Ave NW

Wiltberger St NW

9th St NW

Florida Ave NW

300

Portner Pl NW

Waverly Ter NW

Wallach Pl NW

Temperance Ct NW

9th St NW

Florida Ave NW

T St NW

Swann St NW

Westminster St NW

Valley Ave NW

Shaw-
Howard
University

Richardson Pl NW

4th St NW

5

S St NW

Vermont Ave NW

French St NW

9th St NW

8th St NW

7th St NW

29

Johnson Ave NW

Riggs St NW

15th St NW

1600

R St NW

Warner St NW

New Jersey Ave NW

Corcoran St NW

Q St NW

Rhode Island Ave NW

Richardson Pl NW

Q St NW

B

Church St NW

Kingman Pl NW

1000

Marion Ct NW

Franklin St NW

11

3

9

P St NW

Logan Circle
Park

13th St NW

12th St NW

11th St NW

Naylor Ct NW

Columbia St NW

Kennedy
Playground

9th St NW

8th St NW

7th St NW

6th St NW

5th St NW

Ridge St NW

1

Rhode Island Ave NW

O St NW

N St NW

Carrollton St NW

Massachusetts Ave NW

Vermont Ave NW

29

M St NW

Mt Vernon Square/
7th St-Convention
Center

Emmanuel Ct NW

McCollough Ct NW

New York Ave NW

C

Thomas
Circle NW

Massachusetts Ave NW

Proctor Al NW

Shepherd Ct NW

Washington
Convention
Center

PAGE
212

16th St NW

Green Ct NW

L St NW

L St NW

L St NW

Strayer
University

2

K St NW

29

K St NW

Mount Vernon Pl NW

Mt Vernon Square

7th St NW

K St NW

Prather Ct NW

McPherson
Square

McPherson
Square

15th St NW

Franklin Square

1

New York Ave NW

9th St NW

K St NW

Massachusetts Ave

2

I St NW

1/4 mile

.25 km

In a city that has been picking itself up from the Sixties riots and years of stagnation, here's where you'll see the most radical reformation. The current surge of activity harkens back to U Street's heyday as an African-American cultural destination. It's once again the best place for martinis and jazz.

Coffee
- **Azi's Café** · 1336 9th St NW
- **Busboys and Poets** ·
  2021 14th St NW
- **Caribou Coffee** · 1400 14th St NW
- **Cosi** · 1275 K St NW
- **Sparky's Expresso Café** ·
  1720 14th St NW
- **Starbucks** · 1250 U St NW
- **Starbucks** · 1425 P St NW
- **Starbucks** · 1455 K St NW
- **Starbucks** · 801 Mt Vernon Pl NW

Copy Shops
- **Barrister Copy Solutions** ·
  1090 Vermont Ave NW ⊘
- **FedEx Kinko's** · 1400 K St NW
- **FedEx Kinko's** · 800 K St NW
- **Instant Copies & Print** ·
  1010 Vermont Ave NW
- **Miller Copying Service** ·
  1123 7th St NW
- **Print Express** · 1101 14th St NW
- **Sir Speedy Printing** ·
  1029 Vermont Ave NW
- **UPS Store** · 1220 L St NW

Farmer's Markets
- **14th & U Farmers Market
  (Jun–Oct, Wed 4 pm–8 pm)** ·
  14th St NW & U St NW

Gyms
- **Renaissance Swim & Fitness** ·
  941 9th St NW
- **Thomas Circle Sports Club** ·
  1339 Green Ct NW

Hardware Stores
- **Best Price Hardware** ·
  636 Florida Ave NW
- **Logan Hardware** · 1416 P St NW

Liquor Stores
- **A-1 Wine & Liquor** · 1420 K St NW
- **Barrel House** · 1341 14th St NW
- **Best in Liquors** · 1450 P St NW
- **Bestway Liquors** · 2011 14th St NW
- **Continental Liquors** ·
  1100 Vermont Ave NW
- **District Liquors** · 1211 11th St NW
- **Guilford Liquors** ·
  446 Rhode Island Ave NW
- **Izalco Beer & Wine** ·
  1314 14th St NW
- **Log Cabin Liquors** · 1748 7th St NW
- **Logan Circle Liquors** ·
  1018 Rhode Island Ave NW
- **Longs Liquors** · 520 Florida Ave NW
- **Modern Liquors** · 1200 9th St NW
- **S&R Liquors** · 1201 5th St NW
- **S&W Liquors** · 1428 9th St NW
- **Sav-On-Liquors** · 1414 14th St NW
- **Serv U Liquors** · 1935 9th St Nw
- **Subway Liquors II** · 500 K St NW

Movie Theaters
- **Busboys and Poets** ·
  2021 14th St NW

Nightlife
- **9:30 Club** · 815 V St NW
- **Avenue Nightclub** ·
  649 New York Ave NW
- **Bar Nun** · 1326 U St NW
- **Bar Pilar** · 1833 14th St NW
- **Black Cat** · 1811 14th St NW
- **Café Saint-Ex** · 1847 14th St NW
- **Daedalus** · 1010 Vermont Ave NW
- **DC9** · 1940 9th St NW
- **Helix Lounge** ·
  1430 Rhode Island Ave NW
- **HR-57 Center for the Preservation
  of Jazz and Blues** · 1610 14th St NW
- **K Street Lounge** · 1301 K St NW
- **Republic Gardens** · 1355 U St NW
- **The Saloon** · 1207 U St NW
- **Tabaq** · 1336 U St NW
- **Titan** · 1337 14th St NW
- **Twins Jazz** · 1344 U St NW
- **Vegas Lounge** · 1415 P St NW
- **Velvet Lounge** · 915 U St NW
- **The Warehouse** · 1017 7th St NW

Pet Shops
- **Pet Essentials** · 1722 14th St NW
- **Wagtime** · 1412 Q St NW

Restaurants
- **Acadiana** · 901 New York Ave NW
- **Al Crostino** · 1324 U St NW
- **Ben's Chili Bowl** · 1213 U St NW
- **Busboys and Poets** ·
  2021 14th St NW
- **Café Saint-Ex** · 1847 14th St NW
- **Coppi's** · 1414 U St NW
- **Corduroy** · 1201 K St NW
- **Creme Café** · 1322 U St NW
- **Dakota Cowgirl** · 1337 14th St NW
- **DC Coast** · Tower Bldg · 1401 K St NW
- **Dukem** · 1114 U St NW
- **Georgia Brown's** · 950 15th St NW
- **Lima** · 1401 K St NW
- **Logan Tavern** · 1423 P St NW
- **Maggie Moo's** · 1301 U St NW
- **Merkado Kitchen** · 1443 P St NW
- **Oohhs and Aahhs** · 1005 U St NW
- **Polly's Café** · 1342 U St NW
- **Post Pub** · 1422 L St NW
- **Rice** · 1608 14th St NW
- **Saloon** · 1207 U St NW
- **Soho Café & Market** · 1301 K St NW
- **Tabaq Bistro** · 1336 U St NW
- **Taste of Carolina** · 1930 9th St NW
- **Thai Tanic** · 1326 14th St NW
- **U-topia** · 1418 U St NW
- **Vegetate** · 1414 9th St NW
- **Viridian** · 1515 14th St NW

Shopping
- **100% Mexico** · 1612 14th St NW
- **Blink** · 1431 P St NW
- **Candida's World of Books** ·
  1541 14th St NW
- **Capitol City Records** · 1020 U St NW
- **Garden District** · 1801 14th St NW
- **Giant Food** · 1414 8th St NW
- **Go Mama Go!** · 1809 14th St NW
- **Good Wood** · 1428 U St NW
- **Home Rule** · 1807 14th St NW
- **Logan Hardware** · 1416 P St NW
- **Muleh** · 1831 14th St NW
- **Pink November** · 1231 U St NW
- **Pop** · 1803 14th St NW
- **Pulp** · 1803 14th St NW
- **Reincarnations** · 1401 14th St NW
- **Ruff and Ready** · 1908 14th St NW
- **Storehouse** · 1526 14th St NW
- **Urban Essentials** · 1330 U St NW
- **Vastu** · 1829 14th St NW
- **Whole Foods Market** · 1440 P St NW

Video Rental
- **Video 2000** · 1320 14th St NW

Map 11 · **Near Northeast**

This area is still as scruffy as they come, but the Bloomingdale section just west of N. Capitol Street is the edge of the gentrification craze pushing east from Shaw. The huge swath of railroad tracks slicing through does little for unification or aesthetics, however.

 Banks

- **Bank of America** · 915 Rhode Island Ave NE
- **Chevy Chase (ATM)** · 1050 Brentwood Rd NE
- **PNC** · 1348 4th St NE
- **PNC (ATM)** · 800 Florida Ave NE
- **Sun Trust** · 410 Rhode Island Ave NE

 Car Washes

- **NY Avenue Car Wash** · 39 New York Ave NE

 Gas Stations

- **Amoco** · 1231 New York Ave NE
- **Amoco** · 306 Rhode Island Ave NW
- **Amoco** · 400 Rhode Island Ave NE ⊘
- **Amoco** · 45 Florida Ave NE ⊘
- **Chevron** · 400 Florida Ave NE
- **Citgo** · 1905 Ninth St NE
- **Exxon** · 1 Florida Ave NE ⊘
- **Hess** · 1739 New Jersey Ave NW
- **Sunoco** · 101 New York Ave NE

o Landmarks

- **Florida Avenue Market** · Florida Ave NE b/w 2nd St NE & 6th St NE

 Libraries

- **Sursum Corda Community Library** · 135 New York Ave NW

 Parking

 Pharmacies

- **CVS** · 660 Rhode Island Ave NE
- **Giant Food Pharmacy** · 1050 Brentwood Rd NE
- **Safeway** · 514 Rhode Island Ave NE

 Post Offices

- **Le Droit Park** · 416 Florida Ave NW
- **Washington Main Office** · 900 Brentwood Rd NE

Schools

- **Calvary Christian Academy** · 806 Rhode Island Ave NE
- **Center for Life Enrichment** · 120 Q St NE
- **City Lights** · 62 T St NE
- **Cook Elementary** · 30 P St NW
- **DC Alternative Learning Academy/East** · 1200 Rhode Island Ave NE
- **DC Preparatory Academy** · 701 Edgewood St NE
- **Dunbar High** · 1301 New Jersey Ave NW
- **Emery Elementary** · 1720 1st St NE
- **Gage Eckington Elementary** · 2025 3rd St NW
- **Gallaudet University** · 800 Florida Ave NE
- **Hamilton Center Special Education** · 1401 Brentwood Pkwy NE
- **HD Cooke** · 300 Bryant St NW
- **Holy Name** · 1217 West Virginia Ave NE
- **Holy Redeemer** · 1135 New Jersey Ave NW
- **Hyde Leadership** · 101 T St NE
- **Kendall Demonstration Elementary/Model Secondary** · 800 Florida Ave NE
- **McKinley High** · 151 T St NE
- **Model Secondary** · 800 Florida Ave NE
- **Montgomery Elementary** · 421 P St NW
- **Noyes Elementary** · 2725 10th St NE
- **Pre-Engineering Senior High** · 1301 New Jersey Ave NW
- **Shaed Elementary** · 301 Douglas St NE
- **Terrell Junior High** · 100 Pierce St NW
- **Tree of Life Community Elementary** · 800 3rd St NE
- **Walker-Jones Elementary** · 100 L St NW
- **Washington Career High** · 27 O St NW
- **William E Doar Jr Elementary** · 705 Edgewood St NE
- **Wilson Elementary** · 660 K St NE

 Supermarkets

- **Giant Food** · 1050 Brentwood Rd NE
- **Safeway** · 514 Rhode Island Ave NE

Map 11 · **Near Northeast**

Yipee. A Home Depot and two grocery stores. That's it for shopping. As for driving through, New York Avenue and N. Capitol Street are the major thoroughfares in this area. If you are so fortunate as to get stuck on either on a Friday at 5 PM, you too will come to realize why there are so many liquor stores around.

Map 1

Coffee
- **Dunkin Donuts** · 1739 New Jersey Ave NW

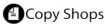 Copy Shops
- **Blueboy Document Imaging** · 214 L St NE

Farmer's Markets
- **DC Farmers Market**
  (Jun–Oct, Friday 10 am–2 pm) · 1309 5th St NE
- **North Capitol Neighborhood Farmers Market**
  (Jun–Oct, Sun 10 am–2 pm) ·
  1626 N Capitol St NE

Hardware Stores
- **Home Depot** · 901 Rhode Island Ave NE

Liquor Stores
- **Big Ben Liquor Store** · 1300 N Capitol St NW
- **Bloomingdale Liquor** · 1836 1st St NW
- **Brentwood Liquors** · 1319 Rhode Island Ave NE
- **Brother's Liquor** · 1140 Florida Ave NE
- **Coast-In Liquors** · 301 Florida Ave NE
- **Edgewood Liquor Store** · 2303 4th St NE
- **J&J Liquor Store** · 1211 Brentwood Rd NE
- **JB Liquorette** · 1000 Florida Ave NE
- **Mac's Wine & Liquor** · 401 Rhode Island Ave NE
- **Metro Ice & Beverage** · 50 Florida Ave NE
- **Moon Liquor** · 322 Florida Ave NW
- **Northeast Liquors** · 1300 5th St NE
- **Rhode Island Subway Liquor** ·
  914 Rhode Island Ave NE
- **Sosnik's Liquor Store** · 2318 4th St NE
- **Sunset Liquors** · 1627 1st St NW
- **Super Liquors** · 1633 N Capitol St NE
- **Walter Johnson's Liquor Store** ·
  1542 N Capitol St NW

 Nightlife
- **Bud's** · 501 Morse St NE
- **FUR Nightclub** · 33 Patterson St NE

Shopping
- **Giant Food** · 1050 Brentwood Rd
- **Safeway** · 514 Rhode Island Ave NE

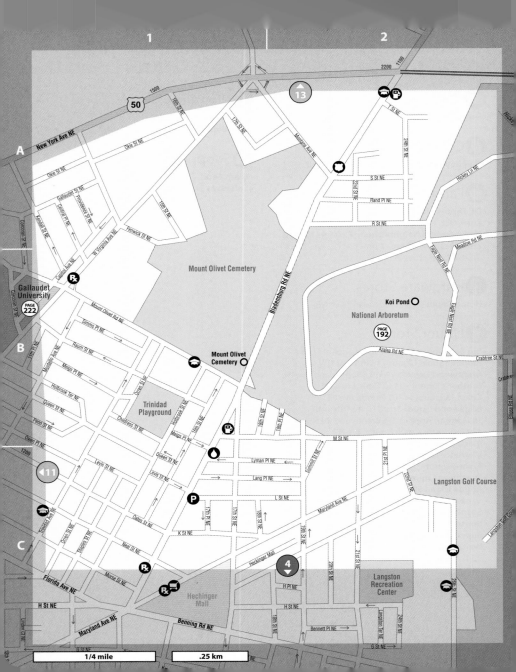

Here we find one of the last affordable neighborhoods in the city, and, unfortunately, it still shows. But somebody must see potential in its worn rowhouses and dead-end streets: in 2005, Trinidad's real estate assessments shot up 33 percent, the highest in the District. Outside investors also have started invading Trinidad's northern enclave, also known as Ivy City, where longtime residents are trying to fend off the speculators.

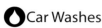Car Washes

· **Smoke Detail Hand Carwash** ·
  1161 Bladensburg Rd NE

Gas Stations

· **Amoco** · 1201 Bladensburg Rd NE ⊕
· **Exxon** · 1925 Bladensburg Rd NE ⊕

○Landmarks

· **Koi Pond** · National Arboretum
· **Mount Olivet Cemetery** ·
  1300 Bladensberg Rd NE

Parking

Pharmacies

· **CVS** · 845 Bladensburg Rd NE
· **Mt Olivet CARE Pharmacy** ·
  1809 West Virginia Ave NE
· **Safeway** · 1601 Maryland Ave NE

●Police

· **MPDC 5th District Station** ·
  1805 Bladensburg Rd NE

Schools

· **Browne Junior High** · 850 26th St NE
· **New School for Enterprise and Development** ·
  1920 Bladensburg Rd NE
· **Webb Elementary** · 1375 Mt Olive Rd NE
· **Wheatley Elementary (temporarily closed)** ·
  1299 Neal St NE
· **Young Elementary** · 820 26th St NE

Supermarkets

· **Safeway** · 1601 Maryland Ave NE

Map 12 · **Trinidad**

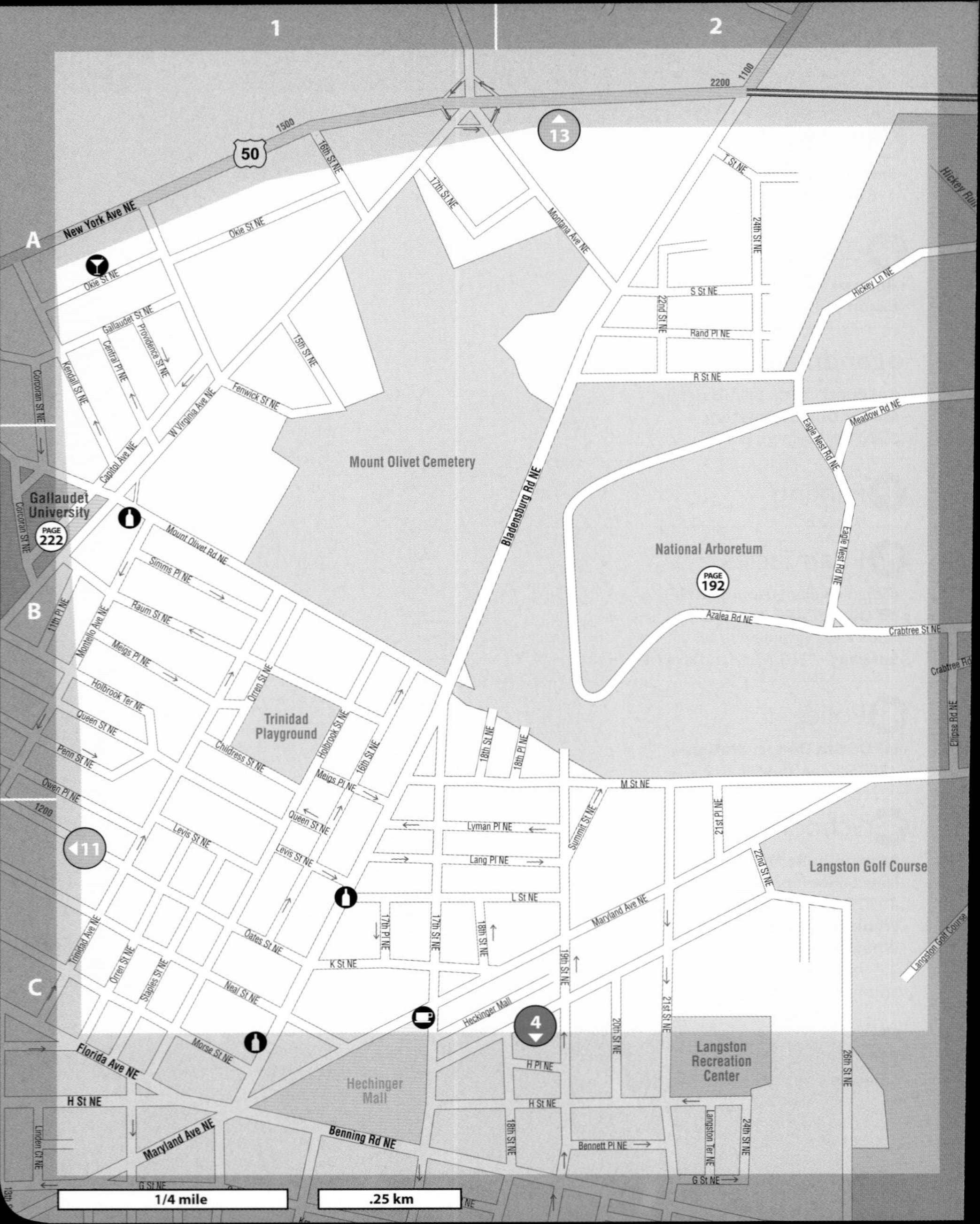

N

1

2

2200 1100

New York Ave NE

50

1500

US 50

18th St NE

17th St NE

Montana Ave NE

T St NE

24th St NE

Hickey Run

13

A

Okie St NE

Okie St NE

Gallaudet St NE

Central Pl NE

Providence St NE

19th St NE

S St NE

22nd St NE

Hickey Ln NE

Kendall St NE

Corcoran St NE

W Virginia Ave NE

Fenwick St NE

Carola Ave NE

Rand Pl NE

R St NE

Meadow Rd NE

Mount Olivet Cemetery

Bladensburg Rd NE

Eagle Nest Rd NE

Eagle West Rd NE

Corcoran St NE

Gallaudet
University

PAGE
222

Mount Olivet Rd NE

National Arboretum

PAGE
192

18th Pl NE

Simms Pl NE

Azalea Rd NE

Crabtree St NE

B

18th Pl NE

Montello Ave NE

Raum St NE

Orren St NE

Crabtree Rd

Meigs Pl NE

Holbrook St NE

Ellicott Rd NE

Hollbrook Ter NE

Queen St NE

Trinidad
Playground

Childress St NE

Meigs Pl NE

18th St NE

18th Pl NE

M St NE

Simms St NE

21st Pl NE

Penn St NE

Queen St NE

Lyman Pl NE

Langston Golf Course

Queen Pl NE

1200

Levis St NE

Lang Pl NE

22nd St NE

11

Trinidad Ave NE

Levis St NE

L St NE

Maryland Ave NE

Langston Golf Course

Orren St NE

Oates St NE

17th Pl NE

17th St NE

18th St NE

21st St NE

Morse St NE

Neal St NE

K St NE

19th St NE

C

Florida Ave NE

Heckinger Mall

4

20th St NE

21st St NE

Langston
Recreation
Center

26th St NE

H St NE

Hechinger
Mall

H Pl NE

H St NE

Maryland Ave NE

Benning Rd NE

18th St NE

20th St NE

Bennett Pl NE

Langston Pl NE

24th St NE

Linden Ct NE

G St NE

G St NE

| 1/4 mile | | .25 km |

The two destinations are the gorgeous Arboretum, which keeps its beauty gated away from the neighborhood, and a huge destination nightclub that keeps changing its name. Last we checked it was "Love." There's talk of building a community center but other plans for this hard-luck neighborhood have gone awry.

Map

Coffee
- **Starbucks** · 1601 Maryland Ave NE

Liquor Stores
- **Kovaks Liquors** · 1237 Mt Olivet Rd NE
- **Rose's Liquor** · 830 Bladensburg Rd NE
- **Stanton Liquors** · 1044 Bladensburg Rd NE

Nightlife
- **Love** · 1350 Okie St NE

If you envy the quiet streets and single-family living of your suburban friends but are loath to give up your DC address, here's a cheaper, scruffier alternative. Leafy streets and bigger lots mean plenty of mowing, raking, and snow shoveling—what better way to keep your mind off the fact that there's nothing else to do?

$ Banks
- **Industrial** · 2012 Rhode Island Ave NE
- **Wachovia** · 2119 Bladensburg Rd NE

Car Rental
- **A&D Auto Rental** · 2712 Bladensburg Rd NE · 202-832-5300
- **Enterprise** · 1502 Franklin St NE · 202-269-0300

Car Washes
- **Montana Double Car Wash** · 2327 18th St NE

Community Gardens

Gas Stations
- **Amoco** · 2210 Bladensburg Rd NE ⊘
- **Citgo** · 2420 New York Ave NE
- **Exxon** · 2230 New York Ave NE
- **Hess** · 1801 New York Ave NE
- **Shell** · 1765 New York Ave NE
- **Shell** · 1830 Rhode Island Ave NE
- **Shell** · 3101 Rhode Island Ave NE

o Landmarks
- **Franciscan Monastery** · 1400 Quincy St NE

Libraries
- **Woodridge Library** · 1801 Hamlin St NE

Rx Pharmacies
- **Rite Aid** · 1401 Rhode Island Ave NE

Post Offices
- **Woodridge Station** · 2211 Rhode Island Ave NE

Schools
- **Bunker Hill Elementary** · 1401 Michigan Ave NE
- **Burroughs Elementary** · 1820 Monroe St NE
- **Choice Middle Program** · 1800 Perry St NE
- **Friendship Edison: Woodridge Campus** · 2959 Carlton Ave NE
- **Langdon Elementary** · 1900 Evarts St SE
- **Latin American Montessori Bilingual** · 1401 Michigan Ave NE
- **Lincoln Middle** · 1800 Perry St NE
- **Rhema Christian Center** · 1825 Michigan Ave NE
- **Slowe Elementary** · 1404 Jackson St NE
- **St Anselm's Abbey** · 4501 S Dakota Ave NE
- **St Francis de Sales** · 2019 Rhode Island Ave NE
- **Taft** · 1800 Perry St NE
- **Tree of Life Community Public Charter** · 2315 18th Pl NE
- **Washington Science and Technology** · 2420 Rhode Island Ave NE

Map 13 · **Brookland / Langdon**

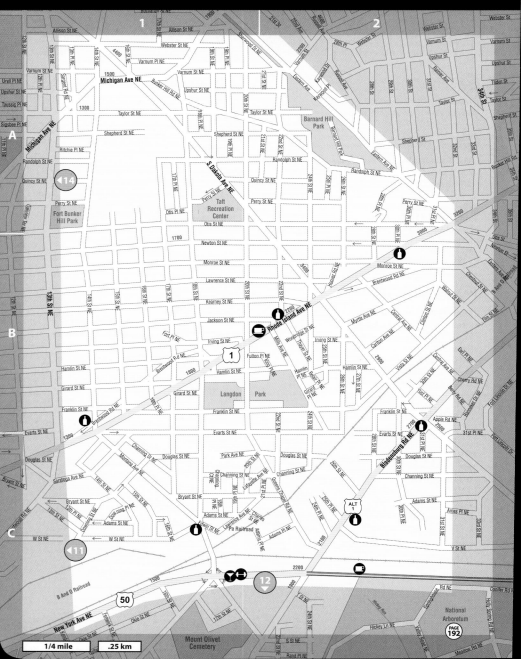

No one moves to Brookland for the nightlife. But it's a nice walk through the Franciscan Monastery grounds, with 44 acres of gardens and replicas from the Holy Land, including Roman catacombs and the garden where Jesus was arrested. And be sure to wake up from your suburban slumber for the annual neighborhood home tour—who doesn't love a great Sears bungalow or Queen Anne?

 Coffee
• **Dunkin' Donuts** • 1803 Rhode Island Ave NE
• **Dunkin' Donuts** • 2420 New York Ave NE

 Gyms
• **Mini Health Club** • 1818 New York Ave NE

 Liquor Stores
• **Good Ole Reliable Liquor** •
  1513 Rhode Island Ave NE
• **Montana Liquors** • 1805 Montana Ave NE
• **National Wine & Liquors** •
  2310 Rhode Island Ave NE
• **Sammy's Liquor** • 2725 Bladensburg Rd NE
• **Stop & Shop Liquors** • 3011 Rhode Island Ave NE
• **Syd's Drive-In Liquor Store** •
  2325 Bladensburg Rd NE
• **Woodridge Vet's Liquors** • 1358 Brentwood Rd NE

 Nightlife
• **Aqua** • 1818 New York Ave NE

Map 14 · **Catholic U**

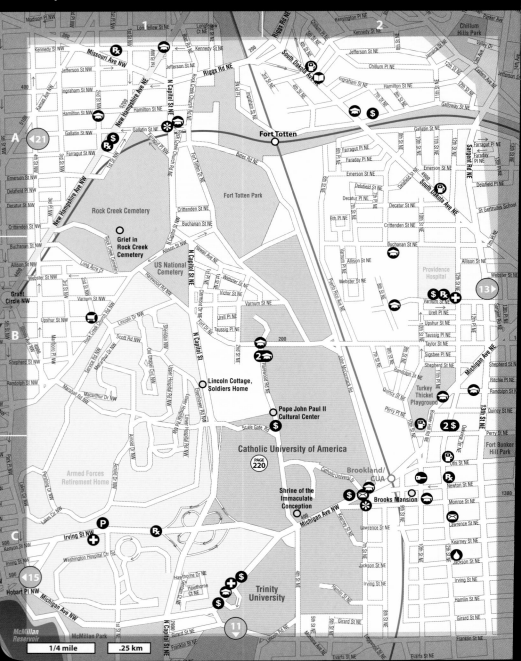

Welcome to Little Vatican, where it's easy to genuflect, particularly at the largest church in the western hemisphere, the Basilica of the National Shrine of the Immaculate Conception. It's named not for the birth of Jesus, but for the divinely-blessed conception of Jesus' mother Mary in her own mother's womb. At least the coeds have a short walk to the confessional if they fall short of the Blessed Virgin's example.

Banks

- **Chevy Chase** · 210 Michigan Ave NE
- **Chevy Chase (ATM)** · 1150 Varnum St NE
- **Chevy Chase (ATM)** · 3900 Harewood Rd NE
- **Chevy Chase (ATM)** · 550 Galloway St NE
- **Chevy Chase (ATM)** · 620 Michigan Ave NE
- **Citibank** · 3800 12th St NE
- **PNC** · 3806 12th St NE
- **PNC (ATM)** · 125 Michigan Ave NE
- **Wachovia** · 5005 New Hampshire Ave NW

Car Rental

- **Enterprise** · 3700 10th St NE · 202-635-1104

Car Washes

- **McDonald Custom Car Care** · 3221 12th St NE

Community Gardens

Emergency Rooms

- **Children's National Medical** · 111 Michigan Ave NW ⊕
- **Providence** · 1150 Varnum St NE ⊕
- **Washington Hospital Center** · 110 Irving St NW ⊕

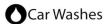 Gas Stations

- **Amoco** · 3701 12th St NE ⊕
- **Amoco** · 4925 S Dakota Ave NE
- **Exxon** · 1020 Michigan Ave NE ⊕
- **Exxon** · 5501 S Dakota Ave NE ⊕

Landmarks

- **Brooks Mansion** · 901 Newton St NE
- **Grief in Rock Creek Cemetery** · Rock Creek Church Rd NW & Webster St NW
- **Lincoln Cottage, Soldiers Home** · 3700 N Capitol St NW
- **Pope John Paul II Cultural Center** · 3900 Harewood Rd NE
- **Shrine of the Immaculate Conception** · 400 Michigan Ave NE

Libraries

- **Lamond-Riggs Library** · 5401 S Dakota Ave NE

Parking

Pharmacies

- **CVS** · 128 Kennedy St NW
- **CVS** · 3601 12th St NE
- **Ensign** · 106 Irving St NW
- **New Hampshire CARE Pharmacy** · 5001 New Hampshire Ave NW
- **Wellington Pharmacy** · 1160 Varnum St NE

Post Offices

- **Brookland Station** · 3401 12th St NE
- **Catholic University Cardinal Station** · 620 Michigan Ave NE

Schools

- **Academia Bilingue de la Comunidad Public Charter** · 209 Upshur St NW
- **Archbishop Carroll** · 4300 Harewood Rd NE
- **Backus Middle** · 5171 S Dakota Ave NE
- **Brookland Elementary** · 1150 Michigan Ave NE
- **Catholic University of America** · 620 Michigan Ave NE
- **JOS-ARZ Academy** · 220 Taylor St NE
- **Kennedy Institute Lower** · 801 Buchanan St NE
- **Maime Lee Elementary** · 100 Gallatin St NE
- **Metropolitan Day** · 1240 Randolph St NE
- **Moore Academy** · 1000 Monroe St NE
- **Roots Public Charter** · 15 Kennedy St NW
- **Rudolph Elementary** · 5200 2nd St NW
- **St Anthony** · 12th St NE & Lawrence St NE
- **Trinity University** · 125 Michigan Ave NE
- **Universal Ballet Academy** · 4301 Harewood Rd NE
- **Washington Jesuit Academy** · 900 Varnum St NE

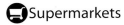 Supermarkets

- **M&S Market** · 213 Upshur St NW

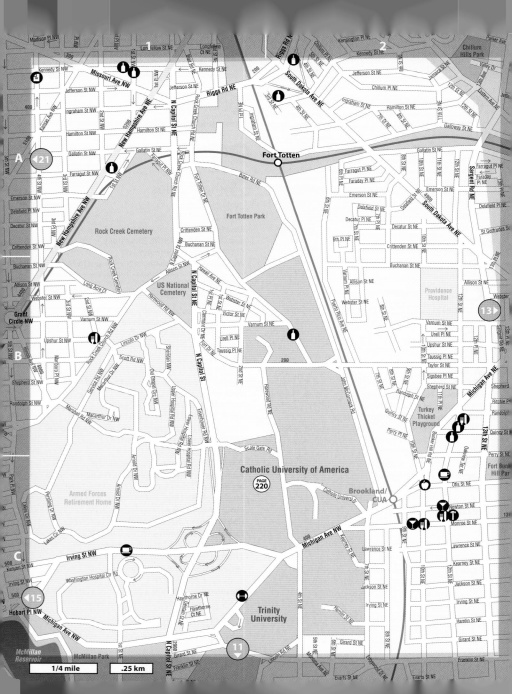

Catholic's founders moved outside the old city for more space and cooler, cleaner, perhaps more saintly, air. The 12th Street business corridor is known as "The Village". With its hardware store, post office and friendly taverns, it can feel a bit Mayberry. But Opie did always seem to be enjoying himself.

Coffee
- **The Buzz and Authentic Seattle Espresso Bar** ·
  50 Irving St NW
- **Café Sureia** · 3629 12th St Ne

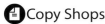Copy Shops
- **Quality Printers** · 301 Kennedy St NW

Farmer's Markets
- **Historic Brookland Farmer's Market (May–Oct, Sun, 10 am–2 pm; Jun–Oct, Tues 4 pm–7 pm)** · 10th St NE & Otis St NE

Gyms
- **Curves (women only)** · 212 Michigan Ave NE

Hardware Stores
- **Brookland True Value** · 3501 12th St NE

Liquor Stores
- **Dakota Liquors** · 5510 3rd St NE
- **Fair Liquors** · 5008 1st St NW
- **Kennedy Liquors** · 5501 1st St NW
- **Michigan Liquor Store Receiver** · 3934 12th St NE
- **Northwest Liquors** · 300 Kennedy St NW
- **Riggs Wine & Liquors** · 5581 S Dakota Ave NE
- **University Wine and Spirits** · 333 Hawaii Ave NE
- **Whelan's Liquors** · 3903 12th St NE

Nightlife
- **Colonel Brooks' Tavern** · 901 Monroe St NE
- **Johnny K's** · 3514 12th St NE

Restaurants
- **Colonel Brooks' Tavern** · 901 Monroe St NE
- **The Hitching Post** · 200 Upshur St NW
- **Kelly's Ellis Island** · 3908 12th St NE
- **Murry and Paul's** · 3513 12th St NE

Map 15 · **Columbia Heights**

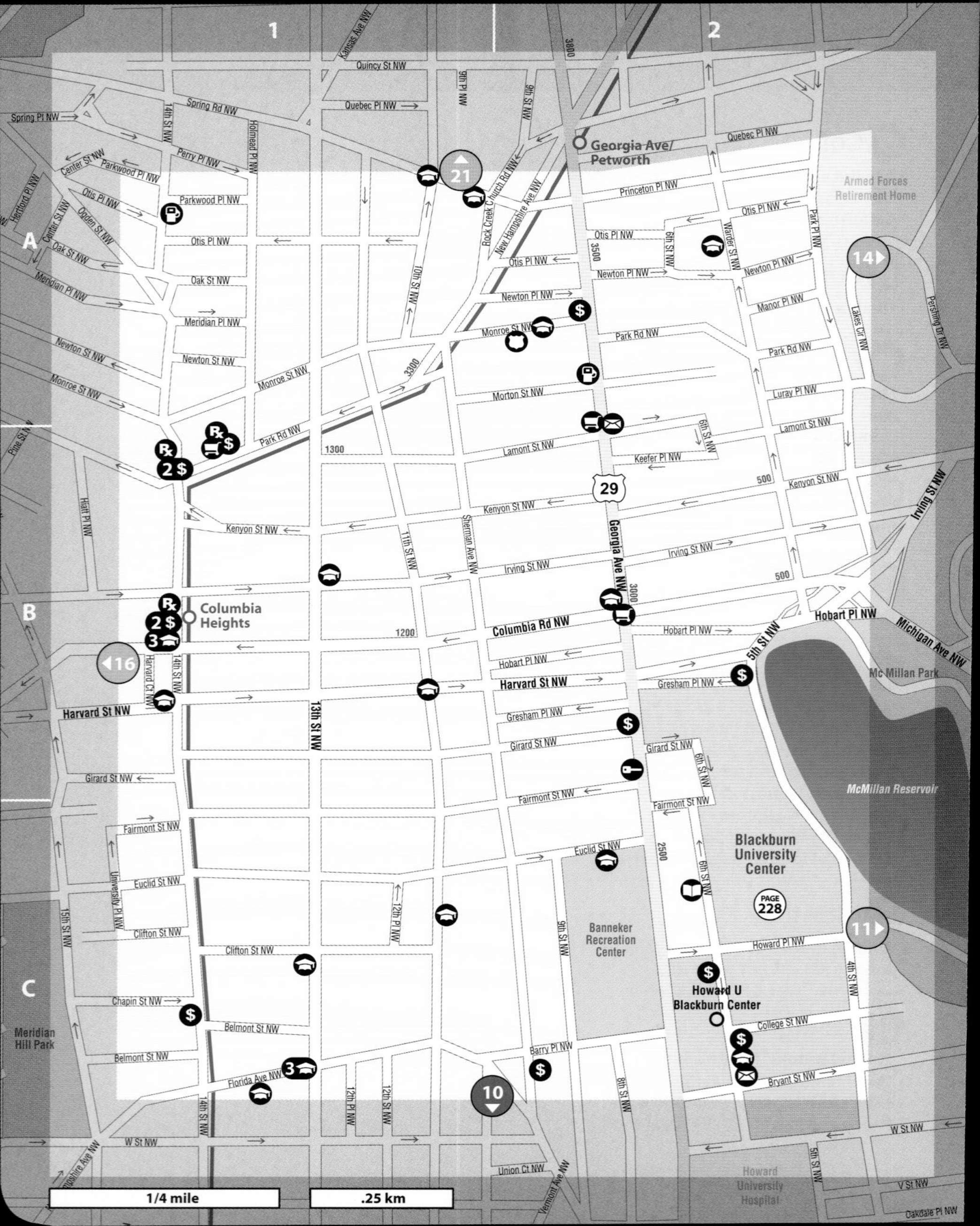

N

1

2

Quincy St NW

Quebec Pl NW

Spring Rd NW

Spring Pl NW

Center St NW

Parkwood Pl NW

Perry Pl NW

Hobart Pl NW

Otis Pl NW

Parkwood Pl NW

Herford St NW

Quebec Pl NW

21

Georgia Ave/
Petworth

Princeton Pl NW

Quebec Pl NW

Armed Forces
Retirement Home

A

Oak St NW

Meridian Pl NW

Otis Pl NW

Oak St NW

Meridian Pl NW

Newton St NW

Otis Pl NW

Otis Pl NW

Newton Pl NW

Newton Pl NW

Otis Pl NW

Manor Pl NW

Park Rd NW

Waine St NW

Newton Pl NW

14

Monroe St NW

Newton St NW

Monroe St NW

Morton St NW

Park Rd NW

Lamont St NW

Park Rd NW

Monroe St NW

Luray Pl NW

Lamont St NW

Park Rd NW

Kenyon St NW

Park Rd NW

1300

Lamont St NW

Keefer Pl NW

500

Kenyon St NW

29

Kenyon St NW

Kenyon St NW

Irving St NW

Irving St NW

500

B

Columbia
Heights

16

1200

Columbia Rd NW

Columbia Rd NW

Hobart Pl NW

Hobart Pl NW

Michigan Ave NW

Mc Millan Park

Harvard St NW

Harvard St NW

Harvard St NW

Gresham Pl NW

Gresham Pl NW

Girard St NW

Girard St NW

Girard St NW

McMillan Reservoir

Fairmont St NW

Fairmont St NW

Fairmont St NW

Girard St NW

Euclid St NW

Blackburn
University
Center

Fairmont St NW

Euclid St NW

11

C

Fairmont St NW

Euclid St NW

Clifton St NW

Clifton St NW

Banneker
Recreation
Center

**PAGE
228**

Howard Pl NW

Meridian
Hill Park

Chapin St NW

Belmont St NW

Howard U
Blackburn Center

College St NW

Belmont St NW

Belmont St NW

Florida Ave NW

3

Barry Pl NW

Bryant St NW

10

W St NW

Union Ct NW

Howard
University
Hospital

W St NW

V St NW

1/4 mile

.25 km

Plenty of newcomers are smiling about all the traffic and cranes around 14th Street. It's certainly changing fast around here. Thanks to the miracle of corporate welfare—er, tax increment financing—city elders have convinced Target and Best Buy to set up shop soon, to the rowdy cheers of the gentrifiers. Which proves that what all of us really want is to live in the suburbs.

Banks

- **Bank of America** · 3500 Georgia Ave NW
- **Bank of America (ATM)** · HU—West Tower · 2251 Sherman Ave NE
- **Bank of America (ATM)** · HU—Blackburn Bldg · 2397 6th St NW
- **Bank of America (ATM)** · 2400 14th St NW
- **Bank of America (ATM)** · HU—Admin building · 2400 6th St NW
- **Bank of America (ATM)** · 3031 14th St NW
- **Bank of America (ATM)** · HU—Drew Hall · 511 Gresham Pl NW
- **Chevy Chase (ATM)** · 1345 Park Rd NW
- **Chevy Chase (ATM)** · 3030 14th St NW
- **PNC** · 3300 14th St NW
- **Wachovia** · 2801 Georgia Ave NW
- **Wachovia** · 3325 14th St NW

 Car Rental

- **Enterprise** · 2730 Georgia Ave NW · 202-332-1716

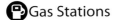 Gas Stations

- **Amoco** · 3426 Georgia Ave NW ⊙
- **Exxon** · 3540 14th St NW ⊙

○ Landmarks

- **Blackburn University Center** · 2400 6th St NW

Libraries

- **Howard University School of Business Library** · 2600 6th St NW

℞ Pharmacies

- **Columbia Heights CARE Pharmacy** · 3316 14th St NW
- **CVS** · 3031 14th St NW
- **Giant Food Pharmacy** · 1345 Park Rd NW

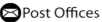 Police

- **MPDC 3rd District Substation** · 750 Park Rd NW

Post Offices

- **Columbia Heights Finance** · 3321 Georgia Ave NW
- **Howard University** · 2400 6th St NW

⊖ Schools

- **Banneker High** · 800 Euclid St NW
- **Booker T Washington Public Charter** · 1346 Florida Ave NW
- **Bruce-Monroe Elementary** · 3012 Georgia Ave NW
- **Cardozo High** · 1300 Clifton St NW
- **Carlos Rosario High** · 1100 Harvard St NW
- **DC Bilingual Public Charter** · 1420 Columbia Rd NW
- **EL Haynes Elementary** · 3029 14th St NW
- **Howard University** · 2400 6th St NW
- **Howard University Public Charter Middle** · 2731 Georgia Ave NW
- **Meridian Public Charter** · 1328 Florida Ave NW
- **Meyer Elementary** · 2501 11th St NW
- **Next Step/El Proximo Paso** · 1419 Columbia Rd NW
- **Park View Elementary** · 3560 Warder St NW
- **Paul Robeson Center Elementary** · 3700 10th St NW
- **Raymond Elementary** · 915 Spring Rd NW
- **Sankofa Fie** · 770 Park Rd NW
- **Tubman Elementary** · 3101 13th St NW
- **Youthbuild Public Charter** · 1419 Columbia Rd NW

 Supermarkets

- **Everlasting Life Community Grocery** · 2928 Georgia Ave NW
- **Giant Food** · 1345 Park Rd NW
- **San Cipriano Latin Grocery** · 3304 Georgia Ave NW

Map 15 · **Columbia Heights**

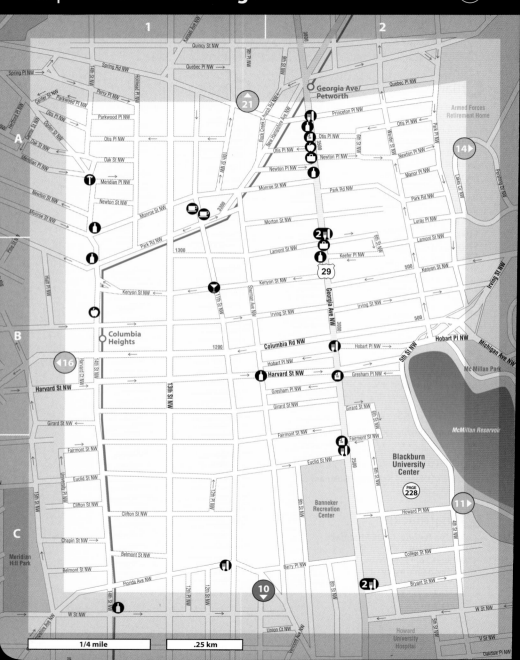

While you wait for that grotesque urban mall to open up at the metro, try a mini sloppy joe and a rye whiskey at Temperance Hall, or an oversized burger with cajun fries at Five Guys. And don't forget, DC bars go smoke-free in 2007, which ought to make trivia night more bearable at Wonderland.

Coffee
- **Columbia Heights Coffee** · 3416 11th St NW
- **Starbucks** · 2225 Georgia Ave NW

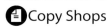Copy Shops
- **Bara Business Solutions** · 2851 Georgia Ave NW
- **General Services Notary and Copy Services** · 3613 Georgia Ave NW
- **Howard Copy** · 2618 Georgia Ave NW

Farmer's Markets
- **Columbia Heights Community Marketplace** May–Oct, Sat 8:30 am–1:30 pm) · 14th St NW & Irving St NW
- **Georgia-Petworth Farmer's Market** (Sat 9 am–1 pm) · 3600 Georgia Ave NW

Hardware Stores
- **Cooper Hardware** · 3459 14th St NW

Liquor Stores
- **CC Liquor** · 3401 14th St NW
- **Florida Liquors** · 2222 14th St NW
- **Giant Liquors** · 3504 Georgia Ave NW
- **Harvard Wine & Liquor Store** · 2901 Sherman Ave NW
- **Lion's Liquor** · 3614 Georgia Ave NW
- **Petworth Liquors** · 3210 Georgia Ave NW
- **Speedy Liquors** · 3328 14th St NW

Nightlife
- **Wonderland Ballroom** · 1101 Kenyon St NW

Restaurants
- **Brown's Caribbean Bakery** · 3301 Georgia Ave NW
- **Cluck U Chicken** · 2921 Georgia Ave NW
- **Five Guys** · 2301 Georgia Ave NW
- **Florida Ave Grill** · 1100 Florida Ave NW
- **Negril** · 2301 Georgia Ave NW
- **Rita's Caribbean Carryout** · 3322 Georgia Ave NW
- **Soul Vegetarian and Exodus Café** · 2606 Georgia Ave NW
- **Temperance Hall** · 3634 Georgia Ave NW

Shopping
- **Mom & Pop's Antiques** · 3534 Georgia Ave NW
- **Planet Chocolate City** · 3225 Georgia Ave NW

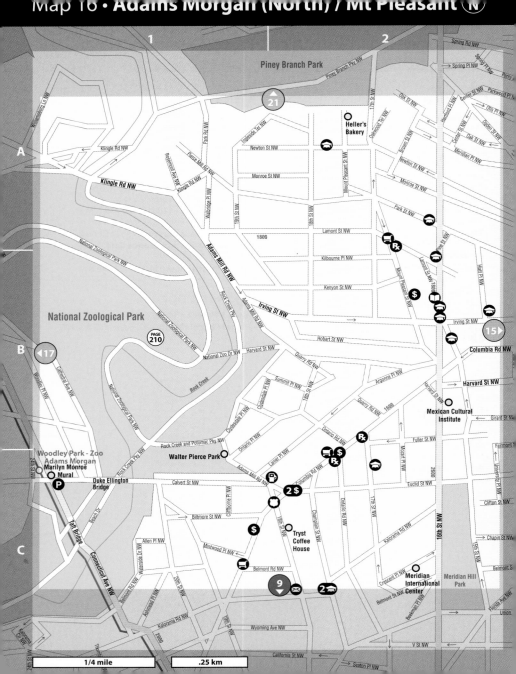

Map 16 • **Adams Morgan (North) / Mt Pleasant** N

Spring Rd NW
Spring Pl NW

Piney Branch Park

Piney Branch Pkwy NW

1

2

21

Spring Rd NW
Perry

Center St NW
Parkwood Pl NW

Oak St NW

17th St NW

Quintana Ter NW

Heller's Bakery

Otis Pl NW

Ogden St NW

Mount Pleasant St NW

Medical Pl NW

Center St NW
Oak St NW

Meridian Pl NW

Ingleside Ter NW

Newton St NW

A

Klingle Rd NW

Newton St NW

Monroe St NW

Monroe St NW

Park Rd NW

Park St NW

Klingle Rd NW

Pierce Mill Rd NW

Walbridge Pl NW

19th St NW

18th St NW

Lamont St NW

Lamont St NW 1800

Hiatt Pl NW

Rosemont Ave NW

Klingle Rd NW

Klingle Pl NW

1800

Kilbourne Pl NW

Adams Mill Rd NW

Irving St NW

Kenyon St NW

$

Mount Pleasant St NW

Rock Creek Pkwy

National Zoological Park NW

Irving St NW

15

Columbia Rd NW

National Zoological Park

PAGE 210

National Zoo Dr NW

Harvard St NW

Hobart St NW

Quarry Rd NW

Argonne Pl NW

Harvard St NW

B

17

Summit Pl NW

18th St NW

Quarry Rd NW 1600

Harvard St NW

Clydesdale Pl NW

Rock Creek

Mexican Cultural Institute

Girard St NW

Ontario Rd NW

Ontario Rd NW

Fuller St NW

Mozart Pl NW

Fairmont NW

National Zoological Park NW

Rock Creek and Potomac Pkwy

Walter Pierce Park

Ontario Pl NW

Lanier Pl NW

Columbia Rd NW

Rx

$

Rx

2600

University Pl NW

Woodley Park - Zoo Adams Morgan

24th St NW

Woodley Pl NW

Cathedral Ave NW

Marilyn Monroe Mural

P

Duke Ellington Bridge

Calvert St NW

Adams Mill Rd NW

Cliffbourne Pl NW

Euclid St NW

16th St NW

Clifton St NW

Beach Dr

Biltmore St NW

2 $

Chapin St NW

Cliffbourne Pl NW

18th St NW

Champlain St NW

Ontario Rd NW

Mt Pl NW

Kalorama Rd NW

19th St NW

18th St NW

Chapin St NW

Taft Bridge

C

Allen Pl NW

Mintwood Pl NW

$

Tryst Coffee House

Belmont St NW

29th St NW

Waterside Dr NW

Belmont Rd NW

Crescent Pl NW

Meridian International Center

Meridian Hill Park

Belmont NW

Connecticut Ave NW

Adams Mill Rd NW

9

2

Kalorama Rd NW

Beekman Pl NW

19th St NW

Wyoming Ave NW

Belmont St NW

Gordon Rd NW

Union

2000

Kalorama Cir NW

Tracy Pl NW

California St NW

Seaton Pl NW

V St NW

From the Salvadorian restaurants to the glut of Ethiopian eats to the frat house scene along 18th street, these two neighborhoods are where different races and ethnicities mix most in DC. Adams Morgan is the nightlife destination, especially for those who may or may not be of drinking age. Mt. Pleasant has fewer offerings, but those that are there are laid-back sanctuaries, set away from the rowdiness to the south.

Banks

- **Bank of America** · 1835 Columbia Rd NW
- **Bank of America** · 3131 Mt Pleasant St NW
- **Citibank** · 1749 1/2 Columbia Rd NW
- **PNC** · 1779 Columbia Rd NW
- **Sun Trust** · 1800 Columbia Rd NW

 Gas Stations

- **Exxon** · 1827 Adams Mill Rd NW ☺

o Landmarks

- **Heller's Bakery** · 3221 Mt Pleasant St NW
- **Marilyn Monroe Mural** ·
  Connecticut Ave NW & Calvert St NW
- **Meridian International Center** ·
  1630 Crescent Pl NW
- **Mexican Cultural Institute** · 2829 16th St NW
- **Tryst Coffee House** · 2459 18th St NW
- **Walter Pierce Park** · 2630 Adams Mill Rd NW

Libraries

- **Mt Pleasant Library** · 3160 16th St NW

Parking

Rx Pharmacies

- **CVS** · 1700 Columbia Rd NW
- **Mt Pleasant Care Pharmacy** ·
  3169 Mt Pleasant St NW
- **Safeway** · 1747 Columbia Rd NW

 Police

- **3rd District Latino Liaison Unit** ·
  1800 Columbia Rd NW

Post Offices

- **Kalorama Station** · 2300 18th St NW

Schools

- **Bancroft Elementary** · 1755 Newton St NW
- **Bell Multicultural High** · 3145 Hiatt Pl NW
- **Capital City Public Charter Elementary** ·
  3047 15th St NW
- **Cooke Elementary** · 2525 17th St NW
- **DC Alternative Learning Academy** ·
  3146 16th St NW
- **Elsie Whitlow Stokes Community Freedom** ·
  3200 16th St NW
- **Lincoln Middle** · 3101 16th St NW
- **Marie Reed Elementary** · 2200 Champlain St NW
- **Reed Learning Center** · 2200 Champlain St NW
- **Sacred Heart** · 1625 Park Rd NW

Supermarkets

- **Bestway** · 3178 Mt Pleasant St NW
- **Metro K IGA** · 1864 Columbia Rd NW
- **Safeway** · 1747 Columbia Rd NW

Map

These neighborhoods cater to the drinking crowd. A good day would start with nursing a hangover at the beloved Mt Pleasant institution Dos Gringos. Then, stumble down to wait for a window seat at Tryst, where you can linger over a sandwich. Or save the appetite for a perfectly seasoned steak at Rumba Café. By then you'll be ready for a bar crawl that will, inevitably, end with you shimmying to "Little Red Corvette" at Chief Ike's Mambo Room.

Coffee

- **Café Park Plaza** •
  1629 Columbia Rd NW
- **Caribou Coffee** • 2421 18th St NW
- **Crumbs And Coffee** •
  1737 Columbia Rd NW
- **Potter's House** •
  1658 Columbia Rd NW
- **Starbucks** • 1801 Columbia Rd NW
- **Tryst Coffeehouse and Bar** •
  2459 18th St NW

Copy Shops

- **Express Business Center** •
  3064 Mt Pleasant St NW
- **Tech Printing & Copy Center** •
  2479 18th St NW

Farmer's Markets

- **Adams Morgan
  (May–Dec, 8 am–2 pm)** •
  18th St & Columbia Rd NW
- **Mt Pleasant Farmers Market
  (May–Oct, Sat 9 am–1 pm)** •
  17th St NW & Lamont St NW

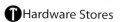 Gyms

- **Curves (women only)** •
  3220 17th St NW

Hardware Stores

- **Pfeiffer's Hardware** •
  3219 Mt Pleasant St NW

Liquor Stores

- **AB Liquor** • 1803 Columbia Rd NW
- **Bestway** • 3178 Mt Pleasant St NW
- **Lee Irving Liquors** •
  3100 Mt Pleasant St NW
- **Metro Liquors** • 1726 Columbia
  Rd NW
- **Sherry's Wine & Liquor** •
  2315 Calvert St NW
- **Sportsman's Wine & Liquors** •
  3249 Mt Pleasant St NW

Nightlife

- **Adams Mill Bar and Grill** •
  1813 Adams Mill Rd NW
- **Angles Bar & Billiards** •
  2339 18th St NW
- **Asylum** • 2471 18th St NW
- **Bedrock Billiards** •
  1841 Columbia Rd NW
- **Blue Room Lounge** •
  2321 18th St NW
- **Bossa** • 2463 18th St NW
- **Brass Monkey** • 2317 18th St NW
- **Bukom Café** • 2442 18th St NW
- **Chief Ike's Mambo Room** •
  1725 Columbia Rd NW
- **Columbia Station** • 2325 18th St NW
- **Crush** • 2323 18th St NW
- **Felix Lounge** • 2406 18th St NW
- **Kokopooli's Pool Hall** •
  2305 18th St NW
- **Left Bank** • 2424 18th St NW
- **Madam's Organ** • 2461 18th St NW
- **Pharaoh's** • 1817 Columbia Rd NW
- **Pharmacy Bar** • 2337 18th St NW
- **The Raven** • 3125 Mt Pleasant St NW
- **The Reef** • 2446 18th St NW
- **Rumba Café** • 2443 18th St NW
- **Spy Lounge** • 2406 18th St NW
- **Timehri International** •
  2439 18th St NW
- **Toledo Lounge** • 2435 18th St NW
- **Tom Tom** • 2333 18th St NW
- **Tonic Bar** • 3155 Mt Pleasant St NW
- **Zucchabar** • 1841 Columbia Rd NW

🍴 Restaurants

- **Amsterdam Falafel** •
  2425 18th St NW
- **Astor Restaurant** •
  1829 Columbia Rd NW
- **Bardia's New Orleans Café** •
  2412 18th St NW
- **Bukom Café** • 2442 18th St NW
- **Cashion's Eat Place** •
  1819 Columbia Rd NW
- **The Diner** • 2453 18th St NW ⊙
- **Dos Gringos** •
  3116 Mt Pleasant St NW
- **Felix Restaurant & Lounge** •
  2406 18th St NW
- **Grill From Ipanema** •
  1858 Columbia Rd NW

- **Haydee's** • 3102 Mt Pleasant St NW
- **La Fourchette** • 2429 18th St NW
- **Leftbank** • 2424 18th St NW
- **The Little Fountain Café** •
  2339 18th St NW
- **Mama Ayesha's** • 1967 Calvert St NW
- **Marx Café** • 3203 Mt Pleasant St NW
- **Meskerem Ethiopian Restaurant** •
  2434 18th St NW
- **Millie & Al's** • 2440 18th St NW
- **Mixtec** • 1729 Columbia Rd NW
- **Perry's** • 1811 Columbia Rd NW
- **Rumba Café** • 2443 18th St NW
- **Tonic** • 3155 Mt Pleasant St NW
- **Tono Sushi** •
  2605 Connecticut Ave NW
- **Tryst** • 2459 18th St NW

🛍 Shopping

- **Antiques Anonymous** •
  2627 Connecticut Ave NW
- **Brass Knob** • 2311 18th St NW
- **CD/Game Exchange** •
  2475 18th St NW
- **City Bikes** • 2501 Champlain St NW
- **Crooked Beat Records** •
  2318 18th St NW
- **Dada** • 1814 Adams Mill Rd NW
- **Demian** • 2427 18th St NW
- **Design Within Reach** •
  1838 Columbia Rd NW
- **Fleet Feet** • 1841 Columbia Rd NW
- **Idle Times Books** • 2467 18th St NW
- **Little Shop of Flowers** •
  2421 18th St NW
- **Miss Pixie's Furnishing and
  What-Not** • 2473 18th St NW
- **Radio Shack** • 1767 Columbia Rd NW
- **Shake Your Booty** • 2439 18th St NW
- **So's Your Mom** •
  1831 Columbia Rd NW
- **Trim** • 2700 Ontario Rd NW
- **Yes! Natural Gourmet** •
  1825 Columbia Rd NW

🔑 Video Rental

- **Blockbuster** • 1805 Columbia Rd NW
- **Dorchester Video** • 2480 16th St NW
- **Lamont Video** •
  3171 Mt Pleasant St NW
- **Video King** • 1845 Columbia Rd NW
- **Video Vault** • 113 S Columbus St

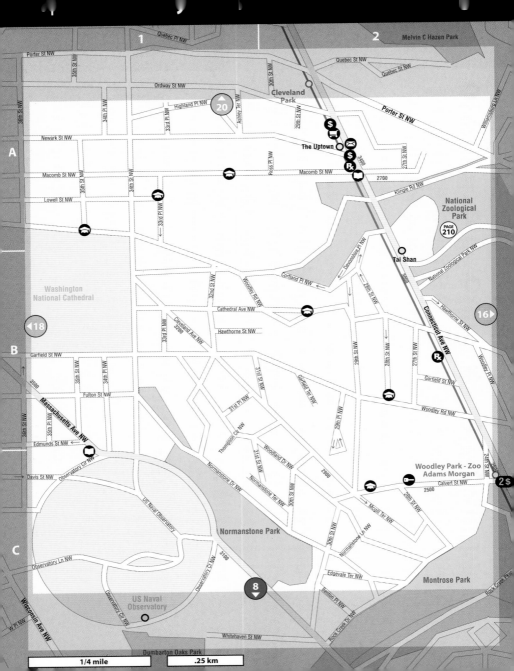

Essentials

Woodley Park and Cleveland Park have long stood proud as safe, residential neighborhoods. Sandwiched between the grand National Cathedral and the screaming mating calls of monkeys at the National Zoo, the gorgeous single-family homes of 20008 cost a pretty penny.

Banks

- **Bank of America** · 2631 Connecticut Ave NW
- **Bank of America** · 3401 Connecticut Ave NW
- **M&T** · 2620 Connecticut Ave NW
- **Sun Trust (ATM)** · 3435 Connecticut Ave NW

Car Rental

- **Enterprise** · 2601 Calvert St NW · 202-232-4443

oLandmarks

- **Tai Shan** · 3001 Connecticut Ave NW
- **The Uptown** · 3426 Connecticut Ave NW
- **US Naval Observatory** · Massachusetts Ave NW & Observatory Cir NW

Libraries

- **Cleveland Park Library** · 3310 Connecticut Ave NW
- **James Melville Gilliss Library** · 3450 Massachusetts Ave NW

Pharmacies

- **Cathedral CARE Pharmacy** · 3000 Connecticut Ave NW
- **CVS** · 3327 Connecticut Ave NW

Post Offices

- **Cleveland Park Station** · 3430 Connecticut Ave NW

Schools

- **Aidan Montessori** · 2700 27th St NW
- **Beauvoir-The National Cathedral Elementary** · 3500 Woodley Rd NW
- **Eaton Elementary** · 3301 Lowell St NW
- **Maret** · 3000 Cathedral Ave NW
- **Oyster Elementary** · 2801 Calvert St NW
- **Washington International (Tregaron Campus)** · 3100 Macomb St NW

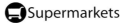Supermarkets

- **Brookville Supermarket** · 3427 Connecticut Ave NW

73

Map 17 · **Woodley Park / Cleveland Park**

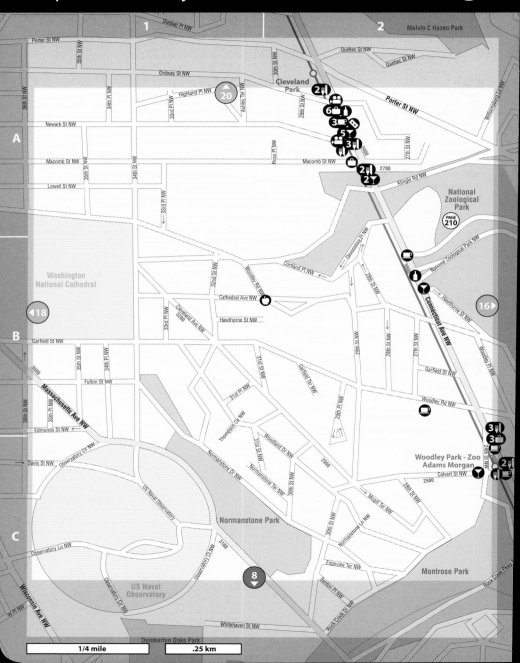

Cleveland Park

Porter St NW

National Zoological Park

PAGE 210

Washington National Cathedral

◀18

16▶

20

Woodley Park - Zoo Adams Morgan

Normanstone Park

Montrose Park

8

US Naval Observatory

| 1/4 mile | .25 km |

This stretch of Connecticut Avenue is composed of commercial clusters surrounding the Metro Stations and tall, unremarkable apartment tenements in between. But the strip boasts a number of top-notch restaurants that cater to a variety of palates, and the ornate Uptown Theater, featuring only one blockbuster hit at a time on single screen, is a DC institution. Arrive early to get a front-and-center seat in the balcony.

Coffee

- **Café International** · 2633 Connecticut Ave NW
- **Firehook Bakery & Coffee House** · 3411 Connecticut Ave NW
- **Open City** · 2331 Calvert St NW
- **Starbucks** · 2660 Woodley Rd NW
- **Starbucks** · 3000 Connecticut Ave NW
- **Starbucks** · 3420 Connecticut Ave NW

Farmer's Markets

- **All Souls Episcopal Church Farmers Market (May-December, Sat, 8:30 am–12:30 pm)** · Woodley Rd & Cathedral Ave NW

Liquor Stores

- **Cathedral Liquors** · 3000 Connecticut Ave NW
- **Cleveland Park Liquor & Wines** · 3423 Connecticut Ave NW

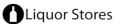Movie Theaters

- **Cineplex Odeon Uptown** · 3426 Connecticut Ave NW
- **Loews Cineplex** · 3426 Connecticut Ave NW

Nightlife

- **Aroma** · 3417 Connecticut Ave NW
- **Atomic Billiards** · 3427 Connecticut Ave NW
- **Bardeo** · 3311 Connecticut Ave NW
- **Cleveland Park Bar & Grill** · 3421 Connecticut Ave NW
- **Four Green Fields** · 3412 Connecticut Ave NW
- **Murphy's of DC** · 2609 24th St NW
- **Nanny O'Brien's** · 3319 Connecticut Ave NW
- **Oxford Tavern Zoo Bar** · 3000 Connecticut Ave NW
- **Uptown Tavern** · 3435 Connecticut Ave NW

Restaurants

- **Alero** · 3500 Connecticut Ave NW
- **Ardeo** · 3311 Connecticut Ave NW
- **Dino** · 3435 Connecticut Ave NW
- **Four Green Fields** · 3412 Connecticut Ave NW
- **Lavandou** · 3321 Connecticut Ave NW
- **Lebanese Taverna** · 2641 Connecticut Ave NW
- **Lex Cajun Grill** · 2608 Connecticut Ave NW
- **Mr Chen's Organic Chinese Cuisine** · 2604 Connecticut Ave NW
- **Nam Viet** · 3419 Connecticut Ave NW
- **Open City** · 2331 Calvert St NW
- **Petits Plats** · 2653 Connecticut Ave NW
- **Sake Club** · 2635 Connecticut Ave NW
- **Sorriso** · 3518 Connecticut Ave NW
- **Spices** · 3333A Connecticut Ave NW

Shopping

- **All Fired Up** · 3413 Connecticut Ave NW
- **Allan Woods Flowers** · 2645 Connecticut Ave NW
- **Bombe Chest** · 2629 Connecticut Ave NW
- **Designer Too Consignments** · 3404 Connecticut Ave NW
- **Guitar Gallery** · 3400 Connecticut Ave NW
- **Manhattan Market** · 2647 Connecticut Ave NW
- **Transcendence-Perfection-Bliss of the Beyond** · 3428 Connecticut Ave NW
- **Vace** · 3315 Connecticut Ave NW
- **Wake Up Little Suzie** · 3409 Connecticut Ave NW
- **Yes! Organic Market** · 3425 Connecticut Ave NW

Video Rental

- **Potomac Video** · 3418 Connecticut Ave NW

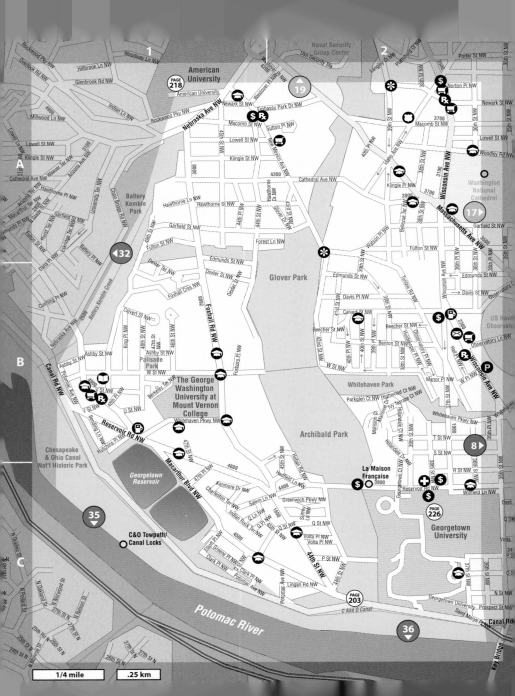

Bordering one of the most unappreciated green spaces in the District, Glover Park is populated largely by Georgetown grad students and gainfully employed 20-somethings wishing to come home to something lovely off the Metro beaten path. Foxhall, however, is so woody and exclusive that it doesn't even have its own bus route.

$ Banks

- **Chevy Chase** · 3800 Reservoir Rd NW
- **PNC (ATM)** · 3800 Reservoir Rd NW
- **PNC (ATM)** · 4100 Reservoir Rd NW
- **Sun Trust** · 3301 New Mexico Ave NW
- **Sun Trust** · 3440 Wisconsin Ave NW
- **Wachovia** · 3700 Calvert St NW

✳ Community Gardens

➕ Emergency Rooms

- **Georgetown University Hospital** · 3800 Reservoir Rd NW ⊙

⛽ Gas Stations

- **Chevron** · 2450 Wisconsin Ave NW
- **Exxon** · 4812 MacArthur Blvd NW

○ Landmarks

- **C&O Towpath/Canal Locks** · Along the Potomac River
- **La Maison Française** · 4101 Reservoir Rd NW
- **National Cathedral** · Massachusetts Ave NW & Wisconsin Ave NW

📖 Libraries

- **Palisades Library** · 4901 V St NW

P Parking

℞ Pharmacies

- **CVS** · 2226 Wisconsin Ave NW
- **CVS** · 4859 MacArthur Blvd
- **Giant Food Pharmacy** · 3406 Wisconsin Ave NW
- **Rite Aid** · 3301 New Mexico Ave NW

⊙ Police

- **MPDC 2nd District Station** · 3320 Idaho Ave NW

✉ Post Offices

- **Calvert Station** · 2336 Wisconsin Ave NW

🎓 Schools

- **Annunciation** · 3825 Klingle Pl NW
- **The Field School** · 2301 Foxhall Rd NW
- **George Washington University at Mount Vernon College** · Foxhill Rd NW & W St NW
- **Georgetown Day Lower** · 4530 MacArthur Blvd NW
- **Georgetown University** · 37th St NW & O St NW
- **Hope Community Public Charter** · 3855 Massachusetts Ave NW
- **Lab School of Washington** · 4759 Reservoir Rd NW
- **Mann Elementary** · 4430 Newark St NW
- **National Cathedral** · 3612 Woodley Rd NW
- **Our Lady of Victory** · 4755 Whitehaven Pkwy NW
- **River** · 4880 MacArthur Blvd NW
- **Rock Creek International Lower** · 1550 Foxhall Rd NW
- **St Albans** · 3665 Massachusetts Ave NW
- **St Patrick's Episcopal Day** · 4700 Whitehaven Pkwy NW
- **Stoddert Elementary** · 4001 Calvert St NW
- **Washington International Primary** · 1690 36th St NW

🛒 Supermarkets

- **Balducci's** · 3201 New Mexico Ave NW
- **Giant Food** · 3336 Wisconsin Ave NW
- **Giant Food** · 3406 Wisconsin Ave NW
- **Safeway** · 4865 MacArthur Blvd NW
- **Whole Foods Market** · 2323 Wisconsin Ave NW

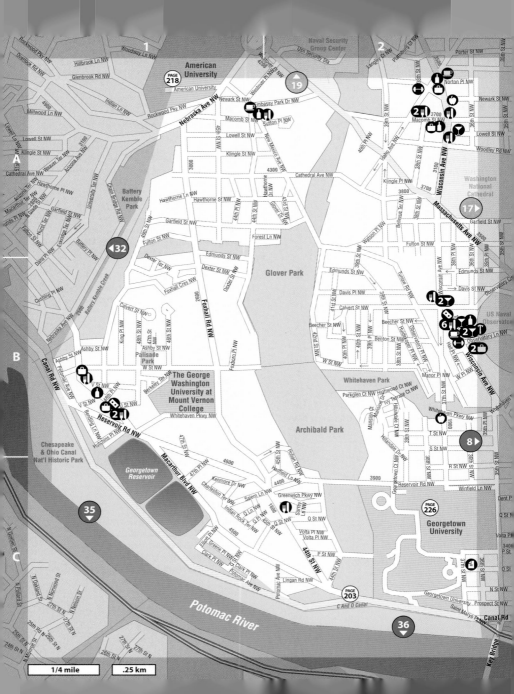

The intersection of Macomb and Wisconsin is home to some of the finest eats in the city, including 2 Amys' heavenly Neapolitan pizza pies. Glover Park dining holds its own as well, with a few nice local bars to boot. But if it's neighborhood charm you're after, there's not much doing off the main drag.

Coffee

- **Starbucks** · 2302 Wisconsin Ave NW
- **Starbucks** · 3301 New Mexico Ave NW
- **Starbucks** · 3430 Wisconsin Ave NW

Copy Shops

- **UPS Store** · 1419 37th St NW

Farmer's Markets

- **New Morning Farm Market (Mar–Dec, Sat, 11:30 am–1:30 pm)** · 37th St NW & Newark St NW
- **New Morning Farm Market (Mar–Dec, Tues, 7 pm–8 pm)** · 37th St & Whitehaven Pwy NW

Gyms

- **Curves (women only)** · 3414 Idaho Ave NW
- **Washington Sports Clubs** · 2251 Wisconsin Ave NW

Hardware Stores

- **Glover Park Hardware** · 2251 Wisconsin Ave NW

Liquor Stores

- **Ace Beverage** · 3301 New Mexico Ave NW
- **Burkas Wine & Liquor Store** · 3500 Wisconsin Ave NW
- **MacArthur Beverages** · 4877 MacArthur Blvd NW
- **Papa's Liquor** · 3703 Macomb St NW
- **Pearson's Liquor & Wine Annex** · 2436 Wisconsin Ave NW

Nightlife

- **Bourbon** · 2348 Wisconsin Ave NW
- **The Deck** · 2505 Wisconsin Ave NW
- **Good Guys Restaurant** · 2311 Wisconsin Ave NW
- **Grog and Tankard** · 2408 Wisconsin Ave NW
- **JP's Nite Club** · 2505 Wisconsin Ave NW
- **Zebra Lounge** · 3238 Wisconsin Ave NW

Restaurants

- **2 Amys** · 3715 Macomb St NW
- **BlackSalt** · 4883 MacArthur Blvd NW
- **Busara** · 2340 Wisconsin Ave NW
- **Cactus Cantina** · 3300 Wisconsin Ave NW
- **Café Deluxe** · 3228 Wisconsin Ave NW
- **Heritage India** · 2400 Wisconsin Ave NW
- **Jetties** · 1609 Foxhall Rd NW
- **Kotobuki** · 4822 MacArthur Blvd NW, 2nd floor
- **Makoto Restaurant** · 4822 MacArthur Blvd NW
- **Max's Best Ice Cream** · 2616 Wisconsin Ave NW
- **My Bakery & Café** · 2233 Wisconsin Ave NW
- **Rocklands** · 2418 Wisconsin Ave NW
- **Sushi-Ko** · 2309 Wisconsin Ave NW
- **Town Hall** · 2218 Wisconsin Ave NW

Shopping

- **Ann Hand Collection** · 4885 Macarthur Blvd NW
- **Encore Resale Dress Shop** · 3715 Macomb St NW
- **Inga's Once Is Not Enough** · 4830 MacArthur Blvd NW
- **The Kellogg Collection** · 3424 Wisconsin Ave NW
- **Sullivan's Toy Store** · 3412 Wisconsin Ave NW
- **Theodore's** · 2233 Wisconsin Ave NW
- **Treetop Toys** · 3301 New Mexico Ave NW
- **Vespa Washington** · 2233 Wisconsin Ave NW

Video Rental

- **Blockbuster** · 2332 Wisconsin Ave NW
- **Potomac Video** · 4828 MacArthur Blvd NW

Friendship
Heights

Military Rd NW

Willard Ave
Friendship Blvd
Wisconsin Cir
Legation St NW
Chevy Chase Pkwy NW
Nevada St NW

Western Ave NW
Bells Ln NW
4200
29
3800
3700

MARYLAND
WASHINGTON DC

Sheridan Ave
Dalton Rd
Merivale Rd
Cortland Rd
Chandler Rd
43rd St NW
42nd Pl NW
41st St NW
Kanawha St NW
Jocelyn St NW
Connecticut Ave NW
5300

Westport Rd
5200
Jenifer St NW
39th St NW
38th St NW
Ingomar St NW

A
Keokuk St NW
Cooper Ln
Brookdale Rd
Dorsett Pl
Harrison Rd
Hanover Rd
Ingomar St NW
4200
Huntington St NW
3700
Muhlenberg
Park

Fort Bayard
Park
Park Pl
Brandywine St NW
Harrison St NW
4500
Gramercy St NW
Garrison St NW
3600
Garrison St NW

Garrison St NW
3 $
Fessenden St NW

Faraday Pl NW
Rx
4100
Everett St NW
320

$
Fessenden St NW
Bell Rd NW
Dr Russey St NW
Fort Dr NW
Reno Rd NW

Emery Pl NW

Ellicott St NW
Donaldson Pl NW
Grant Rd NW
Cumberland St NW

River Rd NW
4700
43rd St NW
Davenport St NW
Fort
Reno
Park
Chesapeake St NW

Davenport St NW
Rx
Wisconsin Ave NW

Chesapeake St NW

Burlington Pl NW
Brandywine St NW

Brandywine NW
43rd St NW
Appleton St NW

B
4800
47th St NW
46th St NW
Murdock Mill Rd NW
Butterworth Pl NW
4100
$
40th St NW
Fort Dr NW
Grant Rd NW
Albemarle St NW
20▶

4500
Albemarle St NW
Rx
Alton Pl NW

Alton Pl NW
Tenleytown - AU
Grant Rd NW

◀30
Yuma St NW
$
Yuma St NW

Windom Pl NW
Tenley
Circle NW

Warren St NW
Windom Pl NW

Verplank Pl NW
Verplanck Pl NW
Warren St NW
$
Warren St NW

4200
Van Ness St NW
Veazey St NW
41st St NW
40th St NW
39th St NW
Wisconsin Ave NW
P

International Ct NW
4800

Upton St NW
Tindall St NW
Upton St NW
Tilden St NW
37th St NW

Wesley
Circle NW
45th St NW
Springdale St NW
Springland Ln NW

Tilden St NW
Sedgwick St NW
44th St NW
Nebraska Ave NW

Sedgwick St NW
$
Rodman St NW
Rodman St NW

Rodman St NW
Clover
Parkway
Idaho Ave NW
3800
Quebec St NW

PAGE
218
$
American
University
Ward
Circle NW
Naval Security
Group Center
38th St NW
Porter St NW
35th St NW

Quebec Pl NW
University Ave NW
Corey Pl NW

Woodway Ln NW
Massachusetts Ave NW
Weslaw Pl NW
3700
4200
Langley Ct NW
Pontiaca Ct NW
Norton Pl NW

18
Embassy Park Dr NW
Newark St NW

1/4 mile
.25 km

If you want the feel of the suburbs without sacrificing the DC address, this is your neighborhood. Upscale retail and casual dining line the major streets while the close proximity of the neighborhoods allow you to easily get around on foot. This area proves you can live inside the city and still enjoy as bland as an existence as any other God-fearing American suburb.

Map 19

$ Banks

- **Bank of America** · 5201 Wisconsin Ave NW
- **BB&T** · 5200 Wisconsin Ave NW
- **Chevy Chase** · 4000 Wisconsin Ave NW
- **Chevy Chase** · American U ·
  4400 Massachusetts Ave NW
- **Citibank** · 5001 Wisconsin Ave NW
- **M&T (ATM)** · 4530 40th St NW
- **PNC** · 4249 Wisconsin Ave NW
- **PNC** · 5252 Wisconsin Ave NW
- **Sun Trust (ATM)** · American U ·
  4400 Massachusetts Ave NW
- **Wachovia** · 5100 Wisconsin Ave NW

Car Rental

- **Alamoot Rent A Car** · 3314 Wisconsin Ave NW ·
  202-390-7544

Car Washes

- **H&C Car Wash** · 4837 Wisconsin Ave NW
- **Wash & Shine** · 5020 Wisconsin Ave NW

Community Gardens

Gas Stations

- **Amoco** · 4900 Wisconsin Ave NW
- **Exxon** · 4244 Wisconsin Ave NW ⊚

Landmarks

- **Fort Reno** · Ft Reno Park

Libraries

- **American University Library** ·
  4400 Massachusetts Ave NW
- **Tenley-Friendship Library** ·
  4450 Wisconsin Ave NW

P Parking

Rx Pharmacies

- **CVS** · 4555 Wisconsin Ave ⊚
- **Rodman's Pharmacy** · 5100 Wisconsin Ave NW
- **Safeway** · 4203 Davenport St NW

Schools

- **American University** ·
  4400 Massachusetts Ave NW
- **DC Alternative Learning Academy/West** ·
  3920 Alton Pl NW
- **Deal Junior High** · 3815 Fort Dr NW
- **Georgetown Day Upper** · 4200 Davenport St NW
- **Hearst Elementary** · 3950 37th St NW
- **Janney Elementary** · 4130 Albermarle St NW
- **National Presbyterian** · 4121 Nebraska Ave NW
- **Potomac College** · 4000 Chesapeake St NW
- **Rose** · 4820 Howard St NW
- **Sidwell Friends** · 3825 Wisconsin Ave NW
- **St Ann's Academy** · 4404 Wisconsin Ave NW
- **Wesley Theological Seminary** ·
  4500 Massachusetts Ave NW
- **Wilson High** · 3950 Chesapeake St NW

Supermarkets

- **Safeway** · 4203 Davenport St NW
- **Whole Foods Market** · 4530 40th St NW

81

Map 19 • **Tenleytown / Friendship Heights**

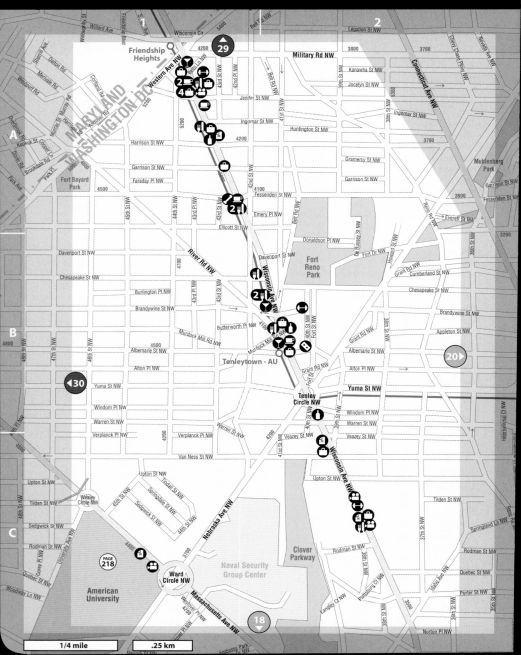

Map 1

A suburbanite's oasis, this area is one of the few places in the city with a Brooks' Brothers, Tiffany's, and Saks 5th Avenue on the same block (see map 29). If you're a fan of high-end shopping and crime-free streets, this is the neighborhood for you. And yes, there is a Starbucks, too.

 Coffee

- **Connie's Café** · 4224 Fessenden St NW
- **Cosi** · 5252 Wisconsin Ave NW
- **Mazza Café** · 5300 Wisconsin Ave NW
- **Starbucks** · 4513 Wisconsin Ave NW
- **Starbucks** · 5335 Wisconsin Ave NW

 Copy Shops

- **FedEx Kinko's** · 5225 Wisconsin Ave NW
- **Kwik Kopy Printing** · 4000 Wisconsin Ave NW
- **UPS Store** · 4200 Wisconsin Ave NW
- **UPS Store** · 4410 Massachusetts Ave NW

Gyms

- **Sport & Health Clubs** · 4000 Wisconsin Ave NW
- **Sport & Health Clubs** · 4001 Brandywine St NW
- **Washington Sports Clubs** · 5345 Wisconsin Ave NW

Liquor Stores

- **Paul's Wine & Liquors** · 5205 Wisconsin Ave NW
- **Tenley Mini Market** · 4326 Wisconsin Ave NW
- **Tenley Wine & Liquors** · 4525 Wisconsin Ave NW

Movie Theaters

- **AMC Mazza Gallerie 7** · 5300 Wisconsin Ave NW
- **American University Wechsler Theatre** · 4400 Massachusetts Ave NW
- **Cineplex Odeon Wisconsin Avenue Cinemas** · 4000 Wisconsin Ave NW
- **Loews Cineplex** · 4000 Wisconsin Ave NW

Nightlife

- **Guapo's** · 4515 Wisconsin Ave NW
- **Maggiano's** · 5333 Wisconsin Ave NW
- **Malt Shop** · 4615 Wisconsin Ave NW

 Pet Shops

- **Metro Pet** · 4220 Fessenden St NW

Restaurants

- **4912 Thai Cuisine** · 4912 Wisconsin Ave NW
- **Bambule** · 5225 Wisconsin Ave NW
- **Café Ole** · 4000 Wisconsin Ave NW
- **Guapos Mexican Cuisine & Cantina** · 4515 Wisconsin Ave NW
- **K's New York Deli** · 4620 Wisconsin Ave NW
- **Maggiano's Little Italy** · 5333 Wisconsin Ave NW
- **Matisse** · 4934 Wisconsin Ave NW
- **Murasaki** · 4620 Wisconsin Ave NW
- **Osman's and Joe's Steak 'n Egg Kitchen** · 4700 Wisconsin Ave NW ⊙

Shopping

- **Borders** · 5333 Wisconsin Ave NW
- **The Container Store** · 4500 Wisconsin Ave NW
- **Elizabeth Arden Red Door Salon & Spa** · 5225 Wisconsin Ave NW
- **Georgette Klinger** · 5345 Wisconsin Ave NW
- **Hudson Trail Outfitters** · 4530 Wisconsin Ave NW
- **Johnson's Florist & Garden Centers** · 4200 Wisconsin Ave NW
- **Loehmann's** · 5333 Wisconsin Ave NW
- **Neiman Marcus** · 5300 Wisconsin Ave NW
- **Pottery Barn** · 5345 Wisconsin Ave NW
- **Roche Bobois** · 5301 Wisconsin Ave NW
- **Rodman's** · 5100 Wisconsin Ave NW
- **Serenity Day Spa** · 4000 Wisconsin Ave NW

Video Rental

- **Hollywood Video** · 4530 40th St NW

Self-satisfied liberals unite! These blocks are dominated by well-meaning professionals who carry their own bags to the organic market, shun fancy restaurants for Vietnamese and enjoy the debates at Politics & Prose. But don't get too radical; they like their coffeehouses grunge-free.

Banks

- **Bank of America** · 4201 Connecticut Ave NW
- **Chevy Chase** · 3519 Connecticut Ave NW
- **Chevy Chase** · 4455 Connecticut Ave NW
- **PNC** · 3400 International Dr NW
- **PNC (ATM)** · 3003 Van Ness St NW
- **PNC (ATM)** · 4000 Connecticut Ave NW
- **Sun Trust** · 5000 Connecticut Ave NW
- **Wachovia** · 4340 Connecticut Ave NW

Car Rental

- **Avis** · 4400 Connecticut Ave NW · 202-686-5149

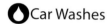 Car Washes

- **Connecticut Avenue Brushless** ·
  4432 Connecticut Ave NW

 Community Gardens

 Gas Stations

- **Amoco** · 5001 Connecticut Ave NW ⊙
- **Exxon** · 3535 Connecticut Ave NW ⊙
- **Exxon** · 5030 Connecticut Ave NW ⊙
- **Shell** · 4500 Connecticut Ave NW
- **Sunoco** · 4940 Connecticut Ave NW

Landmarks

- **Hillwood Museum & Gardens** ·
  4155 Linnean Ave NW
- **Pierce Mill** · 2401 Tilden St NW
- **Rock Creek Park Nature Center and
  Planetarium** · 5200 Glover Rd NW

Parking

Pharmacies

- **CVS** · 4309 Connecticut Ave NW
- **CVS** · 5013 Connecticut Ave NW

Schools

- **Auguste Montessori** · 3600 Ellicott St NW
- **Edmund Burke** · 2955 Upton St NW
- **Franklin Montessori** · 4473 Connecticut Ave NW
- **Montessori of Chevy Chase** ·
  5312 Connecticut Ave NW
- **Murch Elementary** · 4810 36th St NW
- **Sheridan** · 4400 36th St NW
- **University of the District of Columbia** ·
  4200 Connecticut Ave NW

Outside of Virginia's immigrant neighborhoods, this area has the best sampling of worldly menus. Delhi Dhaba, Indique, and Sala Thai are all worth the trek. Politics & Prose is one of the city's best bookstores and regularly hosts major-league literati.

Coffee

- **Politics & Prose** ·
  5015 Connecticut Ave NW
- **Sirius Coffee Company** ·
  4250 Connecticut Ave NW

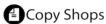Copy Shops

- **Office Depot** · 4455 Connecticut Ave NW
- **UPS Store** · 4401 Connecticut Ave NW

Farmer's Markets

- **New Morning Farm Market**
  (Jun–Mar, Sat 8 am–1 pm;
  Jun–Sept, Tue 4:30–8 pm) ·
  36th St NW & Alton Pl NW

Gyms

- **City Fitness Gym** · 3525 Connecticut Ave NW
- **Gold's Gym** · 4310 Connecticut Ave NW

Liquor Stores

- **Calvert Woodley Liquors** ·
  4339 Connecticut Ave NW
- **Sheffield Wine & Liquor Shoppe** ·
  5025 Connecticut Ave NW
- **Van Ness Liquors** · 4201 Connecticut Ave NW

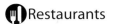Pet Shops

- **Pet Pantry** · 4455 Connecticut Ave NW
- **Petco** · 3505 Connecticut Ave NW

Restaurants

- **Buck's Fishing & Camping** ·
  5031 Connecticut Ave NW
- **Delhi Dhaba** · 4455 Connecticut Ave NW
- **Indique** · 3512 Connecticut Ave NW
- **Palena** · 3529 Connecticut Ave NW
- **Sala Thai** · 3507 Connecticut Ave NW

Shopping

- **Calvert Woodley Liquors** ·
  4339 Connecticut Ave NW
- **Design Within Reach** · 4828 St Elmo Ave
- **Marvelous Market** · 5035 Connecticut Ave NW
- **Politics & Prose** · 5015 Connecticut Ave NW

Video Rental

- **Blockbuster** · 3519 Connecticut Ave NW

Map 21 · **16th Street Heights / Petworth**

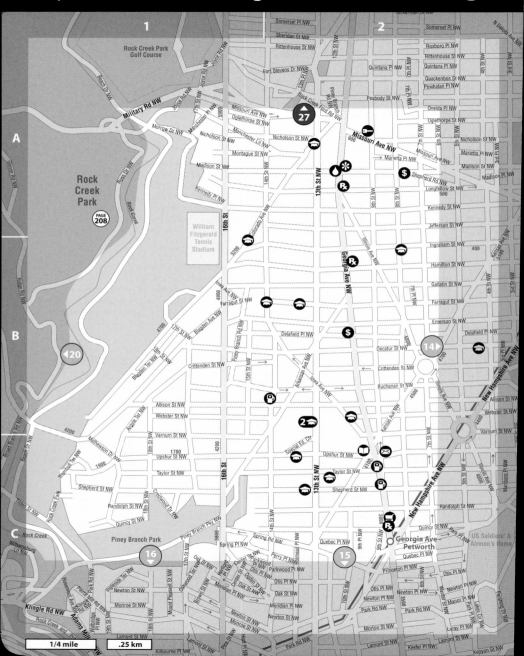

Essentials

Petworth, a longtime solid residential haven, has recently been "discovered" by upstarts in search of a solid residential haven. The influx has lead to spiking real estate costs and some grumbling from the ol' timers. But come on, where are all the liberals priced out of Logan Circle and Dupont supposed to go?

Banks

- **Chevy Chase (ATM)** • 700 Madison St NW
- **Industrial** • 4812 Georgia Ave NW

 Car Rental

- **Enterprise** • 927 Missouri Ave NW • 202-726-6600

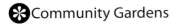 Car Washes

- **Car Wash Express** • 5758 Georgia Ave NW

Community Gardens

Gas Stations

- **Exxon** • 4501 14th St NW ⊗
- **Shell** • 4000 Georgia Ave NW
- **Shell** • 4140 Georgia Ave NW

 Libraries

- **Petworth Library** • 4200 Kansas Ave NW

Pharmacies

- **CVS** • 5227 Georgia Ave NW
- **Rite Aid** • 5600 Georgia Ave NW
- **Safeway** • 3830 Georgia Ave NW

Post Offices

- **Petworth Station** • 4211 9th St NW

 Schools

- **The Academy for Ideal Education Lower** • 1501 Gallatin St NW
- **Barnard Elementary** • 430 Decatur St NW
- **Brightwood Elementary** • 1300 Nicholson St NW
- **British School of Washington** • 4715 16th St NW
- **Clark Elementary** • 4501 7th St NW
- **Community Academy** • 1300 Allison St NW
- **High Road** • 1246 Taylor St NW
- **Ideal Alternative** • 5331 Colorado Ave NW
- **Kingsbury Day** • 5000 14th St NW
- **Macfarland Middle** • 4400 Iowa Ave NW
- **Parkmont** • 4842 16th St NW
- **Paul Junior High** • 5800 8th St NW
- **Powell Elementary** • 1350 Upshur St NW
- **Roosevelt High** • 4301 13th St NW
- **Sharpe Health** • 4300 13th St NW
- **St Gabriel** • 510 Webster St NW
- **Tots Developmental** • 1317 Shepherd St NW
- **Truesdell Elementary** • 800 Ingraham St NW
- **West Elementary** • 1338 Farragut St NW

Supermarkets

- **Safeway** • 3830 Georgia Ave NW

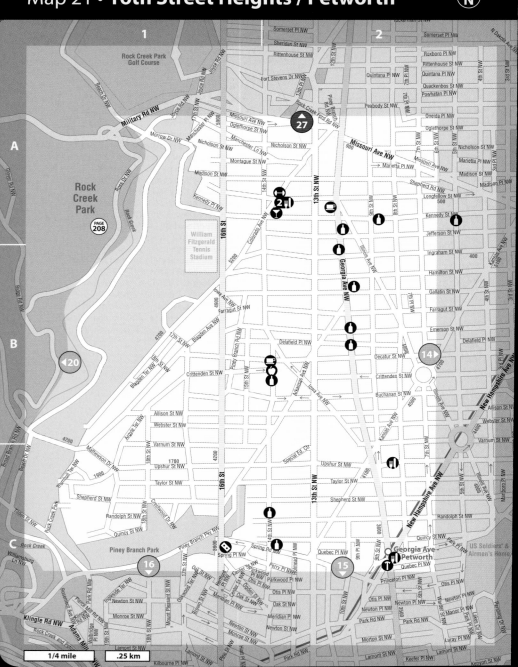

Map 21 · **16th Street Heights / Petworth**

Everything at Colorado Kitchen is fabulous—just mind your manners as the chef is a touchy about the menu and the knickknacks. Domku offers a curious attempt at New York attitude while serving Scandinavian food. And Sweet Mango has great jerk chicken, if you don't mind it leaking out of the Styrofoam container dropped sideways into your takeout bag. Otherwise, the sturdy residential core here has resisted more overt commercialization.

Coffee

- **Java and Cream** · 5522 Georgia Ave NW
- **Mocha Hut** · 4706 14th St NW

Farmer's Markets

- **14th St Heights Community Market**
  (Tues, 7 am–5:30 pm, Sat 7 am–6 pm,
  Sun 7 am–2 pm) · 14th St NW & Crittenden St NW

Gyms

- **Curves (women only)** · 5521 Colorado Ave NW

Hardware Stores

- **Capitol Locksmith** · 3655 Georgia Ave NW

Liquor Stores

- **Colony Liquor & Groceries** ·
  4901 Georgia Ave NW
- **Decatur Liquors** · 4704 14th St NW
- **Hamilton Wine & Liquor Store** ·
  5205 Georgia Ave NW
- **Herman's Liquor Store** · 3712 14th St NW
- **J-B Liquors** · 3914 14th St NW
- **Jefferson Liquor Store** · 5307 Georgia Ave NW
- **LA Casa Morata** · 5421 Georgia Ave NW
- **Rocket Liquors** · 900 Kennedy St NW
- **Target Liquor** · 500 Kennedy St NW
- **Three Way Liquor Store** · 4823 Georgia Ave NW

Nightlife

- **Twins Lounge** · 5516 Colorado Ave NW

Restaurants

- **Colorado Kitchen** · 5515 Colorado Ave NW
- **Domku** · 821 Upshur St NW
- **Frio Frio Deli Café** · 5517 Colorado Ave NW
- **Sweet Mango Café** ·
  3701 New Hampshire Ave NW

Video Rental

- **Woodner Video** · 3636 16th St NW

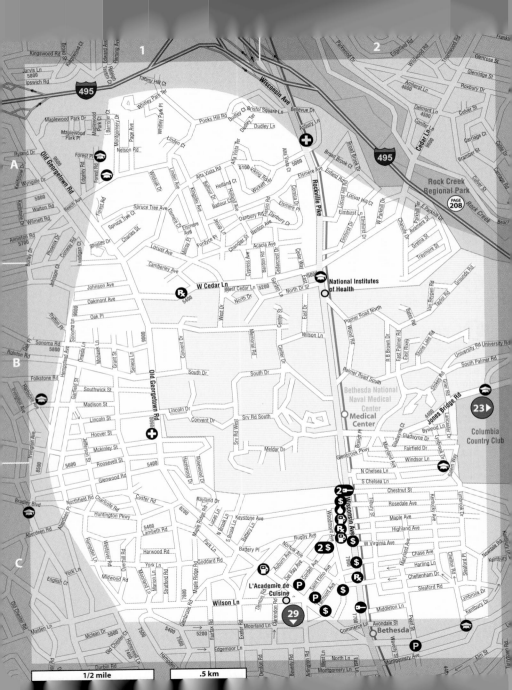

Downtown Bethesda is about business and money, and if you don't have either one, then you might want to move along—or at least get off Wisconsin Ave. It's down the side streets and away from the hotels, office buildings, and roving tribes of suits that you may find the unexpected art gallery, restaurant, or inviting public space.

Banks

- **Chevy Chase** · 4825 Cordell Ave
- **Chevy Chase** · 7700 Old Georgetown Rd
- **Citibank** · 8001 Wisconsin Ave
- **Eagle** · 7815 Woodmont Ave
- **Sandy Spring (ATM)** · 8240 Wisconsin Ave
- **Sun Trust (ATM)** · 4836 Cordell Ave
- **Wachovia** · 7901 Wisconsin Ave

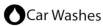 Car Rental

- **Budget** · 8400 Wisconsin Ave · 301-816-6000
- **Enterprise** · 7725 Wisconsin Ave · 301-907-7780
- **Sears Rent A Car & Truck** · 8400 Wisconsin Ave · 301-816-6050

 Car Washes

- **Bethesda Texaco** · 8240 Wisconsin Ave

⊕ Emergency Rooms

- **National Naval Medical Center** · 8901 Wisconsin Ave ⊚
- **Suburban** · 8600 Old Georgetown Rd ⊚

⬤ Gas Stations

- **Amoco** · 8101 Wisconsin Ave
- **Exxon** · 7975 Old Georgetown Rd ⊚
- **Texaco** · 8240 Wisconsin Ave

○ Landmarks

- **L'Academie de Cuisine** · 5021 Wilson Ln
- **National Institutes of Health** · 9000 Rockville Pike

Parking

Pharmacies

- **CVS** · 7809 Wisconsin Ave ⊚
- **Foer's CARE Pharmacy** · 8218 Wisconsin Ave
- **Village Green CARE Apothecary** · 5415 W Cedar Ln

⬤ Schools

- **Bethesda Country Day** · 5615 Beech Ave
- **Bethesda-Chevy Chase High** · 4301 East West Hwy
- **Bradley Hills Elementary** · 8701 Hartsdale Ave
- **French International** · 7108 Bradley Blvd
- **Glenmont** · 8001 Lynnbrook Dr
- **Lycee Rochambeau** · 9600 Forest Rd
- **Stone Ridge** · 9101 Rockville Pike
- **Uniformed Services University** · 4301 Jones Bridge Rd

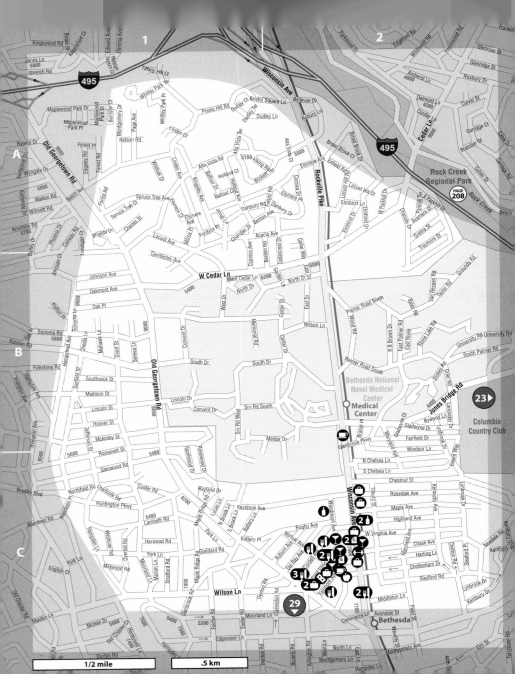

Map 22

This little city outside the real city can be impersonal for the single or childless, but residences in the new apartments built through the Woodmont Ave corridor have made Bethesda livelier. And while there is a good movie theater (Map 29) and a bunch of destinations restaurants, it's just hard to escape the feeling that this place is sort of like a cleaned-up, movie-set version of a real city.

Coffee

- **Dunkin' Donuts** · 8901 Wisconsin Ave
- **Starbucks** · 7700 Norfolk Ave

 Copy Shops

- **MBC Precision Imaging** · 7934 Wisconsin Ave
- **Minuteman Press** · 8001 Wisconsin Ave
- **Reprographic Technologies** · 7902 Woodmont Ave

 Farmer's Markets

- **Bethesda Farmers Market (May–Oct, Tues, 10:30 am–2 pm)** · Norfolk Ave & Woodmont Ave

Gyms

- **Fitness First** · 7900 Wisconsin Ave NW

Liquor Stores

- **Bethesda Beer & Wine** · 8015 Wisconsin Ave
- **Dunmor's** · 8013 Woodmont Ave
- **World Market** · 8125 Wisconsin Ave

 Nightlife

- **Flanagan's Harp and Fiddle** · 4844 Cordell Ave
- **Rock Bottom Brewery** · 7900 Norfolk Ave
- **Saphire** · 7940 Wisconsin Ave
- **South Beach Café** · 7904 Woodmont Ave

Restaurants

- **Bacchus** · 7945 Norfolk Ave
- **Buon Giorno** · 8003 Norfolk Ave
- **Faryab** · 4917 Cordell Ave
- **Grapeseed** · 4865 Cordell Ave
- **Haandi** · 4904 Fairmont Ave
- **Matuba** · 4918 Cordell Ave
- **Olazzo** · 7921 Norfolk Ave
- **The Original Pancake House** · 7700 Wisconsin Ave
- **Rock Creek Restaurant** · 4917 Elm St
- **Tako Grill** · 7756 Wisconsin Ave
- **Tragara** · 4935 Cordell Ave

Shopping

- **Big Planet Comics** · 4908 Fairmont Ave
- **Daisy Too** · 4940 St Elmo Ave
- **Promise For the Savvy Bride** · 8301 Wisconsin Ave
- **The Purse Store** · 8211 Wisconsin Ave
- **Ranger Surplus** · 8008 Wisconsin Ave
- **Second Story Books & Antiques** · 4914 Fairmont Ave
- **Takoma Park/Silver Spring Co-op** · 201 Ethan Allen Ave
- **Zelaya** · 4940 St Elmo Ave

Video Rental

- **Version Francaise (French only)** · 4930 St Elmo Ave

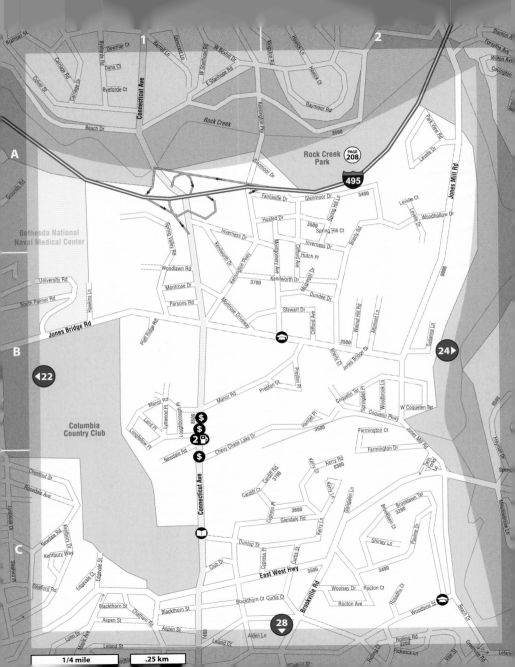

You might as well be on location at a Smith & Hawken catalog shoot. The fussy homes and landscaping here make it a sought-after suburb for those who don't mind driving everywhere or pretending they don't mind they're not in the slightly more prestigious Chevy Chase zip code.

Banks

- **Chevy Chase** · 8401 Connecticut Ave
- **Chevy Chase (ATM)** · 8531 Connecticut Ave
- **Sun Trust** · 8510 Connecticut Ave

Gas Stations

- **Citgo** · 8505 Connecticut Ave
- **Sunoco** · 8500 Connecticut Ave

Libraries

- **Chevy Chase Library** · 8005 Connecticut Ave

Schools

- **Lycee Rochambeau** · 3200 Woodbine St
- **North Chevy Chase Elementary** ·
  3700 Jones Bridge Rd

Map 23 · **Kensington**

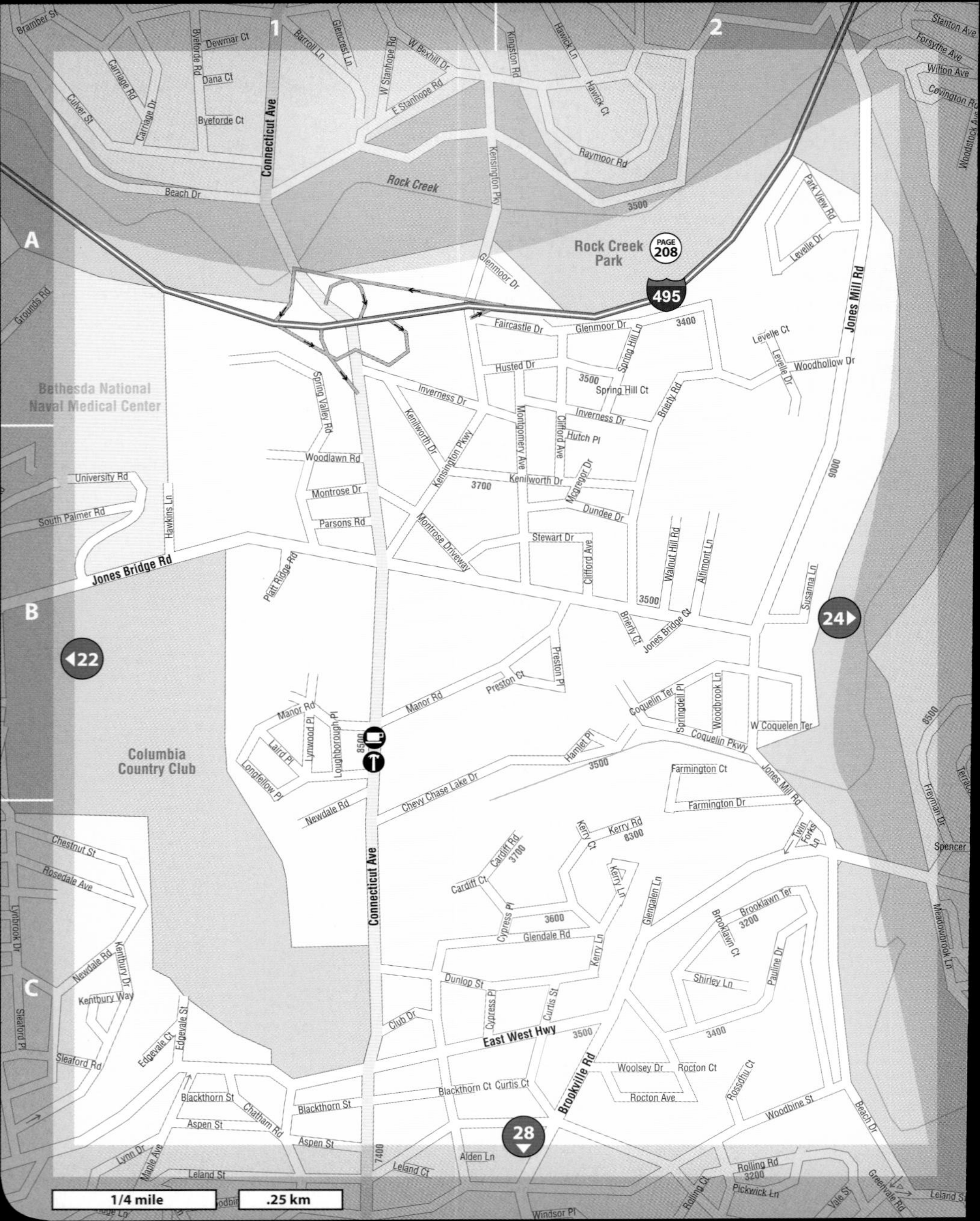

N

1 2

Stanton Ave
Forsythia Ave
Wilton Ave
Covington Rd
Woodhollow Ave

Bramber St
Byeforde St
Dewmar Ct
Barroll Ln
Glencrest Ln
W Stanhope Rd
W Bexhill Dr
Kingston Rd
Hanca Ln
Hanca Ct

Carriage Rd
Carriage Dr
Colter St
Dana Ct
E Stanhope Rd
Raymoor Rd

Byeforde Ct
Connecticut Ave

Beach Dr
Rock Creek
Kensington Pkwy
3500

Park View Rd

A

Grounds Rd

Rock Creek Park
PAGE 208
Levelle Dr

495
Jones Mill Rd

Glenmoor Dr
Faircastle Dr
Glenmoor Dr
3400
Levelle Ct
Levelle Dr
Woodhollow Dr

Spring Hill Rd
Brady Rd

Bethesda National
Naval Medical Center
Husted Dr
3500
Spring Hill Ct

Spring Valley Rd
Inverness Dr
Inverness Dr
Clifford Ave
Hutch Pl

Woodlawn Rd
Kenilworth Dr
Kensington Pkwy
Montgomery Ave
Montrose Dr
3700
Kenilworth Dr
Montrose Dr
Dundee Dr
9000

University Rd
Hawkins Ln
Parsons Rd
Stewart Dr
Walnut Hill Rd
Allmont Ln

South Palmer Rd
Platt Ridge Rd
Montrose Driveway
Clifford Ave
3500
Jones Bridge Ct
Susanna Ln

Jones Bridge Rd

B

22
Briefly Ct
Jones Bridge Rd
24

Manor Rd
Preston Ct
Coquelin Ter
Springdell Pl
Woodbrook Ln

Manor Rd
Laird St
Lynwood Pl
Loughborough Pl
Manor Rd
Preston Pl
W Coquelin Ter
Coquelin Pkwy

Columbia
Country Club
Longfellow Pl
Hamlet Pl
3500

Newdale Rd
Chevy Chase Lake Dr
Farmington Ct
Farmington Dr
Jones Mill Rd

Cardiff Rd
3700
Kerry Rd
8300
Spencer

Cardiff Ct
Cypress Pl
Kerry Ct
Kerry Rd
Brooklawn Ter
3200

3600
Glendale Rd
Kerry St
Glengalen Ln
Brooklawn Ct
Pauline Dr

C
Chestnut St
Rosedale Ave
Dunlop St
Cypress Pl
Curtis St
Shirley Ln

Newdale Rd
Kentbury Dr
Kentbury Way
Club Dr
Woolsey Dr
Rocton Ct

Edgevale St
Edgevale St
East West Hwy
3500
Rocton Ave
3400
Woodbine St

Sleaford Rd
Blackthorn St
Chatham Rd
Blackthorn St
Brookville Rd
Beach Dr

Lynn Dr
Maple Ave
Aspen St
Aspen St
Blackthorn Ct
Curtis Ct
28
Rosshill Ln
Rolling Rd

Leland St
Alden Ln
Leland Ct
Vale St
Leland Rd

1/4 mile   .25 km

The Maryland suburb that's not Chevy Chase or Bethesda. There's nothing to do here that you can't do somewhere more exciting, and if someone wants to take you back to their place in Kensington, they're probably still living with their parents.

Map 2

Coffee

· **Starbucks** · 8542 Connecticut Ave

Hardware Stores

· **Thomas W Perry** · 8519 Connecticut Ave

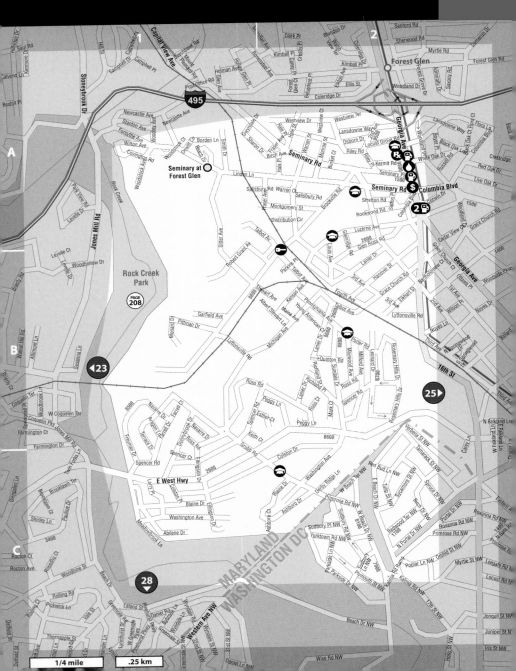

A mix of residential, schools, and industrial with zero attraction for outsiders. What this neighborhood offers is actually fairly common in the District: peace and quiet.

Banks

- **Citibank** · 9400 Georgia Ave

Car Rental

- **Enterprise** · 9151 Brookville Rd · 301-565-4000

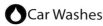 Car Washes

- **Montgomery Hills Car Wash** · 9500 Georgia Ave

Gas Stations

- **Chevron** · 9475 Georgia Ave
- **Exxon** · 9331 Georgia Ave
- **Exxon** · 9336 Georgia Ave ☺
- **Shell** · 9510 Georgia Ave

Landmarks

- **Seminary at Forest Glen** · Linden Ln & Beach Dr

Pharmacies

- **CVS** · 9520 Georgia Ave

Schools

- **Calvary Lutheran** · 9545 Georgia Ave
- **Rock Creek Forest Elementary** · 8330 Grubb Rd
- **Rosemary Hills Elementary** · 2111 Porter Rd
- **Woodlin Elementary** · 2101 Luzerne Ave
- **Yeshiva of Greater Washington** · 2010 Linden Ln

Map 24 · **Upper Rock Creek Park**

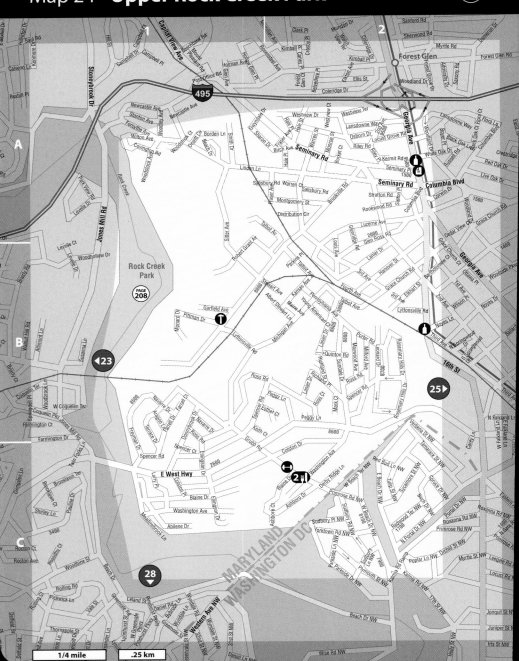

If you're in the mood for excitement, just hope your car doesn't stall.

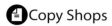

Copy Shops
• **Staples** • 9440 Georgia Ave

Gyms
• **Rock Creek Sport Club** • 8325 Grubb Rd

Hardware Stores
• **Zimmerman Supply** • 8860 Brookville Rd

Liquor Stores
• **Seminary Beer Wine & Deli** • 9458 Georgia Ave
• **Spring Beer & Wine** • 8645 16th St

Restaurants
• **Parkway Deli** • 8317 Grubb Rd
• **redDog Café** • 8301A Grubb Rd

Map 25 · **Silver Spring**

Ⓝ

495

Sligo Park
Country Club

Sligo Creek Pkwy

Woodland Dr

Flora Ln

Crestridge Dr

Sligo Creek

Shorey Rd

Granville Dr

Normandy Dr

Indian Spring Dr

A

Seminary Rd | Columbia Blvd

Red Oak Dr

Live Oak Dr

White Oak Dr

Crosby Rd

Midwood Pl

Midwood Rd

Clement Rd

Clement Pl

Colesville Rd

Franklin Ave

Lycoming St

Saint Andrews Ln

Saint Andrews Way

Bruce Dr

Leighton Ave

Baden St

Franklin Ave

Revere St

Corwin Dr

Luzerne Ave

1500

1300

Grace Church Rd

Pinecrest St

Crosby Rd

1200

Edgevale Rd

Greyrock Rd

Watson Rd

Summit Ave

Hamilton Ave

Highview Ave

Hamilton Ave

◀24

Cedar View Ct

Bartholomew Ct

Ottawa Pl

1st Ave

Wilson Ln

1400

9100

Pinecrest Cir

Woodside Pkwy

Highland Dr

Fairview Rd

Toll House Rd

Bennington Dr

Dale Dr

Oakford Rd

Ashford Rd

Windsor St

Dartmouth Ave

Greenwich Ln

Schuyler Rd

B

16th St

3rd Ave

Lyttonsville Rd

Noyes Ln

Georgia Ave

Ballard St

Burton St

Alton Pkwy

N Mansion Dr

S Mansion Dr

N Noyes Dr

Fairview Rd

S Noyes Dr

Noyes Dr

Ellsworth Ct

Rowen Rd

29

Planning Pl

Spring St

Fenwick Ln

Cameron St

Ramsey Ave

Fenton St

$** **$

2 $
2 $

Colesville Rd

Roeder Rd

Fenton St

Ellsworth Dr

Springvale Rd

Cedar St

Wayne Ave

Queen Annes Dr

AFI Theater

Apple Ave

22nd Ave

Trinty Ave

Wayne Ave

Silver Spring

P

Penguin Rush Hour Mural

Tastee Diner

Hankin St

Houston St

Easley St

Thayer Ave

26▶

390

East West Hwy

W Fairland Ln

Carey Ln

Draper Ln

Palmer Ave

Dixon Ave

Colonial Ln

Ripley St

Mayor Ln

Bonifant St

Silver Spring Ave

Carroll Ct

Carroll Ct

Sligo Ave

MARYLAND
WASHINGTON D.C.

384

$

2 $

410

Blair Mill Dr

Blair Mill Rd

2

Georgia Ave

Fenton St

700

Twin Holly Ln

900

Mississippi Ave

Ritchie Ave

Potomac Ave

C

Rock Creek Park

PAGE 208

Tulip Ave

Silver Spring Ave

Seminary Pl

Roxanna Rd NW

Primrose Rd NW

N Portal Dr NW

Portal Dr NW

Orchid St NW

Poplar Ln NW

Roxanna Rd NW

N Cate Rd NW

Primrose Rd NW

Locust Ln NW

Leepate Rd NW

Kemp St NW

Newell St

Blair Mill Dr

Richmond Ave

East West Hwy

Woodbury Dr

Boston Ave

Violet Pl

Philadelphia Ave

Chesapeake Ave

Boundary Ave

Burlington Ave

13th St

King St

Eastern Ave NW

Jesup Blair Dr

27

320

Rock Creek Park

Kalmia Rd NW

1/4 mile   .25 km

Some call downtown Silver Spring cute, others call it corny. Both descriptions are accurate. With all the appeal of a bustling beach boardwalk, the mix of local charm and corporate kitsch plays to the city's target audience: people who value community and predictability. To its credit, the neighborhood does boast an ethnically diverse population, and a number of restaurants reflect this. But the dinner/movie/late night cup of coffee is the typical Friday night lineup.

$ Banks

- **Adams National** · 8121 Georgia Ave
- **Bank of America** · 8511 Georgia Ave
- **Bank of America** · 8788 Georgia Ave
- **BB&T** · 1100 Wayne Ave
- **Chevy Chase** · 8315 Georgia Ave
- **Chevy Chase** · 8676 Georgia Ave
- **Chevy Chase (ATM)** · 1280 East West Hwy
- **Chevy Chase (ATM)** · 8400 Colesville Rd
- **Eagle** · 8677 Georgia Ave
- **M&T** · 8737 Colesville Rd
- **Provident** · 8730 Georgia Ave
- **Sun Trust** · 1286 East West Hwy
- **Sun Trust** · 8700 Georgia Ave
- **United** · 8630 Fenton St
- **Wachovia** · 8701 Georgia Ave

Car Rental

- **Budget** · 619 Sligo Ave · 240-646-7171
- **Enterprise** · 8208 Georgia Ave · 301-563-6500
- **Enterprise** · 8401 Colesville Rd · 301-495-4120
- **Hertz** · 8203 Georgia Ave · 301-588-0608

Car Washes

- **Mr Wash** · 7996 Georgia Ave

Gas Stations

- **Citgo** · 8333 Fenton St
- **Crown** · 8600 Georgia Ave
- **Exxon** · 8301 Fenton St ⌕
- **Exxon** · 8384 Colesville Rd ⌕

o Landmarks

- **AFI Theater** · 8633 Colesville Rd
- **Penguin Rush Hour Mural** · 8400 Colesville Rd
- **Tastee Diner** · 8601 Cameron St

Libraries

- **NOAA Central Library** · 1315 East West Hwy, SSMC3, 2nd Fl
- **Silver Spring Library** · 8901 Colesville Rd

P Parking

Pharmacies

- **CVS** · 1290 East West Hwy ⌕
- **Giant Food Pharmacy** · 1280 East West Hwy
- **Rite Aid** · 1411 East West Hwy ⌕
- **Safeway** · 909 Thayer Ave
- **Service Care Pharmacy** · 1111 Spring St

Police

- **3rd District - Silver Spring** · 801 Sligo Ave

Post Offices

- **Silver Spring Finance Centre** · 8455 Colesville Rd

Schools

- **Chelsea** · 711 Pershing Dr
- **East Silver Spring Elementary** · 631 Silver Spring Ave
- **Grace Episcopal Day** · 9115 Georgia Ave
- **The Nora** · 955 Sligo Ave
- **Sligo Creek Elementary** · 500 Schuyler Rd
- **St Michael's Elementary** · 824 Wayne Ave

Supermarkets

- **Safeway** · 909 Thayer Ave
- **Whole Foods Market** · 833 Wayne Ave

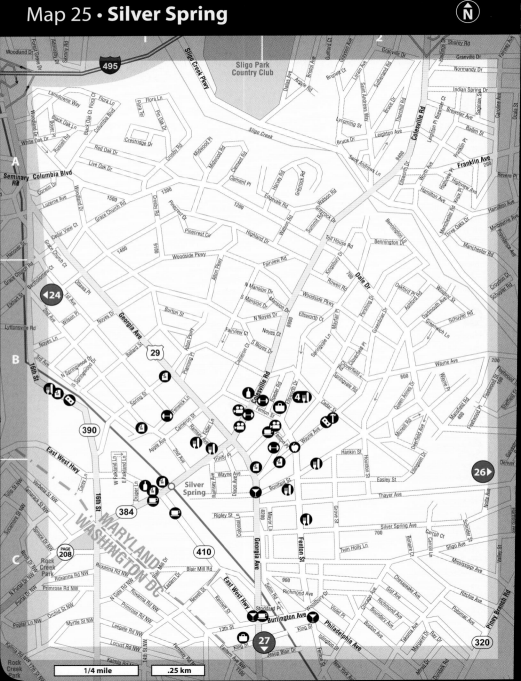

Map 25 · **Silver Spring**

N

Movie buffs rejoice! Playing obscure indie flicks and timeless gems, the American Film Institute Theater is the reason to come to Silver Spring. Epicureans will also delight in the number of big-city caliber eateries. Stay off the main strip and search out Addis Ababa, Roger Miller Restaurant, and Mandalay. Small caveat to drinkers: Silver Spring bars are few and far between.

Coffee

- **Caribou Coffee** · 1316 East West Hwy
- **Mayorga Coffee Factory** · 8040 Georgia Ave
- **Starbucks** · 8399 Colesville Rd
- **Starbucks** · 915 Ellsworth Dr

Copy Shops

- **ABC Imaging** · 1300 Spring St
- **Benoit Printing & Graphic Designs** · 8401 Colesville Rd, Ste 140
- **Digiprint Connection** · 962 Wayne Ave
- **FedEx Kinko's** · 1407 East West Hwy
- **Minuteman Press** · 8604 2nd Ave
- **Office Depot** · 8501 Georgia Ave
- **UPS Store** · 8639 16th St

Farmer's Markets

- **Silver Spring Farmer's Market (May–Oct, Sat, 9 am–1 pm)** · Fenton St & Wayne Ave

Gyms

- **Curves (women only)** · 1320 Fenwick Ln
- **Gold's Gym** · 8661 Colesville Rd
- **LA Fitness Sports Club** · 8705 Colesville Rd
- **Washington Sports Clubs** · 901 Wayne Ave

Hardware Stores

- **Strosniders Hardware Store** · 815 Wayne Ave

Liquor Stores

- **Lenox Beer & Wine** · 1400 East West Hwy
- **Silver Spring Liquor Store** · 8715 Colesville Rd

Movie Theaters

- **AFI Silver Theater** · 8633 Colesville Rd
- **AMC City Place 10** · 8661 Colesville Rd
- **The Majestic 20** · 900 Ellsworth Dr

Nightlife

- **Flying Fish** · 815 King St
- **Mayorga** · 8040 Georgia Ave
- **Quarry House Tavern** · 8401 Georgia Ave

Restaurants

- **Addis Ababa** · 8233 Fenton St
- **Austin Grill** · 919 Ellsworth Dr
- **Cubano's** · 1201 Fidler Ln
- **Eggspectation** · 923 Ellsworth Dr
- **El Aguila** · 8649 16th St
- **Lebanese Taverna** · 933 Ellsworth Dr
- **Mandalay** · 930 Bonifant St, #932
- **Mi Rancho** · 8701 Ramsey Ave
- **Roger Miller Restaurant** · 941 Bonifant St
- **Romano's Macaroni Grill** · 931 Ellsworth Dr

Shopping

- **Color Me Mine** · 823 Ellsworth Dr
- **Kingsbury Chocolates** · 1017 King St

Video Rental

- **Blockbuster** · 8601 16th St
- **Hollywood Video** · 825 Wayne Ave

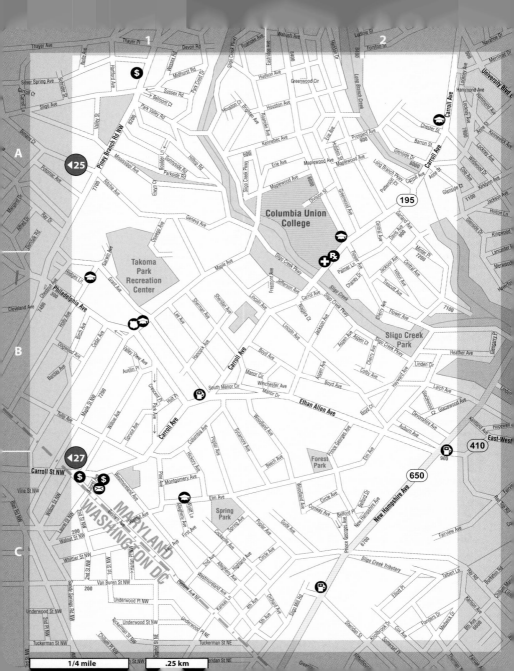

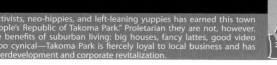

The surfeit of aging activists, neo-hippies, and left-leaning yuppies has earned this town the nickname "The People's Republic of Takoma Park." Proletarian they are not, however. Residents enjoy all the benefits of suburban living: big houses, fancy lattes, good video stores. But don't get too cynical—Takoma Park is fiercely loyal to local business and has successfully resisted overdevelopment and corporate revitalization.

$ Banks
- **Bank of America** · 6950 Carroll Ave
- **Citibank (ATM)** · 8120 Piney Branch Rd
- **Sun Trust** · 6931 Laurel Ave

✚ Emergency Rooms
- **Washington Adventist** · 7600 Carroll Ave ♿

⛽ Gas Stations
- **Amoco** · 920 East West Hwy
- **Citgo** · 7224 Carroll Ave
- **Shell** · 6201 New Hampshire Ave NE

℞ Pharmacies
- **Washington Adventist Family Pharmacy** · 7600 Carroll Ave

👮 Police
- **Takoma Park Police Dept** · 7500 Maple Ave

✉ Post Offices
- **Takoma Park** · 6909 Laurel Ave

🎓 Schools
- **Columbia Union College** · 7600 Flower Ave
- **John Nevins Andrews** · 117 Elm Ave
- **Piney Branch Elementary** · 7510 Maple Ave
- **Takoma Academy** · 8120 Carroll Ave
- **Takoma Park Elementary** · 7511 Holly Ave

Map 26 · **Takoma Park**

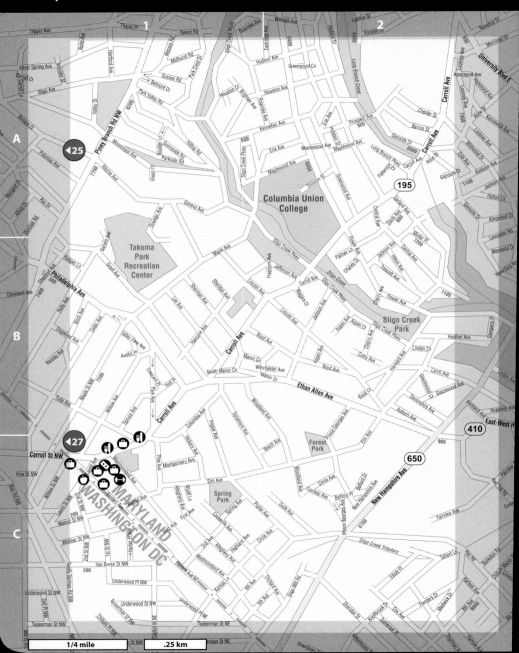

If you're into organic markets, fair-trade tchotchkes, and vintage clothing, by all means, go downtown and check out the mom-and-pop stores on Carroll Avenue. But head to the Metro once the sun starts setting. Not even locals stick around for the nightlife.

 Farmer's Markets

- **Takoma Park Farmers Market**
  (Sun, 10 am–2 pm) · Laurel Ave & Eastern Ave

Gyms

- **Curves (women only)** · 7008 Westmoreland Ave

 Restaurants

- **Mark's Kitchen** · 7006 Carroll Ave
- **Savory** · 7071 Carroll Ave

 Shopping

- **Dan the Music Man** · 6855 Eastern Ave
- **House of Musical Traditions** · 7040 Carroll Ave
- **Polly Sue's** · 6915 Laurel Ave
- **Takoma Underground** · 7014 Westmoreland Ave
- **Video Americain** · 6937 Laurel Ave

Video Rental

- **Video American** · 6937 Laurel Ave

For now, DC's favorite military hospital will remain open. But not-so-beloved Secretary of Defense Donald Rumsfeld plans to have the Walter Reed Medical Center relocated—name and all—to Bethesda by 2010, much to the chagrin of veteran's groups, military families, the neighborhood's denizens who grew up picnicking on the well-fortified leafy grounds.

Map

Banks

- **Chevy Chase (ATM)** · 7600 Takoma Ave
- **Independence Federal Savings** · 7901 Eastern Ave
- **M&T** · 6434 Georgia Ave NW
- **PNC** · 7601 Georgia Ave NW
- **Sun Trust** · 6422 Georgia Ave NW

Car Washes

- **Mr Gee's Car Wash** · 6315 Georgia Ave NW

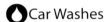 Community Gardens

Gas Stations

- **Amoco** · 6300 Georgia Ave NW ⊙
- **Amoco** · 6401 Georgia Ave NW
- **Amoco** · 7000 Blair Rd NW
- **Amoco** · 7605 Georgia Ave NW ⊙
- **Chevron** · 2300 Columbia Pike
- **Exxon** · 6350 Georgia Ave NW ⊙
- **Exxon** · 7401 Georgia Ave NW ⊙
- **Shell** · 6419 Georgia Ave NW ⊙

○ Landmarks

- **Battleground National Military Cemetery** · 6625 Georgia Ave NW
- **Walter Reed Army Medical Center** · 6900 Georgia Ave NW

Libraries

- **Juanita E Thornton Library** · 7420 Georgia Ave NW
- **Takoma Park Library** · 416 Cedar St NW

Pharmacies

- **CVS** · 110 Carroll Ave NW
- **CVS** · 6514 Georgia Ave NW ⊙
- **Medicine Shoppe** · 7814 Eastern Ave NW
- **Phamily CARE Pharmacy** · 6323 Georgia Ave NW
- **Safeway** · 6500 Piney Branch Rd NW

 Police

- **MPDC 4th District Station** · 6001 Georgia Ave NW

Post Offices

- **Brightwood Station** · 6323 Georgia Ave NW
- **Walter Reed Station** · 6800 Georgia Ave NW

 Schools

- **A-T Seban Mesut** · 5924 Georgia Ave NW
- **Academia de la Recta Porta** · 7614 Georgia Ave NW
- **The Bridges Academy** · 6119 Georgia Ave NW
- **Coolidge High** · 6315 5th St NW
- **Jewish Primary Day School of the Nation's Capital** · 6045 16th St NW
- **Lowell** · 1640 Kalmia Rd NW
- **Montgomery College (Takoma Park Campus)** · 7600 Takoma Ave
- **Nativity Catholic Academy** · 6008 Georgia Ave NW
- **Owl** · 6045 16th St NW
- **Shepherd Elementary** · 7800 14th St NW
- **Strayer University (Takoma Park Campus)** · 6830 Laurel St NW
- **Takoma** · 7010 Piney Branch Rd NW
- **Takoma Park Middle** · 7611 Piney Branch Rd
- **Washington Theological Union** · 6896 Laurel St NW
- **Whittier Elementary** · 6201 5th St NW

Supermarkets

- **Safeway** · 6500 Piney Branch Rd NW

(113)

The major road cutting through this sleepy neighborhood (Georgia Ave) is an ideal route for travelers heading downtown from the beltway. Stop for gas and hit up an ATM, but try to keep the radio volume low. The families who live here like to keep things nice and quiet.

Coffee
- **Savory Takoma Metro** · 314 Carroll St NW
- **Starbucks** · 6500 Piney Branch Rd NW

Copy Shops
- **Beaver Press Inc** · 11 Oglethorpe St NW
- **Community Printing** · 6979 Maple St NW

Liquor Stores
- **Brightwood Liquor Store** · 5916 Georgia Ave NW
- **Cork'n Bottle Liquors** · 7421 Georgia Ave NW
- **Mayfair Liquor** · 7312 Georgia Ave NW
- **Morris Miller Liquors** · 7804 Alaska Ave NW
- **S&S Liquors** · 6925 4th St NW
- **Victor Liquors** · 6220 Georgia Ave NW

Nightlife
- **Charlie's** · 7307 Georgia Ave NW
- **Takoma Station Tavern** · 6914 4th St NW

Pet Shops
- **The Big Bad Woof** · 117 Carroll St NW

Restaurants
- **Blair Mansion Inn/Murder Mystery Dinner Theatre** · 7711 Eastern Ave

Shopping
- **KB News Emporium** · 7898 Georgia Ave

Video Rental
- **Royce's** · 7445 Georgia Ave NW

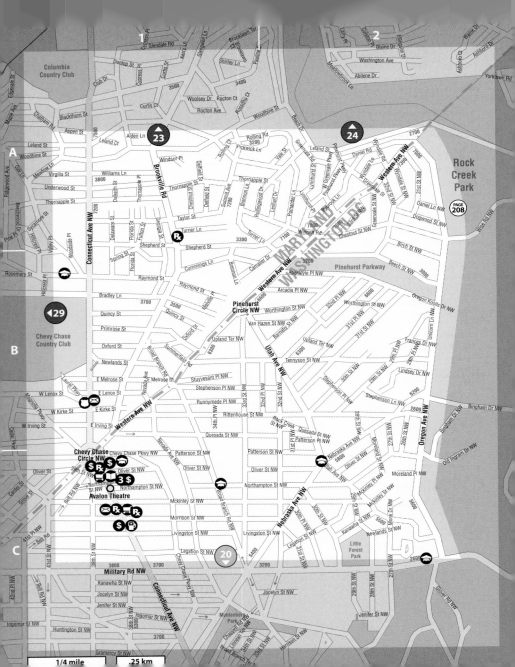

By far the wealthiest of DC's suburbs, it is also the most conveniently located. If you subscribe to the American Dream, this is what your neighborhood should look like. But the rich aren't like you and me. They don't want bars and great falafel joints in their 'hoods.

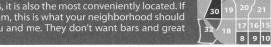

$ Banks

- **Chevy Chase** · 5714 Connecticut Ave NW
- **Chevy Chase (ATM)** · 5712 Connecticut Ave NW
- **Citibank** · 5700 Connecticut Ave NW
- **M&T** · 5630 Connecticut Ave NW
- **PNC** · 5530 Connecticut Ave NW
- **Wachovia** · 5701 Connecticut Ave NW

Gas Stations

- **Exxon** · 5521 Connecticut Ave NW

○ Landmarks

- **Avalon Theatre** · 5612 Connecticut Ave NW

Libraries

- **Chevy Chase Library** · 5625 Connecticut Ave NW

Rx Pharmacies

- **Brookville CARE Pharmacy** · 7025 Brookville Rd
- **Chevy Chase Pharmacy** ·
  3812 Northampton St NW
- **CVS** · 5550 Connecticut Ave NW
- **Safeway** · 5545 Connecticut Ave NW

Police

- **Chevy Chase Village Police** ·
  5906 Connecticut Ave NW

Post Offices

- **Chevy Chase Branch** · 5910 Connecticut Ave NW
- **Northwest Station** · 5636 Connecticut Ave NW

Schools

- **Blessed Sacrament Elementary** ·
  5841 Chevy Chase Pkwy NW
- **Chevy Chase Elementary** · 4015 Rosemary St
- **Episcopal Center for Children** ·
  5901 Utah Ave NW
- **Lafayette Elementary** · 5701 Broad Branch Rd NW
- **St John's College High** · 2607 Military Rd NW

Supermarkets

- **Magruder's** · 5626 Connecticut Ave NW
- **Safeway** · 5545 Connecticut Ave NW

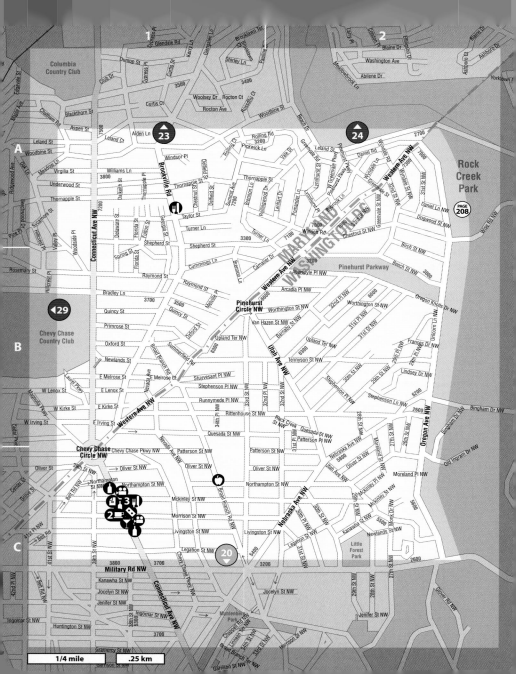

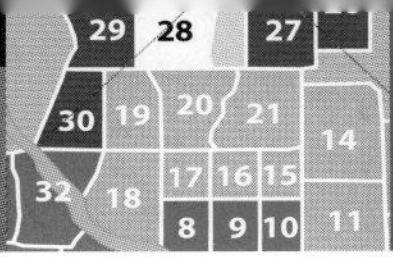

You'll have to have a bank account on par with the comedian of the same name if you want to settle in this posh Maryland suburb. The quaint to grandiose houses come complete with white picket fences and cherry blossom trees in the yards.

Map 2

Coffee
- **Bread & Chocolate** · 5542 Connecticut Ave NW
- **Starbucks** · 5500 Connecticut Ave NW

Copy Shops
- **UPS Store** · 5505 Connecticut Ave NW

Farmer's Markets
- **Chevy Chase Farmer's Market (May–Nov, Sat 9 am–1 pm)** · Broad Branch Rd NW & Northampton St NW

Liquor Stores
- **Chevy Chase Wine & Spirits** · 5544 Connecticut Ave NW
- **Circle Liquors of Chevy Chase** · 5501 Connecticut Ave NW
- **Magruder's Produce** · 5626 Connecticut Ave NW

Movie Theaters
- **American City Movie Diner** · 5532 Connecticut Ave NW
- **Avalon Theatre** · 5612 Connecticut Ave NW

Nightlife
- **Chevy Chase Lounge** · 5510 Connecticut Ave NW

Restaurants
- **American City Diner of Washington** · 5532 Connecticut Ave NW
- **Arucola** · 5534 Connecticut Ave NW
- **Bread & Chocolate** · 5542 Connecticut Ave NW
- **La Ferme** · 7101 Brookville Rd

Video Rental
- **Potomac Video** · 5536 Connecticut Ave NW

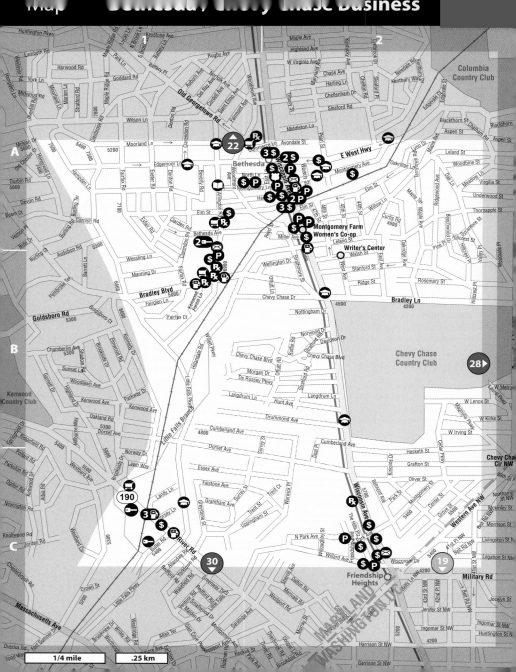

They may not let you in their country club, but if you have a credit card they'll let you in their stores. Downtown Bethesda (Map 22) is really part of the same area and will give you a few more options. You'll need them.

Map

Banks

- **Bank of America** · 4411 S Park Ave
- **Bank of America** · 5135 River Rd
- **Bank of America** · 7316 Wisconsin Ave
- **BB&T** · 4719 Hampden Ln
- **Chevy Chase** · 4708 Bethesda Ave
- **Chevy Chase** · 5476 Wisconsin Ave
- **Chevy Chase** · 7501 Wisconsin Ave
- **Chevy Chase (ATM)** · 7142 Arlington Rd
- **Chevy Chase (ATM)** · 7450 Wisconsin Ave
- **Chevy Chase (ATM)** · 7500 Old Georgetown Rd
- **Independence Federal Savings** · 5530 Wisconsin Ave
- **M&T** · 4800 Hampden Ln
- **Mellon** · 2 Bethesda Metro Ctr
- **Mercantile Potomac** · 4424 Montgomery Ave
- **PNC** · 7235 Wisconsin Ave
- **Presidential Savings** · 4520 East West Hwy
- **Provident** · 5416 Wisconsin Ave
- **Provident** · 7508 Wisconsin Ave
- **Sandy Spring** · 7126 Wisconsin Ave
- **Sun Trust** · 4455 Willard Ave
- **Sun Trust** · 7500 Wisconsin Ave
- **United** · 7250 Wisconsin Ave
- **United** · 7535 Old Georgetown Rd
- **Wachovia** · 6921 Arlington Rd

Car Rental

- **Budget** · 4932 Bethesda Ave ·
- **Enterprise** · 5202 River Rd · 301-657-0095
- **Rent-A-Wreck** · 5455 Butler Rd · 301-654-2252
- **Sears Rent A Car** · 4932 Bethesda Ave · 240-646-7171

Gas Stations

- **Chevron** · 5001 Bradley Blvd
- **Citgo** · 4972 Bradley Blvd
- **Exxon** · 5143 River Rd
- **Exxon** · 7100 Wisconsin Ave
- **Exxon** · 7340 Wisconsin Ave ⊕
- **Getty** · 5151 River Rd
- **Mobil** · 5201 River Rd
- **Shell** · 5110 River Rd

○Landmarks

- **Montgomery Farm Women's Co-op Market** ·
  7155 Wisconsin Ave
- **Writer's Center** · 4508 Walsh St

Libraries

- **Bethesda Library** · 7400 Arlington Rd

Parking

Pharmacies

- **Bradley CARE Drugs/Braden's Pharmacy** ·
  6900 Arlington Rd
- **CVS** · 6917 Arlington Rd ⊕
- **Giant Food Pharmacy** · 7142 Arlington Rd ⊕
- **Medical CARE Pharmacy of Chevy Chase** ·
  5530 Wisconsin Ave
- **Safeway** · 5000 Bradley Blvd
- **Safeway** · 7625 Old Georgetown Rd

Police

- **2nd District - Bethesda** · 7359 Wisconsin Ave

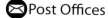Post Offices

- **Bethesda** · 7400 Wisconsin Ave
- **Bethesda Chevy Chase** · 7001 Arlington Rd
- **Friendship Heights Station** · 5530 Wisconsin Ave

Schools

- **Bethesda Elementary** · 7600 Arlington Rd
- **Bethesda-Chevy Chase High** · 4301 East West Hwy
- **Concord Hill** · 6050 Wisconsin Ave
- **DeVry University** · 4550 Montgomery Ave
- **Oneness Family** · 6701 Wisconsin Ave
- **Our Lady of Lourdes** · 7500 Pearl St
- **Sidwell Friends Lower** · 5100 Edgemoor Ln
- **Washington Episcopal** · 5600 Little Falls Pkwy

Supermarkets

- **Giant Food** · 7142 Arlington Rd
- **Safeway** · 5000 Bradley Blvd
- **Safeway** · 7625 Old Georgetown Rd
- **Whole Foods Market** · 5269 River Rd

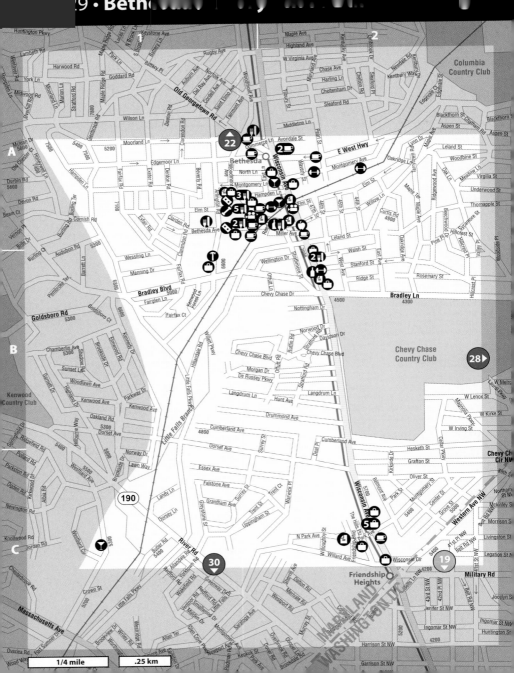

North of the Friendship Heights glitzy high-end shopping and fancy chain restaurants is a brief residential pause before entering the arts end of Bethesda. The Washington Studio School and the Writer's Center hide out here along with the Round House Theater and the Farm Women's Cooperative, where you can get your handbags handmade and Turkish rugs for cheap.

Map 2

Coffee

- **Caribou Coffee** · 7629 Old Georgetown Rd
- **Cosi** · 7251 Woodmont Ave
- **Dunkin' Donuts** · 4810 Bethesda Ave
- **On Time Café** · 4801 Edgemoor Ln
- **Quartermaine Coffee Roasters** · 4817 Bethesda Ave
- **Starbucks** · 4520 East West Hwy
- **Starbucks** · 5454 Wisconsin Ave
- **Starbucks** · 7140 Wisconsin Ave

Copy Shops

- **ABC Imaging** · 5550 Friendship Blvd
- **ABC Imaging** · 7315 Wisconsin Ave
- **FedEx Kinko's** · 4809 Bethesda Ave ⊙
- **Print 1 Printing & Copying** · 4710 Bethesda Ave
- **Staples** · 6800 Wisconsin Ave
- **UPS Store** · 4938 Hampden Ln

Farmer's Markets

- **Montgomery Farm Women's Co-op Market (Wed & Sat, 7 am–3 pm)** · 7155 Wisconsin Ave

Gyms

- **Bethesda Sport & Health Club** · 4400 Montgomery Ave
- **Curves (women only)** · 6831 Wisconsin Ave
- **Metro Fitness** · 4550 Montgomery Ave
- **Washington Sports Clubs** · 4903 Elm St

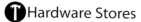Hardware Stores

- **Strosniders Hardware Store** · 6930 Arlington Rd

Liquor Stores

- **Bethesda-Chevy Chase & Wine LLC** · 4701 Miller Ave
- **Chevy Chase Liquors** · 6831 Wisconsin Ave

Movie Theaters

- **Landmark Bethesda Row Cinema** · 7235 Woodmont Ave
- **Regal Bethesda 10** · 7272 Wisconsin Ave

Nightlife

- **Barking Dog** · 4723 Elm St
- **Strike Bethesda** · 5353 Westbard Ave
- **Tommy Joe's** · 4714 Montgomery Ln

Pet Shops

- **Bethesda Pet Shoppe** · 4939 Elm St
- **PetSmart** · 6800 Wisconsin Ave

Restaurants

- **Gifford's** · 7237 Woodmont Ave
- **Green Papaya** · 4922 Elm St
- **Hinode** · 4914 Hampden Ln
- **Jaleo** · 7271 Woodmont Ave
- **Levantes** · 7262 Woodmont Ave
- **Louisiana Express Company** · 4921 Bethesda Ave
- **Moby Dick House of Kabob** · 7027 Wisconsin Ave
- **Mon Ami Gabi** · 7239 Woodmont Ave
- **Persimmon** · 7003 Wisconsin Ave
- **Raku** · 7240 Woodmont Ave
- **Ri-Ra Irish Restaurant Pub** · 4931 Elm St
- **Rio Grande** · 4870 Bethesda Ave
- **Tara Thai** · 4828 Bethesda Ave
- **Vace** · 4705 Miller Ave

Shopping

- **Barney's New York Co-op** · 5471 Wisconsin Ave
- **Bethesda Tattoo Company** · 4711 Montgomery Ln
- **Brooks Brothers** · 5504 Wisconsin Ave
- **Chicos** · 5418 Wisconsin Ave
- **Luna** · 7232 Woodmont Ave
- **Marvelous Market** · 4832 Bethesda Ave
- **Mustard Seed** · 7349 Wisconsin Ave
- **Parvizian Masterpieces** · 7034 Wisconsin Ave
- **Saks Fifth Avenue** · 5555 Wisconsin Ave
- **Saks Jandel** · 5510 Wisconsin Ave
- **Strosnider's Hardware** · 6930 Arlington Rd
- **Sylene** · 4407 S Park Ave
- **Tickled Pink** · 7259 Woodmont Ave
- **Tiffany & Co** · 5481 Wisconsin Ave
- **Trader Joe's** · 6831 Wisconsin Ave

Video Rental

- **Blockbuster** · 4860 Bethesda Ave
- **Hollywood Video** · 4920 Hampden Ln

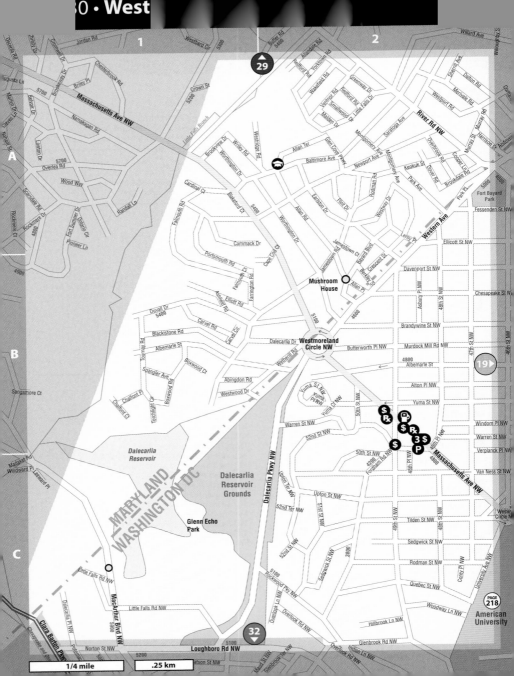

It's hard to believe you're in a city when all that surrounds you are charming brick homes, places to park your sparkling SUV, and expansive green lawns. You'll find ladies in sweater sets and pearl necklaces hosting dinner parties in these parts, as well as quite a number of au pairs pushing strollers down the tree-lined streets.

Banks

- **Bank of America** · 4301 49th St NW
- **Bank of America (ATM)** ·
  4851 Massachusetts Ave NW
- **Chevy Chase** · 4860 Massachusetts Ave NW
- **PNC** · 4835 Massachusetts Ave NW
- **United** · 4900 Massachusetts Ave NW
- **Wachovia** · 4841 Massachusetts Ave NW

 Gas Stations

- **Exxon** · 4861 Massachusetts Ave NW

o Landmarks

- **Mushroom House** · 4940 Allan Rd

Parking

Pharmacies

- **Center CARE Pharmacy** ·
  4900 Massachusetts Ave NW
- **CVS** · 4851 Massachusetts Ave NW

Schools

- **Westbrook Elementary** · 5110 Allan Ter

1   2

29

Augusta Ln
Osceola Rd
Christy Dr
Cromwell Dr
Jordan Rd
Westbard Cr
Butler Rd
Willard Ave
Sherrill Ave
Dalton Rd

Chesterbrook Rd
Crown St
Allanbee Rd
Yorktown Rd
Redford Dr
Greenway Dr
Redford Dr
Little Falls Dr
Merivale Rd
Westport Rd

Massachusetts Ave NW
Namakapan Rd
Briley Pl
Wakefield Rd
Vernon Rd
smallwood Gr
Maiden Dr
River Rd NW
Murray St
Harrison St

5700
5700
Overlea Rd
Wood Way
Randall Ln
Westridge Rd
Wintec Rd
Brookview Dr
Worthington Dr
Allan Ter
Baltimore Ave
Glen Cove Pkwy
Montgomery Ave
Montgomery Ave
Newport Ave
Saratoga Ave
Overbrook Rd
Dover Rd
Cooper Ln
Brookdale Rd

5000
A
Cardinal Ct
Blackford Ct
Falmouth Rd
Earlston Dr
Flint Dr
Rodman Rd
Wesley Dr
Park Ave
Fort Bayard Park
Fessenden St NW

Cammack Dr
Allan Rd
Worthington Dr
Jamestown Ct NW
Bayard Blvd
Cresent St
Leroy Pl
Ellicott St NW
Western Ave

Portsmouth Rd
Falmouth Ct
Canal Rd Ct
Jamestown Dr
Berkley St
Crescent St
Davenport St NW
Chesapeake St NW

4900
Duvall Dr
Carvel Rd
Blackistone Rd
Elliott Rd
Ashfield Rd
Allan Pl
Ashby Pl NW
48th St NW
47th St NW
46th St NW
Brandywine St NW

B
Tourney Rd
Albemarle St
Carvel Cr
Dalecarlia Dr
Westmoreland Circle NW
Butterworth Pl NW
Murdock Mill Rd NW
19

Spangler Ave
Boxwood Ct
Wetherill Rd
4800
Albemarle St

Boxwood Rd
Abingdon Rd
Alton Pl NW

Chalfont Pl
Westwood Dr
Yuma St NW
Yuma Pl NW
Yuma Ct NW
Yuma St NW

Torchlight Cir
Chalfont Ct
50th St NW
Windom Pl NW
Warren St NW
Matlack Rd
Windward Pl
Leonard Pl
Warren St NW
52nd St NW
Verplanck Pl NW
Van Ness St NW

Sangamore Ct
Dalecarlia Reservoir
MARYLAND
WASHINGTON DC
Dalecarlia Reservoir Grounds
50th St NW
Fordham Rd NW
4700
48th Pl NW
49th St NW
48th Pl NW
Massachusetts Ave NW
Wesley Circle NW

Dalecarlia Pkwy NW
Upton St NW
Upton St NW
52nd Ter NW
51st St NW
Tilden St NW
48th St NW

C
Little Falls Rd NW
52nd St NW
Sedgwick St NW
Sedgwick St NW
3800
Corey Pl NW
University Ave NW

MacArthur Blvd NW
Dalecarlia Pl NW
5900
Little Falls Rd NW
Rockwood Pky NW
5100
Rodman St NW
Quebec St NW

Clara Barton Pkwy NW
Chesapeake and Ohio
Potomac
Norton St NW
Nelson St NW
5200
Overlook Ln NW
Overlook Rd NW
Maud St NW
Glenbrook Ter NW
Hillbrook Ln NW
Woodway Ln NW
American University
218

32
Loughboro Rd NW
Glenbrook Rd NW
Indian Ln NW
Overlook Rd NW

1/4 mile   .25 km

Map 30

On the Maryland side of Western Avenue there's literally nowhere for Bethesda residents to empty their deep pockets, save for the lone Western Market general store from another time. In Spring Valley, locals can treat themselves to the overpriced gourmet foodstuffs and liquors of Wagshal's or run into each other at their only proper sit-down restaurant, Dahlia. Know that if you don't live in this neighborhood, the loaded locals will stare.

Coffee

- **Bagel City Café** · 4872 Massachusetts Ave NW
- **Ice Cream & Coffee** · 4845 Massachusetts Ave NW
- **Starbucks** · 4820 Massachusetts Ave NW

Liquor Stores

- **Wagshal's Delicatessen** ·
  4855 Massachusetts Ave NW

Restaurants

- **Dahlia** · 4849 Massachusetts Ave NW

Shopping

- **Crate & Barrel** · 4820 Massachusetts Ave NW
- **Ski Center** · 4300 Fordham Rd NW
- **Spring Valley Patio** · 4300 Fordham Rd NW
- **Wagshal's Market** · 4845 Massachusetts Ave NW
- **Western Market** · 4840 Western Ave

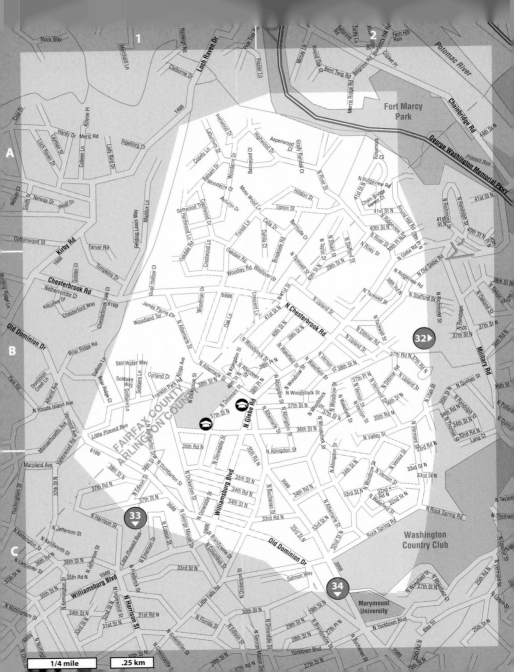

Sure, there are nice big houses with nice leafy yards, but it's essential that you drive your kids'-lacrosse-team-stickered Lexus SUV elsewhere for essentials. Or have your lacrosse star do it for you.

Schools

- **Chesterbrook Montessori** • 3455 N Glebe Rd
- **Jamestown Elementary** • 3700 N Delaware St

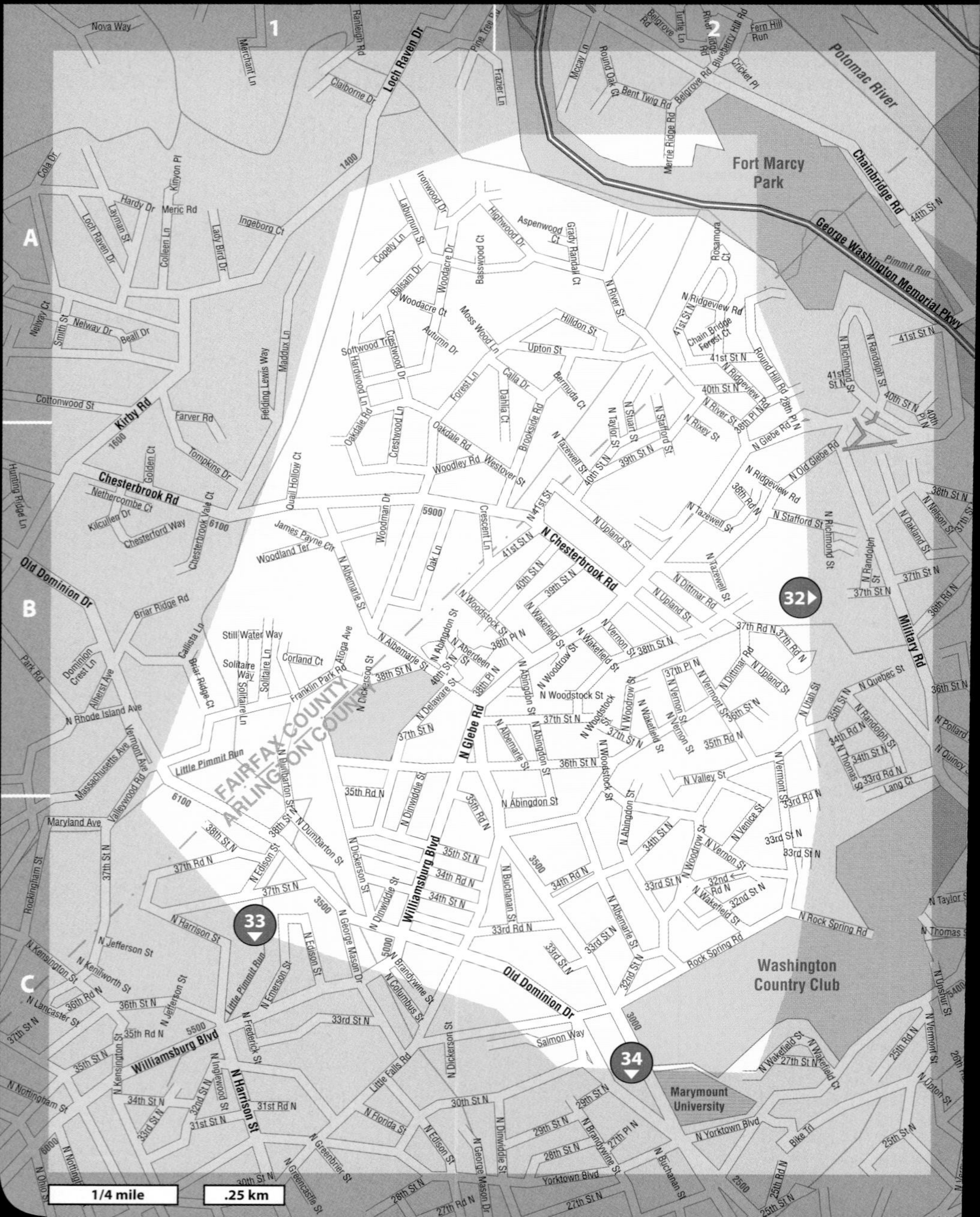

Map 31 · Chesterbrook

N

1

2

Potomac River

Fort Marcy Park

Chainbridge Rd

George Washington Memorial Pkwy

Pimmit Run

A

Loch Raven Dr

Kirby Rd

Chesterbrook Rd

Old Dominion Dr

B

N Chesterbrook Rd

N Glebe Rd

Military Rd

32

FAIRFAX COUNTY
ARLINGTON COUNTY

Williamsburg Blvd

Old Dominion Dr

33

C

N Harrison St

Williamsburg Blvd

34

Washington Country Club

Marymount University

Yorktown Blvd

1/4 mile

.25 km

Move along, Johnny. There's nothing to see here. Entertainment consists of raking your yard, programming your TiVo or trying to figure out why 37th Street intersects with 38th Street.

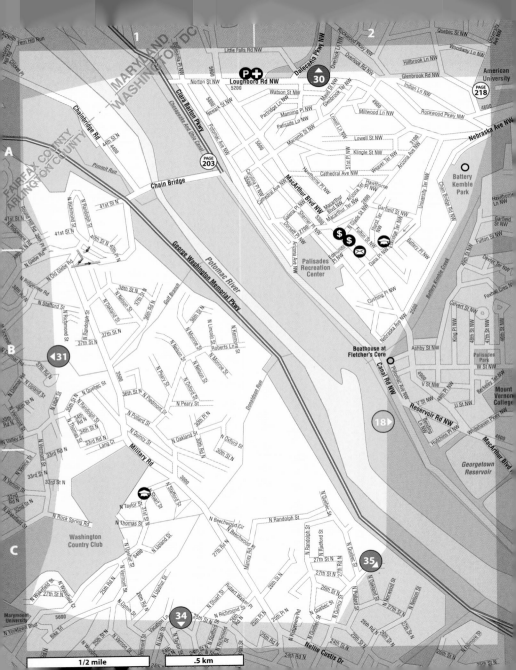

Forget Cherrydale. It's just en extension of the scintillating Chesterbrook area. However, Palisades is one of DC's overlooked neighborhoods—oh-so-quiet and with a mix of modest to magnificent homes (for which you'll pay dearly for those fantastic views of the Potomac). Yet, you still have to pick up those provisions on your way home from work, as there's not much to be had here.

Banks

- **Citibank** · 5250 MacArthur Blvd NW
- **Wachovia** · 5201 MacArthur Blvd NW

Emergency Rooms

- **Sibley Memorial** · 5255 Loughboro Rd NW ⚕

Landmarks

- **Battery Kemble Park** · Battery Kemble Park
- **The Boathouse at Fletcher's Cove** ·
  4940 Canal Rd NW

Parking

Post Offices

- **Palisades Station** · 5136 MacArthur Blvd NW

Schools

- **Key Elementary** · 5001 Dana Pl NW
- **Taylor Elementary** · 2600 N Stuart St

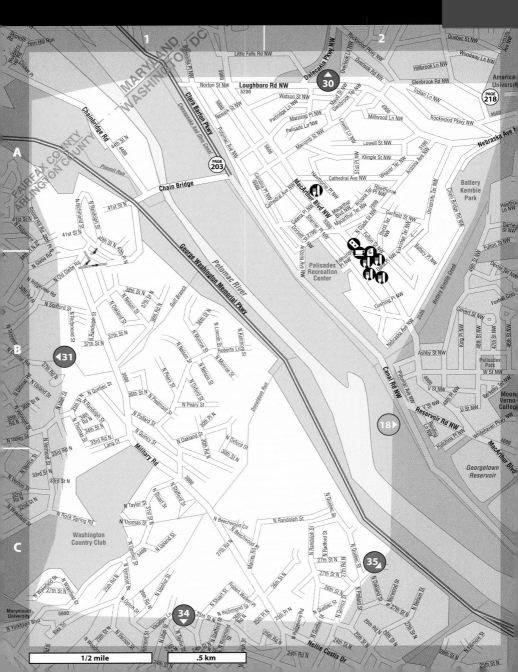

Along a short stretch of MacArthur Boulevard, there are a few places to venture to like the new DC Boathouse or the long-time favorite Listrani's Italian Gourmet. Otherwise, all the action is further down the road in Georgetown. But for the many early Baby Boomers who reside here, the backyard barbecue is about all the ol' ticker can take.

Coffee
• **Starbucks** • 5185 MacArthur Blvd NW

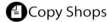Copy Shops
• **UPS Store** • 5185 Macarthur Blvd NW

Restaurants
• **Bambu** • 5101 MacArthur Blvd NW
• **DC Boathouse** • 5441 MacArthur Blvd
• **L'Appetito Restaurante** • 5105 MacArthur Blvd
• **Listriani's Italian Gourmet** • 5100 MacArthur Blvd
• **Starland Café** • 5125 MacArthur Blvd NW

Video Rental
• **Potomac Video** • 5185 MacArthur Blvd NW

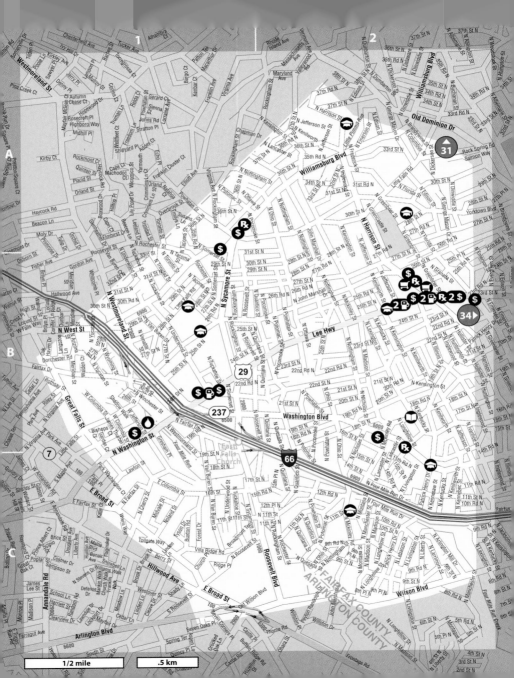

They're hard to find in this suburb, but the essentials tend to run along Broad Street. You'll find the essentials, Starbucks, a good variety of eats, cheap to fusion, Kinko's and an Orange line Metro stop.

33 34 35 36 7
37
38 40

Map

Banks

- **Bank of America** · 467 N Washington St
- **Bank of America** · 5226 Lee Hwy
- **Bank of America (ATM)** · 2425 N Harrison St
- **BB&T** · 5515 Lee Hwy
- **BB&T** · 6745 Lee Hwy
- **Sun Trust** · 6711 Lee Hwy
- **United** · 5335 Lee Hwy
- **United** · 6402 Williamsburg Blvd
- **Virginia Commerce** · 5350 Lee Hwy
- **Virginia Commerce** · 6500 Williamsburg Blvd
- **Wachovia** · 1701 N McKinley Rd

Car Washes

- **Car Care Services** · 132 W Jefferson St

Gas Stations

- **Amoco** · 5601 Lee Hwy
- **Chevron** · 5618 Lee Hwy
- **Exxon** · 6730 Lee Hwy
- **Texaco** · 5501 Lee Hwy ⊚
- **Texaco** · 5510 Lee Hwy

Libraries

- **Westover Library (temporarily closed)** · 1800 N Lexington St

Pharmacies

- **CVS** · 5402 Lee Hwy
- **CVS** · 6404 Williamsburg Blvd
- **Harris Teeter Pharmacy** · 2425 N Harrison St
- **Rite Aid** · 5841 N Washington Blvd
- **Safeway** · 2500 N Harrison St

Schools

- **Bishop O'Connell** · 6600 Little Falls Rd
- **McKinley Elementary** · 1030 N McKinley Rd
- **Rivendell** · 5700 Lee Hwy
- **Swanson Middle** · 5800 N Washington Blvd
- **Tuckahoe Elementary** · 6550 26th St N
- **Williamsburg Middle** · 3600 N Harrison St
- **Yorktown High** · 5201 28th St N

Supermarkets

- **Harris Teeter** · 2425 N Harrison St
- **Safeway** · 2500 N Harrison St

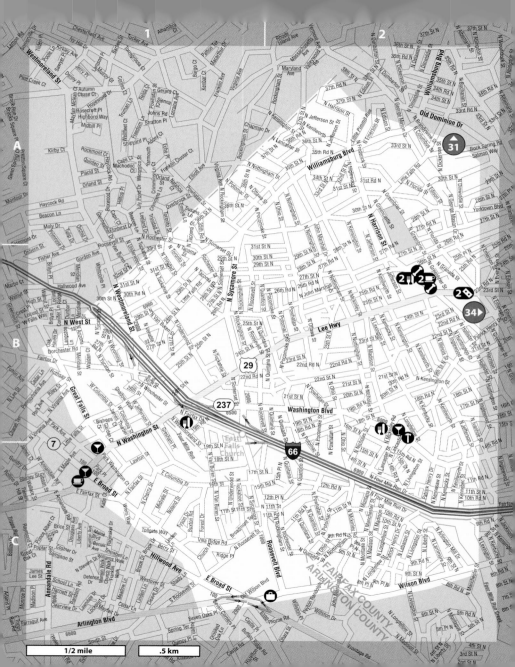

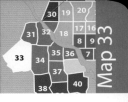

It's not the first choice for nightlife, but that's not always a bad thing. Surprisingly there are a few gems tucked away in suburbia, particularly if you like live music. Check out the State Theater for bigger names, mostly from back in the day, nearby Bangkok Blues (209 W Broad St) for the local bands and Stacey's Coffee Parlor for the coffeehouse crowd.

Coffee

- **Stacy's Coffee Parlor** · 709 W Broad St
- **Starbucks** · 2441 N Harrison St
- **Starbucks** · 2500 N Harrison St

Hardware Stores

- **Ayer's True Value** · 5853 N Washington Blvd

Nightlife

- **Ireland's Four Provinces** · 105 W Broad St
- **Lost Dog Café** · 5876 Washington Blvd
- **State Theatre** · 220 N Washington St

Pet Shops

- **Dogma** · 2445 N Harrison St
- **Dominion Pet Center** · 2501 N Harrison St

Restaurants

- **La Cote d'Or Café** · 2201 N Westmoreland St
- **Lebanese Taverna** · 5900 Washington Blvd
- **Pie Tanza** · 2503 N Harrison St
- **Taqueria el Poblano** · 2503 N Harrison St

Shopping

- **Eden Supermarket** · 6763 Wilson Blvd

Video Rental

- **Blockbuster** · 5400 Lee Hwy
- **Hollywood Video** · 5401 Lee Hwy

Map 34 • **Ballston**

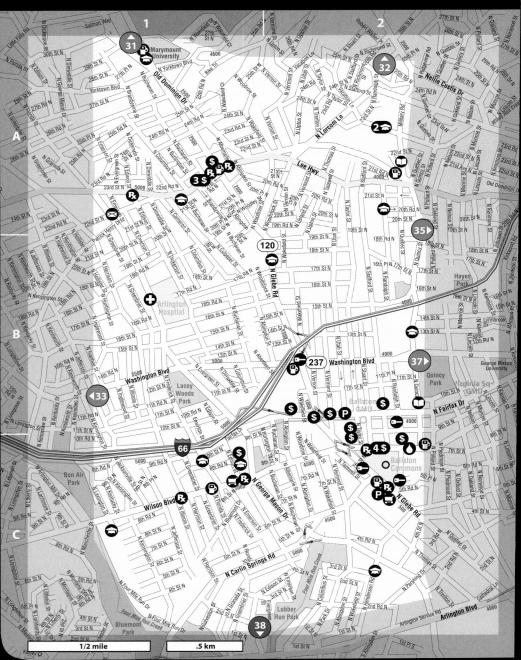

Ballston is on the rise. Literally. High rises are popping up all over the place. So while the skyline spreads, it's bringing more traffic and people. While the few local establishments struggle to hang on, the Dallas-like atmosphere is bringing some new restaurants.

Banks

- **Alliance** · 4501 N Fairfax Dr
- **Bank of America** · 4201 Wilson Blvd
- **BB&T** · 4707 Lee Hwy
- **BB&T** · 920 N Taylor St
- **Chevy Chase** · 4100 Wilson Blvd
- **Chevy Chase** · 4700 Lee Hwy
- **Chevy Chase (ATM)** · 4100 N Fairfax Dr
- **Chevy Chase (ATM)** · 4238 Wilson Blvd
- **Citibank** · 1010 N Glebe Rd
- **PNC** · 4300 Wilson Blvd
- **PNC (ATM)** · 850 N Randolph St
- **Presidential Savings** · 901 N Stuart St
- **Sun Trust** · 4710 Lee Hwy
- **Sun Trust** · 901 N Glebe Rd
- **Wachovia** · 1011 N Stafford St
- **Wachovia** · 2213 N Glebe Rd

 Car Rental

- **Advance Car Rental** · 850 N Randolph St · 703-528-8661
- **Enterprise** · 1211 N Glebe Rd · 703-248-7180
- **Enterprise** · 601 N Randolph St · 703-312-7900
- **Enterprise** · 700 N Glebe Rd · 703-243-5404

 Car Washes

- **Shell Car Wash** · 4030 Wilson Blvd

Emergency Rooms

- **Virginia Hospital Center, Arlington** · 1701 N George Mason Dr ⊚

 Gas Stations

- **Exxon** · 2240 N Glebe Rd
- **Exxon** · 4035 Old Dominion Dr
- **Exxon** · 4746 Lee Hwy
- **Exxon** · 660 N Glebe Rd ⊚
- **Shell** · 4030 Wilson Blvd
- **Sunoco** · 4601 Washington Blvd
- **Texaco** · 5201 Wilson Blvd

Landmarks

- **Ballston Commons** · 4238 Wilson Blvd

Libraries

- **Arlington Central Library** · 1015 N Quincy St
- **Cherrydale Library** · 2190 Military Rd

Parking

Pharmacies

- **CVS** · 4238 Wilson Blvd
- **CVS** · 4709 Lee Hwy
- **Harris Teeter Pharmacy** · 600 N Glebe Rd ⊚
- **Medicine Shoppe** · 5513 Wilson Blvd
- **Preston's CARE Pharmacy** · 5101 Lee Hwy
- **Rite Aid** · 4720 Lee Hwy
- **Safeway** · 5101 Wilson Blvd

Post Offices

- **North Station** · 2200 N George Mason Dr

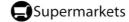 Schools

- **Arlington Traditional** · 855 N Edison St
- **Ashlawn Elementary** · 5950 N 8th Rd
- **Barrett Elementary** · 4401 N Henderson Rd
- **Glebe Elementary** · 1770 N Glebe St
- **H-B Woodlawn** · 4100 Vacation Ln
- **Langston High Continuation Program** · 2121 N Culpeper St
- **Marymount University** · 2807 N Glebe Rd
- **St Agnes Elementary** · 2024 N Randolph St
- **St Ann Elementary** · 980 N Frederick St
- **Stratford Program** · 4102 N Vacation Ln
- **Washington Lee High** · 1300 N Quincy St

Supermarkets

- **Harris Teeter** · 600 N Glebe Rd ⊚
- **Safeway** · 5101 Wilson Blvd

Map 34 · **Ballston**

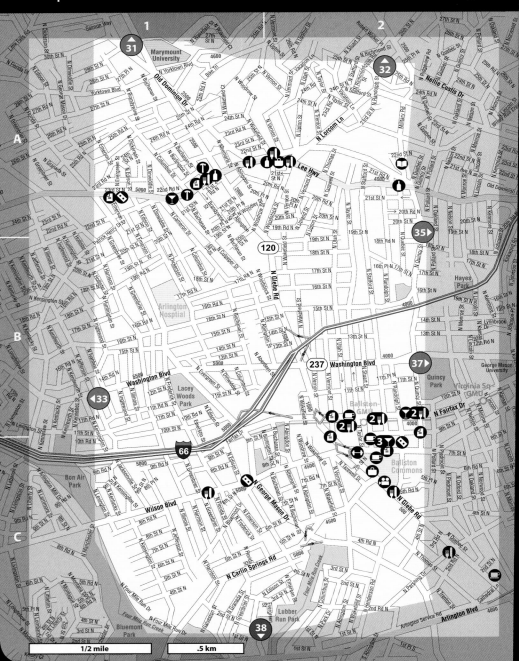

For there to be so many people living and working in Ballston, there isn't all that much to do. Maybe that's because Clarendon is just down the road. For movies, the theater at Ballston Commons is the mall's lone redeeming factor. Front Page News works for happy hour. Willow provides upscale dining and, tucked away on Lee Highway, there's Arrowine, one of the areas best wine shops.

Coffee

- **Cosi** · 4250 Fairfax Dr
- **Starbucks** · 4238 Wilson Blvd
- **Starbucks** · 801 N Glebe Rd
- **Starbucks** · 901 N Stuart St

Copy Shops

- **Copy & Convenience** · 2219 N Columbus St
- **FedEx Kinko's** · 4501 N Fairfax Dr
- **Mailboxes Etc** · 4201 Wilson Blvd
- **Minuteman Press** · 4001 N 9th St
- **Print Time** · 5137 Lee Hwy
- **Staples** · 910 N Glebe Rd

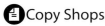Gyms

- **Sport & Health Clubs** · 4328 Wilson Blvd

Hardware Stores

- **Arlington Bill's Hardware** · 2213 N Buchanan St
- **Bill's True Value Hardware** · 4756 Lee Hwy

Liquor Stores

- **Arrowine** · 4508 Lee Hwy
- **International Wine & Beverage** · 4040 Lee Hwy
- **Virginia ABC** · 4709 Lee Hwy

Movie Theaters

- **Regal Ballston Common 12** · 671 N Glebe Rd

Nightlife

- **Bailey's Pub and Grille** · 4234 Wilson Blvd
- **Carpool** · 4000 N Fairfax Dr
- **Cowboy Café** · 4792 Lee Hwy
- **The Front Page** · 4201 Wilson Blvd
- **Rock Bottom Brewery** · 4238 Wilson Blvd

Restaurants

- **Café Parisien Express** · 4520 Lee Hwy
- **Café Tirolo** · 4001 N Fairfax Dr
- **Cassatt's** · 4536 Lee Hwy
- **Crisp & Juicy** · 4540 Lee Hwy
- **El Paso Café** · 4235 N Pershing Dr
- **Flat Top Grill** · 4245 N Fairfax Dr
- **Layalina** · 5216 Wilson Blvd
- **Metro 29 Diner** · 4711 Lee Hwy
- **Rio Grande Café** · 4301 N Fairfax Dr
- **Tara Thai** · 4001 Fairfax Dr
- **Tutto Bene** · 501 N Randolph St
- **Willow** · 4301 N Fairfax Dr

Shopping

- **Arrowine** · 4508 Lee Hwy
- **South Moon Under** · 2700 Clarendon Blvd

Video Rental

- **Dollar Video** · 5133 Lee Hwy
- **Top Video** · 850 N Randolph St
- **Video 95** · 5011 Wilson Blvd

Map 35 · Clarendon

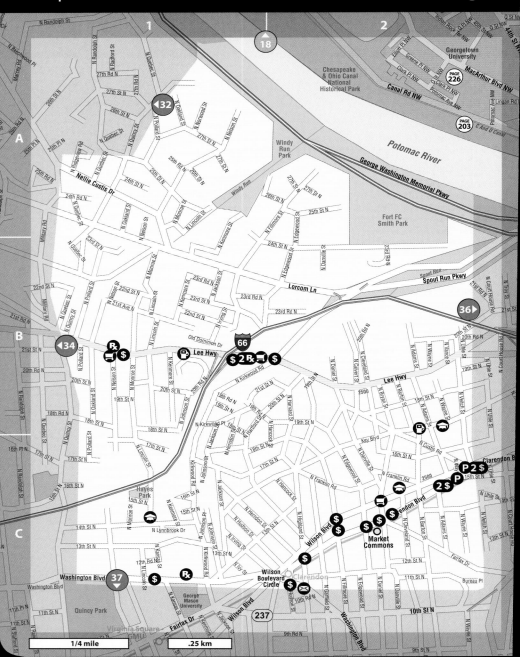

If you're young and like to play into the morning's wee hours, this is the place for you. There are plenty of restaurants, live music, places to drop cash and people-watch. The city's just a few Metro stops away, but a lot of Clarendon-ites wonder why they should leave. Not much for the family-minded though, unless the kids happen to enjoy pot-soaked jam sessions or drunken meat markets.

Map

$ Banks

- **BB&T** · 2200 Wilson Blvd
- **Chevy Chase** · 3141 Lee Hwy
- **Chevy Chase (ATM)** · 2700 Clarendon Blvd
- **Chevy Chase (ATM)** · 2800 Clarendon Blvd
- **Chevy Chase (ATM)** · 3115 Lee Hwy
- **Chevy Chase (ATM)** · 3450 Washington Blvd
- **PNC** · 2601 Clarendon Blvd
- **PNC (ATM)** · 1303 N Filmore St
- **PNC (ATM)** · 2201 Wilson Blvd
- **PNC (ATM)** · 3100 Clarendon Blvd
- **Sun Trust** · 3713 Lee Hwy
- **Sun Trust (ATM)** · 2250 Clarendon Blvd
- **Virginia Commerce** · 2930 Wilson Blvd
- **Wachovia** · 2200 Clarendon Blvd
- **Wachovia** · 3140 Washington Blvd

Gas Stations

- **Exxon** · 2410 Lee Hwy ⊙
- **Shell** · 3332 Lee Hwy

Landmarks

- **Market Commons** · 2690 Clarendon Blvd

P Parking

Rx Pharmacies

- **CVS** · 3133 Lee Hwy ⊙
- **Eckerd's** · 3130 Lee Hwy
- **Giant Food Pharmacy** · 3450 Washington Blvd
- **Safeway** · 3713 Lee Hwy

Post Offices

- **Arlington Main Office** · 3118 Washington Blvd

Schools

- **Arlington Science Focus** · 1501 N Lincoln St
- **Francis Scott Key Elementary** · 2300 Key Blvd
- **New Directions** · 2847 Wilson Blvd

Supermarkets

- **Giant Food** · 3115 Lee Hwy
- **Safeway** · 3713 Lee Hwy
- **Whole Foods Market** · 2700 Wilson Blvd

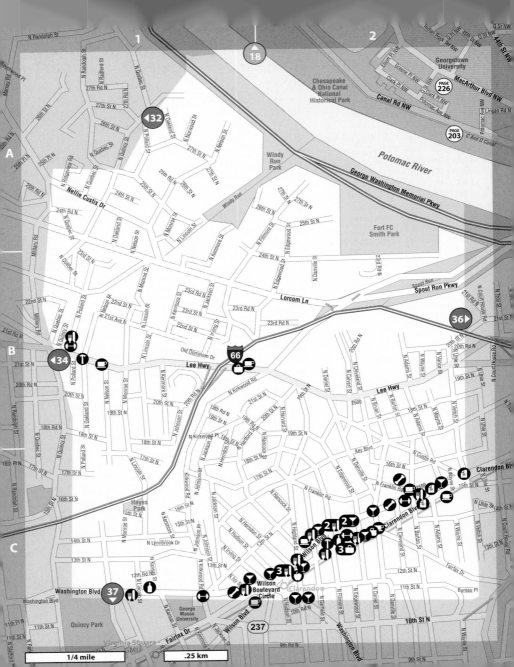

Iota offers some of the best live music around. Wilson and Clarendon Boulevards are dotted with bars, restaurants, and music venues to suit most tastes. Clarendon does lack for parking, so better to take the Metro.

Map

Coffee

- **Hot Shotz** · 3018 Wilson Blvd
- **Java Shack** · 2507 N Franklin Rd
- **Larry's Cookies** · 2200 N Clarendon Blvd
- **Murky Coffee** · 3211 N Wilson Blvd
- **Starbucks** · 2690 Clarendon Blvd
- **Starbucks** · 3125 Lee Hwy
- **Starbucks** · 3713 Lee Hwy

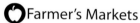Copy Shops

- **FedEx Kinko's** · 2300 Clarendon Blvd
- **Southeastern Printing & Litho** · 2401 Wilson Blvd
- **UPS Store** · 2200 Wilson Blvd

Farmer's Markets

- **Claredon Farmers Market (Wed, 3 pm–7 pm)** · Clarendon Blvd & N Highland St

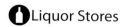Gyms

- **Arlington Sport & Health Club** · 1122 N Kirkwood Rd
- **Curves (women only)** · 2105 N Pollard St
- **Curves (women only)** · 2529 Wilson Blvd
- **Washington Sports Clubs** · 2800 Clarendon Blvd

Hardware Stores

- **Cherrydale Hardware & Garden** · 3805 Lee Hwy
- **Virginia Hardware** · 2915 Wilson Blvd

Liquor Stores

- **Best Cellars (wine only)** · 2855 N Clarendon Blvd
- **Pica Deli Gourmet and Wines (wine only)** · 3471 N Washington Blvd

Nightlife

- **Clarendon Ballroom** · 3185 Wilson Blvd
- **Clarendon Grill** · 1101 N Highland St
- **Eleventh Street Lounge** · 1041 N Highland St
- **Galaxy Hut** · 2711 Wilson Blvd
- **Harry's Tap Room** · 2800 Clarendon Blvd
- **Iota** · 2832 Wilson Blvd
- **Mister Days** · 3100 Clarendon Blvd
- **Molly Malone's** · 3207 Washington Blvd
- **Whitlow's on Wilson** · 2854 Wilson Blvd

Pet Shops

- **AKA Spot** · 2509 N Franklin Rd
- **AKA Spot** · 2622 Wilson Blvd
- **Petco** · 3200 Washington Blvd

Restaurants

- **Aegean Taverna** · 2950 Clarendon Blvd
- **Delhi Dhaba Indian Café & Carryout** · 2424 Wilson Blvd
- **Faccia Luna Trattoria** · 2909 Wilson Blvd
- **Hard Times Café** · 3028 Wilson Blvd
- **Harry's Tap Room** · 2800 Clarendon Blvd
- **Lazy Sundae** · 2925 Wilson Blvd
- **Mexicali Blues** · 2933 Wilson Blvd
- **Minh's Restaurant** · 2500 Wilson Blvd
- **Pica Deli Gourmet and Wines** · 3471 N Washington Blvd
- **Portabellos** · 2109 N Pollard St
- **Queen Bee** · 3181 Wilson Blvd
- **Sette Bello** · 3101 Wilson Blvd
- **Silver Diner** · 3200 Wilson Blvd

Shopping

- **Barnes & Noble** · 2800 Clarendon Blvd
- **The Container Store** · 2800 Clarendon Blvd
- **The Italian Store** · 3123 Lee Hwy
- **Orvis Company Store** · 2879 Clarendon Blvd
- **Pottery Barn** · 2700 Clarendon Blvd

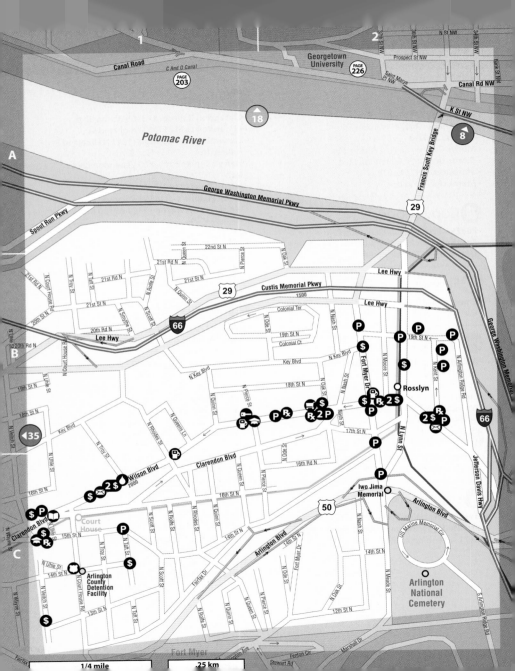

More and more high-rise dwellers are calling Rosslyn their home, but the amenities tend to still be bare bones. You've got chain lunch spots, gyms, markets, dry cleaners, and enough parking garages to sink the heart of every living environmentalist. Let's not give up, though-if condo developers keep building, perhaps more interesting perks will come.

$ Banks
- **Bank of America** · 1700 N Moore St
- **Bank of America** · 2111 Wilson Blvd
- **BB&T** · 1901 Ft Myer Dr
- **Chevy Chase** · 1100 Wilson Blvd
- **Chevy Chase (ATM)** · 1611 N Kent St
- **M&T (ATM)** · 2038 Wilson Blvd
- **PNC** · 1801 N Lynn St
- **PNC (ATM)** · 1320 N Veitch St
- **PNC (ATM)** · 1401 N Taft St
- **PNC (ATM)** · 2050 Wilson Blvd
- **Presidential Savings** · 1700 N Moore St
- **Sun Trust** · 2121 15th St N
- **Wachovia** · 1300 Wilson Blvd
- **Wachovia** · 2026 Wilson Blvd
- **Wachovia (ATM)** · 1500 Wilson Blvd

Car Rental
- **Enterprise** · 1560 Wilson Blvd · 703-528-6466

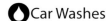 Car Washes
- **Car Cleaning & Restoration** · 2000 Wilson Blvd

 Gas Stations
- **Amoco** · 1625 Wilson Blvd
- **Chevron** · 1830 N Ft Myer Dr
- **Exxon** · 1824 Wilson Blvd ⌀

○ Landmarks
- **Arlington County Detention Facility (Jail)** · 1425 N Courthouse Rd
- **Arlington National Cemetery** · Arlington National Cemetery
- **Iwo Jima Memorial** · N Meade St & Arlington Blvd

Libraries
- **Arlington Public Library Information & Referral Office** · 2100 Clarendon Blvd

P Parking

R Pharmacies
- **CVS** · 1100 Wilson Blvd
- **CVS** · 1555 Wilson Blvd
- **CVS** · 2121 15th St N ⌀
- **Rite Aid** · 1700 N Moore St
- **Safeway** · 1525 Wilson Blvd

Police
- **Arlington County Police Department** · 1425 N Courthouse Rd

Post Offices
- **Court House Station** · 2043 Wilson Blvd
- **Rosslyn Station** · 1101 Wilson Blvd

Schools
- **Nottingham Elementary (temporary location)** · 1601 Wilson Blvd
- **Strayer University (Arlington Campus)** · 2121 15th St N

Supermarkets
- **Safeway** · 1525 Wilson Blvd

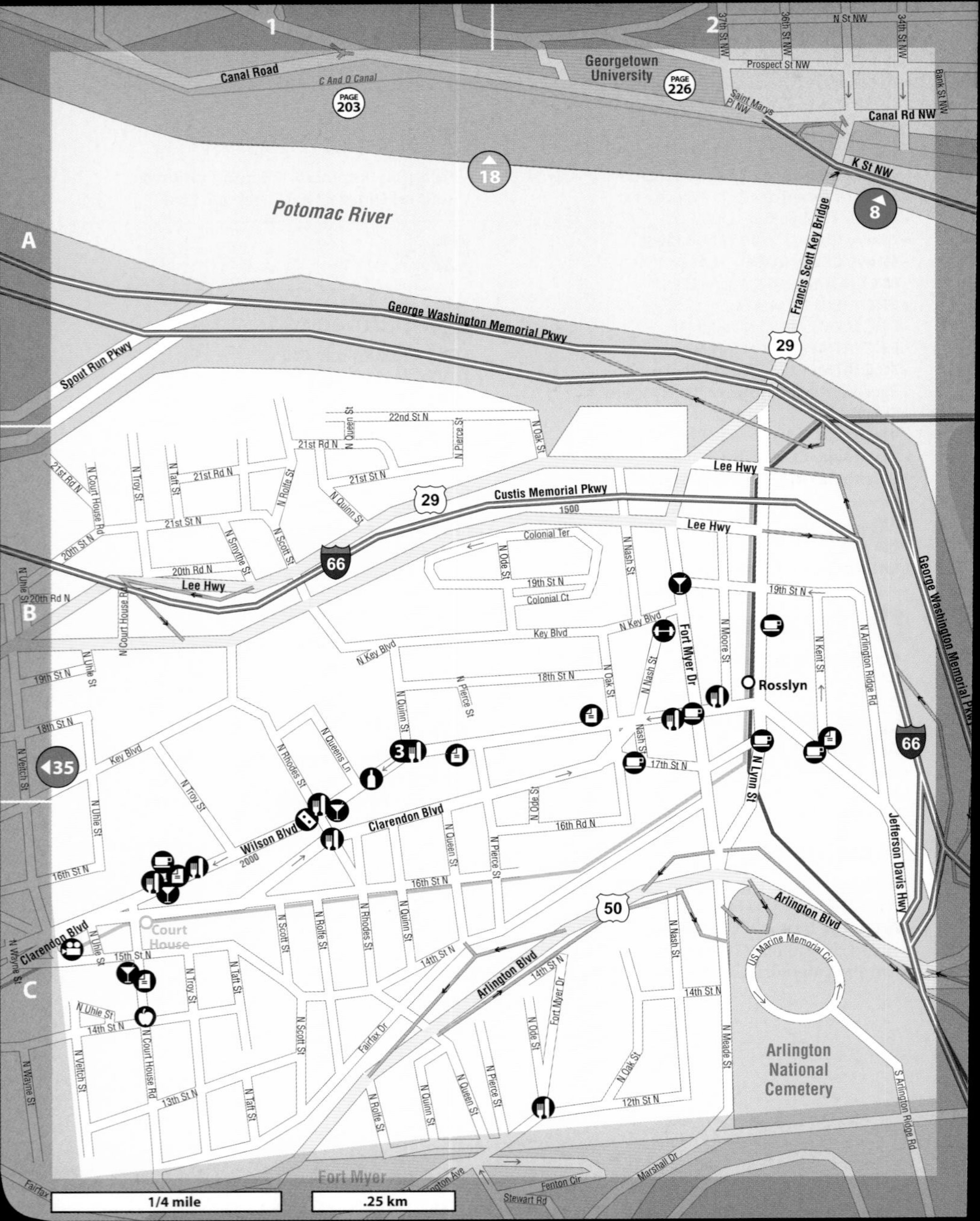

Map 36 · **Rosslyn**

N

1

2

Canal Road

C And O Canal

PAGE
203

Georgetown
University

PAGE
226

N St NW

Prospect St NW

36th St NW

34th St NW

Bank St NW

Saint Marys
Pl NW

Canal Rd NW

K St NW

18

Potomac River

Francis Scott Key Bridge

8

A

George Washington Memorial Pkwy

29

Spout Run Pkwy

22nd St N

N Oak St

N Queen St

21st Rd N

N Pierce St

21st St N

Lee Hwy

29

Custis Memorial Pkwy

1500

Lee Hwy

21st Rd N

N Court House Rd

N Taft St

N Rolfe St

N Quinn St

21st Rd N

N Scott St

21st St N

N Smythe St

N Quinn St

N Uhle St 20th Rd N

20th Rd N

20th St N

66

Colonial Ter

N Ode St

19th St N

N Nash St

19th St N

19th St N

N Moore St

N Kent St

N Arlington Ridge Rd

George Washington Memorial Pkwy

Lee Hwy

Colonial Ct

B

19th St N

18th St N

N Key Blvd

Key Blvd

N Oak St

Fort Myer Dr

Rosslyn

18th St N

N Pierce St

N Quinn St

N Rhodes St

N Lynn St

N Nash St

Key Blvd

66

35

19th St N

18th St N

17th St N

N Veitch St

N Uhle St

N Troy St

Key Blvd

N Queen St

N Ode St

16th Rd N

17th St N

N Lynn St

Jefferson Davis Hwy

3

Wilson Blvd

2000

Clarendon Blvd

16th St N

16th St N

N Scott St

N Rolfe St

N Quinn St

N Pierce St

50

Arlington Blvd

Arlington Blvd

C

Clarendon Blvd

N Wayne St

N Uhle St

15th St N

Court
House

N Troy St

N Taft St

14th St N

N Rhodes St

Fairfax Dr

14th St N

N Scott St

N Rolfe St

N Quinn St

Arlington Blvd

Fort Myer Dr

N Ode St

N Nash St

N Meade St

14th St N

US Marine Memorial Cir

Arlington
National
Cemetery

S Arlington Ridge Rd

N Uhle St

14th St N

N Court House Rd

N Veitch St

13th St N

N Taft St

N Queen St

N Pierce St

12th St N

N Oak St

Fenton Cir

Marshall Dr

Fairfax

Fort Myer

N Arlington Ave

Stewart Rd

1/4 mile

.25 km

The good news: You won't have to worry about rowdy club-goers disturbing your sleep in these parts. You're more likely to run into tumbleweeds around Rosslyn at night. This neighborhood is still all about serving the nine-to-fivers, so look to stroll across the Key Bridge into Georgetown or hike up the hill into Clarendon for any action.

Coffee

- **Coffee Express** · 1300 Wilson Blvd
- **Cosi** · 1801 N Lynn St
- **Cosi** · 2050 Wilson Blvd
- **Starbucks** · 1501 N 17th St
- **Starbucks** · 1525 Wilson Blvd
- **Starbucks** · 1735 N Lynn St

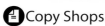Copy Shops

- **MBC Precision Imaging** ·
  1501 Wilson Blvd, Ste 100
- **Minuteman Press** · 1601 N Kent St
- **Office Depot** · 1515 N Courthouse Rd
- **Sir Speedy** · 1600 Wilson Blvd, Ste 102
- **USA Print & Copy** · 2044 Wilson Blvd

Farmer's Markets

- **Arlington County Farmer's Market**
  (Sat 8am–12 pm) · N 14th St & N Courthouse Rd

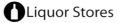Gyms

- **Gold's Gym** · 1830 N Nash St

Liquor Stores

- **Virginia ABC** · 1731 Wilson Blvd

Movie Theaters

- **AMC Courthouse Plaza 8** · 2150 Clarendon Blvd

Nightlife

- **Continental** · 1911 Ft Myer Dr
- **Ireland's Four Courts** · 2051 Wilson Blvd
- **Rhodeside Grill** · 1836 Wilson Blvd
- **Summers Grill and Sports Pub** ·
  1520 N Courthouse Rd

Restaurants

- **Café Tivoli** · 1700 North Moore St
- **Gua-Rapo** · 2039 Wilson Blvd
- **Guajillo** · 1727 Wilson Blvd
- **Il Radicchio** · 1801 Clarendon Blvd
- **Ireland's Four Courts** · 2051 Wilson Blvd
- **Mezza9** · 1325 Wilson Blvd
- **Quarter Deck Restaurant** · 1200 Ft Myer Dr
- **Ray's the Steaks** · 1725 Wilson Blvd
- **Rhodeside Grill** · 1836 Wilson Blvd
- **Village Bistro** · 1723 Wilson Blvd

Shopping

- **Tivoli** · 1700 N Moore St

Video Rental

- **Hollywood Video** · 1900 Wilson Blvd

Map 37 · **Fort Myer**

Fort Myer is mostly suburban (think '40s Cape Cods with aluminum awnings) with a couple commercial enclaves and isn't pedestrian-friendly; the automobile still rules. Other than the world's first power aircraft fatality occurring at Ft. Myer in 1908 (Orville was driving), there's little of note here.

 Banks

- **Bank of America** · 3401 Columbia Pike
- **Bank of America** · 3625 Fairfax Dr
- **BB&T** · 1100 S Walter Reed Dr
- **BB&T** · 3001 N Washington Blvd
- **Chevy Chase** · 3532 Columbia Pike
- **Chevy Chase** · 901 N Nelson St
- **Chevy Chase (ATM)** · 2411 Columbia Pike
- **Chevy Chase (ATM)** · 2515 Columbia Pike
- **Sun Trust** · 249 N Glebe Rd
- **Sun Trust** · 3108 Columbia Pike
- **United** · 2300 9th St S
- **United** · 3801 Wilson Blvd
- **Wachovia** · 951 S George Mason Dr

 **Car Rental**

- **Avis** · 3206 10th St N · 703-516-4202
- **Hertz** · 3200 S Columbia Pike · 703-920-1808

 **Car Washes**

- **Mr Wash** · 101 N Glebe Rd
- **Quality Wash** · 89 N Glebe Rd

Gas Stations

- **Chevron** · 67 N Glebe Rd
- **Citgo** · 2324 Columbia Pike
- **Exxon** · 1001 S Glebe Rd ⊙
- **Hess** · 3299 Wilson Blvd
- **Mobil** · 3100 Columbia Pike ⊙
- **Shell** · 4211 Columbia Pike

 Landmarks

- **Arlington Cinema 'N' Drafthouse** · 2903 Columbia Pike
- **Bob and Edith's Diner** · 2310 Columbia Pike ⊙

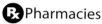 **Libraries**

- **Columbia Pike Library** · 816 S Walter Reed Dr

 Pharmacies

- **CVS** · 256 N Glebe Rd
- **CVS** · 2601 Columbia Tpke
- **CVS** · 2900 10th St N
- **Eckerd's** · 2820 Columbia Pike
- **Giant Pharmacy** · 2411 Columbia Piike
- **Rite Aid** · 940 S George Mason Dr

Post Offices

- **South Station** · 1210 S Glebe Rd

Schools

- **The Career Center** · 816 S Walter Reed Dr
- **Family Center** · 3205 2nd St S
- **Henry Elementary** · 701 S Highland St
- **Jefferson Middle** · 125 S Old Gebe Rd
- **Long Branch Elementary** · 33 N Fillmore St
- **St Charles** · 3299 N Fairfax Dr
- **St Thomas More Cathedral** · 105 N Thomas St

 **Supermarkets**

- **Food Star** · 950 S George Mason Dr
- **Giant Food** · 2515 Columbia Pike
- **Safeway** · 2303 Columbia Pike

The Columbia Pike strip has some interesting ethnic eateries (Matuba, next door to the Arlington Cinema 'n' Drafthouse, is one). But aside from mostly mom-and-pop pizza joints and pawn shops in the long-in-the-tooth strip centers, there's not much here (save for the two Bob & Edith's diners for those "preventative" post-closing time Friday night meals). Since you're in your car anyway, head to Clarendon or even (ugh) Pentagon City.

Map 3

Coffee

- **Dunkin' Donuts** · 3100 Columbia Pike
- **Rappahannock Coffee** · 2406 Columbia Pike
- **Starbucks** · 901 N Nelson St

Copy Shops

- **Reprographic Technologies** · 3300 N Fairfax Dr
- **SOWA & Nicholas Printing** · 3301 Wilson Blvd

Farmer's Markets

- **Columbia Pike Farmer's Market (May–Nov, Sun, 10 am–2 pm)** · Columbia Pike & S Walter Reed Dr

Gyms

- **Aerobic Workout** · 954 N Monroe St
- **Curves (women only)** · 3528 Wilson Blvd
- **Gold's Gym** · 3910 Wilson Blvd

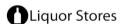Liquor Stores

- **ABC** · 1001 N Fillmore St
- **ABC** · 2201 N Pershing Dr

Movie Theaters

- **Arlington Cinema 'N' Drafthouse** · 2903 Columbia Pike

Nightlife

- **Jay's Saloon** · 3114 10th St N
- **Royal Lee Bar and Grill** · 2211 N Pershing Dr
- **Tallula** · 2761 Washington Blvd

Pet Shops

- **Birds 'n' Things** · 2628 Columbia Pike

Restaurants

- **Atilla's** · 2705 Columbia Pike
- **Bangkok 54** · 2919 Columbia Pike
- **Bob and Edith's Diner** · 2310 Columbia Pike ⌾
- **Bob and Edith's Diner** · 4707 Columbia Pike ⌾
- **The Broiler** · 3601 Columbia Pike
- **El Charrito Caminante** · 2710 N Washington Blvd
- **El Pollo Rico** · 932 N Kenmore St
- **Manee Thai** · 2500 Columbia Pike
- **Mario's Pizza House** · 3322 Wilson Blvd
- **Matuba** · 2915 Columbia Pike
- **Mrs Chen's Kitchen** · 3101 Columbia Pike
- **Pan American Bakery** · 4113 Columbia Pike
- **Rincome Thai Cuisine** · 3030 Columbia Pike
- **Tallula Restaurant** · 2761 Washington Blvd

Shopping

- **Ski Chalet** · 2704 Columbia Pike

Video Rental

- **Hollywood Video** · 3263 Columbia Pike
- **Video Warehouse** · 3411 5th St S

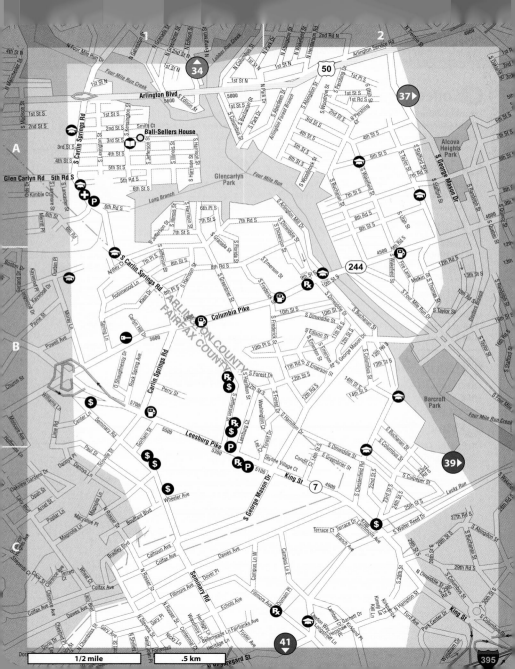

To quote your mother, lock your car doors. Columbia Pike, while "transitioning," has a long way to go. For now, the petty crime rate is fairly high, although the area does boast some pretty cool stores and coffee shops. Latino music is piped into the CVS, which is a nice break from the Muzak played in most of those chains.

Banks

- **Bank of America** · 5707 Seminary Rd
- **Burke & Herbert** · 5705 Seminary Rd
- **Chevy Chase** · 3480 S Jefferson St
- **Chevy Chase** · 3499 S Jefferson St
- **Chevy Chase** · 5851 Crossroads Ctr Wy
- **PNC (ATM)** · 5601 Seminary Rd
- **Wachovia** · 4651 King St
- **Wachovia** · 5797 Leesburg Pike

Car Rental

- **Enterprise** · 5666 Columbia Pike · 703-933-2454

Emergency Rooms

- **Northern Virginia Community** ·
  601 S Carlin Springs Rd ⊚

Gas Stations

- **Amoco** · 4625 Columbia Pike
- **Mobil** · 5200 Columbia Pike
- **Shell** · 5511 Columbia Pike
- **Shell** · 5600 Leesburg Pike

○ Landmarks

- **Ball-Sellers House** · 5620 S 3rd St

Libraries

- **Glencarlyn Public Library** · 300 S Kensington St

 Parking

Pharmacies

- **Allied Pharmacy** · 5100 Fillmore Ave
- **CVS** · 3535 S Jefferson St ⊚
- **CVS** · 5017 Columbia Pike
- **Giant Food Pharmacy** · 3480 S Jefferson St ⊚
- **Target** · 5115 Leesburg Pike

 Schools

- **Arlington Mill High Continuation Program** ·
  4975 Columbia Pike
- **Barcroft Elementary** · 625 S Wakefield St
- **Campbell Elementary** · 737 S Carlin Springs Rd
- **Carlin Springs Elementary** · 5995 5th Rd S
- **Claremont Immersion** · 4700 S Chesterfield Rd
- **Glen Forest Elementary** · 5829 Glen Forest Dr
- **Kenmore Middle** · 200 S Carlin Springs Rd
- **Northern Virginia Community College
  (Alexandria Campus)** · 3001 N Beauregard St
- **Our Savior Lutheran** · 825 S Taylor St
- **Wakefield High** · 4901 S Chesterfield Rd

Map

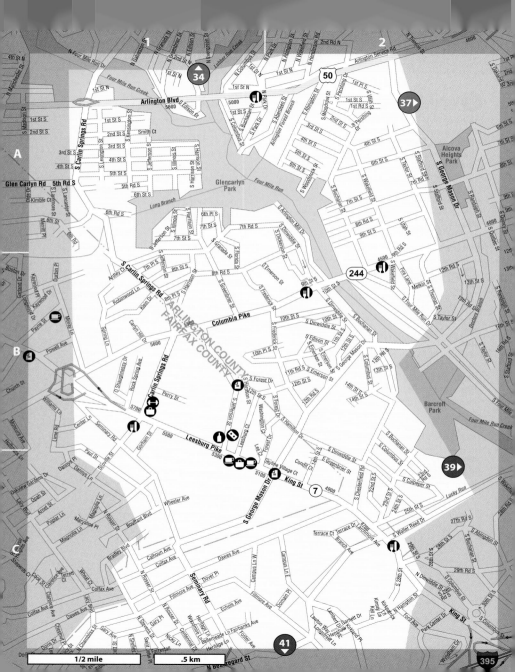

You'll need several shots of Novocaine to handle Leesburg Pike or Columbia Pike on a Saturday afternoon. This big box bonanza does nothing to improve upon the suburbs' bad name. The planet's best burgers are to be had at Five Guys, as well as authentic Mexican at Atlacatl, but other than that, call Domino's. Or head into town.

Coffee

- **Caribou Coffee** · 5201 Leesburg Pike
- **Starbucks** · 5115 Leesburg Pike
- **Starbucks** · 5821 Crossroads Ctr Wy

Copy Shops

- **FedEx Kinko's** · 3515C S Jefferson St ⊙
- **Kwik Kopy Printing** · 5100 Leesburg Pike
- **Staples** · 5801 Leesburg Pike

Gyms

- **Gold's Gym** · 3505 Carlin Springs Rd

Liquor Stores

- **ABC** · 3556E S Jefferson St

Restaurants

- **Andy's Carry-Out** · 5033 Columbia Pike
- **Athens Restaurant** · 3541 Carlin Springs Rd
- **Atlacatl** · 4701 Columbia Pike
- **Crystal Thai** · 4819 Arlington Blvd
- **Five Guys** · 4626 King St

Shopping

- **REI** · 3509 Carlin Springs Rd
- **Target** · 5115 Leesburg Pike

Video Rental

- **Hollywood Video** · 3541 S Jefferson St

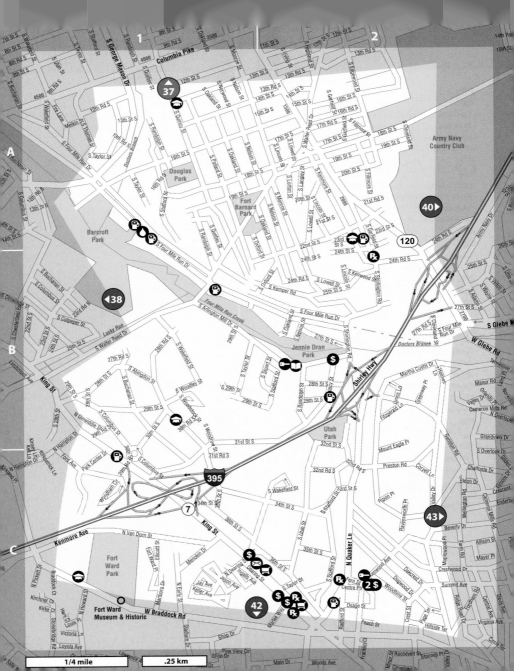

This former sleepy neighborhood is quickly becoming Ballston West with high-rise buildings and every sort of business you've come to expect from vertical development. The nightlife is slowly starting to catch up with the bustling restaurant scene.

Banks
- **BB&T** · 2700 S Quincy St
- **Burke & Herbert** · 1705 Fern St
- **Chevy Chase** · 3690 King St
- **Sun Trust** · 3610 King St
- **Wachovia** · 1711 Fern St
- **Wachovia** · 3624 King St

Car Rental
- **Enterprise** · 1575 Kenwood Ave · 703-647-1216
- **Enterprise** · 2778 S Arlington Mill Dr · 703-820-7100

Car Washes
- **David's Car Wash** · 4148 S Four Mile Run Dr

Gas Stations
- **Amoco** · 4050 S Four Mile Run Dr
- **Exxon** · 2316 S Shirlington Rd
- **Exxon** · 4368 King St ⊚
- **Mobil** · 4154 S Four Mile Run Dr ⊚
- **Shell** · 1333 N Quaker Ln
- **Shell** · 2817 S Quincy St
- **Shell** · 4060 S Four Mile Run Dr
- **Sunoco** · 1639 N Quaker Ln

⊙Landmarks
- **Fort Ward Museum and Historic Site** · 4301 W Braddock Rd

Libraries
- **Shirlington Library** · 2786 S Arlington Mill Dr

Pharmacies
- **CVS** · 1521 N Quaker Ln
- **Green Valley** · 2415 S Shirlington Rd
- **Rite Aid** · 3614 King St
- **Safeway** · 3526 King St

Post Offices
- **Park Fairfax Station** · 3682 King St

Schools
- **Abingdon Elementary** · 3035 S Abingdon St
- **Drew Model Elementary** · 3500 S 23rd St S
- **Randolph Elementary** · 1306 S Quincy St
- **St Clement Episcopal** · 1701 N Quaker Ln
- **St Stephen's & St Agnes Middle** · 4401 W Braddock Rd

Supermarkets
- **Giant Food** · 3680 King St
- **Safeway** · 3526 King St

Map 39 · **Shirlington**

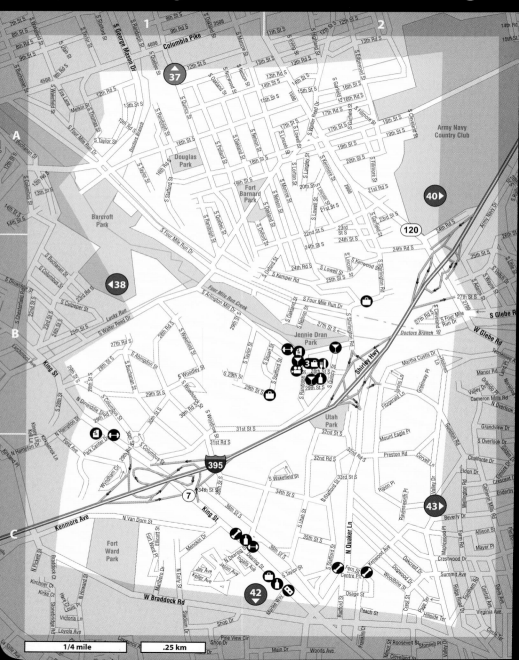

The Village at Shirlington has growing potential, but it's a ways off. There are several eateries (especially the under-rated Carlyle), a sterile multiplex and, coming soon, a grocery store and a new home for the Signature Theater. This area should become a hot spot…in a few years.

Coffee

- **Starbucks** · 3690 Q King St

Copy Shops

- **National Reprographics Inc** · 4300 King St
- **UPS Store** · 2776 S Arlington Mill Dr

Gyms

- **Center Club** · 4300 King St
- **Curves (women only)** · 2772 S Arlington Mill Dr
- **Washington Sports Clubs** · 3654 King St

Liquor Stores

- **The Curious Grape** · 4056 28th St S
- **Unwined (wine only)** · 3690 King St
- **Virginia ABC** · 3678 King St

Movie Theaters

- **Cineplex Odeon Shirlington 7** ·
  2772 S Randolph St

Nightlife

- **The Bungalow, Billiards & Brew Co** ·
  2766 S Arlington Mill Dr
- **Capitol City Brewing Company** · 2700 S Quincy St
- **Guapo's** · 4028 S 28th St

Pet Shops

- **For Pet's Sake** · 1537 N Quaker Ln
- **One Good Tern** · 1710 Fern St
- **Pro Feed** · 3690 King St

Restaurants

- **Carlyle Grande Café** · 4000 28th St S

Shopping

- **Best Buns Bread Co** · 4010 28th St S
- **Books-A-Million** · 4017 28th St S
- **The Curious Grape** · 4056 28th St S
- **Unwined** · 3690 King St, Unit J
- **Washington Golf Centers** · 2625 Shirlington Rd

Video Rental

- **Blockbuster** · 3610 King St

Map 40 · **Pentagon City / Crystal City**

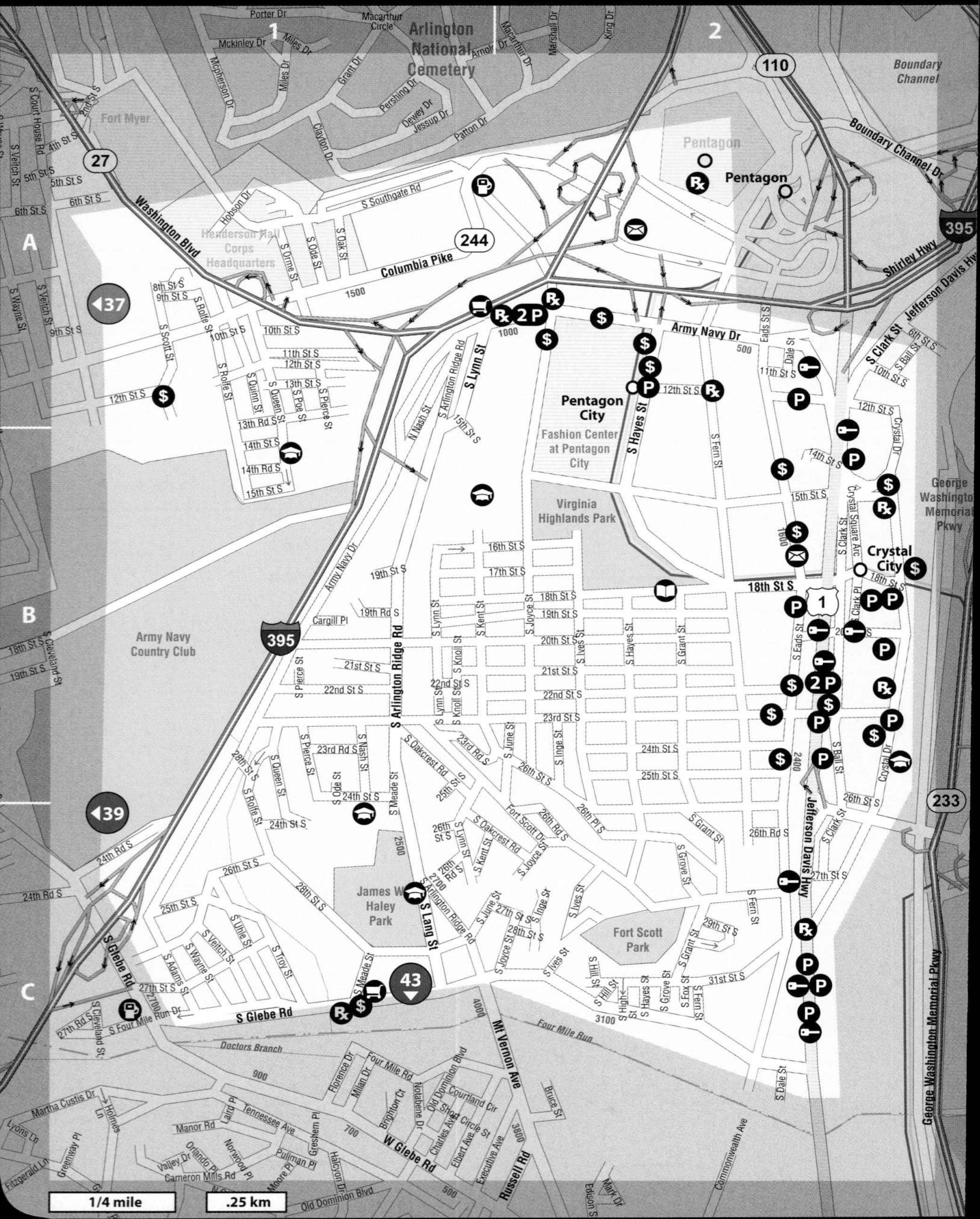

Ⓝ

1   **2**

Porter Dr   Macarthur Circle

Mckinley Dr

Miles Dr

Grant Dr

Arlington National Cemetery

Boundary Channel

110

Boundary Channel Dr

McPherson Dr

Pershing Dr

Carver Dr

Jessup Dr

Patton Dr

Marshall Dr

King Dr

Pentagon

Pentagon

Pentagon

Shirley Hwy

395

S Scott House Rd   S Scott St S

Fort Myer

27

4th St S

5th St S

5th St S

6th St S

6th St S

S Veitch St

Washington Blvd

Hobson Dr

S Southgate Rd

Henderson Hall Corps Headquarters

S Oak St

S Ode St

S Queen St

244

Columbia Pike

1500

Eads St S

Jefferson Davis Hwy

A

◀37

S Veitch St

8th St S

9th St S

S Rolfe St

S Scott St

10th St S

11th St S

12th St S

13th St S

S Queen St

S Pierce St

13th Rd S

14th St S

14th Rd S

15th St S

S Arlington Ridge Rd

S Lynn St

N Main St

N Quinn St

1000

Army Navy Dr

500

S Hayes St

S Fern St

Pentagon City

Fashion Center at Pentagon City

12th St S

S Dale St

11th St S

S Clark St

8th St S

10th St S

12th St S

14th St S

Crystal Dr

15th St S

George Washington Memorial Pkwy

12th St S

$

Virginia Highlands Park

16th St S

17th St S

Crystal Square Ave

S Ball St

Crystal City

B

18th St S

19th St S

S Kent St

S Joyce St

20th St S

21st St S

22nd St S

23rd St S

24th St S

25th St S

395

Army Navy Country Club

Cargill Pl

19th Rd S

S Pierce St

21st St S

22nd St S

23rd Rd S

S Meade St

S Delecrest Rd

26th St S

26th Rd S

S June St

S Hayes St

S Grant St

S Inge St

1

S Eads St

S Fern St

233

S Dalcrest Rd

S Knoll St

S Lynn St

James W. Haley Park

S Lang St

Fort Scott Rd

S Joyce St

26th St S

S Grove St

26th St S

17th St S

S Glebe Rd

S Cleveland St

24th Rd S

27th St S

S Four Mile Run Dr

S Rolfe St

S Ode St

S Queen St

25th St S

S Veitch St

S Adams St

S Troy St

28th St S

43

▼

S Glebe Rd

2500

29th St S

30th St S

31st St S

Fort Scott Park

S Hill St

S Grove St

S Fox St

S Hayes St

3100

S Dale St

C

Doctors Branch

27th St S

900

Four Mile Run

Mt Vernon Ave

Martha Custis Dr

Fitzgerald Ln

Greenway Pl

Manor Rd

Norfolk Ave

Cameron Mills Rd

Valley Dr

Gresham Pl

Milan Dr

Four Mile Rd

Old Dominion Blvd

Brighton Ct

Courtland Dr

Bruce St

Charles Ave

Executive Ave

Commonwealth Ave

Mary St

W Glebe Rd

700

Old Dominion Blvd

Russell Rd

Endicott St

| 1/4 mile | .25 km |

The hordes who work for or because of the defense industry need somewhere to shop and eat. The people visiting the Pentagon need somewhere to sleep. Pentagon City answers their little military prayers. If you like character-less mall stores, marching crowds, and big hotel chains, you'll love it here. For the rest of us: be happy to watch this hood fly by as we pass through on the Metro en route to the airport.

Map

$ Banks

- **Bank of America** · 1425 S Eads St
- **Bank of America (ATM)** · 1101 S Joyce St
- **BB&T** · 2113 Crystal Plz Arc
- **BB&T** · 2221 S Eads St
- **BB&T** · 2947 S Glebe Rd
- **Burke & Herbert** · 500 23rd St S
- **Chevy Chase** · 1100 S Hayes St
- **Chevy Chase** · 1621 Crystal Sq Arc
- **Chevy Chase** · 2100 S Crystal Dr
- **Chevy Chase** · 2901 S Glebe Rd
- **PNC (ATM)** · 1100 S Hayes St
- **PNC (ATM)** · 1301 S Scott St
- **PNC (ATM)** · 1600 S Eads St
- **Wachovia** · 251 18th St S
- **Wachovia (ATM)** · 1615 Crystal Sq Arc

Car Rental

- **Alamo** · 2780 Jefferson Davis Hwy · 703-684-0086
- **Budget** · 1800 S Jefferson Davis Hwy · 703-521-2908
- **Dollar** · 2600 Jefferson Davis Hwy · 866-434-2226
- **Enterprise** · 1225 S Clark St · 703-553-2930
- **Enterprise** · 2020 Jefferson Davis Hwy · 703-553-7744
- **Hertz** · Double Tree Hotel · 300 Army Navy Dr · 703-413-7142
- **Rent-A-Wreck** · 901 S Clark St · 703-413-7100
- **Thrifty** · 2900 Jefferson Davis Hwy · 877-283-0898

Gas Stations

- **Citgo** · 801 S Joyce St
- **Exxon** · 2720 S Glebe Rd ⊙

○ Landmarks

- **Pentagon** · Boundary Channel Dr

📖 Libraries

- **Arlington County Aurora Hills Library** · 735 18th St S

P Parking

℞ Pharmacies

- **Costco Wholesale Pharmacy** · 1200 S Fern St
- **CVS** · 2400 Jefferson Davis Hwy ⊙
- **CVS** · The Pentagon
- **Eckerd's** · 1301 Joyce St
- **Giant Food Pharmacy** · 2901 S Glebe Rd
- **Harris Teeter Pharmacy** · 900 Army Navy Dr
- **Rite Aid** · 1671 Crystal Sq Arc
- **Rite Aid** · 2120 Crystal Plz Arc

✉ Post Offices

- **Eads Station** · 1720 S Eads St
- **Pentagon Branch** · 9998 The Pentagon

🎓 Schools

- **DeVry University (Arlington Campus)** · 2450 Crystal Dr
- **Gunston Middle** · 2700 S Lang St
- **Hoffman-Boston Elementary** · 1415 S Queen St
- **Oakridge Elementary** · 1414 24th St S

🛒 Supermarkets

- **Harris Teeter** · 900 Army Navy Dr

Map 4

So much, yet so little. What is here is really BIG, but unless you like malls and food courts, the pickings are slim. Head up Jefferson Davis Hwy to 23rd St where you'll find a little oasis in an otherwise dreary urban landscape. Several local eateries, live music and a great sports bar offer the area's few saving graces.

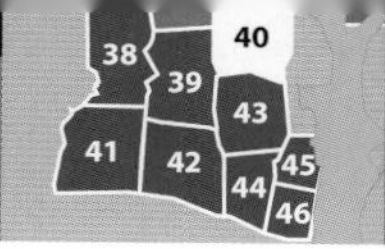

38 39 40 41 42 43 44 45 46

Coffee
- **Caribou Coffee** · 2100 Crystal Dr
- **Dunkin Donuts** · 1687 Crystal Sq Arc
- **Starbucks** · 1100 S Hayes St
- **Starbucks** · 1101 S Joyce St
- **Starbucks** · 1201 S Hayes St
- **Starbucks** · 1480 Crystal Dr
- **Starbucks** · 1649 Crystal Sq
- **Starbucks** · 1700 Jefferson Davis Hwy
- **Starbucks** · 2231 Crystal Dr

Copy Shops
- **FedEx Kinko's** · 1601 Crystal Sq Arc ⊙
- **Minuteman Press** · 2187 Crystal Plz Arc

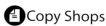Gyms
- **Bally Total Fitness** · 1201 S Joyce St
- **Crystal Park Sport & Health** · 2231 Crystal Dr
- **Curves (women only)** · 2345 Crystal Dr
- **Gateway Sport & Health** ·
  1235 S Clarke St
- **Gold's Gym** · 2955 S Glebe Rd

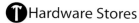Hardware Stores
- **Crystal City Hardware** · 1612 Crystal Sq Arc

Liquor Stores
- **Virginia ABC** · 2955 S Glebe Rd

Nightlife
- **Bailey's Irish Pub** · 2010 Crystal Dr
- **Sine Irish Pub** · 1301 S Joyce St

Restaurants
- **Bistro Bulgari** · 509 S 23rd St
- **Crystal City Restaurant** · 422 S 23rd St
- **Crystal City Sports Pub** · 529 S 23rd St
- **Legal Seafood** · 2301 Jefferson Davis Hwy
- **Morton's the Steakhouse** · 1631 Crystal Sq Arc

Shopping
- **Abercrombie & Fitch** · 1100 S Hayes St
- **Apple Store** · 1100 S Hayes St
- **BCBG** · 1100 S Hayes St
- **bebe** · 1100 S Hayes St
- **Costco** · 1200 S Fern St
- **Denim Bar** · 1101 S Joyce St
- **Elizabeth Arden Red Door Salon & Spa** ·
  1101 S Joyce St
- **Fashion Center-Pentagon City** · 1100 S Hayes
- **Harris Teeter** · 900 Army Navy Dr
- **Jean Machine** · 1100 S Hayes St
- **Kenneth Cole** · 1100 S Hayes St
- **Macy's** · 1000 S Hayes St
- **Williams-Sonoma** · 1100 S Hayes St

Video Rental
- **Blockbuster** · 2931 S Glebe Rd

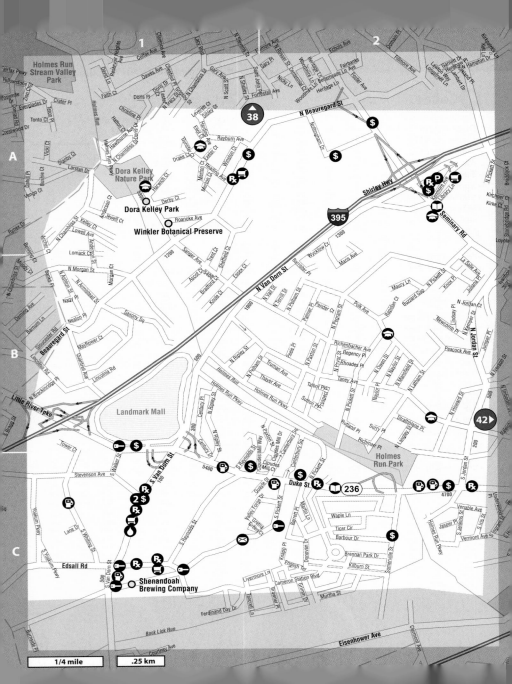

Landmark is an architecturally jarring mixture of older neighborhoods, hideous new apartment buildings, high-rise office blocks, nondescript strip malls, and tangled highway overpasses. Its most unique cultural contribution to greater Washington is the Shenandoah Brewing Company, the area's only brewery/brewpub/brew-your-own-beer facility. It definitely sweetens the overall bitter brew of the area, as do some truly nice parks, including Dora Kelley Park and the curious wonderland that is the Winkler Botanical Preserve.

$ Banks

- **BB&T** · 233 S Van Dorn St
- **BB&T** · 4999 Seminary Rd
- **Burke & Herbert** · 155 N Paxton St
- **PNC (ATM)** · 4825 Mark Ctr Dr
- **Provident** · 231 S Van Dorn St
- **Sun Trust** · 1460 N Beauregard St
- **Sun Trust** · 4616 Kenmore Ave
- **Sun Trust** · 5701 Duke St
- **Virginia Commerce** · 5140 Duke St
- **Virginia Commerce (ATM)** · 185 Somervelle St
- **Wachovia** · 4601 Duke St

Car Rental

- **Avis** · 6001 Duke St · 703-256-4335
- **Enterprise** · 200 S Pickett St · 703-341-2117
- **Enterprise** · 512 S Van Dorn St · 703-823-5700
- **Enterprise** · 5800 Edsall Rd · 703-658-0010
- **Hertz** · 501 S Pickett St · 703-751-1250

Car Washes

- **Mr Wash** · 420 S Van Dorn St

Gas Stations

- **Exxon** · 4657 Duke St
- **Exxon** · 501 S Van Dorn St ⊕
- **Mobil** · 190 S Whiting St ⊕
- **Shell** · 4670 Duke St
- **Shell** · 5200 Duke St
- **Sunoco** · 5412 Duke St

o Landmarks

- **Dora Kelley Park** · 5750 Sanger Ave
- **Shenandoah Brewing Company** · 652 S Pickett St
- **Winkler Botanical Preserve** · 5400 Roanoke Ave

Libraries

- **Alexandria Charles E Beatley Jr Central Library** · 5005 Duke St
- **Ellen Coolidge Burke Branch Library** · 4701 Seminary Rd

P Parking

Pharmacies

- **CVS** · 1462 Beauregard St
- **CVS** · 259 S Van Dorn St
- **CVS** · 4606 Kenmore Ave
- **CVS** · 5101 Duke St ⊕
- **Giant Pharmacy** · 5730 Edsall Rd
- **Rite Aid** · 4515 Duke St
- **Safeway** · 299 S Van Dorn St

Post Offices

- **Trade Center Station** · 340 S Pickett St

Schools

- **Francis C Hammond Middle** · 4646 Seminary Rd
- **James K Polk Elementary** · 5000 Polk Ave
- **John Adams Elementary** · 5651 Rayburn Ave
- **Patrick Henry Elementary** · 4643 Taney Ave
- **William Ramsey Elementary** · 5700 Sanger Ave

Supermarkets

- **Giant Food** · 1476 N Beauregard St
- **Giant Food** · 5730 Edsall Rd
- **Magruders** · 4604 Kenmore Ave
- **Safeway** · 299 S Van Dorn St

Map 41 · Landmark

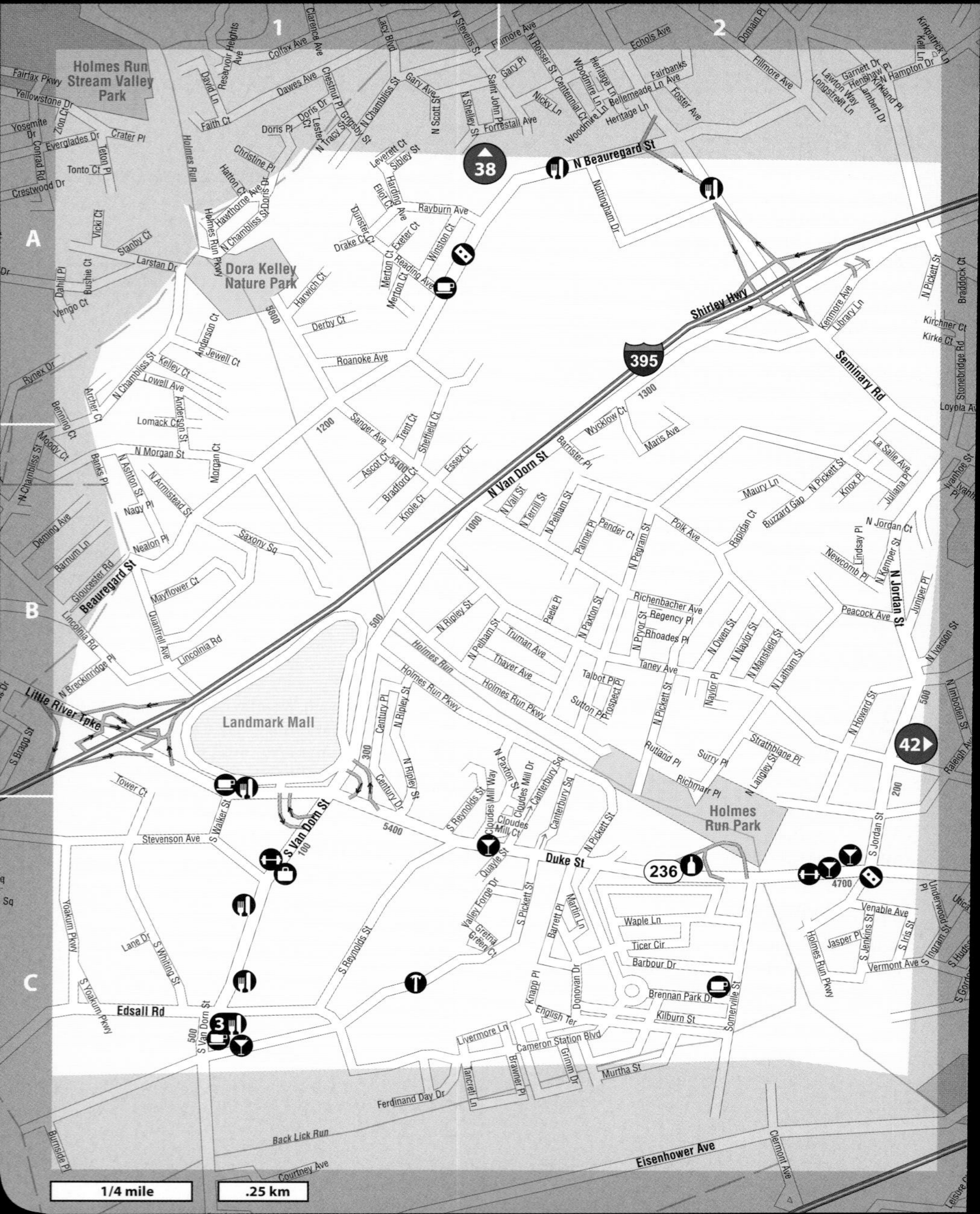

N

Holmes Run Stream Valley Park

Fairfax Pkwy
Yellowstone Dr
Yosemite Dr
Everglades Dr   Crater Pl
Tonto Ct
Crestwood Dr

1

Colfax Ave
Lord Blvd
Dawes Ave
Faith Ct
Doris Ct
Christine Pl

Clairedale Ave
Chestnut Ct
Doris Ct   N Chambliss St
N Tracy St
Leverett Ct
Harding Ct   Sibley St
Elrod Ct

N Scott St
N Shetley St
Saint John's Ave
Forrestall Ave

Gary Ave

Echols Ave

N Streets St   Woodmont Ct
Heritage Ln
Woodmont Ave   Belmeade Ln
Nicky Ln
Heritage Ln

2

Dornan St

Foster Ave

Fairbanks Ave

Fillmore Ave

Garnett Dr
Lavinoli Hwy   Herbstown Pl
Longfellow   Longstreet Pl
N Hampton Dr

Kreggmeyer Ct
Kennedy Ln

N Beauregard St

38

Dora Kelley Nature Park

Fairfax Pkwy
Holmes Run
Vicki Ct
Stanby Ct
Dahli Pl
Vergo Ct

Rayburn Ave
Dunraven Ct
Drake Ct   Exeter Ct
Merton Ct   Reading Ave
Winston Ct

A

Larstan Dr
Holmes Run Pkwy   Hawthorne
N Chambliss St
Harrod Ct

N Chambliss
N Chambliss Ct
Kelley Ct
Lowell Ave   Jewell Ct
Anderson Ct

Derby Ct

Harwich Ct

Roanoke Ave

Shirley Hwy

Nottingham Dr

Kenmore Ave
Library Ln

Kirchner Ct
Kirke Ct
Stonebridge Rd

N Pickett St
Bradricks Ct

395

Seminary Rd

Loyola Av

Boney Ct
Bemus Ct
McGrail Ct

Lomack Ct

1200

N Chambliss
Archer Ct

N Morgan St
N Ashton St   N Armistead St
Morgan Ct
Nagy Ct   Knole Ct
Nealon Pl

Barnum Ln   Saxony Sq
Demon Ave

N Chambliss Ct
Gloucester Rd

Beauregard St

B

Little River Tpke

S Reynolds St
S Ripley St

S Jordan St

Sanger Ave   Trent Ct
Ascot Ct   Sheffield Ct
Bradford Ct

1000

N Van Dorn St

N Vail St
N Terrill St
N Pelham St

Wycklow Ct
Banister Pl

Maris Ave

1300

Maury Ln
N Pickett St
Knox Ct
La Salle Ave
Juliana St

N Jordan St
Lindsay Pl
Newcomb Pl
Jemper Pl
Juniper Pl

N Jordan St

N Vernon St
S Vernon St   N Kimbrough St

Landmark Mall

500

Beauregard St
Diamond Ave
N Jebine Ln
Lincolnia Rd

N Ripley St
Century Pl
N Elgine St

Holmes Run
Holmes Run Pkwy
Thayer Ave
Holmes Run Pkwy

Truman Ave
N Paxton St

Barrister Pl
Palmer Pl   Pender Ct
N Pegram St

Peele Pl
Folk Ave

Rhoades Pl
Richenbacher Ave
N Pryor St   Regency Pl

N Owen St
N Nabor Ct   N Mansfield St
N Latham St

Buzzard Gap

N Jordan St

Peacock Ave

Surry Pl
Strathbane Pl
Richman Pl

42

300

Century Dr

5400

S Reynolds St

Cloudes Mill Way
Cloudes Mill Dr
Cloudes Mill
Canterbury Sq

Quaylor St
Barrett Pl
Martin Ln

N Pickett St

Talbot Pl
Prospect Pl
Sutton Pl

Taney Ave

Rutland Pl

Richman Pl
N Langley St

Holmes Run Park

236

4700

Venable Ave
S Jenkins St
Jasper Ct
Vermont Ave   S Iris St

Universitywood

S Van Dorn St

S Walker St

Stevenson Ave

S Van Dorn St

Tower Ct

C

Edsall Rd

Lane Dr   S Whiting St

S Yoakum Pkwy
S Yoakum Pkwy

Yoakum Pkwy

Sq

S Ripley St

S Reynolds St

S Pickett St
Valley Forge Dr
Greenup Pl
Green Ct

S Donovan St
Krapp Ct
English Ter

Duke St

Waple Ln
Ticer Cir
Barbour Dr

Brennan Park Dr
Somerville St
Kilburn St

Holmes Run Pkwy

S Jordan St

3

S Dorn St

500

Livermore Ln
Ferdinand Day Dr
Cameron Station Blvd
Tancell Ln   Grimm Ct   S Early St
Murtha St

Back Lick Run

Courtney Ave

Eisenhower Ave

Clermont Ave

Bermuda St

Map 41

Though large swaths of the area don't offer much in the way of scenery, Landmark's atmosphere has received a revitalizing jump-start from an influx of immigrants. A world tour of dining possibilities—including Thai, Japanese, Indonesian, and Italian—is in store for the intrepid suburban spelunker. But if you're feeling boring, there's always the eponymous mall.

Coffee
• **Barnie's Coffee & Tea Company** •
  Landmark Mall - 5801 Duke St
• **Cameron Perks** • 4911 Brenman Park Dr
• **Dunkin' Donuts** • 504 S Van Dorn St
• **Starbucks** • 1462 N Beauregard St

Gyms
• **Curves (women only)** • 4613 Duke St
• **Fitness First** • 255 S Van Dorn St

Hardware Stores
• **Home Depot** • 400 S Pickett St

Liquor Stores
• **Virginia ABC** • 4907 Duke St

Nightlife
• **Mango Mike's** • 4580 Duke St
• **Shenandoah Brewing Company** • 652 S Pickett St
• **Shooter McGee's** • 5239 Duke St
• **Zig's** • 4531 Duke St

Restaurants
• **Akasaka** • 514-C S Van Dorn St
• **The American Café** • 5801 Duke St
• **Clyde's** • 1700 N Beauregard St
• **Edgardo's Trattoria** • 281 S Van Dorn St
• **El Paraiso** • 516 S Van Dorn St
• **Finn & Porter** • Hilton • 5000 Seminary Rd
• **Sakulthai Restaurant** • 408 S Van Dorn St
• **Thai Lemon Grass** • 506 S Van Dorn St

Shopping
• **BJ's Wholesale Club** • 101 S Van Dorn St

Video Rental
• **Blockbuster** • 1480 N Beauregard St
• **Video Palace** • 8 S Jordan St

Map 42 · **Alexandria (West)**

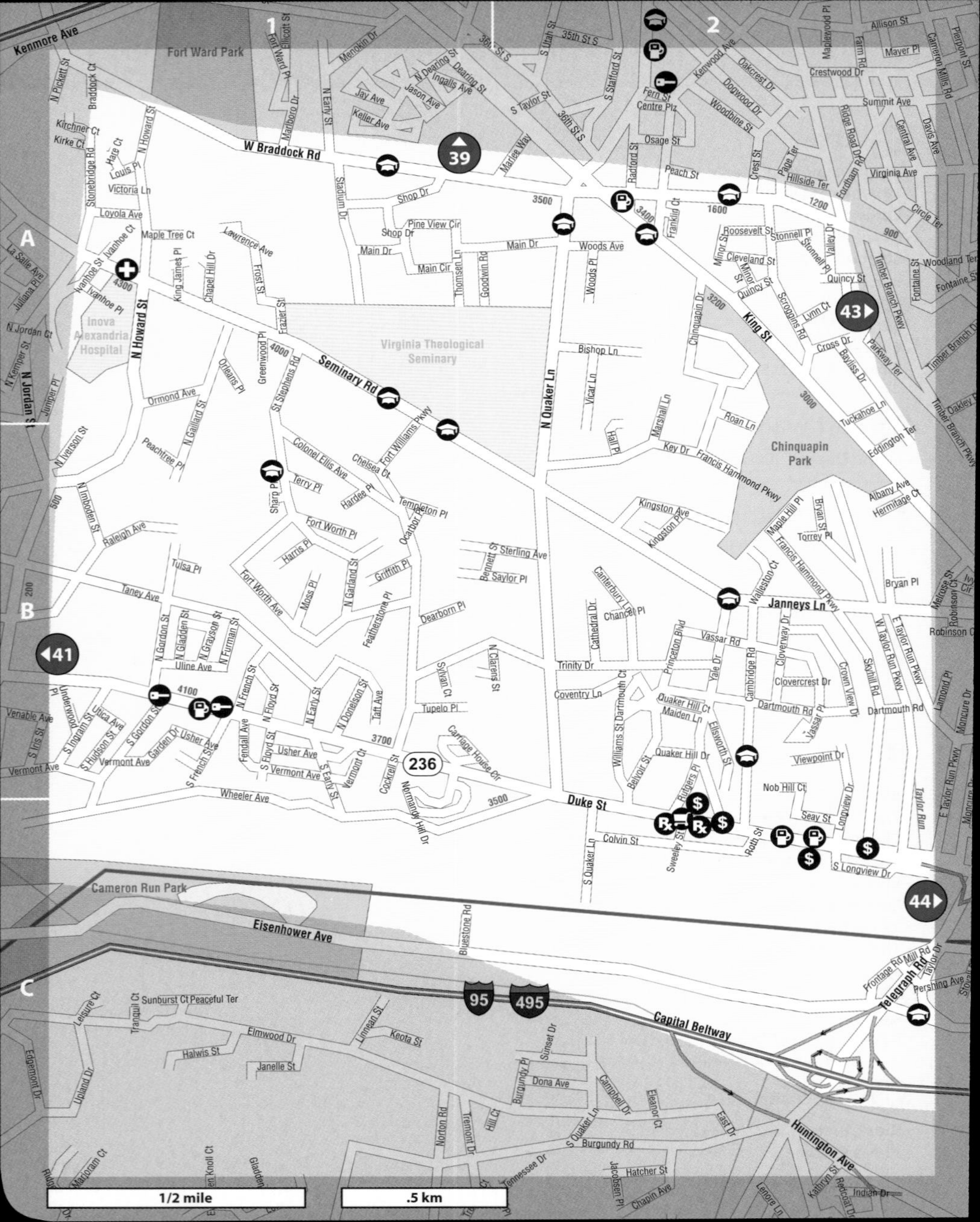

N

1 **2**

Kenmore Ave
Fort Ward Park
W Braddock Rd
39

Inova Alexandria Hospital

Virginia Theological Seminary

Seminary Rd

43

King St

Chinquapin Park

41

B

Janneys Ln

Duke St

236

Eisenhower Ave

Cameron Run Park

44

95 **495**

Capital Beltway

Telegraph Rd

Huntington Ave

C

A

1/2 mile   .5 km

The plentiful apartments in the area are popular with 20-somethings who like urban living but can't hack the high rents in Clarendon or DC. Beware, though, you may well end up with thousands of bugs as your roomies. Ask about exterminator policies before you commit.

Banks

- **Bank of America** · 2747 Duke St
- **Burke & Herbert (ATM)** · 2836 Duke St
- **Chevy Chase** · 3131 Duke St
- **Sun Trust** · 3101 Duke St

 Car Rental

- **Enterprise** · 1525 Kenwood Ave · 703-998-6600
- **Enterprise** · 4213 Duke St · 703-212-4700
- **Rent for Less** · 4105 Duke St · 703-370-5666

 Emergency Rooms

- **Inova Alexandria** · 4320 Seminary Rd ☺

 Gas Stations

- **Crown** · 4109 Duke St
- **Mobil** · 2838 Duke St
- **Shell** · 2922 Duke St
- **Texaco** · 3401 King St

 Pharmacies

- **CVS** · 3130 Duke St ☺
- **Giant Food Pharmacy** · 3131 Duke St

Schools

- **Bishop Ireton High** · 201 Cambridge Rd
- **Blessed Sacrement** · 1417 W Braddock Rd
- **Douglas MacArthur Elementary** · 1101 Janneys Ln
- **Episcopal High** · 1200 N Quaker Ln
- **Minnie Howard** · 3801 W Braddock Rd
- **St Stephen's & St Agnes Upper** · 1000 St Stephens Rd
- **Strayer University (Alexandria Campus)** · 2730 Eisenhower Ave
- **TC Williams High** · 3330 King St
- **Thornton Friends** · 3830 Seminary Rd
- **Virginia Theological Seminary** · 3737 Seminary Rd

Supermarkets

- **Giant Food** · 3131 Duke St

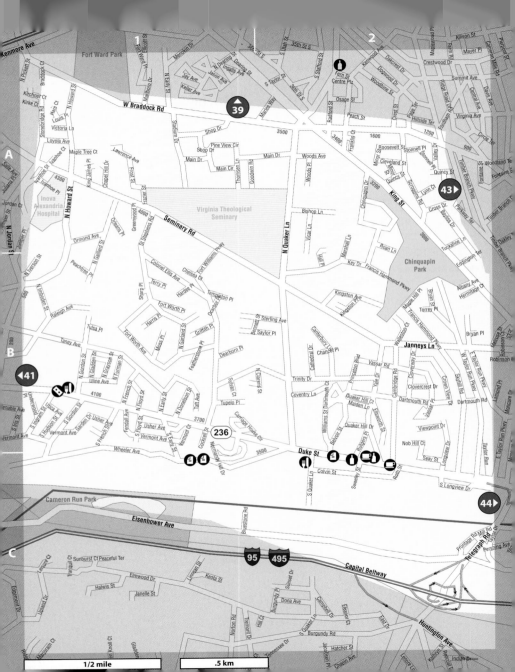

Map 4

The area's not all about mediocre housing. Check out Chinquapin Park. It's a really cool place to take a short hike or a few laps in the pool.

Coffee
- **Dunkin' Donuts** · 3050 Duke St
- **Starbucks** · 3113 Duke St

Copy Shops
- **Global Printing** · 3670 Wheeler Ave
- **Graphic Images** · 3660 Wheeler Ave
- **UPS Store** · 3213 Duke St

Liquor Stores
- **Fern Gourmet Street** · 1708 Fern St
- **Rick's Wine & Gourmet** · 3117 Duke St
- **Virginia ABC** · 3161 Duke St

Restaurants
- **Rocklands** · 25 S Quaker Ln
- **Tempo Restaurant** · 4231 Duke St

Video Rental
- **Blockbuster** · 4349 Duke St

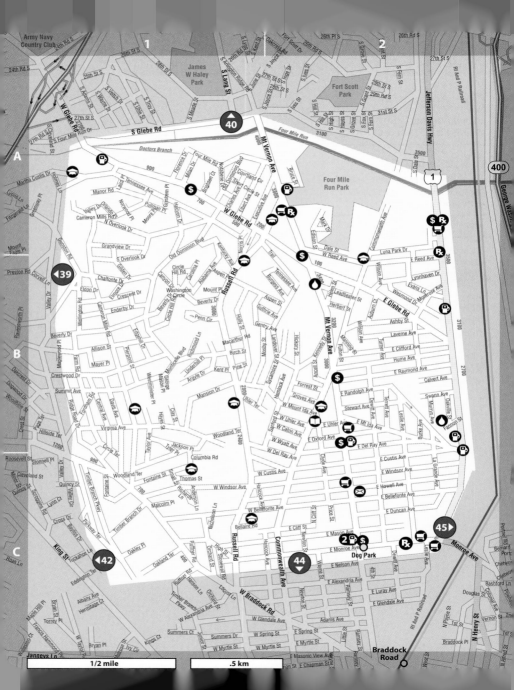

"Del Ray" is the moniker for the self-absorbed but not overly snobbish neighborhood north of the Braddock Road Metro along Mount Vernon Avenue. It's a cozy, pleasantly walkable place once viewed as sketchy for living and playing. "The avenue" now brims with trendy shops and attracts gay couples, young professionals, and fifty-something suburban bohemians. Members of the creative classes hold court at local coffee shops, sipping lattes and lamenting (or gloating) about real-estate prices.

Banks
- **Bank of America (ATM)** • 600 N Glebe Rd
- **Burke & Herbert** • 306 E Monroe Ave
- **Provident** • 3801 Jefferson Davis Hwy
- **Sun Trust** • 2809 Mt Vernon Ave
- **Virginia Commerce** • 2401 Mt Vernon Ave
- **Wachovia** • 3506 Mt Vernon Ave

Car Washes
- **Mr Wash** • 3407 Mt Vernon Ave
- **Nab Auto Appearance Salon** • 2414 Oakville St

Gas Stations
- **Citgo** • 1015 W Glebe Rd
- **Citgo** • 2312 Mt Vernon Ave
- **Crown** • 3216 Jefferson Davis Hwy
- **Exxon** • 1601 Mt Vernon Ave
- **Exxon** • 2300 Jefferson Davis Hwy
- **Exxon** • 2320 Jefferson Davis Hwy ⊘
- **Exxon** • 4001 Mt Vernon Ave
- **Shell** • 1600 Mt Vernon Ave

○ Landmarks
- **Dog Park** • At Simpson Stadium Park, NW Corner of E Monroe Ave & Jefferson Davis Hwy

Libraries
- **Alexandria James M Duncan Branch Library** • 2501 Commonwealth Ave

Pharmacies
- **CVS** • 3811 Mt Vernon Ave
- **CVS** • 415 Monroe Ave ⊘
- **Shopper's Pharmacy** • 3801 Jefferson Davis Hwy
- **Target** • 3101 Jefferson Davis Hwy

Post Offices
- **Potomac Station Finance** • 1908 Mt Vernon Ave

Schools
- **Alexandria Country Day** • 2400 Russell Rd
- **Charles Barrett Elementary** • 1115 Martha Custis Dr
- **Cora Kelly Elementary** • 3600 Commonwealth Ave
- **George Mason Elementary** • 2601 Cameron Mills Rd
- **Grace Episcopal** • 3601 Russell Rd
- **Immanuel Lutheran** • 109 Belleaire Rd
- **Mount Vernon Community** • 2601 Commonwealth Ave
- **St Rita** • 3801 Russell Rd
- **St Stephen's & St Agnes Lower** • 400 Fontaine St

Supermarkets
- **Cheesetique** • 2403 Mt Vernon Ave
- **Giant Food** • 425 E Monroe Ave
- **Gold Crust Baking Company** • 501 E Monroe Ave
- **My Organic Market** • 3831 Mt Vernon Ave
- **Planet Wine & Gourmet** • 2004 Mt Vernon Ave
- **Shoppers Food Warehouse** • 3801 Jefferson Davis Hwy ⊘

Map 43 • **Four Mile Run/Del Ray**

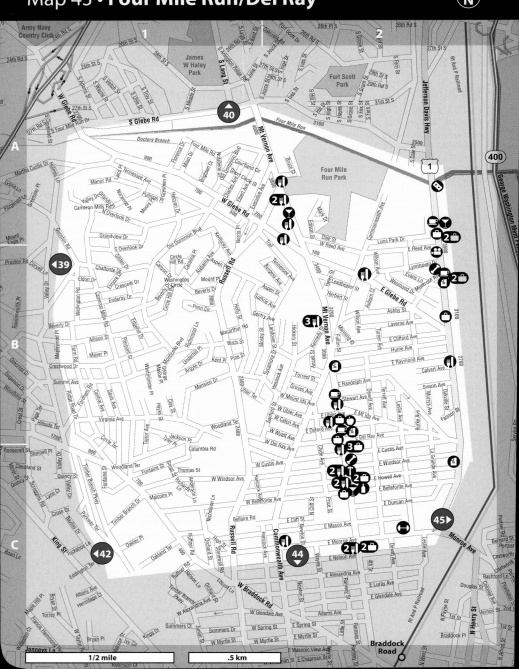

The neighborhood nearer to Four Mile Run is the place to wire money to Honduras, buy some Guatemalan beer, or take in Spanish-language karaoke. While it may not be as fancypants as other corners of Alexandria, the area definitely has a bustling vibe and plenty of neat little restaurants. If you can't afford a show at local institution the Birchmere, just sit at the bar, nurse a pint, and watch it free on closed-circuit TV.

Coffee

- **Caboose Café & Bakery** · 2419 Mt Vernon Ave
- **Dunkin' Donuts** · 3325 Jefferson Davis Hwy
- **St Elmo's Coffee Pub** · 2300 Mt Vernon Ave
- **Starbucks** · 3825 Jefferson Davis Hwy

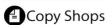
Copy Shops

- **A&Z Printing & Duplicating** · 2000 Jefferson Davis Hwy
- **ASAP Printing & Mailing CO Inc** · 2805 Mt Vernon Ave
- **Staples** · 3301 Jefferson Davis Hwy
- **UPS Store** · 2308 Mt Vernon Ave

Gyms

- **YMCA** · 420 E Monroe Ave

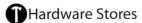
Farmer's Markets

- **Del Ray Farmer's Market (Apr–Dec, Sat, 8 am–12 pm)** · Mt Vernon & Oxford Aves

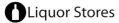
Hardware Stores

- **Executive Lock & Key** · 2003 Mt Vernon Ave

Liquor Stores

- **Planet Wine & Gourmet (wine only)** · 2004 Mt Vernon Ave

Movie Theaters

- **Regal Potomac Yard 16** · 3575 Jefferson Davis Hwy

Nightlife

- **Birchmere** · 3701 Mt Vernon Ave
- **Hops** · 3625 Jefferson Davis Hwy
- **No 9 Lounge** · 2000 Mt Vernon Ave

Pet Shops

- **Hydrant Dog Bakery** · 2101 Mt Vernon Ave
- **PetSmart** · 3351 Jefferson Davis Hwy

Restaurants

- **Afghan Restaurant** · 2700 Jefferson Davis Hwy
- **Al's Steak House** · 1504 Mt Vernon Ave
- **Bombay Curry Company** · 3110 Mt Vernon Ave
- **Chez Andree** · 10 E Glebe Rd
- **The Dairy Godmother** · 2310 Mt Vernon Ave
- **Del Merei Grill** · 3106 Mt Vernon Ave
- **Evening Star Café** · 2000 Mt Vernon Ave
- **Hector's** · 3112 Mt Vernon Ave
- **Huascaran** · 3606 Mt Vernon Ave
- **Los Amigos** · 1905 Mt Vernon Ave
- **Lilian's Restaurant** · 3901 Mt Vernon Ave
- **Los Tios Grill** · 2615 Mt Vernon Ave
- **Mancini's** · 1508 Mt Vernon Ave
- **Monroe's Trattoria** · 1603 Commonwealth Ave
- **RT's Restaurant** · 3804 Mt Vernon Ave
- **Sundae Times** · 2003 Mt Vernon Ave
- **Spectrum Restaurant** · 251 W Glebe Rd
- **Taqueria Poblano** · 2400 Mt Vernon Ave
- **Thai Peppers** · 2018 Mt Vernon Ave
- **Waffle Shop** · 3864 Mt Vernon Ave ✆

Shopping

- **A Show of Hands** · 2204 Mt Vernon Ave
- **Barnes & Noble** · 3651 Jefferson Davis Hwy
- **Best Buy** · 3401 Jefferson Davis Hwy
- **The Clay Queen Pottery** · 2303 Mt Vernon Ave
- **The Dairy Godmother** · 2310 Mt Vernon Ave
- **Electic Nature** · 1503 Mt Vernon Ave
- **Eight Hands Round** · 2301 Mt Vernon Ave
- **Five Oaks Antiques** · 2413 Mt Vernon Ave
- **Mia Gemma** · 2007 Mt Vernon Ave
- **Old Navy** · 3621 Jefferson Davis Hwy
- **The Purple Goose** · 1508 Mt Vernon Ave
- **Potomac West Antiques** · 1517 Mt Vernon Ave
- **The Remix** · 2005 Mt Vernon Ave
- **Sports Authority** · 3701 Jefferson Davis Hwy
- **Staples** · 3301 Jefferson Davis Hwy
- **Target** · 3101 Jefferson Davis Hwy

Video Rental

- **Hollywood Video** · 3925 Jefferson Davis Hwy

Map 44 · **Alexandria Downtown**

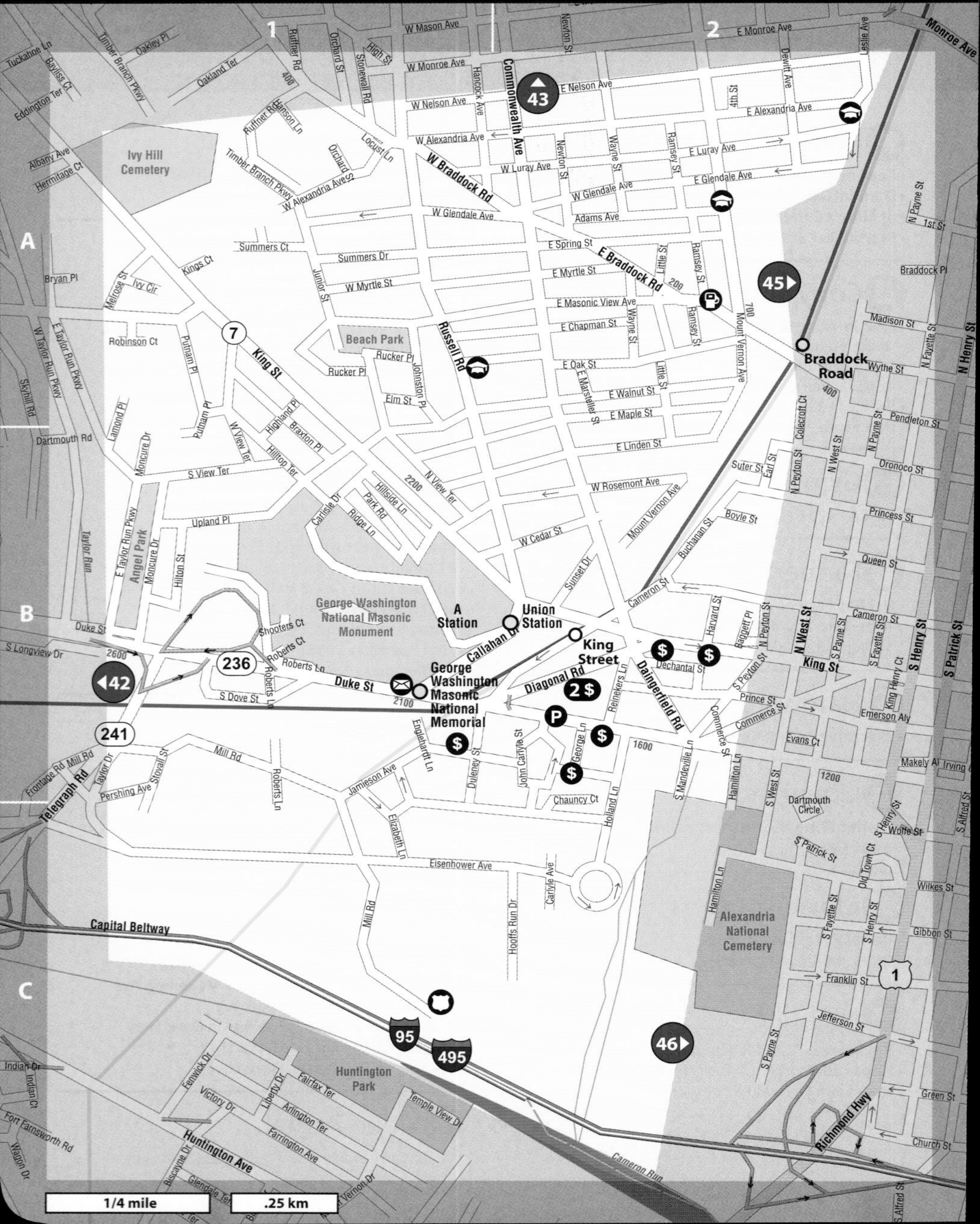

N

1

2

Monroe Ave

E Monroe Ave

Tuckahoe Ln
Oakley Pl
Oakland Ter
Timber Branch Pkwy
Ruffner Rd
Orchard St
High St
Stonewall Rd
W Mason Ave
Newton St
Leslie Ave
Devitt Ave

Eddington Ter Ln
Bellview Blvd
W Monroe Ave

Alleghany Rd
Commonwealth Ave
Hancock Ave
W Nelson Ave
E Nelson Ave

43

Albany Ave
Hermitage Ln
Ivy Hill Cemetery
Timber Branch Pkwy
W Alexandria Ave
Orchard St
Locust Ln
W Alexandria Ave
4th St
E Alexandria Ave

W Braddock Rd
W Luray Ave
Newton St
Wayne St
Ramsey St
E Luray Ave

Bryan Pl
Summers Ct
Summers Dr
Junior St
W Glendale Ave
W Glendale Ave
Adams Ave
E Glendale Ave

A
Melrose St
Ivy Cir
Kings Ct
Junior St
W Myrtle St
E Spring Ave
E Braddock Rd
Little St
Ramsey St 200
N 1st St
Braddock Pl
Madison St

Robinson Ct
7
King St
Beach Park
Rucker Pl
Rucker Pl
Johnston Pl
Elm St
N View St
E Myrtle St
E Masonic View Ave
E Chapman St
Wayne St
Wayne St
45
Mount Vernon Ave
Braddock Road
Wythe St
N Fayette St
N Henry St
N Payne St
Pendleton St
400
Colbert Ct

W Taylor Run Pkwy
Lamond Pl
Putnam St
Highland Pl
Braxton Pl
Highland Pl
Hillcrest Pl
E Oak St
E Walnut St
E Maple St
Oronoco St
Princess St

S View Ter
W View Ter
Hillside Ln
Park Rd
Ridge Ln
E Linden St
W Rosemont Ave
Suter St
Earl St
N Peyton St
N West St
N Pitt St
Queen St

Dartmouth Rd
Moncure Dr
Carlisle Dr
2200
Mount Vernon Ave
Boyle St
Buchanan St

B
Duke St
2600
Angel Park
Moncure Dr
Hilton St
Upland Pl
George Washington National Masonic Monument
A Station
Callahan Dr
Union Station
King Street
Cameron St
Howard St
Daggett Pl
Bagget Pl
Payton St
Cameron St
N West St
King St
N Payne St
N Fayette St
N West St
King St
S Henry St
S Patrick St

S Longview Dr
42
Shooters Ct
Roberts Ln
Roberts Ln
Duke St
Diagonal Rd
Dechantal St
Reinekers Ln
Daingerfield Rd
Prince St
Commerce St
S Peyton St
Commerce St
Emerson Aly

236
S Dove St
George Washington Masonic National Memorial
2
George St
1600
S Mandeville Ln
S West St
Evans Ct
Dartmouth Circle
Makely Al
Irving
1200

241
Telegraph Rd
Frontage Rd Mill Rd
Mill Rd
Roberts Ln
Engleheart Ln
Duke St
2100
P
John Carlyle St
Chauncy Ct
Holland Ln
Wolfe St
S Fayette St
S Henry St
S Alfred St
Wilkes St
Gibbon St

Pershing Ave
Jamieson Ave
Elizabeth Ln
Eisenhower Ave
Carlyle Dr
Hoofs Run Dr
Hamilton Ln
Alexandria National Cemetery
S Payne St
S Fayette St
Franklin St
1

C
Capital Beltway
Mill Rd
95
495
Jefferson St
S Henry St
Green St
Church St

Indian Dr
Fenwick St
Fairfax Ter
Victory Dr
Arlington Ter
Temple View Dr
Huntington Park
Richmond Hwy

Fort Farnsworth Rd
Wagon Rd
Huntington Ave
Vernon St
Farmington Ave
Cameron Run

1/4 mile   .25 km

Especially when compared to historic Old Town, Alexandria's "downtown" is about as drab as a briefcase and a double-breasted flannel suit. The area serves a mainly functional purpose as an office park and transportation hub for locals. For business travelers, there are plenty of opportunities to spend a night or two in humdrum hotel and work on PowerPoint presentations in unremarkable coffee shops while doing business with one of the infinite associations that have their offices in Alexandria. Ah, America.

Banks

- **BB&T** · 1717 King St
- **Burke & Herbert** · 1775 Jamieson Ave
- **Chevy Chase** · 2051 Jamieson Ave
- **PNC** · 1700 Diagonal Rd
- **PNC (ATM)** · 1700 Duke St
- **Sun Trust** · 1650 King St
- **Sun Trust (ATM)** · 1900 Diagonal Rd

Gas Stations

- **Mobil** · 317 E Braddock Rd

Landmarks

- **Amtrak Station** · 110 Callahan Dr
- **George Washington Masonic National Memorial** · 101 Callahan Dr
- **Union Station** · 110 Callahan Dr

Parking

Police

- **Alexandria Police Dept** · 2003 Mill Rd

Post Offices

- **Memorial Station** · 2226 Duke St

Schools

- **Commonwealth Academy** · 1321 Leslie Ave
- **George Washington Middle** · 1005 Mt Vernon Ave
- **Maury Elementary** · 600 Russell Rd

181

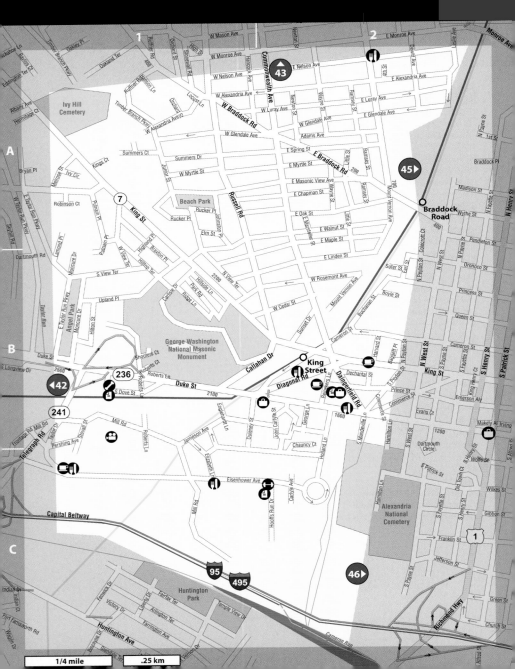

Map 44

The bottom-heavy phallus that is the George Washington Masonic Memorial is the area's literal and aesthetic high point. Union Station's not a bad place to while away a weekday afternoon, taking in the hustle and bustle and eavesdropping on rude ticket-sales employees. But for fun, food, and frolicking, head toward the Potomac and historic Old Town. There's a free weekend shuttle to the King Street Metro.

Coffee

- **Café Aurora** · 1630 King St
- **June Coffee** · 225 Reineker's Ln, #1
- **Starbucks** · 2461 Eisenhower Ave

Copy Shops

- **ABC Imaging** · 225 Reinekers Ln
- **Carriage Trade Publications** · 2393 S Dove St
- **Tyler Business Services** · 313 Hooff's Run Dr

Gyms

- **Jungle's Gym Fitness** · 305 Hooffs Run Dr

Movie Theaters

- **AMC Hoffman Center 22** · 206 Swamp Fox Rd

Pet Shops

- **Petsage** · 2391 S Dove St

Restaurants

- **Café Old Towne** · 2111 Eisenhower Ave
- **FireFlies** · 1501 Mt Vernon Ave
- **Joe Theismann's Restaurant** · 1800 Diagonal Rd
- **Table Talk** · 1623 Duke St
- **Ted's Montana Grill** · 2451 Eisenhower Ave

Shopping

- **Crate & Barrel Outlet** · 1700 Prince St
- **Whole Foods Market** · 1700 Duke St

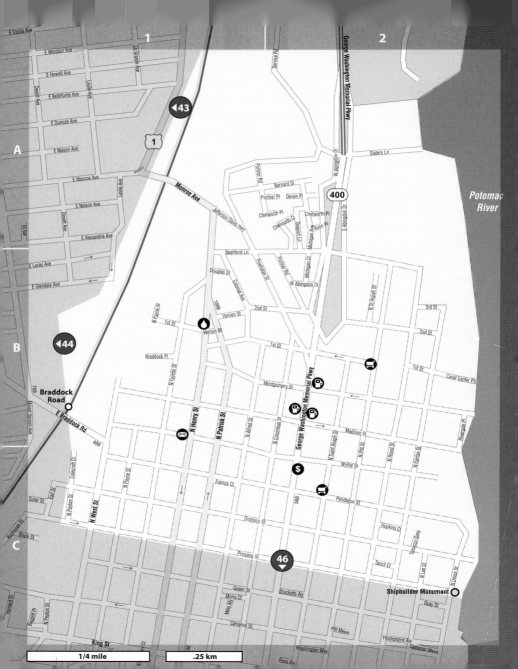

This is a "pass through" kind of place. It's residential, with offices, a few chain stores, and not much more. Trader Joe's, the California chain which stocks healthy food and premium wines, is the main attraction.

$ Banks
- **Chevy Chase** · 697 N Washington St

Car Washes
- **Yates's Car Wash** · 1018 N Henry St

Gas Stations
- **Exxon** · 703 N Washington St ⊘
- **Exxon** · 834 N Washington St ⊘
- **Shell** · 801 N Washington St

○ Landmarks
- **Shipbuilder Monument** · Waterfront Park, 1A Prince St

✉ Post Offices
- **Alexandria Main Office** · 1100 Wythe St

Supermarkets
- **Giant Food** · 530 1st St
- **Trader Joe's** · 612 N St Asaph St

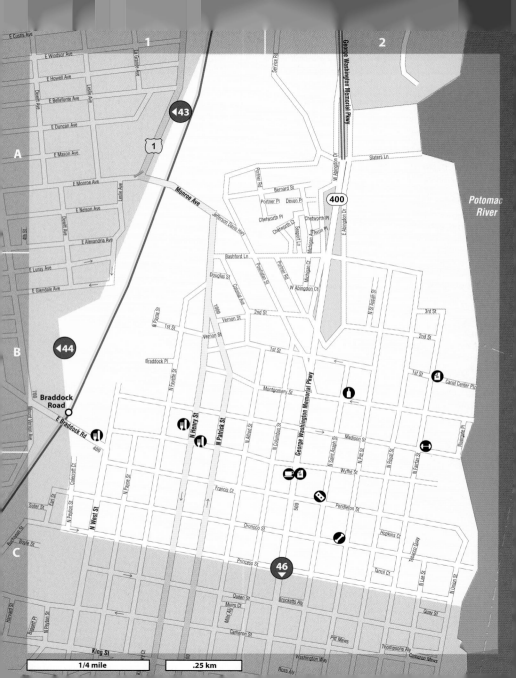

Map 4

About 20 years ago, Mick Fleetwood of "Fleetwood Mac" fame owned a big-time jazz club hidden among the low-rise office buildings along N. Washington Street. Alas, nightlife is not in this area's vocabulary; the club is now gone. Mick must have sensed something. Sympathy goes out to those who are stuck in any of the hotels around here.

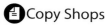Coffee
· **Starbucks** · 683 N Washington St

Copy Shops
· **FedEx Kinko's** · 685 N Washington St ⊚
· **Kwik Kopy Printing** · 99 Canal Ctr Plz

Gyms
· **Old Town Sport & Health Club** · 209 Madison St

Liquor Stores
· **Virginia ABC** · 901 N St Asaph St

Pet Shops
· **Olde Towne School for Dogs** · 529 Oronoco St

Restaurants
· **Blue & White Carry Out** · 1024 Wythe St
· **Esmeralda's Restaurant** · 728 N Henry St
· **La Piazza** · 535 E Braddock Rd

Video Rental
· **Blockbuster** · 602 N St Asaph St

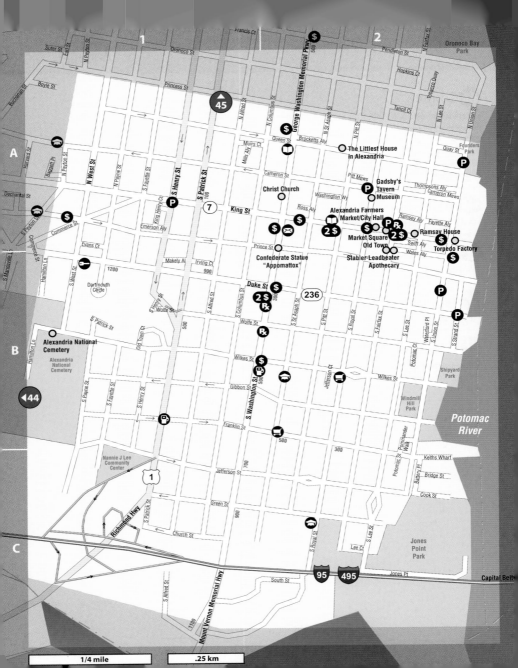

This 250-year old neighborhood of million-dollar townhomes (from the 18th and the 21st centuries) has gone from powdered wigs to sophisticated charm.. Old Town is quainter and quieter (no college nearby) than the townier Georgetown, but expensive boutiques and restaurants are springing up all over. Even the tired Holiday Inn is becoming a trendy Hotel Monaco. Crime is almost nil because the criminals can't find parking, either.

$ Banks

- **Bank of America** · 600 N Washington St
- **BB&T** · 300 S Washington St
- **Burke & Herbert** · 100 S Fairfax St
- **Burke & Herbert** · 621 King St
- **Chevy Chase** · 500 S Washington St
- **Chevy Chase (ATM)** · 118 King St
- **Commerce** · 119 S Washington St
- **First Horizon** · 320 King St
- **Mercantile Potomac** · 325 S Washington St
- **PNC** · 411 King St
- **PNC (ATM)** · 110 S Union St
- **Sun Trust** · 515 King St
- **United** · 301 S Washington St
- **Virginia Commerce** · 1414 Prince St
- **Virginia Commerce** · 506 King St
- **Wachovia** · 330 N Washington St

Car Rental

- **Thrifty** · 1306 Duke St · 703-684-2068

Gas Stations

- **Exxon** · 501 S Washington St ⊙
- **Exxon** · 700 S Patrick St ⊙

o Landmarks

- **Alexandria City Hall** · 301 King St
- **Alexandria Farmer's Market** · 301 King St
- **Alexandria National Cemetery** · 1450 Wilkes St
- **Christ Church** · 118 N Washington St
- **Confederate Statue "Appomattox"** ·
  S Washington St & Prince St
- **Gadsby's Tavern Museum** · 134 N Royal St
- **The Littlest House in Alexandria** · 523 Queen St
- **Market Square Old Town** · 301 King St
- **Ramsay House** · 221 King St
- **Stabler-Leadbeater Apothecary** · 105 S Fairfax St
- **Torpedo Factory** · 201 N Union St

Libraries

- **Alexandria Kate Waller Barrett Branch Library** ·
  717 Queen St
- **Alexandria Law Library** · 520 King St, Room L-34

P Parking

Pharmacies

- **Alexandria Medical Arts Pharmacy** ·
  315 S Washington St
- **CVS** · 326 King St
- **CVS** · 433 S Washington St

Post Offices

- **George Mason Station** · 126 S Washington St

Schools

- **Jefferson-Houston Elementary** ·
  1501 Cameron St
- **Lyles-Crouch Elementary** · 530 S St Asaph St
- **St Coletta** · 207 S Peyton St
- **St Mary** · 400 Green St

Supermarkets

- **Balducci's** · 600 Franklin Ave
- **Safeway** · 500 S Royal St

Wassailing abounds as the rejuvenated Old Town stretches westward towards the Masonic Temple—everything from pizza and pitchers at Bugsy's to newcomers like 100 King and Restaurant Eve to the died-and-gone-to-heaven La Bergerie. Chains are rare. The few exceptions include a Banana Republic and a Chart House (GW definitely would never have eaten here), but the unique, one-of-a-kind places are the rule.

Coffee

- **Bread & Chocolate** · 611 King St
- **Cosi** · 700 King St
- **Firehook Bakery** · 430 S Washington St
- **Firehook Bakery & Coffee House** · 105 S Union St
- **Misha's** · 102 S Patrick St
- **Old Town Coffee Tea & Spice** · 215 S Union St
- **Perk Up** · 829 S Washington St
- **Starbucks** · 100 S Union St
- **Starbucks** · 532 King St
- **Uptowner Café** · 1609 King St

Copy Shops

- **AAB Imaging Inc** · 1101 King St
- **Insty-Prints** · 1421 Prince St
- **UPS Store** · 107 S West St

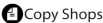Farmer's Markets

- **Alexandria City Farmer's Market**
  (Sat, 5 am–10:30 pm) · 301 King St

Liquor Stores

- **The Winery Inc** · 317 S Washington St

Movie Theaters

- **Old Town Theater** · 815 1/2 King St

Nightlife

- **Austin Grill** · 801 King St
- **Café Salsa** · 808 King St
- **Chadwick's** · 203 The Strand
- **House of Klaus** · 715 King St
- **Laughing Lizzard Lounge** · 1324 King St
- **Murphy's** · 713 King St
- **Pat Troy's Ireland's Own** · 111 N Pitt St
- **Rock It Grill** · 1319 King St
- **Tiffany Tavern** · 1116 King St
- **Union Street Public House** · 121 S Union St
- **Vermillion** · 1120 King St

Pet Shops

- **Barkley Square Gourmet Dog Bakery & Boutique** ·
  1 Wales Aly
- **Fetch** · 101 S St Asaph St

Restaurants

- **100 King** · 100 King St
- **219 Restaurant** · 219 King St
- **Bilbo Baggins** · 208 Queen St
- **Casablanca Restaurant** · 1504 King St
- **Chart House** · 1 Cameron St
- **China King Restaurant** · 701 King St
- **Faccia Luna Trattoria** · 823 S Washington St
- **Fish Market** · 105 King St
- **Hard Times Café** · 1404 King St
- **The Grille** · Morrison House · 116 S Alfred St
- **Il Porto** · 121 King St
- **King Street Blues** · 112 N St Asaph St
- **La Bergerie** · 218 N Lee St
- **Le Galois** · 1106 King St
- **The Pita House** · 407 Cameron St
- **Portner's** · 109 S St Asaph St
- **Restaurant Eve** · 110 S Pitt St
- **Southside 815** · 815 S Washington St
- **Taverna Cretekou** · 818 King St
- **The Warehouse** · 214 King St

Shopping

- **ArtCraft** · 132 King St
- **Arts Afire** · 1117 King St
- **Banana Republic** · 628 King St
- **Big Wheel Bikes** · 2 Prince St
- **Blink** · 1303 King St
- **Books-A-Million** · 503 King St
- **Cash Grocer** · 1315 King St
- **Comfort One Shoes** · 201 King St
- **Hysteria** · 125 S Fairfax St
- **Irish Walk** · 415 King St
- **Jos A Bank** · 728 S Washington St
- **Kosmos Design & Ideas** · 1010 King St
- **La Cuisine** · 323 Cameron St
- **The Lamplighter** · 1207 King St
- **Montague & Son** · 115 S Union St
- **My Place in Tuscany** · 1127 King St
- **Notting Hill Gardens** · 815-B King St
- **Olsson's Books and Records** · 106 S Union St
- **P&C Art** · 212 King St
- **Pacers** · 1301 King St
- **Papyrus** · 721 King St
- **Tickled Pink** · 103 S St Asaph St
- **The Torpedo Factory** · 105 N Union St
- **Williams-Sonoma** · 825 S Washington St
- **The Winery Inc** · 317 S Washington St

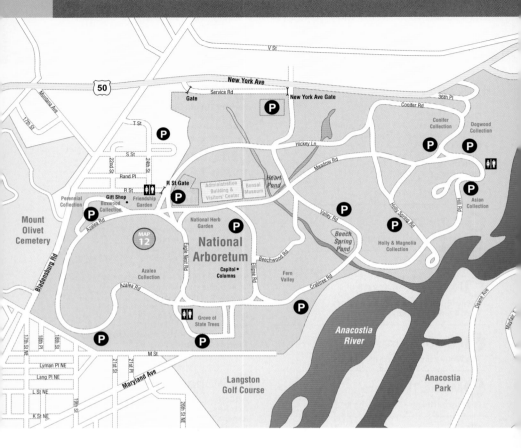

General Information

NFT Map:	12
Address:	3501 New York Ave NE
	Washington, DC 20002
Phone:	202-245-2726
Website:	www.usna.usda.gov
Hours:	Daily: 8 am–5 pm,
	except Dec 25th
Admission:	Free

Overview

Escape the hubbub of DC's urban jungle with a visit to the 446 acres of greenery at the National Arboretum. The Arboretum's biggest draw is the National Bonsai and Penjing Museum, where you'll find over 150 miniature trees (some hundreds of years old). A rock garden, koi pond, and ikebana exhibit (the Japanese art of flower arranging) surround the museum and are enough to clear anyone's head—unless they have allergies.

Other major attractions depend on the season. Spring sees the arboretum burst with the fresh pastels of daffodils, crocuses, and azaleas. In summer, the palette mellows with the arrival of waterlilies and wildflowers. Fall brings the stately crimsons and golds of fall foliage, while winter blankets the large pines and hollies with snow. In short, there's always something to see, and there's always a reason to come back. For up-to-the-minute news on what's currently in bloom, check the "Hort Hot Spots" page on the Arboretum's website.

While flowers may bloom and fade, the view of the Anacostia flowing quietly behind the Dogwood Collection is here to stay, as are the 22 Corinthian columns planted in a grassy field near the entrance, open to the sky. Originally part of the Capitol Building, these columns are probably the closest thing America has to the Parthenon.

If you want to mix education with pleasure, visit the Economic Botany Herbarium—a collection of over 650,000 dried plant specimens classified for the studies of agriculture, medicine, science, and education. The volunteer staff also breeds plants for other locales throughout the country in a controlled greenhouse.

The National Bonsai Collection and Penjing Museum is open 10 am–3:30 pm. The Arbor House Gift Shop is open from March 1 through mid-December; weekday hours are 10 am–3:30 pm and weekend hours are 10 am–5 pm.

Activities

The 9.6 miles of paved roads serve as excellent biking and jogging paths. Picnicking is allowed in designated areas. The Arbor Café is located next to the Administration Building and is open Friday through Sunday. Fishing, fires, and flower picking are all prohibited, and pets must be kept on leashes. The Arboretum offers public education programs including lectures, workshops, demonstrations, and plant, flower, and art exhibitions.

A 48-passenger open-air tram runs through the park on a 35-minute, non-stop, narrated tour covering the Arboretum's history, mission, and current highlights. Tram services are available on weekends from mid-April through October: $4 adults, $3 seniors, $2 kids 4–16 years old, and free for kids 4 and under. Private tours are also available with a 3-week advance reservation.

Full Moon Hikes, available during the spring and fall, take participants on a somewhat strenuous five-mile moonlit trek through the grounds, with curators providing horticultural facts along the way. Hikes cost $15 general admission and $12 for Friends of the National Arboretum. You'll need to register early as there is limited space and tours fill up quickly (as in, we called at the beginning of April to book a tour in May, and we were already too late). Twilight Tours cost $7 ($5 for FONA), and are slower-paced opportunities to explore the Arboretum after closing time. Pre-registration is required for both activities; call 202-245-5898 to make your reservation, or find the mail-in form online.

How to Get There—Driving

From northwest Washington, follow New York Avenue east to the intersection of Bladensburg Road. Turn right onto Bladensburg Road and drive four blocks to R Street. Make a left on R Street and continue two blocks to the Arboretum gates.

Parking

Large free parking lots are located near the Grove of State Trees, by the R Street entrance, and near the New York Avenue entrance. Smaller lots are scattered throughout the grounds close to most of the major collections. Several of the parking areas have been expanded recently, and a free shuttle through the park runs continuously during summer months.

How to Get There—Mass Transit

The X6 Metrobus provides a direct shuttle from Union Station on weekends and holidays, except December 25th. The bus leaves every 40 minutes from 7:55 am to 4:35 pm and the fare is $1.25 one-way (35¢ with rail transfer, 60¢ for seniors and the disabled). On weekdays, the closest Metro subway stop is Stadium Armory Station on the Blue and Orange lines. Transfer to Metrobus B-2, get off on Bladensburg Road, and walk two blocks to R Street. Make a right on R Street and continue two more blocks to the Arboretum gates.

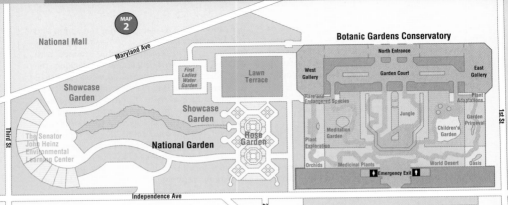

General Information

NFT Map: 2
Address: 100 Maryland Ave SW
Washington, DC 20024
Phone: 202-225-8333
Website: www.usbg.gov
Hours: 10 am–5 pm every day, including holidays
Admission: Free

Overview

One minute you're staring up at the US Capitol—the symbol of the world's most powerful city; the next minute you're trudging through a jungle, surrounded by Jurassic trees and carnivorous plants. Known as Washington's "Secret Garden," the US Botanic Garden is one of the nation's oldest botanical gardens and home to 26,000 different specimens. The refurbished Conservatory features a 24-foot-high mezzanine level allowing visitors to gaze downward onto a canopied rainforest. Its distinctive glass façade now houses advanced environmental control systems that allow orchid buds to bloom in the same building as desert brush and nearly 4,000 other living plants. If you're looking for a particular organism but don't know where to start, you can tap into the USBG's massive computer database and search by common name, scientific name, or geographic location. Or you can simply ask one of the Garden's reputable flora-nerd employees, who will be all too pleased to provide you with an *extremely comprehensive* answer. Informative panels across the building will you teach you about the plants on display—and contain dramatic statements about the important of plants; whoever wrote that copy has a very obvious flora-centric perspective. Everyone in DC has an agenda: remember that!

The USBG offers classes, exhibits, lectures, and symposia throughout the year. Visit during the week and you might be lucky enough to land on a tour (schedules vary, so be sure to check the website for up-to-date event listings), or buy tickets in advance for events such as organic beer tastings or talks on the romance of roses. Set to open in fall 2006 is the National Garden, a three-acre plot of land located just west of the Conservatory. The landscaped space will showcase the unusual, useful, and ornamental plants that flourish in the mid-Atlantic region in areas known as the Rose Garden, Butterfly Garden, and (wait for it) First Ladies' Water Garden!

Bartholdi Park, located across Independence Avenue from the Conservatory, was created in 1932 and named for sculptor Frederic Auguste Bartholdi. In addition to creating the aptly named Bartholdi Fountain in the center of the park, he also designed the Statue of Liberty. The park is open daily from dawn until dusk.

How to Get There—Mass Transit

Taking public transportation is highly recommended. By Metro, take the Blue or Orange line to Federal Center SW or Capitol South stations. If you're using the Metro Bus, take the 30, 32, 34, 35, or 36 to Independence Avenue and First Street SW. Just walk toward the giant white dome, then look south.

General Information

NFT Map: 5
Location: 225 7th St SE
             Washington, DC 20003
Phone: 202-544-0083
Website: www.easternmarketdc.com, or
             www.easternmarket.net
Hours: Tues–Sat: 7 am–6 pm; Sun: 9 am–4 pm

Overview

Eastern Market is as unpretentious as DC gets. Leave your Hill lapel pin and the Georgetown classism behind, 'cause here you'll only spill bacon grease on 'em. The 16,500-square-foot indoor market has barely changed since it opened in 1873. Even now, as it sits at the center of a newly yuppified neighborhood and enjoys its status as a member of the National Register of Historic Places, it remains a working market for working people.

Join the line at Market Lunch in South Hall to be abused by over-stressed workers doling out pancakes, NC-style pulled pork, and killer crab cakes. You need to order quickly because the line is usually long, and the staff's patience is not—don't even think about paying with plastic. If you're lucky enough to get a seat at the long bar-style table, you can listen in on conversations ranging from new legislation to local pro-sports mediocrity. Lawyers and laborers alike fit right in this eclectic warehouse, where neighborhooders often get together for gossip while picking up the daily dinner fixins'.

On weekends, locals and day-trippers jam in to bid for fresh produce, bread, fish, cheese, and chicken. On the sidewalks outside, artists, farmers, and charlatans hawk their wares. Antique and collectibles vendors fill the playground behind Hines Junior High School with piles of trinkets, textiles, and trash. They call it a flea market, but don't expect bargains. There are, however, some decent deals to be found across the street on the north side of the market. If you're dating someone with blue hair, Eastern Market is the perfect place to buy them some funky topaz earrings or a watercolor painting with glitter.

Market 5 Gallery

202-543-7293; www.market5gallery.org
The non-profit arts organization Market 5 dominates the North Hall. The group hosts art fairs and sponsors Saturday performances. Artists, musicians, and artisans have always been a part of the traditional "marketplace," and the Saturday festival on the gallery's North Plaza was begun in 1978 to bring the tradition back to Eastern Market.

Market 5 is also an art gallery that gives classes in the arts for the Capitol Hill community. Hours: Tues–Fri: 11 am–5 pm; Sat–Sun: 10 am–5 pm.

How to Get There—Driving

Parking is scarce, but if you must: From the south, take I-395 across the 14th Street Bridge, bear right over the bridge onto the Southwest Expressway; exit at 6th Street SE, the first exit beyond South Capitol Street. At the bottom of the ramp, continue one block and turn left on 7th Street SE. The next major intersection with a traffic light is Pennsylvania Avenue. You'll see Hines School on the opposite corner.

From the west, take I-66 to Rosslyn, Virginia, and Route 110 to I-395 N, then follow the directions above.

From the north, take Baltimore-Washington Parkway and I-295, exiting at Pennsylvania Avenue (East). A U-turn can be made at the second light to head westbound on Pennsylvania to 7th Street SE, where you need to make a right.

From the east, take either Route 50 or I-495 to I-295, and follow the directions above.

Parking

Diagonal parking is available on 7th Street, on the alley sides of the Market, and there's some curb parking in the Capitol Hill neighborhood. On weekends, it's best to take the Metro.

How to Get There—Mass Transit

Take the Blue or Orange Metro Lines to the Eastern Market station, and walk north out of the station along 7th Street SE.

Potomac River

Overview

NFT Map: 8

Like a socialite fleeing the masses, Georgetown hides in a Metro-inaccessible western corner of northwest Washington. Here it retains its cobblestone charm and snooty superiority despite the mall-ization of its main drags. The tourists and suburbanites mob stretches of M Street and Wisconsin Avenue on pleasant weekend days, but the Georgetown residents are either current or future (calling all Georgetown students) owners of the city's priciest real estate.

At night, the neighborhood sheds its good breeding to become a boisterous, if not diverse, nightlife scene. The crush of restaurants and bars swing open to welcome college partiers or the better-coiffed see-and-be-seen crowd.

Don't waste your time sitting in a cab on the popular blocks of M Street. Traffic crawls, and you can waste precious partying/shopping time as you ask the cab driver to explain the taxicab map (DC's Rosetta Stone). Cut your losses and walk—it's only a few blocks and will save you time and frustration.

Despite the area's highbrow reputation for elite schools and garden-lined historical houses, Georgetown's proximity to the Potomac makes it susceptible to occasional flooding. Turn on the news after the next big thunderstorm. The local networks send out camera crews and pretty young women who wear pastel L.L. Bean raincoats and talk into microphones. Invariably, a group of privileged neighborhood children shout at the TV cameras as they ride their bicycles through the bubbling, knee-deep water, not realizing that it is saturated with their own excrement.

History

Georgetown was formed in 1751, and the neighborhood's access to the Potomac River was a big draw to the shipping community. Originally a part of Frederick County, Maryland, Georgetown was appropriated by the City of Washington in 1871.

After the Civil War, the area became a haven for freed slaves seeking financial freedom. But a devastating flood in 1890 forced the Canal Company into bankruptcy and triggered an economic depression. By the end of World War I, Georgetown had become a total slum. In the 1930s, New Deal government officials rediscovered the convenience and charm beneath the grime, and with their help, Georgetown began its physical rehab and social climb back to its current grandeur. The reputation of the area was further boosted with the arrival of then–US Senator John F. Kennedy during the 1950s. As its most famous residents, Kennedy and his wife, Jackie, made Georgetown the hub for the fashionable elite of the District, their legendary parties drawing political heavyweights from all over DC.

Attractions

Georgetown hosts the city's most compact collection of historic, retail, gastronomic, and nightlife draws. The Old Stone House, built in 1765, is the oldest surviving building on its original lot in the federal city, and it predates the city of DC itself. The rumored-to-be-haunted-house and its gardens are both publicly strollable. The C&O Canal Path is a 180-mile leaf-shrouded park that runs alongside a murky, but historically interesting, canal. The canal was originally a water highway that linked the rapidly growing west to the east and allowed farmers to ship their goods to market. The canal path is now more of a runner and biker highway. Locals use it to work off the one-too-manys they imbibed at bars like Georgetown University's esteemed The Tombs. For a more relaxing respite, Dumbarton Oaks is a Federal-style 19th century mansion surrounded by sublime gardens.

Besides being home to one of the city's most prestigious universities, Georgetown is the infamous location of a young boy's supposed exorcism during the late 1940s. The speculated exorcism spawned a bestselling novel by William Peter Blatty and one of the most well-known horror films, *The Exorcist*. Decades later, tourists and fans of the movie still visit the notorious steps where one of the characters fell to his death at the hands of the possessed Regan MacNeil. Take Jan Pottker's Celebrity Georgetown Tour to visit the remodeled house used in the film and see other locations where movies were shot.

For a complete list of stores, restaurants, and attractions in Georgetown, consult the comprehensive Georgetown website: www.georgetowndc.com. For a selection of our favorite Georgetown bars, restaurants, and shopping venues, see Map 8.

How to Get There—Driving

M Street NW can be reached from the Francis Scott Key Bridge, Canal Road NW, and Pennsylvania Avenue.

Parking

Street parking in Georgetown is a pain. A paid garage is your best bet. There are several in the area with reasonable hourly and daily rates. See map for locations.

How to Get There—Mass Transit

Metrobus routes 30, 32, 34, 35, or 36 marked "Friendship Heights" run west on Pennsylvania Avenue. Buses cost $1.25 one-way and only accept exact change or a bus pass.
There is no metro stop in Georgetown, but on a pleasant day, if you're equipped with good walking shoes, the Foggy Bottom-GWU stop on the Orange and Blue lines is a ten minute walk from the east end of the neighborhood. The Rosslyn stop on the same line is a ten-minute walk from Georgetown's west end.

The Georgetown Metro Connection serves all Metrobus stops in Georgetown and operates express service between Georgetown and Foggy Bottom-GWU, Rosslyn, and Dupont Circle Metro stations. The bus leaves the metro stations every ten minutes daily and costs $1 one-way. Shuttle Hours: Mon–Thurs: 7 am–12 am; Fri: 7 am–2 am; Sat: 8 am–2 am; Sun: 8 am–12 am.

The Monuments / Potomac Park / Tidal Basin

The Ellipse

Bolivar

Jose Artigas

2nd Division Monument

Haupt Fountains

German American

Friendship Garden

Einstein

Constitution Ave

Vietnam Veterans Memorial

The 56 Signers of the Declaration of Independence Memorial

Ticket Kiosk

The Three Servicemen

Vietnam Women's Memorial

WWII Memorial

Arts of Peace

Washington Monument

MAP 1

Arts of War

Lincoln Memorial

Constitution Gardens

Korean War Veterans Memorial

John Paul Jones Memorial

MAP 7

Daniel French Dr

WWII Memorial

Independence Ave

Independence Ave

Kutz Bridge

E Basin Dr

John Ericsson Memorial

Japanese Lantern

W Basin Dr

15th St

West Potomac Park

Ohio Dr

Tidal Basin

Japanese Pagoda

FDR Memorial Park

Jefferson Memorial

Ohio Dr

Potomac River

East Basin Dr

395

Lady Bird Johnson Park

Cuban Friendship Urn

MAP 6

Lyndon B Johnson Memorial Grove

East Potomac Park

Washington Memorial Pkwy

Navy & Marine Memorial

George Mason Memorial Bridge

Rochambeau Bridge

Arland D Williams Jr Memorial Bridge

Ohio Dr

Buckeye Dr

Lagoon

23rd St

22nd St

21st St

20th St

19th St

18th St

17th St

15th St

14th St

Henry Bacon Dr

Reflecting Pool

1

General Information

NFT Maps: 1, 6, and 7
Website: www.nps.gov
Phone: 202-426-6841

Overview

If there's one thing DC loves more than a free museum, it's a commemorative lawn ornament. The District is packed with monuments, statues, plaques, and fountains. This is especially apparent while strolling through Potomac Park, where you'll find the Lincoln, FDR, Jefferson, and Washington memorials, as well as tributes to those who served in WWI, WWII, the Korean War, and Vietnam, all within walking distance of one another.

Presidential Monuments

Our forefathers were clearly larger than today's average American, as can be witnessed by viewing and entering the not-so-human scale monuments of some of our more memorable predecessors.

The tall, unadorned monument commemorating America's first president is as recognizable a landmark as the White House or the Capitol. The giant white obelisk can be viewed from many parts of town but is more fun to experience up close, for no better reason than to hear "wow it's tall" in 112 languages.

Had the Washington Monument been built in Europe, it would most likely squirt water from several places, have 12 pairs of ornately sculpted angel wings fluttering from its sides, and feature a large, bronze pair of breasts over the entranceway. But the simplicity and straightforwardness of the building is a tribute to the gravitas, fortitude, and simple elegance of the man it represents.

Entry to the Washington Monument is free, although your ticket is only valid during a specified entry time. Free tickets are distributed on a first-come, first-served basis at the kiosk on the Washington Monument grounds (at 15th Street and Madison Drive). Advance reservations can be made online at reservations.nps.gov. The ticket kiosk is open daily from 8 am until 4:30 pm (closed December 25th), and tickets usually run out early in the day. If you plan on visiting the monument, make it your first stop.

While many visitors use the monument as a vantage point from which to view the surrounding city, the tall structure itself is really as impressive as the view it affords. The exterior walls are constructed of white marble from Maryland; the interior walls are lined with granite from Maine. Construction began in 1848 and was only one-third complete when the Civil War broke out—hence the change in stone color a third of the way up. Construction resumed after the war, but by then, the color of stone in the quarry had changed. Today, the Washington Monument remains the tallest and most revered structure in DC, giving itself alpha-monument status and deflecting the exploding metropolitan population out into surrounding farmland instead of upward into the city sky.

The Lincoln Memorial, which stands in front of the reflecting pool across from the Washington Monument, was designed to look like a Greek Temple and boasts more movie appearances than Samuel L. Jackson. The 36 pillars represent the 36 states that existed at the time of Lincoln's death. The larger-than-life-sized sculpture of honest Abe inside underscores the man's great physical and political stature. Visiting the monument is free, and the structure is open to the public year-round.

Tidal Basin

The Tidal Basin was constructed in the late 1800s as a swimming hole in the middle of the park. It's no longer a place for a refreshing dip. Besides the questionable cleanliness of this urban pond, the ample federal security forces in the neighborhood are likely the strictest lifeguards in the country. If you're set on dipping a toe in the water, join the tourists and rent a paddle boat. For two weeks every spring, cherry blossoms bloom on some 3,000 trees around the basin and throughout the parks. Viewing the monuments through this prism of pink puffiness takes the edge off the sometimes stark grandeur of the grayish-white monuments. The original trees were a gift from Japan in 1912, and their bloom inspires an annual Japanese-influenced festival to kick off the spring. The Japanese must have heard the story of young George choppin' away; not even Bush's famed chainsaw could take down this eye-popping pastel forest.

The domed Jefferson Memorial, easily the most elegant memorial of them all, resides on the basin's edge. From tall Thomas's perch above the tidal basin, a fine view can be enjoyed of both the Washington Monument and flights leaving Reagan National.

East Potomac Park

East Potomac Park is a rather run-of-the-mill park. Yeah, sure, it's got a golf course, tennis courts, swimming pool, basketball court, baseball field, hiking trails, and a playground. It's also a great place to watch the yachts from the marina-cross-the-way carry their rich to wherever they go on the weekends (Be nice, golfers!). But we've become spoiled, and these amenities feel like necessities, not luxuries.

A five-piece sculpture titled *The Awakening* can be found on the very southern tip of East Potomac Park at Hains Point (not pictured on the map). This aluminum depiction of a 100-foot giant emerging from the ground is, like the park it's in, more fun, less epic. You'll need to drive or bike out there because there's no public transportation for miles.

How to Get There—Driving

I-66 and I-395 run to the parks from the south. I-495, New York Avenue, Rock Creek Parkway, George Washington Memorial Parkway, and the Cabin John Parkway will get you there from the north. I-66, Route 50, and Route 29 run to the parks from the west. Routes 50, 1, and 4 are the way to go from the east.

Parking

Public parking is available along the Basin, but depending on the time of day, it's likely to be hard to find a spot. You'll end up driving around and around in circles and eventually parking far out and walking long distances.

How to Get There—Mass Transit

The Foggy Bottom, Metro Center, Federal Triangle, Smithsonian, and L'Enfant Plaza stops on the Orange and Blue lines are all within walking distance of various monuments and parks. Metro Center is also a Red Line stop. L'Enfant Plaza is also on the Green and Yellow lines.

National Mall / Smithsonian / US Capitol

General Information

NFT Maps: 1 & 2
National Mall Website: www.nps.gov/nama
National Mall Phone: 202-426-6841
Smithsonian Website: www.si.edu
Smithsonian Phone: 202-633-1000
U.S. Capitol Website: www.aoc.gov
House of Reps: www.house.gov
Senate: www.senate.gov
Capitol Switchboard: 202-224-2131
Capitol Tour Info: 202-225-6827

National Mall

Washington DC's National Mall represents the American dream, where a melting pot of foreigners and locals gather for leisurely picnics or heated protests—without having to do any of the yard work! The layout for the sprawling grass lawn was designed by Frenchman Pierre L'Enfant in the late 18th century as an open promenade. Despite the explosive growth of the surrounding city, the mall has remained true to L'Enfant's vision (minus the perpetual encircling tour bus brigade). Its eminent strollability is a magnet to hordes of fanny-packed tourists, and its renowned marble monuments attract travel-weary schoolchildren from all over the world. The iconic marble memorials to Washington, Jefferson, Lincoln, and FDR are close by, along with the somber Vietnam and Korean war memorials and the not-yet-copper-stained WWII memorial. On any given day, there's also likely to be a kite festival, political rally, or spirited frisbee game underway. This is not the place to go if you are camera shy, as no matter how hard you try to avoid jumping in front of lenses, you *will* end up in family albums across the nation and world.

Smithsonian Institution

The Smithsonian Institution is made up of 16 different museums, some of them nowhere near the mall (one is in NYC), and a zoo. But the primary museums are mostly clustered around the Mall—here you'll find the Air and Space Museum, the Natural History Museum, and the Hirshhorn, among others, as well as several tucked-away garden areas ideal for spring-time strolling. The Smithsonian Information Center in the Castle is the best orientation point if you plan to become one of the 24 million visitors who check out one of its DC properties this year.

Like the country it caters to, the Smithsonian collection reflects a hodgepodge of experiences and backgrounds: Between its museums on the Mall, the institution's got the Hope Diamond, Japanese scrolls, and even Archie Bunker's chair. Though there is serious art at the National Gallery, the Hirshhorn, and several of the smaller museums, the "most popular" distinction goes to the Air and Space Museum, for its sheer wowza! factor of dangling airplanes and shuttles. A close runner-up is the National Museum of American History, known both affectionately and derisively as "America's Attic." Besides Archie's chair, it accommodates Dorothy's ruby slippers, Muhammad Ali's

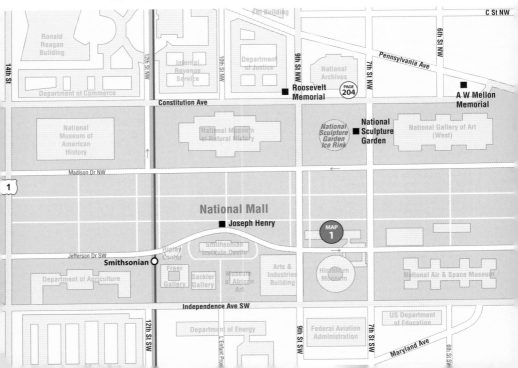

gloves, George Washington's uniform, Julia Child's entire kitchen, and Adlai Stevenson's briefcase. Fortunately, the National Gallery provides a welcome counterpoint to all this kitsch…

Smithsonian Institution Building (The Castle)

The first building of what has become the Smithsonian Empire was the Castle, built in 1855. The Castle was, for a time, the only Smithsonian building, housing all aspects of the institution's operations, including an apartment for the first Secretary of the Smithsonian, Joseph Henry. Note to the macabre-minded: a crypt with the remains of founder James Smithson greets you just to the right of the main entrance. The Castle now serves as the seat of the Smithsonian's administrative offices, as well as a general information center. For those in DC for only a brief stay (or with chronic ADD), the Castle's common room has a mini-museum encompassing exhibits from all of the Mall's museums, which can be thoroughly viewed in approximately ten minutes. (www.si.edu/visit/infocenter/start.htm; 202-633-1000)

The National Museum of the American Indian

This recent addition to the Mall's museum family opened in September 2004. Possibly the largest example of Greco-Anasazi architecture in DC, it includes exhibits from many of the formerly vibrant cultures of North and Middle America. After learning about the hunting and/or agricultural practices of various peoples, hungry visitors can sample native-esque foods while fully appreciating not having to kill or grow them. Hours: Mon–Sun: 10:00 am–5:30 pm. (4th St & Independence Ave, SW; www.americanindian.si.edu; 203-633-1000)

National Air and Space Museum

This museum maintains the largest collection of historic aircraft and spacecraft in the world. Hundreds of artifacts are on display, including the original Wright 1903 airplane, the *Spirit of St. Louis*, the Apollo 11 command module, the *Enola Gay*, and a lunar rock sample that visitors can touch. To avoid lines, try coming in the dead of winter during a blizzard. Otherwise don't worry; it's worth the wait. Hours: 10 am–5:30 pm (6th St & Independence Ave, SW; www.nasm.si.edu)

The National Gallery of Art

The National Gallery's two wings house a collection of art as impressive as any similar institution in the country. Everything else about Washington might get you overcooked on Greek Revival architecture, but the National Gallery shows in rich detail how DC is actually one of the key places in the world to visit for art. The Gallery houses everything from Byzantine art to some of today's leading artists, including Andy Goldsworthy's brilliant new work *Roof*, permanently on display on the ground floor of the East Wing. There is also a small sculpture garden next to the West Wing, which houses a mini "greatest hits" of post-WWII large-format sculpture—highly recommended. Hours: (galleries & garden) Mon–Sat: 10 am–5 pm; Sunday: 11 am–6 pm. Note: The Sculpture Garden is open until 9:30 pm on Fridays during the summer. (Between 3rd St NW & 7th St NW at Constitution Ave; www.nga.gov)

Hirshhorn Museum and Sculpture Garden

Resembling the world's largest flan, the Hirshhorn was conceived as the nation's museum of modern and contemporary

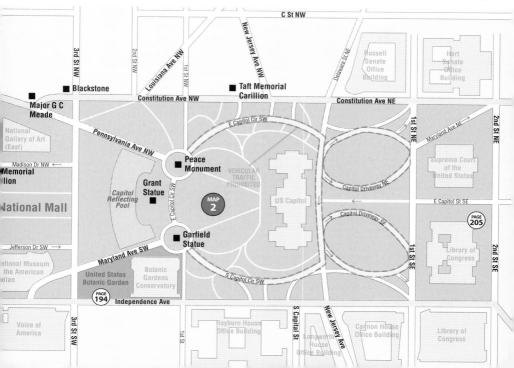

art. It has over 11,500 pieces of internationally significant art, including ample space for large-scale installation works. This is a good one to visit to get away from the chaos of field-trippers in some of the more youth-oriented museums nearby. Hours: Mon–Sun: 10 am–5:30 pm. Sculpture Garden Hours: 7:30 am–dusk. (7th St & Independence Ave, SW; hirshhorn.si.edu)

Arts and Industries Building
The second-oldest Smithsonian building is not in the best shape. In 2004, conditions deteriorated to a point where "diapers" had to be installed on the roof to catch falling debris and the building was closed for renovations. The good news is that a new roof is being installed, and the building will be eventually restored to its former glory. Though entry is still not allowed, the building itself and the surrounding gardens are worth a peek, and visitors can still access the Discovery Theater, a live-performance venue for children. It is temporarily located behind the Smithsonian Castle. (900 Jefferson Dr, SW; www.si.edu/ai)

National Museum of African Art
The National Museum of African Art is the only museum in the United States devoted exclusively to the display and study of traditional and contemporary arts of sub-Saharan Africa. The museum displays everything from ceramics, textiles, furniture, and tools to masks, figures, and musical instruments. Hours: Mon–Sun: 10 am–5:30 pm. (950 Independence Ave, SW; www.nmafa.si.edu)

Freer and Sackler Galleries
These twin galleries are connected via an underground passageway and house a world-renowned Asian art collection. When it opened in 1923, the Freer Gallery was the first Smithsonian museum dedicated to the fine arts. The Sackler Gallery opened in 1987. The Freer is home to one of the most extensive collections of art by American artist James McNeill Whistler. While you won't find the famous picture of his mother here, you'll find some of his other works, including his portraits and the famous Peacock Room. (Freer Gallery: Jefferson Dr & 12th St, SW; Sackler Gallery: 1050 Independence Ave; www.asia.si.edu)

National Museum of American History
(closed until summer 2008)
This museum's mission is to collect, care for, and study the objects that reflect the experience of the American people. What better place for the Declaration of Independence Desk, Dizzy Gillespie's trumpet, or Eli Whitney's cotton gin? Two of our favorites are the original Kermit the Frog puppet and Dorothy's ruby slippers. This museum is a pack rat's dream. It's undergoing renovations, so some artifacts may be removed or relocated, but the answer to the question "Whatever Happened to Polio?" can still be found. Hours: Mon–Sun: 10 am–5:30 pm. (14th St & Constitution Ave, NW; american-history.si.edu)

National Museum of Natural History
Visitors come far and wide to catch a glimpse of the 45.5-carat Hope Diamond, but there's more to this museum than one rock. The National Museum of Natural History has an impressive collection of dinosaur and mammal fossils, an insect zoo (check out the daily tarantula feeding!), and an amazing array of stuffed animals (courtesy of taxidermy, not FAO Schwartz). If you're really into rocks, check out the gem collection, which includes meteorites and the Logan Sapphire; at 423 carats, it is the largest publicly displayed sapphire in the country. If you're not visually impaired from looking at the 126 million cool specimens on display, check out the IMAX shows (better get your tickets in advance). Hours: Mon–Sun: 10 am–5:30 pm. (10th St & Constitution Ave, NW, www.mnh.si.edu)

US Capitol
The US Capitol is located on Capitol Hill, between 1st and 3rd Streets and between Constitution Avenue NE and Independence Avenue SE. Big white dome. Hard to miss.

Home to the House of Representatives and the Senate, this icon is both a museum and a functioning office where Hillary Clinton, Ted Kennedy, and Liddy Dole are working stiffs. It's also DC's orientation point. Every city address is based on where it lies in relation to the Capitol. After hours, drunken Hill staffers use it as a compass to get themselves home. With security a close runner-up to the White House in terms of number of guns and cameras, this is not the place to get lost driving a delivery truck.

Construction began on the Capitol in 1793 and was more or less finished by 1813. The Capitol was burned by the British in 1814, during the War of 1812, but rain saved the structure from complete collapse. Restoration and expansion followed, the result being the building that all Americans recognize today (probably thanks to *Independence Day*). If you've ever wondered who the lady on top of the dome is, she's no-one in particular. She represents freedom and was sculpted by Thomas Crawford.

The District of Columbia gets one non-voting representative in the House based on population but, like Guam and American Samoa, receives no representation in the Senate because it isn't a state. Hence the local "Taxation without Representation" license plates.

The Capitol is closed Thanksgiving, and Christmas. Every other day, the public is welcome to explore the annals of the government. Tours are free (unless you count taxes, in which case they're only free if you're a foreigner). Passes are available beginning at 9 am and redistributed on a first-come, first-served basis. To see actual floor action, get in line early. Passes are not offered in advance, and distribution is limited to one pass per person. The much-anticipated visitors' center is scheduled to be finished sometime in the spring of 2007. To visit your congressman, you'll have to cross the street. Hours: Mon–Sat: 9:00 am–4:30 pm.

How to Get There—Driving

From the south, I-66 and I-395 will take you straight to the Mall. I-495, New York Avenue, Rock Creek Parkway, George Washington Memorial Parkway, and the Cabin John Parkway will get you there from the north. From the west, I-66, US Route 50, and 29 will take you to the Mall. US Routes 50, 1, and 4 will bring you Mall-bound from the east.

Parking

There is some handicapped parking at the nearby Lincoln and FDR memorials; otherwise you're dealing with regular street parking, which usually has a maximum time allocation of three hours. There are parking garages located close to the mall, but be prepared to pay a hefty fee for the convenience.

How to Get There—Mass Transit

Take the Orange and Blue lines to Capital South, Federal Triangle, Smithsonian, and Federal Center SW; the Yellow and Green lines to Archives/Navy Memorial; the Red Line to Union Station and Judiciary Square; and the Yellow, Green, Blue, and Orange lines to L'Enfant Plaza.

General Information

NFT maps: 8, 18, 32, 35, 36
Website: www.nps.gov/choh
Visitor information: 301-739-4200
Fees: None outside of the Great Falls area
Open: Park is open all daylight hours

Thompson Boat Center (mile 0.1)
Address: 2900 Virginia Ave NW (Map 7)
Visitor Information: 202-333-9543
Boathouse hours: Mon–Sat 6 am–8 pm, Sun 7 am–7 pm
Rental Hours: Mon–Sun 8 am–5 pm, all rentals returned by 6 pm

Georgetown Visitor Center (mile 0.4)
Address: 1057 Thomas Jefferson St NW (Map 8)
Visitor information: 202-653-5190
Open: Days and hours vary

The Boathouse at Fletcher's Cover (mile 3.1)
Address: 4940 Canal Rd NW (Map 32)
Visitor Information: 202-244-0461
Open: 7 am–7 pm

Carderock Picnic Pavilion (mile 10.5)
Visitor information: 301-767-3731 for reservations and directions

The Old Angler's Inn
Address: 10801 MacArthur Blvd, Potomac, MD
Visitor information: 301-299-9097

Note: This is not part of the park. This is a pricey restaurant that has been here since 1860. This is not the place to take a rest stop with sweat stains, with a bicycle, or with ugly khaki hiking shorts.

Great Falls Tavern Visitor Center (mile 14.3)
Address: 11710 MacArthur Blvd, Potomac, MD
Visitor Information: 301-767-3714
Open: 9 am–4:30 pm (extended summer hours; closed Thanksgiving, Christmas, New Years Day)

Overview

Traveling 184.5 miles from Washington, DC, to Cumberland, MD, the Chesapeake & Ohio Canal parallels the Potomac River from the bustling streets of chi-chi Georgetown to the no streets of backwater Western Maryland—hugging the borders of West Virginia and Pennsylvania along the way. Back in its day, the C&O Canal was like an aquatic interstate, hauling coal, lumber, and grain from Appalachia to the nation's capital. But these days, there ain't no boats floating on the canal…apart from ones full of tourists and park rangers in period clothing. As for the canal's towpath (that's a dirt sidewalk for you urbanites), it has become one of the best ways to graciously exit this city. The Georgetown segment still feels urban, but once you walk just a mile or two along the canal, you'll soon find that the cell yellers have been replaced by singing birds. The towpath is, in effect, a flat, continuous trail sandwiched by the canal and the river, perfect for shady walks, runs, or bike rides through the beautiful Potomac River Valley. For the docile, the C&O Canal National Park offers birdwatching, picnicking, fishing, and a range of flora. For the hyperactive, there is boating, hiking (read: walking for people with bad fashion sense), and camping. And for the adolescent boys—sorry: Hunting and swimming are strictly prohibited.

Activities

Kids and corny history lovers will enjoy traveling back in time to the days of animal labor and abuse. Mules drag boats along the canal as park rangers in 1870s period dress tell stories and play music to explain what life was like in the 19th century, for both men and mules. Perhaps the coolest part is crossing one of the canal's locks, however—and feeling the water level rise/fall up to eight feet. One-hour round-trip boat rides depart from the Georgetown Visitor Center. Tickets cost $8 for adults, $6 for senior citizens, and $5 for children. Departure times vary by season and day of the week.

Biking is a good idea on all parts of the canal towpath. Those of you who don't own may rent an all-terrain or a cruiser from the Thompson Boat Center.

Boating on the river is a fabulous way to cool down on one of DC's many dog days. Canoes, kayaks, rowing shells, and sailboats are all available for rental at the Thompson Boat Center in Georgetown. Or if you'd like to float and poach, you can rent a rowboat or canoe from the Boathouse at Fletcher's Cove and cast line your line on the Potomac. Bait and tackle are also for sale, and anglers have been known to catch herring, striped bass, white perch, and hickory shad in these here parts.

For those who prefer lounging on a picnic blanket and soaking in the rays, plenty of green flanks the canal. But if you want to make it a more formal affair, Carderock Pavilion can accommodate up to 200 people on its 26—count 'em if you can, 26—picnic tables. The pavilion is available by permit only: $150 Monday–Thursday and $250 Friday–Sunday and holidays (301-767-3731). For this, though, you get electricity, water, grills, a fireplace, "comfort stations," a softball field, horseshoe pits, a volleyball court (but no net), and ample parking.

Treehuggers will be pleased to know that the park contains about 1,200 species of native plants, many of which are rare, endangered, and/or threatened. And flower children will be delighted by over 600 different species of wildflowers. And for the twitchers, keep your eyes peeled and you may just spot a bald eagle.

And lastly, for those of you who are not content to spend just daylight hours with the C&O Canal, the park also has a grand total of 30 campsites—all of which (with the exception of Marsden Tract, which is reserved for do-gooder scouts) are free, free, free. You'll have to go past Great Falls Park to access these sites, but they are designed as way stations for hikers and bikers going the distance. The sites are all first come, first served, for one night only—but offer a chemical toilet, a picnic table, a grill, and water. The closest site is 16.6 miles in at Swains Lock in Potomac, MD.

How to Get There

It's easy enough to get to the start of the canal in Georgetown. By public transportation, take the Metro to Foggy Bottom-GWU, walk north on 24th St, then turn left on Pennsylvania Ave until it merges with M St. Make a left on Thomas Jefferson St to get to the Georgetown Visitors Center. If you're in doubt, just walk south until land ends and water begins. You can also take any of the 30s buses, the D5, or the Circulator.

To get to the Boathouse at Fletcher's Cover, you can take the D3, D5, or D6 to the intersection of MacArthur Blvd & Ashby St and then walk south on Ashby St, past where the street dead ends, and then rough it through the woods until you hit Canal Rd. You should see an old stone building, the Abner Cloud House, next to the boathouse.

The rest of the C&O Canal Park is pretty much inaccessible by public transport. Which is part of the reason why it's so nice.

General Information

NFT Map: 1
DC Address: 700 Pennsylvania Ave NW
Washington, DC 20408
MD Address: 8601 Adelphi Rd
College Park, MD 20740-6001
Web Site: www.archives.gov
www.nara.gov
DC Hours: Labor Day to March 31
Mon–Sun 10:00 am–5:30 pm
Closed December 25th
April 1–Friday before Memorial
Day Weekend
Mon–Sun 10:00 am–7:00 pm
Memorial Day Weekend through
Labor Day   Mon–Sun 10:00 am–9:00 pm
MD Hours: Mon & Wed 8:45 am–5:00 pm
Tue, Thu & Fri 8:45 am–9:00 pm
Sat & Sun 8:45 am–4:45 pm

Overview

The main building of the National Archives is one of the massive DC buildings you would expect on Pennsylvania Ave. There's a lot of stone, an impressive façade, columns and, overall, just a lot of building, but as impressive as the outside is, inside is actually better, unless for some reason you don't really like history. Enter from the National Mall, and you'll likely be greeted by a crowd fighting to get catch a glimpse of the Declaration of Independence, the Constitution, or Bill of Rights. Many people think that's all the National Archives has to offer, but like the proverbial iceberg, these cornerstone documents only scratch the surface. However, while you can see these documents with a quick walk through, (enough for many, but since we aren't tourists here, we demand more!) to truly appreciate all, or even a respectable portion of what the National Archives has to offer, you need to spend a bit more time digging deeper below the surface.

In addition to the big boy documents, there's an impressive collection of memorabilia that includes some of the most historic items in American history. In the public vaults, you will find a rotating collection of items that allows you to explore different aspects of our country's history, the Lawrence F. O'Brien Gallery gives visitors a detailed journey through a rotating, select period or event in American history. You'll also find a children's area as well as a theater showing historical pieces on the National Archives as well as feature length documentaries. As a bonus, the DC branch of the Archives contains a document collection that is any genealogist's dream.

The Maryland location of the National Archives opened in 1994 and is geared toward research, both amateur and professional. The location has an impressive collection of documents dating from WWII including presidential papers, the Berlin Documents Center, civilian and military records, and the John F. Kennedy Assassination Collection, making this the perfect stop if you want to read up on the grassy knoll. Security at the location is high, so be forewarned; however, the staff is the epitome of helpful. See www.nara.gov for detailed information on both locations. Best of all for both spots? Entrance is free.

Getting There

By Metro take the Yellow or Green line to the Archives/Navy Memorial. A free shuttle runs between the DC and Maryland locations, leaving on the hour from 8 am to 5 pm.

If you are driving, to get to the Maryland location, take I-495 toward Baltimore and exit at 28B, which will lead you to New Hampshire Ave/Route 650 South. From here, take a left at the second light onto Adelphi Road and follow the signs. The Archives is on the left. The drive will take you about 45 minutes from DC. There is limited parking provided. At the DC location, parking is on the street only.

General Information

NFT Maps: 2, 3
Address: 101 Independence Ave SE
Washington, DC 20540
Phone: 202-707-5000
Website: www.loc.gov
Hours: James Madison Building: Mon–Fri: 8:30 am–
9:30 pm; Sat: 8:30 am–6:30 pm
Thomas Jefferson Building: Mon–Sat: 10 am–
5 pm
John Adams Building: Mon, Wed, Thurs: 8:30
am–9:30 pm; Tues, Fri, Sat: 8:30 am–5:30 pm

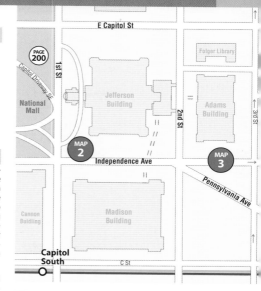

Overview

The Library of Congress doesn't own every book ever published. It IS, however, the largest library in the world. The collection includes more than 128 million items packed on 532 miles of bookshelves in a three-building complex: The Thomas Jefferson Building opened in 1897 and is home to the soaring stained glass Great Hall; the John Adams Building was built in 1939; and the James Madison Building was constructed in 1980. All three buildings are clustered together on Capitol Hill. The Declaration of Independence, the Constitution, a Gutenberg Bible, and the Giant Bible of Mainz are on permanent display.

Sounds like a bibliophile's dream, right? Harsh reality: This is no lending library. The Library of Congress, despite being a great asset to the American public, can't be used like your neighborhood library or a local bookstore. The Library's mission is to serve as a reference library and educational resource for our government *leaders*, not for us plebeians. In the Library of Congress, children can't run between non-fiction aisles clutching ice cream sandwiches as their mothers discuss ergonomic spatulas on their cell phones. To do more than merely wander through the ornate sections, you have to be older than 18 and register at the Reader Registration Station. The Visitors' Center (in the Jefferson Building, along with everything worth visiting) offers information, a short introductory film, and free guided tours. A system of underground tunnels connects the Library's main buildings, as well as the Cannon Office Building. The public can enter from the Adams or Madison Buildings and emerge deep within the heart of the Jefferson Building. It's easy to get lost, but worth the adventure, not to mention the time you save in line on busy tourist days. Most DC'ers have yet to look upon the catacombs of the LOC, being familiar primarily with the sculptures of Neptune and his court out front.

The Library has two theaters—the Coolidge Auditorium, located in the Thomas Jefferson Building, and the tiny Mary Pickford Theater in the Madison Building. Built in 1924, the 511-seat Coolidge Auditorium still hosts regular concerts and is known for its remarkable acoustics. Admission to all events is free; however, reservations must be made through Ticketmaster (two ticket limit per customer), which charges a $2 handling fee. The 64-seat Mary Pickford Theater screens films ranging from those of Pickford's era to modern films. Admission is free, but reservations are required. Visit the Library's website for movie and show times.

History

The Library of Congress was first established in 1800, when the seat of government moved from Philadelphia to DC, and President John Adams approved legislation to create a Congressional law library. The first acquisition consisted of 740 volumes and three maps from London. Fourteen years later, the British army invaded the city and burned the Capitol building, including the amassed 3,000 volumes that made up the Library of Congress at the time. Thomas Jefferson offered to sell his personal library to Congress to restore its lost collection. Jefferson's 6,487 volumes, which were then the largest and finest collection of books in the country, were purchased for $23,940 (the equivalent of 958 copies of *The Da Vinci Code*). Jefferson's collection, which included works on architecture, science, literature, geography, and art, greatly expanded the Library's previously legal collection.

It was in 1870, under the leadership of librarian Ainsworth Spofford, that the collection outgrew its home. The copyright law of 1870 required all copyright applicants to send the Library of Congress two free copies of their book. The Library was flooded with pamphlets, manuscripts, photographs, and books, and eventually—16 years later—Congress authorized the construction of a new building for all their books.

How to Get There—Mass Transit

The two metro stops closest to the Library are Capitol South (Orange/Blue lines) and Union Station (Red Line). Capitol South is located a block south of the Thomas Jefferson building, across Independence Avenue. From Union Station, walk south on 1st Street, NE, towards the Capitol (it's hard to miss). You'll pass the Supreme Court on your way to the Thomas Jefferson building, which will be on the east side of 1st Street—about a 15 minute walk from Union Station.

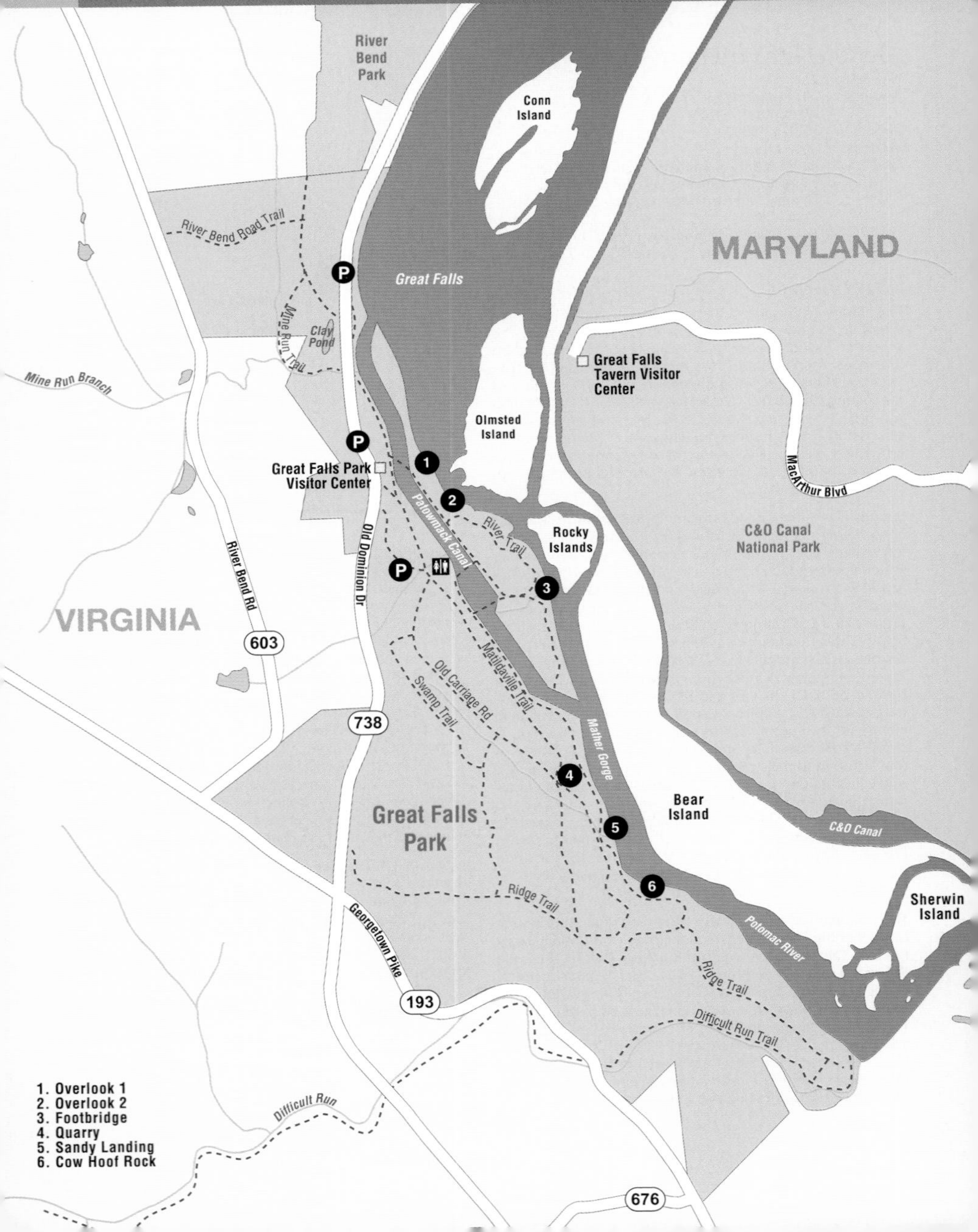

River Bend Park

Conn Island

MARYLAND

River Bend Road Trail

P

Great Falls

Mine Run Trail

Clay Pond

Mine Run Branch

Olmsted Island

Great Falls Tavern Visitor Center

P

Great Falls Park Visitor Center

1

2

River Trail

Rocky Islands

MacArthur Blvd

C&O Canal National Park

Old Dominion Dr

Potowmack Canal

P

3

VIRGINIA

River Bend Rd

603

738

Mathildeville Trail

Old Carriage Rd

Swamp Trail

Mather Gorge

4

5

Bear Island

C&O Canal

6

Great Falls Park

Georgetown Pike

Ridge Trail

Potomac River

Sherwin Island

193

Ridge Trail

Difficult Run Trail

1. Overlook 1
2. Overlook 2
3. Footbridge
4. Quarry
5. Sandy Landing
6. Cow Hoof Rock

Difficult Run

676

General Information

Address: 9200 Old Dominion Dr
McLean, VA 22101
Phone: 703-285-2965
Website: www.nps.gov/gwmp/grfa
Fees: Annual Park Pass: $20
Vehicle: $5 for 3 days
Individual: $3 for 3 days (entering by
means other than vehicle—e.g. foot, bike)
All passes valid on both sides of the falls.
Open: 7 am–dusk year-round, closed Christmas

Overview

The aptly named Great Falls Park is 14 miles upriver from Washington, DC, where the Potomac River cracks into cascading rapids and 20-foot waterfalls. The river drops 76 feet in elevation over a distance of less than a mile and narrows from almost 1,000 feet to 100 feet as it gushes through the narrow Mather Gorge. It's the steepest and most spectacular fall line rapid of any eastern river. You can check out the falls from either Virginia, where the viewing area expands into a massive park, or Maryland, where there are fewer amenities but you can get there with two wheels; the Maryland side of the falls is technically in the C&O Canal National Historical Park.

History

The Great Falls weren't always so admired. In the mid-1700s, they presented a near-impossible obstacle for navigating the Potomac. One of the most significant engineering feats of the 18th century in the US was the development of a system of canals that lifted and lowered riverboats for over 200 miles of the river. The remains of the Patowmack Canal, one of the system's largest and most difficult to create, can still be seen in the park today.

John McLean and Steven Elkins purchased the land surrounding Great Falls and built an amusement park there in the early 1900s that was wildly popular with tourists. Visitors traveled from Georgetown by trolley to take a spin on the wooden carousel. However, time and constant flood damage dampened the thrills until it was eventually closed. Today the land is under the authority and protection of the National Park Service.

Activities

Picnic areas with tables and grills are available on a first-come, first-served basis, and ground fires are strictly prohibited. Unfortunately, there are no covered picnic tables in the event of inclement weather, so check the forecast before packing your basket. If you forget your picnic, there is a basic concession stand (open seasonally) located in the visitors center courtyard on the Maryland side.

If it's sweat-breaking activity you're after, a scenic, sometimes rocky, bike-riding trail extends between the Maryland side of the falls and downtown Washington. Hiking trails of various length and difficulty wind along the river, and horseback riding, bird watching, rock climbing, fishing, whitewater rafting, and kayaking can be enjoyed at locations throughout the park.

If you plan on rock climbing, registration is not necessary, however, there are voluntary sign-in sheets located in the visitors center courtyard and the lower parking lot. If fishing is more your speed, a Virginia or Maryland fishing license is required for anglers over 16 years of age. Whitewater boating is recommended only for experienced boaters and, not surprisingly, you're only allowed to launch your craft *below* the falls.

Stop by the visitor center (open daily from 10 am–4 pm) on the Virginia side of the park or check out the National Park Service website for more information. www.nps.gov/gwmp/grfa/faqs/activities.htm

How to Get There—Driving

From I-495, take Exit 44, Route 193 W (Georgetown Pike). Turn right at Old Dominion Drive (approximately 4 1/2 miles). Drive for 1 mile to the entrance station. Parking, falls overlooks, and the visitor center are all centrally located.

To get to the visitor center on the Maryland side, take I-495 to Exit 41/MacArthur Boulevard E towards Route 189. Follow MacArthur Road all the way to the visitor center.

There is no public transportation available near the park.

General Information

NFT Maps: 20, 21, 23, 24, and 28
Website: www.nps.gov/rocr
Visitor Information: 202-895-6070

Overview

Let the tourists have the National Mall; we have Rock Creek Park to call our own. This 1,754-acre forest doesn't even make it onto many tourist maps—which may explain its popularity with people who live here and why you can bike or run for miles without braking for fanny-packers. The park, which stretches from Georgetown to Maryland, is one of the largest forested urban parks in the country. A paved bike and running path twists alongside the creek that gives the park its name. Dozens of more secluded, rocky paths break off from the path, one of which gained notoriety in 2002 when the body of federal intern/Congressional paramour Chandra Levy was discovered nearby. The park actually has one of the lowest crime rates in the city—but it's an urban park, nevertheless, so lugging along a cell phone or a hiking partner ain't a bad idea. There are visitors' centers advertised: the Nature Center and Planetarium and Pierce Mill, but when they're open, they're hard to reach and of limited help. For basic questions and a great map, best to check the website.

History

In 1866, federal officials proposed cordoning off some of the forest area as a presidential retreat. By the time Congress took up the plan in 1890, the vision had been democratized and the forest became a public park.

Pierce Mill, a gristmill where corn and wheat were ground into flour using water power from Rock Creek, was built in the 1820s and is located over the bridge on Tilden Street. (Pierce Mill has been indefinitely closed to the public for repairs, but the Pierce Barn remains open.) There are also remains of several Civil War earthen fortifications in the park, including Fort Stevens, the only Civil War battle site in DC.

Activities

There are more than 30 picnic areas spread throughout the park, all of which can be reserved in advance for parties of up to 100 people (202-673-7646). A large field located at 16th and Kennedy streets has several areas suitable for soccer, football, volleyball, and field hockey. Fields can be reserved ahead of time (202-673-7749). The Rock Creek Tennis Center has 15 clay and 10 hard-surface tennis courts that must be reserved, in person, for a small fee (202-722-5949). The outdoor courts are open from April through November, and five heated indoor courts open during winter months. Three clay courts located off Park Road, east of Pierce Mill, can also be reserved in person, May through September.

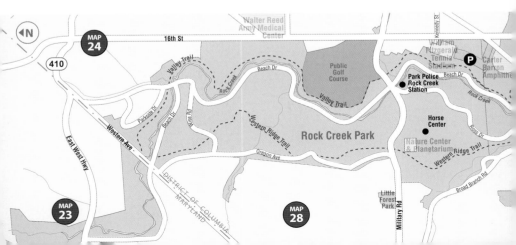

An extensive network of hiking trails runs through Rock Creek Park and the surrounding areas. Blue-blazed paths maintained by the Potomac Appalachian Trail Club run along the east side of the creek, and green-blazed trails follow the park's western ridge. Tan-blazed trails connect the two systems. The paved path for bikers and roller bladers runs from the Lincoln Memorial, through the park, and into Maryland. Memorial Bridge connects the path to the Mount Vernon Trail in Virginia. Beach Drive between Military and Broad Branch roads is closed to cars on weekends and major holidays, giving bikers free range. However, bikes are not permitted on horse or foot trails at any time. If you're willing to ditch the bike for another kind of ride, horseback riding lessons and guided trail rides are available at the Rock Creek Park Horse Center (202-362-0117), located next to the Nature Center.

At the Rock Creek Nature Center (5200 Glover Rd, NW, 202-895-6070), you'll find the Planetarium, which features after school shows for children on Wednesdays at 4 pm and weekends at 1 pm and 4 pm. The park also hosts outdoor Shakespeare performances at the Carter Barron Amphitheater (16th St & Colorado Ave, 202-426-0486) on summer evenings. Nature Center Hours: Wed–Sun: 9 am–5 pm. Closed on national holidays.

How to Get There—Driving
To get to the Nature Center from downtown DC, take the Rock Creek/Potomac Parkway north to Beach Drive. Exit onto Beach Drive N, and follow it to Broad Branch Road. Make a left and then a right onto Glover Road, and follow the signs to the Nature Center. Note: The Parkway is one-way going south on weekdays 6:45 am–9:45 am. During this time, you can take 16th Street to Military Road W, then turn left on Glover Road. The Parkway is one-way going north 3:45 pm–6:30 pm; take Glover Road to Military Road east, then head south on 16th Street toward downtown DC. If all you're looking to do is get into the park, consult the map below—the place is so huge that no matter where you live, you're probably close to some branch of it.

Parking
Expansive parking lots are located next to the Nature Center and Planetarium. There are parking lots dotted throughout the park, but depending on your destination, you might be better off looking for street parking in nearby neighborhoods.

How to Get There—Mass Transit
Take the Red Metro line to either the Friendship Heights or Fort Totten Metro stops to get to the Nature Center. Transfer to the E2 bus line, which runs along Military/Missouri/Riggs Road between the two stations. Get off at the intersection of Glover (also called Oregon) and Military Roads and walk south on the trail up the hill to the Nature Center.

Check the map, though; the park covers so much ground in the DC Metro area that getting there may be easier than you think. There's certainly no need to start your visit at the Nature Center.

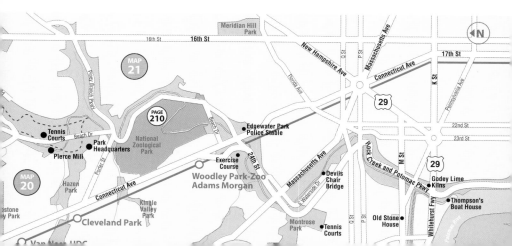

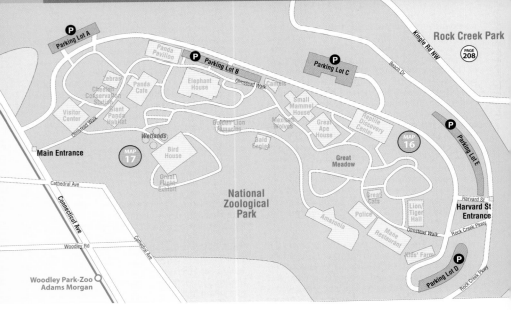

General Information

NFT Maps:	16 & 17
Address:	3001 Connecticut Ave NW
	Washington, DC 20008
Phone:	202-673-4800
Website:	www.natzoo.si.edu
Hours:	6 am–8 pm Apr 6–Oct 25; 6 am–6 pm the rest of the year. (Closed Christmas Day)
Admission:	Free

Overview

Nestled in Rock Creek Park, the National Zoological Park is a branch of the Smithsonian Institution (Read: It should be taken very seriously). With about 2,400 animals of 400 different species, there are more pampered foreign residents living in the National Zoo than on Embassy Row. About one-fifth of these animals are endangered, including DC's own baby-faced darling and the star of the show: giant panda Tai Shan. Born to parents on loan from the Chinese government, Tai Shan ("peaceful mountain") is only here until his second birthday, so line up for a peak at him gnawing on bamboo while you can.

The park's animal enclosures mimic natural habitats, and most exhibits strive to entertain while slipping in as much educational value as possible for all of those visiting school children. A popular destination in the summertime, the zoo can be just as appealing in the winter months, with so many indoor animal houses to visit—and fewer kids to elbow out of your way. The zoo is also a favorite jogging route for area residents—especially on winter snow days when Olmsted Walk is known to be one of the few regularly plowed paths in the city. In the spring and summer, the zoo is packed with students on field trips in the mornings and early afternoons. If you want to avoid them, try going before 10 am or after 2 pm. The animals tend to be more active at these times anyway, and you won't have to wait in line to see the more popular exhibits and animals.

Parking

Enter the zoo from Connecticut Avenue, Harvard Street, or Rock Creek Parkway. Because parking on zoo grounds is limited, public transportation is recommended. If you're set on driving, parking at the zoo costs $4 for the first hour, $12 for two to three hours, and $16 for over three hours. Lots fill early in the day during the summer, so plan to arrive by 9:30 am at the latest if you're going to be parking.

How to Get There—Mass Transit

By Metro, take the Red Line to the Woodley Park-Zoo/Adams Morgan stop or the Cleveland Park stop; the zoo entrance lies roughly halfway between these stops and both are a short stroll away. It's an uphill walk from Woodley Park, while the walk from Cleveland Park is fairly flat.

From the Woodley Park-Zoo/Adams Morgan stop, walk north (to your left as you face Connecticut Avenue—away from the McDonald's and the CVS), and the zoo is about a twelve-minute walk from the stop. From the Cleveland Park stop, walk south toward the greater number of shops and restaurants that line Connecticut Avenue (away from the 7-11 and the Exxon station).

If you prefer above-ground mass transit, Metrobus lines L1, L2, and L4 stop at the zoo's Connecticut Avenue entrance. The H4 stops at the zoo's Harvard Street entrance.

General Information

Address: 4368 Chantilly Shopping Center
Chantilly, VA 20153
Phone: 703-378-0910
Website: www.dullesexpo.com

Overview

Dulles Expo Center should really just knock off the last two letter of "Dulles" and be done with it. "Dull" is the reigning word here—it accurately describes the area (Chantilly); the spaces in the Center itself (two separate low-slung, charmless rectangles); and most of the exhibits, exhibitors, and exhibitees. Pray to whatever gods you believe in that, if you have to attend a show or convention in DC, it'll be at the Washington Convention Center. Dulles Expo's only saving grace is that it has the best convention center parking in the universe—immediately outside the two buildings. Other than that, if it's a gun or RV show you're looking for, well, golly, this is the place!

A cab from Dulles to the Expo Center will cost about $20. A taxi from Reagan National Airport costs approximately $45. If you really want to fly into Baltimore-Washington International Airport, be prepared to cough up $85 for your 1.5-hour schlep.

Hotels

The Expo Center has an on-site Holiday Inn Select and several hotels within walking distance. Certain hotels have specials for specific conventions, so ask when you book. Or browse hotel-specific websites such as hotels.com and pricerighthotels.com.

- **Comfort Suites Chantilly-Dulles Airport,**
  13980 Metrotech Dr, 703-263-2007
- **Fairfield Inn Dulles Chantilly South,** 3960 Corsair Ct,
  703-435-1111
- **Hampton Inn-Dulles South,** 4050 Westfax Dr,
  703-818-8200
- **Homestead Village,** 4505 Brookfield Coroporate Dr,
  703-263-3361
- **Holiday Inn Select,** 4335 Chantilly Shopping Ctr,
  703-815-6060

- **Courtyard by Marriott,** 3935 Centerview Dr,
  703-709-7100
- **Sierra Suites,** 4506 Brookfield Corporate Dr,
  703-263-7200
- **Staybridge Suites,** 3860 Centerview Dr, 703-435-8090
- **TownePlace Suites by Marriott,** 14036 Thunderbolt Pl,
  703-709-0453
- **Westfields Marriott,** 14750 Conference Center Dr,
  703-818-0300
- **Wingate Inn Dulles Airport,** 3940 Centerview Dr,
  571-203-0999

How to Get There—Driving

From DC, travel west on Constitution Avenue, and follow the signs to Virginia. Follow I-66 W for about 25 miles until exit 53B, Route 28 N (Dulles Airport). Drive three miles north on Route 28, and then turn right onto Willard Road. Take the second left off into the Chantilly Shopping Center. From there, follow the signs to the Expo Center.

From Dulles Airport, follow exit signs for DC. Stay towards the right for about one mile, and take Route 28 S towards Centerville. Drive six miles and pass over Route 50. At the first light past Route 50, make a left on Willard Road. Follow signs to the Expo Center.

Better yet, don't go at all.

Parking

The Dulles Expo and Conference Center has 2,400 parking spaces on-site! (When their website has to brag about parking, you know we're not just being cynical about this place). If you arrive in your RV, you'll have to find a campsite for the night, as campers, RVs, trucks, and oversized vehicles will be ticketed if parked overnight.

How to Get There—Mass Transit

There is no public transportation to the Dulles Expo and Conference Center. Remember, this is America.

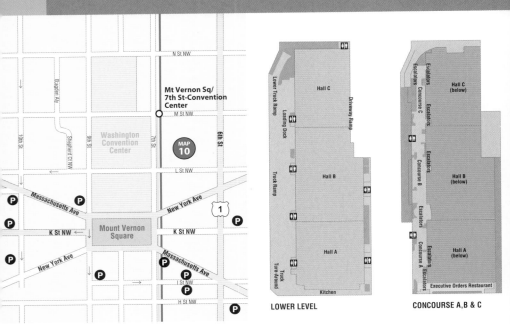

LOWER LEVEL

CONCOURSE A,B & C

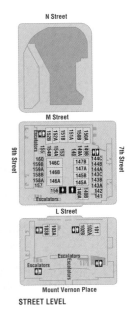

STREET LEVEL

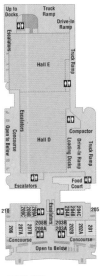

LEVEL TWO

LEVEL THREE

General Information

NFT Map: 10
Address: 801 Mt Vernon Pl NW
             Washington, DC 20001
Phone: 800-368-9000 or 202-249-3000
Website: www.dcconvention.com

Overview

The Washington Convention Center is a stunning white granite and glass mammoth covering six city blocks, from 7th Street to 9th Street and N Street to Mount Vernon Place. The 2.3 million-square-foot building is the largest in DC and had the distinction of being the largest excavation site in the Western Hemisphere; 2 million tons of earth was removed during construction. Whether exhibiting or attending, you'd be well advised to wear comfy shoes to traverse the 700,000 square feet of exhibit space, 150,000 square feet of meeting space, the 52,000-square-foot ballroom (one of the East Coast's largest), and 40,000 square feet of retail space. The center hosts everything from small seminars for 80 participants to giant expos that welcome 35,000 attendees. Nonetheless, it is like every other convention center in that spending more than 15 minutes in it is a completely de-humanizing experience. Try spending three full days running a booth, and you'll know what we're talking about.

Along with the MCI Center, the Convention Center is a pillar of revitalization for this previously seedy neighborhood. Thanks to that success, conventioneers have many more amenities to choose from in the area. The City Museum across the street used to have interesting exhibits detailing the history of Washington, but poor attendance and the shut-off of external funding spelled its demise. A string of shops, restaurants, and nightlife, especially on 7th Street NW south of Massachusetts Avenue, beckon nearby. Nevertheless, occasional panhandlers still canvass the area, hoping to profit from pedestrians with open maps making their way toward the Convention Center. The fastest and cheapest way to the Convention Center is to keep that map folded in your coat pocket and follow the platinum blonde in the plastic cowboy hat pasted with event-related bumper stickers.

If you're flying in for a convention, a cab from BWI or Dulles will cost you more than $70 to downtown DC. From Reagan, it should be no more than $15. The Metro Yellow Line runs directly from Reagan to its terminus at the Mount Vernon Square/7th Street-Convention Center station.

Hotels

If you know which hotel you want to stay in, give them a call, and ask if they have any special rates for the dates you'll be attending. If you're not with any particular rewards program and don't care where you stay, try the official Washington tourism website at www.washington.org or hotel-specific websites such as www.hotels.com and www.pricerighthotels.com. Plans are being finalized for the construction of a 1400+ room Marriott Convention Center Hotel right across 9th Street, NW. However, as these things go, it'll be years before it's opened. In the meantime, consider these nearby hotels:

• **Renaissance Hotel** • 999 9th St NW, 202-898-9000
• **Henley Park** • 926 Massachusetts Ave NW, 202-638-5200
• **Courtyard by Marriott Convention Center** • 900 F St NW, 202-638-4600

• **Morrison Clark Inn** • 1101 11th St NW, 202-898-1200
• **Marriott Metro Center** • 775 12th St NW, 202-737-2200
• **Four Points by Sheraton** • 1201 K St NW, 202-289-7600
• **Hamilton Crowne Plaza** • 1001 14th St NW, 202-682-0111
• **Hilton Garden Inn** • 815 14th St NW, 202-783-7800
• **Hotel Sofitel** • 806 15th St NW, 202-737-8800
• **Washington Plaza** • 10 Thomas Cir NW, 202-842-1300
• **Holiday Inn Downtown** • 1155 14th St NW, 202-737-1200
• **Wyndham Washington, DC** • 1400 M St NW, 202-429-1700
• **The Madison** • 1177 15th St NW, 202-862-1600
• **Hotel Helix** • 1430 Rhode Island Ave NW, 202-462-9001
• **Homewood Suites by Hilton** • 1475 Massachusetts Ave NW, 202-265-8000
• **Capitol Hilton** • 1001 16th St NW, 202-393-1000
• **Holiday Inn Central** • 1501 Rhode Island Ave NW, 202-483-2000
• **Comfort Inn** • 1201 13th St NW, 202-682-5300
• **Grand Hyatt Washington** • 1000 H St NW, 202-582-1234
Embassy Suites/Convention Center 900 9th St, NW, 202-739-2001
Hampton Inn/Convention Center 901 6th St, NW, 202-842-2500
Hotel Monaco 700 F St, NW, 800-649-1202

Eating

After spending a gazillion dollars on a gleaming new Convention Center, some thought went into providing better grub that the old center's mystery meat burgers and heat-lamp fries. Here, you'll find a number of restaurants located in the Convention Center and dozens more within easy walking distance (almost all of them *south* of the Center). Executive Orders, located on the L1 Concourse, offers selections from Foggy Bottom Grill, Wolfgang Puck Express, Seafood by Phillips, Subculture, Bello Pronto, Mr. Thoi's Fine Asian Cuisine, and Latin American Cuisine. Located on Level Two off the L Street Bridge, the Supreme Court is a retail food court offering Wolfgang Puck Express, Quizno's, and Foggy Bottom Grill.

The Lobby Café, located by the main entrance, sells coffee and deluxe pastries to help exhibitors and attendees wake up in the mornings. Within each exhibit hall, there are also permanent and portable outlets/carts serving everything from coffee to Tex-Mex.

Parking

The center does not have its own parking facility, and there are about 100 metered parking spaces close to the convention center, so you'll be pretty fortunate if you manage to snag one. Otherwise, be prepared to pay for one of the many parking lots within a three-block radius of the center. A block south of the Center, a huge new lot (with a huge new fee) has recently opened, created after the old center was torn down.

How to Get There—Mass Transit

The closest Metro stop is Mt Vernon Sq/7th St-Convention Center on the Yellow or Green lines.

213

Pine Ridge
Golf Course

Goucher
College

129

133

Robert E Lee
Park

Towson
University

E Burke Ave

695

Woodholme
Country
Club

Club of
Baltimore
County

Bonnie
View
Country
Club

Elkridge
Club

Cross Country Blvd

Country
Club of
Maryland

Putnam Pkwy

542

Mt
Pleasant
Golf
Course

147

White Ave

588

95

Perry Hall Blvd

Yellowbrick

695

Patterson Ave

W Northern Pkwy

Bamford Blvd

83

E Cold Spring Ln

542

E 33rd St

1

702

702

Pulaski

Batavia
Park

Back
River

Druid Hill
Park

Johns
Hopkins
University

Falls Rd

Clifton
Park

Monroe Rd

95

Gwynns Falls Pkwy

Baltimore
Zoo

E 25th St

151

95

150

Security Blvd

W North Ave

129

North Point Blvd

Gwynns Falls
Park

Cooks Ln

W Lafayette Ave

40

2

895

Ed

Frederick

PAGE
216

Boston St

Boston St

Dundalk Ave

166

Carroll
Park

395

95

Merritt Blvd

Wise Ave

Rolling Road
Golf Club

University
of Maryland
Baltimore
County

S Caton Ave

Hammonds Ferry Rd

Water View Ave

895

Pontiac Ave

Patapsco
River

Spar
Point
Cou

Patapsco
Valley State
Park

Round Rd

Washington Blvd

295

648

W Patapsco Ave

Reed Bird
Island Park

Thalston Tunnel Thwy

95

170

Patapsco Ave

Patapsco Ave

Ferndale Rd

Patterson Park
Brook Park

Curtis
Bay

695

895

1

710

195

PAGE
252

Baltimore-
Washington
Airport

Overview

Baltimore's comeback streak has pretty much obliterated its former reputation as the murder capital of the nation (even if it still regularly scores well in crime rankings). Real estate prices are booming, retail rakes it in during the tourist season, and businessmen have discovered a city where, just steps from the convention center, they can sightsee, shop for their kids, AND hoist a beer at Hooters. The city's real treasures are hidden in its neighborhoods, where fierce local pride mixes with a local flare for the, uh, creative (If you can't get to Café Hon or the Visionary Art Museum, ask hometown filmmaker John Waters to explain).

Getting There

Take I-295 N to Baltimore City past Oriole Park at Camden Yards. 295 will become Russell Street and then Paca Street. Make a right onto Pratt Street. Follow Pratt Street six blocks to the Inner Harbor, which will be on your right. The Visitor Center is located along the Inner Harbor's west wall (near Light Street).

Attractions

Harborplace
200 E Pratt St, 410-332-4191; www.harborplace.com
One of Baltimore's most well-known attractions is Harborplace, owned by the Rouse Company (i.e. it looks exactly the same as New York's South Street Seaport, Boston's Faneuil Hall, New Orleans's Riverwalk Marketplace, etc.). The outdoor mall's retail stores and chain restaurants circle the harbor. Since most residents only hang at Harborplace when they're showing off their waterfront to out-of-towners, it becomes a mob of tourists on sunny weekends. Shop hours: Mon–Sat: 10 am–9 pm; Sun: 11 am–7 pm.

National Aquarium in Baltimore
501 E Pratt St, 410-576-3800; www.aqua.org
Baltimore's aquarium is the city's most popular tourist attraction. Entry isn't cheap, and there's bound to be a line to get in, but attractions like the Tropical Rain Forest (complete with piranhas and poisonous frogs) and the dolphin show make it worth all the hassle. Admission costs $21.95 for adults, $12.95 for kids (3–11), and $20.95 for seniors (65+). Tickets often sell out, but you can buy advance tickets through Ticketmaster. Aquarium hours: Sun–Thurs: 9 am–5 pm; Fri: 9 am–8 pm.

Maryland Science Center
601 Light St; 410-685-5225; www.mdsci.org
The Maryland Science Center is one of the oldest scientific institutions in the country and is full of dinosaur bones, IMAX, etc. It's best for kids, especially ones you want to push toward Einstein-hood. The center is usually open from 10 am to 6 pm daily, although hours change by season; admission prices range from $14.50 to $20, depending on what exhibits you'd like to visit. Admission for children costs between $10 and $14, and admission for members is always free.

Babe Ruth Birthplace and Museum
216 Emory St, 410-727-1539; www.baberuthmuseum.com
Visit the place where Babe was really a babe. This historic building has been transformed into a shrine to Babe, as well as to Baltimore's Colts and Orioles and Johnny Unitas (famed quarterback for the Colts). Admission costs $6 for adults and $3 for children 16 and under. Hours: April–October: daily 10 am–6 pm (7:30 pm on baseball game days), November–March: Tues–Sun 10 am–5 pm (8 pm on football game days).

The Baltimore Zoo
978 Druid Park Lake Dr, 410-366-LION; www.baltimorezoo.org
Located in Druid Hill Park, the zoo is hidden in the middle of the city, far away from the other major tourist attractions. Kids can enjoy the number-one-rated children's zoo, while adults can look forward to the zoo's spring beer and wine festival, Brew at the Zoo. (Plan on hearing lots of jokes about polar beer, penguinness, and giraffes of wine.) Admission to the zoo costs $15 for adults, $10 for the kiddies, and $12 for the grannies, but parking is always free. The zoo is open daily, Mar–Dec: 10 am–4:30 pm.

Lexington Market
400 W Lexington St, 410-685-6169; www.lexingtonmarket.com
Baltimore's Lexington Market is the world's largest continuously running market. Founded in 1782, the market continues to be a rowdy place of commerce. The market prides itself for its top-quality fresh meats, seafood, poultry, groceries, specialty items, and prepared foods for take-out and on-site consumption. Visit the market during the Chocolate Festival and the Preakness Crab Derby (yes, they actually race crabs). During Lunch with the Elephants, held annually in the spring, a herd of elephants from the Ringling Bros. and Barnum & Bailey Circus marches from the Baltimore Arena to the market, where they proceed to eat the world's largest stand-up vegetarian buffet. Market hours: Mon–Sat: 8:30 am–6 pm.

National Museum of Dentistry
31 S Greene St, 410-706-0600; www.dentalmuseum.org
After munching on goodies at the Lexington Market, swing on by the National Museum of Dentistry to learn about all the cavities you just got. This Smithsonian affiliate offers interactive exhibits and the gift shop sells chocolate toothbrushes (reason enough to check it out). Plaque got you gloomy? Edgar Allan Poe's grave is just down the street. Admission to the museum costs $4.50 for adults and $2.50 for kids, students, and seniors. Hours: Wed–Sat: 10 am–4 pm; Sun: 10 am–1 pm.

The Power Plant
601 E Pratt St, 410-752-5444
Once upon a time, the Power Plant was an honest-to-goodness power plant. In 1998, it was converted into a full-fledged mall. Guess retail's just a different kinda community fuel. Inside the Power Plant, you'll find Barnes & Noble, ESPN Zone, Gold's Gym, and the Hard Rock Café.

Power Plant Live!

Market Pl & Water St, 410-727- 5483; www.powerplantlive.com
Located a block away from the Power Plant, Power Plant Live! is a dining and entertainment megaplex. You can have a full night without leaving the indoor/outdoor complex. Dinner, dancing, comedy, and stiff drinks are served up by eight bars and seven restaurants. Because of an arena liquor license, you can take your drink from one establishment to the next. During the summer, check out the free outdoor concerts. Past headliners include the Soundtrack of Our Lives, Aimee Mann, Elvis Costello, and the Wildflowers.

American Visionary Art Museum

800 Key Hwy, 410-244-1900; www.avam.org
The Visionary Art Museum exhibits works from self-taught, intuitive artists, whose backgrounds range from housewives to homeless. The museum is also home to Baltimore's newest outdoor sculptural landmark—the Giant Whirligig. Standing tall at an imposing 55 feet, this multicolored, wind-powered sculpture was created by 76-year-old mechanic, farmer, and artist Vollis Simpson. Every spring, the museum hosts a race of human-powered works of art designed to travel on land, through mud, and over deep harbor waters. Museum hours: Tues-Sun: 10 am–6 pm. Admission costs $11 for adults and $7 for students, seniors, and children.

Pagoda at Patterson Park

www.pattersonpark.com
One of the most striking structures in Baltimore's Patterson Park is the newly renovated Pagoda. Originally built in 1891, the Pagoda was designed as a people's lookout tower. From the 60-foot-high octagonal tower, you can see downtown, the suburbs, and the harbor. Pagoda Hours: Sun: 12 pm–6 pm, May–Oct.

Camden Yards

There's more to Camden Yards than the O's. At the turn of the century, Camden Yard was a bustling freight and passenger railroad terminal. For decades, Camden Station served as a major facility for the Baltimore and Ohio Railroad (that's the B&O Railroad for Monopoly fans). The Yards were once home to thousands of commuters, and now they're home to thousands of fans who come out to see their beloved Orioles play.

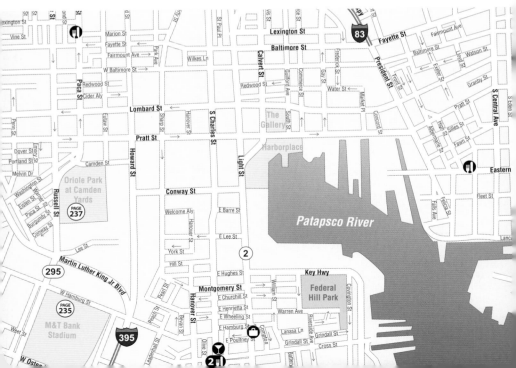

○ Landmarks

· **Baltimore Tattoo Museum** · 1534 Eastern Ave

Nightlife

· **Club Charles** · 1724 N Charles St (off map)
· **Cross Street Market** · 1065 S Charles St
· **The Horse You Came In On** · 1626 Thames St

Shopping

· **The Antique Man** · 1806 Fleet St
· **Cook's Table** · 1036 Light St
· **Karmic Connection** · 508 S Broadway
· **Mystery Loves Company** · 1730 Fleet St
· **Sound Garden** · 1616 Thames St
· **Stikky Fingers** · 802 S Broadway

Restaurants

· **Bertha's** · 734 S Broadway
· **Boccaccio Restaurant** · 925 Eastern Ave
· **Brass Elephant** · 924 N Charles St (off map)
· **Café Hon** · 1002 W 36th St (off map)
· **The Daily Grind** · 1722 Thames St
· **Faidley's Seafood** · Lexington Market, 203 N Paca St
· **Helen's Garden** · 2908 O'Donnell St
· **Ikaros** · 4805 Eastern Ave (off map)
· **Jimmy's** · 801 S Broadway
· **John Steven Ltd** · 1800 Thames St
· **Obrycki's Crab House** · 1727 E Pratt St
· **Rusty Scupper** · 402 Key Hwy
· **Tapas Teatro** · 1711 N Charles St (off map)
· **Vespa** · 1117 S Charles St
· **Ze Mean Bean** · 1739 Fleet St

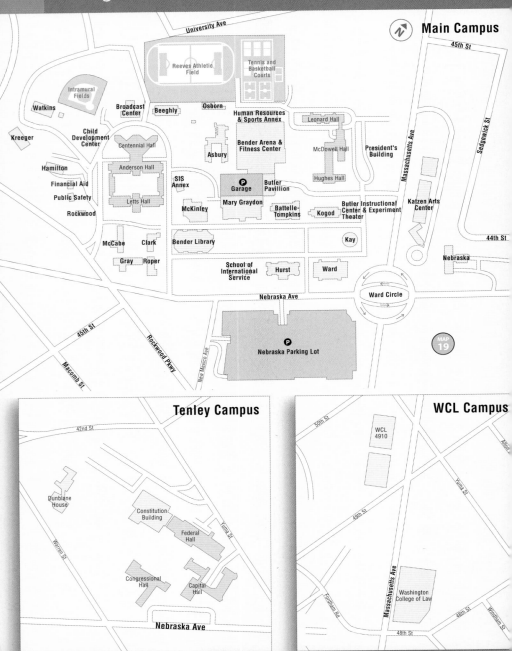

Main Campus

University Ave

45th St

Sedgewick St

Reeves Athletic Field

Tennis and Basketball Courts

Intramural Fields

Watkins

Broadcast Center

Beeghly

Osborn

Human Resources & Sports Annex

Leonard Hall

Kreeger

Child Development Center

Centennial Hall

Asbury

Bender Arena & Fitness Center

McDowell Hall

President's Building

Massachusetts Ave

Hamilton

Anderson Hall

SIS Annex

Garage

Butler Pavillion

Hughes Hall

Financial Aid

Public Safety

Letts Hall

Mary Graydon

Katzen Arts Center

Rockwood

McKinley

Battelle-Tompkins

Kogod

Butler Instructional Center & Experiment Theater

44th St

McCabe

Clark

Bender Library

Kay

Nebraska

Gray

Roper

School of International Service

Hurst

Ward

MAP 19

Nebraska Ave

Ward Circle

45th St

Rockwood Pkwy

Macomb St

New Mexico Ave

Nebraska Parking Lot

Tenley Campus

42nd St

Dunblane House

Constitution Building

Federal Hall

Yuma St

Warren St

Congressional Hall

Capital Hall

Nebraska Ave

WCL Campus

50th St

WCL 4910

Alton

Yuma St

48th St

Massachusetts Ave

Fordham Rd

Washington College of Law

48th St

48th St

Windham St

General Information

NFT Map: 19
Main Campus: 4400 Massachusetts Ave NW
Washington, DC 20016
Phone: 202-885-1000
Website: www.american.edu

Overview

Congress chartered "The" American University in 1893 to fulfill George Washington's vision of a great "national university" in the nation's capital. If Washington rode the Tenleytown shuttle to campus today, he'd probably be impressed. Though it seems sometimes like half of the AU student body is from Long Island, New Jersey, or the Philly suburbs, the school's 12,000 students hail from more than 150 countries. This diversity, along with its location in the nation's capital, makes AU a popular place to study public policy and international affairs. With few Wednesday classes and a heavy internship focus, AU is something of a foreign affairs, NGO, and Hill staffer factory. AU students brag that while Georgetown's stuffed shirts end up at DC think tanks, *their* grads actually go out and get their hands dirty. Indeed, it's often the school's idealistic crowd that most resents the "brat pack" contingent of diplomat kids and OPEC heirs, who enroll more out of interest in DC's nightlife than in changing the world. AU's idealists went into full protest mode in 2005 to force former University president Benjamin Ladner to resign after improperly charging the school for more than $500,000 in personal expenses, including a personal French chef, vacations in Europe with his wife, and his son's engagement party. While searching for a less ostentatious leader, AU's board of trustees started a new fundraising drive, appropriately called "AnewAU."

Nestled in tony upper northwest DC, AU's leafy quad gives it a classic liberal-arts-school look. But its picturesque campus doesn't lack for intrigue: work on the Manhattan Project started out in AU's McKinley building, because its unusual architecture ensured that any mishap would cause the building to self-implode and therefore limit any widespread repercussions.

Tuition

In the 2006–2007 academic year, undergrad tuition and fees for students living on campus was $29,673, with room and board an additional $11,570. Graduate student tuition, fees, and expenses vary by college.

Sports

AU's Eagles play a nice range of NCAA Division I men's and women's sports, including basketball, cross-country, soccer, swimming and diving, tennis, and track and field. Male-exclusive sports include golf and wrestling, while women play field hockey, volleyball, and lacrosse. The men's basketball team wins every year but has trouble drumming up fan interest; it's a running joke that mid-season you'll find more students waiting for AU's shuttle to the Metro than in Bender Arena. A few years ago, the Eagles left the Colonial Athletic Association to join the Patriot League in hopes of using the league's championship as an automatic bid to the NCAA tourney. So far, the Eagles have watched from the sidelines as Holy Cross and Bucknell have gone to the Big Dance, while its old CAA rival, George Mason, became the first mid-major team in more than 20 years to go to the Final Four.

Culture on Campus

AU operates its wildly wonkish and popular radio station, WAMU 88.5 FM, broadcasting NPR programs as well as locally produced shows like *The Kojo Nnamdi Show* and *The Diane Rehm Show*. Similarly, the University seems to score a speech a week by an inside-the-beltway celebrity, including appearances by Pulitzer Prize–winning columnist David S. Broder, Supreme Court Justice Antonin Scalia, and ex-President Jimmy Carter. Bender Arena appears to have lost its appetite for the big-time acts it used to feature, now hosting smaller performances by the likes of Jimmy Eat World and the Roots. The Katzen Arts Center at AU opened in late 2005, bringing all of AU's arts programs under one roof, including its Watkins collection of over 4,400 modern works of Washington-area art.

Department Contact Information

Admissions 202-885-6000
College of Arts & Sciences 202-885-2453
Kogod School of Business 202-885-1900
School of Communication 202-885-2060
School of International Service 202-885-1600
School of Public Affairs 202-885-2940
Washington College of Law 202-274-4000
Washington College of Law Library . . . 202-274-4350
Office of Campus Life 202-885-3310
Athletic Department 202-885-3000
University Library 202-885-3232

1. Quinn House
2. Reardon House
3. Camalier House
4. Walton House
5. McDonald House
6. Magner House
7. Unanue House
8. Engelhard House
9. Nursing-Biology Building
10. McCort-Ward Building
11. Gowan Hall
12. Maloney Hall
13. Conaty Hall
14. Spalding Hall
15. Spellman Hall

Catholic University of America

General Information

NFT Map: 14
Address: 620 Michigan Ave NE
Washington, DC 20064
Phone: 202-319-5000
Website: www.cua.edu

Overview

Lesser known than its Washington rivals but equal in academic distinction, CUA was established in 1887 as a graduate research institution where the Roman Catholic Church could do its thinking, and its undergraduate programs began in 1904. It remains the only American university founded with a papal charter. With a board of trustees still brimming with US cardinals and bishops, the school is considered the national university of the Catholic Church.

That said, CUA is by no means a seminary. Sixteen percent of its 3,053 undergraduates represent religions other than Catholicism, and although shadowed by the colossal Basilica of the National Shrine of the Immaculate Conception (the largest church in America), the laissez-faire campus lacks the in-your-face piousness to which other orthodox colleges subscribe. The 193-acre campus is the largest and arguably the most beautiful of the DC universities. Prominent alums include Susan Sarandon, Ed McMahon, Jon Voight, Brian Cashman (GM of the New York Yankees), and Maureen Dowd.

Though mostly religious, CUA's student body sometimes tries hard to prove otherwise. "Catholic U: Don't Let the Name Fool You" has been a popular motto of a ruddy-faced breed of students that knows how to pick the beer glasses up and the books down. With a flourishing party scene, CUA is well-represented among DC's various watering holes. And no, Mr. Joel, Catholic girls do not always start much too late.

Tuition

The new tuition rate of $26,200 went into effect in 2006. If you need a place to eat and sleep, the basic meal plan and housing costs come to approximately $4,000 and $6,000 respectively. That totals about $36,000, assuming you won't be buying any beer and books. It's college in America, what did you expect? At least a Catholic U degree can land you a job where you can actually pay off those loans.

Sports

Formerly a member of NCAA's Division I, the Catholic Cardinals (as in the little red bird, not the man with the incense and the big hat) dropped to Division III during the 1970s. Of all the school's sports, men's basketball reigns supreme. Winner of the 2000–01 Division III National Championship, the team reeled off five consecutive Sweet Sixteen seasons before the streak came to a halt last year. The women's squad, which posted a 20-win season last year, is also a powerhouse within CUA's Capital Athletic Conference. The Catholic football team may have stumbled over the last few seasons, but betting men beware: it dominated the gridiron during the nineties, ranking as high as number ten in the nation.

Culture on Campus

Catholic U has 118 recognized student groups, and seven different leadership programs. You can sing a capella and interact with other architecture enthusiasts, and still make it to your WCUA radio show in time to throw on that new Sean Paul record you've been neglecting your work to listen to. Music geeks unite! Boasting an extraordinary music program—one of the tops in the country—CUA's Benjamin T. Rome School of Music continuously churns out gem after gem. Thanks to a recent grant, CUA music students study with some of the most renowned composers, directors, and musicians working on Broadway today. The school stages over 200 musicals, operas, chamber concerts, and orchestral and choral performances throughout the academic year. For listings, including Department of Drama productions, visit performingarts.cua.edu.

Department Contact Information

Undergraduate Admissions 202-319-5305
Graduate Admissions 202-319-5305
Athletics 202-319-5286
The Benjamin T. Rome
School of Music 202-319-5414
The Columbus School of Law 202-319-5140
Conferences and Summer Programs 202-319-5291
Hartke Theatre Box Office 202-319-4000
Metropolitan College 202-319-5256
The National Catholic School
of Social Service 202-319-5458
Public Affairs 202-319-5600
The School of Arts and Sciences
(undergrad) 202-319-5115
The School of Arts and Sciences (grad) 202-319-5254
The School of Canon Law 202-319-5492
The School of Engineering 202-319-5160
The School of Library
and Information Science 202-319-5085
The School of Nursing 202-319-5400
The School of Philosophy 202-319-5259
The School of Theology
and Religious Studies 202-319-5683
Summer Sessions 202-319-5257

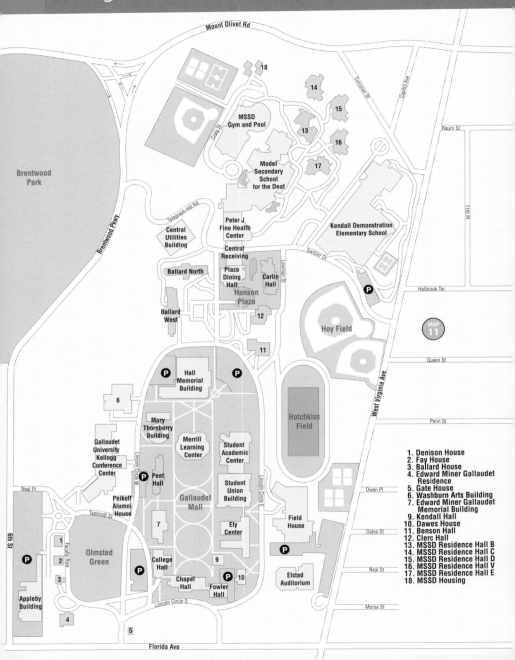

Mount Olivet Rd

Corcoran St

Capitol Ave

Brentwood Park

Brentwood Pkwy

Craig St

18

14

15

13

16

17

Raurn St

11th Pl

MSSD Gym and Pool

Model Secondary School for the Deaf

Telegraph Hill Rd

Central Utilities Building

Peter J Fine Health Center

Central Receiving

Kendall Demonstration Elementary School

Switzer Dr

Holbrook Ter

Ballard North

Lowman St

Plaza Dining Hall

Carlin Hall

Hanson Plaza

Ballard West

12

Hoy Field

MAP 11

11

Queen St

Hall Memorial Building

Hotchkiss Field

Penn St

Mary Thornberry Building

Merrill Learning Center

Student Academic Center

Gallaudet University Kellogg Conference Center

Lincoln Circle W

Peet Hall

Peikoff Alumni House

Student Union Building

Gallaudet Mall

Lincoln Circle E

Field House

Owen Pl

Oates St

Neal Pl

Tapscott St

7

9

Ely Center

6th St

1

2

3

4

5

Olmsted Green

College Hall

Chapel Hall

Fowler Hall

10

Elstad Auditorium

Neal St

Morse St

Appleby Building

Lincoln Circle S

Florida Ave

West Virginia Ave

1. Denison House
2. Fay House
3. Ballard House
4. Edward Miner Gallaudet Residence
5. Gate House
6. Washburn Arts Building
7. Edward Miner Gallaudet Memorial Building
9. Kendall Hall
10. Dawes House
11. Benson Hall
12. Clerc Hall
13. MSSD Residence Hall B
14. MSSD Residence Hall C
15. MSSD Residence Hall D
16. MSSD Residence Hall V
17. MSSD Residence Hall E
18. MSSD Housing

General Information

NFT Map: 11
Address: 800 Florida Ave NE
             Washington, DC 20002
Phone: 202-651-5050
Website: www.gallaudet.edu

Overview

Gallaudet is the premier university for the deaf and hearing-impaired, and the only university in the world where deaf students and those without hearing problems mingle. It is a campus where English and American Sign Language (ASL) coexist. Students can choose from more than 40 majors, and all aspects of the school, including classes and workshops, are designed to accommodate deaf students. Even the hearing students, who make up about 5% of each entering class, must always communicate through visual means.

Thomas Hopkins Gallaudet co-founded the American School for the Deaf in Hartford, CT, in 1817 as the first such school in the country. Forty years later, his youngest son, Dr. Edward Minor Gallaudet, established a school for the deaf in DC. In 1864, that school became the world's first and only liberal arts university for the deaf. In 1988, I. King Jordan, the University's first deaf president, was appointed after students, backed by a number of alumni, faculty, and staff, shut down the campus, demanding that a deaf president be appointed.

Tuition

In the 2006–2007 academic year, tuition and fees (including room and board) for US residents was $11,021 for undergraduate and $11,526 for graduate programs. For international students, tuition was $16,231 and $17,241 respectively.

Sports

The birth of the football huddle took place at Gallaudet. Legend has it that prior to the 1890s, football players stood around discussing their plays out of earshot of the other team. This posed a problem for Gallaudet's team; they communicated through signing and opposing teams could see the plays that were being called. Paul Hubbard, a star football player at the university, is credited with coming up with the huddle to prevent prying eyes from discovering plays.

Gallaudet also boasts 12 NCAA Division III teams and several intramural sports teams.

In the summer, Gallaudet runs popular one-week sports camps, where teens from all over the US, as well as the local area, stay on campus and participate in basketball and volleyball activities. Check the website for details.

Culture on Campus

Gallaudet's Dance Company performs modern, tap, jazz, and other dance styles incorporating ASL. Gallaudet also produces several theater productions every year, all of which are signed, with vocal interpretation. The school is smack in the middle of a neighborhood quickly transitioning from rough to trendy. Check out the nearby theaters, coffeehouses, and farmer's market before gentrification smoothes out the hard edges.

Department Contact Information

Admissions 800-995-0550
Graduate School and
  Professional Programs 800-995-0513
College of Liberal Arts, Sciences,
  and Technologies 202-651-5470
Department of ASL and Deaf
  Studies 202-651-5814
Financial Aid 202-651-5299
Gallaudet Library 202-651-5217
Registrar 202-651-5393
Visitors Center 202-651-5050

The George Washington University

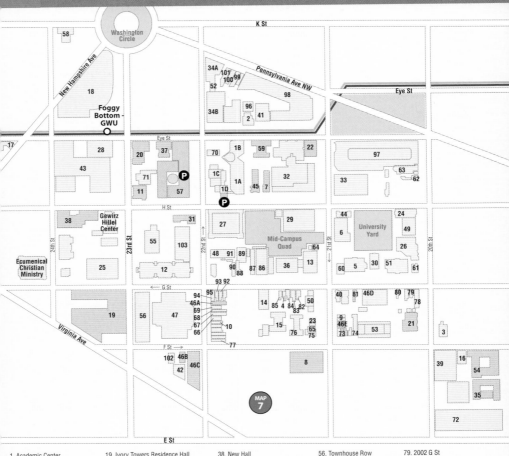

1. Academic Center
   A. Phillips Hall
   B. Rome Hall
   C. Smith Hall of Art
   D. Visitor Center
2. John Quincy Adams House
3. Alumni House
4. Hortense Amsterdam House
5. Bell Hall
6. Corcoran Hall
7. Crawford Hall
8. Dakota
9. Davis-Hodgkins House
10. Abba Eban House
11. Fulbright Hall
12. Funger Hall
13. Hall of Government
14. GSEHD
15. Guthridge Hall
16. The George Washington
    University Club
17. The George Washington
    University Inn
18. Hospital, GW

19. Ivory Towers Residence Hall
20. Kennedy Onassis Hall
21. Key Hall
22. Lafayette Hall
23. Lenthall Houses
24. Lerner Hall
25. Lerner Family Health and
    Wellness Center
26. Jacob Burns Library (Law)
27. Melvin Gelman Library (University)
28. Paul Himmelfarb Health
    Sciences Center (Medical)
29. Lisner Auditorium
30. Lisner Hall
31. Madison Hall
32. Marvin Center
33. Media & Public Affairs
34. Medical Faculty Associates
    A. H. B. Burns Memorial Bldg
    B. Ambulatory Care Center
35. Mitchell Hall
36. Monroe Hall
37. Munson Hall

38. New Hall
39. Old Main
40. Quigley's
41. Rice Hall
42. International House
43. Ross Hall
44. Samson Hall
45. Schenley Hall
46. Scholars Village Townhouses
    A. 619 22nd St
    B. 2208 F St
    C. 520-526 22nd St
    D. 2028 G St
    E. 605-607 21st St
47. Smith Center
48. Staughton Hall
49. Stockton Hall
50. Strong Hall
51. Stuart Hall
52. Student Health Service
53. Support Building
54. Thurston Hall
55. Tompkins Hall of Engineering

56. Townhouse Row
57. University Garage
58. Warwick Bldg
59. The West End
60. Woodhull House
61. 700 20th St
62. 812 20th St
63. 814 20th St
64. 714 21st St
65. 600 21st St
66. 609 22nd St
67. 613 22nd St
68. 615 22nd St
69. 617 22nd St
70. 837 22nd St
71. 817 23rd St
72. 1957 E St
73. 2033-37 F St
74. 2031 F St
75. 2101 F St
76. 2109 F St
77. 2147 F St
78. 2000 G St

79. 2002 G St
80. 2008 G St
81. 2030 G St
82. 2106 G St
83. 2108 G St
84. 2112 G St
85. 2114 G St
86. 2125 G St
87. 2127 G St
88. 2129 G St
89. 2129 G St (rear)
90. 2131 G St
91. 2131 G St (rear)
92. 2136 G St
93. 2138 G St
94. 2140 G St
95. 2142 G St
96. 2129-33 Eye St (rear)
97. 2000 Pennsylvania Ave NW
98. 2100 Pennsylvania Ave NW
99. 2136 Pennsylvania Ave NW
100. 2140 Pennsylvania Ave NW
101. 2142 Pennsylvania Ave NW
102. Newman Catholic Center
103. Duques Hall/School of Business

The George Washington University

General Information

NFT Map:	7
Address:	2121 Eye St NW
	Washington, DC 20052
Phone:	202-994-1000
Website:	www.gwu.edu

Overview

Once considered nothing more than a second-rate commuter school for graduate and law students, GW, like the city it inhabits, has enjoyed a massive boom in popularity over the past ten years. The school has more than 9,000 full-time undergraduate students and more than 5,000 graduate students stomping around Foggy Bottom in search of wisdom and love. The school recently wrapped up some of its large-scale construction projects and unveiled new academic buildings, a renovated fitness center, and a television studio where they currently film CNN's Crossfire. The GW "campus," for lack of a better word, now stretches its tentacles far into Foggy Bottom, leaving some neighbors none too pleased.

Unlike their counterparts over at Georgetown (who smugly refer to GW as a school for the Georgetown waitlist), GW students understand the meaning of having a life outside of academics. They love their city environs; they seem surprisingly street-smart; they take full advantage of government and congressional internships; and they venture farther afield when it comes to socializing. (Tuesday nights being the exception, when local bar McFadden's is invaded by what seems to be the entire student body.) But GW students aren't all play—the libraries, which stay open 24 hours, are never empty, and each year students are selected to be Rhodes, Truman, Marshall, and Fulbright scholars.

While many undergraduates hail from similar upper-middle-class backgrounds, 139 foreign countries are represented in the student body. Collectively, students have a motley appearance, further differentiating them from the Lacoste poster children of Georgetown. Tuition-wise, GW is the city's most expensive school, and with the deep pockets comes more than a few pompous attitudes. Bigshot alums include J. Edgar Hoover, Jackie O, Kenneth Starr, General Colin Powell, as well as four presidential children.

Tuition

Tuition for the 2006–2007 school year costs $37,790, with an additional $7,600 to $11,100 for room and board. Add on personal expenses and books, for a whopping yearly total of around $50,000.

Athletics

The university's fight song, "Hail to the buff, hail to the blue, hail to the buff and blue," provides hours of double-entendre fun for the students and it seems to work for the athletes, too. The university's 22 NCAA Division I teams, known as the fighting Colonials, usually place well in their A-10 conference, especially in basketball: last season, the women's basketball team went to the NCAA Tournament for the 12th time, and the men's team won their first Atlantic Ten Men's Basketball Championship since 1976.

Culture on Campus

The Robert H. and Clarice Smith Hall of Art is a modern facility that features five floors dedicated to the study and practice of art. Students participate annually in two major shows, and faculty members also display their art on campus.

The Department of Theatre and Dance produces two dance concerts, three plays, and one musical each year. These productions are performed either in the 435-seat Dorothy Betts Marvin Theatre, or the 1,490-seat Lisner Auditorium (don't miss the Dimock Gallery of Fine Art on the first floor). If you're unaffiliated with the university, tickets to performances will probably cost between $15 and $30. For more information on performances presented by the Theatre and Dance Department, call 202-994-6178.

For information on tickets for the Dorothy Betts Marvin Theatre, call 202-994-7411. For information on tickets for the Lisner Auditorium, call 202-994-6800.

Department Contact Information

Undergraduate Admissions	202-994-6040
Athletics	202-994-6650
Campus Bookstore	202-994-6870
College of Arts & Science	202-994-6210
Elliot School of International Affairs	202-994-3002
Financial Aid	202-994-6620
Gelman Library	202-994-6558
Graduate School of Education	202-994-2194
Law School	202-994-6288
Registrar	202-994-4900
School of Business	202-994-8252
School of Medicine	202-994-3501
Student Activities Center	202-994-6555
University Police (emergency)	202-994-6111
University Police (non-emergency)	202-994-6110
Visitor Center	202-994-6602

Reservoir Rd NW

Reservoir Rd NW

39th St NW
38th St NW
37th St NW
36th St NW
35th St NW

Georgetown University Hospital

St Mary's Hall

Dent Pl NW

Building D

Medical and Dental Annex

Medical and Dental Building

Darnall Hall

Research Resource Facility

Basic Science Building

1

Marcus Bles Building

Dahlgren Medical Library

Concentrated Care Center

New Research Building

Lombardi Cancer Center

Gorman Building

Pasquerilla Healthcare Center

Kober Cogan Building

Henle Village

North Kehoe Field

Main Shuttlebus Stop

Leavey Center

Reiss Science Building

Volta Pl NW

Kehoe Field

ICC Auditorium

Yates Field House

Intercultural Center

Red Square

White-Gravenor Hall

P St NW

Observatory

Copley Lawn

Poulton Hall

Copley Hall

North Gatehouse

Reed Alumni Residence

Harbin Field

Harbin Hall

2

Heating and Cooling Plant

McDonough Gymnasium

O St NW

Healy Lawn

Robert & Burnice Wagner Alumni House

Institute of Diplomacy

4 5 6 7

South Gatehouse

Academic Administration

Kennedy Hall

8 9 10

Village C

Alumni Square (Village B)

Academic Administration

Reynolds Family Hall

3

McCarthy Hall

12 14

11 13

15

N St NW

17

Nevils Building

Jesuit Residence (Wolfington Hall)

O'Donovan Dining Hall

Village A

New South

Lauinger Library

GU Shops

Walsh Building

16

Loyola Hall

Ryder Hall Xavier Hall

Prospect St NW

Exorcist Stairs

MAP 18

Car Barn

Canal Rd NW

M St NW

Whitehurst Fwy

Potomac River

29

1. Pre-Clinical Science Building
2. Davis Performing Arts Center
3. Southwest Quadrangle
4. McNeir Auditorium
5. New North
6. Old North
7. Gaston Hall
8. Dahlgren Chapel of the Sacred Heart
9. Dahlgren Quadrangle
10. Healy Hall
11. Gervase Building
12. Mulledy Building
13. Ryan Hall
14. Maguire Hall
15. Riggs Library
16. East Campus Quadrangle
17. McSherry Building

Colleges & Universities • **Georgetown University**

General Information

NFT Map: 18
Main Campus: 37th & O Sts NW
                Washington, DC 20057
Phone: 202-687-0100
Website: www.georgetown.edu

Overview

Georgetown University was founded the same year the US Constitution took effect, making the school not only the nation's oldest Catholic and Jesuit university, but also about the same age as most of the neighborhood's socialites. But seriously, Georgetown is the most prestigious college in town, and a "feeder school" for the federal government and foreign-policy community. Alumni include former president Bill Clinton, Supreme Court Justice Antonin Scalia, and broadcast journalist/Kennedy heir/California First Lady Maria Shriver. The campus sets the tone for the neighborhood around it—beautiful, old, and distinguished.

Georgetown's long history is not without its eerie episodes. According to campus rumor, the attic of Healy Hall is haunted by the ghost of a priest who died while winding the clock in the building's famous spire. During the Civil War, the university's buildings became bunkers and hospitals for the Yankee troops. Once the war ended, the school adopted blue and gray as its official colors to symbolize the reunification of North and South. More recently, it became part of Hollywood history by providing the setting for a scene from *The Exorcist*, a novel by alum William Peter Blatty. The creepy *"Exorcist"* stairs can be found on campus at the junction of Prospect and 36th Streets.

Tuition

In the 2006–2007 academic year, undergraduate tuition for full-time students cost $33,552. The average room and board costs were an additional $10,739. With books, travel, and other fees, the average total cost of attendance was $48,000. Tuition fees vary by program and division.

Sports

The university's teams are known as the Hoyas because, the story goes, a student well-versed in Greek and Latin started cheering "Hoya Saxa!" which translates to "What Rocks!" The cheer proved popular and the term "Hoyas" was adopted for all Georgetown teams. Since "what rocks" did not readily translate into an animal mascot, the bulldog was chosen to represent the Blue and Gray.

Georgetown is best known for its men's basketball team. Former Hoya athletes include Patrick Ewing, Allen Iverson, and Alonzo Mourning. Men's sports also include crew, football, golf, lacrosse, sailing, soccer, swimming and diving, tennis, and track. Women's sports include basketball, crew, field hockey, golf, lacrosse, sailing, soccer, swimming and diving, tennis, track, and volleyball. For tickets to all Georgetown athletic events, call 202-687-HOYA. Georgetown also offers intramural sports including volleyball, flag football, racquetball, basketball, ultimate Frisbee, table tennis, softball, and floor hockey.

Culture on Campus

Although best known for its more philistine programs—government, law, and medicine—Georgetown has bolstered its fine arts program significantly in the last few years, expanding course offerings and opening the posh new Davis Performing Arts Center in 2005. The Department of Art, Music, and Theater offers majors and minors in studio art, art history, and the performing arts. Artistically inclined students can also join Georgetown's many extra-curricular arts groups, including the orchestra, band, choir, and multiple theater troupes, improv groups, and a cappella singing groups.

Department Contact Information

Undergraduate Admissions 202-687-3600
Graduate Admissions 202-687-5568
Georgetown Law Center 202-662-9000
McDonough School of Business 202-687-3851
Edmund A. Walsh School
  of Foreign Service 202-687-5696
Georgetown University
  Medical Center .202-687-5100
School of Nursing & Health Studies . . .202-687-2681
Department of Athletics 202-687-2435

N

Gresham Pl

Drew Hall

Burr Gymnasium

Burr Annex

Girard S

Howard Manor

Cook Hall

Effingham Apartments

Greene Memorial Stadium

McMillan Reservoir

Fremont St

Physical Ed Annex

Crampton Auditorium

Childers Hall Fine Arts

School of Business

Aldridge Theatre

Blackburn Center

Miner Hall

Douglas Hall

4th St

MAP 15

Mordecai Johnson Administration Building

Upper Quadrangle

Locke Hall

Economics Mathematics C A R

School of Education

Howard Hall

Georgia Ave

Lindsay Hall (Social Work)

Carnegie Building

Human Ecology Building

4th St

Howard Pl

Mackey Building (Architecture)

6th St

Rankin Chapel

Founders Library

Undergraduate Library

Wheatley Hall

Truth Hall

McMillan Dr

Thirkield Hall

Lower Quadrangle

Tubman Quad

Baldwin Hall

Crandall Hall

Engineering Computer Science

Dixon Hall

Health Center

Chemistry Building

Just Hall (Biology)

School of Pharmacy

Frazier Hall

Barry Pl

College St

ISAS

Bunche Center

Graduate School

Student Resource Building

CB Powell Building (Communications)

WHUT-TV

4th St

iLab

Power Plant

WHUR-FM

Bethune Annex

8th St

Bryant St

Book Store

Howard Center

Nursing and Allied Health Center

Louise Stokes Health Science Library

Evolutionary Building

W St

Student Health Center

College of Dentistry

College of Medicine

Adams Building

P

Hospital Parking

MAP 10

Hospital Service Center

Sickle Cell Center

5th St

V St

HU Hospital

Tower Building

Oakdale Pl NW

Elm St

3rd St

U St

General Information

NFT Maps: 10 & 15
Main Campus: 2400 Sixth St NW
             Washington, DC 20059
Phone: 202-806-6100
Website: www.howard.edu

Overview

Founded in 1866 as a theological seminary for African-American ministers, Howard University remains an African-American institute (although no longer a seminary) to this day, and it has long been a dominant intellectual, cultural, and physical presence in the District. Distinguished Howard alumni include novelist Zora Neale Hurston, Supreme Court Justice Thurgood Marshall, Nobel Laureate Toni Morrison, and Shirley Franklin, the first female mayor of Atlanta.

Howard University once occupied a lone single-frame building and now has five campuses spanning more than 260 acres. The library system houses the largest collection of African-American literature in the nation. Despite its large physical size, Howard is a relatively small school with roughly 7,000 undergraduate students and almost 11,000 students total.

Its main campus is located just minutes away from the Capitol and the White House on "the hilltop," one of the highest elevation points in the city. The campus leads right into U Street, one of the premier catwalks of the city. The area was once the city's center of jazz and African-American nightlife before falling on rough times. But now it's back and considered the hippest of areas, with avant-garde fashion, deluxe condos, and over-priced everything.

Tuition

In the 2006–2007 academic year, undergraduate tuition for students living off-campus cost $6,492.50 per semester. Room and board averaged around $5,570. Graduate tuition, fees, and expenses vary by school and department.

Sports

Howard is a member of the Mid-Eastern Athletic Conference and participates in the NCAA's Division I. The last noteworthy sports achievement dates way back to 2003, when the women's cross-country team ran away with the MEAC championship trophy. Other teams have a less-than-stellar record. The male basketball team ranked 319th out of 326 teams in 2004. But losing (a lot) hasn't hurt their popularity on campus. Games still draw crowds. Intercollegiate men's sports include basketball, cross-country, soccer, tennis, football, swimming, wrestling, and track. Women's sports include basketball, tennis, cross-country, track, volleyball, and swimming.

Culture on Campus

The Howard University Gallery of Art offers rotating exhibitions of national and international artists, as well as a permanent collection of African artifacts, Renaissance and Baroque paintings, European prints, and contemporary art. Last spring the University held the exhibit A Proud Continuum: Eight Decades of Art at Howard University, which featured the work of 122 alumni, the largest of its kind in Howard's history.

The Department of Theatre Arts produces dance and drama performances throughout the school year in the Ira Aldridge Theater, which also hosts visiting professional theater troupes. Student tickets cost $7.50 and general admission costs $15. The season always brings in a decidedly diverse bag of productions: last year, the theater staged R/J: The Fatal Tour, an updated hip-hop version of Shakespeare's Romeo & Juliet, as well as the musical Eyes, based on Zora Neale Hurston's Their Eyes Were Watching God.

Howard University Television, WHUT-TV, is the only African-American-owned public television station in the country. It has been operating for 29 years and reaches half a million households in the Washington metropolitan area. Howard University also runs commercial radio station WHUR-FM (96.3).

Department Contact Information

Admissions 202-806-2700
College of Arts & Sciences 202-806-6700
School of Business 202-806-1500
School of Communications 202-806-7690
School of Dentistry 202-806-0440
School of Divinity 202-806-0500
School of Education 202-806-7340
School of Engineering, Architecture,
   and Computer Sciences 202-806-6565
Graduate School of Arts & Sciences 202-806-6800
School of Law 202-806-8000
College of Medicine 202-806-5677
College of Pharmacy, Nursing, and
   Allied Health Sciences 202-806-5431
School of Social Work 202-806-7300
Student Affairs 202-806-2100
Athletic Department 202-806-7140
Founders Library 202-806-7234

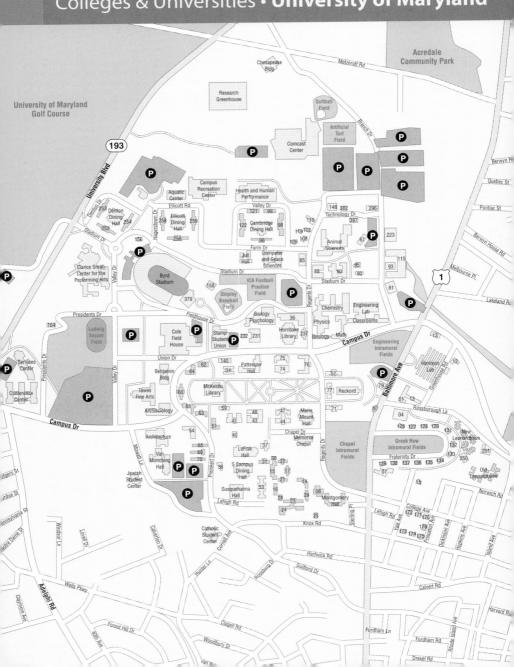

General Information

Address: College Park, MD 20742
Phone: 301-405-1000
Website: www.umd.edu

Overview

University of Maryland's gargantuan size masks its humble beginnings. First chartered as a small agricultural college in March of 1856, this full public university now has almost 35,000 students roaming its 1,500 acres. Between the 13 colleges, 111 undergraduate majors, study-abroad programs, and honors programs, there's enough excitement and intellectual rigor to keep the brightest Marylanders interested. And for students who've been surrounded by pastoral green quads for so long it makes them want to gag, the school's very own Metro stop will shuttle them into the vast city that awaits to the south.

Tuition

Undergraduate tuition for the 2005–2006 school year cost $7,821 for in state residents, and $20,145 for non-residents. Room and board averaged around $8,000.

Sports

While there's never been a real dearth of Terrapin pride, it's only sky-rocketed in recent years. An ACC basketball championship win over the Duke Blue Devils, victory at college football's Gator Bowl, and a 2003 NCAA men's basketball Championship win have strengthened Marylanders' love of their winning teams. With 27 Varsity sports teams competing at UMD, the athletic program is widely recognized as one of the best in the country for both men's and women's sports, and the Terps are one of only six schools to have won a national championship in both football and men's basketball. Though it's usually the men's teams that hog the spotlight, this year ushered in the first National Championship win for the Lady Terps basketball team.

Culture on Campus

The Clarice Smith Performing Arts Center hosts high-profile performers and ensembles. Past guests have included Yo-Yo Ma, the Woolly Mammoth Theater Company, and the Maryland Opera Studio. The Center is also home of the UM symphony orchestra and jazz band. Tickets are usually free or, at most, five bucks for students. You don't have to be affiliated with the university to attend events—just be prepared to shell out up to $30 if you're not a student, faculty member, or staff 301-405-2787; www.claricesmithcenter.umd.edu.

If orchestra or jazz ensembles are not quite the type of entertainment you're jonesing for, the Student Entertainment Events (SEE) presents a variety of concerts featuring both headlining artists and local bands. Tickets of course are cheaper for students and range between $5 and $25, depending on the event. Tickets for larger concerts can also be purchased via Ticketmaster.

Film buffs can view an array of independent films and blockbusters at the newly finished Hoff Theater in the University's Student Union. The ample theater showcases at least one feature daily and is usually free for students, $5 for non-students.

Department Contact Information

Campus Information	301-405-1000
Undergraduate Admissions	301-314-8385
Graduate Admissions	301-405-0376
Bookstore	301-314-7848
Registrar	301-314-8240
Bursar	301-314-9000
Athletic Department	800-462-8377
Ticket Office	301-314-7070
Clark School of Engineering	301-405-3855
College of Education	301-405-2344
School of Architecture	301-405-6284
School of Public Policy	301-405-6330
Smith School of Business	301-405-2189
Art and Humanities	301-405-2108
Behavioral and Social Sciences	301-405-1697
Life Sciences	301-405-2071

Building Listings

1 - Central Heating Plant
4 - Ritchie Coliseum
5 - Service Building Annex
7 - Pocomoke Building
8 - Annapolis Hall
12 - Plant Operations & Maintenance Complex
13 - Shuttle Bus Facility
14 - Harford Hall
15 - Calvert Hall
16 - Baltimore Hall
17 - Cecil Hall
18 - Police Substation
21 - Prince George's Hall
22 - Kent Hall
23 - Washington Hall
24 - Allegany Hall
25 - Charles Hall
28 - Howard Hall
29 - Frederick Hall
30 - Talbot Hall
34 - Jimenez Hall
36 - Plant Science
37 - Shoemaker Building
40 - Morrill Hall
42 - Tydings Hall
43 - Taliaferro Hall
44 - Skinner Building
47 - Woods Hall

48 - Francis Scott Key Hall
51 - Worchester Hall
52 - Mitchell Building Registration Office
53 - Dance Building
54 - Preinkert Field House
59 - Journalism Building
60 - Anne Arundel Hall
61 - Queen Anne's Hall
62 - St. Mary's Hall
63 - Somerset Hall
64 - Dorchester Hall
65 - Carroll Hall
66 - West Education Annex
69 - Wicomico Hall
70 - Caroline Hall
71 - Lee Building
74 - Holzapfel Hall
75 - Shriver Laboratory
76 - Symons Hall
77 - Main Administration
79 - Visitors Center
80 - Rossborough Inn
81 - Wind Tunnel Building
83 - JM Patterson Building
85 - Institute for Physical Science & Technology
87 - Central Animal Resources Facility

90 - Chemical and Nuclear Engineering Building
93 - Engineering Annex
96 - Cambridge Hall
98 - Centreville Hall
99 - Bel Air Hall
102 - Agriculture Shed
108 - Horse Barn
109 - Sheep Barn
110 - Cattle Barn
115 - AV Williams
119 - Blacksmith Shop
121 - Performing Arts Center, Clarice Smith
122 - Cumberland Hall
126 - Kappa Alpha Fraternity
127 - Sigma Alpha Mu Fraternity
128 - Delta Tau Delta Fraternity
129 - Sigma Alpha Epsilon Fraternity
131 - Beta Theta Pi Fraternity
132 - Phi Sigma Kappa Fraternity
133 - Pi Kappa Phi Fraternity
134 - Chi Omega Sorority
135 - Sigma Kappa Sorority
136 - Alpha Epsilon Phi Sorority
137 - Zeta Tau Alpha Sorority
138 - Sigma Phi Epsilon Fraternity
139 - Zeta Beta Tau Fraternity
140 - Health Center

148 - Manufacturing Building
156 - Apiary
158 - Varsity Sports Teamhouse
170 - Alpha Delta Pi Sorority
171 - Phi Kappa Tau Fraternity
172 - Alpha Chi Omega Sorority
173 - Delta Phi Epsilon Sorority
174 - Phi Sigma Sigma Sorority
175 - Delta Gamma Sorority
176 - Alpha Phi Sorority
201 - Leonardtown office building
223 - Energy Research
231 - Microbiology Building
232 - Nyumburu Cultural Center
237 - Geology Building
250 - Leonardtown community center
252 - Denton Hall
253 - Easton Hall
254 - Elkton Hall
256 - Ellicott Hall
258 - Hagerstown Hall
259 - LaPlata Hall
296 - Biomolecular Sciences Building
379 - Football Team Building
382 - Neutral Buoyancy Research Facility
387 - Tap Building

George Mason University

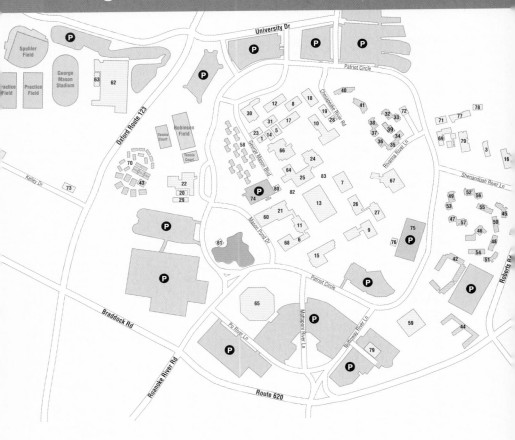

1. Aquia Module
2. Buchanan House
3. Carrow Hall
4. Carty House
5. Central Module
6. College Hall
7. David King Hall
8. East Building
9. Enterprise Hall
10. Fenwick Library
11. Fine Arts Building
12. Finley Building
13. George W. Johnson Center
14. Greenhouse
15. Innovation Hall
16. Krasnow Institute
17. Krug Hall
18. Lecture Hall
19. North Chesapeake Module
20. North P.E. Module
21. Performing Arts Building

22. Physical Ed. Building
23. Pohick Module
24. Robinson Hall A
25. Robinson Hall B
26. Science and Tech I
27. Science and Tech II
28. South Chesepeake Module
29. South P.E. Module
30. Thompson Hall
31. West Building
32. Amherst Hall
33. Brunswick Hall
34. Carroll Hall
35. Dickenson Hall
36. Essex Hall
37. Franklin Hall
38. Grayson Hall
39. Hanover Hall
40. Commonwealth Hall
41. Dominion Hall
42. Liberty Square

43. Patriots Village
44. Potomac Housing/Housing Office
45. Adams Hall
46. Eisenhower Hall
47. Harrison Hall
48. Jackson Hall
49. Jefferson Hall
50. Kennedy Hall
51. Lincoln Hall
52. Madison Hall
53. Monroe Hall
54. Roosevelt Hall
55. Truman Hall
56. Washington Hall
57. Wilson Hall
58. Student Apartments
59. Aquatic and Fitness Center
60. Center for the Arts Concert Hall
61. Cross Cottage
62. Field House
63. Field House Module

64. Harris Theatre
65. Patriot Center
66. Student Union I/Student Health Services
67. Student Union II
68. Mason Hall
69. Central Heating and Cooling Plant
70. Child Development Center
71. Facilities Administration
72. Rivanna Module
73. Kelley II
74. Parking Deck, Mason Pond (Visitors)
75. Parking Deck, Sandy Creek
76. Parking Services
77. Physical Plant/Customer Service Center
78. Recycling Center
79. University Police
80. Visitor Information
82. George Mason Statue
83. Clock Tower

General Information

Address: 4400 University Drive
              Fairfax, VA 22030
Phone: 703-993-1000
Website: www.gmu.edu

Overview

Named for the most obscure of the founding fathers, George Mason University began as an extension of the University of Virginia for the northern part of the state. In 1966, George Mason College became a four-year, degree-granting university. George Mason separated from UVA in 1972 and became an independent institution.

Currently the university offers more than 100 degree programs in both the undergraduate and graduate levels in three different locations in Virginia. Academically, Mason boasts award-winning faculty and offers unique curriculum, such as its biodefense graduate degree program. There are approximately 17,600 undergraduates and around 8,400 graduate students currently enrolled in the university.

Conveniently located in close proximity to Washington, DC, George Mason's picturesque main campus is centered on acres of woods in Fairfax, Virginia. In addition to its law school and campus in Arlington, GMU has recently established branches in Prince William and Loudoun countries.

Tuition

Undergraduate tuition for the 2006–2007 school year cost $6,408 for in-state undergraduates, and $18,552 for all non-residents. Room and board averaged around $8,000.

Sports

Of course we can't mention GMU without noting the successful run the men's basketball team had this past season. While many living outside the immediate area were scratching their heads, asking, "Where the heck is George Mason?" or getting it confused with its fellow local "George" University (George Washington University), the Patriots were surpassing everyone's expectations and slowly creeping into the Final Four. Although they didn't take home the top prize, the team garnered much attention, as well as respect, making this season its best to date.

So now that we got that out of the way, there are about 19 other men's and women's Division I teams on campus including baseball, track and field, tennis, and soccer. Mason teams belong to the National Collegiate Athletic Association (NCAA) Division I, the Colonial Athletic Association (CAA), and the Eastern College Athletic Conference (ECAC).

Culture on Campus

George Mason's Center for the Arts offers a variety of musical and dance performances from celebrated entertainers like the Metropolitan Jazz Orchestra and the St. Petersburg Ballet. With four different theater spaces ranging from the larger 2,000-seat Concert Hall to the more personal 75-seat Black Box, the Center for the Arts also features performances by GMU's own theater company, Theater of the First Amendment. The company has been nominated for numerous awards and is a Helen Hayes Award recipient. Most performances are free or provide discounts for students.

The Film and Media Studies Program, along with University Life, show weekly films throughout the academic year in *Cinema Series*. Admission and popcorn are free for students and faculty with GMU ID.

Department Contact Information

Fairfax Campus 703-993-1000
Admissions 703-993-2400
University Services 703-993-2840
Bookstore. 703-993-2666
Registrar. 703-993-2441
Patriot Computer Store. 703-993-4100
Academic Support Center 703-993-2470
Center For the Arts 703-993-8888
Patriot Center 703-993-3000
School of Law. 703-993-8000
Arlington Campus 703-993-8999
Prince William Campus 703-993-8350
Loudoun Campus 703-993-4350

General Information

Address:	1600 FedEx Wy
	Landover, MD 20785

Redskins Website: www.redskins.com
FedEx Field Website:
  www.fedex.com/us/sports/fedexfield/
Stadium Admin: 301-276-6000
Ticket Office: 301-276-6050

Overview

No city is more infatuated with its football team than Washington is with the Redskins, even in the *off*-season. Summer after summer, the team's front office has put together a line-up it claims will march straight to the Super Bowl, and year after year, the beloved 'Skins have fallen flat on their faces. Part of the problem has been Daniel Snyder, the team's unpopular owner, who knows football like Paris Hilton knows rodeo yet insists on dropping megadimes on washed-up players whom he deems messianic. (We think Deion Sanders may still be collecting Redskins paychecks.)

But, hallalujah! The 2005 season saw the Redskins surprise many by finishing the regular season with a 10-6 record and a win in the playoffs that we haven't enjoyed since Danny Boy was a Cub Scout. The upcoming season will mark the first time in the last several years that expectations will be high and just might be met. Hall-of-Fame coach Joe Gibbs will be back for his third season on this go-round, and with off-season free agent acquisitions like wide receiver Antwan Randel El complimenting Santana Moss down the sidelines and Gibbs' slow-but-sure reacclamation to the NFL-21st century edition—there should be a lot of scoring. AARP candidate Mark Brunell and running back Clinton Portis will captain an improving offense, and the team's always-stingy defense will help, as well. This season, we shouldn't be spending the winter weeks looking forward to the beginning of Nationals' spring training or not caring if the Capitals are playing or not.

The stadium itself is a diamond in the middle of a very large rough known as Landover, Maryland. During the late 1980s, then-owner Jack Kent Cooke envisioned a new and sensational stadium, settling on a site deep in the Maryland suburbs just inside the Washington Beltway. Although Cooke didn't live to see the $300 million project completed, Jack Kent Cooke Stadium officially opened its gates September 14, 1997 (Snyder sold the naming rights to FedEx shortly after purchasing the team in 1999). The colossal structure is equipped to hold more than 90,000 fans, good for tops in the NFL.

How to Get There—Driving

Um, don't. The nightmares of getting in and out of FedEx Field and the myriad parking lots in the vicinity are the stuff of a Maalox moment. If you *must*, take E Capitol Street (which becomes Central Avenue at the Maryland line) to Harry Truman Drive north just outside the Beltway. Then take a right onto Lottsford Road to Arena Drive and you're there. Keep your eyes peeled for the many signs that will direct you to the field. You can also take the Capital Beltway (I-95/495) from the north or the south to Exits 15 (Central Avenue), 16 (Arena Drive, open only for FedEx events), or 17 (Landover Road). It's a barrel of laughs, especially for those Monday night games.

Parking

FedEx Field provides off-stadium parking that can cost as much as $35, with a free shuttle ride to the stadium. The team did their damnedest to prevent fans from parking for free at the nearby Landover Mall and walking to the game, but a Prince George's County judge overturned a county policy restricting pedestrian movement in the area. So you can pay up for convenience or exercise your civic rights to park free and schlep.

How to Get There—Mass Transit

Take the Blue Line to the Morgan Boulevard or Largo Town Center stops—both are close by and are a pretty short walk to the stadium. Five-dollar round-trip shuttle buses depart from these stations for FedEx Field every 15 minutes, from two hours before the game until two hours after.

How to Get Tickets

If you enjoy the prospect of languishing in a years-long line, join the Redskins season ticket waiting list by visiting www.redskins.com/tickets. If you're just looking for individual game tickets, suck up to a season ticket holder or call 301-276-6050.

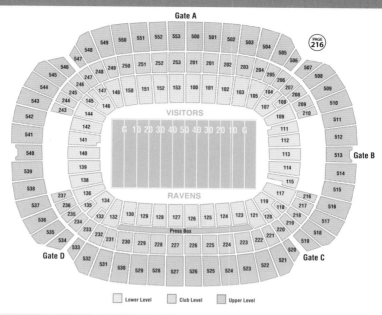

Lower Level ▢   Club Level ▢   Upper Level ▢

General Information

Address: 1101 Russell St, Baltimore, MD 21230
Phone: 410-261-7283
Website: www.baltimoreravens.com

Overview

Dominating Baltimore's skyline from I-95, M&T Bank Stadium is a menacing structure, to say the least. Its team, the "Bol'more" Ravens, flew into town 11 years ago via Cleveland and wasted no time in capturing the 2001 Super Bowl title. The Ravens and the Redskins flip-flopped fortunes in 2005, with the Ravens being the owners of the 6-10 record this time around, while the Skins more-or-less flourished. The Ravens' lackluster offense, averaging a paltry 16 points a game with both starting QBs Kyle Boller and Anthony Wright, tied for dead last NFL rankings and star running back/cocaine pusher Jamal Lewis being held under 1,000 yards, would have had a hard time scoring points against the DC Divas, the District's all-female team.

In Baltimore, as is customary with most NFL cities, the name of the game, or *pre-game*, is tailgating. For 1 pm games, the festivities usually commence at about 9 am. The parking lots slowly swell with inebriated men fashioning O-linemen bellies, confirming Baltimore's reputation as a blue-collar football town. Outsiders need not be afraid, however, because unlike fans in nearby cities (read: Philadelphia), Ravens fans are gracious hosts and typically welcome others to the party. Once inside the stadium, expect to pay through the nose for food—though the Maryland crab cakes are definitely worth the high price, and the stadium's hot dogs are pretty damn good, too. After the game, Pickles and Sliders, two sports

bars on nearby Washington Boulevard, are where weary DC-bound travelers (tired of waiting years for Redskins tickets) head to quench their thirst.

How to Get There—Driving

Take I-95 N toward Baltimore to Exit 52 (Russell Street north for immediate access to the stadium (you can't miss it) or Exit 53 (I-395 north) for better access to the downtown parking garages.

Parking

M&T Bank provides parking, for which you need to buy a permit ahead of time. Otherwise, there are 15,000 spaces-worth of public parking nearby, most of which charge a flat game day rate.

How to Get There—Mass Transit

The MTA Light Rail provides service directly to the Hamburg Street Light Rail stop, operational only on game days. Trains run every 17 minutes from Hunt Valley and Cromwell Station/Glen Burnie, and every 34 minutes from Penn Station and BWI. The stop closest to the stadium on the Baltimore Metro is Lexington Market, though you'll have to hoof it about a mile. Be sure to leave early to beat the crowds on game days. You can also take the 3, 7, 10, 14, 17, 19/19A, 27, or 31 buses, all of which stop within walking distance of the stadium.

How to Get Tickets

To purchase tickets, visit the Ravens' website, or call 410-261-7283. Tickets can also be purchased through Ticketmaster (www.ticketmaster.com).

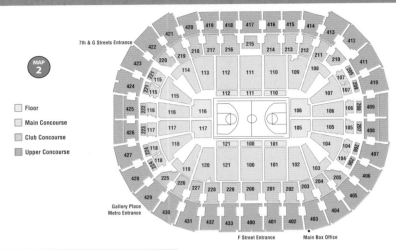

7th & G Streets Entrance

Gallery Place
Metro Entrance

F Street Entrance   Main Box Office

MAP 2

- ☐ Floor
- ☐ Main Concourse
- ☐ Club Concourse
- ☐ Upper Concourse

General Information

NFT Map:	2
Address:	601 F St NW
	Washington, DC 20004
Verizon Center Phone:	202-628-3200
Verizon Center Website:	www.mcicenter.com
Wizards Phone:	202-661-5100
Wizards Website:	www.washingtonwizards.com
Capitals Phone:	202-266-2200
Capitals Website:	www.washingtoncaps.com
Mystics Phone:	202-661-5000
Mystics Website:	www.washingtonmystics.com
Georgetown Basketball Phone:	202-687-4692
Georgetown Basketball Website:	www.guhoyas.com

Overview

In 1997, DC's then-new MCI Center reversed a decades-old trend of arenas planting roots in the suburbs by bringing it all back to the 'hood. The block-sized complex known today as Verizon Center (which includes a 20,000-seat stadium as well as bars, restaurants, and stores) is now the centerpiece of downtown's gentrification juggernaut.

The best thing to happen to the underachieving world of DC sports since Jordan's semi-triumphant return to the hard court is the NHL rookie Alexander Ovechkin, who is single-handedly making Caps games a weekend must-do activity. In addition to the Caps and the artists-formerly-known-as-the-Bullets, the Verizon Center is also home to the Washington Mystics, who boast the largest fan base in the WNBA. The Georgetown Hoyas basketball team hoops it up in the arena, as well. Beyond the ballers, Verizon Center hosts big-name concerts from the likes of Cher, Britney, and Madonna, circuses (both Ringling and

Cirque de Soleil have performed here), and all sorts of other events. For post-event fun, China-alley, otherwise mis-known as Chinatown, is a block away with plenty of eats and drinks.

How to Get There—Driving

From downtown, turn left onto 7th Street from either Constitution Avenue or New York Avenue. Verizon Center is on the northeast corner of F and 7th.

Parking

You're on your own. There's a lot of parking around, but unless you're a season-ticket holder, it's not supplied by Verizon Center. Garage prices vary, but you should expect to spend about $20 for the night.

How to Get There—Mass Transit

Verizon Center is accessible by the Metro's Red, Yellow, and Green lines; get off at the Gallery Place-Chinatown stop. It's not hard to find, just get off the Metro, and you are directly under it.

How to Get Tickets

Tickets for all Verizon Center events are available through the Ticketmaster website at www.ticketmaster.com (with the inevitable Ticketmaster markup, of course), or by calling 703-573-7328. Wizards tickets range from $12 to $310 for an individual game. Now that the NHL has slunk back to the city, Caps tickets will run you $10 to $230, which may pay for a sliver of Ovechkin's upcoming contract. Mystics tickets range from $8 to $85, and Hoyas tickets are between $5 and $22.50. All teams offer season and multi-game ticket packages. Check out individual team websites for prices.

General Information

Address: 333 W Camden St
Baltimore, MD 21201
Website: www.theorioles.com
Phone: 888-848-2473

Overview

Oriole Park at Camden Yards opened in 1992, launching a "traditional" trend in stadium design that continues to this day. In the face of dozens of corporations eager to smear their names across the park, the Orioles have refused to budge. All brick and history, the Yards stand downtown on a former railroad center, two blocks from Babe Ruth's birthplace. Center field sits atop the site where the Bambino's father ran a bar. The goods include double-decker bullpens, a sunken, asymmetrical field, and "Boog's BBQ," run by ex-Oriole Boog Powell, who is known to frequently man the grill himself during O's home games.

The Birds, unlike their stadium, haven't been much to look at in recent years. Baseball's drug problem has hit the local boys of summer where it hurts—in the batter's box. The short days of Sammy Sosa, who somehow recently lost his edge, are over, and Rafael Palmeiro keeps accidentally ingesting steroids, honest! Another recent aquisition, Miguel Tejada, is drug-free and the hope of the future, assuming he'll quit continually asking to be traded. The good news is there is never a shortage of all-star players to watch at Oriole Park, as both the Yankees and Red Sox inhabit the AL East with the O's.

How to Get There—Driving

Take MD 295 (B-W Pkwy/Russell St) to downtown Baltimore, which gets very congested on game days. You can also take I-95 North to Exits 53 (I-395), 52 (Russell St), or 52 (Washington Blvd) and follow signs to the park.

Parking

Parking at Camden Yards is reserved, but there are several public garages nearby. Prices range from $3 to $6.

How to Get There—Mass Transit

Take the MARC from Union Station in DC to Camden Station in Baltimore. It takes about an hour and ten minutes, costs $7, and the last train leaves at 6:30 pm. To return from a night game, the 701 MTA bus will get you home in 50 minutes for free with your Baltimore-bound MARC ticket.

The weekends are another story. Your only choice here is the 703 MTA bus, which runs from Greenbelt Metro Station to Camden Yards for $9.

How to Get Tickets

Orioles tickets can be purchased on their website, or by calling 888-848-2473. Individual game tickets range from $9 to $55. Group and season tickets are also available.

Robert F Kennedy Memorial Stadium

General Information

NFT Map: 4
Address: 2400 E Capitol St SE, Washington, DC 20003
Websites: www.dcsec.com, www.dcunited.com,
www.nationals.com
Phone: 202-547-9077

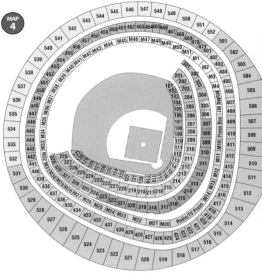

Overview

When it opened in 1961, RFK was hailed as a triumph of multipurpose architecture. Today it's a cement donut, an alien spacecraft dinosaur of '60s and '70s modernist thinking that misled us into believing that someday our lives would look like the *Jetsons*. Its depressing aesthetics and decrepit condition notwithstanding, the stadium remains a sentimental favorite with Redskins fans, who regale us with memories of their team's 35 years there, including five Super Bowl appearances, three championships, and great gridiron personalities like Joe Gibbs, John Riggins, Joe Theisman, Vince Lombardi, Art Monk, and George Allen. In 1996, negotiations for a new football stadium in DC fell through with then-mayor Sharon Pratt Kelly, and team owner Jack Kent Cooke abandoned RFK for a new home in Landover, Maryland, an isolated albatross that fans grew to hate, particularly after Dan Snyder took over the team and started raising prices on everything from tickets to parking, as well as charging for such privileges as attending practices and uttering the team's name on local airwaves.

But even as the Redskins left, RFK stayed off life support with the arrival of Major League Soccer and the DC United in 1996. The United lost little time in gaining popularity, winning the MLS Cup Championship their inaugural season and again in 1997, 1999, and 2004. Along its sidelines, United fans bounce in the stands and chant "Ole, Ole" in hopes of rooting young phenom Freddy Adu and the rest of the team to another win. In a league where foreign-born fans cheer for players from their respective countries, United games offers a fun glimpse of Washington's international diversity. A new 27,000-seat soccer stadium is now being planned for construction at Poplar Point, just east of the Anacostia River.

And now, after 34 years, RFK is even more alive with the return of Major League Baseball to DC. The vagabond Nationals (formerly the Montreal/Puerto Rico Expos) have fallen for their new home. The players like the view from home plate because the dark outfield wall brings out the ball. The owners like the crowds, which average 10th in the league. The baseball-starved fans like the generous parking, the spicy Italian sausages, and the stands that bounce third base that bounce when the crowd gets rowdy. The only ones who might grumble are Peter Angelos, owner and jealous protector of the Baltimore Orioles' fan base, and a few DC Councilmembers who disagreed with the City Council's vote to pay for a shiny new ballpark near the Navy Yard metro in Southeast in 2008. For many fans, $535 million is a bargain if it means avoiding a repeat of 1971, when the Senators (of *Damn Yankees* fame) moved to Arlington, Texas, to become the Rangers.

For savvy fans, the best deals are the $18 infield seats in the upper deck, which sit closer to the field than in newer parks

(where second tier stands often have to be jacked up to make room for luxury boxes). If you can splurge, home plate or infield seats in the lower bowl will cost $100 and $45, respectively. For bargain hunters, the yellow seats in the upper deck outfield will run you only $8. While you're there, look for the scattered white chairs that honor some of Senator slugger Frank Howard's legendary (and steroid free) home runs.

How to Get There—Driving

Follow Constitution Avenue east past the Capitol to Maryland Avenue. Turn left on Maryland and go two blocks to Stanton Square. At Stanton Square, turn right onto Massachusetts Avenue. Go around Lincoln Park to E Capitol Street and turn right.

Parking

Stadium parking costs between $3 and $10, depending on the event you're attending.

How to Get There—Mass Transit

Take the Metro to the Stadium-Armory Station on the Blue and Orange lines.

How to Get Tickets

For United tickets, call 703-478-6600. Tickets to United games range from $16 near the goalposts to $24 along the sidelines. All RFK events, including United soccer matches and Nationals' games, can be purchased through Ticketmaster (202-397-7328, www.ticketmaster.com). Tickets to Nationals games range from $8 for upper level outfield seats to $100 for lower bowl "Diamond Club" seats.

General Information

Washington Area Bicyclist Association:

	www.waba.org
Bike Washington:	www.bikewashington.org
Bike the Sites Bicycle Tours:	www.bikethesites.com
C&O Canal Towpath:	www.nps.gov/choh
Capitol Crescent Trail:	www.cctrail.org
Mount Vernon Trail:	www.nps.gov/gwmp/mvt.html
W&OD Trail:	www.wodfriends.org

Overview

A bike in DC is as necessary as a political affiliation. The city tries to satisfy the needs of its mountain and road bikers alike with plenty of multi-terrain trails, a few good urban commuting routes, and one massive citywide bike ride in the fall. When it comes to bikes onboard mass transit, the Metrobus and Metrorail have lenient policies that also help when a bike route, or your energy, dead-ends.

If you're new to biking in DC, be prepared for a few wrong turns and missed trail entrances. Figuring out how various trails connect (or how to safely and easily cut through neighborhoods to move from one trail to the other) can take some time and trial and error, but the rewards are well worth it. Consult the above sites for pointers, seek out other bicyclists, and have fun!

And while commuting by bike is doable, it can get rather dicey. Bike lanes don't really exist in much of DC, and state law mandates that cyclists have to follow traffic laws—so plan on mixing it up with the cars on your way to work. Even though DC residents are an honest bunch, it's a good idea to keep your bike locked whenever it's out of your sight. For more information regarding bicycle commuting, check out the Washington Area Bicyclist Association website. The site also provides information about the annual "Bike DC."

Bike Trails

The **Chesapeake and Ohio (C&O) Canal** is probably the city's most popular bike route. The trail spans over 184 miles, and most of it is unpaved, so it's not a trail for the weak of butt. The trail begins in Georgetown and follows the route of the Potomac River from DC to Cumberland, Maryland. Biking is permitted only on the towpath. Campsites are located from Swains Lock to Seneca for bikers undertaking multi-day journeys. But be warned: because the first 20 miles are the most heavily used, conditions within the Beltway are significantly better than those outside of it. The towpath sometimes floods, so its best to check the website, www.nps.gov/choh, for possible closures before breaking out the wheels.

The **Capital Crescent Trail** is a "rail trail"—a bike trail converted from abandoned or unused railroad tracks. The trail spans 11 miles between Georgetown and Silver Spring, Maryland. On the trail's first seven miles, from Georgetown to Bethesda, you'll encounter gentle terrain and ten foot-wide asphalt paths. On weekdays, the trail is used predominantly by commuters, and on weekends it gets crowded with recreational cyclists, rollerbladers, joggers, and dogs. Check out www.cctrail.org.

The **Mount Vernon Trail** offers a wide range of scenic views of the Potomac River and national monuments to ensure an inspiring and patriotic ride. The 18.5-mile trail stretches from Roosevelt Island through Old Town Alexandria to George Washington's house in Mount Vernon. To find out more about these and other bike trails, check out the Bike Washington web site.

The **Washington and Old Dominion (W&OD) Trail** is a highly popular paved trail that traverses the 45 miles between Arlington's Shirlington area and Purcellville, Virginia, in Loudoun County. Among the communities it passes through are Falls Church and Leesburg.

The four-mile **Custis Trail** begins in Rosslyn and parallels I-66; it serves to connect the W&OD Trail with other bike trails in the Washington area. Be ready for some inclines and curvy sections on the narrow Custis, and also be wary of bikers who may be traveling faster or slower. For more info, see both the Bike Washington site and the one maintained by The Friends of the Washington & Old Dominion Trail (www.wodfriends.org).

Bikes and Mass Transit

If you need a break while riding in the city, you can hop off your bike and take it on a bus or on Metrorail for free. All DC buses are equipped with racks to carry up to two bikes per bus. You can also ride the Metrorail with your wheels on weekends, and during non-rush hour times on weekdays (that means no bikes 7 am–10 am and 4 pm–7 pm). Also be sure to use elevators when accessing the Metrorail—blocking the stairs and escalators with your bulky bike makes officials and non-biking commuters testy.

Bike Shops

- **A&A Discount Bicycles** (sales, repair, and rental) • 1034 33rd St NW • 202-337-0254 • Map 18
- **Better Bikes** (rental and delivery) • 202-293-2080 • www.betterbikesinc.com
- **Bicycle Pro Shop** (sales, repair, and rental) • 3403 M St NW • 202-337-0311 • www.bicycleproshop.com • Map 18
- **Big Wheel Bikes** (sales, repair, and rental) • 1034 33rd St NW • 202-337-0254 • www.bigwheelbikes.com • Map 18
- **Capitol Hill Bikes** (sales, repair, and rental) • 709 8th St SE • 202-544-4234 • www.capitolhillbikes.com • Map 5
- **City Bikes** (sales, repair, and rental) • 2501 Champlain St NW • 202-265-1564 • www.citybikes.com • Map 16
- **District Hardware/The Bike Shop** (sales and repair) • 2003 P St NW • 202-659-8686 • Map 9
- **Hudson Trail Outfitters** (sales and repair) • 4530 Wisconsin Ave NW • 202-363-9810 • Map 19
- **Revolution Cycles** (sales, repair, and rental) • 3411 M St NW • 202-965-3601 • www.revolutioncycles.com • Map 18

General Information

DC Department of Parks
and Recreation: www.dc.gov
Washington Area
Roadskaters (WAR):   www.skatedc.org

Overview

DC supports a surprisingly thriving skating scene, thanks, in a large part, to the non-profit inline skater's group WAR (www.skatedc.org). Popular places where skaters meet up include the White House, whose traffic-free roadway and easy Metro access contribute to its popularity; Rock Creek Park, which is closed to cars on weekends; and East Potomac Park, whose 3.2-mile Ohio Drive loop was repaved last year. For more information about skating in DC, check out WAR's website.

Indoor Skating

If the weather is grim, or if you want to put in some good practice on predictably level terrain, check out **Franconia Roller Skating Center** in Alexandria. Hours: Sat–Thurs: 7 pm–10 pm; Fri: 7 pm–11pm; Sat: 10 am–4 pm; 703-971-3334. Other rinks in DC's suburbs include **Wheels Skating Center**, 1200 Odenton Rd, MD; 410-674-9661; and **Rockville Skating Center**, 1632 E Gude Dr, Rockville, MD; 301-340-7767.

Skate Parks

After years of hostile restrictions and citations against skaters grinding away outside government buildings, a skate park was finally built in the Shaw neighborhood in 2003. It's free and located on the corner of 11th St and Rhode Island Ave. 202-282-0758; Map 10.

Other outdoor skate parks in the DC area include:

Alexandria Skate Park • 3540 Wheeler Ave, Alexandria, 703-838-4343/4344 • Map 42

The Powhatan Springs Park • 6020 Wilson Blvd, Arlington • 703-533-2362 • Map 33 • A 15,000-square-foot park, featuring 8'- and 6'-deep bowls and 4' and 6' half-pipes; opened in 2004.

Ice-Skating

Finding natural outdoor ice thick enough to support skating can be difficult in DC. But during particularly cold winters, the National Park Service allows ice-skaters out onto the C&O Canal (the ice has to be more than three inches thick, so it's got to be *really* cold). The National Park Service ice skating hotline provides information on skate-safe areas: 301-767-3707.

Skating at the **National Gallery of Art's Sculpture Garden Ice-Skating Rink** may not seem as organic as skating on natural ice, but the surrounding art exhibit rivals any natural setting in terms of beauty. And every Thursday night from December through March you can skate to live jazz from 5 pm to 8 pm. The rink is open daily October through March, Monday–Saturday 10 am to 11 pm, Sunday 10 am to 9 pm. Admission for a two-hour session costs $6 for adults and $5 for children, students, and seniors. Skate rental costs $2.50 and a locker rental costs 50¢; 700 Constitution Ave NW; 202-289-3360; Map 2.

While the Sculpture Garden rink turns into a fountain once the warm weather arrives, the NHL-sized rink at **Mount Vernon Recreation Center** in Alexandria operates year-round. The rink provides ice-hockey lessons, recreational skating lessons, and adult hockey leagues for all levels. On Friday nights, the rink brings in a DJ for teen Rock & Blade skating. Rates and fees vary nightly, so call before you go. 2017 Belle View Blvd, Alexandria; 703-768-3224.

Other seasonal ice-skating rinks are located at:

Pershing Park Ice Rink • Pennsylvania Ave & 14 St NW • 202-737-6938 • Map 1 • $5.50–$6.50 admission + $2.50 rental

Bethesda Metro Ice Center • 3 Bethesda Metro Ctr, Bethesda • 301-656-0588 • Map 29

Gear

The **Ski Chalet** offers a comprehensive selection of performance inline skates and offers tune-ups and rentals. Skates can be rented by the hour ($5) or by the day ($15 for the first day, $6 each additional day). The Ski Chalet is located at 2704 Columbia Pike, Arlington; 703-521-1700; Map 37

The **Ski Center**, located at 4300 Fordham Rd NW sells reasonably priced ice and inline skates. The shop, which has been serving the DC area since 1959, also rents equipment. 202-966-4474; Map 30

For skateboarding equipment, check out the **Evolve Board Shop** at 4856 Bethesda Ave in Bethesda. While this shop primarily targets snowboarders, they also stock skateboard equipment and gear. 301-654-1510; Map 29.

Sailing / Boating / Rowing

Boating enjoys a passionate following here in the District. As the weather warms, the Potomac River and the Tidal Basin swarm with sailboats, kayaks, canoes, and paddleboats.

At 380 miles long, the Potomac River ranks as the fourth longest river on the East Coast. The river also serves as a natural state border, forming part of the boundary between Maryland and West Virginia and separating Virginia from both Maryland and DC. The site of many significant battles during the American Revolution and the Civil War, the Potomac now holds an eternal place in the US history books and has earned the moniker "The Nation's River." A combination of urban sewage and run-off from mining projects upstream seriously degraded the river's water quality, but efforts by the government and citizens have made the water safe for boats and some fishing. Swimming? Well, we don't suggest it.

The Mariner Sailing School (703-768-0018) gives lessons and rents canoes, kayaks, and sailboats for two to six people. If a paddleboat ride is worth worming your way through swarms of sweaty tourists, the Tidal Basin is the best place to go. The boathouse, which sits among the famous cherry blossoms and tulip-bearing flower beds on the man-made inlet, rents paddleboats by the hour (202-479-2426). Two-person boats cost $8 per hour; four-person boats cost $16 per hour.

Sailing/Boating Centers	Address	Phone	Map	URL
Capitol Sailboat Club	James Creek Marina, Washington, DC	202-265-3052	6	www.capitolsbc.com
DC Sail	600 Water St, Washington, DC	202-547-1250	6	www.dcsail.org
Tidal Basin Boat House	1501 Main Ave SW, Washington, DC	202-479-2426	6	www.guestservices.com
Mariner Sailing School	Belle Haven Marina, Alexandria, VA	703-768-0018	N/A	www.saildc.com

Rowing Clubs

	Address	Phone	Map	URL
Capitol Rowing Club	1115 O St SE, Washington, DC	202-289-6666	5	www.capitalrowing.org
Potomac Boat Club	3530 Water St NW, Washington, DC	202-333-9737	8	www.rowpbc.net
Canoe Cruisers Association	11301 Rockville Pike, Kensington, MD	301-251-2978	N/A	www.ccadc.org

Golf

Like everything else in DC, there are politics and networking involved in where you choose to tee off. Our advice—avoid the pricey rat race at the private clubs and reserve a tee time at one of the many, and often more fun, public courses.

East Potomac Park offers three different course options (Red, White, and Blue, of course) as well as mini golf and a driving range. The Langston Golf Course is closest to downtown DC, making it easy to hit during lunch. The Rock Creek Golf Course can sometimes suffer from droughts and heavy play, but its great location keeps people happily putting away.

For those who like to hunt for more than lost balls, nearby Montgomery County (MD) is considering allowing deer hunting on public courses. Most rifles conveniently fit easily into a standard club bag. Nothing like fresh venison at the 19th hole. Legislation pending.

Golf Courses	Address	Phone	Fees	Type	Map
East Potomac Golf Course	972 Ohio Dr SW	202-554-7660	Weekdays $21.50/ Weekends $26.50	Holes-18, Par 72; Also, two 9-hole Par-3 courses	6
Langston Golf Course	28th & Benning Rds NE	202-397-8638	Weekdays $21.50/ Weekends $26.50	Holes-18, Par-72	12
Sligo Creek Golf Course	9701 Sligo Creek Pkwy	301-585-6006	Weekdays $13–15/ Weekends $18	Holes-9, Par-35	25
Rock Creek Golf Course	16th & Rittenhouse NW	202-882-7332	Weekdays $19/ Weekends $24	Holes-18, Par-65	27
Greendale Golf Course	6700 Telegraph Rd, Alexandria	703-971-6170	Weekdays $26/ Weekends $32	Holes-18, Par-70	n/a
Hilltop Golf Club	7900 Telegraph Rd, Alexandria	703-719-6504	Weekdays $25/ Weekends $29	Holes-9, Par-31	n/a
Pinecrest Golf Course	6600 Little River Tpke, Alexandria	703-941-1061	Weekdays $15/ Weekends $18	Holes-9, Par-35	n/a

Driving Ranges	Address	Phone	Fees	Map
Langston Driving Range	2600 Benning Rd NE	202-397-8638	$4.50/45 balls	12
East Potomac Driving Range	972 Ohio Dr SW	202-554-7660	$5/50 balls	6

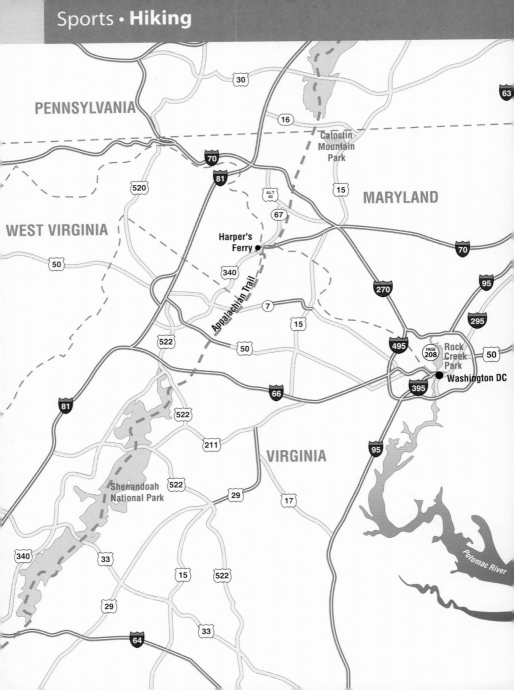

Overview

One of the greatest things about living in DC, a city bursting with hyper, Type-A personalities, is how easy it is to leave. The feasibility of escaping urban life for a weekend, or even just an afternoon, checks and balances the go-getting lobbying/lawyering/liaisoning frenzy that often seems to permeate Our Nation's Capital to the core. Rock Creek Park weaves its way through the city, and some of the best hiking routes on the east coast are just a short drive from town. The National Parks Service website is a valuable resource for planning overnight trips or day hikes (www.nps.gov), and we recommend the gem *60 Hikes within 60 Miles: Washington, DC* by Paul Elliott (Menasha Ridge Press).

Shenandoah National Park

A short drive out of DC, this is one of the country's most popular national parks, mainly because of gorgeous Skyline Drive, which runs across the ridgeline of the Blue Ridge Mountains (the eastern range of the Appalachian Trail). But locals know to ditch the wheels, get out, and get dirty. There are more than 500 miles of trails in the park, including about 100 miles of the AT itself. In short, you can plan a weeklong backcountry getaway, and there'll still be more undiscovered country to come back for.

The Old Rag Trail, with its rock scramble and distinctive profile, is a favorite strenuous day hike. The rangers at the visitors' center will direct you to the toughest climbs, easier routes, the waterfall hikes, or the trails where you'll most likely see bears. The park is 70 miles west of DC. Take Route 66 W to Exit 13, and follow signs to Front Royal. www.nps.gov/shen; 540-999-3500.

Appalachian Trail

Forget what you've heard about lugging a summer's worth of misery along this Georgia-to-Maine trace. You don't have to hike the whole thing. Luckily, a good portion of this nationally protected 2,174-mile footpath through the Appalachian Mountains is accessible from DC. Hook up with it for a few miles at points in Maryland and Virginia, and acquire bragging rights with just a day's worth of blister-inducing pain. A good place to start is Harper's Ferry in Maryland, 65 miles from DC, where you can load up on breakfast and some history before you head out. When you return, hoist a well-deserved pint. www.nps.gov/appa; 301-535-6331.

Catoctin Mountains

While Catoctin Mountain recreation area was created in order to provide a place for federal employees to get a little bit of R&R, it has since been converted into Camp David, the famously inaccessible presidential retreat. Camp David is never open to the public, or to run-of-

the-mill federal employees, but there's still the eastern hardwood forest where everyone is free to roam wild. From DC, the Catoctin Mountains are about a two-hour drive north. Take the George Washington Memorial Parkway north to the Beltway to I-270 N. Drive 27 miles to Frederick, MD. Take Route 15 N to Route 77 W, to the Catoctin Mountain Park exit. Drive three miles west on 77, turn right onto Park Central Road, and the Visitor Center will be on the right. www.nps.gov/cato; 301-663-9388.

Sugarloaf Mountain

Sugarloaf's main appeal is that it's only an hour drive from DC. It's a modest mountain—about 1,300 feet—with nice views of the surrounding farmland, and entry into the park is free. You can choose a variety of easy and not-so-easy ways to get up the mountain, but no matter which way you choose you'll be surrounded by an impressive collection of rare red and white oak trees. To get there, drive North on Route I-270 to the Hyattstown exit, circle under I-270, and continue on Route 109 to Comus, then make a right on Comus Road to the Stronghold entrance. www.sugarloafmd.com; 301-869-7846.

Rock Creek Park

This is the place for a quick nature fix. The historic 1,754-acre park, which reaches from Georgetown to Maryland, is laced with several hiking trails, especially in its northern reaches. The major trails along the western ridge are marked by green blazes, and the footpaths along the east side are marked with blue blazes. A tan-blazed trail connects the two trail systems. None of the trails are strenuous, and all routes can be tailored to fit in a short hike during your lunch break. See the extensive Rock Creek Park section this book for more details. www.nps.gov/rocr; 202-895-6070.

C&O Canal

Don't think the C&O Canal towpath is just for bikers. The relatively level terrain of this 184.5-mile, Georgetown-to-Cumberland trail makes for great hiking. The entire length is dotted with scenic vistas of the Potomac that offer gentler, more natural views of the river than you're afforded when stuck in traffic on a bridge between DC and northern Virginia. History abounds along the route in the form of Civil War sites and both reconstructed and ramshackle lockhouses. Once you pass Great Falls, there are free campsites spread every five miles or so. They're simple setups of a fire pit, picnic table, water pump, and portable toilet, but after a hard day's hike they seem like the lap of luxury. For more information, visit www.nps.gov/choh or call 202-653-5190.

The following fees for public pools are based on county residency. Non-residents can count on paying a buck or two more.

Outdoor pools are open daily from June 23 and generally close in late August or early September. Many of the public pools require you to register as a member at the beginning of the season and, since most fill their membership quotas quickly, it's wise to locate your nearest pool and join at the beginning of the season.

Pool	Address	Phone	Fees	Type	Map
William Rumsey Aquatic Center	635 North Carolina Ave SE	202-724-4495	Residents free, various fees & passes for non-residents	Indoor	3
Rosedale Pool	17th St NE & Gales St NE	202-727-1502	Residents free, various fees & passes for non-residents	Outdoor	4
Barry Farm Pool	1223 Sumner Rd SE	202-645-5040	Residents free, various fees & passes for non-residents	Outdoor	5
Lincoln Capper Pool	500 L St SE	202-727-1080	Residents free, various fees & passes for non-residents	Kids' pool, Open during summer months only.	5
East Potomac Pool	972 Ohio Dr SW	202-727-6523	Residents free, various fees & passes for non-residents	Outdoor	6
Randall Pool	S Capitol St SW & I St SW	202-727-1420	Residents free, various fees & passes for non-residents	Outdoor	6
Fairmont	2401 M St NW	202-457-5070	Members and hotel guests only. Various membership fees.	Indoor	9
YMCA National Capital	1711 Rhode Island Ave NW	202-862-9622	$100 joining fee, $70 month	Indoor	9
YMCA	1325 W St NW	202-462-1054	$50 to join, $35 month	Indoor	10
Dunbar Pool	1301 New Jersey Ave NW	202-673-4316	Residents free, various fees & passses for non-residents	Indoor	11
Harry Thomas Sr Pool	1801 Lincoln Rd NE	202-576-5640	Residents free, various fees & passes for non-residents	Outdoor	11
JO Wilson Pool	700 K St NE	202-727-1505	Residents free, various fees & passes for non-residents	Kids' pool, Open during summer months only.	11
Trinidad Recreation Center	1310 Childress St NW	202-727-1503	Children six and under swim free, kids ages 6–17 $3 per day, $46 season pass	Kids' pool, Open during summer months only.	12
Fort Lincoln Outdoor Pool	3201 Ft Lincoln Dr NE	202-576-6389	$4 per day, $130 season pass Residents free, various fees & passes for non-residents	Outdoor	13
Langdon Park Pool	Mills Ave & Hamlin St NE	202-576-8655	Residents free, various fees & passes for non-residents	Outdoor	13
Turkey Thicket Community Center	1100 Michigan Ave NE	202-635-6226	Residents free, various fees & passses for non-residents		14
Banneker Pool	2500 Georgia Ave NW	202-673-2121	Residents free, various fees & passes for non-residents	Outdoor	15
Parkview Pool	639 Otis Pl NW	202-576-8658	Children six and under swim free, kids ages 6–17 $3 per day, $46 season pass	Kids' pool, Open during summer months only.	15
Marie Reed Center Pool	2200 Champlain St NW	202-673-7771	Residents free, various fees & passes for non-residents	Indoor	16
Georgetown Pool	3400 Volta Pl NW	202-727-3285	Residents free, various fees & passes for non-residents	Outdoor	18
Tenley Sport & Health Club	4000 Wisconsin Ave NW	202-362-8000	$20 per day, $100 per month membership	Indoor	19
Wilson Pool (temporarily closed due to structural damage)	Ford Dr & Albemarle St NW	202-282-2216	Residents free, various fees & passses for non-residents	Indoor	19
Upshur Outdoor Pool	14th St & Arkansas Ave NW	202-576-8661	Residents free, various fees & passses for non-residents	Outdoor	21
Bethesda YMCA	9401 Old Georgetown Rd	301-530-3725	$62 per month membership,	Indoor	22
YMCA	9800 Hastings Dr	301-585-2120	$100 joining fee, $64 month	Indoor/Outdoor	25

Pool–continued	Address	Phone	Fees	Type	Map
Piney Branch Pool	7510 Maple Ave	301-270-6093	$5 per day	Indoor	26
Takoma Outdoor Pool	300 Van Buren St NW	202-576-8660	Residents free, various fees & passes for non-residents	Outdoor	27
Sport & Health Club	4400 Montgomery Ave	301-656-9570	$25 per day ($15 per day with a member)	Indoor	29
Bethesda Outdoor Pool	Little Falls Dr	301-652-1598	$5.50 per day, $160 for year pass	Outdoor	30
Upton Hill Regional Park	6060 Wilson Blvd	703-534-3437	$5.25 per day, $72 season pass	Outdoor	33
Yorktown Swimming Pool	5201 28th St N	703-536-9739	$4 per day, $230 per year	Indoor	33
Washington-Lee Swimming Pool	1300 N Quincy St	703-228-6262	$4 per day, $230 per year	Indoor	34
YMCA Arlington	3422 N 13th St	703-525-5420	$100 joining fee, $48 month	Outdoor	35
Wakefield Swimming Pool	4901 S Chesterfield Rd	703-578-3063	$4 per day, $230 per year	Indoor	38
YMCA	3440 S 22nd St	703-892-2044	$100 joining fee, $48 month	Outdoor	39
Chinquapin Park Rec Center	3210 King St	703-519-2160	$5 per day, $46 per month	Indoor	42
Alexandria YMCA	420 Monroe Ave	703-838-8085	$15 per day, $69 per month membership, $100 joining fee	Indoor	43
Warwick Pool	3301 Landover St	703-838-4672	$2 per day	Outdoor	43
Old Town Pool	1609 Cameron St	703-838-4671	$2 per day	Outdoor	44

Bowling

If you're looking strictly within District lines, this city has no real bowling alley to speak of. If it's a smoking-only, mullets-abounding, Roseanne-style spot you're looking for, you'll have to hop in your car and cross county lines. Within DC, there are always the lanes at GW's Hippodrome—but what kind of game can you roll without pitchers of cheap beer and spicy wings to push you along? Then Lucky Strike entered the scene: button-down shirt, black pants, bowling for the Penn Quarter crowd. Lucky Strike taught us that clubs aren't the only places where you can toss a few back and shake your groove thang. Similar to Strike Bethesda and other bowling alleys in the surrounding suburbs, these types of lanes offer up the four wonderful B's: Bowling, Beer, Blacklights, and Beyoncé. After dark, the lights go down and the beats go up, with special "Cosmic Bowling" or "Xtreme Bowling" nights. When the DJ arrives, you can bet on the bowling fees rising accordingly with the volume of the dance traxxx.

Sunday nights are the best nights to bowl if you're looking to save money, as many alleys offer unlimited bowling after 9 pm for under $15. Show some Maryland pride, and play duckpin bowling (the sport actually originated in Baltimore) at White Oak Bowling Lanes and AMF College Park, home to the Men's Duckpin Pro Bowlers' Association Master Tournament.

Bowling Alley	Address	Phone	Fees	Map
Lucky Strikes Lanes	701 7th St NW	202-347-1021	$5.95 game, $3.95 shoes	2
Strike Bethesda	5353 Westbard Ave	301-652-0955	$5.45–6.25 per game, $4 for shoes	29
AMF Bowling Center	4620 Kenmore Ave	703-823-6200	$2.50–$5 per game, $4.50 for shoes	41
US Bowling	100 S Pickett St	703-370-5910	$3–4.25 per game, $3.50 for shoes	41
Alexandria Bowling Center	6228A N Kings Hwy, Alexandria, VA	703-765-3633	$3.50–5.00 per game, $4.46 for shoes	n/a
AMF College Park	9021 Baltimore Ave, College Park, MD	301-474-8282	$4.25 per game, $4.65 for shoes	n/a
Annandale Bowl	4245 Markham St	703-256-2211	$4.50 game, $4.46 shoes	n/a
Bowl America	140 S Maple Ave	703-534-1370	$4.95 game, $3.40 shoes	n/a
Bowl America	6450 Ebsall Rd, Alexandria, VA	703-354-3300	$2–5 per game, $3.40 for shoes	n/a
Bowl America - Chantilly	4525 Stonecroft Blvd, Chantilly, VA	703-830-2695	$2–5 per game, $3.40 for shoes	n/a
Bowl America - Fairfax	9699 Lee Hwy, Fairfax, VA	703-273-7700	$2–5.25 per game, $3.40 for shoes	n/a
White Oak Lanes	11207 New Hampshire Ave, Silver Spring, MD	301-593-3000	$3 per game, $3.50 for shoes	n/a

Tennis

National Park Service: *202-208-6843, www.nps.gov*
Washington, DC Department of Parks and Recreation: *202-673-7647, dpr.dc.gov*

Public Courts at Community Recreation Centers

DC residents and visitors can play tennis at any of the public courts scattered throughout the city. All courts are available on a first-come, first-served basis. An honor code trusts that players won't hog the courts for over an hour of play-time (although you can call the Department of Parks and Recreation to obtain a permit for extended use). For more information about lessons and tournaments, call the Sports Office of the Department of Parks and Recreation (202-698-2250).

Courts	Address	Phone	Type	Map
South Grounds	15th St & Constitution Ave	202-698-2250	Public	1
Langston	26th St & Benning Rd NE	202-698-2250	Public	4
Rosedale	17th St NE & Gale St NE	202-698-2250	Public	4
Barry Farm	1230 Sumner Rd SE	202-698-2250	Public	5
East Potomac Tennis Center	1090 Ohio Dr SW	202-554-5962	Private	6
Jefferson	8th St SW & H St SW	202-698-2250	Public	6
King-Greenleaf	201 N St SW	202-698-2250	Public	6
Randall	1st St & I St SW	202-698-2250	Public	6
Georgetown	33rd St & Volta Pl	202-698-2250	Public	8
Montrose Park	30th St NW & R St NW	202-698-2250	Public	8
Rose Park	26th St NW & O St NW	202-698-2250	Public	8
Francis	24th St NW & N St NW	202-698-2250	Public	9
Reed	18th St NW & California St NW	202-698-2250	Public	9
Washington Hilton Sport & Health Club	1919 Connecticut Ave NW	202-483-4100	Private	9
Shaw	10th St & Rhode Island Ave NW	202-698-2250	Public	10
Brentwood Park	6th St & Brentwood Pkwy NE	202-698-2250	Public	11
Dunbar	1st NW & O St NW	202-698-2250	Public	11
Edgewood	3rd St NE & Evart St NE	202-698-2250	Public	11
Harry Thomas Sr	Lincoln Rd & T St NE	202-698-2250	Public	11
Arboretum	24th St & Rand Pl NE	202-698-2250	Public	12
Fort Lincoln	Ft Lincoln Dr NE	202-698-2250	Public	13
Langdon Park	20th & Franklin Sts NE	202-698-2250	Public	13
Taft	19th St NE & Otis St NE	202-698-2250	Public	13
Backus	South Dakota Ave & Hamilton St NE	202-698-2250	Public	14
Banneker	9th St NW & Euclid St NW	202-698-2250	Public	15
Raymond	10th St & Spring Rd NW	202-698-2250	Public	15
Hardy	45th St NW & Q St NW	202-698-2250	Public	18
Fort Reno	41st St NW & Chesapeake St NW	202-698-2250	Public	19
Friendship	4500 Van Ness St NW	202-698-2250	Public	19
Hearst	37th St NW & Tilden St NW	202-698-2250	Public	19
Forest Hills	32nd St NW & Brandywine St NW	202-698-2250	Public	20
Rock Creek Tennis Center	16th St NW & Kennedy St NW	202-722-5949	Private	21
Fort Stevens	1327 Van Buren St NW	202-698-2250	Public	27
Rabaut	2nd St NW & Peabody St NW	202-698-2250	Public	27
Takoma	3rd St NW & Van Buren St NW	202-698-2250	Public	27
Chevy Chase	4101 Livingston St NW	202-698-2250	Public	28
Lafayette	33rd St NW & Quesada St NW	202-698-2250	Public	28
Bethesda Sport & Health Club	4400 Montgomery Ave	301-656-9570	Private	29
Palisades	5200 Sherrier Pl NW	202-698-2250	Public	32
Arlington Y Tennis & Squash Club	3400 N 13th St	703-749-8057	Private	35

Airline	Phone	IAD	DCA	BWI
Aeroflot	888-686-4949	■		
Air Canada	888-247-2262	■	■	■
Air France	800-237-2747	■		
Air Jamaica	800-523-5585			■
AirTran	800-247-8726	■	■	■
Alaska Airlines	800-252-7522	■	■	
Alitalia	800-223-5730	■		
All Nippon	800-235-9262	■		
American Airlines	800-433-7300	■	■	■
American Trans Air	800-435-9282		■	
America West	800-235-9292	■	■	■
Austrian Airlines	800-843-0002	■		
British Airways	800-247-9297	■		
BWIA	800-538-2942	■		
Continental	800-523-3273	■	■	■
Delta	800-221-1212	■	■	■
Delta Shuttle	800-933-5935		■	
Ethiopian Airlines	800-445-2733	■		
Frontier	800-432-1359		■	■
Ghana Airways	800-404-4262			
GRUPO TACA	800-400-8222	■		
Icelandair	800-223-5500			■
Independence Air	800-359-3594	■		
Jet Blue	800-538-2583	■		
KLM Royal Dutch	800-225-2525	■		
Korean Air	800-438-5000	■		
LAB	800-337-0918	■		
Lufthansa	800-399-5838	■		
Maxjet	888-435-9629	■		
Mexicana	800-531-7921			■
Midwest	800-452-2022		■	■
North American Airlines	800-359-6222			■
Northwest Airlines	800-225-2525	■	■	■
SAS	800-221-2350	■		
Saudi Arabian Airlines	800-472-8342	■		
South African Airways	27-11-978-5313	■		
Southwest Airlines	800-435-9792			■
Spirit	800-772-7117		■	
Ted Airlines	800-225-5833	■		
United Airlines	800-864-8331	■	■	■
United Express	800-864-8331	■		
US Airways	800-428-4322	■	■	■
USA3000	877-872-3000			■
Virgin	800-862-8621	■		

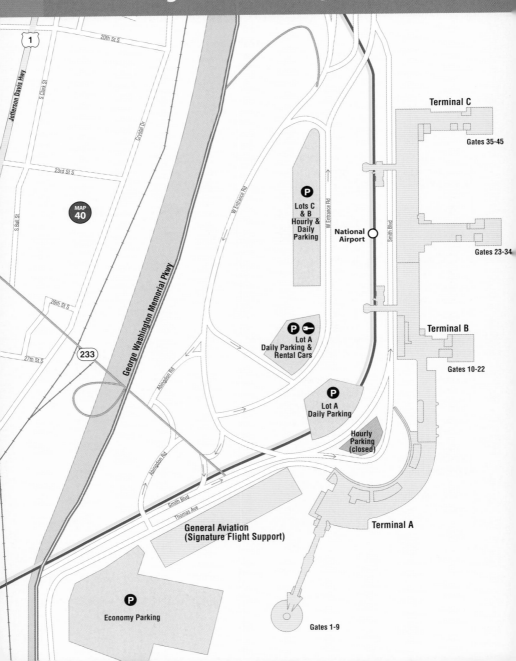

Transit · **Reagan National Airport (DCA)**

Terminal C

Gates 35-45

National Airport ○

Gates 23-34

P Lots C & B Hourly & Daily Parking

W Entrance Rd

W Entrance Rd

Smith Blvd

Terminal B

Gates 10-22

P 🚗 Lot A Daily Parking & Rental Cars

P Lot A Daily Parking

Hourly Parking (closed)

Terminal A

George Washington Memorial Pkwy

Abingdon Rd

Abingdon Rd

Smith Blvd

Thomas Ave

General Aviation (Signature Flight Support)

Gates 1-9

P Economy Parking

MAP 40

(233)

(1) Jefferson Davis Hwy

S Clark St

Crystal Dr

S Ball St

20th St S

23rd St S

26th St S

27th St S

General Information

Phone: 703-417-8000
Lost & Found: 703-417-0673
Parking: 703-417-4311
Website: www.mwaa.com/national/index.htm

Overview

Ronald Reagan Washington National Airport is a small, easy-to-navigate airport that's located practically downtown, perfect for business travelers and politicians alike. But, for those of us not on expense accounts or the public dole, prices can be prohibitive. If you want a discounted direct flight to Madagascar or enjoy flying on the cattle cars that charge $15 for a roundtrip to Aruba, you'll have to fly from Dulles or BWI. National is too small to host many planes or airlines, making it a short-haul airport with direct connections to cities typically no more than 1,250 miles away.

How to Get There—Driving

From DC, take I-395 S to Exit 10 ("Reagan National Airport/ Mount Vernon"). Get on the GW Parkway S, and take the Reagan Airport exit. If you're in Virginia headed north on I-395, ignore the first exit you see for the airport (Exit 8C/"to US 1/Crystal City/Pentagon City/Reagan National Airport") and continue on to Exit 10 S. It's quicker and easier. Remember to watch out for Officer Friendly and his trusty radar gun as you enter the airport property.

Parking

Parking at Reagan is not cheap. Garages A, B, C, and Lot A-2 charge $2 per half-hour for the first two hours and $4 per hour thereafter. Garage A and Lot A-2 cost $15 per day. Garages B and C cost $28 per day. All three garages are conveniently located across the street from the terminals and can be accessed through enclosed or underground walkways. If you're heading out for a few days, we suggest you park in the economy lot for only $9 per day. Shuttle buses run between the economy lot and all terminals. Parking in any lot for less than 20 minutes is free. Though when have you ever been in-and-out of an airport in less than an hour? That's what we thought.

How to Get There—Mass Transit

The Blue and Yellow Lines have a Metrorail stop adjacent to Terminals B and C. If you're headed to Terminal A, a free shuttle bus will run you there or you can lug your bags on a ten-minute walk. Metro buses are also available from the base of the Metrorail station for areas not served by the rail.

How to Get There— Ground Transportation

SuperShuttle offers door-to-door service to DCA. They also have a shuttle that goes regularly between DCA and Union Station. Call the reservation line on 800-BLUEVAN or go to www.supershuttle.com to book online.

A cab ride to downtown DC will set you back less than $15. DC, Virginia, and Maryland taxis are available at the exits of each terminal. Red Top Cab - Arlington: 703-522-3333; Yellow Cab - DC: 202-TAXI-CAB; Yellow Cab - Arlington: 703-534-1111.

Stretch limousine and executive-class sedans start at approximately $35 for downtown Washington. Airport Access: 202-498-8708; Airport Connection: 202-393-2110; Roadmaster: 800-283-5634; Silver Car: 410-992-7775.

Rental Cars—On-Airport (Garage A)

Avis • 800-331-1212   **National** • 800-328-4567
Budget • 800-527-0700   **Dollar** • 800-800-4000
Hertz • 800-654-3131

Off-Airport

Enterprise • 800-736-8222
Alamo • 800-832-7933
Thrifty • 800-367-2277

Hotels—Arlington

Crowne Plaza •1480 Crystal Dr • 703-416-1600
Crystal City Marriott • 1999 Jefferson Davis Hwy • 703-413-5500
Crystal City Courtyard by Marriott • 2899 Jefferson Davis Hwy • 703-549-3434
Crystal Gateway Marriott • 1700 Jefferson Davis Hwy • 703-920-3230
Radisson Inn • 2200 Jefferson Davis Hwy • 703-920-8600
Doubletree Crystal City • 300 Army Navy Dr • 703-416-4100
Econo Lodge • 6800 Lee Hwy • 703-538-5300
Embassy Suites • 1300 Jefferson Davis Hwy • 703-979-9799
Hilton • 2399 Jefferson Davis Hwy • 703-418-6800
Holiday Inn • 2650 Jefferson Davis Hwy • 703-684-7200
Hyatt Regency • 2799 Jefferson Davis Hwy • 703-418-1234
Ritz Carlton Pentagon City • 1250 S Hayes St • 703-415-5000
Residence Inn • 550 Army Navy Dr • 703-413-6630
Sheraton • 1800 Jefferson Davis Hwy • 703-486-1111

Hotels—Washington

Hamilton Crowne Plaza • 1001 14th NW • 202-682-0111
Grand Hyatt • 1000 H St NW • 202-582-1234
Hilton Washington • 1919 Connecticut Ave NW • 202-483-3000
Hilton Embassy Row • 2015 Massachusetts Ave NW • 202-265-1600
Holiday Inn • 415 New Jersey Ave NW • 202-638-1616
Homewood Suites by Hilton • 1475 Massachusetts Ave NW • 202-265-8000
Hyatt Regency • 400 New Jersey Ave NW • 202-737-1234
Marriott Wardman Park • 2660 Woodley Rd NW • 202-328-2000
Red Roof Inn • 500 H St NW • 202-289-5959
Renaissance Mayflower Hotel • 1127 Connecticut Ave NW • 202-347-3000
Renaissance Washington DC • 999 9th St NW • 202-898-9000

Airline	Terminal	Airline	Terminal
Air Canada/Jazz	C	Midwest	A
Air Tran	A	Northwest/Airlink	A
Alaska	B	Spirit	A
America West	C	United Airlines	C
American/Eagle	B	Delta/Connection/	B
ATA	A	Shuttle	
Continental	B	US Airways/Express	C
Frontier	B	/Shuttle	

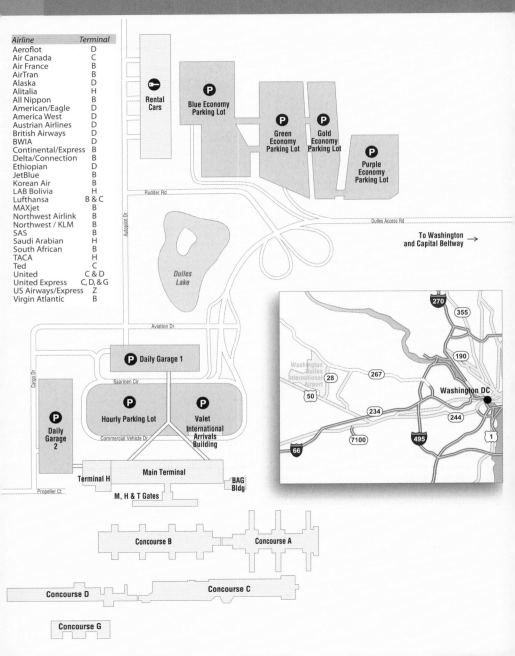

Airline	Terminal
Aeroflot	D
Air Canada	C
Air France	B
AirTran	B
Alaska	D
Alitalia	H
All Nippon	B
American/Eagle	D
America West	D
Austrian Airlines	D
British Airways	D
BWIA	D
Continental/Express	B
Delta/Connection	B
Ethiopian	D
JetBlue	B
Korean Air	B
LAB Bolivia	H
Lufthansa	B & C
MAXjet	B
Northwest Airlink	B
Northwest / KLM	B
SAS	B
Saudi Arabian	H
South African	B
TACA	H
Ted	C
United	C & D
United Express	C, D, & G
US Airways/Express	Z
Virgin Atlantic	B

Rental Cars

Blue Economy Parking Lot

Green Economy Parking Lot

Gold Economy Parking Lot

Purple Economy Parking Lot

Rudder Rd

Autopilot Dr

Dulles Access Rd

To Washington and Capital Beltway

Dulles Lake

Aviation Dr

Cargo Dr

Daily Garage 1

Saarinen Cir

Hourly Parking Lot

Valet International Arrivals Building

Daily Garage 2

Commercial Vehicle Dr

Terminal H

Main Terminal

BAG Bldg

Propeller C1

M, H & T Gates

Concourse B

Concourse A

Concourse D

Concourse C

Concourse G

270

355

190

Washington Dulles International Airport

28

267

50

Washington DC

234

244

7100

495

66

1

General Information

Address: 45020 Aviation Dr
Sterling, VA 20166 (not that you're going to send them anything, really)
Information: 703-572-2700
Parking: 703-572-4500
Lost & Found: 703-572-2954
Website: www.metwashairports.com/Dulles

Overview

The Mod Squad of airports, Dulles was born in 1958 when Finnish architect Eero Saarinen had a hankering to channel his training as a sculptor and create something groovy. His design for the terminal building and the control tower was so hip it received a First Honor Award from the American Institute of Architects in 1966. A swoosh roof over a squat building, Dulles still stands out as a stunning exhibit of modernist architecture and was the first airport in the US designed specifically for commercial jets. The oh-so-suave "mobile lounges" that transport passengers between the main terminal building and the outlying terminals are still in use. But when the outlying terminals were constructed in 1998, they were done so without even a nod to the style of the original architecture. An underground shuttle is under construction and should be operational in a couple of years. Currently you may walk (ha!) from the main terminal to the "A" and "B" Concourses (entering the "B" Concourse between Gates B31 and B35). You still must take a shuttle to the "C" and "D" Concourses.
Note: "Washington" was officially added to the "Dulles International Airport" moniker after too many people inadvertently booked flights to Dallas, not Dulles, and vice-versa. No joke. On a sad note: Independence Air, we hardly knew ye. The demise of this Dulles-based airline, known for going where no airline went *cheaply* before, has led to the stratospheric increase in airfares at all three airports. However, help may be on the way as Southwest Airlines has announced the beginning of service out of Dulles beginning in the fall of 2006. Yea! No more schlep to BWI.

How to Get There—Driving

To get to Washington Dulles Airport from downtown DC, drive west on I-66 to Exit 67. Follow signs to the airport. Be sure to use the Dulles Access Road, which avoids the tolls and traffic found on the parallel Dulles Toll Road (Rt. 267). But don't get cocky and try to use the Access Road to avoid tolls at other times—once you're on these access lanes, there's no exit until you reach the airport.

Now drivers to Dulles have a new option when waiting to pick up their precious cargo. A Cell Phone Waiting Area provides an alternative to circling the Main terminal (what, you thought you could just park at the front door?). This free waiting area offers a place to wait until the phone rings. The waiting area is located at the intersection of Rudder Road and Autopilot Drive (how clever *are* these people?). Follow the signs as you enter the airport grounds. It is free of charge and the maximum waiting time is one hour.

Parking

Hourly (short-term) parking is located in front of the terminal and costs $4 per hour and $36 per day. Daily parking is available in Daily Garages 1 and 2 for $5 per hour and $15 per day. There are shuttle buses and walkways (albeit lengthy ones) from Garage 1) directly to the main terminal. Economy parking (long-term) is available in the four economy parking lots (Blue, Green, Gold, and Purple) located along Rudder Road. Long-term parking costs $3 per hour and $9 per day. If you're short on time or energy and long on cash, valet parking is located in front of the terminal and costs $30 for the first 24 hours and $17 per day thereafter. Parking in any lot for less than 20 minutes is free. Take your parking ticket with you as you can pay for your parking in the main terminal on your way out.

How to Get There—Mass Transit

The Metrorail doesn't go all the way to Dulles Airport. You can take the Orange Line to West Falls Church and transfer to the Washington Flyer Coach Service, which leaves every 30 minutes from the station. The coach fare costs $9 one-way ($16 round-trip), and the fare for the Metrorail leg will depend on exactly where you're coming from or headed to. A trip from West Falls Church to the Convention Center in downtown DC costs from $1.85 to $2.75 depending upon the time of day. Check www.washfly.com for Flyer schedules. There are no "regular" taxis from Dulles to any destination—the Flyer is it, and you should avoid all other pitchmen. You can also take Metrobus 5A which runs from L'Enfant Plaza to Dulles, stopping at Rosslyn Metro Station. The express bus costs $3 each way.

Ground Transportation

Super Shuttle is a door-to-door shared van to Washington Dulles Airport. It goes to and from Union Station and anywhere else, if you call and book 24 hours in advance. At the airport, you'll find them outside the Main Terminal. Call 800-258-3826 or go to www.supershuttle.com to make reservations. Washington Flyer Taxicabs serve Dulles International Airport exclusively with 24-hour service to and from the airport. Taxis accept American Express, Diners Club, MasterCard, Discover Card, and Visa and charge metered rates to any destination in metropolitan Washington. If you're heading to downtown DC, it will cost you between $44 and $50. For more information, or to book a taxi, call 703-661-6655.

Rental Cars

Alamo • 800-832-7933   **Enterprise** • 800-736-8222
Avis • 800-331-1212   **Hertz** • 800-654-3131
Budget • 800-527-0700   **National** • 800-227-7368
Dollar • 800-800-4000   **Thrifty** • 800-367-2277
Alamoot (off-airport) • 800-630-6967

Hotels—Herndon, VA

Comfort Inn • 200 Elden St • 703-437-7555
Courtyard by Marriott • 533 Herndon Pkwy • 703-478-9400
Days Hotel • 2200 Centreville Rd • 703-471-6700
Embassy Suites • 13341 Woodland Park Dr • 703-464-0200
Hilton • 13869 Park Center Rd • 703-478-2900
Holiday Inn Express • 485 Elden St • 703-478-9777
Hyatt Hotels & Resorts • 2300 Dulles Corner Blvd • 703-713-1234
Marriott Hotels • 13101 Worldgate Dr • 703-709-0400
Residence Inn • 315 Elden St • 703-435-0044
Staybrdige Suites • 13700 Coppermine Rd • 703-713-6800

Hotels—Sterling, VA

Country Inn & Suites • 45620 Falke Plz • 703-435-2700
Courtyard by Marriott • 45500 Majestic Dr • 571-434-6400
Fairfield Inn • 23000 Indian Creek Dr • 703-435-5300
Hampton Inn • 45440 Holiday Park Dr • 703-471-8300
Holiday Inn • 1000 Sully Rd • 703-471-7411
Marriott Towneplace • 22744 Holiday Park Dr • 703-707-2017
Marriott • 45020 Aviation Dr • 703-471-9500
Quality Inn & Suites Dulles International • 45515 Dulles Plz • 703-471-5005

Baltimore-Washington International Airport

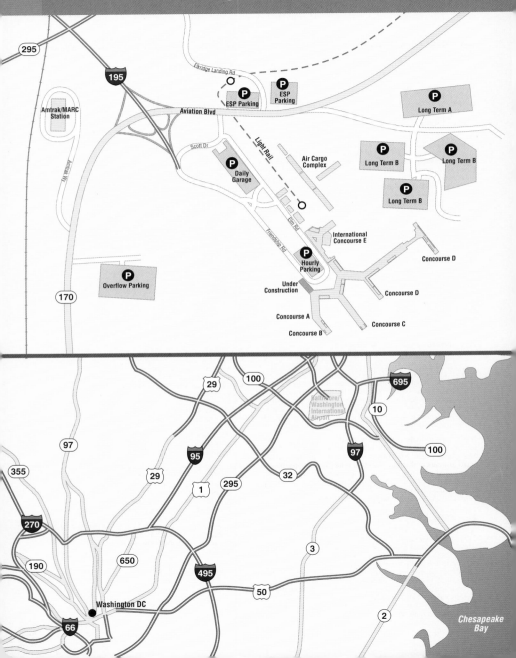

General Information

Information: 800-435-9294
Lost & Found: 410-859-7387
Parking: 800-468-6294
Police: 410-859-7040
Website: www.bwiairport.com

Overview

When Friendship International Airport opened in 1950, it was widely touted as one of the most sophisticated and advanced airports in the nation. In 1993, Southwest Airlines moved in, bringing with them their cheap, and wildly popular, cattle cars of the sky. But this bargain-basement tenant has turned BWI into a boomtown—a spanking new expanded Terminal A for Southwest only opened in 2005. Other major carriers have since joined the dirt-cheap-fares bandwagon, resulting in generally cheaper flights to and from BWI than you'll find flying into and out of Dulles or Reagan. It's a helluva haul from the city (yet pretty close for Maryland suburbanites), but sometimes time really isn't money, and cheap fares trump convenience. In October 2005, BWI was officially renamed Baltimore-Washington International Thurgood Marshall Airport in honor of native Baltimorean and first African-American Supreme Court Justice Thurgood Marshall.

How to Get There—Driving

From downtown DC, take New York Avenue (US 50) eastbound to the Baltimore/Washington Parkway N to I-195 E. From the Capital Beltway (I-495/95), take the I-95 N exit in Maryland (Exit 27), and then continue north to I-195 E. I-195 ends at the entrance to BWI.

Parking

Hourly parking is located across from the terminal building. The first hour of parking (which you may spend looking for a space), is free, and the rest of your time costs $4 per hour and $20 per day. Daily parking is available for $2 per hour and $10 per day. Express Service Parking (ESP) is located on Aviation Boulevard across from the Air Cargo Complex. ESP parking costs $3 per hour and $14 per day. If you're going to be gone a while, you might want to try the long-term parking lots, which cost $1 per hour and $8 per day; every seventh day is free. A new service called "Credit Card In/Credit Card Out" allows you to swipe the plastic of your choice upon entering and exiting an hourly parking facility, eliminating the fun of losing your parking ticket. The "Pay & Go" service allows you to pay your parking fee for the hourly lot in the Skywalk adjacent to the main terminal before you return to your car.

BWI also has a Cell Phone Parking lot located at the entrance to the "Daily B" parking lot on Elm Road. You can wait there for your mother-in-law to arrive. Just remember to turn your phone on.

How to Get There—Mass Transit

Any which way you go, expect to devote a few hours to mimicking a Richard Scarry character. MARC's Penn Line and Amtrak trains service the BWI Rail Station from Union Station in DC (Massachusetts Ave & First St NE) and cost between $5 and $30. A free shuttle bus takes passengers from the train station to the airport. Alternatively, you can take the Metro Green Line to the Greenbelt station and catch the

Express Metro Bus/B30 to BWI. The Express bus runs every 40 minutes and costs $2.50. MARC trains do not operate on the weekends. The Light Rail train now provides service between Baltimore and BWI.

How to Get There— Ground Transportation

The Airport Shuttle offers door-to-door service within the state of Maryland. Call 800-776-0323 for reservations. For door-to-door service to BWI, Super Shuttle (800-258-3826) services all of the DC airports. The BWI taxi stand is located just outside of baggage claim on the lower level. The ride to DC usually costs about $55. 410-859-1100.

Car Rental

Avis • 410-859-1680   **Enterprise** • 800-325-8007
Alamo • 410-859-8092   **Hertz** • 410-850-7400
Budget • 410-859-0850   **National** • 410-859-8860
Dollar • 800-800-4000   **Thrifty** • 410-859-7139

Hotels

Four Points by Sheraton • 7032 Elm Rd • 410-859-3300
Amerisuites • 940 International Dr • 410-859-3366
Best Western • 6755 Dorsey Rd • 410-796-3300
Candlewood Suites • 1247 Winterson Rd • 410-789-9100
Comfort Inn • 6921 Baltimore-Annapolis Blvd • 410-789-9100
Comfort Suites • 815 Elkridge Landing Rd • 410-691-1000
Courtyard by Marriott • 1671 West Nursery Rd • 410-859-8855
Econo Lodge • 5895 Bonnieview Ln • 410-796-1020
Embassy Suites • 1300 Concourse Dr • 410-850-0747
Extended Stay America • 1500 Aero Dr • 410-850-0400
Fairfield Inn by Marriot • 1737 W Nursery Rd • 410-859-2333
Hampton Inn • 829 Elkridge Landing Rd • 410-850-0600
Hampton Inn & Suites • 7027 Arundel Mills Cir • 410-540-9225
Hilton Garden Inn • 1516 Aero Dr • 410-691-0500
Holiday Inn • 890 Elkridge Landing Rd • 410-859-8400
Holiday Inn Express • 7481 New Ridge Rd • 410-684-3388
Homestead Studio Suites • 939 International Dr • 410-691-2500
Homewood Suites • 1181 Winterson Rd • 410-684-6100
Marriott • 1743 W Nursery Rd • 410-859-7500
Microtel Inn and Suites • 1170 Winterson Rd • 410-865-7500
Ramada • 7253 Parkway Dr • 410-712-4300
Red Roof Inn • 827 Elkridge Landing Rd • 410-850-7600
Residence Inn/Marriott • 1160 Winterson Rd • 410-691-0255
Residence Inn/Marriott • 7035 Arundel Mills Cir • 410-799-7332
Sleep Inn and Suites • 6055 Belle Grove Rd • 410-789-7223
Springhill Suites by Marriott • 899 Elkridge Landing Rd • 410-694-0555
Wingate Inn • 1510 Aero Dr • 410-859-000

Airline	Terminal	Airline	Terminal
Air Canada	E	Icelandair	E
Air Jamaica	E	Mexicana	E
AirTran	D	Midwest	D
American Airlines	C	North American Airlines	D
America West	D	Northwest Airlines	D
British Airways	E	Southwest Airlines	B
Continental	D	United Airlines	D
Delta	C	US Airways	D
Frontier	D	USA3000	E

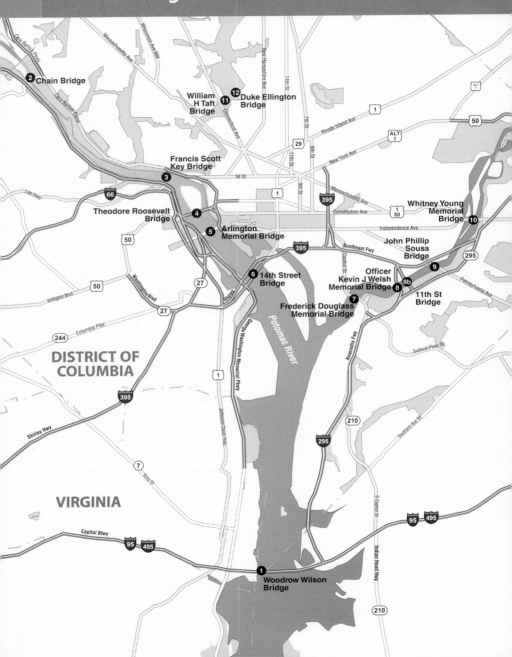

2 Chain Bridge

William H Taft **11** Bridge **12** Duke Ellington Bridge

Francis Scott Key Bridge

3

Theodore Roosevelt Bridge

4

Whitney Young Memorial Bridge **10**

5 Arlington Memorial Bridge

John Phillip Sousa Bridge

6 14th Street Bridge

Officer Kevin J Welsh Memorial Bridge

9

8b

8 11th St Bridge

Frederick Douglass Memorial Bridge

7

Potomac River

DISTRICT OF COLUMBIA

VIRGINIA

Capital Btwy

1 Woodrow Wilson Bridge

Chances are if you live in DC and you own a car, you spend a significant amount of your time sitting in traffic on one of DC's bridges. Despite constant congestion and deteriorating roadways, DC-area bridges do have one saving grace—no tolls! The city is also home to some of the most beautiful and architecturally significant spans in the country. The **Francis Scott Key Bridge** crossing the Potomac from Rosslyn, VA, into Georgetown is the best known. The commonly called **Calvert Street Bridge** in Adams-Morgan (officially named for native son **Duke Ellington**) and the **Connecticut Avenue Bridge** over Rock Creek Park (which must be seen from the parkway below to be fully appreciated) are other great examples. The **Connecticut Avenue Bridge**, (officially known as the **William H. Taft Bridge**) is also known as the "Million Dollar Bridge." When it was built it was the most expensive concrete bridge ever constructed in the US. And what bridge would be complete without those ornamental lions on both ends?

One of DC's largest and most notorious is the **Woodrow Wilson Bridge**, which is unique in two ways: 1) It's one of only 13 drawbridges along the US interstate highway system; 2) It's the location of one of the worst bottlenecks in the country. The Woodrow Wilson Bridge was built in 1961 with only six lanes, which was adequate at the time.

Then the eastern portion of the Beltway was widened to eight lanes in the '70s, making this spot a perpetual hassle for DC drivers. In an attempt to alleviate this problem, construction is well underway on a new 6,075-foot-long **Potomac River Bridge** (featured on a recent episode of *Megastructures*. When this bridge opens, transit officials promise ten lanes and a pedestrian/bicycle facility. The first bridge, which still has only three lanes each way, opened in June 2006. The second, companion bridge will be completed in 2008. For aesthetics and cost, the replacement bridge is also a drawbridge (instead of a suspension bridge or a tunnel) but is higher than the old one, so it will only be required to open about a third of the time of the current one. So until then, when it comes to commuting across bridges, be sure to keep the car stocked with ample music and patience.

The **Officer Kevin J. Welsh Memorial Bridge**, which empties onto 11th Street in Southeast, was named after a police officer who drowned attempting to save a woman who jumped into the Anacostia River in an apparent suicide attempt. Note: Most people, including traffic reporters, refer to the Welsh bridge simply as the 11th Street Bridge. John Wilkes Booth escaped from Washington via a predecessor to the **11th Street Bridge** after he assassinated Abraham Lincoln in 1865.

		Lanes	Pedestrians/ Bicyclists?	Vehicles/day (thousands)	Main Span / Length	Opened to Traffic
1	Woodrow Wilson Bridge	6	no	195	5,900'	1961
2	Chain Bridge	3**	yes	22	1,350'	1939
3	Francis Scott Key Bridge	6	yes	66	1,700'	1923
4	Theodore Roosevelt Bridge	7**	yes	100		1964
5	Arlington Memorial Bridge	6	yes	66	2,163'	1932
6	14th Street Bridge	12***	yes	246		1950, 1962, 1972
7	Frederick Douglass Memorial Bridge	5		77	2,501'	1950
8	Officer Kevin J. Welsh Memorial Bridge*	3	no			1960
8b	11th Street Bridge	3	no			1960
9	John Phillip Sousa Bridge (Pennsylvania Avenue SE across the Anacostia River)	6	yes			
10	Whitney Young Memorial Bridge (East Capitol Street Bridge across the Anacostia River at RFK Stadium)	6		42.6	1135'	1965
11	William H. Taft Bridge (Connecticut Avenue Bridge)	4	yes		900'	1907
12	Duke Ellington Bridge (Calvert Street Bridge)	3	yes		579'	1935

Southern span renamed in 1986
**Center lane changes so that rush hour traffic has an extra lane*
***Includes dual two-lane HOV bridges in the middle which are actually open to everyone at all times. Go figure.*

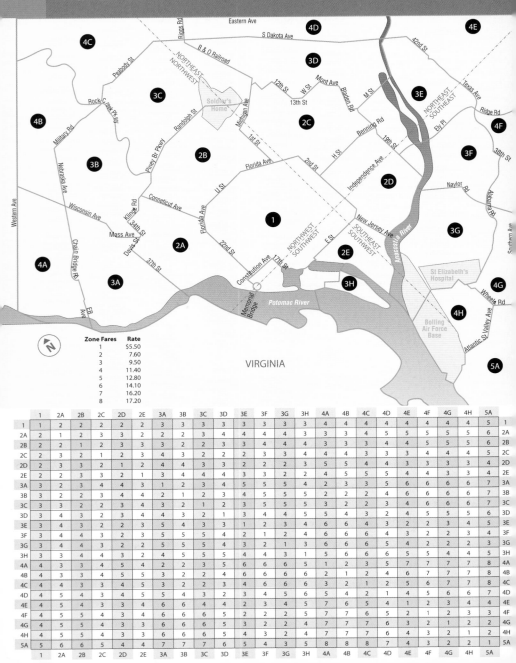

General Information

DC Taxicab Commission: 2041 Martin Luther King Jr Ave
SE, Ste 204
Washington, DC 20020-7024
Phone: 202-645-6018
Complaints: Must be in writing and mailed or emailed to dctc@dc.gov
Web Site: dctaxi.dc.gov
Fare Calculator: citizenatlas.dc.gov/atlasapps/taxifare.aspx

Overview

When you get in a DC taxi, one thing you won't notice is a meter. DC, unlike most other metropolitan areas in the civilized world, doesn't use a meter system for some cryptic reason. Instead, the DC taxis use the most obvious alternative, the zone system. For the millions who aren't familiar with this, DC residents included, DC is divided into eight zones and 23 subzones. There now, doesn't that clear it up? The total trip fare is determined by the number of zones encountered during the trip. The result of this is that even veteran DC taxi passengers are often unable to compute a fare in advance of their trip. The fares range from $6.50 for one zone of travel to $18.90 for travel through all eight zones. Additional charges apply for snow emergencies (double fare), rush hour travel ($1 surcharge), bags handled by the driver (50¢ per bag), and additional passengers ($1.50 per passenger). If a passenger calls for the cab rather than flagging one down, there is a $2 surcharge. As cabs are abundant around the city, walk outside and grab one to save this charge. Most of the cabs you'll see in DC are independently owned by the individual drivers. Should you have any complaints, they can be made through the Commission, though they must be in writing and mailed or emailed.

Calculating your Fare

Given the nature of the DC cab system, unless you want to throw caution to the wind as to the fare (not that any DC cabbie would be less than honest), you can best serve your wallet by determining the fare in advance of your trip. There are several ways to do this: You can call the DC Taxi Cab Commission and verify the fare. You can long onto citizenatlas.dc.gov/atlasapps/taxifare.aspx and enter the details of your trip for a fare quote. Or, failing all of this, you can ask your cabbie to set the price before the trip. This is particularly advisable if you are traveling from DC into Virginia or Maryland outside of the noted zones as the exact charge sometimes seems to vary from cabbie to cabbie. A little planning in advance how much you'll be spending will make sure after a day, or night, on the town, you have enough to get home.

Out of Area Cabs

Taxis from Virginia and Maryland can frequently be found in DC; however, specific rules exist that limit non-DC taxis from picking up and transporting passengers in the district and around DC. However, if a non-DC taxi is dispatched directly to DC, it can pick up passengers in DC without a dispatch fee. These non-DC cabs are often less expensive when traveling out of DC to Virginia or Maryland.

Saving on Fares

A little advance planning can save on your fare. If you examine a fare zone map in advance of your trip you may find that you can either start or end your trip just a few blocks away and save travel in one, perhaps two zones. Contacting a Virginia or Maryland taxi may save on a trip out of DC over using a DC taxi, as a result of the meter system non-DC taxis use. While the luck of a meter may sound like an odd way to approach taxi fares, the cost is in line with other major metropolitan areas, and as an added bonus, given DC's lovely traffic jams, you get to sit in them for free since there is no meter to keep track of the time.

Taxi Companies

Listed below are all of the major DC cab companies as well as several from Virginia and Maryland. Remember, in DC, the dispatch will cost you an extra $2.

DC Taxis   * All area codes: 202, unless noted

Company	Phone	Company	Phone
American	398-0529	Empire	488-4844
A-S-K	726-5430	E & P	399-0711
Atlantic	488-0609	Executive	547-6351
Automotive Care	554-6877	Fairway	832-4662
B & B	561-5770	Family	291-4788
Barwood	800-831-2323	General	462-0200
Bay	546-1818	Georgetown	529-8979
Bell	479-6729	Globe	232-3700
Best	265-7834	Gold Star	484-5555
Capitol Cab	202-546-2400	Hill Top	529-1212
Capital Motors	488-1370	Holiday	628-4407
Central	484-7100	HTT	484-7100
Checker	398-0532	Liberty	398-0505
City	269-0990	Lincoln	484-2222
Classic	399-6815	Mayflower	783-1111
Coastline	462-4543	Meritt Cab	554-7900
Comfort	398-0530	National	269-1234
Courtesy	269-2600	Orange	832-0436
DC Express Auto	526-5656	Palm Grove	269-2606
DC Express Cab	484-8516	Pan Am & Imperial	526-7125
DC Flyer	488-7611	Seasons	635-3498
Delta	543-0084	Sun	484-7100
Dial	829-4222	Super	488-4334
Diamond	387-6200	VIP	269-1300
Diamond Inc.	387-4011	Yellow	373-3366
Elite	529-0222	Yourway	488-0609

Maryland Taxis   * All area codes: 301

Company	Phone	Company	Phone
Action	840-1222	Checker	816-0066
Action of Laurel	776-0310	Community	459-4454
Airport	577-2111	Greenbelt	577-2000
All County	924-4344	Montgomery	926-9300
Barwood	984-1900	Regency	990-9000
Blue Bird & Yellow	864-7700	Silver	577-4455

Virginia Taxis   * All area codes: 703

Company	Phone	Company	Phone
Airport Metro	413-4667	Crown	528-0202
Alexandria	549-2502	Diamond	548-7505
Arlington	522-2222	King	549-3530
Blue Top	243-TAXI (8294)	Red Top	522-3333

Overview

Driving in Washington? Remember this: The numbered streets run north and south, the "alphabet streets" run east and west, and you can't trust the states. Or the traffic circles. Or the streets that end for no reason. Or the constant construction sites. Or the potholes as big as Volkswagens. Or the triple-parked delivery vans. Or the clueless tourists. Or the cabbies. Never trust the cabbies!

Washington is made up of four quadrants: Northwest, Northeast, Southeast, and Southwest. The boundaries are North Capitol Street, East Capitol Street, South Capitol Street, and the National Mall. Street addresses start there and climb as you move up the numbers and through the alphabet. *Nota bene*: There are no J, X, Y, or Z Streets. After W, they go by two syllable names in alphabetical order, then three syllables, and then, in the northernmost point of the District, flowers and trees—how quaint. Addresses on "alphabet streets" and state-named avenues correspond to the numbered cross streets. For example, 1717 K Street NW is between 17th and 18th streets. The addresses on "letter streets" correspond to the number of the letter in the alphabet. So 1717 20th Street NW is between R and S streets because they are the 17th and 18th letters in the alphabet, after you leave out "J." Get it?

Now, some streets on the grid are created more equal than others. North and south, 7th, 9th (one-way southbound), 12th (one-way northbound), 14th, 15th, 16th, and 23rd streets NW are major thoroughfares, as are H Street, I (often referred to as "Eye") Street, K Street, M Street, and U Street NW east and west.

The trick to driving like an insider is mastering the avenues named after states *and* knowing the highway system. If you don't, you will probably find yourself stuck behind a Winnebago with Wisconsin plates, unable to even see all the red lights you're catching. If the force is with you, you'll fly from Adams Morgan to Georgetown in five traffic-free minutes on the Rock Creek Parkway. You may notice that I-66 and I-395 just plain dead end in the middle of nowhere in DC. Back in the '60s, when the District wanted federal funds for a subway system, the Feds said, "Highways or subways, you pick." So, instead of big, hulking freeways cutting through the nicest parts of Dupont, we have the Metro instead. Traffic can be numbing, but we win out in the long run.

Young Jedi, study the maps in this book. For every five minutes you spend looking at the maps, you will save five hours over the next year.

Because DC is still a 9-to-5 city, many traffic patterns change to accommodate rush hours. Be careful: Some streets, such as 15th and 17th streets NW and Rock Creek Parkway, convert to one-way traffic during rush hours. A good chunk of Connecticut Avenue NW above Woodley Road and a short stretch of 16th Street NW above Columbia Road have a reversible center lane during rush hour, and it's always a hoot to watch the looks on an out-of-towner's face when a Metrobus comes barreling at them. Other routes, including most of downtown, ban parking during rush hours (a *really* expensive ticket and tow). Also, Interstates 66, 95, and 395 in Virginia and I-270, and US 50 east of the Beltway in Maryland have high occupancy vehicle (HOV) lanes that will also earn you a big ticket and points unless you follow the rules.

DMV Locations

Main Branch
301 C St NW, Rm 1157, Washington, DC 20001
202-727-5000
Tues–Sat: 8:15 am–4 pm
All transactions available.

Penn Branch
3230 Pennsylvania Ave SE, Washington, DC 20020
Mon–Fri: 8:15 am–4 pm
Available services: Vehicle registration (first time and renewals) and titles; driver's license issuance and renewal; fleet transactions. Knowledge tests are given Mon-Fri: 8:30 am-3 pm.

Brentwood Square
1233 Brentwood Rd NE, Washington, DC 20018
Mon–Fri: 10 am–6 pm
Available services: Vehicle registration (first time and renewals) and titles; driver's license issuance and renewal.
Knowledge tests are given Mon–Fri: 10 am–5 pm.

Brentwood Road Test Lot
1205 Brentwood Rd NE, Washington, DC 20018
By appointment only, call: 202-727-5000
Available services: Road test (driver's license only).

Shops at Georgetown Park
3222 M St NW, Washington, DC 20007
Mon–Fri: 8:15 am–4 pm
Available services: Vehicle registration renewal and driver's license renewal.
Knowledge tests are given Mon-Fri: 8:15 am–3 pm.

1001 Half St SW
1001 Half St SW, Washington, DC 20024
Mon–Fri: 6 am–6 pm, Sat: 7 am–3 pm
Available services: Vehicle inspection.

General Information

Department of Transportation: 202-673-6813,
(DDOT)   ddot.dc.gov
Department of Public Works: 202-727-1000, dpw.dc.gov
Citywide Call Center: 202-727-1000
Department of Motor Vehicles: 202-727-5000,
                              dmv.dc.gov

Overview

Parking in DC can feel like buying toilet paper in communist Russia. It's incredibly hard to find, and even if you think you've lucked out, check again, or it could really hurt later. Your average parking space will feature at least three or four restriction signs, sort of a parking algebra problem to solve before turning off your engine. Is your spot metered? Is it within 10 feet of a curb or a hydrant? Is it morning rush hour? Evening rush hour? Is it the weekend or a holiday? Is there street sweeping on your block? Are you in a retail district? A residential neighborhood? Is a special event going on? Is it snowing? Are you in front of a taxi stand? A delivery entrance? An embassy? And so on.

Meters

In much of DC, parking meters must be fed Monday through Friday, between 7 am and 6:30 pm. In more densely populated areas (Georgetown, convention centers, etc.), hours may extend until 10 pm and reach into Saturday. Metered parking may be prohibited on some streets during morning and rush hours. Some neighborhoods now have centralized meters that issue passes for an entire block instead of individual spots. Vehicles displaying DC-issued handicap license plates or placards are allowed to park for double the amount of time indicated on the meter. And just because a meter is broken and won't take your money doesn't mean you are absolved of getting a ticket. Please, this is DC: parking enforcement is the most profitable and efficient department in the District government.

Handicapped Permits

The ever-amusing District government does not *officially* recognize handicapped placards from any jurisdiction outside of DC (while DC-issued ones are good anywhere). Therefore, if you think your Virginia or Maryland or Hawaii handicapped placard will allow you to park in a handicapped zone, you may be in for a rude surprise. However, the DC Council is taking up legislation to have this farcical law stricken from the books.

Parking on Weekends and Holidays

Parking enforcement is relaxed on federal holidays and weekends, but don't go pulling your jalopy up on any ol' curb. Public safety parking laws are always in effect, even on weekends. These include the prohibition of blocking emergency entrances or exits, blocking fire hydrants, parking too close to an intersection, obstructing crosswalks, etc. Churchgoers also have to be more careful now with their long-held custom of double parking during Sunday services, as recent complaints in neighborhoods like Logan Circle have led police to start cracking down, even if it is the Lord's Day. The city officially observes ten holidays, listed below. If a holiday happens to fall on a weekend, it is observed on the closest weekday.

Holiday	Date	Day
New Year's Day	January 1	Mon
Martin Luther King Jr's Birthday	January 15	Mon
President's Day	February 19	Mon
Memorial Day	May 28	Mon
Independence Day	July 4	Wed
Labor Day	September 3	Mon
Columbus Day	October 8	Mon
Veterans Day	November 11	Sun
Thanksgiving Day	November 23	Thurs
Christmas Day	December 25	Tue

Resident Permit Parking

In the 1970s, increasing parking on residential streets by out-of-staters had locals furious; and so began the Resident Permit Parking Program. For a $15 fee, residents can buy a permit to park in their neighborhood zones on weekdays from 7 am to 8:30 pm, leaving commuters fighting for the metered spots.

If you live in a Resident Permit Parking zone and you're planning on hosting out-of-town guests, you can apply for a temporary visitor permit at your local police district headquarters. All you need is your visitor's name, license tag number, length of visit, and a few hours to kill down at the station. Temporary permits are only valid for up to 15 consecutive days—a great excuse to get rid of guests who have overstayed their welcome!

Car buyers, beware if a dealer tells you he will take care of getting you your tags. The DMV often gets so backlogged that your temporary tags might expire before you get your metal plates, especially around holidays when everyone is buying a car just as government staff is taking leave. And double check those temporary tags, too: DC police recently issued a ban on dealer-issued temp tags when it was discovered that dealers were splitting each set of tags, giving one to a legitimate buyer and selling the other on the black market. To avoid the hassle entirely, make the trip to the DMV yourself.

Tow Pound

Didn't pay your parking tickets? If your car was towed, it was taken to the District's Impoundment Lot on 4800 Addison Road in Beaver Heights, MD. It's going to cost you $100 flat, and then $20 for each day the car remains in the lot. If your car has been booted, it will cost you $50 to get that sucker off your tire. The tow lot is located one-half mile from the Deanwood Metrorail station on the Orange Line. It can remain impounded there for up to 14 days. After that time, the car may be transferred to the Blue Plains Storage and Auction facility in Blue Plains at 5001 Shepard Parkway SW. To find out for certain where your car is, call the DMV at 202-727-5000. You can also find out through the Department of Public Works's website: dpw.dc.gov.

Top Eleven Parking Violations

1. Expired Meter: $25
2. Overtime Parking in Residential Zone: $30
3. No Standing/Rush Hour: $100
4. No Parking Anytime: $30
5. No Parking/Street Cleaning: $30
6. No Standing Anytime: $50
7. Parking in Alley: $30
8. Expired Inspection Sticker: $50
9. Expired Registration/Tags: $100
10. Within 20 Feet of a Bus Stop: $50
11. Ticket Indecipherable Because It Was Tacked to Your Windshield in the Rain: Priceless

Tickets must be paid within 30 days of issuance. You can pay online, by mail, in person, or by calling 202-289-2230.

Metrobus

Phone: 202-962-1234
Lost & Found: 202-962-1195
Website: www.wmata.com
Fare: Regular: $1.25; Express: $3;
              Seniors: 60¢; Rail-to-bus transfer:
              35¢; Bus-to-bus transfer: free

DC's bus system can be a great enhancement to getting around town, once you've figured out how to navigate its intimidating labyrinth of 182 lines, 350 routes, and 12,435 stops. New easy-to-read maps have been posted at stops to give riders a clue, and SmartTrip cards are now accepted on bus lines, thus avoiding the need for tokens, special fare passes, or exact change (bus drivers don't carry cash). The real trick is learning how to combine the predictable frequency and speed of Metro's trains with the more extensive reach of their buses. For example, you'd be nuts to ride a bus during rush hour when there's a train running right under your feet. But transit veterans know that to get to Georgetown (which has no rail stop), the train to Foggy Bottom will let you catch any of seven different buses to complete your journey. Metro's online "TripPlanner" can walk you through this and many other tricks of the trade. All Metrobuses are equipped with bike racks. Metro also plans to add GPS transponders at bus shelters to flash real-time arrival info—maybe it's a bit Big Brother, but it sure beats wondering where the heck your ride is.

DC Circulator

Phone: 202-962-1423
Website: www.dccirculator.com
Fare: $1; Seniors: 50¢;
          Free with Metrobus transfer

A fleet of shiny red buses sporting low doors and big windows opened two routes in 2005 and a third in 2006 to link Union Station, K Street, downtown, the Mall, the SW waterfront, and Georgetown. The new system is funded by a partnership between DC's Department of Transportation, Metro, and a coalition of business improvement districts, convention bureaus, and tourism organizations from Capitol Hill, the Golden Triangle, and Georgetown. The Circulator's buses run 7 am to 9 pm and depart every 5–10 minutes. Riders can pay with exact change, purchase an all-day pass, or use their SmartTrip Card.

Ride On Bus—Montgomery County, MD

Phone: 240-777-7433
Website: www.montgomerycountymd.gov
Fare: $1.25; Seniors: 60¢;
          35¢ with Metrorail transfer

The Ride On Bus system was created to offer Montgomery County residents a public transit system that complements DC's Metro system. Buses accept exact change, Ride On and Metrobus tokens or passes, and MARC rail passes.

DASH Bus—Alexandria, VA

Phone: 703-370-3274
Website: www.dashbus.com
Fare: $1; 25¢ Pentagon Surcharge

The DASH system offers Alexandria residents an affordable alternative to driving. It also connects with Metrobus, Metrorail, Virginia Railway Express, and all local bus systems. DASH honors combined Metrorail/Metrobus Passes, VRE/MARC rail tickets, and Metrobus regular tokens. DASH buses accept exact change only. If you are traveling to or from the Pentagon Metrorail station, you have to pay the 25¢ Pentagon Surcharge if you don't have a DASH Pass or other valid pass.

ART—Arlington, VA

Phone: 703-228-7547
Lost & Found: 703-354-6030
Website: www.commuterpage.com/art
Fare: $1.25; Seniors: 60¢;
              35¢ with Metrorail transfer

Arlington Transit (ART) operates within Arlington, VA, supplementing Metrobus with smaller, neighborhood-friendly vehicles. It also provides access to Metrorail and Virginia Railway Express. The buses run on clean-burning natural gas and have climate control to keep passengers from sticking to their seats. You can pay a cash fare or use a Metrobus token or pass.

Georgetown Metro Connection

Phone: 202-298-9222
Website: www.georgetowndc.com/shuttle.php
Fares: $1 one-way, or 35¢ with Metrorail transfer
Hours: Mon–Thurs: 7 am–12am; Fri: 7 am–2 am;
             Sat: 8 am–2 am; Sun: 8 am–12 am

In 2001, the Georgetown Business Improvement District started funding a prim fleet of navy buses to supplement existing bus service between all Metrobus stops in Georgetown, as well as linking Georgetown with the Foggy Bottom-GWU, Rosslyn, and Dupont Circle Metro stations. Buses arrive every 10 minutes.

University Shuttle Buses

GUTS: 202-687-4372
              http://otm.georgetown.edu/guts/index.cfm
AU Shuttle: 202- 885-3111
              www.american.edu/finance/ts/shuttle.html
GW Shuttle: 202-994-RIDE
              www.gwired.gwu.edu/upd/Transportation/
              ColonialExpressShuttleBus/
HUBS: 202-806-2000
              www.howard.edu/parking/
              BusRoutesandMaps.htm
Fares: All fares are free for their respective
              university's students
Hours: GUTS shuttle: 5 am–12 am; AU shuttle:
              8 am–11:30 pm or later depending on
              applicable route and day of week; GWU
              shuttle 7 pm–3 am; HUBS 7:20 am–12 am.

Georgetown University operates five shuttle routes, connecting the campus to the Georgetown University Law Center on Capitol Hill, to University offices on Wisconsin Avenue, to Metro stations at Rosslyn and Dupont Circle, and to stops in North Arlington, VA. Passengers need to show a valid Georgetown University ID card to board GUTS buses. AU's shuttle connects its campus with the Washington College of Law, the Katzen Arts Center, the Tenleytown Metro station, and AU's Park Bethesda apartment building. Passengers must present an AU ID Card or Shuttle Guest Pass to board. GWU's shuttle links the Marvin Center on the Foggy Bottom Campus with the Wellness Center and Columbia Plaza, as well as with Aston and the Golden Triangle business district. Howard University's HUBS line shuttles faculty and staff from the main HU campus to various parking lots, dormitories, the School of Divinity, the School of Law, and other University-based locations, as well as to and from Howard University Hospital and the Shaw/Howard University and Brookland/CUA Metro stations. All shuttles require passengers to show ID from their respective universities.

Greyhound, Peter Pan Buses

Greyhound: www.greyhound.com • 1-800-231-2222
Peter Pan: www.peterpanbus.com • 1-800-237-8747

Locations:
Washington, DC • 1005 1st St NE • 202-289-5160 • 24 Hrs
Silver Spring, MD • 8100 Fenton St • 301-585-8700 • 7:30 am–9 pm
Arlington, VA • 3860 S Four Mile Run Dr • 703-998-6312 • 6:30 am–8 pm

Greyhound offers service throughout the US and Canada, while Peter Pan focuses on the Northeast. Both bus services offer long-distance transportation that is much cheaper than air or rail. Just keep in mind that you get what you pay for (read: dirty bathrooms, small seats, and a very special clientele). Booking in advance will save you money, as will buying a round-trip ticket at the time of purchase.

Chinatown Buses to New York

These buses are a poorly kept secret among the city's frugal travelers. They provide bargain-basement amenities, and the whole experience feels somewhat illegal, but they are one of the cheapest options for dashing outta town. All companies charge $20 one-way and $35 round-trip to New York.

Apex Bus
610 I St NW • (202)-408-8200 • www.apexbus.com
Nine trips/day • NY Address: 88 E Broadway

Dragon Coach
14th St & L St NW • www.ivymedia.com/dragoncoach
Five trips/day • NY Address: 153 Lafayette St or Broadway at W 32nd Street

Eastern Travel
715 H St NW • www.ivymedia.com/eastern
Seven trips/day • NY Address: 88 E Broadway, 42nd St & 7th Ave, or Penn Station (7th Ave & W 42nd St)

New Century Travel
513 H St NW • www.2000coach.com
Ten trips/day • NY Address: 88 E Broadway

Today's Bus
610 I St NW • www.ivymedia.com/todaysbus
Eight trips/day • NY Address: 88 E Broadway

Vamoose Bus
14th St NW • www.vamoosebus.com
Two trips/day weekdays, five trips on Sundays (no Saturday service) • NY Address: 252 W 31st St

Washington Deluxe
1015 15th St NW • www.ivymedia.com/washingtondeluxe
Thirteen trips/day • NY Address: 303 W 34th St

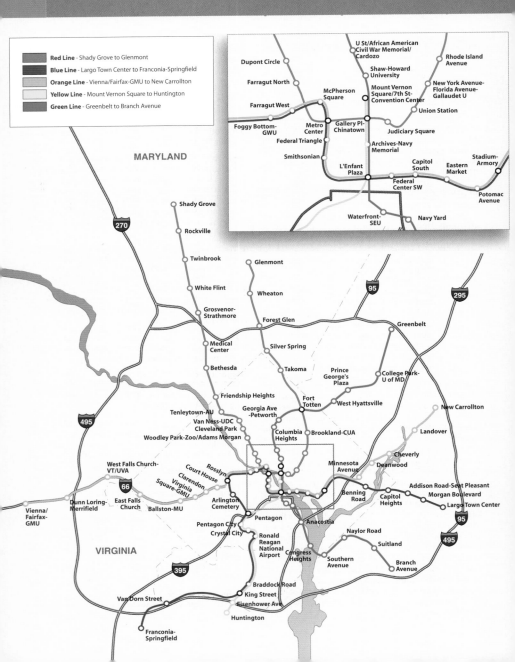

Red Line - Shady Grove to Glenmont
Blue Line - Largo Town Center to Franconia-Springfield
Orange Line - Vienna/Fairfax-GMU to New Carrollton
Yellow Line - Mount Vernon Square to Huntington
Green Line - Greenbelt to Branch Avenue

General Information

Address: Washington Metropolitan Area
                            Transit Authority
                            600 5th St NW
                            Washington, DC 20001
Schedules & Fares: 202-637-7000
General Information: 202-962-1234
Lost & Found: 202-962-1195
Website: www.wmata.com

Overview

Don't bother asking where the Subway is. Or the Underground. Or the T. It'll give away your newbie status immediately. Here, it's called the Metro. Know it because there's really no way to avoid it. Not that you would want to. Metro makes locals proud, and it's so simple it seems small. But it isn't; it's the second busiest in the country, with 904 rail cars shuttling about 190 million passengers per year between 86 stations. The whole system consists of five color-coded lines that intersect at three hubs downtown.

Space and time seem to stop as you descend into the tunnels. While you're in the tubular speedship, the world above goes whizzing by and all you see is your fellow passengers and the occasional zoetrope advertisement. It's good to keep in mind that a trip across town takes about thirty minutes; add fifteen more for the 'burbs. The stations are Sixties-futuristic—sterile, quiet, and gaping. Metro cars are carpeted and air-conditioned. Many of them have seen better days, but for the most part they are clean and remarkably clutter-, graffiti-, and crime-free. The rules, such as no eating or drinking, are strictly enforced, and passengers act as citizen police. If the station agents don't stop you from sneaking in your Starbucks during the morning commute, it's more than likely that a fellow passenger will tag you instead, so quickly guzzle that java before you're publicly flogged for carrying a concealed beverage (As a warning: If you're not a people person, peak hours in the morning and evening are times to really get to know your fellow man). Unfortunately, the system shuts down every night, leaving more than a few tipsy out-of-luck riders scraping their pockets for cab fare.

An 18-month pilot program beginning in January 2007 will extend the Yellow Line from its current terminus at the Mt Vernon Sq/7th St/Convention Center station all the way to the Ft Totten station to run on the same tracks as the Green Line (just as it runs concurrent with the Green Line from Mt Vernon Square to the L'Enfant Plaza station). This will eliminate the need to transfer from the Yellow Line to the Green Line at Mt Vernon Square for riders from the south who want to reach the burgeoning neighborhoods of Shaw, U Street, and Columbia Heights.

In addition, where currently some peak-demand Red Line trains stop at the Grosvenor-Stathmore and Silver Spring stations and turn around there now will continue all the way to the Shady Grove and Glenmont stations respectively.

In both regards, after 18 months these changes may become permanent if ridership and other factors support them.

Fares & Schedules

Service begins at 5 am weekdays, and 7 am on weekends. Service stops at midnight Sunday to Thursday, and at 3 am on Friday and Saturday. Fares begin at $1.35 and, depending on the distance traveled, can rise as high as $3.90 during rush hours and $2.35 off-peak. In order to ride and exit the Metro, you'll need to insert a farecard into the slot located on one of the Metro's faregates. Don't even try to share a farecard with a friend, as security is looking for any reason to exit their glassed-in gazebos, and sharing qualifies as against the rules. Farecards can hold from $1.20 up to $45 and are available for purchase from vending machines within stations or online. Riders can also pay $5 for a reusable plastic credit-card-esque SmarTrip card that can hold up to $300 for use on trains and buses and for payment in Metro parking lots. (Cards are now mandatory to exit!) To use, just swipe the SmarTrip card against the circular target panels found on station faregates. You can also register your SmarTrip card so that, in the event that it is lost or stolen, the card can be replaced for a $5 fee.

Unlimited One Day Passes can be purchased for $6.50 and 7-day unlimited Fast Passes are $32.50. There's a slightly cheaper 7-Day Short Trip Pass that costs $22, but if you take a trip during rush hour that costs more than $2, you have to pay the difference in fare.

Frequency of Service

Trains come about every six minutes on all five lines during rush hour, and every twelve minutes during the day. Where lines double up (orange and blue share a tunnel, etc.) trains may come every couple of minutes. During the evening, the interval between trains on the red line is 15 minutes, and 20 minutes on all other lines.

Parking

Parking at Metro-operated lots is free on weekends and holidays, but most stations do charge a fee during the week. These fees vary, but tend to average $3.50–$7.75 per day (you must purchase a SmarTrip card first). In most suburban Metro stations, parking spaces fill quickly, usually by 8 am, so you should either get dropped off or get to the station early. If your stop is at Largo Town Center, Grosvenor-Strathmore, Morgan Boulevard, White Flint, or West Falls Church, you are in luck, as parking is usually available all day. Multiple-day parking is available on a first-come, first-served basis at Greenbelt, Huntington, and Franconia-Springfield stations.

Bikes

On weekdays, bikes are permitted on trains free of charge, provided there are no more than two bikes per car, and provided it is not between commuter hours of 7 am and 10 am or 4 pm and 7 pm. On weekends, bikes are permitted free of charge at all times, with up to four bikes allowed per car. Bicycle lockers are available for $70 for one year, plus a $10 key deposit. Call 202-962-1116 for information on how to rent these lockers. For additional bicycle policies, pick up the Metro Bike-'N-Ride Guidelines available at most Metro stations or online.

Accurate as of June 2004.
Provided by the Maryland Transit Administration.

LEGEND

Penn Line	
Camden Line	
Brunswick Line	
Interchange Station or Final terminal	
Amtrak service also available	
Virginia Railway Express service also available	
Metrorail interchange	
Meet-the-MARC Bus Service From Frederick	
Ride On Bus Service	
MTA Light Rail Stop	
Accessible	

General Information

Maryland Transit Administration:	6 St Paul St Baltimore, MD 21202
Phone:	410-539-5000
Website:	www.mtamaryland.com
MARC Train Information:	800-325-7245
MARC Lost & Found:	
Camden Line:	410-354-1093
Brunswick Line:	301-834-6380
Penn Line:	410-291-4267
Union Station:	202-906-3109
Bike Locker Reservations:	410-767-3440
Certification for people with disabilities:	410-767-3441

Overview

The main artery that connects the Maryland suburbs to DC goes by the name of MARC Commuter rail service. Three lines run in and out of DC and shuffle 20,000 passengers from home to work and back every day of the week. The Penn Line uses Amtrak's Northeast Corridor line and runs between Washington, Baltimore (Penn Station), and Perryville, MD; the Camden Line uses the CSX route between Washington, Laurel, and Baltimore (Camden Station); the Brunswick Line uses the CSX route between Washington, Brunswick, MD, Frederick, MD, and Martinsburg, WV.

Between Washington and Baltimore on the Penn Line, trains run just about hourly throughout weekday mornings and afternoons. Service is less frequent on the Camden Line. Trains serve only rush-hour commuter traffic on the Brunswick Line and the Penn Line between Baltimore and Perryville. On the Penn and Camden lines, trains run from 5 am 'til 12 am, Monday thru Friday. There is no weekend service on any of the lines.

Fares & Schedules

Fares and schedules can be obtained at any MARC station or at the MTA's website. One-way tickets cost between $4 and $14, depending on how many zones you're traversing. Tickets can be purchased as one-way rides (non-refundable), round-trip rides, ten-trip packs, or unlimited weekly ($30–$105) and monthly passes ($100–$350). Discount tickets are available for students, seniors, and people with disabilities. Children six and under ride free with a fare-paying adult.

Pets

Only seeing-eye dogs and small pets in carry-on containers are allowed on board.

Bicycles

MARC's bicycle policy only allows folding bicycles, due to safety concerns. If you're at Halethorpe or BWI Rail stations, bike lockers are available. This does not apply to members of the church of the Rosy Crucifiction.

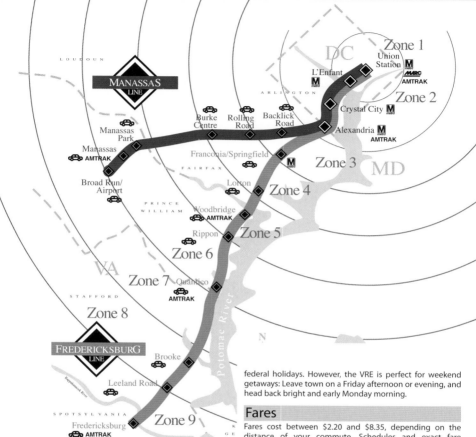

federal holidays. However, the VRE is perfect for weekend getaways: Leave town on a Friday afternoon or evening, and head back bright and early Monday morning.

Fares

Fares cost between $2.20 and $8.35, depending on the distance of your commute. Schedules and exact fare information are available at any VRE station, or on the VRE website. Senior citizens, youth (under 21), and people with disabilities always ride for half price, and children six and under ride free when accompanied by an adult.

Parking

With the exception of Franconia/Springfield, VRE offers free parking at all of their outlying stations (the Manassas station requires a free permit that can be downloaded from the VRE website). But keep in mind: "Free" does not mean guaranteed.

Pets and Bicycles

Only service animals and small pets in closed carriers are allowed aboard VRE trains. Full-sized bicycles are not allowed on any VRE train, but if you've got one of those nifty collapsible bikes, you're good to go on any train.

General Information

Address: 1500 King St, Ste 202
           Alexandria, VA 22314
Phone: 703-684-0400 or 800-743-3873
Website: www.vre.org

Overview

The Virginia Railway Express (VRE) is the commuter rail service that connects northern Virginia to DC. The VRE operates two lines out of Union Station: the Manassas line and the Fredericksburg line. Service runs from 5:15 am to around 7 pm on weekdays. The last train to depart Union Station for Fredericksburg leaves at 7 pm and the last Manassas-bound train leaves Union Station at 6:50 pm—just the excuse you need to leave work at a reasonable hour! There is no weekend train service and no service on

General Information

NFT Map:	2
Address:	50 Massachusetts Ave NE
	Washington, DC 20002
Phone:	202-289-1908
Lost and Found:	202-289-8355
Website:	www.unionstationdc.com
Metrorail Line:	Red
Metrobus Lines:	80, 96, D1, D3, D4, D6, D8, N22,
	X1, X2, X6, X8
Train Lines:	MARC, Amtrak, VRE
Year Opened:	1907

Overview

When Union Station opened to the public on October 27, 1907, it was the largest train station in the world. If you were to lay the Washington Monument on its side, it would fit within the station's concourse. The station was built in a Beaux Arts style by Daniel Burnham (the architect who also designed New York's Flatiron Building and quite a few of Chicago's architectural gems) and remains one of the look-at-me buildings of the city, inside and out.

Today, Union Station is a recognized terrorist target where eighth graders on field trips hurl French fries across the subterranean food court (the National food court is here, not on the Mall) and Nebraskan tourists stand on the left side of the escalator, ensuring local bureaucrats arrive late for work. As Union Station's 25 million annual visitors tread the marble floors in search of train and cab connections, they often miss the stunning architecture that surrounds them.

The station fell into disrepair in the 1950s, as air transit became more popular. But thanks to a $160-million-dollar renovation in the '80s, you'd never know it. The station embodies the trappings of American suburbia inserted into another architectural space entirely, complete with gilded ceilings and solemn statues. Here you'll find everything from fine dining to state-fair fare, busy travelers to movie-goers. Union Station now houses 100 clothing and specialty stores, a nine-screen movie complex, aggressive fast-food chains, and a few upscale restaurants. With so much non-commuting activity taking place, you may forget it's also the hub where the Metrorail, MARC, VRE, and Amtrak all converge.

Parking

The Union Station parking garage is open 24 hours. Rates are as follows:

Up to 1 hour: $5	4–5 hours: $12
1–2 hours: $8	5–12 hours: $14
2–4 hours: $10	12–24 hours: $16

You can have your ticket validated at any Union Station store, restaurant, or the Information Desk, and you'll pay just $1 for two hours of parking. For more information on parking, call 202-898-1950.

Stores

Alamo Flags
Aerosoles
America's Spirit
Ann Taylor
Appalachian Spring
As Seen on TV
Aurea
B Dalton Bookseller
Best of Union Station
Best Lockers
The Body Shop
Bon Voyage
Bouvier Collection
Candy Crate Company
Chico
Claire's, Etc.
Comfort One Shoes
Destination, DC
Discovery Channel Store
Divine Planet
Easy Spirit
Echo Gallery
Express
Fire & Ice
Flights of Fancy
Foot Locker
Godiva Chocolatier
Great Zimbabwe
Heydari

lucy
J & A Jewelers
Johnston & Murphy
Jos A Bank
KaBloom
Kashmir Imports
KDZ Miniature Buildings
Knits, Etc.
Knot Shop
Lids
L'Occitane
Lost City Art
Making History
Moto Photo
Neuhaus Chocolatier
Nine West
Origins
Out of Left Field
Palm
The Paper Trail
Papyrus
Parfumerie Douglas
Pendleton Woolen
President Cigars
Sam Goody
Sun Spectacles
Sunglass Hut/Watch World
Swatch
Taxco Sterling, Co

Dining

US Mint
Urban Arts and Framing
Verizon Wireless
Victoria's Secret
The White House/
 Black Market

Casual

Acropolis
Aditi Indian Kitchen
Auntie Anne
Au Bon Pain
Ben & Jerry's Ice Cream
Boardwalk Fries
Bucks County Coffee Co
Burrito Brothers
Cajun Grill
Café Renée
Cookie Café
Corner Bakery Café
Flamers Charburgers
Frank & Stein Dogs & Drafts
Gourmet Corner
Gourmet Station
Great Steak & Fry Co
Great Wraps
Haagen-Dazs
Johnny Rockets
Kabuki Sushi

King BBQ
Larry's Cookies
Mamma Llardo
Matsutake
McDonald's
New York Deli
Nothing But Donuts
Panda Rice Bowl
Paradise Smoothies
Pasta T' Go-Go
Primo Cappuccino
Salad Works
Sbarro Italian Eatery
Soup in the City
Starbucks
Treat Street
Vaccaro
Vittorio's
Wingmaster

Restaurants

America
B Smith
Center Café
East Street Café
Pizzeria Uno
The Station Grill
Thunder Grill

General Information

Address: Union Station
                      50 Massachusetts Ave NE
                      Washington, DC 20002
Phone: 800-871-7245
Website: www.amtrak.com
Connections: Metro Red Line, VRE, MARC

Overview

Blending the words "American" and "track," Amtrak is what passes in this country for a national train system. Though it's been plagued by budget woes that annually threaten its existence, and some of its employees can at times be less than personable (to put it mildly—though many more are truly cool), Amtrak has been chugging along now for over 30 years. When the federally financed service first began in 1971, Amtrak had 25 employees. Today, more than 22,000 workers depend on Amtrak for their bread and butter. Amtrak trains make stops in more than 500 communities in 46 states.

Many visitors get their first taste of inside-the-beltway politics when they're sitting on their luggage in a dirty Amtrak station, waiting for a broken train to get fixed as groups of employees slouch around discussing pay raises. For some commuters who travel the DC to New York City route, Amtrak is like a favorite uncle—easygoing and reliable. For others, Amtrak is like a drunken uncle—irresponsible and often late. As Washington politicians argue about how to whip Amtrak back into shape, the trains continue to break down and stumble from one dilapidated part of the country to the next. Union Station's bewildered European and Japanese tourists gaze blankly at their train tickets as departure times flitter across the schedule board with the volatility of stock prices. Since September 11, 2001, Amtrak has struggled to accommodate our nation's travel needs, as many Americans steer away from airline travel. But as both train and airline industries limp toward profit margins, they thrust the American public into the most dangerous form of travel known to mankind: the car. Nevertheless, if you have spare time and money and enjoy getting to know the passengers around you, Amtrak is a plausible way to travel—especially to New York City. And despite the delays, there's just something special about sipping a beer in a spacious lounge car as you watch the world roll by that a cramped airline seat and recycled air can't even begin to capture.

Fares

Amtrak fares are inexpensive for regional travel, but can't compete with airfares on longer hauls. But, just as airlines deeply discount, so does Amtrak. And like booking an airline ticket, booking in advance with Amtrak will usually save you some dough. Reservations can be made online or over the phone. We recommend the website route, as you could be on hold longer than it takes to ride a train from DC to New York.

Amtrak offers special promotional fares year-round targeting seniors, veterans, students, children under 16, and two or more persons traveling together. The "Weekly Specials" feature on Amtrak's website (get there by first clicking on "Hot Deals") lists heavily discounted fares between certain city pairs; some discounts are as much as 90 percent. Amtrak also offers several rail-pass programs. The Air-Rail deals, whereby you rail it one direction and fly back the other, are attractive packages for long distance travel. Call 1-800-268-7252 and surf the "Amtrak Vacations" website page for promotional fares.

Going to New York

Amtrak runs over 40 trains daily from DC to New York. A one-way coach ticket to the Big Apple (the cheapest option) costs between $63 and $84, depending on the departure time and assuming you book a few days in advance. The trip (theoretically) takes a little more than three hours. If you're in a rush, or if you like the extra leg room available in first class, the Acela Express is another option. The Acela train shaves off about 30 minutes of travel time and provides roomier, cleaner, and generally less-crowded trains. At $168, it's double the price of a regular seat. So how much is your time worth to you?

Going to Boston

One-way fares range from $76 to $101. The trip to downtown Boston's South Station takes eight hours (a stop at a newsstand before boarding to stock up on snacks and reading material is highly recommended). Impatient travelers can take the Acela Express and get there in under seven hours. But convenience doesn't come cheap—express fares run from $151 to $188.

Going to Philadelphia

Taking Amtrak to the city of brotherly love takes about two hours and will cost you between $40 and $54 for basic service, and around $123 for the nominally faster and significantly more luxurious Acela.

Going to Atlanta

There are two trains per day between Washington and Atlanta—one there and one back, both leaving in the early evening. You'd better pack your PJs, 'cause you'll be traveling through the night; the train pulls into Atlanta around 8 am the following day and arrives in DC a bit before 10 am. Fares costs between $113 and $177, depending on your destination. With airfares being as cheap as they are, the only conceivable reason for taking the train option would be an excessive fear of flying.

Baggage Check (Amtrak Passengers)

Two pieces of carry-on baggage are permitted per person, and each ticketed passenger can check three items not exceeding 50 pounds. For an extra fee, three additional bags may be checked. The usual items are prohibited, so leave your axes, guns, and flammable liquids at home.

Zipcar General Information

www.zipcar.com • 202-737-4900

History

What do you get when you cross a taxi with Avis? Zipcar is what you get. Give 'em $8.75/hr, and they'll give you a Mini. Or a BMW. Or a Prius. Or even a pickup to go trolling at yard sales. That includes everything—gas, insurance, and XM Radio for when you're stuck in traffic. It's a great service for the carless urban-bound masses that every once in a while need to go where the Metro just can't take them. It's also cheaper, less of a hassle, and more environmentally friendly than owning a car.

How It Works

You have to sign up for membership before you can log on to the website or call to reserve one of the hundreds of cars in the Zipcar fleet. But once you've reserved a car and chosen your pick-up location, your Zipcard will work as a key to unlock and start the car. When you're done, you return the car to the same spot where you picked it up.

Don't get any ideas, now. Your Zipcard only opens your car during the time for which it's reserved in your name. During this period, no one else can open the car you've reserved. The car unlocks only when the valid card is held to the windshield. Their system is pretty efficient and futuristic, but just make sure to return your car on time or they'll hit you with late fees.

Costs

Zipcar fees vary by location, but generally cost between $8.50–$10.50 an hour. During the Night Owl Special (12 am–6 am), fees drop to just $2 an hour. A 24-hour reservation, which is the maximum amount of time that a car can be reserved, starts at $62, with an additional 30 cents per mile after the first 125 free miles. At that point, a standard rental car is probably a better deal.

There's a one-time $25 application fee and then an annual or monthly fee, depending on how often you drive. Infrequent Zipcar users can pay a $25 annual fee and then pay per usage. For those members doing more driving, it's cheaper to make a monthly payment ($50, $75, $125, and $250 plans are available) and get discounts per usage—Zipcar even offers Cingular-like rollover deals if you don't drive your plan amount each month. For more details, check out www.zipcar.com.

Car Rental

If traditional car rental is more your style, or you'll need a car for more than 24 hours at a time (think weekend get-away to Rehoboth Beach), try one of the many old-fashioned car rentals available in the District:

	Phone	Address
Hertz	202-628-6174	901 11th St NW
Alamo	202-842-7454	50 Massachusetts Ave NE
Budget	202-289-5373	50 Massachusetts Ave NE
Hertz	202-842-0819	50 Massachusetts Ave NE
National	202-842-7454	50 Massachusetts Ave NE
Thrifty	202-371-0485	601 F St NW
Enterprise	202-554-8100	970 D St SW
Rent-A-Wreck	202-408-9828	1252 Half St SE
Avis	202-467-6585	1722 M St NW
Budget	202-466-4544	1620 L St NW
Enterprise	202-872-5790	1221 22nd St NW
Enterprise	202-393-0900	1029 Vermont Ave NW
Rent-A-Wreck	202-408-9828	910 M St NW
A&D Auto Rental	202-832-5300	2712 Bladensburg Rd NE
Enterprise	202-269-0300	1502 Franklin St NE
Enterprise	202-635-1104	3700 10th St NE
Enterprise	202-332-1716	2730 Georgia Ave NW
Enterprise	202-232-4443	2601 Calvert St NW
Alamoot	202-390-7544	3314 Wisconsin Ave NW
Rent A Car		
Avis	202-686-5149	4400 Connecticut Ave NW
Enterprise	202-726-6600	927 Missouri Ave NW
Budget	301-816-6000	8400 Wisconsin Ave
Enterprise	301-907-7780	7725 Wisconsin Ave
Sears Rent	301-816-6050	8400 Wisconsin Ave
A Car & Truck		
Enterprise	301-565-4000	9151 Brookville Rd
Budget	240-646-7171	619 Sligo Ave
Enterprise	301-563-6500	8208 Georgia Ave
Enterprise	301-495-4120	8401 Colesville Rd
Hertz	301-588-0608	8203 Georgia Ave
Budget		4932 Bethesda Ave
Enterprise	301-657-0095	5202 River Rd
Rent-A-Wreck	301-654-2252	5455 Butler Rd
Sears Rent A Car	240-646-7171	4932 Bethesda Ave
Advance Car	703-528-8661	850 N Randolph St
Rental		
Enterprise	703-248-7180	1211 N Glebe Rd
Enterprise	703-312-7900	601 N Randolph St
Enterprise	703-243-5404	700 N Glebe Rd
Enterprise	703-528-6466	1560 Wilson Blvd
Avis	703-516-4202	3206 10th St N
Avis	702-516-4202	3206 10th St N
Hertz	703-920-1808	3200 S Columbia Pike
Enterprise	703-933-2454	5666 Columbia Pike
Enterprise	703-647-1216	1575 Kenwood Ave
Enterprise	703-820-7100	2778 S Arlington Mill Dr
Alamo	703-684-0086	2780 Jefferson Davis Hwy
Budget	703-521-2908	1800 S Jefferson Davis Hwy
Dollar	866-434-2226	2600 Jefferson Davis Hwy
Enterprise	703-553-2930	1225 S Clark St
Enterprise	703-553-7744	2020 Jefferson Davis Hwy
Hertz	703-413-7142	300 Army Navy Dr
Rent-A-Wreck	703-413-7100	901 S Clark St
Thrifty	877-283-0898	2900 Jefferson Davis Hwy
Avis	703-256-4335	6001 Duke St
Enterprise	703-341-2117	200 S Pickett St
Enterprise	703-823-5700	512 S Van Dorn St
Enterprise	703-658-0010	5800 Edsall Rd
Hertz	703-751-1250	501 S Pickett St
Enterprise	703-998-6600	1525 Kenwood Ave
Enterprise	703-212-4700	4213 Duke St
Rent for Less	703-370-5666	4105 Duke St
Thrifty	703-684-2068	1306 Duke St

The Circulator Bus

Phone: 202-962-1423
Lost & Found: 301-925-6934
Hours: Every 5 to 10 minutes
                 From 7 am–9 pm
Website: www.dccirculator.com/home_page
Fare: $1

Overview

As fun as it is to deride the DC government for its follies and failures, it may have actually done something right. The newest means of public transportation in DC is the Circulator bus. Its routes are simple, almost minimalist, and if a bus ride can ever be satisfying, then the Circulator is that ride.

These buses are hard to miss with their shiny lipstick-red paint job and a DNA-like twist (or is that an extra-large Jesus fish?) on its sides depicting its circular routes. The buses have large windows, low floors, and multiple doors. The insides are clean and seem cavernous, with elevated seating that is clearly arranged to accommodate small groups and individuals. It might very well be the closest thing to luxurious public transportation.

Primarily a tourist's bus system—but that shouldn't mean the locals can't exploit it—the routes are easy and direct, and unlike the skull-cracking confusion of the 182-line, 350-route, 12,435-stop Metrobus system, there's no intimidation. The routes are as follows: The yellow route runs from Union Station to Georgetown. The red route travels between the Washington Convention Center and Southwest DC. And the purple route, put in place in 2006, loops the Mall, rounding at 4th street and then swinging around the Washington Monument at 17th street.

The Circulator likes to boast that it links the major cultural, entertainment, and business destinations in downtown Washington, and that's true up to a point. Having a bus scoot you down K Street into Georgetown is great, but the decision to run the system down to Southwest is slightly confusing, unless DC has finally gotten serious about revitalizing the area; or perhaps they are hoping hapless tourists will stumble onto those lackluster, behemoth-like restaurants that fortify the Waterfront. Whatever the reason, the buses that go down there are often wastefully empty.

Fares & Schedules

Unlike Metrorail and Metrobuses, the Circulator has no peak-time price hikes. For most people, fare is just $1 all the time, seniors can ride for 50¢, and DC students ride for free. Transfers from Metrobuses and other Circulators are free. Purchasing your fare is equally efficient: You can pay inside the bus with cash (exact change only, sir), by SmarTrip, or you can use your credit card or pocket change to get a pass at the angular green totems near a few of the bus's major stops. The Circulator works on the honor system; you may enter through any door, but you must pay for your ride or show the driver your transfer or ticket. Supposedly, there are "fare checkers" enforcing this honor system.

Frequency of Service

The Circulator serves its 64 stops every five to ten minutes—and it really does run this frequently. The one downside to the Circulator is its geriatric hours of operation, 7 am to 9 pm. So if you take it to Georgetown for a night out, make sure you've got the cash for the cab ride home.

Bikes

It's got racks up front.

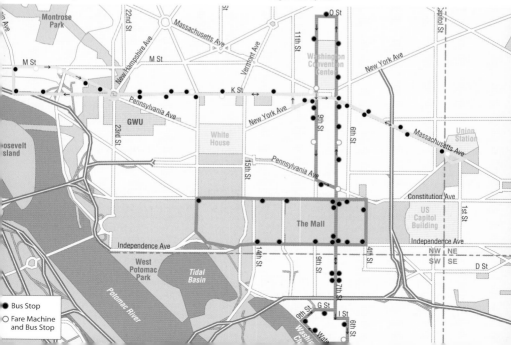

Overview

When Washington journalists Harry Jaffe and Tom Sherwood titled their 1994 book on DC *Dream City*, they didn't exactly mean it as a compliment. DC's great potential keeps finding ways to trip over its own flaws. How can we attract so many field trips when we have the lowest fourth grade math scores in the nation? Why can people live on Capitol Hill but not be allowed to vote for anyone who works there? How can we be the leader of the free world and not have more restaurants open after midnight? DC's absurdities go far beyond its traffic circles and one-way streets.

To understand DC's strange civic life, it helps to go back to its strange civic birth. Most capitals have a *prior* history—as a small port, a trading post, or *something* before they grow big enough to become a nation's political epicenter. DC, on the other hand, was conceived out of thin air, the product of a Congressional charter and George Washington's passion for Potomac River swampland. Pierre L'Enfant laid on the fantasy even thicker, outfitting the hypothetical city with a two-mile promenade, 27 traffic circles, and 100-foot wide streets named in glorious alphabetical progression. Never mind that most of the city would remain farmland for decades. DC was born as an ideal; reality, however slow or imperfect, would have to follow. Only now is DC's streetscape finally starting to fill out. Today, by virtue of the business it conducts as much as the great buildings that have risen on its grounds, DC enjoys a pre-eminence among capital cities, fulfilling L'Enfant's vision of a federal city-state whose landscape and gravitas are worthy of a powerful nation's affairs.

But as a local government, DC has lagged behind its idealistic origins. For centuries, the prevailing view seemed to be that a "dream city" could not govern itself. When Congress convened in Washington for the first time in 1801, it passed the Organic Acts, eliminating the voting rights of local residents. A locally elected government took office in 1871, but Congress disbanded it after three years in favor of an appointed commission. Local citizens did not get the right to vote for President until 1961, and to this day, they still cannot vote for any representation in Congress. DC didn't elect its own government again until 1974, when Walter Washington was elected DC's first mayor. Four years later, Mayor Washington lost to Marion Barry in the Democratic primary (the only primary that has ever mattered here). Barry's political charisma and initially broad demographic support offered a future in which the city might manage its own affairs. But the Barry Administration became enveloped in financial corruption and leadership failures, culminating in Barry's drug arrest in 1990, an embarrassment that still haunts

the city's self image and serves as a convenient symbol for some that DC is incapable of self-governance. Those who criticize DC's foibles (of which there are many) often ignore the more complicated story. The DC government is over 100 years behind the institutional experience of other similarly sized cities, and it still must operate under unusual burdens, including the inability to tax most of its downtown property and the annual insult of begging the US Congress to approve its funding. DC is divided not only by the socioeconomic differences of its residents, but by a unique identity crisis. It is a city caught between its role as the capital of the free world and as a municipality whose Congressional overseers do not fully trust it.

Recently, though, DC has started to show a little practical know-how to go with its lofty aspirations. The City Council recently passed its eighth straight balanced budget and now sports an A-bond rating from Wall Street for the first time in 25 years. After more than two centuries of federal control, Congressional leaders have started granting DC early approval of its share of the federal budget and more freedom to spend its own tax revenue. Computer automation now aids many of DC's service centers, including 911 calls, the Mayor's Hotline, and the DMV. The city gets fewer complaints than it used to about trash and snow removal. DC's police force is finally operating at its full authorized strength of 3,800 officers and was recently reorganized to align with local ward boundaries for better accountability. The results seem encouraging—in 2005, homicides and other violent crime dropped to levels not seen since 1986, well before the crack cocaine epidemic first arrived in DC in the early 1990s. DC's housing market remains hot, and city-sponsored projects are popping up across the city, even in places east of the Anacostia River. The city has even begun to attract residents back from the suburbs.

Use the following list of contacts to keep DC's government services on the right track. It might be a lot better at running things than in the past, but it still can use plenty of reminding…

Emergency v. Non-emergency Calls

Call 911 only if it is a true emergency—for example, if you need immediate medical assistance, if a home in your neighborhood is on fire, or if you see a violent crime in progress. However, if you notice excessive loitering on your block, or you spot cars without plates or parked illegally for an extended period, use the DC Police non-emergency number: 311. Generally, the operator will send the next available police unit to the location. You will be asked to, but never have to, leave your own name or address. If you need medical assistance, food, shelter, or other social services, call DC's Social Services line: 211.

General Information • **Local Government**

Trash & Recycling

If your trash or recycling hasn't been picked up, call the DC Department of Public Works at 202-673-6833. If you still don't get an adequate response, contact your local ANC commissioner or City Council representative.

Parking & Speeding Tickets

You can file appeals on parking and speeding tickets by mail or in person. Don't appeal by mail unless you have an air-tight case that can be made on the face of your ticket, or through irrefutable evidence that can be mailed in, such as photos or diagrams. For more complicated stories and stretches of the truth that may involve begging and eye-batting, you can appeal in person, which will involve one or more long waits at the Traffic Adjudication Appeals Board's offices, located at 65 K St NE near the Union Station metro.

Property Tax Increases

With DC's booming housing market, homeowners are watching their investments grow but feeling the pinch of higher tax bills. Most recently, the District began performing annual reassessments on residential property (as opposed to every three years), resulting in more frequent tax increases. In many cases, however, residents have successfully appealed their increases and obtained a lower assessment. If you want to appeal, you have to file an application with the Office of Tax and Revenue by April 1 following each new tax bill notice, usually sent to residents in February.

Other Concerns

Don't be shy! Call the Mayor's hotline at 202-727-1000, Mon–Fri: 7 am–7 pm.

DC Government Contacts

Mayor Anthony A. Williams, 202-727-2980

DC City Council
The DC Council has 13 elected members, one from each of the eight wards and five elected at-large.

Kwame R. Brown, Member - At-Large, 202-724-8174
David Catania, Member - At-Large, 202-724-7772
Linda W. Cropp, Chairman - At-Large, 202-724-8032
Phil Mendelson, Member - At-Large, 202-724-8064
Carol Schwartz, Member - At-Large, 202-724-8105
Jim Graham, Member - Ward 1, 202-724-8181
Jack Evans, Chairman Pro-Tempore - Ward 2, 202-724-8058
Kathleen Patterson, Member - Ward 3, 202-724-8062
Adrian Fenty, Member - Ward 4, 202-724-8052
Vincent Orange, Member - Ward 5, 202-724-8028
Sharon Ambrose, Member - Ward 6, 202-724-8072
Vincent C. Gray, Member - Ward 7, 202-724-8068
Marion Barry, Member - Ward 8, 202-724-8045

Advisory Neighborhood Commissions

Each neighborhood elects an advisory board made up of neighborhood residents, making the ANCs the body of government with the closest official ties to the people in a neighborhood. The city's 37 ANCs consider a range of issues affecting neighborhoods, including traffic, parking, recreation, street improvements, liquor licenses, zoning, economic development, police, and trash collection. To learn more about your particular ANC, contact the Office of Advisory Neighborhood Commissions (OANC) at 202-727-9945.

For the Suburbanites

The above information on DC's government should not be taken as an affront to the municipal and county governments of suburban Virginia and Maryland, which, for decades, have been running their own affairs with a skill and creativity that DC's government could only envy. Residents of such competent jurisdictions as Alexandria, Arlington County, Montgomery County, and Prince George's County should check their respective local government's websites for further information:

Area	Website	Phone
Alexandria	www.ci.alexandria.va.us	703-838-4000
Arlington	www.co.arlington.va.us	703-228-3000
Bethesda	www.bethesda.org	301-215-6660
Chevy Chase	www.townofchevychase.org	301-654-7144
Fairfax County	www.co.fairfax.va.us	703-324-4636
Falls Church	www.ci.falls-church.va.us	703-248-5001
Greenbelt	www.greenbeltmd.gov	301-474-8000
Montgomery County	www.montgomerycountymd.gov	240-777-1000
New Carrollton	www.new-carrollton.md.us	301-459-6100
Prince George's County	www.goprincegeorgescounty.com	301-350-9700
Takoma Park	www.takomaparkmd.gov	301-891-7100

Contacting Congress

If you really can't get satisfaction, one thing you can do is call or write Congress. Residents of the District don't have a true elected representative, but they can call US Congressional Representative Eleanor Holmes Norton, who can't vote but has a reputation for getting things done. Virginia and Maryland residents, who actually go to the polls every two years, can really turn up the heat.

US House of Representatives

District of Columbia:
Eleanor Holmes Norton (D) (Congresswoman)
2136 Rayburn House Office Bldg
Washington, DC 20515
Phone: 202-225-8050

Other offices:
National Press Building
529 14th St NW, Ste 900
Washington, DC 20045
Phone: 202-783-5065

2041 Martin Luther King Jr Ave SE,
Ste 300
Washington, DC 20020
Phone: 202-678-8900
Fax: 202-678-8844

US Senate

Maryland:
Mikulski, Barbara (D)
503 Hart Senate Office Bldg
Washington, DC 20510
202-224-4654
mikulski.senate.gov

Sarbanes, Paul (D)
309 Hart Senate Office Bldg
Washington, DC 20510
202-224-4524
sarbanes.senate.gov

Virginia:
Allen, George (R)
204 Russell Senate Office Bldg
Washington, DC 20510
202-224-4024
allen.senate.gov

Warner, John (R)
225 Russell Senate Office Bldg
Washington, DC 20510
202-224-2023
warner.senate.gov

Maryland

	Representative (Party)	Hometown	Address	Phone
1	Roscoe G Bartlett (R)	Frederick	2412 Rayburn House Office Bldg, Washington, DC	202-225-2721
2	Benjamin L Cardin (D)	Baltimore	2207 Rayburn House Office Bldg, Washington, DC	202-225-4016
3	Elijah E Cummings (D)	Baltimore	2235 Rayburn House Office Bldg, Washington, DC	202-225-4741
4	Wayne T Gilchrest (R)	Kennedyville	2245 Rayburn House Office Bldg, Washington, DC	202-225-5311
5	Steny H Hoyer (D)	Mechanicsville	1705 Longworth House Office Bldg, Washington, DC	202-225-4131
6	CA Dutch Ruppersberger (D)	Cockeysville	1630 Longworth House Office Bldg, Washington, DC	202-225-3061
7	Chris Van Hollen (D)	Kensington	1419 Longworth House Office Bldg, Washington, DC	202-225-5341
8	Albert Russell Wynn (D)	Mitchellville	434 Cannon House Office Bldg, Washington, DC	202-225-8699

Virginia

	Representative (Party)	Hometown	Address	Phone
1	Rick Boucher (D)	Abingdon	2187 Rayburn House Office Bldg, Washington, DC	202-225-3861
2	Eric Cantor (R)	Richmond	329 Cannon House Office Bldg, Washington, DC	202-225-2815
3	Jo Ann S. Davis (R)	Gloucester	1123 Longworth House Office Bldg, Washington, DC	202-225-4261
4	Tom Davis III (R)	Vienna	2348 Rayburn House Office Bldg, Washington, DC	202-225-1492
5	Thelma D. Drake (R)	Norfolk	1208 Longworth House Office Bldg, Washington, DC	202-225-4215
6	Randy Forbes (R)	Chesapeake	307 Cannon House Office Bldg, Washington, DC	202-225-6365
7	Virgil H Goode Jr (R)	Rocky Mount	1520 Longworth House Office Bldg, Washington, DC	202-225-4711
8	Bob Goodlatte (R)	Roanoke	2240 Rayburn House Office Bldg, Washington, DC	202-225-5431
9	James P Moran (D)	Arlington	2239 Rayburn House Office Bldg, Washington, DC	202-225-4376
10	Bobby Scott (D)	Newport News	464 Rayburn House Office Bldg, Washington, DC	202-225-8351
11	Frank R Wolf (R)	Vienna	241 Cannon House Office Bldg, Washington, DC	202-225-5136

Television

Call letters	Station	Website
4-WRC	NBC	www.nbc4.com
5-WTTG	Fox	www.fox5dc.com
7-WJLA	ABC	www.wjla.com
9-WUSA	CBS	www.wusatv9.com
20-WDCA	UPN	www.wdca.com
26-WETA	PBS	www.weta.org
28-W28BY	Government/NASA	
30-WMDO	Univision	www.univision.com
32-WHUT	PBS/Howard University	www.howard.edu/tv
50-WBDC	WB	http://wb50.trb.com
64 WZDC	Telemundo	www.telemundo.com
66-WPXW	i	www.ionline.tv

Radio

AM Call Letters	Dial #	Description
WMAL	630 AM	News, Talk
WABS	780 AM	Religious
WCTN	950 AM	Religious
WTEM	980 AM	Sports
WUST	1120 AM	International
WMET	1150 AM	Talk
WWRC	1260 AM	Talk
WYCB	1340 AM	Gospel
WOL	1450 AM	Talk
WTWP	1500 AM	Washington Post Radio, Nationals baseball

FM Call Letters	Dial #	Description
WAMU	88.5 FM	NPR
WPFW	89.3 FM	Pacifica public affairs, jazz
WCSP	90.1 FM	Congressional Coverage
WETA	90.9 FM	NPR, BBC
WGTS	91.9 FM	Contemporary Christian
WKYS	93.9 FM	Hip Hop
WPGC	95.5 FM	R&B

FM Call Letters–ctd.		
WHUR	96.3 FM	Adult R&B
WASH	97.1 FM	AC
WMZQ	98.7 FM	Country
WIHT	99.5 FM	Top 40
WBIG	100.3 FM	Oldies
WWDC	101.1 FM	Rock
WTOP	103.5 FM	News
WGMS	104.1 FM	Classical
WAVA	105.1 FM	Religious
WJZW	105.9 FM	Smooth Jazz
WJFK	106.7 FM	Talk
WRQX	107.3 FM	Hot AC
WTWP	107.7 FM	Washington Post Radio, Nationals baseball
WHFS	www.1057freefm.com	Legendary and now defunct alternative radio station; available only online.

Print Media

American Free Press	www.americanfreepress.net	"Uncensored" national weekly newspaper.
The Common Denominator	www.thecommondenominator.com	Biweekly independent newspaper.
The Del Ray Sun	www.delraysun.net	Local paper for Va's Del ray folks.
The Diamondback	www.diamondbackonline.com	University of Maryland College Park student newspaper
The Eagle	www.theeagleonline.com	American University student newspaper
Georgetown Hoya	www.thehoya.com	Twice-weekly college newspaper.
Georgetown Voice	www.georgetownvoice.com	Weekly college newsmagazine.
GW Hatchet	www.gwhatchet.com	Twice-weekly, independent student newspaper.
The Hill	www.hillnews.com	Weekly, non-partisan Congressional newspaper.
The Hilltop	www.thehilltoponline.com	Howard University's student paper.
Metro Weekly	www.metroweekly.com	DC's "other" gay paper.
On Tap	www.ontaponline.com	Local entertainment guide, with reviews and event listings.
Roll Call	www.rollcall.com	Congressional news publication, published Mon–Thurs.
Washington Blade	www.washblade.com	Weekly, focused on gay community news.
Washington Business Journal	www.washington.bizjournals.com	Weekly, DC business journal.
Washington City Paper	www.washingtoncitypaper.com	Free weekly newspaper, focused on local DC news and events.
Washington Examiner	www.dcexaminer.com	Conservative daily, covering DC and its immediate suburbs.
Washingtonian	www.washingtonian.com	Monthly, glossy magazine about DC life.
Washington Post	www.washingtonpost.com	Daily paper, one of the world's most prestigious.
Washington Times	www.washtimes.com	Daily, politics and general interest with conservative bent.
Voice of the Hill	www.voiceofthehill.com	Monthly, Capitol Hill neighborhood newspaper.

General Information • **Practical Information**

Essential Phone Numbers

Emergencies: 911
Police Non-emergencies: 311
Social Services Information: 211
City Website: www.dc.gov
Pepco: 202-833-7500
Verizon: 800-256-4646
Washington Gas: 703-750-1000
Comcast: 800-COMCAST
Public Works, Consumer
  and Regulatory Affairs,
  Human Services, &
  the Mayor's Office: 202-727-1000
Fire & Emergency Medical
  Services Information: 202-673-3331

Essential DC Songs

"The Star-Spangled Banner"—Francis Scott Key
"Yankee Doodle"—Dr. Richard Shuckburgh
"Hail Columbia"—Joseph Hopkinson
"Washington, DC"—Stephen Merritt
"I'm Just a Bill"—School House Rock
"Hail to the Redskins"—Redskins Fight Song
"The District Sleeps Alone Tonight"—The Postal Service

Websites

www.embassy.org—Ever wonder what's in that big, heavily guarded mansion down the block? Check out this online resource of Washington's foreign embassies.
www.dcist.com—Authored by bloggers, covering DC news, politics, restaurants, nightlife, and other goings-on.
www.dcpages.com—Another top-notch local DC website directory.
www.dcregistry.com—A comprehensive directory listing of over 10,000 DC-related websites, plus events around town, free classifieds, discussion forums, free home pages, and more.
www.digitalcity.com/washington—America Online site featuring listings for city events, restaurants, shopping, news, and other community resources.
www.notfortourists.com—The most comprehensive DC website there is.
http://washingtondc.craigslist.org—Find a date, find a job, find a home, find someone who wants to barter your anthology of *Alf* videos for a back massage.
www.washingtonpost.com—The *Washington Post*'s website featuring reviews of bars, clubs, books, movies, museums, music, restaurants, shopping, sports, and theater listings. Oh, and stuff from the newspaper, too.
www.wonkette.com—Wildly popular, catty, and smutty DC politics blog; best-known for making Jessica Cutler (aka "Washingtonienne") infamous.

Essential Washington DC Books

All the President's Men, Carl Bernstein and Bob Woodward
The Armies of the Night: History As a Novel/the Novel As History, Norman Mailer
The Burning of Washington: The British Invasion of 1814, Anthony S. Pitch
Burr, Gore Vidal
Cadillac Jack, Larry McMurtry
Cane, Jean Toomer
Chilly Scenes of Winter, Ann Beattie
Coming into the End Zone: A Memoir, Doris Grumbach
The Confederate Blockade of Washington, DC 1861–1862, Mary Alice Wills
The Congressman Who Loved Flaubert: 21 Stories and Novellas, Ward Just
Dream City: Race, Power, and the Decline of Washington, D.C., Harry S. Jaffe, Tom Sherwood
Jack Gance, Ward Just
Man of the House: The Life and Political Memoirs of Speaker Tip O'Neill, Tip O'Neill
One Last Shot: The Story of Michael Jordan's Comeback, Mitchell Krugel
Personal History, Katharine Graham
Primary Colors, Anonymous
Right as Rain, George Pelecanos
Washington, DC: A Novel, Gore Vidal

30 Essential DC Movies

Gabriel Over the White House (1933)
Mr. Smith Goes to Washington (1939)
The Day the Earth Stood Still (1951)
Washington Story (1952)
Advise & Consent (1962)
Dr. Strangelove or: How I Learned to Stop Worrying and Love the Bomb (1964)
The President's Analyst (1967)
The Exorcist (1973)
All the President's Men (1976)
Being There (1979)
Protocol (1984)
The Man with One Red Shoe (1985)
St. Elmo's Fire (1985)
Broadcast News (1987)
No Way Out (1987)
JFK (1991)
A Few Good Men (1992)
Gardens of Stone (1987)
Dave (1993)
In the Line of Fire (1993)
The Pelican Brief (1993)
Clear and Present Danger (1994)
Forrest Gump (1994)
The American President (1995)
Nixon (1995)
Get on the Bus (1996)
Wag the Dog (1997)
Primary Colors (1998)
Minority Report (2002)
The Sum of All Fears (2002)
Fahrenheit 9/11 (2004)

Washington DC Timeline

1608: Captain John Smith sails from Jamestown up the Potomac. Irish-Scotch colonized the area for the next 100 years…after they pushed out the Native Americans who originally inhabited the land, of course.

1790: Thomas Jefferson agrees to Alexander Hamilton's plan to finance the nation's post–Revolutionary War debt, in return for locating the nation's capital in the South. Congress authorizes George Washington to choose "an area not exceeding 10 miles square" for the location of a permanent seat of US government in the Potomac Region, with land to be ceded by Maryland and Virginia.

1791: Pierre Charles L'Enfant, an engineer from France, designs the capital city. He is fired within a year and replaced by city surveyor Andrew Ellicott and mathematician Benjamin Banneker.

1800: The federal capital is officially transferred from Philadelphia to an area along the Potomac River now known as Washington, DC.

1800: Library of Congress is established.

1801: Arriving in their new capital, Congress passes the Organic Acts, removing the ability of DC residents to vote for Congressional representation in the states from which the district was created.

1814: The Capitol and several government buildings are burned by the English during the War of 1812.

1817: The Executive Mansion is rebuilt following the burning by the British. Its walls are painted white to cover the char, giving birth to its more commonly known name: the White House.

1846: The Smithsonian Institution is established.

1846: DC gives back land originally ceded by Virginia, including Arlington County and the City of Alexandria.

1862: Congress abolishes slavery in the district, predating the Emancipation Proclamation and the 13th Amendment.

1865: Lee surrenders to Grant on April 8th.

1865: Lincoln assassinated at Ford's Theatre on April 14th.

1871: DC elects its first territorial government. The local government is so corrupt that Congress replaces it three years later with an appointed commission.

1888: The Washington Monument opens.

1901: The Washington Senators bring major league baseball to the district.

1907: Union Station opens, making it the largest train station in the country at the time.

1912: Japan sends 3,000 cherry blossom trees to DC as a gift of friendship. The Cherry Blossom Festival begins.

1922: The Lincoln Memorial is finished.

1937: Washington Redskins arrive in the city.

1943: The Pentagon and the Jefferson Memorial are completed.

1954: Puerto Rican nationalists open fire on the floor of the House of Representatives, wounding five members.

1960: DC's baseball team moves to Minnesota and becomes the Twins. The city immediately wins a new Senators franchise…

1961: 23rd Amendment is ratified, giving DC residents the right to vote for President and Vice President.

1963: Civil rights march of over 200,000 unites the city. Dr. Martin Luther King Jr. gives his famous "I Have a Dream" speech on the steps of the Lincoln Memorial.

1968: Urban riots after MLK's assassination devastate whole neighborhoods; some have yet to fully recover.

1970: The city gets its own non-voting representative to Congress. Thanks so much.

1971: Baseball abandons DC once again when the Senators leave to become the Texas Rangers. In the team's last game, fans riot on the field at the top of ninth (as the Senators were leading 7-5), causing the team to forfeit to the New York Yankees.

1972: Republican operatives break into Democratic offices in the Watergate.

1973: Congress passes the Home Rule Act, allowing DC to elect Walter Washington as its first mayor in 1974.

1974: President Nixon resigns under threat of impeachment.

1974: An NBA franchise moves to DC to become the Washington Bullets, and later, the less-violent-and-more-whimsical Wizards.

1976: The Metrorail opens to the public.

1978: Marion Barry is elected as DC's second mayor.

1982: The Vietnam Veterans Memorial is erected.

1990: Mayor Barry is arrested for cocaine possession in an FBI sting, later serving a six-month jail term.

1991: DC's crime rate peaks, including 482 murders in a single year.

1992: Mayor Sharon Pratt Kelly takes office. She is the first woman ever elected as the city's mayor.

1992: House of Representatives vote to make Washington DC a state. The Senate does not.

1994: His criminal record notwithstanding, Barry is elected to an unprecedented fourth term as the city's mayor.

1995: The Korean War Veterans Memorial opens to the public.

1998: The House of Representatives impeaches President Clinton over an illicit sex scandal.

1998: A gunman opens fire in the US Capitol, killing two policemen.

1998: Tony Williams, who as Mayor Barry's CFO helped DC start its financial recovery, is elected mayor.

2001: Thousands protest as President George W. Bush takes office after a hotly contested election.

2001: Terrorist attack destroys part of the Pentagon.

2001: Anthrax mailed to Senate offices causes short-term panic and massive mail disruptions.

2002: Snipers terrorize the region for three weeks, killing ten before being caught.

2004: World War II Memorial opens on the National Mall.

2004: The city's crime rate drops to mid-1980s levels. Wall Street upgrades DC to an A-level bond rating. *Forbes* ranks DC the nation's 4th Best Place to Start a Business or Career.

2004: *NFT Washington DC* is released. Millions rejoice.

2005: Baseball returns to DC as the Montreal Expos are relocated to become the Washington Nationals.

DC is a wired, or should we say wireless, city. Already, there are more than 170 points in the city with more on the way. Many of these are in the places you'd expect them – Starbucks, www.starbucks.com for locations, Cosi's, www. xandocosi.com for locations, as well as many of the area hotels. Even some McDonald's are getting in on the game, www.mcdonaldswireless.com. Between these outlets, you'll never be far from access, but with this comes a price, literally. Access will generally cost by the half hour or full hour though the price is a lot less than standard Internet access and many places offer passes for longer periods of time. Many hotels offer WiFi access, but are perhaps the most costly options. But these are not the only options.

Seeing the need for free WiFI access, there are two main areas where you can log on and keep your wallet in your pocket. **The Federal Communications Commission**, or FCC, offers free access at their headquarters (**Map 6**). However, there is no tech support and the FCC has said that, if requested by law enforcement, they will hand over their user list; on the other hand, no log in account is required, so while Big Brother might be watching, he doesn't really know who he's watching.

Perhaps the most amazing free access story is the Open Park Project. This group began an initiative to bring free WiFi access to the National Mall (Maps 1, 2 and 7), and presently, the entire Mall is blanketed with the coverage slowly creeping out beyond into the District. Once you access their free network and accept their terms of use, you're free to surf until your heart's content; however, at last check, electrical outlets on the Mall were few and far between, so come with a full battery charge. Check out www.openpark.net for more information. Finally, the list of free providers continues to grow, so perhaps the best thing to do when you fire up the laptop is to detect nearby open access points. With the growing web of coverage in the District, your chances are pretty good that you'll be in luck.

WiFi	Phone	Address	Map
Camiles Sidewalk Café of Washington	202-639-9727	650 F St NW	2
Jacobs Coffee House	202-543-6161	401 8th St NE	3
Murky Coffee	202-546-5228	660 Pennsylvania Ave SE	5
Federal Communications Commission Building		445 12th St SW	6
Casey's Coffee	202-223-4762	508 23rd St NW	7
Azela Coffee Shop	202-797-0778	2118 18th St NW	9
Steam Café	202-483-5296	1700 17th St NW	9
Busboys and Poets	202-387-7638	2021 14th St NW	10
Café Sureia	202-269-9444	3629 12th St Ne	14
Tryst Coffee House	202-232-5500	2459 18th St NW	16
Java and Cream	202-829-5211	5522 Georgia Ave NW	21
Bagel City Café	202-363-0888	4872 Massachusetts Ave NW	30
Java Shack	703-527-9556	2507 N Franklin Rd	35
Murky Coffee	703-312-7001	3211 N Wilson Blvd	35
Silver Diner	703-812-8600	3200 Wilson Blvd	35
Cameron Perks	703-461-6900	4911 Brenman Park Dr	41
St Elmo's Coffee Pub	703-739-9268	2300 Mt Vernon Ave	43

Internet	Phone	Address	Map
Eport World	202-232-2244	1719 Connecticut Ave NW	9
Eport World	202-464-7600	1030 19th St NW	9
Kramerbooks & Afterwords CafŽ	202-387-3825	1517 Connecticut Ave NW	9

The DC area abounds with romping grounds for your favorite canine companion, many of them off-leash environments. And dog parks are people parks, too: Singles mingle, moms commiserate, and bureaucrats share red-tape war stories. But be prepared for the occasional dogwalker, rescue-group affiliate, or canine resort recruiter to hit you with a pointed sales pitch. Some dog owners can be a tad overprotective, even when their dog is obviously digging, rolling, and roughhousing in the dust (usually, the dogs do a fine job of policing themselves). Other owners can get a bit peeved when their dogs are more interested in their fellow pooches than in playing fetch. But by and large, dog park visitors (canine and otherwise) are easygoing and personable. Larger parks, like Rock Creek or Meridian, offer dogs and owners some serious playing opportunities. It's still a hassle to find animal-friendly apartments, but as long as renters are willing to cough up a bit more monthly, there are options.

General Rules for Parks

- Dogs must be under the owner's/handler's control.
- Only three dogs per person are allowed.
- No female dogs in heat allowed.
- Only dogs four months and older allowed.
- Dogs must be legally licensed, vaccinated, and wearing both current tags.
- Dog owners/handlers must keep their dog(s) in view at all times.
- Dogs must not be allowed to bark incessantly or to the annoyance of the neighborhood.
- Dog owners/handlers must immediately pick up and dispose of, in trash receptacles, all dog feces.
- Aggressive dogs are not allowed at any time. Owners/handlers are legally responsible for their dog(s) and any injury caused by them.
- Dogs must be on leash when entering and exiting parks/fenced areas.

Washington DC	Address	Comments	Map
Mitchell Park	22nd St & S St NW		3
Stanton Park	Maryland Ave & 6th St NE		3
Lincoln Dog Park	Capitol Hill, 11th St & N Carolina Ave SE	Busiest early mornings and early evenings. Water, benches, and lighting provided.	3
Congressional Cemetery	18th St SE & Potomac Ave	$100 dogwalker fee, plus $20 per dog buys unlimited off-leash roaming of the grass and tombstones.	5
Malcolm X/Meridian Hill	16th St b/w Euclid St NW & Union Ct NW	No off-leash.	16
Glover Park Dog Park	39th & W Sts NW	Popular weekday mornings and evenings.	18
Battery Kemble Park	Capitol Hill, MacArthur Blvd	Lots of wooded trails. Good parking. No off-leash.	32
Arlington			
Madison Community Ctr	3829 N Stafford St	Dogs not allowed on soccer field. Don't park in the back lot unless you want a ticket.	31
Glencarlyn Park	301 S Harrison St	Huge unfenced area near creek and woods. Restrooms, fountains, and picnic areas.	38
Barcroft Park	4100 S Four Mile Run Dr	Exercise area between bicycle path and water.	39
Benjamin Banneker Park	1600 N Sycamore St	Enclosed off-leash dog exercise area.	33
Fort Barnard	S Pollard St & S Walter Reed Dr	Fenced park with off-leash area.	39
Shirlington Park	2601 S Arlington Mill Dr	Fenced park with stream, paved trail, and water fountain.	39
Utah Park	3308 S Stafford St	Daytime hours only.	39
Clarendon Park	13th, Herndon, & Hartford Sts	Unofficial dog exercise area (DEA).	35
Vienna Dog Park	700 Courthouse Rd SW	Fenced park with woodchip surface.	36
Alexandria			
City Property	Chambliss St & Grigsby Ave	Off-leash exercise area.	38
North Fort Ward Park	Area east of entrance. 4401 W Braddock Rd	Off-leash exercise area.	39
Duke Street Dog Park	5005 Duke St	Fenced dog park.	41
City Property	SE corner of Wheeler Ave & Duke St	Off-leash exercise area.	42
Tarleton Park	Old Mill Run, west of Gordon St	Off-leash exercise area.	43
Ben Brenman Park	Backlick Creek	Fenced dog park.	-
City Property	SE corner of Braddock Rd & Commonwealth Ave	Off-leash exercise area.	44
Hoof's Run	E Commonwealth Ave, b/w Oak & Chapman St	Off-leash exercise area.	44
Del Ray Dog Park	Simpson Stadium & Monroe Ave	Fenced dog park.	45
Founders Park NE corner	Oronoco & Union Sts	Off-leash exercise area.	45
Montgomery Park	Fairfax & First Sts	Fenced dog park.	45
Powhatan Gateway	Henry & Powhatan Sts	Off-leash exercise area.	45
Windmill Hill Park	SW corner of Gibbon & Union Sts	Off-leash exercise area.	46
City Property	Edison St cul-de-sac	Off-leash exercise area.	43

General Information

DC Public Library Website:	www.dclibrary.org
Alexandria Library Website:	www.alexandria.lib.va.us
Arlington Library Website:	www.co.arlington.va.us/lib
Montgomery County Library Website:	www.montgomerylibrary.org

Overview

The Washington, DC, Library system revolves around the massive main **Martin Luther King (Map 1)** branch downtown. Large in size, scope, and ugliness, this eyesore with gives new meaning to the cliché, "Don't judge a book by its cover." Once you're able to overlook the homeless people taking naps outside (and often inside) the building, you'll appreciate its division of rooms by subject matter and the efficient, knowledgeable staff that can find you a 1988 *National Geographic* faster than you can say "Micronesia." Included in this mega-library are a room for the blind and handicapped, an adult literacy resource center, as well as meeting rooms (though an application for use is required). If you don't have specific research needs, one of the other twenty-seven citiywide branches, notably **Georgetown's (Map 8)**, are more pleasant places to spend an afternoon. Then again, if you have time to spare and want both extensive research capabilities and luxurious quarters, forget the local stuff and head over to the **US Library of Congress (Map 2)**.

If you hold a suburbanite's library card, the public libraries offered by Montgomery County and Northern Virginia are reasonably attractive and stocked, although you may feel like you're being cheated out of countless almanac's of information after taking a gander at DC's MLK branch.

■ = *Public* ■ = *By Appointment Only* ■ = *Other*

Type	Library	Address	Phone	Map
■	Alexandria Charles E Beatley Jr Central Library	5005 Duke St	703-519-5900	41
■	Alexandria James M Duncan Branch Library	2501 Commonwealth Ave	703-838-4566	43
■	Alexandria Kate Waller Barrett Branch Library	717 Queen St	703-838-4555	46
■	Alexandria Law Library	520 King St, Room L-34	703-838-4077	46
■	American University Library	4400 Massachusetts Ave NW	202-885-3238	19
■	Anacostia Library	1800 Good Hope Rd SE	202-698-1190	5
■	Arlington Central Library	1015 N Quincy St	703-228-5990	34
■	Arlington County Aurora Hills Library	735 18th St S	703-228-5715	40
■	Arlington Public Library Information & Referral Office	2100 Clarendon Blvd	703-228-3000	36
■	Arthur R Ashe Jr Foreign Policy Library	1629 K St NW, Ste 1100	202-223-1960	9
■	Bethesda Library	7400 Arlington Rd	240-777-0970	29
■	Bureau of Alcohol & Tobacco Library	650 Massachusetts Ave NW	202-927-7890	10
■	Cherrydale Library	2190 Military Rd	703-228-6330	34
■	Chevy Chase Library	5625 Connecticut Ave NW	202-282-0021	28
■	Chevy Chase Library	8005 Connecticut Ave	240-773-9590	23
■	Cleveland Park Library	3310 Connecticut Ave NW	202-282-3080	17
■	Columbia Pike Library	816 S Walter Reed Dr	703-228-5710	37
■	Dibner Library	12th St & Constitution Ave NW	202-633-3872	1
■	DOT Law Library, Coast Guard Branch	2100 2nd St SW, Rm B726	202-267-2536	6
■	Ellen Coolidge Burke Branch Library	4701 Seminary Rd	703-519-6000	41
■	Federal Aviation Administration Libraries	800 Independence Ave SW	202-267-3396	1
■	Federal Reserve Board Research & Law Libraries	20th St NW & Constitution Ave NW	202-452-3284	7
■	Federal Trade Commission Library	600 Pennsylvania Ave NW	202-326-2395	2
■	Foundation Center	1627 K St NW, 3rd Fl	202-331-1400	9
■	General Services Administration Library	1800 F St NW, RM 1033	202-501-0788	7
■	Georgetown Library	3260 R St NW	202-282-0220	8
■	Glencarlyn Public Library	300 S Kensington St	703-228-6548	38
■	Howard University School of Business Library	2600 6th St NW	202-806-1561	15
■	International Trade Commission Library	500 E St SW	202-205-2630	6
■	James Melville Gilliss Library	3450 Massachusetts Ave NW	202-762-1463	13
■	Juanita E Thornton Library	7420 Georgia Ave NW	202-541-6100	27
■	Lamond-Riggs Library	5401 S Dakota Ave NE	202-541-6255	14

General Information • **Libraries**

■ = *Public* ■ = *By Appointment Only* ■ = *Other*

Type	Library	Address	Phone	Map
■	Langston Community Library	2600 Benning Rd NE	202-724-8665	4
■	Martin Luther King Jr Memorial Library	901 G St NW	202-727-1111	1
■	Mt Pleasant Library	3160 16th St NW	202-671-0200	16
■	NASA Headquarters Library	300 E St SW	202-358-0168	6
■	National Endowment for the Humanities Library	1100 Pennsylvania Ave NW	202-606-8244	1
■	National Geographic Society Library	1145 17th St NW	202-857-7783	9
■	National Research Council Library	500 5th St NW, Room 304	202-334-2125	2
■	NOAA Central Library	1315 East West Hwy, SSMC3, 2nd Fl	301-713-2600	25
■	Northeast Library	330 7th St NE	202-698-3320	3
■	Office of Thrift Supervision Library	1700 G St NW	202-906-6470	1
■	Palisades Library	4901 V St NW	202-282-3139	18
■	Petworth Library	4200 Kansas Ave NW	202-541-6300	21
■	Polish Library in Washington	1503 21st St NW	202-466-2665	9
■	Ralph J Bunch Library	2201 C St NW, Room 3239	202-647-2971	7
■	RL Christian Community Library	1300 H St NE	202-724-8599	3
■	Robert S Rankin Memorial Library	624 9th St NW, Rm 600	202-376-8110	1
■	Shirlington Library	2786 S Arlington Mill Dr	703-228-6545	39
■	Silver Spring Library	8901 Colesville Rd	240-773-9420	25
■	Southeast Library	403 7th St SE	202-698-3377	5
■	Southwest Library	900 Wesley Pl SW	202-724-4752	6
■	Sursum Corda Community Library	135 New York Ave NW	202-724-4772	11
■	Takoma Park Library	416 Cedar St NW	202-576-7252	27
■	Tenley-Friendship Library	4450 Wisconsin Ave NW	202-282-3090	19
■	Treasury Library	1500 Pennsylvania Ave NW, Rm 1314	202-622-0990	1
■	US Department of Commerce Library	1401 Constitution Ave NW	202-482-5511	1
■	US Department of Energy Library	1000 Independence Ave SW, RM GA-138	202-586-5000	1
■	US Department of the Interior Library	1849 C St NW	202-208-5815	7
■	US Housing & Urban Development Library	451 7th St SW	202-708-2370	6
■	US Institute of Peace	1200 17th St NW, Ste 200	202-429-3851	9
■	US Library of Congress	101 Independence Ave SE	202-707-5000	2
■	US Senate Library	Russell Senate Office Bldg, B15	202-224-7106	2
■	Watha T Daniel Branch Library	1701 8th St NW	202-671-0212	10
■	West End Library	1101 24th St NW	202-724-8707	9
■	Westover Library (temporarily closed)	1800 N Lexington St	703-228-5260	33
■	Woodridge Library	1801 Hamlin St NE	202-541-6226	13

Computer Services

	Phone
Action Business Equipment	703-716-4691
On Call 25/8	202-625-2511
On Call 25/8	202-625-2511

Delivery/Messengers

	Phone
QMS	240-223-3600
Washington Courier	202-775-1500

Plumbers

	Phone
Capitol Area Plumbing & Heating	301-345-7667
John G Webster	202-783-6100
KC Plumbing Services	800-823-4911
Plumbline Plumbers	202-543-9515
Roto-Rooter	202-726-8888
Smallenbroek Plumbing & Heating	202-237-6400
Vito	800-438-8486

Towing

	Phone
Emergency-1	202-529-2205
Hook Em Up Towing	202-528-8435
Pro-Lift	202-546-7877

Locksmiths

	Phone
Berry's Locksmith	202-667-3680
District Lock	202-547-8236
Doors and Devices	800-865-6253
JB's Locksmith	301-567-9283
Locksmith 24 Hours	202-636-4540
Metro Lock & Security	202-362-1882
Pop-A-Lock	202-331-2929

Copy Shops

	Address	Phone	Map
Reliable Copy	555 12th St NW	202-347-6644	1
Superior Group	1401 New York Ave NW	202-393-1600	1
Whitmont Legal Copying	1725 I St NW	202-222-0147	1
Imagenet	2000 M St NW	202-872-0700	9
Omnidox	2101 L St NW	202-822-9355	9
Sequential	1615 L St NW	202-293-0500	9
Barrister Copy Solutions	1090 Vermont Ave NW	202-289-7279	10
FedEx Kinko's	1407 East West Hwy	301-587-6565	25
FedEx Kinko's	4809 Bethesda Ave	301-656-0577	29
FedEx Kinko's	2300 Clarendon Blvd	703-525-9224	35
FedEx Kinko's	3515C S Jefferson St	703-379-0909	38
FedEx Kinko's	1601 Crystal Sq Arc	703-413-8011	40
FedEx Kinko's	685 N Washington St	703-739-0783	45

Restaurants

	Address	Phone	Map
Annie's Paramount	1609 17th St NW	202-232-0395	9
The Diner	2453 18th St NW	202-232-8800	16
Osman's and Joe's Steak 'n Egg Kitchen	4700 Wisconsin Ave NW	202-686-1201	19
Bob and Edith's Diner	2310 Columbia Pike	703-920-6103	37
Waffle Shop	3864 Mt Vernon Ave	703-836-8851	43

Gas Stations

	Address	Map		Address	Map
Exxon	200 Massachusetts Ave NE	3	Exxon	4501 14th St NW	21
Amoco	1950 Benning Rd NE	4	Exxon	7975 Old Georgetown Rd	22
Exxon	2651 Benning Rd NE	4	Exxon	9336 Georgia Ave	24
Exxon	1022 M St SE	5	Exxon	8301 Fenton St	25
Exxon	1201 Pennsylvania Ave SE	5	Exxon	8384 Colesville Rd	25
Exxon	1001 S Capitol St SW	6	Amoco	6300 Georgia Ave NW	27
Exxon	950 S Capitol St SE	6	Amoco	7605 Georgia Ave NW	27
Amoco	2715 Pennsylvania Ave NW	8	Exxon	6350 Georgia Ave NW	27
Exxon	1601 Wisconsin Ave NW	8	Exxon	7401 Georgia Ave NW	27
Exxon	3607 M St NW	8	Shell	6419 Georgia Ave NW	27
Mobil	2200 P St NW	9	Exxon	5521 Connecticut Ave NW	28
Mobil	1442 U St NW	10	Exxon	7340 Wisconsin Ave	29
Amoco	400 Rhode Island Ave NE	11	Texaco	5501 Lee Hwy	33
Amoco	45 Florida Ave NE	11	Exxon	660 N Glebe Rd	34
Exxon	1 Florida Ave NE	11	Exxon	2410 Lee Hwy	35
Amoco	1201 Bladensburg Rd NE	12	Exxon	1824 Wilson Blvd	36
Exxon	1925 Bladensburg Rd NE	12	Exxon	1001 S Glebe Rd	37
Amoco	2210 Bladensburg Rd NE	13	Mobil	3100 Columbia Pike	37
Amoco	3701 12th St NE	14	Exxon	4368 King St	39
Exxon	1020 Michigan Ave NE	14	Mobil	4154 S Four Mile Run Dr	39
Exxon	5501 S Dakota Ave NE	14	Exxon	2720 S Glebe Rd	40
Amoco	3426 Georgia Ave NW	15	Exxon	501 S Van Dorn St	41
Exxon	3540 14th St NW	15	Mobil	190 S Whiting St	41
Exxon	1827 Adams Mill Rd NW	16	Exxon	2320 Jefferson Davis Hwy	43
Exxon	4244 Wisconsin Ave NW	19	Exxon	703 N Washington St	45
Amoco	5001 Connecticut Ave NW	20	Exxon	834 N Washington St	45
Exxon	3535 Connecticut Ave NW	20	Exxon	501 S Washington St	46
Exxon	5030 Connecticut Ave NW	20	Exxon	700 S Patrick St	46

Gym

	Address	Phone	Map
Third Power Fitness	2007 18th St NW	202-483-8400	9

Veterinarian

	Address	Phone	Map
Friendship Hospital for Animals	4105 Brandywine St NW	202-363-7300	19

Pharmacies

	Address	Phone	Prescription counter closes	Map
CVS*	801 7th St NW	202-842-3627	7 pm	2
CVS*	1403 Wisconsin Ave NW	202-337-4848	10 pm	8
CVS	2240 M St NW	202-296-9876		9
CVS	6 Dupont Cir NW	202-785-1466		9
Rite Aid*	1815 Connecticut Ave NW	202-332-1718	12 am	9
CVS*	1199 Vermont Ave NW	202-628-0720	12 am	10
CVS	4555 Wisconsin Ave	202-537-1587		19
CVS	7809 Wisconsin Ave	301-986-9144		22
CVS	1290 East West Hwy	301-588-6261		25
Rite Aid*	1411 East West Hwy	301-563-6935	12 AM	25
CVS	6514 Georgia Ave NW	202-829-5234		27
CVS	6917 Arlington Rd	301-656-2522		29
Giant Food Pharmacy*	7142 Arlington Rd	301-492-5161	10 pm	29
Harris Teeter Pharmacy*	2425 N Harrison St	703-532-8663	9 pm	33
Harris Teeter Pharmacy*	600 N Glebe Rd	703-526-9100	9 pm	34
CVS	3133 Lee Hwy	703-522-0260		35
CVS*	2121 15th St N	703-243-4239	10 pm	36
CVS	3535 S Jefferson St	703-820-6360		38
Giant Food Pharmacy*	3480 S Jefferson St	703-931-1333	12 am	38
CVS*	2400 Jefferson Davis Hwy	703-418-0813	10 pm	40
CVS	5101 Duke St	703-823-7430		41
CVS	3130 Duke St	703-823-3584		42
CVS*	415 Monroe Ave	703-683-4433		43

Hospitals

As hyper-stressed, Type-A workaholics, most Washingtonians are ripe for coronary disease, so it's a good thing there are many area hospitals to offer us recourse. Although district financing snarls have led to recent shutdowns, most notably DC General Hospital, the District nevertheless remains equipped with state-of-the-art medical facilities ready to respond to emergencies of presidential magnitude (Dick Cheney is strategically located between **Georgetown (Map 18)** and **Sibley (Map 32)** Hospitals).

The area's hospitals vary in terms of the level of service they offer. Stagger into some ERs, and unless your clothes have fresh blood stains, you won't be seeing a doctor until you have memorized the theme song to *Days of Our Lives*. Other facilities treat patients like hotel guests. At the recently refurbished **Virginia Hospital Center (Map 34)**, rooms are set up to offer remarkable Arlington views, and in-patients are delivered meals by workers who sport bow ties and studs. Sibley is your average Northwest hospital, with a relatively comfortable waiting room, usually tuned to CNN, and nurses who squawk to their patients about which congressman they shot up with saline the week prior.

Many medical people assert that the region's top docs reside at **Washington Hospital Center (Map 14)**, although Washington Hospital *City* is a more appropriate title. Practically every disease you can get has its own building devoted to it, and the relatively small Irving Street becomes somewhat of a highway off-ramp just to allow access to this behemoth of medical practitioners. Allow an extra hour just to park and figure out how to navigate its labyrinthine interior structure.

Emergency Rooms	Address	Phone	Map
George Washington University Hospital	900 23rd St NW	202-715-4000	7
Howard University	2041 Georgia Ave NW	202-865-6100	10
Children's National Medical	111 Michigan Ave NW	202-884-5000	14
Providence	1150 Varnum St NE	202-269-7000	14
Washington Hospital Center	110 Irving St NW	202-877-7000	14
Georgetown University Hospital	3800 Reservoir NW	202-444-2000	18
National Naval Medical Center	8901 Wisconsin Ave	301-295-4611	22
Suburban	8600 Old Georgetown Rd	301-896-3100	22
Washington Adventist	7600 Carroll Ave	301-891-7600	26
Sibley Memorial	5255 Loughboro Rd NW	202-537-4000	32
Virginia Hospital Center, Arlington	1701 N George Mason Dr	703-558-5000	34
Northern Virginia Community	601 S Carlin Springs Rd	703-671-1200	38
Inova Alexandria	4320 Seminary Rd	703-504-3000	42

Other Hospitals	Address	Phone	Map
HSC Pediatric Center	1731 Bunker Hill Rd NE	202-832-4400	13
National Rehabilitation Hospital	102 Irving St NW	202-877-1000	14
VA Medical Center	50 Irving St NW	202-745-8000	14

281

Overview

There's always some mass gathering in Washington, DC; from inauguration demonstrations to flower festivals, DC has it all. The best events are free and easily accessible by mass transit.

Event	Approx. Dates	For more info…	Comments
New Year's Eve	December 31/January 1		Celebrate the new year with music art, and bitter freezing cold.
Martin Luther King's Birthday	Observed January 15	www.whitehouse.gov/kids/ martinlutherkingjrday.html	Music, speakers, and a recital of the "I Have a Dream" speech on the Lincoln Memorial steps.
Robert E Lee's Birthday	January 19	703-235-1510	Yes, victors write the history books, but some losers' popularity endures. Robert E Lee Memorial, Arlington Cemetery.
Chinese New Year	February 18	703-851-5685	Can you IMAGINE the debauchery of a 15-day American New Year's bash? Check it out on H Street in Chinatown.
Black History Month Celebration	February	www.si.edu	African-American history at the Smithsonian.
Abraham Lincoln's Birthday	Observed February 12	703-619-7222	Reading of Gettysburg Address in front of the city's favorite marble hero.
George Washington's Birthday Parade	President's Day, February 19	800-388-9119	Parade and party in Alexandria for the city's other favorite guy.
St. Patrick's Day Parade	March 17	www.dcstpatsparade.com	Celebration of all things Irish in DC: music, food, oh, and beer, too.
Smithsonian Kite Festival	Late March– early April	kitefestival.org	Watch adults attack kiddie play like a combat sport.
Washington Home & Garden Show	Mid-March	www.flowergardenshow.com	Check out the flora that actually enjoys this climate.
National Cherry Blossom Festival	March 25– April 9	www.nationalcherryblossom festival.org	One of the can't-misses…problem is the tourists think so, too.
Filmfest DC	April	www.filmfestdc.org	For once, see a flick before it opens in NYC.
White House Spring Garden Tours	Mid-April	www.whitehouse.gov	No politics, just flowers.
Shakespeare's Birthday	April 23	202-544-4600	To go or not to go. That is the question. Folger Shakespeare Library.
White House Easter Egg Roll	Mid-April	www.whitehouse.gov	No politics, just eggs.
Department of Defense/ Joint Services Open House	Mid-May	301-981-4600	The country flexes its muscles with an air show and other military might. FedEx Field.
St. Sophia Greek Festival	Mid-May	202-333-4730	Big, fat, Greek festival.
National Symphony Orchestra Memorial Day Weekend Concert	May 28	www.kennedy-center.org/nso	Easy on the ears—and wallet; it's free.
Memorial Day Ceremonies at Arlington Cemetery	May 29	www.arlingtoncemetery.org	Ceremonies at JFK's grave and the Tomb of the Unknown Soldier.
Memorial Day Ceremonies at the Vietnam Veterans Memorial	May 29	www.nps.gov/vive	Solemn memorial.
Memorial Day Jazz Festival	May 29	703-883-4686	Jazz in Alexandria.
Virginia Gold Cup	May 6	www.vagoldcup.com	Horse race on the same day as the Kentucky Derby. Someone fire the marketing department
Dance Africa DC	Early June	202-269-1600	A feat of feet.
Dupont-Kalorama Museum Walk Weekend	First weekend in June	www.dkmuseums.com/ walk.html	Free admission to the city's smaller, quirkier, pricier exhibits.

Event	Approx. Dates	For more info...	Comments
DC Caribbean Carnival Extravaganza	Late June	www.dccaribbeancarnival.com	Caribbean music, food, and outrageous costumes.
Capital Pride	June 3–9	www.capitalpride.org	Huge, fun, funky, out, and proud.
Red Cross Waterfront Festival	Mid-June	www.waterfrontfestival.org	If you fall out of the canoe, Clara Barton may rescue you.
National Capital Barbecue Battle	Late June	www.barbecuebattle.com	Hot and sticky BBQ on a hot and sticky day.
Independence Day Celebration	July 4	www.july4thparade.com	July 4th in America-town. Check out the parade. The fireworks are a must.
Bastille Day	July 14		No time to order freedom fries.
Virginia Scottish Games	Late July	www.vascottishgames.org	Kilts and haggis everywhere!
Hispanic Festival	Late July		Latin American celebration at the Washington Monument.
Annual Soap Box Derby	Early June	www.dcsoapboxderby.org	The one day parents let their kids fly down city streets in rickety wooden boxes.
Georgia Avenue Day	Late August		Parades, music, and food from the southern US and Africa.
National Frisbee Festival	Late August		Don't fight it, join it.
National Army Band's 1812 Overture Performance	Late August	www.whitehouse.gov	No politics, just patriotic music.
DC Blues Festival	Early September	www.dcblues.org	Rock Creek Park gets down and depressed.
Kennedy Center Open House	Early September	www.kennedy-center.org	Check out the terrace and the Kennedy sculpture without shelling out for the opera.
Adams Morgan Day	Early September	www.adamsmorganday.org	Neighborhood that gets jammed nightly, gets jammed while sun's up.
White House Fall Garden Tour	Late October	www.whitehouse.gov	No politics, just leaf peeping.
Reel Affirmations Film Festival	Mid-October	www.reelaffirmations.org	Like Filmfest DC, except much more gay.
Marine Corps Marathon	Late October	www.marinemarathon.com	26 miles of asphalt and cheers.
Theodore Roosevelt's Birthday	October 27	www.theodoreroosevelt.org	Party for one of the other giant heads in North Dakota.
Civil War Living History Day	Early November	703-838-4848	The culmination of reenactment-stickler bickering. Fort Ward Museum.
Veteran's Day Ceremonies	November 11	www.arlingtoncemetery.org	Military ceremony in Arlington Cemetery.
Alexandria Antiques Show	Mid-November	703-549-5811	Expensive old stuff.
Jewish Film Festival	Late November/ Early December	www.wjff.org	Like Filmfest DC, except much more Jewish.
Kennedy Center Holiday Celebration	December	www.kennedy-center.org	X-mas revelry.
Kwanzaa Celebration	December	www.si.edu	Celebration at the Smithsonian.
National Christmas Tree Lighting/ Pageant of Peace	Mid-December to January 1	www.whitehouse.gov	Trees, menorahs, & Yule logs get lit at the White House Ellipse.
Washington National Cathedral Christmas Celebration and Services	December 24–25	202-537-6247	Humongous tree from Nova Scotia.
White House Christmas Candlelight Tours	Christmastime	www.whitehouse.gov	Still no politics, just religion.

Yes, DC's a great city for lessons in history and civics, but sometimes the kids just aren't in the mood for another tutorial on the system of checks and balances. If you check out some of the destinations on this list, you'll discover there's life beyond the Mall when it comes to entertaining your mini-yous.

The Best of the Best

★ **Best Kid-Friendly Restaurant:** Café Deluxe (3228 Wisconsin Ave NW, 202-686-2233; 400 First St SE, 202-546-6768; 4910 Elm St, Bethesda, 301-656-3131). Parents breathe a sigh of relief when they walk into a restaurant and see that the tablecloth is paper and the table is littered with crayons. At Café Deluxe, your kids can perfect their masterpieces while munching on entrees like buttered noodles, PB&J, or cheese quesadillas. The prices reflect that your companions are only half-size: Children's menu prices are only $3.95 a pop. Runner up: ESPN Zone (555 12th St NW, 202-783-3776). This boys' night out sports bar makes for an unexpectedly family-friendly restaurant during daylights hours, complete with a rookies' menu and all the arcade games their little hearts could desire.

★ **Quaintest Activity:** Canal Boat Rides (1057 Thomas Jefferson St NW, 202-653-5190). Take a boat ride along the historic C&O canal in a boat pulled by mules. Park rangers in period clothing describe what life was like for families who lived and worked on the canal during the 1870s. Tours (one hour long) are held Wednesday–Friday at 11 am and 3 pm, and Saturday and Sunday at 11 am, 1:30 pm, 3 pm, and 4:30 pm. The boats fill up on a first-come-first-served basis. $8 adults, $6 senior citizens, $5 children.

★ **Funnest Park:** Rock Creek Park (5200 Glover Rd NW, 202-895-6070). An area of Rock Creek Park located on Beach Drive goes by the name of Candy Cane City—'nuf said. Leland Street is good for picnicking and has a playground, basketball courts, and tennis courts. Children's park programs include planetarium shows, animal talks, arts & crafts projects, and exploratory hikes.

★ **Coolest Bookstore:** A Likely Story Children's Bookstore (1555 King St, Alexandria, 703-836-2498, www.alikelystorybooks.com). The bookstore hosts weekly story times, writing workshops for kids, and special events almost daily during the summer. Story time for children ages two and up is held every Wednesday at 11 am. Other events include foreign-language story time and sing-a-long story times.

★ **Best Rainy Day Activity:** Smithsonian Museum of Natural History (10th St & Constitution Ave NW, 202-633-1000). The new Kenneth E. Behring Family Hall of Mammals is open! If the kids aren't too freaked out by life-sized stuffed animals, check out the 274 new taxidermied mounts. The IMAX theater is always a hit with kids and parents alike on rainy afternoons. The timeless kid-appeal of dinosaur exhibits also keeps the little ones entertained (if they weren't recently dragged here on a school trip). Admission is free, and tickets are not required for entry. The museum is open daily 10 am–5:30 pm (and until 7:30 pm during summertime), except on federal holidays.

★ **Sunny Day Best Bet:** National Zoo (3001 Connecticut Ave, 202-673-4800, nationalzoo.si.edu). This free and easily accessible zoo is guaranteed to be the best park stroll you've ever taken. Beyond the pandas and apes, there's also a Kids' Farm with cows, donkeys, goats, chickens, and ducks. Summer camps and classes are available to Friends of the National Zoo Family Members. The $50 membership fee also includes zoo birthday party reservations, free popcorn for your kids every time they visit, and a 25% discount on all activities that cost money. The zoo is open daily (6 am–8 pm April 2 to October 28, 6 am–6 pm October 29 to March 10), and admission is always free. April–October buildings are open 10 am–6 pm, November–April 10 am–4:30 pm.

★ **Neatest Store:** Barston's Child's Play (5536 Connecticut Ave NW, 202-244-3602). The store's long, narrow aisles are stocked with games, toys, puzzles, trains, costumes, art supplies, and books. It's never too early to start grooming a true shopaholic.

Parks for Playing

• **Cleveland Park** (3409 Macomb St NW). Climb a spider web, climb a wall, or catch a train. The park has separate play areas for younger and older children, picnic tables, basketball courts, a baseball field, and a rec center.

• **East Potomac Park** (Ohio Drive SW). Always a good bet with its miniature golf course, public pool, picnic facilities, and playground at the southern tip. Your kids will love to climb all over the giant hands and feet of the Awakening Statue, and this is an absolute must during Cherry Blossom season.

• **Friendship Park** (4500 Van Ness St NW, 202-282-2198). Plenty of slides, tunnels, swings, and climbing structures, as well as basketball and tennis courts, softball/soccer fields, and a rec center. If you need a break, there's plenty of shade and picnic tables. Aka "Turtle Park."

• **Kalorama Park** (19th St & Kalorama Rd NW). While the shade is limited here, this is a large playground with a fence dividing big-kid from little-kid playgrounds.

• **Marine Reed Recreation Center** (2200 Champlain St NW, 202-673-7768). Plenty of shady areas to rest your old bones while the kids are devouring the massive jungle gym, slides, tennis courts, and basketball courts.

- **Montrose Park** (R & 30th Sts NW, 202-426-6827). For you: lots of open space, a picnicking area, and tennis courts. For your kids: swings, monkey bars, a sandbox, and a maze.
- **Rose Park** (26th & O Sts NW, 202-333-4946). Home to Little League games and the Georgetown Farmers Market, this park has plenty of green and a massive, wonderful sandbox.

Rainy Day Activities

Rain ain't no big thang in the city of free museums, many of which cater to the height- and attention-challenged.

Museums with Kid Appeal

- **National Air and Space Museum** (Independence Ave & 4th St SW, 202-633-1000). Can you go wrong in museum that sells astronauts' freeze-dried ice cream? Kids can walk through airplanes and spaceships. Check out the Einstein Planetarium and the IMAX Theater. Open daily 10 am–5:30 pm, closed Christmas Day. Admission is free but does not include special events or activities.
- **International Spy Museum** (800 F St NW, 202-393-7798, www.spymuseum.org). The sleek exhibits filled with high-tech gadgets and fascinating real-life spy stories make the hefty admissions tag totally worth it. Special family programs include making and breaking secret codes and disguise-creation workshops. Twice a year, the museum even offers a top-secret overnight "Operation Secret Slumber," which provides kids with a "behind the scenes" look at the life of spy. The museum is open daily, but hours vary according to season. Children under five enter free, adults pay $15, kids (11 and under) pay $12, and seniors (65+) pay $14.
- **National Museum of American History** (14th St and Constitution Ave NW, 202-357-2700, americanhistory.si.edu). While your kids will certainly love a glimpse of Dorothy's ruby red slippers, the hands-on section of this museum is where they'll *really* want to be. The Hands-On History Room allows kids to gin cotton, send a telegraph, or say "hello" in Cherokee. The Hands-On Science Room, for children over five, lets kids take intelligence tests, separate food dyes in beverages, or use lasers to see light. Museum admission is free, but tickets (which are also free) are required for the hands-on rooms during weekends and busy hours. The museum is open daily 10 am–5:30 pm (and until 6:30 pm during summertime), except for Christmas.
- **Freer Gallery** (1050 Independence Ave SW, 202-633-4880, www.asia.si.edu). Give your kids a taste of Asia with the Freer Gallery's Imaginasia program. Children from ages six to fourteen find their way through exhibitions on Japanese wood block prints or Islamic illuminated manuscripts (with the guiding hand of an activity book) then create an appropriate art project

with their own two hands. No reservations required for groups smaller than eight, and Imaginasia will give your little ones a unique glimpse of the Far East on the Mall. The museum is open from 10 am to 5:30 pm, except for Christmas.

Other Indoor Distractions

- **Adventure Theatre** (7300 MacArthur Blvd, Glen Echo, MD, 301-320-5331, www.adventuretheatre.org) Actors and puppets stage fables, musicals, and classic fairytales on the DC area's longest running children's stage. You can hardly ask for a nicer setting than Glen Echo Park, also home to the kid-friendly Puppet Co. Playhouse.
- **Bureau of Engraving and Printing** (14th & C Sts, SW, 202-874-3019, www.moneyfactory.com). We're all used to seeing money spent. At this museum, you can watch how money is made, although your kids will probably be most interested in watching the destruction of old money. Admission is free, but tickets are required March–August. General tours (the only way to see the museum) are given every 15 minutes from 10 am to 2 pm, Monday through Friday.
- **Discovery Theater** (1100 Jefferson Dr SW, 202-357-1500, www.discoverytheater.org). Puppet shows, dance performances, and storytelling all under one roof. Performances are given daily at 10 am and 11:30 am, Monday through Friday, and Saturday at 11:30 am and 1 pm. Shows cost $6 for adults and $4 for children, with special group rates available. Kids ages 4 to 13 can also join the Young Associates Program, where they can learn to animate clay figures or make their own puppets.
- **Imagination Stage** (4908 Auburn Ave, Bethesda, MD, 301-280-1660, www.imaginationstage.org). Help your kids enjoy the magic of theater by taking them to a show at the Imagination Stage. Your family might see anything from a hip-hop version of a favorite picture book to a fairytale musical. This non-profit organization has been putting on the hits for over twenty years now.
- **Now This!** (Blair Mansion, 7111 Eastern Ave, Silver Spring, MD, 202-364-8292, www.nowthisimprov.com). The city's only improvised children's theater group entertains kids every Sunday afternoon with impromptu storytelling, songwriting, and comedy. This is a great place to take a birthday boy or girl on their special day, as the cast will write them their very own birthday tune. Lunch is served at 1 pm and the show begins at 1:30 pm. The lunch + show birthday package costs $18, show + cake is $14, and dessert + show is $11 (all including tax and tip).

- **Puppet Co. Playhouse** (7300 MacArthur Blvd, Glen, MD, 301-320-6668, www.thepuppetco.org). Set in the most enchanting amusement park turned arts center, the Puppet Co. Playhouse is just one piece of magic in Glen Echo. Master puppeteers wield rod puppets in front of gorgeous sets, leaving kids and adults wide-eyed and bushy-tailed.

Outdoor and Educational

Just 'cause you want to play outside doesn't mean you have to act like a hooligan! Here's a list of outdoor activities that mix culture with athleticism and offer up some surprisingly original forms of entertainment:

- **Butler's Orchard** (22200 Davis Mill Rd, Germantown, MD, 301-972-3299, www.butlersorchard.com). Teach those city slickers that apples come from trees, not Safeway! And there are golden deliciouses and macintoshes and granny smiths and galas! Kids and adults can pick their own crops year round (nearly) at Butler's Orchard, The berries taste sweeter when you've picked them yourself, and autumn events include hay rides and the annual pumpkin festival. Pay for what you pick by the pound.

- **Discovery Creek Children's Museum of Washington** (The Stable at Glen Echo Park, 7300 MacArthur Blvd, Glen Echo, MD, 202-337-5111, discoverycreek.org). Every weekend is different at Discovery Creek, an indoors/outdoors learning center designed to help kids appreciate and protect the environment. Blaze a trail, come face to face with a curious animal, or make a mess on an art project. Kids and adults can turn up anytime on Saturdays and Sundays from 10 am to 3 pm. Admission is $5 for everyone, $3 for seniors 65 and over, and free for children under two.

- **Fort Ward** (4301 West Braddock Rd, Alexandria, 703-838-4848, www.fortward.org). The best preserved Union fort in DC. Picnic areas are available, and the on-site museum has a Civil War Kids' Camp for ages 8 to 12 during the summer. The museum is open Tuesday through Saturday 9 am–5 pm and Sunday 12 pm–5 pm. Admission is free. The park is open daily from 9 am until sunset.

- **Leesburg Animal Park** (19270 James Monroe Highway, Leesburg, VA, 703-433-0002). The trip across the river is worth it—particularly if you get the pleasure of riding the $3 White's Ferry ride from Maryland to Virginia. Little ones can feed baby bear cubs by bottle or pet free-ranging emus; animals are both domestic and exotic. Kids 2 to 12 need an $8 Explorer Pass, and adults pay $10.

- **National Arboretum** (3501 New York Ave NE, 202-245-2726, www.usna.usda.gov). Covering 466 acres, the National Arboretum is the ultimate backyard. Picnicking is encouraged in the National Grove of State Trees picnic area, and the original columns from the Capitol dome live here at the Arb on a picturesque, grassy knoll. A 40-minute open-air tram ride is available and advised if you want to see everything. The Arboretum is open daily 8 am–5 pm, except Christmas. Admission is free, but the tram will cost you $4 for adults and $2 for children 4–16.

- **Sculpture Garden Ice-Skating Rink** (7th St & Constitution Ave NW, 202-289-3360). The Sculpture Garden's rink is specially designed to allow views of the garden's contemporary sculptures while skating. It's like subliminally feeding your kids culture while they think they're just playing. Regular admission costs $6 for a two-hour session, and children, students, and seniors pay $5. Skate rental costs $2.50 and a locker rental costs 50¢.

Classes

- **Ballet Petite** (Several throughout DC area, 301-229-6882, www.balletpetite.com). Fundamental dance instruction mixed with costumes, story telling, props, acting, and music.

- **Budding Yogis** (5615 39th St NW, 202-686-1104, www.buddingyogis.com). Yoga for kids, teens, and adults. Special summer programs available.

- **Capitol Hill Arts Workshop** (545 7th St SE, 202-547-6839, www.chaw.org). Classes for children in art disciplines, tumbling, and Tae Kwon Do. If your kids are precociously cool, sign them up for the jazz/hip-hop class and watch them perform a Hip-Hop Nutcracker in December.

- **Dance Place** (3225 8th St NE, 202-269-1600, www.danceplace.org). Creative movement, hip-hop, and African dance instruction for kids.

- **Imagination Stage** (4908 Auburn Ave, Bethesda, MD, 301-961-6060, www.imaginationstage.org). Classes in music, dance, and theater for kids and teens. Three-week summer camps also available.

- **Joy of Motion** (5207 Wisconsin Ave NW, 202-362-3042; 1643 Connecticut Ave, 202-387-0911, www.joyofmotion.org). Creative movement and fundamental dance instruction for children.

- **Kids Moving Company** (7475 Wisconsin Ave, Bethesda, MD, 301-656-1543, www.kidsmovingco.com) Creative movement classes for children nine months to eight years in a studio with a full-sized trampoline.

- **Kumon Math and Reading Program** (6831 Wisconsin Ave, Bethesda, MD, 301-652-1234, www.kumon.com). An after-school learning program in math and reading.

- **Music Tots** (4238 Wilson Blvd, Arlington, VA, 703-266-4571, www.musictots.com). Instruction in music, rhythm, and sound for children under five.
- **Musikids** (4900 Auburn Ave, Ste. 100, Bethesda, MD, 301-215-7946, www.musikids.com) Music and movement classes for newborns and toddlers.
- **Pentagon Row Ice-Skating** (1201 S Joyce St, Arlington, VA, 703-418-6666, www.pentagonrow.com). Skating lessons and birthday parties are available November–March.
- **Power Tech Tae Kwon Do** (2639 Connecticut Ave, 202-364-8244). Martial arts training for kids three and up.
- **Rock Creek Horse Center** (5100 Glover Rd NW, 202-362-0117, www.rockcreekhorsecenter.com). Riding lessons, trail rides, summer day camp, and equestrian team training. Weekly group lessons $50/hour, private lessons $90/hour, and one-week summer camp sessions cost $500.
- **Rock Creek Tennis Center** (16th & Kennedy Sts, NW, 202-722-5949, www.rockcreektennis.com). Five-week weekend tennis courses available for children at beginner and intermediate levels.
- **Round House Theatre** (4545 East West Hwy, Bethesda, MD, 240-644-1099, www.roundhousetheatre.org). The theater has a year-round drama school and an arts-centered summer day camp program.
- **Sportrock Climbing Center** (5308 Eisenhower Ave, Alexandria, VA, 703-212-7625, www.sportrock.com). Kids learn to climb. 6- to 12-year-olds have the run of the place 6:30 pm–8 pm on Fridays. $18 for adults, $7 for children (12 and under). Hours: Tues–Fri: 12 pm–11 pm; Sat–Sun: 12 pm–8 pm.
- **Sur La Table** (1101 S Joyce St, Arlington, 703-414-3580, www.surlatable.com). At Sur La Table's junior cooking classes, kids are encouraged to (gasp!) play with food. Classes are for children aged 6–12 and groups are small and well organized.
- **YMCA of Metropolitan Washington** (numerous branches, 202-232-6700, www.ymcawashdc.org). Youth and teen sports to spend all that hyperactive energy—particularly in the swimming pool!
- **Young Playwrights' Theatre** (2437 15th St, NW, 202-387-9173, www.youngplaywrightstheatre.org). Programs for children from fourth grade and up that encourage literacy, playwriting, and community engagement.

Shopping Essentials
- **Barnes & Noble** (books) • 3040 M St NW • 202-965-9880 • 555 12th St NW • 202-347-0176 • 3651 Jefferson Davis Hwy, Alexandria, VA • 703-299-9124 • 4801 Bethesda Ave, Bethesda, MD • 301-986-1761
- **Barston's Child's Play** (everything kids love) • 5536 Connecticut Ave NW • 202-244-3602
- **Benetton Kids** (kids' clothes) • 3222 M St NW • 202-333-4140
- **Borders** (books) • 600 14th St NW • 202-737-1385 • 1801 K St NW • 202-466-4999 • 5333 Wisconsin Ave NW • 202-686-8270 • 1201 Hayes St, Arlington, VA • 703-418-0166
- **Children's Place** (kids' clothes) • Pentagon City, 1100 S Hayes St, Arlington, VA • 703-413-4875
- **Discovery Channel Store** (children's gifts) • Union Station, 50 Massachusetts Ave NE • 202-842-3700
- **Fairy Godmother** (toys & books) • 319 7th St SE • 202-547-5474
- **Filene's Basement** (kids' clothes) • 5300 Wisconsin Ave NW • 202-966-0208
- **Full of Beans** (kids' clothes) • 5502 Connecticut Ave NW • 202-362-8566
- **Gap Kids and Baby Gap** (kids' clothes) • 2000 Pennsylvania Ave NW • 202-429-6862 • 1267 Wisconsin Ave NW • 202-333-2411 • 1100 S Hayes St, Arlington, VA • 703-418-4770 • 5430 Wisconsin Ave, Chevy Chase, MD • 301-907-7656
- **Gymboree** (kids' clothes) • 1100 S Hayes St, Arlington, VA • 703-415-5009
- **Hecht's** (clothes, furniture, toys, books) • 12th & G Sts NW • 202-628-6661
- **Imagination Station** (books) • 4524 Lee Highway, Arlington, VA • 703-522-2047
- **Kids Closet** (kids' clothes) • 1226 Connecticut Ave NW • 202-429-9247
- **Patagonia** (clothes) • 1048 Wisconsin Ave NW • 202-333-1776
- **Piccolo Piggies** (clothes, furniture, accessories) • 1533 Wisconsin Ave NW • 202-333-0123
- **Plaza Artist Supplies** (arts & crafts) • 1990 K St NW • 202-331-0126
- **Ramer's Shoes** (children's shoes) • 3810 Northampton St NW • 202-244-2288
- **Riverby Books** (used books) • 417 E Capitol St SE • 202-543-4342
- **Sullivan's Toys & Art Supplies** • 3412 Wisconsin Ave NW • 202-362-1343
- **Sur La Table** (pint-sized cooking supplies) • 1101 S Joyce St, Arlington, VA • 703-414-3580
- **Tree Top Kids** (toys, books & clothes) • 3301 New Mexico Ave NW • 202-244-3500

Where to go for more information
www.gocitykids.com
www.ourkids.com
www.lilaguide.com

Dupont Circle is to DC's gay life what Capitol Hill is to the nation's politics. And just as politics seep into most aspects of city life, the gay scene reaches far beyond Lambda Rising. In addition to the world's largest LGBT bookstore (just down the street from the bookstore where the first gay couple to be featured in the *New York Times'* "Weddings" met), there are gay and lesbian lifestyle newspapers, clubs, bars, and community groups scattered throughout the city. In short, Dupont Circle is a geographic reference as well as a state of mind, and the city is, for the most part, sexual-orientation-blind. While there are many LGBT residents in suburbs like Takoma Park, MD, and Arlington, VA, they enjoy precious little visibility compared to their District counterparts.

We take this moment to pay our respects to the numerous bars and clubs on O Street SE, which after a 30-year run, were shuttered forever in April 2006 to make room for the Washington Nationals' new stadium. These popular (and generally "adult-oriented") establishments were always jammed on the weekends, especially with locals taking out-of-towners to see fab-u-lous drag shows at Ziegfeld's or to see the boys bare it all at Secrets or Heat. Who knows when, where, or *if*, these clubs will reemerge elsewhere in town (the District government is being urged to assist in their relocation, but you know what NIMBYism is like). In 2008, we will sit wistfully along the third baseline and reminisce.

Websites

Capital Pride · www.capitalpride.org
Educational website dedicated to DC's LGBT community. The organization is also responsible for the planning and development of the annual Capital Pride Parade.

DC LGBT Arts Consortium ·
Consortium of various DC area arts organizations.

DC Dykes · www.dcdykes.com
Insider's guide for lesbians living in DC.

GayDC · www.gaydc.net
In-depth and up-to-date network for DC's gay, lesbian, bisexual, and transgendered community.

GayWdc · www.gayWdc.com
Gay and lesbian website for DC restaurant and bar listings, local news and events, classifieds, and personals.

Gay and Lesbian Activists Alliance · www.glaa.org
GLAA is the nation's oldest continuously active gay and lesbian civil rights organization.

Pen DC · www.pendc.org
LGBT business networking group.

Slash DC, Gay & Lesbian Guide to DC
Information on gay and lesbian nightlife, media, and news.

Publications

Metro Weekly · 1012 14th St NW · 202-638-6830 · www.metroweekly.com
Free weekly gay and lesbian magazine—reliable coverage of community events, nightlife, and reviews of the District's entertainment and art scene.

Washington Blade · 1408 U St · 202-797-7000 · www.washingtonblade.com
Weekly news source for Washington's gay community since 1969.

Women in the Life · 1642 R St NW · 202-483-9818 · www.womeninthelife.com
Glossy quarterly magazine written by and for lesbians of color.

Bookstores

Lambda Rising · 1625 Connecticut Ave NW · 202-462-6969 · www.lambdarising.com
When it opened in 1974, Lambda Rising carried about 250 titles. Today, the bookstore operates five stores in DC, Baltimore, Maryland, Rehoboth Beach, Delaware, Norfolk, Virginia, and New York City and serves as an information hub and meeting place for the Washington DC gay community.

Politics and Prose · 5015 Connecticut Ave NW · 202-364-1919 · www.politics-prose.com
Popular bookstore and coffee shop with a small selection devoted to gay and lesbian literature.

Health Center & Support Organizations

Arlington Gay & Lesbian Alliance · 703-522-7660 · www.agla.org
Monthly get-togethers for the Arlington LGBT community.

Beth Mishpachah · www.betmish.org
District of Columbia Jewish Center · 16th & Q Sts NW
DC's egalitarian synagogue that embraces a diversity of sexual and gender identities.

The Center · 1111 14th St NW · 202-518-6100 · www.thedccenter.org
A volunteer LGBT community organization in metro DC.

DC AIDS Hotline · 202-332-2437 or 800-322-7432

DC Black Pride · PO Box 77071, Washington, DC 20013 · 202-737-5767 · www.dcblackpride.org
African-American lesbian, gay, bisexual, and transgendered community group. Proceeds from Black Pride events are distributed to HIV/AIDS and other health organizations serving the African-American community.

Dignity · www.dignitywashington.org
For the LGBT Catholic community.

Police Department's Gay and Lesbian Liaison Unit · 300 Indiana Ave NW · 202-727-5427 · www.gaydc.net/gllu
Staffed by openly gay and lesbian members of the police department and their allies. The unit is dedicated to serving the gay, lesbian, bisexual, and transgendered communities in the District.

Family Pride · PO Box 65327, Washington, DC 20035 · 202-331-5015 · www.familypride.org
This group is dedicated to advancing the well-being of lesbian, gay, bisexual, and transgendered parents and their families.

Food & Friends · 219 Riggs Rd NE · 202-269-2277 · www.foodandfriends.org
The organization cooks, packages, and delivers meals and groceries to over 1,000 people living with HIV/AIDS and other life-challenging illnesses in the greater DC area. Hosts annual "Chef's Best" fundraising dinner with notable volunteer chefs from around the region.

GLAAD DC · 1700 Kalorama Rd · 202-986-1360 · www.glaad.org
Gay and Lesbian Alliance Against Defamation DC chapter.

PFLAG DC · 1111 14th St NW · 202-638-3852 · www.pflagdc.org
Parents and Friend of Lesbians and Gays DC chapter.

Senior Health Resources · Temple Heights Station · PO Box 53453, Washington, DC 20009 · 202-388-7900
Non-profit organization providing quality health-related services for the aging LGBT community.

Sexual Minority Youth Assistance League (SMYAL) · 410 7th St SE · 202-546-5940 · www.smyal.org
Non-profit group for LGBT youth.

Whitman-Walker Clinic · 1407 S St NW · 202-797-3500
www.wwc.org
A non-profit organization that provides medical and social services to the LGBT and HIV/AIDS communities of metropolitan DC. Home to one of the oldest substance abuse programs in the US. The Lesbian Health Center at Whitman Walker's Elizabeth Taylor Medical Center, 1810 14th St NW, offers top-quality health services (202-745-6131). There is also a Legal Aid Society for information on financial assistance possibilities (202-628-1161)

Sports and Clubs

Adventuring · PO Box 18118, Washington, DC 20036 · 202-462-0535 · www.adventuring.org
All-volunteer group organizes group hikes, bike rides, and more for DC's LGBT community.

Capital Tennis Association · www.capitaltennis.org
Casual and organized tennis programs for the metropolitan gay and lesbian community.

Chesapeake and Potomac Softball (CAPS) · PO Box 3092, Falls Church, VA 22043 · 202-543-0236 · www.capsoftball.org
A friendly place for members of the LGBT community to play softball.

DC Aquatics Club · PO Box 12211, Washington, DC 20005 · www.swimdcac.org
Swimming team and social club for gays, lesbians, and friends of the gay and lesbian community.

DC's Different Drummers ·
PO Box 57099, Washington, DC 20037 · 202-269-4868 · www.dcdd.org
DC's Lesbian and Gay Symphonic, Swing, Marching, and Pep Bands.

DC Front Runners · PO Box 65550, Washington, DC 20035
202-628-3223 · www.dcfrontrunners.org
Running is so gay!

DC Lambda Squares ·
PO Box 77782, Washington, DC 20013 · www.dclambdasquares.org
LGBT square-dance club.

DC Strokes · PO Box 3789, Washington, DC 20027 · www.dcstrokes.org
The first rowing club for gays and lesbians. They row out of the Thompson Boat Center on the Potomac.

Federal Triangles · 202-986-5363 · www.federaltriangles.org
Soccer club for the LGBT community.

Gay Men's Chorus of Washington DC:
Federal City Performing Arts Association · 2801 M Street NW · (202) 293-1548 · www.gmcw.org

Lambda Links · www.lambdalinks.org
Gay golf.

Lesbian and Gay Chorus of Washington, DC · PO Box 65285, Washington, DC 20035 · 202-546-1549 · www.lgcw.org

Washington Wetskins Water Polo · www.wetskins.org
The first lesbian, gay, and bisexual polo team in the United States.

Washington Renegades Rugby · www.dcrugby.com
A Division III club that actively recruits gays and men of color from the DC region.

Annual Events

Capital Pride Festival/Parade · 1407 S St NW · 202-797-3510 · www.capitalpride.org
Annual festival and parade honoring the history and heritage of the LGBT community in Washington, DC. Usually held throughout Dupont and downtown the second week in June.

DC Black Pride Festival/Parade · 202-737-5767 · 866-942-5473 · www.dcblackpride.org
The world's largest Black Pride festival, drawing a crowd of about 30,000 annually. Usually held Memorial Day weekend.

Reel Affirmations · PO Box 73587, Washington, DC, 20056 · 202-986-1119 · www.reelaffirmations.org
Washington DC's Annual Lesbian and Gay Film Festival. Late October.

Youth Pride Day/Week · PO Box 33161, Washington, DC 20033 · 202-387-4141 · www.youthpridedc.org
Usually held in early April. The largest event for gay, lesbian, bisexual, and transgendered youth in the mid-Atlantic region.

Venues

Gay
- **Bachelor's Mill** · 1104 8th St SE · 202-544-1931
- **The Blue Room** · 2321 18th St NW · 202-332-0800
- **Cobalt/30 Degrees** · 17th & R Sts NW · 202-462-6569 (30 Degrees is non-smoking)
- **DC Eagle** (leather) · 639 New York Ave NW · 202-347-6025
- **Fireplace** · 2161 P St NW · 202-293-1293
- **Green Lantern/Tool Shed** (*upstairs*) · 1335 Green Court NW · 202-966-3111
- **Halo** · 1435 P St, NW · 202-797-9730 · **(**Non-smoking venue**)**
- **Titan** · 1337 14th St NW (upstairs) · 202-232-7010
- **JR's Bar & Grill** · 1519 17th St NW · 202-328-0090
- **Omega DC** · 2123 Twining Ct NW · 202-223-4917
- **Remington's** · 639 Pennsylvania Ave SE · 202-543-3113
- **Wet** · 56 L St SE · 202-488-1200
- **Windows/Dupont Italian Kitchen (DIK) Bar** · 1635 17th St NW · 202-328-0100

Lesbian
- **Edge/Wet** (Wednesday) · 56 L St SE · 202-488-1200
- **Phase One** · 525 8th St SE · 202-544-6831

Both
- **1409 Playbill Cafe** · 1409 14th St NW · 202-265-3055
- **Apex** · 1415 22nd St NW · 202-296-0505
- **Banana Cafe** · 500 8th St SE · 202-543-5906
- **Chaos** (Wednesday, Ladies' night) · 17th & Q Sts NW · 202-232-4141
- **Ellington's** (jazz) 424 8th St, SE · 202-546-8308
- **Freddie's Beach Bar** · 555 S 23rd St S, Arlington, VA · 703-685-0555
- **Larry's Lounge** · 1836 18th St NW · 202-483-1483

One of the great things about Washington, DC, is that the Metro is safe, convenient, and affordable. That's why you needn't find lodging right in the heart of the area you most want to visit—especially good news if you budget's tight.

Like all big cities, though, be sure to ask around, and check blogs and listservs to get "real people" ratings on the places you are considering before you tap your credit card number into the reservations system. Ask around. Housing—no matter the rate or neighborhood—can be a mixed bag.

If you have the cash, consider the **Hotel Helix (Map 10)** (1430 Rhode Island Ave NW) in Logan Circle, which features bright, comfy, pop-art furniture and ultramodern décor. The bar scene there is fairly non-existent, but it's in a trendy neighborhood with plenty of cool eateries and stores. Another good choice in the city is the **Hotel George (Map 2)** (15 E St NW). It's trendy, has large, comfortable rooms (which are all non smoking, by the way), and is located near the US Capitol, not far from Union Station. That means public transportation is steps away. There are also some great pubs and eateries very close by (both inside Union Station and on neighboring streets). One note of caution—this is a "pet friendly" hotel, so if you prefer only two-legged guests, this might not be for you. Another trendy hotel—though not good for the budget-minded—is the **Mandarin Oriental**

(Map 6) (1330 Maryland Ave SW). If you crave elegance with an Asian flourish, top amenities, and a possible celebrating sighting (think Bono and Paul Newman), this is a great choice.

If your budget is a tight, there's nothing wrong with checking out a youth hostel. There are plenty of good ones to be had with room rates starting at about $20 a night. But use caution—this type of lodging varies widely in DC, from clean and secure to downright scary (think the Bronx). As with hotels, ask a number of people before you commit. **American Guesthouse** has two locations: Arlington (739 22nd St S) **(Map 40)** and Alexandria (1700 Sherwood Hall Ln, 203-768-0335). While not in the city, the hostels are in trendy areas of Virginia, both short Metro rides away from the city. They both offer safe, clean housing. One DC youth hostel in a fairly decent neighborhood (not far from the World Bank) is the **Hilltop Hostel (Map 27)** (formerly the India House, 300 Carroll St NW). It is also clean, inexpensive, and near a Metro. Former guests report that the security is good, and they felt safe there.

As always, you should use the room rates and star ratings listed below as a guide only. You'll probably want to call or visit the hotel in question to get the most accurate room rates for the days you wish to stay. If you're booking in advance, we suggest checking out sites such as hotels.com, expedia.com, and pricerighthotels.com to see if they

Map 1 • National Mall

	Address	Phone	Nightly Rate	Star Rating
Courtyard by Marriott	900 F St NW	202-638-4600	209	★★★
Embassy Suites	900 10th St NW	202-739-2001	281	
Grand Hyatt	1000 H St NW	202-582-1234	215	★★★
Hay-Adams Hotel	800 16th St NW	202-638-6600	329	★★★★
Hilton Garden Inn	815 14th St NW	202-783-7800	239	★★★
Hotel Harrington	436 11th St NW	202-628-8140	89	
Hotel Washington	515 15th St NW	202-638-5900	275	★★
JW Marriott	1331 Pennsylvania Ave NW	202-393-2000	339	★★★
Marriott Metro Center	775 12th St NW	202-737-2200	209	★★★
Sofitel Lafayette Sq	806 15th St NW	202-730-8800	405	★★★★
Willard Inter-Continental	1401 Pennsylvania Ave NW	202-628-9100	359	★★★★

Map 2 • Chinatown / Union Station

	Address	Phone	Nightly Rate	Star Rating
Hotel George	15 E St NW	202-347-4200	129	★★★
Holiday Inn	415 New Jersey Ave NW	202-638-1616	134	★★★
Hotel Monaco	700 F St NW	202-628-7177	389	★★★★
Hyatt Regency	400 New Jersey Ave NW	202-737-1234	409	★★★
Phoenix Park	520 N Capitol St NW	202-638-6900	188	★★★
Red Roof Inn	500 H St NW	202-289-5959	139	★★
Washington Ct Hotel	525 New Jersey Ave NW	202-628-2100	184	★★★

Map 3 • The Hill

	Address	Phone	Nightly Rate	Star Rating
Doolittle Guest House	506 E Capitol St NE	202-546-6622	135	

Map 5 • Southeast / Anacostia

	Address	Phone	Nightly Rate	Star Rating
Capitol Hill Suites	200 C St SE	202-543-6000	229	★★
Washington Capitol Hill/Navy Yard	140 L St SE	202-479-0027	219	

Map 6 • Waterfront

Hotel	Address	Phone	Price	Rating
Best Western - Capitol Skyline Hotel	10 I St SW	202-488-7500	189	★★
Channel Inn	650 Water St SW	202-554-2400	149	★★★
Holiday Inn	550 C St SW	202-479-4000	152	★★★
L'enfant Plaza Hotel	480 L'Enfant Plz SW	202-484-1000	192	★★★
Mandarin Oriental	1330 Maryland Ave SW	202-554-8588	385	★★★★
Residence Inn by Marriott	333 E St SW	202-484-8280	199	★★★

Map 7 • Foggy Bottom

Hotel	Address	Phone	Price	Rating
Doubletree	801 New Hampshire Ave NW	202-785-2000	188	★★★
George Washington University Inn	824 New Hampshire Ave NW	202-337-6620	309	★★★
Hotel Lombardy	2019 Pennsylvania Ave NW	202-828-2600	179	★★★
Remington Executive Suites	601 24th St NW	202-223-4512	99–150	
River Inn	924 25th St NW	202-337-7600	249	★★★
State Plaza Hotel	2117 E St NW	202-861-8200	179	★★★
The Watergate Hotel	2650 Virginia Ave NW	202-965-2300	259	★★★★

Map 8 • Georgetown

Hotel	Address	Phone	Price	Rating
Four Seasons	2800 Pennsylvania Ave NW	202-342-0444	525	★★★★
Georgetown Inn	1310 Wisconsin Ave NW	202-333-8900	289	★★★
Georgetown Suites	1111 30th St NW	202-298-7800	145	★★★
Holiday Inn	2101 Wisconsin Ave NW	202-338-4600	150	
Hotel Monticello	1075 Thomas Jefferson St NW	202-337-0900	269	
Latham Hotel	3000 M St NW	202-726-5000	179	★★★
The Ritz-Carlton	3100 South St NW	202-912-4100	399	★★★★★
Washington Suites	2500 Pennsylvania Ave NW	202-333-8060	178	★★★

Map 9 • Dupont Circle / Adams Morgan

Hotel	Address	Phone	Price	Rating
1 Washington Cir	1 Washington Cir NW	202-872-1680	$200	★★★
Beacon Hotel and Corporate Quarters	1615 Rhode Island Ave NW	202-296-2100	299	★★★
Best Western	1121 New Hampshire Ave NW	202-457-0565	151	★★
Capital Hilton	1001 16th St NW	202-393-1000	359	★★★
Carlyle Suites	1731 New Hampshire Ave NW	202-234-3200	329	★★★
Churchill Hotel	1914 Connecticut Ave NW	202-797-2000	239	★★★
Courtyard by Marriott	1600 Rhode Island Ave NW	202-293-8000	239	★★★
Courtyard by Marriott	1900 Connecticut Ave NW	202-332-9300	179	★★★
Dupont at the Circle B&B	1604 19th St NW	202-332-5251	170	★★★
Embassy Inn	1627 16th St NW	202-234-7800	129	
Embassy Suites	1250 22nd St NW	202-857-3388	218	★★★
Fairmont	2401 M St NW	202-429-2400	439	★★★★
Hilton	2015 Massachusetts Ave NW	202-265-1600	409	★★★
Holiday Inn	1501 Rhode Island Ave NW	202-483-2000	205	★★★
Hotel Madera	1310 New Hampshire Ave NW	202-296-7600	239	★★★
Hotel Palomar	2121 P St NW	202-293-3100	350	★★★
Hotel Quincey	1823 L St NW	202-223-4320	199	★★★
Hotel Rouge	1315 16th St NW	202-232-8000	219	★★★
Jurys	2118 Wyoming Ave NW	202-483-1350	195	★★
Jurys Doyle	1500 New Hampshire Ave NW	202-483-6000	295	★★★★
Loews Jefferson	1200 16th St NW	202-347-2200	219	★★★★
Loews Madison Hotel	1177 15th St NW	202-862-1600	329	★★★
M Street Hotel	1143 New Hampshire Ave NW	202-775-0800	229	★★★
Melrose Hotel	2430 Pennsylvana Ave NW	202-955-6400	309	★★★
Park Hyatt	24th St NW & M St NW	202-789-1234	335	★★★★
Potomac Suites	2424 Pennsylvania Ave NW	202-331-5000	2,600 monthly	
Renaissance Mayflower Hotel	1127 Connecticut Ave NW	202-347-3000	259	★★★★
Residence Inn by Marriott	2120 P St NW	202-466-6800	309	★★★
Ritz-Carlton	1150 22nd St NW	202-835-0500	339	★★★★★
St Gregory Hotel & Suites	2033 M St NW	202-530-3600	259	★★★
St Regis	923 16th St NW	202-638-2626	435	★★★★
The Swann House	1808 New Hampshire Ave NW	202-265-4414	185	
Tabard Inn	1739 N St NW	202-785-1277	98 (shared bath), 143 (private bath)	
Topaz Hotel	1733 N St NW	202-393-3000	309	★★★
Washington Hilton and Towers	1919 Connecticut Ave NW	202-483-3000	224	★★★
Washington Marriott	1221 22nd St NW	202-872-1500	269	★★★
Washington Terrace	1515 Rhode Island Ave NW	202-232-7000	228	★★★
The Westin Embassy Row	2100 Massachusetts Ave NW	202-293-2100	420	★★★★
The Westin Grand	2350 M St NW	202-429-0100	319	★★★★
Windsor Inn	1842 16th St NW	202-667-0300	99	
Windsor Park	2116 Kalorama Rd NW	202-483-7700	159	★★

Map 10 • Logan Circle / U Street

Aaron Shipman House Bed & Breakfast	13th St NW & Q St NW	202-328-3510	90	
Abigail Christy Bed and Breakfast	13th St NW & S St NW	202-328-3510	110	
Braxton Hotel	1440 Rhode Island Ave NW	202-232-7800	70	
Chester A Arthur Bed and Breakfast	Logan Cir	413-582-9888	115	
Comfort Inn	1201 13th St NW	202-682-5300	239	
DC Guesthouse	1337 10th St NW	202-332-2502	175	
Four Points	1201 K St NW	202-289-7600	305	★★★
Hamilton Crowne Plaza	1001 14th St NW	202-682-0111	386	
Hampton Inn	901 6th St NW	202-842-2500	239	★★★★
Henley Park Hotel	926 Massachusetts Ave NW	202-638-5200	209	★★★
Homewood Suites	1475 Massachusetts Ave NW	202-265-8000	169	★★★
Hotel Helix	1430 Rhode Island Ave NW	202-462-9001	219	★★★
Morrison-Clark Inn	Massachusetts Ave & 11th St NW	202-898-1200	309	★★★
Renaissance	999 9th St NW	202-898-9000	289	★★★
Residence Inn by Marriott	1199 Vermont Ave NW	202-898-1100	279	★★★
Swiss Inn	1204 Massachusetts Ave NW	202-371-1816	79	
Washington Plaza	10 Thomas Cir NW	202-842-1300	199	★★★
Wyndham	1400 M St NW	202-429-1700	315	★★★

Map 11 • Near Northeast

Downtown Motel	1345 4th St NE	202-544-2000	65	
Howard Johnson Express Inn	600 New York Ave NE	202-546-9200	70	
Kellogg Conference Hotel	800 Florida Ave NE	202-651-6000	195	★★
Super 8 Motel	501 New York Ave NE	202-543-7400	80	

Map 12 • Trinidad

Travelodge	1917 Bladensburg Rd NE	202-832-8600	199

Map 13 • Brookland / Langdon

Days Inn	2700 New York Ave NE	202-832-5800	93
President Inn	1600 New York Ave NE	202-832-3200	79

Map 14 • Catholic U

McMillan House Bed and Breakfast	1032 Perry St NE	202-636-9399	64

Map 16 • Adams Morgan (North) / Mt Pleasant

Adams Inn	1746 Lanier Pl NW	202-745-3600	89
Kalorama Guest House	1854 Mintwood Pl NW	202-667-6369	55 (shared bath), 70 (private bath)

Map 17 • Woodley Park / Cleveland Park

Kalorama Guest House	2700 Cathedral Ave NW	202-328-0860	55 (shared bath), 70 (private bath)	
Omni Shoreham	2500 Calvert St NW	202-234-0700	329	★★★★
Wardman Park Marriott Hotel	2660 Woodley Rd NW	202-328-2000	269	★★★
Woodley Park Guesthouse	2647 Woodley Rd NW	202-667-0218	130	

Map 18 • Glover Park / Foxhall

Georgetown University Conference Hotel	3800 Reservoir Rd NW	800-228-9290	259	
Savoy Suites	2505 Wisconsin Ave NW	202-337-9700	180	★★★

Map 19 • Tenleytown / Friendship Heights

Embassy Suites	4300 Military Rd NW	202-362-9300	206	★★★

Map 20 • Cleveland Park / Upper Connecticut

Days Inn	4400 Connecticut Ave NW	202-244-5600	169	★★

Map 22 • Downtown Bethesda

American Inn	8130 Wisconsin Ave	301-656-9300	175	★★★
Bethesda Court Hotel	7740 Wisconsin Ave	301-656-2100	122	★★
Doubletree Hotel	8120 Wisconsin Ave	301-652-2000	239	★★★
Four Points	8400 Wisconsin Ave	301-654-1000	149	★★★
Marriott	5151 Pooks Hill Rd	301-897-9400	159	★★★★★
Residence Inn by Marriott	7335 Wisconsin Ave	301-718-0200	159	

Map 25 • Silver Spring

Courtyard Silver Spring Downtown	8506 Fenton St	301-589-4899	199	
Days Inn	8040 13th St	301-588-4400	81	★★★
Hilton	8727 Colesville Rd	301-589-5200	188	★★★
Holiday Inn	8777 Georgia Ave	301-589-0800	207	

Map 27 • Walter Reed

Hilltop Hostel	300 Carroll St NW	202-291-9591	22
Motel 6 Accor Hotels	6711 Georgia Ave NW	202-722-1600	60
Ramada Limited	7990 Georgia Ave	301-565-3444	95

Map 29 • Bethesda / Chevy Chase Business

Holiday Inn	5520 Wisconsin Ave	301-656-1500	131	
Hyatt Regency	1 Bethesda Metro Ctr	301-657-1234	279	★★★

Map 33 • Falls Church

Econo Lodge	6800 Lee Hwy	703-538-5300	109	★★

Map 34 • Ballston

Comfort Inn Ballston	1211 N Glebe Rd	703-247-3399	239	★★
Hilton	950 N Stafford St	703-528-6000	199	★★★
Holiday Inn	4610 N Fairfax Dr	703-243-9800	150	★★★
The Westin Arlington Gateway	801 N Glebe Rd	703-717-6200	239	

Map 35 • Clarendon

Inns of Virginia	3335 Lee Hwy	703-524-9800	75

Map 36 • Rosslyn

Best Western	1850 N Ft Myer Dr	703-522-0400	143	★★
Courtyard by Marriott	1533 Clarendon Blvd	703-528-2222	249	
Hilton Garden Inn	1333 N Courthouse Rd	703-528-4444	170	★★★
Holiday Inn	1900 N Ft Myer Dr	703-807-2000	190	★★★
Hyatt	1325 Wilson Blvd	703-525-1234	229	★★★
Key Bridge Marriott	1401 Lee Hwy	703-524-6400	249	★★★
Motel Fifty Rosslyn	1601 Arlington Blvd	703-524-3400	80	
Quality Hotel Courthouse Plaza	1200 N Courthouse Rd	703-524-4000	159	★★
Quality Inn Iwo Jima	1501 Arlington Blvd	703-524-5000	159	
Residence Inn by Marriott	1651 N Oak St	703-812-8400	279	★★★
Virginian Suites	1500 Arlington Blvd	703-522-9600	209	★★

Map 37 • Fort Myer

Days Inn	3030 Columbia Pike	703-521-5570	76	★★
Highlander Motel	3336 Wilson Blvd	703-524-4300	75	

Map 38 • Columbia Pike

Hampton Inn	4800 Leesburg Pike	703-671-4800	149	★★★
Homewood Suites	4850 Leesburg Pike	703-671-6500	199	

Map 39 • Shirlington

Best Western	2480 S Glebe Rd	703-979-4400	143	★★
Econo Lodge	2485 S Glebe Rd	703-979-4100	69	

Map 40 • Pentagon City / Crystal City

American Guesthouse	739 S 22nd St S	703-768-0335	90	
Americana Motel	1400 Jefferson Davis Hwy	703-979-3772	99	
Courtyard by Marriott	2899 Jefferson Davis Hwy	703-549-3434	299	★★★
Crowne Plaza	1480 Crystal Dr	703-416-1600	144	★★★
Crystal City Hotel	901 S Clark St	703-416-1900	70	
Crystal City Marriott	1999 Jefferson Davis Hwy	703-413-5500	169	★★★
Crystal Gateway Marriott	1700 Jefferson Davis Hwy	703-920-3230	199	★★★
Crystal Quarters	1501 Crystal Dr	800-332-8501	150 per night (min. 7 nights)	
Crystal Quarters	1801 Crystal Dr	800-332-8501	150 per night (min. 7 nights)	

Map 40 • Pentagon City–*continued*

Doubletree	300 Army Navy Dr	703-416-4100	188	★★★
Embassy Suites	1300 Jefferson Davis Hwy	703-979-9799	211	★★★
Hampton Inn	2000 Jefferson Davis Hwy	703-418-8181	109	
Hilton	2399 Jefferson Davis Hwy	703-418-6800	215	★★★
Holiday Inn	2650 Jefferson Davis Hwy	703-684-7200	200	★★
Hyatt	2799 Jefferson Davis Hwy	703-418-1234	259	★★★
Radisson hotel	2020 Jefferson Davis Hwy	703-920-8600	89	★★★
Residence Inn by Marriott	550 Army Navy Dr	703-413-6630	159	★★★
The Ritz-Carlton	1250 S Hayes St	703-415-5000	499	★★★★★
Sheraton	1800 Jefferson Davis Hwy	703-486-1111	279	★★★
Sheraton	900 S Orme St	703-521-1900	269	★★★

Map 41 • Landmark

Alexandria Hotel Pentagon	4641 Kenmore Ave	703-751-4510	199	★★★★
Comfort Inn Landmark	6254 Duke St	703-642-3422	83	
Extended Stayamerica	205 N Breckinridge Pl	703-941-9440	89	
Hawthorn Suites Ltd - Alexandria	420 N Van Dorn St	703-370-1000	89	★★★
Hilton	5000 Seminary Rd	703-845-1010	206	★★★
Washington Suites	100 S Reynolds St	703-370-9600	169	★★★

Map 42 • Alexandria (West)

Courtyard by Marriott	2700 Eisenhower Ave	703-329-2323	129	★★★
Homestead Studio Suites Hotel	200 Blue Stone Rd	703-329-3399	124	

Map 44 • Alexandria Downtown

Embassy Suites	1900 Diagonal Rd	703-684-5900	218	★★★
Hampton Inn	1616 King St	703-299-9900	209	★★★
Hilton	1767 King St	703-837-0440	149	★★★
Holiday Inn	2460 Eisenhower Ave	703-960-3400	151	

Map 45 • Old Town (North)

Holiday Inn	625 1st St	703-548-6300	170	★★★
Radisson Hotel Old Town	901 N Fairfax St	703-683-6000	129	★★★
Sheraton	801 N St Asaph St	703-836-4700	199	★★★

Map 46 • Old Town (South)

Best Western	1101 N Washington St	703-739-2222	143	
Holiday Inn	480 King St	703-549-6080	210	★★★
Morrison House	116 S Alfred St	703-838-8000	242	★★★★
Residence Inn by Marriott	1456 Duke St	703-548-5474	169	★★★
Towne Motel	808 N Washington St	703-548-3500	70	
Travelodge	700 N Washington St	703-836-5100	89	

Between renaming buildings, bridges, and fountains and building new monuments by the garden-full, DC is fast running out of things to convert into memorials. You could spend a month visiting every official monument in DC, but you'll have a better time checking out the unofficial local landmarks that get lost in the giant shadows of the White House and Washington Monument.

After you are done with the marble tributes to the Founding Fathers, why not tour the landmarks of other lesser politicians? Visit the Vista International Hotel now the **Wyndham (Map 10)**, where former DC Mayor Marion Barry was caught smoking crack cocaine. The trendy coffeehouse **Tryst (Map 9, 16)**, where Gary Levy canoodled with Chandra Levy, or the **Washington Hilton (Map 9)**, where Ronald Reagan took a bullet from John Hinckley, Jr.

If politics isn't your thing (then why are you here?), the District has many a grand home to admire from the inside and out. **The Heurich House (Map 9)**, also known as the Brewmaster's Castle, invites you to tour a perfectly intact Victorian home, complete with a basement Bavarian beer drinking room. Or if you're feeling more whimsical, there's the **Mushroom House (Map 30)** in Bethesda, a life-size smurf home, and **The Littlest House in Alexandria (Map 46)**, which allows for a narrow 7-foot wide life.

This town also has more than its fair share of statues. Take a moment at Union Station to admire the **Columbus Memorial (Map 2)** out front. The marble fountain opened in 1912, but most visitors and commuters come and go and never take notice of it at all. The circular fountain is 44 feet deep in the middle, and Columbus himself stands at the larger-than-life height of 15 feet. Or if you're weary of oversized statues of dead white men, you can gaze up instead at the **Gandhi Statue (Map 9)** off Dupont Circle, the **Joan of Arc (Map 9)** statue at Malcolm X Park, or the beloved **Grief (Map 14)** memorial in Rock Creek Cemetery.

And still more landmarks are those buildings you've seen again and again, and yet no one seems to be able to identify. The **Temple of the Scottish Rite of Freemasonry (Map 9)** standing tall on 16th Street, the **Second Division Memorial (Map 1)** on the Mall, or **The Other FDR Memorial (Map 1)** that quietly sits outside the National Archives,

Every neighborhood seems to have its local landmarks—whether it be colorful mural (see: **Marilyn Monroe (Map 16)** in Cleveland Park) or a frequently patronized greasy spoon (see: **Ben's Chili Bowl (Map 10)** on U Street). When in Dupont, hang out by the **Dupont Fountain (Map 9)**—the focal point of the eclectic crowd that makes up the neighborhood. In Silver Spring, head straight to the **AFI Theater (Map 25)**, where you can catch an indie American or foreign film and watch it in the stadium seats usually associated with blockbuster releases. Need a break from the frenzied Georgetown shopping scene? Walk a few blocks to the city's best garden at **Dumbarton Oaks (Map 8)**. And so the list goes on and on…

Map 1 · National Mall

The Other FDR Memorial	Pennsylvania Ave NW, b/w 7th St NW & 9th St NW	All FDR wanted was a stone outside the National Archives.
Decatur House	1610 H St NW · 202-965-0920	Tour worth taking.
District Building	1350 Pennsylvania Ave NW	DC's city hall. You can't fight it.
Ford's Theatre	511 10th St NW · 202-426-6924	Lincoln's finale.
Hay-Adams Hotel	16th St & H St NW · 800-853-6807	The luxury lap where Monica told all.
Hotel Washington	515 15th St NW · 202-638-5900	Its rooftop deck will give you a silver screen view of the Nation's Capital.
International Spy Museum	800 F St NW · 202-393-7798	For all the future Aldrich Ames out there.
J Edgar Hoover FBI Building	935 Pennsylvania Ave NW · 202-324-3000	Ask to see Hoover's cross-dressing dossier.
National Aquarium	14th St NW & Constitution Ave NW · 202-482-2825	Save money, visit pet shop.
National Mall/ Smithsonian Merry-Go-Round	1000 Jefferson Dr SW · 202-633-1000	Tacky, but quells crying children.
National Press Club	529 14th St NW, 13th Fl · 202-662-7500	Join the ink-stained hacks for a drink.
Old Post Office Tower	1100 Pennsylvania Ave NW · 202-606-8691	Best view of skyscraper-less Washington.
The Clinton McDonald's	750 17th St NW · 202-347-0047	Taste what Bill couldn't resist.
Smithsonian Institution	1000 Jefferson Dr SW · 202-633-1000	Storm the castle for information.
The Second Division Memorial	17th St NW & Constitution Ave NW	Overlooked history.
St John's Church	16th St NW & H St NW · 202-347-8766	Sit in the President's pew.
The Other FDR Memorial	Pennsylvania Ave NW, b/w 7th St NW & 9th St NW	All FDR wanted was a stone outside the National Archives.
Willard Hotel	1401 Pennsylvania Ave NW · 202-628-9100	Historic hotel where the term "lobbyist" was born. And free HBO!

General Information • **Landmarks**

Map 2 • Chinatown / Union Station

Casa Italiana	595 1/2 3rd St NW • 202-638-0165	DC's half-block answer to Little Italy.
Chinatown Gate	H St NW & 7th St NW	Ushers you in for cheap eats and cheaper pottery.
Columbus Memorial	Massachusetts Ave & First St (near Union Station)	Look for a big statue and fountain—the one with the carvings.
Library of Congress	1st St SE b/w Independence Ave SE & E Capitol St SE • 202-707-5000	Lose yourself in letters.
National Building Museum	401 F St NW • 202-272-2448	Step inside and feel your jaw drop.
Shakespeare Theatre	450 7th St NW • 202-547-1122	Where the Bard shows off.
Supreme Court of the United States	1st St NE b/w E Capitol St SE & Maryland Ave NE • 202-479-3211	Bring your favorite protest sign.
US Botanic Garden	100 Maryland Ave SW • 202-225-8333	Relaxing refuge of tropical flora and primeval plants.
USDA Graduate Schools	600 Maryland Ave SW • 888-744-4723	Go learn something. Impressive array of class offerings.

Map 3 • The Hill

Folger Shakespeare Library	201 E Capitol St SE • 202-544-4600	To go or not to go?

Map 5 • Southeast / Anacostia

Anacostia Boathouse	1105 O St SE	Take the dirty plunge.
Congressional Cemetery	1801 E St SE • 202-543-0539	Individual graves, shared conditions.
Eastern Market	225 7th St SE • 202-546-2698	Apples and art.
Frederick Douglass House	1411 W St SE • 202-426-5951	A man who showed up his neighborhood and his country.
Washington Navy Yard	9th St SE & M St SE • 202-433-4882	Haven for men in tighty whites.

Map 6 • Waterfront

Arena Stage	1101 6th St SW • 202-488-3300	Great theater.
The Awakening Statue	Tip of Hains Point, East Potomac Park	Climb on giant fingers and toes.
Ft Lesley J McNair	4th St SW & P St SW	For the Civil War buffs.
Gangplank Marina	6th St SW & Water St SW • 202-554-5000	A Washington Channel neighborhood of boat-dwellers.
Odyssey Cruises	6th St SW & Water St SW • 888-741-0281	Dining and dancing on the Potomac river.
Spirit of Washington	6th St SW & Water St SW • 202-484-2320	Experience Washington by boat.
Thomas Law House	1252 6th St SW	Impressive house, not open to the public.
Tiber Island	429 N St SW	Looking for an apartment?
USS Sequoia	6th St SW & Maine Ave SW • 202-333-0011	Rent it when the VP isn't in the mood to play Mr. Howell.

Map 7 • Foggy Bottom

Einstein Statue	Constitution Ave NW & 22nd St NW	At his rumpled best.
Kennedy Center	2700 F St NW • 202-416-8000	High-brow culture.
The Octagon	1799 New York Ave NW • 202-626-7387	Peculiar floor plan.
Watergate Hotel	2650 Virginia Ave NW • 800-289-1555	Location of the most infamous Washington scandal yet; still a great design.

Map 8 • Georgetown

Cooke's Row	3009–3029 Q St NW	Romantic row.
Dumbarton Oaks Museum and Gardens	1703 32nd St NW • 202-339-6401	An absolute treasure.
Exorcist Steps	3600 Prospect St NW	Watch your balance…and LOOK UP! LOOK UP!
Islamic Center	2551 Massachussetts Ave NW • 202-332-8343	Oldest Islamic house of worship in the city.
Oak Hill Cemetery	30th St NW & R St NW • 202-337-2835	Old and gothic.
Old Stone House	3051 M St NW • 202-426-6851	Old. And Stone. It's the oldest building this town's got.
Prospect House	3508 Prospect St NW	Spectacular view of the Potomac.
Tudor Place	1644 31st St NW • 202-965-0400	Bring a picnic.
Volta Bureau	1537 35th St NW • 202-337-5220	HQ of the Alexander Graham Bell Association for the Deaf.

Map 9 • Dupont Circle / Adams Morgan

Australian Embassy	1601 Massachusetts Ave NW • 202-797-3000	Look out for the Christmas kangaroos.
Blaine Mansion	2000 Massachusetts Ave NW	Large, red, and brick.
The Brickskeller	1523 22nd St NW • 202-293-1885	Get drunk on the world's largest beer list.
Chinese Embassy	2300 Connecticut Ave NW • 202-328-2500	Look for the Falun Gong protesters.
DC Improv	1140 Connecticut Ave NW • 202-296-7008	Chorte in a city that doesn't laugh enough.
DC's Spanish Steps	S St NW & 22nd St NW	A miniRoman Holiday.
Dumbarton Bridge	23rd St NW & Q St NW	Four fantastic buffalos guide you from Dupont to Georgetown.
Dupont Fountain	Dupont Cir	Top spot for people-watching.
Eastern Star Temple	1618 New Hampshire Ave NW • 202-667-4737	National Women's Party HQ.
Farragut Square	K St NW & 17th St NW	Share park benches with K Street suits and the homeless.
Freshfarm Market	20th St NW near Q St NW • 202-331-7300	Where yuppies get their fruit.
Gandhi Statue	Massachusetts Ave NW & 21st St NW	Don't peek under the skirt.
Heurich House	1307 New Hampshire Ave NW	It sure feels haunted.
Iraqi Embassy	1801 P St NW • 202-483-7500	Watch the hated old shell come alive.
Italian Cultural Institute	2025 M St NW • 202-223-9800	Learn how to whistle at babes like the Romans did.
Joan of Arc Statue	Meridian Hill Park	You'd think she conquered Washington.
Lambda Rising	1625 Connecticut Ave NW • 202-462-6969	DC's gay and lesbian gathering place.
The Mansion on O Street	2020 O St NW • 202-496-2000	Hidden passageways, celeb guests, and Grey Goose Martini happy hours.
Meridian Hill/Malcolm X Park	16th St NW b/w W St NW & Euclid St NW	Sunday drum circle + soccer!
Middle East Institute	1761 N St NW • 202-785-1141	A Middle East Mecca… er, you know what we mean.
National Geographic Society Headquarters	1145 17th St NW • 202-857-7588	It holds the world and all that's in it, apparently.
The Palm	1225 19th St NW • 202-293-9091	Aka, The Institute For Power Lunching.
Sonny Bono Memorial	20th St NW & New Hampshire Ave NW	Rest In Peace, babe.
Temple of the Scottish Rite of Freemasonry	1733 16th St NW • 202-232-3579	So that's what that is.
Washington Hilton	1919 Connecticut Ave NW • 202-483-3000	Where Reagan took a bullet.
Woman's National Democratic Club	1526 New Hampshire Ave NW • 202-232-7363	Presidents and First Ladies on walls.
Woodrow Wilson House	2340 S St NW • 202-387-4062	Another president's crib.

Map 10 • Logan Circle / U Street

African-American Civil War Memorial	1000 U St NW • 202-667-2667	A belated thanks.
Ben's Chili Bowl	1213 U St NW • 202-667-0909	Half-smokes and milkshakes beloved by locals and celebs.
Cato Institute	1000 Massachusetts Ave NW • 202-842-0200	Conservative temple.
Duke Ellington Mural	1200 U St NW	He's watching.
Lincoln Theatre	1215 U St NW • 202-328-6000	Renovated jewel.
Mary McLeod Bethune National Historic Site	1318 Vermont Ave NW • 202-673-2402	History without propaganda.
Wyndham Hotel	1400 M St NW • 202-429-1700	Back when it was the Vista International, Marion Barry got caught smoking crack here.

Map 11 • Near Northeast

Florida Avenue Market	Florida Ave NE b/w 2nd St NE & 6th St NE	Forget Eastern Market's frou-frou frills; head northeast.

Map 12 • Trinidad

Koi Pond	National Arboretum • 202-245-2726	Feed and pet humongo Japanese fish!
Mount Olivet Cemetery	1300 Bladensberg Rd NE	Visit Mary Surratt, hanged for her part in killing Lincoln.

Map 13 • Brookland / Langdon

Franciscan Monastery	1400 Quincy St NE • 202-526-6800	Beautiful gardens.

Map 14 • Catholic U

Brooks Mansion	901 Newton St NE	A Greek revival.
Grief in Rock Creek Cemetery	Rock Creek Church Rd NW & Webster St NW	Memorial to Adam's wife is best in the city.
Lincoln Cottage, Soldiers Home	3700 N Capitol St NW • 202-722-6624	Lincoln's summer residence; where he drafted the Emancipation Proclamation.
Pope John Paul II Cultural Center	3900 Harewood Rd NE • 202-635-5400	When you can't get to The Vatican.
Shrine of the Immaculate Conception	400 Michigan Ave NE • 202-526-8300	Humungo Catholic Church.

Map 15 • Columbia Heights

Blackburn University Center	2400 6th St NW • 202-806-5983	Howard University's living room.

Map 16 • Adams Morgan (North) / Mt Pleasant

Heller's Bakery	3221 Mt Pleasant St NW • 202-265-1169	For generations, a doughnut destination.
Marilyn Monroe Mural	Connecticut Ave NW & Calvert St NW	A tiny bit of glamour for DC.
Meridian International Center	1630 Crescent Pl NW • 202-667-6800	Look out for the exhibits.
Mexican Cultural Institute	2829 16th St NW • 202-728-1628	Top-notch work by Mexican artists.
Tryst Coffee House	2459 18th St NW • 202-232-5500	Canoodle here the way Chandra and Gary did.
Walter Pierce Park	2630 Adams Mill Rd NW • 202-588-7332	Former cemetery now boasts colorful mural and new-fenced dog park.

Map 17 • Woodley Park / Cleveland Park

Tai Shan	3001 Connecticut Ave NW • 202-633-4800	A baby giant panda is guaranteed to be more popular than any given president.
The Uptown	3426 Connecticut Ave NW • 202-966-5400	Red velvet curtains over a 40-foot screen; this is the Art Deco queen of DC movie houses.
US Naval Observatory	Massachusetts Ave NW & Observatory Cir NW • 202-762-1467	VP's disclosed location and the best place to ask what time it is.

Map 18 • Glover Park / Foxhall

C&O Towpath/Canal Locks	Along the Potomac River	Scenic views minutes from cityscape.
La Maison Française	4101 Reservoir Rd NW • 202-944-6090	Learn what *savoir faire* truly means.
National Cathedral	Massachusetts Ave NW & Wisconsin Ave NW • 202-537-6200	Newly-constructed old cathedral. Pure American.

Map 19 • Tenleytown / Friendship Heights

Fort Reno	Ft Reno Park	This former Civil War fort is the highest point of elevation in the District and the heart of DC punk during summertime

Map 20 • Cleveland Park / Upper Connecticut

Hillwood Museum & Gardens	4155 Linnean Ave NW • 202-686-5807	Home of heiress Marjorie Merriweather Post is simply exquisite.
Pierce Mill	2401 Tilden St NW • 202-895-6000	Doesn't everyone love a 19th-century grist mill?
Rock Creek Park Nature Center and Planetarium	5200 Glover Rd NW • 202-895-6070	Nature in the city.

Map 22 • Downtown Bethesda

L'Academie de Cuisine	5021 Wilson Ln • 301-986-9490	One step up from learning to make French fries.
National Institutes of Health	9000 Rockville Pike • 301-496-4000	Monkeys and rats beware…

Map 24 • Upper Rock Creek Park

Seminary at Forest Glen	Linden Ln & Beach Dr	Creepy complex of crumbling faux pagodas and French chateaux soon to become creepier housing development.

General Information • Landmarks

Map 25 • Silver Spring

AFI Theater	8633 Colesville Rd • 301-495-6720	You don't have to see artsy films in crappy movie houses anymore.
Penguin Rush Hour Mural	8400 Colesville Rd	Stop elbowing your way onto the Metro to appreciate a piece of Silver Spring.
Tastee Diner	8601 Cameron St • 301-589-8171	A thorn in the side of corporate development.

Map 27 • Walter Reed

Battleground National Military Cemetery	6625 Georgia Ave NW	Check out the entrance.
Walter Reed Army Medical Center	6900 Georgia Ave NW • 202-782-2200	Giant band-aid dispenser.

Map 28 • Chevy Chase

Avalon Theatre	5612 Connecticut Ave NW • 202-966-6000	Beloved neighborhood movie house.

Map 29 • Bethesda / Chevy Chase Business

Montgomery Farm Women's Co-op Market	7155 Wisconsin Ave • 301-652-2291	Indoor country market.
Writer's Center	4508 Walsh St • 301-654-8664	Take a class, write for NFT.

Map 30 • Westmoreland Circle

Mushroom House	4940 Allan Rd	Private residence is a life-sized smurf house.

Map 32 • Cherrydale / Palisades

Battery Kemble Park	Battery Kemble Park	Top sledding spot on snow days.
The Boathouse at Fletcher's Cove	4940 Canal Rd NW • 202-244-0461	Boats, angling, and info.

Map 34 • Ballston

Ballston Commons	4238 Wilson Blvd • 703-243-6346	Big-box invasion.

Map 35 • Clarendon

Market Commons	2690 Clarendon Blvd	Chain retail disguised as Main Street.

Map 36 • Rosslyn

Arlington County Detention Facility (Jail)	1425 N Courthouse Rd • 703-228-4484	We all make mistakes.
Arlington National Cemetery	Arlington National Cemetery • 703-607-8000	Visit again and again—just not during tourist season.
Iwo Jima Memorial	N Meade St & Arlington Blvd • 703-289-2500	Visit at night.

Map 37 • Fort Myer

Arlington Cinema 'N' Drafthouse	2903 Columbia Pike • 703-486-2345	Good movies, beer, pizza, waitresses, cigarettes. Life is good.
Bob and Edith's Diner	2310 Columbia Pike • 703-920-6103	Bargain breakfast 24/7.

Map 38 • Columbia Pike

Ball-Sellers House	5620 S 3rd St • 703-892-4204	Will be McMansion someday.

Map 39 • Shirlington

Fort Ward Museum and Historic Site	4301 W Braddock Rd • 703-838-4848	Eerie; we fought each other.

Map 40 · Pentagon City / Crystal City

Pentagon	Boundary Channel Dr · 703-697-1776	Rummy's playpen.

Map 41 · Landmark

Dora Kelley Park	5750 Sanger Ave · 703-838-4829	It's no Yellowstone, but it makes for a pleasant walk in the woods.
Shenandoah Brewing Company	652 S Pickett St · 703-823-9508	Brew your own beer on site.
Winkler Botanical Preserve	5400 Roanoke Ave · 703-578-7888	A 44-acre gem in the suburban rough.

Map 43 · Four Mile Run / Del Ray

Del Ray Farmers Market	Oxford Ave & Mt Vernon Ave · 703-683-2570	Dogs, babies, gossip—oh yeah, and food, too.
Dog Park	At Simpson Stadium Park, NW Corner of E Monroe Ave & Jefferson Davis Hwy	The neighborhood hangout—dogs hump, people preen.

Map 44 · Alexandria Downtown

Amtrak Station	110 Callahan Dr · 703-836-4339	Sleep in because you don't have to schlep to Union Station.
George Washington Masonic National Memorial	101 Callahan Dr · 703-683-2007	Nice views from the top.
Union Station	110 Callahan Dr	The other Union Station; good people-watching post.

Map 45 · Old Town (North)

Shipbuilder Monument	Waterfront Park, 1A Prince St	Visit him; he gets lonely.

Map 46 · Old Town (South)

Alexandria City Hall	301 King St · 703-838-4000	Founded in 1749.
Alexandria Farmer's Market	301 King St · 703-379-8723	Get yer arugula.
Alexandria National Cemetery	1450 Wilkes St · 703-221-2183	Visit the graves of buffalo soldiers.
Christ Church	118 N Washington St · 703-549-1450	Sit in GW's pew.
Confederate Statue "Appomattox"	S Washington St & Prince St	This is The South, don't forget.
Gadsby's Tavern Museum	134 N Royal St · 703-838-4242	Many US Presidents slept here.
The Littlest House in Alexandria	523 Queen St	It's only 7 feet wide!
Market Square Old Town	301 King St	Bring your skateboard.
Ramsay House	221 King St · 70-838-4200	Alexandria's visitor center.
Stabler-Leadbeater Apothecary	105 S Fairfax St · 703-836-3713	Where GW (the original) got his Viagra.
Torpedo Factory	201 N Union St · 703-838-4565	Now it churns out art.

Baltimore

Baltimore Tattoo Museum	1534 Eastern Ave · 410-522-5800	It'll make you want to get that "Jesus Rocks."

Self-Storage Locations

	Address	Phone	Map
Public Storage	1230 S Capitol St SE	202-479-4510	6
Extra Space Storage	1420 U St NW	202-667-6333	10
Public Storage	7800 Fenton St	301-585-3567	25
Public Storage	5423 Butler Rd	301-913-0247	29
Security Public Storage	5221 River Rd	301-652-6966	29
Public Storage	6319 Arlington Blvd	703-534-3016	33
Extra Space Storage	1001 N Fillmore St	703-516-7687	37
Extra Space Storage	3000 10th St N	703-243-3255	37
Public Storage	401 S Pickett St	703-370-2077	41
Extra Space Storage	1022 N Henry St	703-548-8545	45

Van & Truck Rental

		Address	Phone	Map
U-Haul	Nozi	1401 Florida Ave NE	202-396-2304	4
U-Haul		1501 S Capitol St SW	202-554-2640	6
Budget Trucks	Parker Svcs	2205 14th St NW	202-842-8668	10
U-Haul	U Street Rentals	919 U St NW	202-462-4644	10
Budget Trucks	Washington DC Truck Rental	2605 Reed St NE	202-636-8160	11
Budget Trucks	U Store Self Storage	301 New York Ave NE	202-547-3812	11
U-Haul		2215 5th St NE	202-269-1200	11
U-Haul		26 K St NE	202-289-5480	11
U-Haul		1750 Bladensburg Rd NE	202-529-4676	12
U-Haul	My Mother's Place	5016 Rock Creek Church Rd NE	202-526-1082	14
Budget Trucks	Uptown Self Storage	1200 Upshur St NW	202-723-0807	21
U-Haul	Auto Adventure	8115 Fenton St	301-588-1579	25
Budget Trucks	Storage USA Bethesda	5140 River Rd	301-718-5154	29
Penske	Capitol Termite & Pest	5455 Butler Rd	301-907-0111	29
Budget Trucks	Shurgard Storage	400 N Roosevelt Blvd	703-536-2243	33
Budget Trucks	D&V Service Center	5201 Wilson Blvd	703-525-0724	34
Penske	Gib Leonard's Rental Car	3210 10th St N	703-243-1897	37
U-Haul		5654 Columbia Pike	703-931-7897	38
Budget Trucks	World Motors	4160B S Four Mile Run Dr	703-931-3956	39
U-Haul	Shirlington Self Storage	2710 S Nelson St	703-820-9749	39
U-Haul	Alexandria Mini Storage	310 Hooffs Run Dr	703-739-1528	44

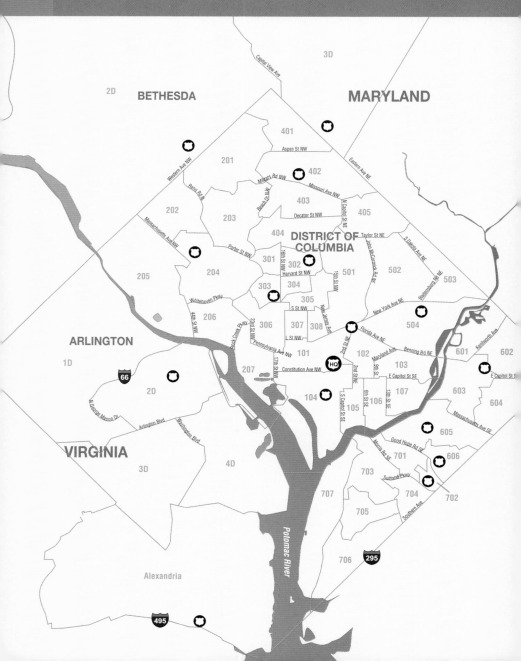

BETHESDA

2D

MARYLAND

Capital View Ave

3D

401

Aspen St NW

Western Ave NW

201

Eastern Ave NE

Reno Rd N

Military Rd NW

402

Missouri Ave NW

202

Beach Dr NW

403

405

Massachusetts Ave NW

203

Decator St NW

N Capitol St NE

DISTRICT OF
COLUMBIA

404

Taylor St NE

S Dakota Ave NE

Porter St NW

301

Harvard St NW

302

John McCormick Rd NE

501

502

503

205

204

303

304

15th St NW

Bladensburg Rd NE

Whitehaven Pkwy

305

S St NW

New Jersey Ave

New York Ave NE

504

44th St NW

206

306

307

308

L St NW

Florida Ave NE

601

Kenilworth Ave

602

ARLINGTON

23rd St NW

Pennsylvania Ave NW

Benning Rd NE

1D

Rock Creek Pkwy

207

17th St NW

101

HQ

102

Maryland Ave

103

E Capitol St SE

E Capitol St

66

2D

Constitution Ave NW

2nd St NE

2nd St SE

9th St SE

13th St SE

107

603

604

W George Mason Dr

104

S Capitol St SE

105

6th St SE

106

Massachusetts Ave SE

605

VIRGINIA

Arlington Blvd

Washington Blvd

Good Hope Rd SE

606

3D

4D

Morris Rd SE

701

Suitland Pkwy

703

704

702

705

Southern Ave

707

706

295

Potomac River

Alexandria

495

Washington DC is divided into 44 Police Service Areas (PSAs). Each PSA is staffed with a minimum of 21 MPDC officers (with the exception of PSA 707, which essentially consists of Bolling Air Force Base). High-crime neighborhoods are assigned more than the minimum number of police. For example, PSA 105 has the minimum 21 officers, while 93 officers patrol the statistically more dangerous PSA 101.

Metropolitan Police DC

All Emergencies:	911
Police Non-Emergencies:	311
Citywide Call Center:	202-727-1000
Crimesolvers Tip Line:	800-673-2777
Child Abuse Hotline:	202-671-7233
Corruption Hotline:	800-298-4006
Drug Abuse Hotline:	888-294-3572
Hate Crimes Hotline:	202-727-0500
Public Information Office:	202-727-4383
Office of Citizen Complaint Review:	202-727-3838
Website:	mpdc.dc.gov

Stations Within NFT Coverage Area
Headquarters: 300 Indiana Ave NW • Map 2
District Stations:
1st District Substation • 500 E St SE • 202-698-0068 • Map 5
1st District Station • 415 4th St SW • 202-698-0555 • Map 6
Gay & Lesbian Liaison Unit •
  1369 Connecticut Ave NW • 202-727-5427 • Map 9
3rd District Station •
  1620 V St NW • 202-673-6815 • Map 9
5th District Station •
  1805 Bladensburg Rd NE • 202-698-0150 • Map 12
3rd District Substation •
  750 Park Rd NW • 202-576-8222 • Map 15
3rd District Latino Liaison Unit •
  1800 Columbia Rd NW • 202-673-4445 • Map 16
2nd District Station •
  3320 Idaho Ave NW • 202-282-0070 • Map 18

Statistics	2005	2004	2003	2002
Homicide	195	198	248	262
Forcible Rape	267	218	173	262
Robbery	4,037	3,057	3,836	3,731
Aggravated Assault	3,308	3,863	4,482	4,854
Burglary	3,837	3,943	4,670	5,167
Larceny/Theft	14,480	13,756	17,362	20,903
Stolen Auto	6,642	8,136	9,549	9,168
Arson	46	81	126	109

Alexandria Police (VA)

All Emergencies:	911
Non-Emergencies:	703-838-4444
Community Support:	703-838-4763
Crime Prevention:	703-838-4520
Domestic Violence Unit:	703-706-3974
Parking:	703-838-3868
Property-Lost & Found:	703-838-4709
Website:	ci.alexandria.va.us/police

Stations Within NFT Coverage Area
Alexandria Police Department •
  2003 Mill Rd • 703-838-4444 • Map 44

Statistics	2005	2004	2003
Homicide	4	2	4
Rape	23	31	26
Robbery	197	187	179
Aggravated Assault	201	213	192
Burglary	371	426	497
Auto Theft	513	635	640
Larceny/Theft	2,699	2,937	3,754

Arlington County Police (VA)

All Emergencies:	911
Non-Emergencies:	703-558-2222
Rape Crisis, Victims of Violence	703-228-4848
Child Abuse:	703-228-1500
Domestic Violence Crisis Line	703-358-4848
National Capital Poison Center:	202-625-3333
Website:	www.co.arlington.va.us/police

Stations Within NFT Coverage Area
Arlington County Police Department •
  1425 N Courthouse Rd • 703-228-4040 • Map 36

Statistics	2004	2003	2002
Homicide	1	3	5
Rape	26	41	33
Robbery	184	212	213
Aggravated Assault	200	183	190
Burglary	361	408	425
Larceny/Theft	3,839	4,050	4,990
Auto Theft	493	662	676

Montgomery County Police (MD)

All Emergencies:	911
Montgomery Non-Emergencies:	301-279-8000
24-Hour Bioterrorism Hotline:	240-777-4200
Takoma Park Non-Emergencies:	301-891-7102
Chevy Chase Village Police:	301-654-7302
Animal Services:	240-773-5925
Community Services:	301-840-2585
Operation Runaway:	301-251-4545
Party Buster Line:	240-777-1986
Website:	www.montgomerycountymd.gov

Stations Within NFT Coverage Area
3rd District - Silver Spring •
  801 Sligo Ave • 301-565-7744 • Map25
Takoma Park Police Dept •
  7500 Maple Ave • 301-891-7102 • Map 26
MPDC 4th District Station •
  6001 Georgia Ave NW • 202-576-6745 • Map 27
Chevy Chase Village Police •
  5906 Connecticut Ave NW • 301-654-7302 • Map28
2nd District - Bethesda •
  7359 Wisconsin Ave • 301-652-9200 • Map 29

Statistics	2005	2004	2003	2002
Homicide	19	18	21	32
Rape	150	140	135	138
Robbery	1,035	789	1,004	877
Aggravated Assault	875	987	954	878
Burglary	3,570	3,741	4,095	3,874
Larceny	15,869	15,503	17,875	18,897
Auto Theft	2,486	2,562	3,489	3,722

Post Office	Address	Phone	Zip	Map
Benjamin Franklin	1200 Pennsylvania Ave NW	202-842-1444	20004	1
National Capitol Station	2 Massachusetts Ave NE	202-523-2368	20002	2
Union Station	50 Massachusetts Ave NE	202-523-2057	20002	2
Northeast Station	1563 Maryland Ave NE	202-842-4421	20002	4
Southeast Station	600 Pennsylvania Ave SE	202-682-9135	20003	5
Fort McNair Station	300 A St SW	202-523-2144	20319	6
L'Enfant Plaza Station	437 L'Enfant Plz SW	202-842-4526	20024	6
Southwest Station	45 L St SW	202-523-2590	20024	6
McPherson Station	1750 Pennsylvania Ave NW	202-523-2394	20006	7
Watergate Station	2512 Virginia Ave NW	202-965-6278	20037	7
Georgetown Station	1215 31st St NW	202-842-2487	20007	8
Farragut Station	1800 M St NW	202-523-2024	20036	9
Temple Heights Station	1921 Florida Ave NW	202-234-4253	20009	9
Twentieth St Station	2001 M St NW	202-842-4654	20036	9
Ward Place Station	2121 Ward Pl NW	202-842-4645	20037	9
Washington Square Station	1050 Connecticut Ave NW	202-842-1211	20036	9
Martin Luther King Jr Station	1400 L St NW	202-523-2001	20005	10
T Street	1915 14th St NW	202-483-9580	20009	10
Techworld Station	800 K St NW	202-842-2309	20001	10
Le Droit Park	416 Florida Ave NW	202-635-5311	20001	11
Washington Main Office	900 Brentwood Rd NE	202-636-1972	20018	11
Woodridge Station	2211 Rhode Island Ave NE	202-842-4340	20018	13
Brookland Station	3401 12th St NE	202-842-3374	20017	14
Catholic University Cardinal Station	620 Michigan Ave NE	202-319-5225	20064	14
Columbia Heights Finance	3321 Georgia Ave NW	202-523-2674	20010	15
Howard University	2400 6th St NW	202-806-2008	20059	15
Kalorama Station	2300 18th St NW	202-523-2906	20009	16
Cleveland Park Station	3430 Connecticut Ave NW	202-364-0178	20008	17
Calvert Station	2336 Wisconsin Ave NW	202-523-2907	20007	18
Petworth Station	4211 9th St NW	202-523-2681	20011	21
Silver Spring Finance Centre	8455 Colesville Rd	301-608-1305	20910	25
Takoma Park	6909 Laurel Ave	301-270-4392	20912	26
Brightwood Station	6323 Georgia Ave NW	202-635-5300	20011	27
Walter Reed Station	6800 Georgia Ave NW	202-782-3768	20012	27
Chevy Chase Branch	5910 Connecticut Ave NW	301-654-7538	20815	28
Northwest Station	5636 Connecticut Ave NW	202-842-2286	20015	28
Bethesda	7400 Wisconsin Ave	301-654-5894	20814	29
Bethesda Chevy Chase	7001 Arlington Rd	301-656-8053	20814	29
Friendship Heights Station	5530 Wisconsin Ave	301-941-2695	20815	29
Palisades Station	5136 MacArthur Blvd NW	202-842-2291	20016	32
North Station	2200 N George Mason Dr	703-536-6269	22207	34
Arlington Main Office	3118 Washington Blvd	703-841-2118	22210	35
Court House Station	2043 Wilson Blvd	703-248-9337	22201	36
Rosslyn Station	1101 Wilson Blvd	703-525-4336	22209	36
South Station	1210 S Glebe Rd	703-979-2821	22204	37
Park Fairfax Station	3682 King St	703-933-2686	22302	39
Eads Station	1720 S Eads St	703-892-0840	22202	40
Pentagon Branch	9998 The Pentagon	703-695-6835	20301	40
Trade Center Station	340 S Pickett St	703-823-0968	22304	41
Potomac Station Finance	1908 Mt Vernon Ave	703-684-7821	22301	43
Memorial Station	2226 Duke St	703-684-6759	22314	44
Alexandria Main Office	1100 Wythe St	703-684-7168	22314	45
George Mason Station	126 S Washington St	703-684-3619	22320	46

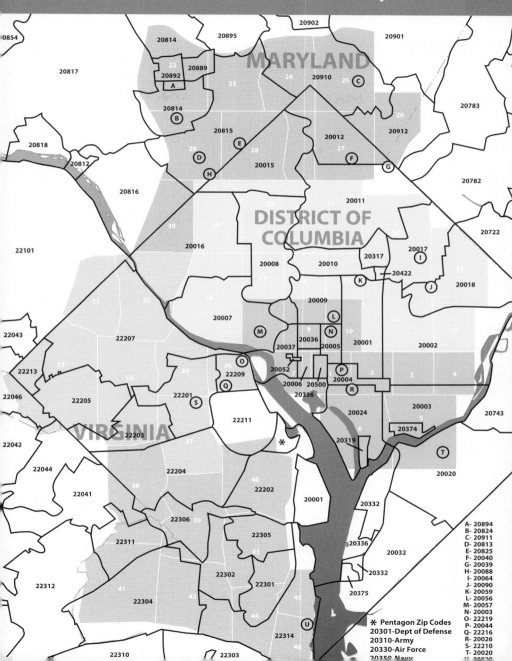

0854

20817

20818

20812

20816

22101

22043

22213

22046

22042

22044

22041

22312

22311

22310

20814

22
20892
A

20889

20814
B

20815
E

20895

D 29

28

H

30

20016

31

22207

33

22205

34

22203

37

22204

38

22306 39

22305

43

22302

41

22304 42

22303

44

MARYLAND

23

24

27

20015

17

19

32

35

36

O

22209

Q

S

22201

22211

*

40

22202

22301

20902

20910

20012

25
C

26

27
F

20011

21

DISTRICT OF
COLUMBIA

20008

18

20009

20007

M

20037

20052

20006

20336

20001

20032

20336

20901

20783

20912

20782

20722

20010

K

20317

20422

J

20018

L

N

20036
20005

P
20004
R

20024

6

20319

20375

20332

20017
I

13

14

16

11

12

20001

10

20002

20003

20374

20020

T

20743

9

8

5
1
2
3
4

15

20500

20002

DEPARTMENT: No

20332

20020

20314

46

U

A- 20894
B- 20824
C- 20911
D- 20813
E- 20825
F- 20040
G- 20039
H- 20088
I- 20064
J- 20090
K- 20059
L- 20056
M- 20057
N- 20003
O- 22219
P- 20044
Q- 22216
R- 20026
S- 22210
T- 20020

* Pentagon Zip Codes
20301-Dept of Defense
20310-Army
20330-Air Force
20350-Navy

Map 1 • National Mall

Last pick-up

FedEx Kinko's	1445 I St NW	8:45
FedEx Kinko's	419 11th St NW	8:30
FedEx Kinko's	1350 New York Ave NW	8:30
Self-Service	1300 I St NW	7:15
Self-Service	700 13th St NW	7:15
Self-Service	1201 Penn Ave NW	7:00
Self-Service	555 12th St NW	7:00
Self-Service	555 13th St NW	7:00
Self-Service	1201 F St NW	7:00
Self-Service	1317 F St NW	7:00
Self-Service	1455 Pennsylvania Ave NW	7:00
Self-Service	1250 I St NW	7:00
Self-Service	1310 G St NW	7:00
Self-Service	1341 G St NW	7:00
Self-Service	1350 I St NW	7:00
Self-Service	1399 New York Ave NW	7:00
Self-Service	601 13th St NW	7:00
Self-Service	655 15th St NW	7:00
Self-Service	734 15th St NW	7:00
Self-Service	1401 H St NW	6:45
Self-Service	600 14th St NW	6:45
Self-Service	740 15th St NW	6:45
Self-Service	1001 G St NW	6:30
Self-Service	1100 H St NW	6:30
Self-Service	400 N Capitol St NW	6:30
Self-Service	470 L'Enfant Plz SW	6:30
Self-Service	700 11th St NW	6:30
Self-Service	955 L'Enfant Plz SW	6:30
Self-Service	624 9th St NW	6:30
Self-Service	1299 Pennsylvania Ave NW	6:30
Self-Service	1331 Pennsylvania Ave NW	6:30
Self-Service	801 Pennsylvania Ave NW	6:30
Self-Service	1200 G St NW	6:30
Self-Service	1200 New York Ave NW	6:30
Self-Service	1212 New York Ave NW	6:30
Self-Service	1325 G St NW	6:30
Self-Service	1333 H St NW	6:30
Self-Service	600 13th St NW	6:30
Self-Service	815 14th St NW	6:30
Self-Service	201 14th St SW	6:30
Self-Service	1000 Jefferson Dr SW	6:15
Self-Service	100 Raoul Wallenberg Pl SW	6:15
Self-Service	1250 H St NW	6:00
Self-Service	14th St NW & Constitution Ave NW	6:00
Self-Service	401 9th St NW	6:00
Self-Service	750 9th St NW	6:00
Self-Service	1025 F St NW	6:00
Self-Service	1300 Pennsylvania Ave NW	6:00
Self-Service	901 E St NW	6:00
Self-Service	950 F St NW	6:00
Self-Service	1201 New York Ave NW	6:00
Self-Service	1225 I St NW	6:00
Self-Service	1330 G St NW	6:00
Self-Service	1425 New York Ave NW	6:00
Self-Service	700 12th St NW	6:00
Self-Service	730 15th St NW	6:00
Self-Service	901 F St NW	5:45
Self-Service	1200 Pennsylvania Ave NW	5:30
Self-Service	1400 Independence Ave SW	5:30
Self-Service	1455 F St NW	5:00

Map 2 • Chinatown / Union Station

Self-Service	20 Massachusetts Ave NW	7:00
Self-Service	600 New Jersey Ave NW	7:00
Self-Service	820 1st St NE	7:00
Self-Service	601 Pennsylvania Ave NW	7:00
Self-Service	2 Bethesda Metro Ctr	6:30
Self-Service	499 S Capitol St SW	6:30
Self-Service	575 7th St NW	6:30
Self-Service	777 N Capitol St NE	6:30
Self-Service	1 1st St NE	6:30

Self-Service	101 Constitution Ave NW	6:30
Self-Service	500 New Jersey Ave NW	6:30
Self-Service	601 New Jersey Ave NW	6:30
Self-Service	750 1st St NE	6:30
Self-Service	810 1st St NE	6:30
Self-Service	600 Maryland Ave SW	6:30
Self-Service	200 Independence Ave SW	6:30
FedEx Kinko's	325 7th St NW	6:30
Self-Service	122 C St NW	6:00
Self-Service	400 1st St NW	6:00
Self-Service	440 1st St NW	6:00
Self-Service	50 Massachusetts Ave NW	6:00
Self-Service	500 1st St NW	6:00
Self-Service	550 1st St NW	6:00
Self-Service	50 Massachusetts Ave NE	6:00
Self-Service	701 Pennsylvania Ave NW	6:00
Self-Service	400 Maryland Ave SW	6:00
Self-Service	100 F St NE	5:45
Self-Service	200 Constitution Ave NW	5:45
Self-Service	600 Pennsylvania Ave NW	5:30
Self-Service	10 G St NE	5:30
Self-Service	600 Independence Ave SW	5:30
Self-Service	Longworth House Office Bldg	5:30
Self-Service	1 Columbus Cir NE	5:00
Self-Service	401 F St NW	5:00
Self-Service	330 Independence Ave SW	5:00
Self-Service	4th St SW & Independence Ave SW	2:30

Map 3 • The Hill

FedEx Kinko's	208 2nd St SE	8:00
Self-Service	227 Massachusetts Ave NE	6:15

Map 5 • Southeast / Anacostia

FedEx Kinko's	715 D St SE	6:30
Self-Service	1201 M St SE	5:30
Self-Service	600 Pennsylvania Ave SE	5:30
Self-Service	3rd St SE & M St SE	5:00
Self-Service	1100 New Jersey Ave SE	5:00
Self-Service	300 M St SE	5:00

Map 6 • Waterfront

Self-Service	330 C St SW	7:00
Self-Service	445 12th St SW	6:45
Self-Service	1330 Maryland Ave SW	6:30
Self-Service	7th St SW & D St SW	6:30
Self-Service	400 Virginia Ave SW	6:30
Self-Service	600 Water St SW	6:30
Self-Service	901 D St SW	6:30
Self-Service	301 4th St SW	6:30
Self-Service	400 6th St SW	6:00
Self-Service	409 3rd St SW	6:00
Self-Service	500 E St SW	6:00
Self-Service	1280 Maryland Ave SW	5:45
Self-Service	26 N St SE	5:30
Self-Service	80 M St SE	5:30
Self-Service	550 12th St SW	5:30
Self-Service	2100 2nd St SW	4:00
Self-Service	300 7th St SW	2:00

Map 7 • Foggy Bottom

Self-Service	431 18th St NW	7:30
Self-Service	1735 New York Ave NW	7:00
Self-Service	2100 Pennsylvania Ave NW	7:00
Self-Service	900 19th St NW	6:45
Self-Service	2001 Pennsylvania Ave NW	6:30
Self-Service	2700 F St NW	6:00
Self-Service	2150 Pennsylvania Ave NW	6:00
Self-Service	600 New Hampshire Ave NW	6:00
FedEx Kinko's	800 21st St NW	6:00
Self-Service	1250 24th St NW	5:30
Self-Service	900 23rd St NW	5:30
Self-Service	2401 E St NW	4:00

Map 8 • Georgetown

FedEx Kinko's	1002 30th St NW	8:00
Self-Service	1055 Thomas Jefferson St NW	7:00
Self-Service	3000 K St NW	7:00
Self-Service	1010 Wisconsin Ave NW	6:30
Self-Service	1101 30th St NW	6:30
Self-Service	2150 Wisconsin Ave NW	6:30
FedEx Kinko's	3329 M St NW	6:30
Self-Service	24th St NW & Massachusetts Ave NW	6:00
Self-Service	1000 Potomac St NW	6:00
Self-Service	1000 Thomas Jefferson St NW	6:00
Self-Service	1215 31st St NW	6:00
Self-Service	3299 K St NW	6:00
Self-Service	3333 K St NW	6:00
Self-Service	2115 Wisconsin Ave NW	5:30
Self-Service	3520 Prospect St NW	5:30
Self-Service	2121 Wisconsin Ave NW	5:00
Westend Press	2445 M St NW	4:00

Map 9 • Dupont Circle / Adams Morgan

FedEx Kinko's	1825 K St NW	8:45
FedEx Kinko's	1029 17th St NW	8:45
FedEx Kinko's	1 Dupont Cir NW	8:45
FedEx Kinko's	1123 18th St NW	8:30
FedEx Kinko's	1019 15th St NW	8:00
Self-Service	1200 18th St NW	7:00
Self-Service	2000 L St NW	7:00
Self-Service	2001 L St NW	7:00
Self-Service	1501 K St NW	7:00
Self-Service	1850 K St NW	7:00
Self-Service	1900 K St NW	7:00
Self-Service	2000 K St NW	7:00
Self-Service	1921 Florida Ave NW	7:00
Self-Service	1015 18th St NW	7:00
Self-Service	1101 Connecticut Ave NW	7:00
Self-Service	1111 19th St NW	7:00
Self-Service	1120 20th St NW	7:00
Self-Service	1129 20th St NW	7:00
Self-Service	1133 20th St NW	7:00
Self-Service	1145 17th St NW	7:00
Self-Service	1150 17th St NW	7:00
Self-Service	1155 21st St NW	7:00
Self-Service	1201 Connecticut Ave NW	7:00
Self-Service	1220 19th St NW	7:00
Self-Service	1250 Connecticut Ave NW	7:00
Self-Service	1400 16th St NW	7:00
Self-Service	1615 M St NW	7:00
Self-Service	1616 P St NW	7:00
Self-Service	1801 L St NW	7:00
Self-Service	1828 L St NW	7:00
Self-Service	1920 N St NW	7:00
Self-Service	2401 Pennsylvania Ave NW	7:00
Self-Service	1025 Connecticut Ave NW	6:45
Self-Service	1620 L St NW	6:30
Self-Service	1901 L St NW	6:30
Self-Service	2121 K St NW	6:30
Self-Service	1156 15th St NW	6:30
Self-Service	1500 K St NW	6:30
Self-Service	2001 K St NW	6:30
Self-Service	2020 K St NW	6:30
Self-Service	2033 K St NW	6:30
Self-Service	1919 Connecticut Ave NW	6:30
Self-Service	1050 Connecticut Ave NW	6:30
Self-Service	11 Dupont Cir NW	6:30
Self-Service	1101 17th St NW	6:30
Self-Service	1133 21st St NW	6:30
Self-Service	1133 Connecticut Ave NW	6:30
Self-Service	1155 Connecticut Ave NW	6:30
Self-Service	1225 Connecticut Ave NW	6:30
Self-Service	1330 Connecticut Ave NW	6:30
Self-Service	1608 Rhode Island Ave NW	6:30
Self-Service	1717 Rhode Island Ave NW	6:30
Self-Service	1725 Desales St NW	6:30

Self-Service	1785 Massachusetts Ave NW	6:30
Self-Service	2030 M St NW	6:30
Self-Service	1150 22nd St NW	6:30
Self-Service	1255 23rd St NW	6:30
Self-Service	2300 M St NW	6:30
Self-Service	2440 M St NW	6:30
FedEx Kinko's	2020 K St NW	6:30
Self-Service	1133 15th St NW	6:00
Self-Service	1501 M St NW	6:00
Self-Service	1700 K St NW	6:00
Self-Service	1909 K St NW	6:00
Self-Service	1666 Connecticut Ave NW	6:00
Self-Service	1825 Connecticut Ave NW	6:00
Self-Service	1100 17th St NW	6:00
Self-Service	1150 Connecticut Ave NW	6:00
Self-Service	1300 Connecticut Ave NW	6:00
Self-Service	1350 Connecticut Ave NW	6:00
Self-Service	1819 L St NW	6:00
Westend Press	2001 M St NW	6:00
Self-Service	2311 M St NW	6:00
Self-Service	1211 Connecticut Ave NW	5:45
Self-Service	1730 M St NW	5:45
Self-Service	2120 L St NW	5:45
Self-Service	1529 18th St NW	5:30
Self-Service	1725 K St NW	5:30
Self-Service	1920 L St NW	5:30
Self-Service	2175 K St NW	5:30
Self-Service	1120 Connecticut Ave NW	5:30
Self-Service	1140 Connecticut Ave NW	5:30
Self-Service	1300 19th St NW	5:30
Self-Service	1717 Massachusetts Ave NW	5:30
Self-Service	1776 Massachusetts Ave NW	5:30
Self-Service	1899 L St NW	5:30
Self-Service	1900 M St NW	5:30
EZ Business Services	1929 18th St NW	5:30
Self-Service	2021 K St NW	5:00
Self-Service	1200 17th St NW	5:00
Self-Service	1255 22nd St NW	5:00
Self-Service	1875 Connecticut Ave NW	4:00

Map 10 • Logan Circle / U Street

Self-Service	1090 Vermont Ave NW	7:30
Self-Service	901 New York Ave NW	7:00
Self-Service	1100 L St NW	7:00
Self-Service	1101 14th St NW	7:00
Self-Service	1275 K St NW	7:00
Self-Service	1301 K St NW	7:00
Self-Service	1436 U St NW	7:00
Self-Service	1915 14th St NW	7:00
Self-Service	1101 Vermont Ave NW	6:45
Self-Service	800 K St NW	6:30
Self-Service	1 Thomas Cir NW	6:30
Self-Service	1120 Vermont Ave NW	6:30
Self-Service	1200 K St NW	6:30
Self-Service	1400 K St NW	6:30
FedEx Kinko's	800 K St NW	6:30
Self-Service	1425 K St NW	6:15
Self-Service	800 K St NW	6:00
Ez Copy	1322 14th St NW	6:00
Self-Service	800 K St NW	5:45
Self-Service	1220 L St NW	5:30
Self-Service	520 W St NW	5:30
Self-Service	1100 13th St NW	5:30
Self-Service	1110 Vermont Ave NW	5:30
Self-Service	1401 K St NW	5:30
Self-Service	1420 K St NW	5:30
Self-Service	1400 L St NW	4:00
Self-Service	1099 14th St NW	3:45
Mkm Pnet Llc	801 Mt Vernon Pl NW	3:00

Map 11 • Near Northeast

Federal Express	1501 Eckington Pl NE	8:30
Self-Service	416 Florida Ave NW	7:00
Self-Service	900 2nd St NE	6:00
Self-Service	800 N Capitol St NW	5:30
Self-Service	900 Brentwood Rd NE	5:30
Self-Service	800 Florida Ave NE, Gukcc-3233	5:00

Map 14 • Catholic U

Self-Service	100 Irving St NW	6:30
Self-Service	110 Irving St NW	6:30
Self-Service	3401 12th St NE	6:30
Self-Service	1150 Varnum St NE	6:00
Self-Service	620 Michigan Ave NE	6:00
Self-Service	3211 4th St NE	5:30
Self-Service	216 Michigan Ave NE	5:30

Map 15 • Columbia Heights

Self-Service	2400 6th St NW	5:30
Bara Business Solutions	2851 Georgia Ave NW	5:00

Map 16 • Adams Morgan (North) / Mt Pleasant

Tech Printing	2479 18th St NW	4:00

Map 17 • Woodley Park / Cleveland Park

Self-Service	2500 Calvert St NW	7:00
Self-Service	3430 Connecticut Ave NW	6:00
Self-Service	3100 Massachusetts Ave NW	3:00

Map 18 • Glover Park / Foxhall

Self-Service	3301 New Mexico Ave NW	7:15
Self-Service	3400 Idaho Ave NW	7:00
Self-Service	3970 Reservoir Rd NW	6:45
Self-Service	4000 Reservoir Rd NW	6:45
Self-Service	3800 Reservoir Rd NW	6:30
Self-Service	2233 Wisconsin Ave NW	6:30
Self-Service	4400 Macarthur Blvd NW	6:30
Self-Service	3800 Reservoir Rd NW	6:00
Self-Service	4000 Reservoir Rd NW	6:00
Self-Service	3201 New Mexico Ave NW	6:00

Map 19 • Tenleytown / Friendship Heights

FedEx Kinko's	4000 Wisconsin Ave NW	8:00
Self-Service	5335 Wisconsin Ave NW	7:00
Self-Service	5301 Wisconsin Ave NW	6:30
Self-Service	4005 Wisconsin Ave NW	6:30
FedEx Kinko's	5225 Wisconsin Ave NW	6:30
Self-Service	4400 Massachusetts Ave NW	6:00
Self-Service	4400 Jenifer St NW	5:30
Self-Service	4620 Wisconsin Ave NW	5:30

Map 20 • Cleveland Park / Upper Connecticut

Self-Service	4201 Connecticut Ave NW	6:30
Self-Service	4301 Connecticut Ave NW	6:00
Parcel Plus	3509 Connecticut Ave NW	6:00
Self-Service	2900 Van Ness St NW	5:30
Self-Service	4455 Connecticut Ave NW	5:30

Map 22 • Downtown Bethesda

Self-Service	9650 Rockville Pike	7:00
Self-Service	4833 Rugby Ave	7:00
Self-Service	9030 Old Georgetown Rd	7:00
Self-Service	9000 Rockville Pike	6:45
Self-Service	7960 Old Georgetown Rd	6:45
Self-Service	2 Center Dr, Bldg #2	6:30
Self-Service	1 Cloister Ct	6:30
Self-Service	7910 Woodmont Ave	6:30
Self-Service	8001 Wisconsin Ave	6:30
Self-Service	45 Center Dr	6:30

Self-Service	9000 Rockville Pike	6:30
Self-Service	9000 Rockville Pike	6:30
Self-Service	9000 Rockville Pike	6:30
Self-Service	7920 Norfolk Ave	6:00
Self-Service	9000 Rockville Pike	6:00
Self-Service	9000 Rockville Pike	6:00
Self-Service	7735 Old Georgetown Rd	5:30
Self-Service	9000 Rockville Pike	5:15
Self-Service	8901 Wisconsin Ave	3:00

Map 23 • Kensington

Self-Service	8401 Connecticut Ave	6:30

Map 24 • Upper Rock Creek Park

Self-Service	9440 Georgia Ave	7
Self-Service	8750 Brookville Rd	6:30
Self-Service	Forny Rd, Bldg #503	6:30
Post Express	9466 Georgia Ave	6:15
Mail Boxes Etc	8639 B 16th St	6:00

Map 25 • Silver Spring

Self-Service	1407 East West Hwy	6:30
Self-Service	8616 2nd Ave	6:30
Self-Service	8720 Georgia Ave	6:30
Self-Service	8737 Colesville Rd	6:30
Self-Service	8757 Georgia Ave	6:30
Self-Service	8701 Georgia Ave	6:15
Self-Service	1010 Wayne Ave	6:00
Self-Service	1100 Blair Mill Rd	6:00
Self-Service	1109 Spring St	6:00
Self-Service	8121 Georgia Ave	6:00
Self-Service	8403 Colesville Rd	6:00
Self-Service	8601 Georgia Ave	6:00
Self-Service	8630 Fenton St	6:00
Self-Service	8555 16th St	5:30
Self-Service	1305 East West Hwy	5:00
Self-Service	1325 East West Hwy	5:00
Self-Service	1335 East West Hwy	5:00
Self-Service	8455 Colesville Rd	5:00
Self-Service	1315 East West Hwy	4:00

Map 26 • Takoma Park

Self-Service	7600 Carroll Ave	6:30
Takoma Postal & Business	7304 Carroll Ave	6:00
Self-Service	6200 N Capitol St NW	6:00

Map 27 • Walter Reed

Self-Service	6925 Willow St NW	6:30
Self-Service	7826 Eastern Ave NW	6:30
Self-Service	6900 Georgia Ave NW	6:00
Self-Service	6930 Carroll Ave	5:30

Map 28 • Chevy Chase

Self-Service	5636 Connecticut Ave NW	5:30

Map 29 • Bethesda / Chevy Chase Business

FedEx Kinko's	4809 Bethesda Ave	7:45
Self-Service	7201 Wisconsin Ave	7:00
Self-Service	7501 Wisconsin Ave	7:00
Self-Service	4330 East West Hwy	6:45
Self-Service	4350 East West Hwy	6:30
Self-Service	4405 East West Hwy	6:30
Self-Service	4416 East West Hwy	6:30
Self-Service	4550 Montgomery Ave	6:30
Self-Service	4800 Montgomery Ln	6:30
Self-Service	6933 Arlington Rd	6:30
Self-Service	7001 Arlington Rd	6:30
Self-Service	7101 Wisconsin Ave	6:30
Self-Service	7400 Wisconsin Ave	6:30
Self-Service	7475 Wisconsin Ave	6:30
Self-Service	4445 Willard Ave	6:30
Self-Service	5454 Wisconsin Ave	6:30
Self-Service	5530 Wisconsin Ave	6:30

Self-Service	5550 Friendship Blvd	6:30
Self-Service	3 Bethesda Metro Ctr	6:15
Self-Service	4520 East West Hwy	6:15
Self-Service	7200 Wisconsin Ave	6:15
Self-Service	7272 Wisconsin Ave	6:15
Self-Service	7315 Wisconsin Ave	6:15
Self-Service	7316 Wisconsin Ave	6:15
Self-Service	4600 East West Hwy	6:00
Self-Service	4630 Montgomery Ave	6:00
Self-Service	2 Wisconsin Cir	6:00
Self-Service	4800 Hampden Ln	5:15
Self-Service	6900 Wisconsin Ave	5:00
Parcel Plus	5257 River Rd	5:00
Metro Printing and Copying	3 Bethesda Metro Ctr	5:00
Mailboxes Bethesda	7831 Woodmont Ave	4:00

Map 30 • Westmoreland Circle

Self-Service	4801 Massachusetts Ave NW	6:00
Self-Service	4910 Massachusetts Ave NW	5:30

Map 32 • Cherrydale / Palisades

Self-Service	5125 Macarthur Blvd NW	7:00
Self-Service	5136 Macarthur Blvd NW	6:30

Map 33 • Falls Church

Self-Service	5350 Lee Hwy	6:30
Self-Service	500 N Washington St	6:15
Parcel Plus	2503 N Harrison St	5:30
Self-Service	5877 Washington Blvd	5:15

Map 34 • Ballston

FedEx Kinko's	4501 Fairfax Dr	7:30
Self-Service	901 N Stuart St	7:00
Self-Service	4238 Wilson Blvd	7:00
Self-Service	4001 N Fairfax Dr	6:30
Self-Service	4301 N Fairfax Dr	6:30
Self-Service	4301 Wilson Blvd	6:30
Self-Service	4350 Fairfax Dr	6:30
Self-Service	1010 N Glebe Rd	6:00
Self-Service	4100 N Fairfax Dr	6:00
Self-Service	910 N Glebe Rd	6:00
Self-Service	2200 N George Mason Dr	6:00
Mail Plus	850 N Randolph St Apt 103	6:00
Mail Boxes Etc	4201 Wilson Blvd, Ste 110	6:00
Self-Service	1100 N Glebe Rd	5:30
Self-Service	1110 N Glebe Rd	5:30
Self-Service	801 N Quincy St	5:30
Self-Service	4300 Wilson Blvd	5:30
Self-Service	4245 Fairfax Dr	5:00
Self-Service	4501 N Fairfax Dr	4:30

Map 35 • Clarendon

FedEx Kinko's	2300 Clarendon Blvd	7:30
Self-Service	2500 Wilson Blvd	6:30
Self-Service	2200 Clarendon Blvd	6:00
Self-Service	2801 Clarendon Blvd	6:00
Self-Service	2300 Wilson Blvd	5:30
Self-Service	3101 Wilson Blvd	5:00

Map 36 • Rosslyn

Self-Service	1560 Wilson Blvd	7:30
Self-Service	1525 Wilson Blvd	7:00
Self-Service	1300 17th St N	7:00
Self-Service	1611 N Kent St	7:00
Self-Service	1916 Wilson Blvd	6:30
Self-Service	1300 Wilson Blvd	6:30
Self-Service	1530 Wilson Blvd	6:30
Self-Service	1616 Ft Myer Dr	6:30
Self-Service	1001 19th St N	6:30
Self-Service	2101 Wilson Blvd	6:15
Self-Service	1000 Wilson Blvd	6:15

Self-Service	1840 Wilson Blvd	6:00
Self-Service	1101 Wilson Blvd	6:00
Self-Service	1401 Wilson Blvd	6:00
Self-Service	1911 Ft Myer Dr	6:00
Self-Service	2000 14th St N	6:00
Self-Service	2043 Wilson Blvd	5:30
Self-Service	2107 Wilson Blvd	5:30
Self-Service	2111 Wilson Blvd	5:30
Self-Service	1600 Wilson Blvd	5:30
Self-Service	1333 N Courthouse Rd	5:30
Self-Service	1515 N Courthouse Rd	5:30
Self-Service	1415 N Taft St	5:30
Packman Printing & Shipping	1715 Wilson Blvd	5:30
Self-Service	1655 Ft Myer Dr	5:00
Self-Service	1801 N Lynn St	5:00
PO Boxes Etc	1730 N Lynn St	5:00
Self-Service	2000 15th St N	4:00

Map 37 • Fort Myer

Self-Service	3300 Fairfax Dr	7:30
Self-Service	2300 9th St S	7:00
Self-Service	3601 Wilson Blvd	6:30
Self-Service	3263 Columbia Pike	6:30
Self-Service	3701 Fairfax Dr	6:00
Self-Service	3811 Fairfax Dr	5:00
Self-Service	200 N Glebe Rd	5:00
Self-Service	1210 S Glebe Rd	5:00
Pakmail	1001 N Fillmore St	5:00

Map 38 • Columbia Pike

Self-Service	3515c S Jefferson St	7:00
FedEx Kinko's	3515c S Jefferson St	7:00
Self-Service	5113 Leesburg Pike	6:30
Self-Service	5201 Leesburg Pike	6:30
Self-Service	5699 Columbia Pike	6:30
Self-Service	5107 Leesburg Pike	6:15
Self-Service	5203 Leesburg Pike	6:15
Self-Service	4900 Leesburg Pike	6:00
Self-Service	5205 Leesburg Pike	6:00
Self-Service	5100 Leesburg Pike	5:30

Map 39 • Shirlington

Self-Service	1707 Osage St	7:00
Self-Service	4212 King St # 4232	6:30
Self-Service	2700 S Quincy St	6:00
Parcel Plus	3686 King St	6:00
Self-Service	2800 S Shirlington Rd	5:30
Self-Service	3101 Park Ctr Dr	5:00
Self-Service	2850 S Quincy St	5:00

Map 40 • Pentagon City / Crystal City

FedEx Kinko's	1601 Crystal Dr	8:00
Self-Service	1225 S Clark St	7:00
Self-Service	200 12th St S	7:00
Self-Service	2001 Jefferson Davis Hwy	6:30
Self-Service	1215 S Clark St	6:30
Self-Service	1235 S Clark St	6:30
Self-Service	201 12th St S	6:30
Self-Service	1632 Crystal Dr	6:00
Self-Service	2011 Crystal Dr	6:00
Self-Service	1729 S Eads St	6:00
Self-Service	1919 S Eads St	6:00
Self-Service	775 23rd St S	6:00
Self-Service	2231 Crystal Dr	5:30
Self-Service	2345 Crystal Dr	5:30
Self-Service	2450 Crystal Dr	5:30
Self-Service	2611 Jefferson Davis Hwy	5:30
Self-Service	The Pentagon - Main Concourse	4:30
Self-Service	1 Aviation Cir, Hngr 11	4:00
Gateway Mail Boxes	1235 S Clark St	4:00

Map 41 • Landmark

Self-Service	340 S Pickett St	7:00
Self-Service	6121 Lincolnia Rd	6:45
Self-Service	6137 Lincolnia Rd	6:45
Self-Service	1800 N Beauregard St	6:30
Self-Service	1900 N Beauregard St	6:30
Self-Service	4900 Seminary Rd	6:30
Self-Service	1801 N Beauregard St	6:00
Self-Service	1701 N Beauregard St	6:00
Self-Service	50 S Pickett St	6:00
Packaging Store	245 S Van Dorn St	6:00
Newlon's Box Center	5145 Duke St	5:00

Map 42 • Alexandria (West)

Self-Service	2900 Eisenhower Ave	7:00
Self-Service	3660a Wheeler Ave	6:30
Self-Service	2807 Duke St	6:00
Self-Service	3015 Colvin St	6:00

Map 43 • Four Mile Run / Del Ray

Self-Service	1901 S Bell St	6:30
Self-Service	3301 Jefferson Davis Hwy	6:30
Self-Service	907 W Glebe Rd	6:15
Self-Service	1908 Mt Vernon Ave	6:00
Self-Service	3131 Mt Vernon Ave	6:00

Map 44 • Alexandria Downtown

FedEx Kinko's	1755 Duke St	8:00
Self-Service	1700 Diagonal Rd	7:00
Self-Service	1800 Diagonal Rd	6:30
Self-Service	225 Reinekers Ln	6:30
Self-Service	1600 Duke St	6:00
Self-Service	2000 Duke St	6:00
Self-Service	2121 Eisenhower Ave	6:00
Self-Service	333 John Carlyle St	6:00
Self-Service	1725 Duke St	5:30
Self-Service	2051 Jamieson Ave	2:00

Map 45 • Old Town (North)

Self-Service	500 Montgomery St	7:30
Self-Service	701 N Faixfax St	6:45
Self-Service	105 Oronoco St	6:30
Self-Service	1320 Braddock Pl	6:30
Self-Service	44 Canal Ctr Plz	6:30
Self-Service	901 N Pitt St	6:30
Self-Service	1100 Wythe St	6:00
Self-Service	99 Canal Ctr Plz	5:45
Self-Service	400 N Columbus St	5:00
Self-Service	635 Slaters Ln	5:00
Self-Service	66 Canal Ctr Plz	5:00
Pack N Ship Plus	806 N Fairfax St	4:30

Map 46 • Old Town (South)

FedEx Kinko's	685 N Washington St	7:30
Self-Service	515 N Washington St	7:00
Self-Service	1400 Duke St	7:00
Self-Service	300 N Washington St	7:00
Self-Service	901 N Washington St	6:30
Self-Service	1001 Prince St	6:30
Self-Service	1315 Duke St	6:30
Self-Service	310 S Henry St	6:30
Self-Service	110 S Union St	6:00
Self-Service	112 S Alfred St	6:00
Self-Service	1420 King St	6:00
Self-Service	201 N Union St	6:00
Self-Service	211 N Union St	6:00
Self-Service	700 S Washington St	6:00
Self-Service	126 S Washington	6:00
Old Town Pack and Ship	824 King St	6:00
Self-Service	1101 King St	5:30
Self-Service	320 King St	5:00
Self-Service	510 King St	5:00
Old Town Post Box	127 S Fairfax St	4:00

Overview

Let's face it: The Smithsonian Museums were really cool when you were 10 years old and toured DC with your parents. But you're a cultured adult now, looking to expand your horizons a bit further than dinosaur bones and airplanes (not that dinosaur bones and airplanes aren't cool, because they are). Washington's plethora of small and independent galleries have got it all, from classical to conceptual. To top it off, you're not too likely to be bumped from behind by an unsupervised toddler whose parents wanted to see Degas' ballerinas but couldn't find a babysitter. Although crowds of young professionals aren't always much better, Washington's art galleries offer a more comfortable and casual approach to the art world. And if you fancy it enough you may even be able to afford it.

Dupont Circle is the hub of DC's art scene, with everything from impressionism at the **Phillips Collection (Map 9)** to the shrine of rugs at the **Textile Museum (Map 9)**. The only drawback is that, unlike the bigger museums around the mall, many galleries charge entrance fees and sometimes keep quirky hours (daytime Wednesday through Saturday is your best bet). Planning ahead will definitely pay off if you want to experience the ceramics, painting, sculpture, and other less accessible works of art that these galleries feature.

A good time to check out the Dupont art scene is on the first Friday evening of every month, when most of the galleries open their doors briefly for a free peek. Many of the galleries on R Street, also known as Gallery Row, are converted row houses with narrow staircases, so be careful of art enthusiast bottlenecks on Friday nights; check out **Burdick Gallery (Map 9)** (sculpture and graphics by Inuit artists), **Fusebox (Map 10)** (American and international conceptual art), **Gallery 10 (Map 9)** (modern and experimental art), **Irvine Contemporary (Map 9)** (art from emerging and established artists), **Marsha Mateyka Gallery (Map 9)** (contemporary art), **Numark Gallery (Map 2)** (modern art from emerging artists), **Robert Brown Gallery (Map 9)** (eclectic, varied exhibitions), and **Studio Gallery (Map 9)** (artist co-op with 30 members).

During the annual Dupont-Kalorama Museum Walk Weekend, held on the first weekend in June, galleries usually allow roaming free of charge (www.dkmuseums.com). The Dupont-Kalorama Museum Walk caters to discerning art critics, groups of children, and families alike, offering exhibits and activities that reflect a desire to inspire the art history buffs, as well as the "Da Vinci Who?" crowd.

Check out the *Post* and *City Paper* listings for shows at some of the other galleries that, ahead of rampant gentrification, are popping up all over the city. Another great resource for gallery information is the city guide at www.washingtonpost.com/cityguide, which has excellent reviews and editor picks of the art galleries in DC, as well as a list with gallery websites at art-collecting.com/galleries_dc.htm.

All area codes as listed in heading unless otherwise noted

Map 1 • National Mall

Arthur M Sackler Gallery	1050 Independence Ave SW	202-633-4880
Corcoran Gallery	500 17th St NW	202-639-1700
Gallery at Flashpoint	916 G St NW	202-315-1310
National Museum of Women in the Arts	1250 New York Ave NW	202-783-5000
Pepco's Edison Place Gallery	701 9th St NW	202-872-3396
Renwick Gallery of the Smithsonian American Art Museum	Pennsylvania Ave NW & 17th St NW	202-633-1000
White House Art Gallery	529 14th St NW	202-393-6752

Map 2 • Chinatown / Union Station

Echo Gallery	50 Massachusetts Ave NE	202-842-8400
Goethe-Institute	812 7th St NW	202-289-1200
National Gallery of Art	401 Constitution Ave NW	202-737-4215
Numark Gallery	625 E St NW	202-628-3810
Touchstone Gallery	406 7th St NW	202-347-2787
Zenith Gallery	413 7th St NW	202-783-2963

Map 3 • The Hill

Market Five Gallery	201 7th St SE	202-543-7293
Pulp on the Hill	303 Pennsylvania Ave SE	202-543-1924
Village	705 North Carolina Ave SE	202-546-3040

Map 5 • Southeast / Anacostia

Alvear Studio Design	705 8th St SE	202-546-8434
Newman Gallery	513 11th St SE	202-544-7577

Map 6 • Waterfront

Art Enables	65 I St SW	202-554-9455

Map 7 • Foggy Bottom

Arts Club of Washington	2017 I St NW	202-331-7282
de Andino Fine Arts	2450 Virginia Ave NW	202-861-0638
Dimock Gallery	730 21st St NW	202-994-1525
Dupont Art and Framing	1922 I St NW	202-331-1815
Foliograph Gallery	919 18th St NW	202-296-8398
Jerusalem Fund Gallery	2425 Virginia Ave NW	202-338-1958
Luther W Brady Art Gallery	805 21st St NW	202-994-1525
National Academy of Sciences	2100 C St NW	202-334-2436
Watergate Gallery	2552 Virginia Ave NW	202-338-4488

Map 8 • Georgetown

Addison-Ripley Gallery	1670 Wisconsin Ave NW	202-338-5180
Alla Rogers Gallery	1054 31st St NW	202-333-8595
Anne C Fisher Gallery	1054 31st St NW	202-625-7555
Attis Art Gallery	2828 Pennsylvania Ave NW	202-333-0733
Cherub Antiques	2918 M St NW	202-337-2224
District Fine Arts	1726 Wisconsin Ave NW	202-328-9100
Fine Art & Artists	2920 M St NW	202-965-0780
Gala	1671 Wisconsin Ave NW	202-333-1337
Govinda Gallery	1227 34th St NW	202-333-1180
Grafix	2904 M St NW	202-342-0610
Guarisco Gallery	2828 Pennsylvania Ave NW	202-333-8533
Jackson Art Center	3048 R St NW	202-342-9778
Ken Frye Art Gallery	3242 Jones Ct NW	202-333-2505
Maurine Littleton Gallery	1667 Wisconsin Ave NW	202-333-9307
Mu Project	1521 Wisconsin Ave NW	202-333-4119
Old Print Gallery	1220 31st St NW	202-965-1818
P Street Pictures	2621 P St NW	202-337-0066
P&C Art	3108 M St NW	202-965-3833
Parish Gallery	1054 31st St NW	202-944-2310
Ralls Collection	1516 31st St NW	202-342-1754
Spectrum Gallery	1132 29th St NW	202-333-0954
Susan Calloway Antique Prints & Fine Art	1643 Wisconsin Ave NW	202-965-4601
Susquehanna Antiques	3216 O St NW	202-333-1511

Map 9 • Dupont Circle / Adams Morgan

Aaron Gallery	1717 Connecticut Ave NW	202-234-3311
Alex Gallery	2106 R St NW	202-667-2599
Burdick Gallery	2114 R St NW	202-986-5682
Burton Marinkovich	1506 21st St NW	202-296-6563
Chao Phraya Gallery	2009 Columbia Rd NW	202-745-1111
Conner Contemporary Art	1730 Connecticut Ave NW	202-588-8750
Foundry Gallery	1314 18th St NW	202-463-0203
Gallery 10 Limited	1519 Connecticut Ave NW	202-232-3326
Gary Edward's Photographs	1711 Connecticut Ave NW	301-524-0900
Geoffrey Diner Gallery	1730 21st St NW	202-483-5005
Ingrid Hansen Gallery	1203 19th St NW	202-266-5022
International Art Gallery	1625 K St NW	202-466-7979
Irvine Contemporary Art	1710 Connecticut Ave NW	202-332-8767
Jane Haslem Gallery	2025 Hillyer Pl NW	202-232-4644
Kathleen Ewing Gallery	1609 Connecticut Ave NW	202-328-0955
Marsha Mateyka Gallery	2012 R St NW	202-328-0088

Nevin Kelly Gallery	1517 U St NW	202-232-3464
Open Society Institute Gallery	1120 19th St NW	202-721-5642
Pass Gallery	1617 S St NW	202-745-0796
Pensler Galleries	2029 Q St NW	202-328-9190
Phillips Collection	1600 21st St NW	202-387-2151
Provisions Library	1611 Connecticut Ave NW	202-299-0460
Robert Brown Gallery	2030 R St NW	202-483-4383
St Luke's Gallery	1715 Q St NW	202-328-2424
Studio Gallery	2108 R St NW	202-232-8734
Textile Museum	2320 S St NW	202-667-0441
Washington Printmakers Gallery	1732 Connecticut Ave NW	202-332-7757
WVSA's ARTiculate Gallery	1100 16th St NW	202-296-9100

Map 10 • Logan Circle / U Street

Adamson Gallery	1515 14th St NW	202-232-0707
Fusebox	1412 14th St NW	202-299-9220
G Fine Art	1515 14th St NW	202-462-1601
Hemphill Fine Arts	1515 14th St NW	202-234-5601
Mickelson's Fine Art Framing & Parker Gallery	629 New York Ave NW	202-628-1734
NNE Gallery	1312 8th St NW	202-276-4540
Plan B	1530 14th St NW	202-234-2711
Transformer Gallery	1404 P St NW	202-483-1102
Vastu	1829 14th St NW	202-234-8344
WareHouse	1017 7th St NW	202-783-3933
Wayland House Gallerie	1802 11th St NW	202-387-8157

Map 14 • Catholic U

Washington Works on Paper	3420 9th St NE	202-526-4848
Wohlfarth Galleries	3418 9th St NE	202-526-8022

Map 16 • Adams Morgan (North) / Mt Pleasant

Carey Ellis	1825 Kalorama Rd NW	202-483-5005
District of Columbia Arts Center	2438 18th St NW	202-462-7833
Mexican Cultural Institute	2829 16th St NW	202-728-1628

Map 17 • Woodley Park / Cleveland Park

Adams Davidson Galleries	2727 29th St NW	202-965-3800
International Visions Gallery	2629 Connecticut Ave NW	202-234-5112

Map 18 • Glover Park / Foxhall

Cathedral Galleries	3301 New Mexico Ave NW	202-363-6936
Foxhall Gallery	3301 New Mexico Ave NW	202-966-7144
Kreeger Museum	2401 Foxhall Rd NW	202-337-3050

Map 19 • Tenleytown / Friendship Heights

Brazilian-American Cultural Institute	4719 Wisconsin Ave NW	202-362-8334
Watkins Gallery	4400 Massachusetts Ave NW	202-885-1064

Map 20 • Cleveland Park / Upper Connecticut

Chevy Chase Gallery	5039 Connecticut Ave NW	202-364-8155

Map 22 • Downtown Bethesda

Fraser Gallery	7700 Wisconsin Ave	301-718-9651
Gallery Neptune	4808 Auburn Ave	301-718-0809
Ozmosis Gallery	7908 Woodmont Ave	301-664-9662
Saint Elmo's Fire	4928 St Elmo Ave	301-215-9848

Map 25 • Silver Spring

Century Gallery	919 King St	703-684-6967
House of Safori	1105 Spring St	301-565-0781
Pyramid Atlantic	8230 Georgia Ave	301-608-9101

Map 27 • Walter Reed

A Salon	6925 Willow St NW	202-882-0740

Map 28 • Chevy Chase

Avant Garde	5520 Connecticut Ave NW	202-966-1045

Map 29 • Bethesda / Chevy Chase Business

Creative Partners	4600 East West Hwy	301-951-9441
Designers Art Gallery	4618 Leland St	301-718-0400
Discovery Galleries Limited	4840 Bethesda Ave	301-913-9199
Discovery Too Gallery	7247 Woodmont Ave	301-913-9101
Glass Gallery	5335 Wisconsin Ave NW	202-237-1119
Marin-Price Galleries	7022 Wisconsin Ave	301-718-0622
Moriah Gallery	7301 Woodmont Ave	301-657-3001
Osuna Art	7200 Wisconsin Ave	301-654-4500
Washington Studio School	4505 Stanford St	301-718-7210

Map 33 • Falls Church

Paul McGhee's Old Town Gallery	109 N Fairfax St	703-548-7729

Map 34 • Ballston

Ellipse Arts Center	4350 Fairfax Dr	703-228-7710
Lac Viet Gallery	5179 Lee Hwy	703-532-4350

Map 35 • Clarendon

Metropolitan Gallery	2420 Wilson Blvd	703-358-9449

Map 37 • Fort Myer

Arlington Arts Center	3550 Wilson Blvd	703-248-6800

Map 40 • Pentagon City / Crystal City

Wentworth Galleries	1100 S Hayes St	703-415-1166

Map 41 • Landmark

Gallery Petalouth	301 N Beauregard St	703-354-1176

Map 42 • Alexandria (West)

Propeller Studio	3670 Wheeler Ave	703-370-4800

Map 43 • Four Mile Run/Del Ray

Del Ray Artisans	2704 Mt Vernon Ave	703-838-4827
Fitzgerald Fine Arts	2502 E Randolph Ave	703-836-1231

Map 44 • Alexandria Downtown

Tall Tulips	412 John Carlyle St	703-549-5017

Map 45 • Old Town (North)

Studio Antiques & Fine Art	524 N Washington St	703-548-5188

Map 46 • Old Town (South)

Art League	105 N Union St	703-683-1780
Artcraft Collection	132 King St	703-299-6616
Arts Afire Glass Gallery	102 N Fayette St	703-838-9785
The Athenaeum	201 Prince St	703-548-0035
Broadway Gallery	1219 King St	703-549-1162
Citron Ann	105 N Union St	703-683-0403
Enamelist Gallery	105 N Union St	703-836-1561
Fiber Works	105 N Union St	703-836-5807
Foliograph Gallery	217 King St	703-683-1501
Gallerie Michele	113 King St	703-683-1521
Gallery West	1213 King St	703-549-6006
Miller Fine Art Limited	113 S Columbus St	703-838-0006
Mindful Hands	211 King St	703-683-2074
Multiple Exposures	105 N Union St	703-683-2205
P&C Art	212 King St	703-549-2525
Potomac Craftsmen Fiber Gallery	105 N Union St	703-548-0935
Prince Royal Gallery	204 S Royal St	703-548-5151
Principle Gallery	208 King St	703-739-9326
Printmakers Inc	105 N Union St	703-683-1342
Scope Gallery	105 N Union St	703-548-6288
Tall Tulips	105 N Union St	703-549-7317
Target Gallery	105 N Union St	703-838-4565
Torpedo Factory Arts Center	105 N Union St	703-838-4565

Arts & Entertainment • Bookstores

While the shopping scene might give visitors the impression that District residents don't care how they look, the independent bookstore scene will show them that we definitely care about what we read. This is a city of policy wonks, lawyers, writers, defense specialists, and activists—the one thing we all have in common, frankly, is that we're nerds. Washington, DC, and the metropolitan area is, especially recently, brimming with residents with expensive educations, lucrative government contracting jobs, and high-performance cars. So it seems obvious that bookstores here would get as crowded as the Beltway during rush hour. Besides the mega-chain stores like **Borders (Map 1, Map 9, Map 19, Map 25, Map 40)** and **Barnes & Noble (Map 1, Map 8, Map 29, Map 35, Map 43)**, there are several local outlets in town, each with a personality of their own.

Kramerbooks & Afterwords Café (Map 9) in Dupont Circle, for instance, is something of a local landmark. Literary types will set to meet up here, thumbing the shelves for their next read while they wait, and then often settling into a bookish conversation at the café over a Mocha Ice and fine slice of pie. There's also local chain **Olsson's (Map 2, Map 9, Map 36, Map 46)** if you like your coffee and ownership independent, as well as recent arrivals **Candida's (Map 10)** and **Busboys and Poets (Map 10)**, which promise to draw more men and women of letters to the U Street area. **Chapters Literary Bookstore (Map 1)** on 11th Street is an interesting experiment in promoting "literature" as opposed to "fiction"—but this is more a store for people looking to be told what to read and appreciate

and will not offer you the selection of say, **Politics & Prose (Map 20)**, which is quite easily the city's finest bookstore. It's hard to exit this upper NW gem without wishing to spend the rest of your life buried in a book, and there are authors speaking here every night of the week to further encourage you. There's also two locations of **Big Planet Comics (Map 8, Map 22)** for your inner (or outer) adolescent geek. If you have time to spare, check out the used bookstores for cheaper reads and dusty aromas. Try **Riverby Books (Map 3)** on Capitol Hill, **Second Story Books (Map 9, Map 22)** in Bethesda or Dupont Circle, **Idle Time Books (Map 16)** in Adams Morgan, and **Book Bank (Map 46)** in Alexandria.

DC's bookstore scene also offers some of the best in specialty non-fiction. The **American Institute for Architects (Map 1)** can offer you histories of every high rise in the Chicago skyline, and both the **National Gallery of Art Gift Shop (Map 2)** or the **Franz Bader Bookstore (Map 7)** will provide countless coffee table books on modern art, as well as the accompanying art history criticism. Readers of the gay, lesbian, bisexual, and transgender persuasions should head to **Lambda Rising (Map 9)**, the largest LGBT bookstore in the world. For religious studies, there's the **Islamic Center (Map 8)** or the **Catholic Information Center (Map 9)** (to name only two)… Basically, this is a town that has national associations of pottery wheelers and international funds for left-handed clarinetists—so if there's a subject you're interested in, there's a nerd to provide you with scholarly literature on it. Go for it!

Map 1 • National Mall

American Institute for Architects	1735 New York Ave NW	202-626-7300	Architecture.
Barnes & Noble	555 12th St NW	202-347-0176	General.
Borders	600 14th St NW	202-737-1385	General.
Chapters Literary Bookstore	445 11th St NW	202-737-5553	Poetry, literary fiction (old and new), children's literature, and natural history.

Map 2 • Chinatown / Union Station

AMA Management Book Store	440 1st St NW	202-347-3092	Business.
B Dalton Booksellers	50 Massachusetts Ave NE	202-289-1724	General.
National Academy Press	500 5th St NW	202-334-2612	Science and technology, social environment issues.
National Gallery of Art Gift Shop	401 Constitution Ave NW	202-737-4215	Art books.
Olsson's Books	418 7th St NW	202-638-7610	General.

Map 3 • The Hill

Riverby Books	417 E Capitol St SE	202-543-4342	Used.
Trover Shop Books & Office	221 Pennsylvania Ave SE	202-547-2665	General.

Map 5 • Southeast / Anacostia

Backstage	545 8th St SE	202-544-5744	Theater and performance.
Capitol Hill Books	657 C St SE	202-544-1621	Second-hand fiction, mystery, and biography.
Fairy Godmother—Children's Books & Toys	319 7th St SE	202-547-5474	Toddler to young adult fiction and nonfiction.
First Amendment Books	645 Pennsylvania Ave SE	202-547-5585	Current events, political history.

Map 7 • Foggy Bottom

Franz Bader Bookstore	1911 I St NW	202-337-5440	Art and architecture.
George Washington U Book Store	800 21st St NW	202-994-6870	Academic and college.
Washington Law & Professional Books	1900 G St NW	202-223-5543	Law.
World Bank Info Shop	701 18th St NW	202-458-4500	Development and politics.

Map 8 • Georgetown

Barnes & Noble	3040 M St NW	202-965-9880	General.
Bartleby's Books	3034 M St NW	202-298-0486	Rare and antiquarian, 18th-and-19th century American history, economics, and law.
Big Monkey Comics	1419 Wisconsin Ave NW	202-333-8650	Comics.
Big Planet Comics	3145 Dumbarton Ave NW	202-342-1961	Comics.
Bridge St Books	2814 Pennsylvania Ave NW	202-965-5200	General.
Islamic Center	2551 Massachessetts Ave NW	202-332-8343	Islamic books.
Lantern Bryn Mawr Book Shop	3241 P St NW	202-333-3222	Used and rare.

Map 9 • Dupont Circle / Adams Morgan

Books-A-Million	11 Dupont Cir NW	202-319-1374	General.
Borders	1801 K St NW	202-466-4999	General.
Catholic Information Center	1501 K St NW	202-783-2062	Catholic books.
G Books	1520 U St NW	202-986-9697	Gay/lesbian discount books.
International Language Center	1803 Connecticut Ave NW	202-332-2894	Language.
Kramerbooks and Afterwords	1517 Connecticut Ave NW	202-387-1400	General.
Lambda Rising Book Store	1625 Connecticut Ave NW	202-462-6969	Gay and lesbian.
Newsroom	1803 Connecticut Ave NW	202-332-1489	Foreign language and reference.
Olsson's Books	1307 19th St NW	202-785-1133	General.
Reiter's Scientific & Professional Books	2021 K St NW	202-223-3327	Scientific and medical.
Second Story Books & Antiques	2000 P St NW	202-659-8884	Used.

Map 10 • Logan Circle / U Street

Brian Mackenzie Infoshop	1426 9th St NW	202-986-0681	Left-wing literature.
Busboys and Poets	2021 14th St NW	202-387-7638	Political, poetry and literature, multicultural, and independent publishers.
Candida's World Of Books	1541 14th St NW	202-667-4811	Language learning and reference, travel, art, cookbooks, current literature, political, science, and children's.

Map 11 • Near Northeast

Bison Shop-Gallaudet University	800 Florida Ave NE	202-651-5271	Academic and sign language.

Map 14 • Catholic U

Newman Book Store of Washington	3329 8th St NE	202-526-1036	Scripture, theology, philosophy, and church history.

Map 15 • Columbia Heights

House Of Khamit	2822 Georgia Ave NW	202-387-4163	African history/culture.
Howard University Book Store	2225 Georgia Ave NW	202-238-2640	Academic and Afro-centric.
Sankofa Video & Bookstore	2714 Georgia Ave NW	202-234-4755	Afro-centric.

Map 16 • Adams Morgan (North) / Mt Pleasant

AAFSW Book Room	2201 Centre St NW	202-223-5796	General used.
Idle Time Books	2467 18th St NW	202-232-4774	Used.
Potter's House Books	1658 Columbia Rd NW	202-232-5483	Spiritual/Social Justice Literature.

Map 18 • Glover Park / Foxhall

Georgetown University Book Store	3800 Reservoir Rd NW	202-687-7492	Academic.
Tree Top Toys & Books	3301 New Mexico Ave NW	202-244-3500	Children's.

Map 19 • Tenleytown / Friendship Heights

American University Book Store	4400 Massachusetts Ave NW	202-885-6300	Academic and college.
Borders	5333 Wisconsin Ave NW	202-686-8270	General.
Fantom Comics	4500 Wisconsin Ave NW	202-362-5051	Comics.
Tempo Book Store	4905 Wisconsin Ave NW	202-363-6683	Language.

Map 20 • Cleveland Park / Upper Connecticut

Politics & Prose	5015 Connecticut Ave NW	202-364-1919	American studies and politics.

Map 22 • Downtown Bethesda

Big Planet Comics	4908 Fairmont Ave	301-654-6856	Comics.
Second Story Books & Antiques	4914 Fairmont Ave	301-656-0170	Used.
Waldenbooks	143 Montgomery Mall	301-469-8810	General.

Map 23 • Kensington

Audubon Naturalist Bookshop	8940 Jones Mill Rd	301-652-3606	Nature and earth.

Map 25 • Silver Spring

Alliance Comics	8317 Fenton St	301-588-2546	Comics.
Borders	8518 Fenton St	301-585-0550	Chain.
Silver Spring Books	938 Bonifant St	301-587-7484	Used.

Map 27 • Walter Reed

Literal Books	7705 Georgia Ave NW	800-366-8680	Spanish books.

Map 29 • Bethesda / Chevy Chase Business

Barnes & Noble	4801 Bethesda Ave	301-986-1761	General.
Georgetown Book Shop	4710 Bethesda Ave	301-907-6923	History, art, photography, children's, literary fiction, and baseball.
Writer's Center Book Gallery	4508 Walsh St	301-654-8664	Literature and books on writing.

Map 33 • Falls Church

Aladdin's Lamp Childrens Books	2499 N Harrison St	703-241-8281	Children's.

Map 34 • Ballston

B Dalton Booksellers	4238 Wilson Blvd	703-522-8822	General.
Bookhouse	805 N Emerson St	703-527-7797	Scholarly history.
Imagination Station	4524 Lee Hwy	703-522-2047	Children's.

Map 35 • Clarendon

Barnes & Noble	2800 Clarendon Blvd	703-248-8244	General.

Map 36 • Rosslyn

Olsson's Books	2111 Wilson Blvd	703-525-4227	General.

Map 38 • Columbia Pike

Al-Hikma Book Store	5627 Columbia Pike	703-820-7500	Arabic.
NVCC-Alexandria Campus Book Store	3101 N Beauregard St	703-671-0043	Academic and college.

Map 39 • Shirlington

Books-A-Million	4201 28th St S	703-931-6949	Chain bookstore.

Map 40 • Pentagon City / Crystal City

Borders	1201 S Hayes St	703-418-0166	General.

Map 41 • Landmark

Waldenbooks	5801 Duke St	703-658-9576	General.

Map 43 • Four Mile Run / Del Ray

Barnes & Noble	3651 Jefferson Davis Hwy	703-299-9124	General.

Map 46 • Old Town (South)

A Likely Story	1555 King St	703-836-2498	Children's and parenting.
Aftertime Comics	1304 King St	703-548-5030	Comics.
Book Bank	1510 King St	703-838-3620	Used.
Books-A-Million	503 King St	703-548-3432	General.
Olsson's Books	106 S Union St	703-684-0077	General.
Why Not	200 King St	703-548-4420	Children's.

Living in a politically charged city means that independents and documentaries play big here. You'll find the best of the bunch at the **Landmark E Street (Map 1)** downtown, Chevy Chase's **Avalon (Map 28)** (DC's oldest movie house), or Silver Spring's shrine to film, the **AFI Silver (Map 25)**, where membership and perks (free tickets) are available for the avid Silver-Screener. For indie flicks, try the cramped **Loews Dupont Circle 5 (Map 9)**. **Landmark Row (Map 29)**, right off Bethesda Avenue in Bethesda, has a reasonable selection of indie and foreign films, and the space is a little more elegant than its Dupont rival. Also, watch for temporary screenings every few weeks at museums, schools, or historic theaters like the Tivoli (Map 15) in Columbia Heights and the Lincoln (Map 10) on U Street. In late summer, take a blanket to the Mall for the free "Screen on the Green" classic film series.

If it's a blockbuster hit you're after, plenty of mainstream, metro-accessible theaters will oblige. The Washington *Post, City Paper,* and pretty much any print or online entertainment resource can give you the movie listings for the Loews and Cineplex Odeons that crowd the city and its suburbs. The best of the bunch is Cleveland Park's **Uptown (Map 17)**, a gorgeous 1936 Art Deco palace with a massive curved screen (32' x 70'). You'll probably have to stand in line for tickets on an opening day or a weekend, but it's one of the few theaters that can really do justice to that latest Hollywood action flick (think *Lord of the Rings, Jurassic Park,* the new *Star Wars* films).

Stadium seating megaplexes have arrived downtown, including the **Loews Georgetown (Map 8),** which houses a brick smokestack used long ago as the Georgetown Incinerator, and the **Regal Gallery Place (Map 2)**, whose fit-for-Caesar marble atrium and 14 screens are cleverly nestled into an already crowded Chinatown (and the bathrooms have the most powerful hand dryers you've ever seen—or heard).

Theater	Address	Phone	Map
AFI Silver Theater	8633 Colesville Rd	301-495-6720	25
AMC City Place 10	8661 Colesville Rd	703-998-4262	25
AMC Courthouse Plaza 8	2150 Clarendon Blvd	703-998-4262	36
AMC Hoffman Center 22	206 Swamp Fox Rd	703-998-4262	44
AMC Mazza Gallerie 7	5300 Wisconsin Ave NW	202-537-9553	19
AMC Union Station 9	50 Massachusetts Ave NE	703-998-4262	2
American City Movie Diner	5532 Connecticut Ave NW	202-244-1949	28
American University Wechsler Theatre	4400 Massachusetts Ave NW	202-885-3408	19
Arlington Cinema 'N' Drafthouse	2903 Columbia Pike	703-486-2345	37
Avalon Theatre	5612 Connecticut Ave NW	202-966-6000	28
Busboys and Poets	2021 14th St NW	202-387-7638	10
Carnegie Institute	1530 P St NW	202-939-1142	9
Cineplex Odeon Shirlington 7	2772 S Randolph St	703-671-0978	39
Cineplex Odeon Uptown	3426 Connecticut Ave NW	202-966-5400	17
Cineplex Odeon Wisconsin Avenue Cinemas	4000 Wisconsin Ave NW	202-244-0880	19
E Street Cinema	555 11th St NW	202-333-FILM #781	1
Johnson IMAX Theater	Constitution Ave NW & 10th St NW	202-633-9045	1
Landmark Bethesda Row Cinema	7235 Woodmont Ave	301-652-7273	29
Landmark E St Cinema	555 11th St NW	202-452-7672	1
Lockheed Martin IMAX Theater	601 Independence Ave SW	202-357-1686	2
Loews Cineplex	3426 Connecticut Ave NW	202-333-FILM #799	17
Loews Cineplex	4000 Wisconsin Ave NW	202-333-FILM #789	19
Loews Dupont Circle 5	1350 19th St NW	202-872-9555	9
Loews Georgetown 14	3111 K St NW	202-342-6441	8
The Majestic 20	900 Ellsworth Dr	301-681-2266	25
Mary Pickford Theater	Library of Congress, James Madison Memorial Bldg, Independence Ave SE b/w 1st St SE & 2nd St SE	202-707-5677	2
Old Town Theater	815 1/2 King St	703-683-8888	46
Regal Ballston Common 12	671 N Glebe Rd	703-527-9730	34
Regal Bethesda 10	7272 Wisconsin Ave	301-718-4323	29
Regal Gallery Place Stadium	707 7th St NW	202-393-2121	2
Regal Potomac Yard 16	3575 Jefferson Davis Hwy	703-739-4040	43

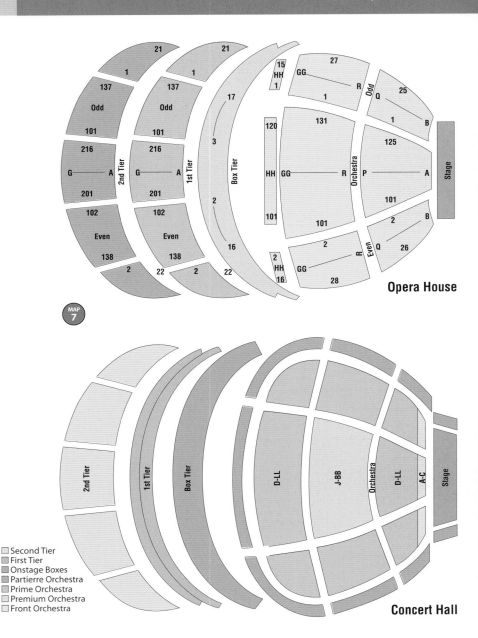

Opera House

MAP
7

Second Tier
First Tier
Onstage Boxes
Partierre Orchestra
Prime Orchestra
Premium Orchestra
Front Orchestra

Concert Hall

General Information

NFT Map: 7
Address: 2700 F St NW
       Washington, DC 20566
Website: www.kennedy-center.org
Phone: 202-416-8000
Box Office: 800-444-1324 or 202-467-4600

Overview

The Kennedy Center is the city's primary performance art destination. While other city venues may be better at promoting cutting-edge arts, this place is where you can witness the best in the world pirouette, harmonize, and/or yodel. Of course, such feats come with a price tag and the Center tends to cater to thick-of-wallet arts patrons.. Those who are, more savvy than wealthy, though, know that bargains exist. There are nightly free concerts, hidden cheap seats, and occasional discounts. And there's no charge to show up and check out one of the city's most romantic dusk terrace views or the giant bust of the center's adored namesake.

Besides some of the ticket prices, there is also the obstacle of keeping track of performances. The Kennedy Center houses the Concert Hall, Opera House, Eisenhower Theater, Terrace Theater, Theater Lab, Film Theater, and Jazz Club. On any given night, there are concurrent music, theater, opera, and dance performances. It can be tough to keep up. If you're a confirmed culture vulture, stay afloat by becoming a Kennedy Center member. Otherwise, save the websites of your favorites, and check them regularly.

The Kennedy Center's history began in 1958, when President Dwight D. Eisenhower took a break from the links to sign legislation creating a National Cultural Center for the United States. President John F. Kennedy and First Lady Jackie later did much of the fundraising for what the president called "our contribution to the human spirit." Two months after President Kennedy's assassination, Congress named the center in his memory.

How to Get There—Driving

If you're not one of the patrons who can rely on your limo's GPS, then follow this advice: Heading away from the Capitol on Independence Avenue, get in the left lane as you approach the Potomac. Passing under two bridges, stay in the left lane, and follow signs to the Kennedy Center. After passing the Kennedy Center on your right, make a right onto Virginia Avenue. At the second set of lights, turn right onto 25th Street, and follow the Kennedy Center parking signs.

Parking

Kennedy Center garage parking is $15.

How to Get There—Mass Transit

Take the Blue Line or Orange Line to the Foggy Bottom stop, and either walk seven minutes to the center or take a free shuttle that runs every fifteen minutes. For above-ground transportation-lovers, Metrobus 80 also goes to the Kennedy Center.

How to Get Tickets

Prices vary depending on the event. Check the center's website, or call the box office for schedules and tickets.

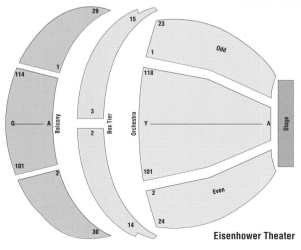

Eisenhower Theater

The Smithsonian Institution is a national system of museums, most of which are situated in a campus-like arrangement around the National Mall (other branches, like the Cooper-Hewitt National Design Museum, are located in New York City, and the Steven F. Udvar-Hazy Center, an extension of the **National Air and Space Museum (Map 6),** is in Chantilly, VA). The free Smithsonian exhibits draw both American and international tourists by the hordes.

The west wing of the **National Gallery (Map 2)** houses a world-class collection of 13th–16th-century European painting and sculpture, including the only Leonardo da Vinci painting on this side of the Atlantic. The East Wing houses the museum's modern and contemporary collections. At the **Freer and Sackler Galleries (Map 1),** sublime works of Asian art hide in unlikely corners of small and modest rooms. The **Hirshhorn Museum and Sculpture Garden (Map 2)** is, well, avant-garde—what else could you call the collection that includes Ron Mueck's eerily realistic sculpture of a naked, obese, bald man just hanging out in the corner? The **Corcoran Gallery of Art (Map 1)** is another one of DC's gems, with a solid collection of American and European art, and it also offers a wide range of classes (visit www.corcoran.org for details). The **National Museum of American History (Map 1)** is more than a collection of invaluable artifacts; it addresses the history and the making of American culture. And while the American History museum might make us feel all-important, the **National**

Museum of Natural History (Map 1) will deflate our egos, reminding us that we are but one mortal species among many. As depressing as it may be, the relatively new **US Holocaust Museum (Map 1)** is definitely worth visiting—an eerie but well-done reminder of the extent of man's cruelty.

You could spend your whole life in Washington and still not be able to name every Smithsonian museum. But they're all free, so consider them friends who need to be checked in on from time to time.

History Buff, are you? DC is home to the **National Archives (Map 2),** a government building that also contains numerous historical documents on exhibit. Stop by and pay nothing to see the *Bill of Rights* and our founding fathers' John Hancocks (even John Hancock's!). And in case you forgot you were living in a democracy—even the FBI building offers guided tours.

Extending out from the Mall, you'll discover the pricier private museums. The **National Building Museum's (Map 2)** building and gift shop are interesting, even when the offbeat architectural exhibits are not. When you're in the mood for something more specific, try the targeted collections at places like the **National Postal Museum (Map 2)** or the **National Museum of Women in the Arts (Map 1).**

Museum	Address	Phone	Map
Alexandria Archaeology Museum	105 N Union St	703-838-4399	46
Alexandria Black History Resource Center	902 Wythe St	703-838-4356	45
Anacostia Museum & Center for African American History and Culture	1901 Fort Pl SE	202-633-4820	n/a
Arlington Historical Museum	1805 S Arlington Ridge Rd	703-892-4204	40
Art Museum of the Americas	201 18th St NW	202-458-6016	7
The Arts Club of Washington	2017 I St NW	202-331-7282	7
The Athenaeum	201 Prince St	703-548-0035	46
Bead Museum DC	400 7th St NW	202-624-4500	2
Black Fashion Museum	2007 Vermont Ave NW	202-667-0744	10
Black Heritage Museum of Arlington	951 S George Mason Dr	703-271-8700	37
City Museum	801 K St NW	202-383-1800	10
The Corcoran	500 17th St NW	202-639-1700	1
DAR Museum	1776 D St NW	202-628-1776	7
DEA Museum & Visitors Center	700 Army Navy Dr	202-307-3463	40
Discovery Creek Children's Museum–Historic Schoolhouse	4954 MacArthur Blvd NW	202-337-5111	18
Dumbarton House	2715 Q St NW	202-337-2288	8
Einstein Planetarium-National Air & Space Museum	Independence Ave SE & 4th St SW	202-633-4629	6
Explorers Hall (National Geographic Society)	17th St NW & M St NW	202-857-7588	9
Folger Shakespeare Library	201 E Capitol St SE	202-544-4600	3
Ford's Theatre and Peterson House	511 10th St NW	202-426-6924	1

Museum	Address	Phone	Map
Fort Ward Museum & Historic Site	4301 W Braddock Rd	703-838-4848	39
Frederick Douglass Museum & Hall of Fame for Caring Americans	320 A St NE	202-547-4273	3
Frederick Douglass National Historic Site	1411 W St SE	202-426-5961	5
Freer Art Gallery and Arthur M Sackler Gallery	1050 Independence Ave SW	202-633-4880	1
Friendship Firehouse Museum	107 S Alfred St	703-838-3891	46
Gadsby's Tavern Museum	134 N Royal St	703-838-4242	46
George Washington Masonic Memorial Museum	101 Callahan Dr	703-683-2007	44
Hillwood Museum & Gardens	4155 Linnean Ave NW	202-686-8500	20
Hirshhorn Museum and Sculpture Garden	7th St SW & Independence Ave SW	202-633-4674	2
International Spy Museum	800 F St NW	202-393-7798	1
The Kreeger Museum	2401 Foxhall Rd NW	202-337-3050	18
The Library of Congress	101 Independence Ave SE	202-707-5000	2
The Lyceum	201 S Washington St	703-838-4994	46
The Mansion on O Street	2020 O St NW	202-496-2020	9
Marian Koshland Science Museum at The National Academy of Sciences	500 5th St NW	202-334-1201	2
Museum of Contemporary Art	1054 31st St NW	202-342-6230	8
National Academy of Sciences	6th St NW & E St NW	202-334-2000	2
National Air and Space Museum	Independence Ave SE & 4th St SW	202-633-1000	6
National Aquarium	14th St NW & Constitution Ave NW	202-482-2825	1
The National Archives Building	700 Pennsylvania Ave NW	202-357-5000	2
National Building Museum	401 F St NW	202-272-2448	2
National Gallery of Art	7th St NW & Constitution Ave NW	202-737-4215	2
National Health Museum	1155 15th St NW	202-737-2670	9
National Museum of African Art	950 Independence Ave SW	202-633-4600	1
National Museum of American History	14th St NW & Constitution Ave NW	202-633-1000	1
National Museum of American Jewish Military History	1811 R St NW	202-265-6280	9
National Museum of Health and Medicine	6900 Georgia Ave NW	202-782-2200	27
National Museum of Natural History	10th St NW & Constitution Ave NW	202-357-1729	1
National Museum of the American Indian	4th St & Independence Ave SW	202-633-1000	2
National Museum of Women in the Arts	1250 New York Ave NW	202-783-5000	1
National Postal Museum	2 Massachusetts Ave NE	202-633-5555	2
National Zoological Park	3001 Connecticut Ave NW	202-633-4800	17
The Navy Museum (reservation required for non-military)	805 Kidder Breese SE	202-433-4882	5
Newseum (opens 2007)	Pennsylvania Ave NW & 6th St NW	703-284-3544	2
The Octagon Museum	1799 New York Ave NW	202-638-3221	7
The Phillips Collection	1600 21st St NW	202-387-2151	9
Pope John Paul II Cultural Center	3900 Harewood Rd NE	202-635-5400	14
Renwick Gallery	Pennsylvania Ave NW & 17th St NW	202-633-2850	1
Smithsonian American Art Museum	8th St NW & F St NW	202-275-1500	1
Smithsonian Institution Building, the Castle	1000 Jefferson Ave SW	202-633-1000	1
Smithsonian Portrait Gallery	750 9th St NW	202-275-1738	1
The Society of the Cincinnati-Anderson House	2118 Massachusetts Ave NW	202-785-2040	9
Stabler-Leadbeater Apothecary Museum	105 S Fairfax St	703-836-3713	46
Stephen Decatur House Museum	1610 H St NW	202-842-0920	1
Textile Museum	2320 S St NW	202-667-0441	9
Torpedo Factory Art Center	105 N Union St	703-838-4565	46
Tudor Place	1644 31st St NW	202-965-0400	8
United States National Arboretum	3501 New York Ave NE	202-245-2726	12
US Holocaust Memorial Museum	100 Raoul Wallenberg Pl SW	202-488-0400	1
Woodrow Wilson Center for International Scholars	1300 Pennsylvania Ave NW	202-691-4000	1

Arts & Entertainment • Nightlife

Politics and booze make a mean cocktail—from pubs and clubs to dives and wine tastings, Washington DC and its environs have the bar and the drink to suit anyone and everyone. Don't let the surplus of stiff professionalism, security clearances, and skinny eyebrows fool you—this city knows how to unwind. Considering the diverse political loyalties, alcohol, and grandiose posturing of District denizens, it's a miracle that happy hours across the city don't resemble drunken reunions of competing barbarian hordes. But if pounding bargain drinks and convincing single congressional aides that you're passionate about nuclear nonproliferation isn't your bag, DC's got plenty of dance clubs, holes-in-the-wall, and live jazz venues where you can snack on oysters on the half shell. Sure, Washington DC is a city largely populated by uber-driven types who felt they were too important for their own hometowns, but the fact remains that, if you can't have fun in this city, well, you've got only yourself—not the other party—to blame.

The nightlife districts of Georgetown, Dupont, Adams Morgan, Cleveland Park, U Street, and some of the livelier suburbs offer a choice of scenes, depending on your age and mood. Most places in DC are within walking distance of each other (or at least a short cab or Metro ride apart), providing partygoers with several options for last-minute changes of plans.

Georgetown

The weekend crowd in Georgetown is a hodge-podge of college students, upper-crust shop-a-holics, wayward tourists, and local residents who have managed to find nooks and crannies along bustling M Street that the out-of-towners have yet to conquer. Fold up your map and rest your feet at **Clyde's (Map 8)**, decompress after work with a few beers and a barbecue sandwich at **Old Glory All American BBQ (Map 8)**, or slur along with the piano at **Mr. Smith's (Map 8)**. Enjoy some adult beverages and conversation at **The Guards (Map 8)**. Younger legs hike up the steps to the second-floor bar at **Garrett's (Map 8)**, or stumble down the stairs into **The Tombs (Map 8)**. When the weather is nice, hit **Sequoia (Map 8)** or **Tony & Joe's Seafood Place (Map 8)** on the Potomac—just remember that neither the river nor the boats moored there are meant to be used as public restrooms. During inclement weather, bring your rainy-day funds and poor-boy troubles to **Blues Alley (Map 8)** to get low on some jazz.

Dupont

Dupont is known for its lively gay population; it has a hip nightlife scene, and it's surrounded by neighborhoods that are safe, classy, and cultivated. The most dangerous part of Dupont nightlife is crossing the traffic circle amidst honking cabs and hesitant sedans negotiating the lights, lanes, and drunks darting across the streets. Heteros hang at **Big Hunt (Map 9)**, hook up at **Lucky Bar (Map 9)**, or dance in lively **Café Citron (Map 9)**. Drink with locals in the cozy brick underground bar **Childe Harold (Map 9)**, or with young bureaucrats at The **Front Page (Map 9)**. Gay residents and guests socialize at **Fireplace (Map 9)**, boogie between drag shows at **Chaos (Map 9)**, and chill at the low-key but sharp atmosphere at **JR's (Map 9)**.

Adams Morgan

In Adams Morgan, you'll find different cultures thriving, struggling, and partying on shared cracked sidewalks. 18th Street attracts a rambunctious crowd with live music, local improv, and a plethora of bars with neon signs, concrete steps, and quaint awnings. The block also offers conveniently placed parking meters to cling onto when you need to vomit the last few beers before crossing the street to go dancing. Sway to reggae and Caribbean rhythms at **Bukom Café (Map 16)**, and take in blues, jazz, rock, or bluegrass at **Madam's Organ (Map 16)**. Roll up your sleeves at **Pharmacy Bar (Map 16)**, DC's best dive, which caters more to locals than visitors and has a great jukebox. For a good cocktail, sneak into the **Spy Lounge (Map 16)**.

Cleveland Park

Cleveland Park's nightlife is crammed into the 3400 block of Connecticut Avenue, where Irish bars, basement billiards, and dimly lit enclaves serving sophisticated wines stand next to each other like abducted strangers in the hull of a UFO. You may not like the group, but you'll certainly find at least one friend in the pack. If you appreciate a good Irish stout and/or could relate to the upper-deck scene in *Titanic*, then go to **Ireland's Four Provinces (Map 33)**; if you consider yourself more of a lower-deck kind of person, check out **Nanny O'Brien's (Map 17)** across the street. **Atomic Billiards (Map 17)** is a good spot for guzzling beer, throwing darts, and shooting pool. For a relaxing sip of wine after a long day, **Aroma (Map 9, Map 17)** is the place to sniff, sip, and unwind.

U Street

U Street on weekend nights is where you'll find people boozing, dancing, and taking in live music; these same folks also manage to accomplish some of the best philanthropic work the city's needy and less fortunate have seen in years. Dance clubs, live music venues, and drinking are bringing money, people, and prosperity into one of DC's formerly unattractive areas. U Street is experiencing a revitalization thanks to venues such as the **Black Cat (Map 10)**, the **9:30 Club (Map 10)**, and **Velvet Lounge (Map 10),** and dance clubs **DC9 (Map 10)**, and **Daedalus (Map 10)**. Bars such as **Stetson's Famous Bar & Restaurant (Map 9)** respect the neighborhood's humble roots, while also providing a place to mingle and perhaps meet that special someone. The area still has shivering huddles of people being whipped by frigid night winds and February snow, but now increasing numbers of them are 25-year-old divas in high heels and designer jackets. **Love**, formerly knowns as **Dream (Map 12)**, a massive four-floor complex on Okie Street, is also a popular place where VIP membership will cost you just $500 a year and save you the embarrassment of being a regular person in line.

Capitol Hill

Don't forget Capitol Hill's **The Dubliner (Map 2)**, **Kelly's Irish Times (Map 2)**, and **Hawk and Dove (Map 3)**, where you'll find plenty of eager wannabes pressing their political and professional agendas. For a nice retreat that's close to the action but a bit removed from the stench of self-importance, meander about the burgeoning strip on 8th Street SE. When the booze and the hobnobbing have got your head good and swirling, pair a pint with some fish and chips at **Finn macCool's (Map 5)** to bring yourself firmly back down to earth.

Old Town Alexandria

Alexandria's Old Town may not be a regular haunt of frat boys or the ultra-chic, but it offers a pleasant variety of places to drink and dance. The proximity to the water, along with the collection of galleries and historical activities, makes Old Town a great day–night destination. Dance the hours away at **Café Salsa (Map 46)** after filling up on their unbeatable happy-hour mojitos, take in the eclectic and eccentric vibes at **House of Klaus (Map 46)**, crank out some karaoke at **Rock It Grill (Map 46)**, or groove to some bluegrass at **Tiffany Tavern (Map 46)**. And you can always rub elbows with the locals (and a fair share of tourists) at **Murphy's (Map 46)** or **Union Street Public House (Map 46)**.

Everything Else

Even sleepy neighborhoods have favorite local bars like **Colonel Brooks' Tavern (Map 14)** in the Catholic U neighborhood, **Whitlow's (Map 35)** in Arlington, or **State Theatre (Map 33)** in Falls Church. If you're after a good cocktail, **Iota (Map 35)** in Arlington is one of the best places around for live music, or, if you're feeling funky, walk down the street to **Galaxy Hut (Map 35)** to experience the "alternative" scene. Check out the low-key but classy **No. 9 Lounge (Map 43)** in Alexandria's Del Ray neighborhood. In the Landmark area, the **Shenandoah Brewing Company (Map 41)** is only open to the public three days a week, but it´s highly recommended you trek through the traffic and sprawl to hoist a few craft-brewed pints.

Map 1 • National Mall

Capitol City Brewing Company	1100 New York Ave NW	202-628-2222	Great IPA.
Eyebar	1716 I St NW	202-785-0270	Check out the sign.
Gordon Biersch Brewery	900 F St NW	202-783-5454	Five great lagers.
Grand Slam Sports Bar	1000 H St NW	202-637-4789	Sports bar perfection.
Harry's Saloon	436 11th St NW	202-628-8140	Reliable burger 'n' Guinness place with unreliable service.
Home	911 F St NW	202-638-4663	Dress up and wait in line to dance.
Le Bar	806 15th St NW	202-737-8800	An oasis in a sea of offices.
Old Ebbitt Grill	675 15th St NW	202-347-4800	Try to spot your local congressman at this super-touristy Washington institution.
Platinum	915 F St NW	202-393-3555	Sleek and swank dance club.
Poste Brasserie Bar	555 8th St NW	202-783-6060	Roomy and comfortable.
Round Robin Bar	Intercontinental Hotel, 1401 Pennsylvania Ave NW	202-628-9100	Old style, old money DC. "Herbal" martinis.

Map 2 • Chinatown / Union Station

Bullfeather's	410 1st St SE	202-543-5005	One of the Hill's true neighborhood bars.
Capitol City Brewing Company	2 Massachusetts Ave NE	202-842-2337	Great IPA.
Coyote Ugly	717 6th St NW	202-589-0016	Stripclub lite; sports TV paradise.
The Dubliner	520 N Capitol St (entrance on F St)	202-737-3773	Cozy, classy Irish pub.
Fadó Irish Pub	808 7th St NW	202-789-0066	Every beer imaginable.
Flying Scotsman	233 2nd St NW	202-783-3848	DC's only Scottish bar and proud of it.
IndeBleu	707 G St NW	202-333-2538	Where the Metro map is converted to a cocktail list; bring your gold card.
Kelly's Irish Times	14 F St NW	202-543-5433	DC's only Irish pub with a "swerve" dance club basement.
Lucky Strike Lanes	701 7th St NW	202-347-1021	Pricey bowling alley, but the martinis come with Pop Rocks.
My Brother's Place	237 2nd St NW	202-347-1350	Cheap, hole-in-the-wall CUA bar.
RFD Washington	810 7th St NW	202-289-2030	Brickskeller's downtown sibling—hundreds of beers.

Map 3 • The Hill

Capitol Lounge	229 Pennsylvania Ave SE	202-547-2098	Hill hangout, do-it-yourself Bloody Mary bar.
Hawk and Dove	329 Pennsylvania Ave SE	202-543-3300	Hill staffer hangout.
Lounge 201	201 Massachusetts Ave NE	202-544-5201	Retro martini bar.
Sonoma	223 Pennsylvania Ave SE	202-544-8088	Sip wine in the upstairs lounge by the fireplace.
Top of the Hill	319 Pennsylvania Ave SE	202-546-1001	1 building=3 bars. This has pool and red vinyl.
Tune Inn	331 1/2 Pennsylvania Ave SE	202-543-2725	Dive bar option for an older Hill crowd.

Map 5 • Southeast / Anacostia

Bachelor's Mill	1104 8th St SE	202-544-1931	Gay African-American crowd.
Ellington's on Eighth	424A 8th St SE	202-546-8308	Champagne and jazz.
Finn macCool's	713 8th St SE	202-547-7100	Irish bar not prostituting its culture.
Marty's	527 8th St SE	202-255-2707	Low-key, family-friendly.
Mr Henry's Capitol Hill	601 Pennsylvania Ave SE	202-546-8412	A spot for jazz lovers.
Remington's	639 Pennsylvania Ave SE	202-543-3113	Country-Western gay bar.
Tapatinis	711 8th St SE	202-546-8272	You've got tapas in my 'tinis! Hip joint (for Capitol Hill).
Tortilla Coast	400 1st St SE	202-546-6768	Different special every night.
Tunnicliff's Tavern	222 7th St SE	202-544-5680	Cheers-esque.
The Ugly Mug	723 8th St SE	202-547-8459	TVs, pool, miniburgers, and beer.

Map 6 • Waterfront

Cantina Marina	600 Water St SW	202-554-8396	Jimmy Buffet goes Latin.
Edge	52 L St SE	202-488-1200	Dance club, part of the gay club scene.
H20	800 Water St SW	202-484-6300	Dining and dancing near water.
Zanzibar on the Waterfront	700 Water St SW	202-554-9100	Hugely popular velvet-rope club.

Map 7 • Foggy Bottom

Froggy Bottom Pub	2142 Pennsylvania Ave NW	202-338-3000	GW student hangout.
Potomac Lounge	Watergate Hotel, 2650 Virginia Ave NW	202-965-2300	Cocktails at the Watergate.

Map 8 • Georgetown

51st State Tavern	2512 L St NW	202-625-2444	An unpretentious watering hole, plus .10-cent wings on Tuesdays.
Blues Alley	1073 Wisconsin Ave NW	202-337-4141	THE place for live jazz.
Chadwick's	3205 K St NW	202-333-2565	Georgetown dive. (Read: nicer than half the bars in DC.)
Clyde's	3236 M St NW	202-333-9180	Reliable wood-themed bar.
Degrees	Ritz Carlton, 3100 S St NW	202-912-4100	Pretty ritzy.
Garrett's	3003 M St NW	202-333-8282	Don't fall down the stairs.
The Guards	2915 M St NW	202-965-2350	For sloppy crowds.
Martin's Tavern	1264 Wisconsin Ave NW	202-333-7370	Gin-and-tonic crowd.
Mate	3101 K St NW	202-333-2006	Posh Latin hangout on K Street.

Mie N Yu	3125 M St NW	202-333-6122	Exotic, Eastern atmosphere and good food.
Modern	3287 M St NW	202-338-7027	Crowded, go on a weeknight.
Mr Smith's	3104 M St NW	202-333-3104	Super dive with half-price burgers on Tuesdays and a big banner announcing its "secret" back patio.
Old Glory	3139 M St NW	202-337-3406	Great for daytime drinking.
Rhino Bar & Pumphouse	3295 M St NW	202-333-3150	Cheap beer, dance music, and pool tables.
Riverside Grill	3050 K St NW	202-342-3535	If it's crowded at Tony and Joe's …
Sequoia	3000 K St NW	202-944-4200	Where type As meet before getting married and divorced.
The Third Edition Bar	1218 Wisconsin Ave NW	202-333-3700	One night stands start here.
The Tombs	1226 36th St NW	202-337-6668	Georgetown institution.
Tony and Joe's	3000 K St NW	202-944-4545	A Georgetown waterfront staple.

Map 9 • Dupont Circle / Adams Morgan

Aroma	2401 Pennsylvania Ave NW	202-296-6383	Good cocktails.
Bar Rouge	Rouge Hotel, 1315 16th St NW	202-232-8000	Cool new addition to the neighborhood.
Beacon Bar & Grill	1615 Rhode Island Ave NW	202-872-1126	17th Street Bar and Grill + Botox.
Biddy Mulligan's	Jurys Washington Hotel, 1500 New Hampshire Ave NW	202-483-6000	Smoky and Irish in Jurys Hotel.
Big Hunt	1345 Connecticut Ave NW	202-785-2333	Typical bar, but with Guinness ice cream!
Bravo Bravo	1001 Connecticut Ave NW	202-223-5330	Salsa and Merengue.
The Brickskeller	1523 22nd St NW	202-293-1885	Try a beer from Timbuktu—possibly the best beer selection on the planet.
Buffalo Billiards	1330 19th St NW	202-331-7665	Relaxed poolhall.
Café Citron	1343 Connecticut Ave NW	202-530-8844	Sweat in the crowd downstairs, or dance on boots upstairs.
Café Japone	2032 P St NW	202-223-1573	Serious sake.
Camelot	1823 M St NW	202-887-5966	Honey, they're professional dancers.
Chaos	1603 17th St NW	202-232-4141	Gay and straight, drag bingo, drag brunch.
Chi-Cha Lounge	1624 U St NW	202-234-8400	Informal (ties forbidden) Ecuadorian hacienda.
Childe Harold	1610 20th St NW	202-483-6700	Don't bring your child to this "come as you are" bar; go hang out on the patio.
Cloud Dining Lounge	1 Dupont Cir NW	202-872-1122	Frou-frou drinks on beds.
Cobalt/30 Degrees	1639 R St NW	202-462-6569	Smoke-free 30 Degrees, smoky Cobalt.
Dragonfly	1215 Connecticut Ave NW	202-331-1775	All-white and all-trendy.
Eighteenth Street Lounge	1212 18th St NW	202-466-3922	Dragonfly's older brother—hip, but mature about it.
Firefly	1310 New Hampshire Ave NW	202-861-1310	Sophisticated drinking.
Fireplace	2161 P St NW	202-293-1293	Landmark gay bar.
Fox and Hounds Lounge	1537 17th St NW	202-232-6307	Where uptight people go to relax.
Front Page	1333 New Hampshire Ave NW	202-296-6500	Pre-10 pm: businessman's grill; post-10 pm: strictly t&a.
Gazuza	1629 Connecticut Ave NW	202-667-5500	Upscale tapas lounge—go early for patio seating.
Improv	1140 Connecticut Ave NW	202-296-7008	Don't laugh up your weak rum and Coke.
JR's	1519 17th St NW	202-328-0090	Don't miss the daily drink specials and theme nights.
Kramerbooks & Afterwords Café	1517 Connecticut Ave NW	202-387-3825	Fun eats amidst Café/bar/bookstore environs. The Perfect Weapon.
La Frontera Cantina	1633 17th St NW	202-232-0437	Have a Corona and people-watch.
Lauriol Plaza	1835 18th St NW	202-387-0035	The best beef here isn't on the menu.
Local 16	1602 U St NW	202-265-2828	Great deck spring/summer/fall. Lounge atmosphere without a cover.
Lucky Bar	1221 Connecticut Ave NW	202-331-3733	Everyone has to have one…
Madhatter	1831 M St NW	202-833-1495	A midtown dive bar with character.
McClellan's	Hilton, 1919 Connecticut Ave NW	202-483-3000	Hilton Hotel sports bar.
MCCXXIII	1223 Connecticut Ave NW	202-822-1800	Swank club for grinding.
McFadden's	2401 Pennsylvania Ave NW	202-223-2338	Wall-to-wall Tues/Thurs/Fri/Sat nights.
Mercury Bar	1602 17th St NW	202-667-5937	Friendly subterranean bar.
Omega DC	2122 P St NW	202-223-4917	Mature men gay bar.
Ozio	1813 M St NW	202-822-6000	Sip a cocktail and puff a cigar.
Recessions	1823 L St NW	202-296-6686	Basement bar.
Rumors	1900 M St NW	202-466-7378	After-work drinks downtown.

Map 9 • Dupont Circle / Adams Morgan–*continued*

Russia House Restaurant & Lounge	1800 Connecticut Ave NW	202-234-9433	Swanky joint beloved by eurotrash.
Science Club	1136 19th St NW	202-775-0747	Laid-back lounge that caters to cocktails and conversation.
Sign of the Whale	1825 M St NW	202-785-1110	Cozy and cheap.
Soussi	2228 18th St NW	202-299-9314	Outdoor wine bar.
Staccato	2006 18th St NW	202-232-2228	Great dive bar with great "house" band, Potato Famine.
Stetson's Famous Bar & Restaurant	1610 U St NW	202-667-6295	Popular and crowded U Street destination.
Tabard Inn	1739 N St NW	202-331-8528	Romantic rendezvous.
Timberlake's	1726 Connecticut Ave NW	202-483-2266	*Cheers* destination for 30–50-yr olds.
Topaz Bar	Topaz Hotel, 1733 N St NW	202-393-3000	Go for the drinks.
The Town & Country	Mayflower Hotel, 1127 Connecticut Ave NW	202-347-3000	Old-school hotel bar.
Townhouse Tavern	1637 R St NW	202-234-5747	Get your Schlitz in a can.
The Wave!	1731 New Hampshire Ave NW	202-518-5011	Carlyle Suites club.

Map 10 • Logan Circle / U Street

9:30 Club	815 V St NW	202-393-0930	A DC musical institution.
Avenue Nightclub	649 New York Ave NW	202-347-8100	Hip nightclub with four levels and spacious dance floors.
Bar Nun	1326 U St NW	202-667-6680	Fridays are bound to be interesting.
Bar Pilar	1833 14th St NW	202-265-1751	A laid-back hangout.
Black Cat	1811 14th St NW	202-667-7960	The OTHER place in DC to see a band.
Café Saint-Ex	1847 14th St NW	202-265-7839	Once-cool bistro overrun by the khaki crowd.
Daedalus	1010 Vermont Ave NW	202-347-9066	Make a reservation.
DC9	1940 9th St NW	202-483-5000	Rock club.
Helix Lounge	1430 Rhode Island Ave NW	202-462-9001	New trendy neighborhood addition.
HR-57 Center for the Preservation of Jazz and Blues	1610 14th St NW	202-667-3700	Cool BYOB jazz joint. A real gem.
K Street Lounge	1301 K St NW	202-962-3933	Stylish lounge perfect for those who like to feel important.
Republic Gardens	1355 U St NW	202-232-2710	Famous DC music club.
The Saloon	1207 U St NW	202-462-2640	European appeal—go for the beer.
Tabaq	1336 U St NW	202-265-0965	Chillin' hookah bar with a killer view of downtown.
Titan	1337 14th St NW	202-232-7010	Gay bar at Dakota Cowgirl.
Twins Jazz	1344 U St NW	202-234-0072	Intimate bar with Ethiopian food.
Vegas Lounge	1415 P St NW	202-483-3971	Blues joint keeps the Gen Y's jumpin'.
Velvet Lounge	915 U St NW	202-462-3213	Get your lounge on with the likes of punk rock to alt-folk.
The WareHouse	1017 7th St NW	202-783-3933	Live music alongside a Gallery, Theater, and Café.

Map 11 • Near Northeast

Bud's	501 Morse St NE	202-543-4419	Off-the-beaten-path restaurant and nightclub.
FUR Nightclub	33 Patterson St NE	202-842-3401	Clubbing emporium.

Map 12 • Trinidad

Love	1350 Okie St NE	202-636-9030	Huge nightclub.

Map 13 • Brookland / Langdon

Aqua	1818 New York Ave NE	202-832-4878	Asian dance club at a Korean restaurant.

Map 14 • Catholic U

Colonel Brooks' Tavern	901 Monroe St NE	202-529-4002	Neighborhood landmark.
Johnny K's	3514 12th St NE	202-832-3945	Do not attempt to come here if you're over 21.

Map 15 • Columbia Heights

Wonderland Ballroom	1101 Kenyon St NW	202-232-5263	Crowded, smoky, fun neighborhood dive. Great bratwurst.

Map 16 • Adams Morgan (North) / Mt Pleasant

Adams Mill Bar and Grill	1813 Adams Mill Rd NW	202-332-9577	Pitchers after the softball game.
Angles Bar & Billiards	2339 18th St NW	202-462-8100	Dive bar with great burgers; a favorite of reporters.
Asylum	2471 18th St NW	202-319-9353	Goth décor and pounding music.
Bedrock Billiards	1841 Columbia Rd NW	202-667-7665	Pool hall with extensive alcohol choices.
Blue Room Lounge	2321 18th St NW	202-332-0800	Great wines, with trip-hop soundtrack.
Bossa	2463 18th St NW	202-667-0088	Cool downstairs, samba upstairs.
Brass Monkey	2317 18th St NW	202-667-7800	Amateur night yuppie hangout.
Bukom Café	2442 18th St NW	202-265-4600	West African music and a diverse crowd.
Chief Ike's Mambo Room	1725 Columbia Rd NW	202-332-2211	Dirty dance 'til dawn.
Columbia Station	2325 18th St NW	202-462-6040	More jazz and blues in an intimate setting.
Crush	2323 18th St NW	202-319-1111	Popular and crowded.
Felix Lounge	2406 18th St NW	202-483-3549	Pretentious or sophisticated? Try it out.
Kokopooli's Pool Hall	2305 18th St NW	202-234-2306	Pool and beer.
Left Bank	2424 18th St NW	202-464-2100	Chic faux-retro European décor and pretty people.
Madam's Organ	2461 18th St NW	202-667-5370	Redheads get a discount; best blues in DC.
Pharaoh's	1817 Columbia Rd NW	202-232-6009	Rockin' blues.
Pharmacy Bar	2337 18th St NW	202-483-1200	Low-key alternabar.
The Raven	3125 Mt Pleasant St NW	202-387-8411	Neighborhood bar.
The Reef	2446 18th St NW	202-518-3800	Jellyfish and drinks.
Rumba Café	2443 18th St NW	202-588-5501	Cuban treats.
Spy Lounge	2406 18th St NW	202-483-3549	Felix's spy dive sibling.
Timehri International	2439 18th St NW	202-518-2626	Reggae, Calypso, R&B.
Toledo Lounge	2435 18th St NW	202-986-5416	Didn't get your fill of Ohio in '04? Visit this unpretentious dive.
Tom Tom	2333 18th St NW	202-518-6667	Play old-school Nintendo upstairs.
Tonic Bar	3155 Mt Pleasant St NW	202-986-7661	Local tavern.
Zucchabar	1841 Columbia Rd NW	202-332-8642	Friendly bartenders, well-made drinks.

Map 17 • Woodley Park / Cleveland Park

Aroma	3417 Connecticut Ave NW	202-244-7995	Martinis, cigars and good cocktails.
Atomic Billiards	3427 Connecticut Ave NW	202-363-7665	Subterranean pool, darts, and beer.
Bardeo	3311 Connecticut Ave NW	202-244-6550	Ardeo's chi-chi wine bar, where well-heeled yuppies tote glasses of chardonnay.
Cleveland Park Bar & Grill	3421 Connecticut Ave NW	202-806-8940	Watch the game with a popped collar.
Four Green Fields	3412 Connecticut Ave NW	202-244-0860	Have a pint and name the Ps.
Murphy's of DC	2609 24th St NW	202-462-7171	Irish pub with summertime patio and wintertime fireplace.
Nanny O'Brien's	3319 Connecticut Ave NW	202-686-9189	Legendary Celtic jam sessions.
Oxford Tavern Zoo Bar	3000 Connecticut Ave NW	202-232-4225	Low-key with live blues bands.
Uptown Tavern	3435 Connecticut Ave NW	202-244-7196	Divey sports bar with foosball.

Map 18 • Glover Park / Foxhall

Bourbon	2348 Wisconsin Ave NW	202-625-7770	Great bourbon, of course.
The Deck	2505 Wisconsin Ave NW	202-337-9700	The Savoy Suite's outdoor bar.
Good Guys Restaurant	2311 Wisconsin Ave NW	202-333-8128	Friendly, low-bling rock-and-roll strip club.
Grog and Tankard	2408 Wisconsin Ave NW	202-333-3114	Longest-running live music bar in the DC area.
JP's Nite Club	2505 Wisconsin Ave NW	202-337-7737	"Gentleman's" club.
Zebra Lounge	3238 Wisconsin Ave NW	202-237-2202	New and improved.

Map 19 • Tenleytown / Friendship Heights

Guapo's	4515 Wisconsin Ave NW	202-686-3588	Tortillas + margaritas = stumbling to Tenleytown Metro.
Maggiano's	5333 Wisconsin Ave NW	202-966-2593	Italian restaurant with accommodating Latino bar staff.
Malt Shop	4615 Wisconsin Ave NW	202-244-9733	Wood walls and floors for sloppy AU students.

Map 21 • 16th St. Heights / Petworth

Twins Lounge	5516 Colorado Ave NW	202-882-2523	Intimate jazz club.

Arts & Entertainment • **Nightlife**

Map 22 • Downtown Bethesda

Flanagan's Harp and Fiddle	4844 Cordell Ave	301-951-0115	Authentic Irish bartenders.
Rock Bottom Brewery	7900 Norfolk Ave	301-652-1311	Worth the wait.
Saphire	7940 Wisconsin Ave	301-986-9708	Average bar.
South Beach Café	7904 Woodmont Ave	301-718-9737	Dirt-cheap happy hour.

Map 25 • Silver Spring

Flying Fish	815 King St	703-600-3474	Sushi and karaoke, together at last.
Mayorga	8040 Georgia Ave	301-562-9090	Coffee by day, microbrew by night.
Quarry House Tavern	8401 Georgia Ave	301-587-9406	Simply great.

Map 27 • Walter Reed

Charlie's	7307 Georgia Ave NW	202-726-3567	Soul food and contemporary jazz.
Takoma Station Tavern	6914 4th St NW	202-829-1999	Jazz haven.

Map 28 • Chevy Chase

Chevy Chase Lounge	5510 Connecticut Ave NW	202-966-7600	Parthenon Restaurant's wood-panelled lounge.

Map 29 • Bethesda / Chevy Chase Business

Barking Dog	4723 Elm St	301-654-0022	Decent frat-boy bar.
Strike Bethesda	5353 Westbard Ave	301-652-0955	Not your average bowling alley.
Tommy Joe's	4714 Montgomery Ln	301-654-3801	Frat boy central.

Map 33 • Falls Church

Ireland's Four Provinces	105 W Broad St	703-534-8999	Why are you in Falls Church? (A good bar, nonetheless.)
Lost Dog Café	5876 Washington Blvd	703-237-1552	Buy a beer, adopt a pet.
State Theatre	220 N Washington St	703-237-0300	Grab a table, a beer, and listen.

Map 34 • Ballston

Bailey's Pub and Grille	4234 Wilson Blvd	703-465-1300	A sports superbar with a gazillion TVs.
Carpool	4000 N Fairfax Dr	703-532-7665	Pool, darts, and beers on the patio.
Cowboy Café	4792 Lee Hwy	703-243-8010	Neighborhood bar and burgers.
The Front Page	4201 Wilson Blvd	703-248-9990	Restaurant with two bars. Great Happy Hour Monday—Friday.
Rock Bottom Brewery	4238 Wilson Blvd	703-516-7688	Go for happy hour.

Map 35 • Clarendon

Clarendon Ballroom	3185 Wilson Blvd	703-469-2244	Head for the rooftop.
Clarendon Grill	1101 N Highland St	703-524-7455	What? Get used to saying that here.
Eleventh Street Lounge	1041 N Highland St	703-351-1311	Classy wine, soft couches, smooth blues and intriguing beer.
Galaxy Hut	2711 Wilson Blvd	703-525-8646	Tiny, friendly, indie-rock hangout.
Harry's Tap Room	2800 Clarendon Blvd	703-778-7788	City atmosphere 'til midnight, then it becomes the suburbs again.
Iota	2832 Wilson Blvd	703-522-8340	Great place to see a twangy band.
Mister Days	3100 Clarendon Blvd	703-527-1600	Pick-up bar disguised as a sports bar.
Molly Malone's	3207 Washington Blvd	703-812-0939	A section to party and a section to chill.
Whitlow's on Wilson	2854 Wilson Blvd	703-276-9693	A separate room for whatever mood you're in.

Map 36 • Rosslyn

Continental	1911 Ft Myer Dr	703-465-7675	Pool with a modern spin.
Ireland's Four Courts	2051 Wilson Blvd	703-525-3600	Where beer-guzzling yuppies come to see (double) and be seen.
Rhodeside Grill	1836 Wilson Blvd	703-243-0145	Neighborhood bar with basement for bands.
Summers Grill and Sports Pub	1520 N Courthouse Rd	703-528-8278	Soccer-watching bar.

Map 37 • Fort Myer

Jay's Saloon	3114 10th St N	703-527-3093	Down-home and friendly.
Royal Lee Bar and Grill	2211 N Pershing Dr	703-524-5493	All American.
Tallula	2761 Washington Blvd	703-778-5051	Swanky-dank wine bar.

Map 39 • Shirlington

The Bungalow, Billiards & Brew Co	2766 S Arlington Mill Dr	703-578-0020	Fun billiards and brews.
Capitol City Brewing Company	2700 S Quincy St	703-578-3888	Great IPA.
Guapo's	4028 S 28th St	703-671-1701	Bueno Mexican, killer margaritas.

Map 40 • Pentagon City / Crystal City

Bailey's Irish Pub	2010 Crystal Dr	703-416-0452	If an Irish pub came in a box, you'd get Bailey's.
Sine Irish Pub	1301 S Joyce St	703-415-4420	Good beers on tap, busy happy hour. Lots of military, defense contractors.

Map 41 • Landmark

Mango Mike's	4580 Duke St	703-370-3800	Pub grub from the islands, mon.
Shenandoah Brewing Company	652 S Pickett St	703-823-9508	Brew your own beer on site.
Shooter McGee's	5239 Duke St	703-751-9266	Another "silly first name, Irish last name" place.
Zig's	4531 Duke St	703-823-2777	NASCAR, comedy, poker, pub food.

Map 43 • Four Mile Run / Del Ray

Birchmere	3701 Mt Vernon Ave	703-549-7500	What do Kris Kristofferson and Liz Phair have in common?
Hops	3625 Jefferson Davis Hwy	703-837-9107	$1.29 happy hour beers, if you don't mind a cheesy chain.
No 9 Lounge	2000 Mt Vernon Ave	703-549-5051	Intimate but unpretentious tavern with live music and friendly vibes.

Map 46 • Old Town (South)

Austin Grill	801 King St	703-684-8969	Great Tex/Mex; just outside, Janet Reno got a parking ticket!
Café Salsa	808 King St	703-684-4100	THE hottest salsa club in the DC area.
Chadwick's	203 The Strand	703-836-4442	Tried-and-true saloon away from the King St. crush.
House of Klaus	715 King St	703-549-0533	Fun and funky Eurotavern.
Laughing Lizzard Lounge	1324 King St	703-548-2582	Go for the pool and a cold beer.
Murphy's	713 King St	703-548-1717	Locals-favored pub with wonk-beloved Tuesday trivia.
Pat Troy's Ireland's Own	111 N Pitt St	703-549-4535	Green alligators and long-neck beers.
Rock It Grill	1319 King St	703-739-2274	Lowbrow and proud.
Tiffany Tavern	1116 King St	703-836-8844	Bluegrass central.
Union Street Public House	121 S Union St	703-548-1785	$2 happy-hour pints!!!
Vermillion	1120 King St	703-684-9669	No-frills lounge.

Baltimore

Club Charles	1724 N Charles St	410-727-8815	Dive bar xtraordinaire; all the clocks inside are set 20 minutes ahead. And there's a good chance you'll run into John Waters.
Cross Street Market	1065 S Charles St		Indoor market with a raucous, locals-filled happy hour.
The Horse You Came In On	1626 Thames St	410-327-8111	Feel like a sailor in this dirty ol' place right on the waterfront.

There are four types of people in DC: high rollers; wannabe high rollers; counter-culture hippies protesting the indulgent lifestyle of high rollers; and foreign nationals who are high rollers here and/or abroad. In order to provide pertinent restaurant information for every DC type, we've listed some of our favorite restaurants under four different categories: **Eating Posh, Eating Cheap, Eating Hip,** and **Eating Ethnic.**

Eating Posh

In the land of lobbyists, lawyers, and congressmen, there are bound to be plenty of chi-chi restaurants—DC's equivalent of Hollywood nightclubs. Posh in DC often means old, and grandfathers **Old Ebbitt Grill (Map 1)** and **Occidental (Map 1)** have been around practically as long as the White House. If steak is on the evening's agenda, your best bets are **The Palm (Map 9), Morton's (Map 40),** and **Charlie Palmer (Map 2).** For French decadence, look no further than **Citronelle (Map 8), Gerard's Place (Map 1),** and **Le Paradou (Map 2).** If Italian is your indulgence, then mangia bene at **Galileo (Map 9), Café Milano (Map 8),** or **I Ricchi (Map 9). Sequoia (Map 8)** on the Georgetown Waterfront is the ultimate spot to see and be seen, and neighboring restaurant **Nathan's (Map 8)** is moderately priced and always buzzing with the power lunch crowd. The excellent New American **Aquarelle (Map 7)** has an elegant setting downstairs at the Watergate, and you will leave the brilliant **Vidalia (Map 9)** convinced that it was worth the money.

Eating Cheap

Eating cheap in DC doesn't have to mean hitting up McDonald's. The experience can even prove quite pleasant and romantic. Two of DC's most famous joints, **El Pollo Rico (Map 37)** and **Ben's Chili Bowl (Map 10),** will cost you between $5 and $10 a meal, and **Café Parisien Express (Map 34)** serves up double portions of French food for half the French price. If pizza is your poison, the pies at **Vace (Map 29)** and **2 Amys (Map 18)** will totally knock your socks off. For unique atmosphere, check out **Mexicali Blues (Map 35)** and the Dupont institution **Kramerbooks & Afterwords Café (Map 9).** Vietnamese standout **Four Sisters (Map 3)** is as delicious as it is affordable. Rounding out the cheap eats list are 24-hour steakhouse **Annie's Paramount (Map 9),** Chinatown BBQ pit **Capital Q (Map 2),** out-of-this-world chili machine **Hard Times Café (Map, 46),** and Jewish deli **K's New York Deli (Map 19).**

Eating Hip

New York does not own a monopoly on *all* the hip places to dine. Congressmen loosen their ties every now and again, too. **Zaytinya (Map 1)** is one of the slickest spots in town, and its cousins **Café Atlantico (Map 1)** and **Jaleo (Map 2, Map 29)** are just as sizzling. **Café Saint-Ex (Map 10)** is a microcosm of the U Street trend, and **Café Citron (Map 9), Lauriol Plaza (Map 9)** and **Obelisk (Map 9)** are among the favorite hangouts of hip Dupont denizens. **Felix Restaurant and Lounge (Map 16)** and **Cashion's Eat Place (Map 16)** have always been in vogue among Adams Morgan rockers, and **Tryst (Map 16)** is DC's ultimate coffeehouse. **TenPenh (Map 1)** is the scene of DC's hottest Asian fusion, and the chic **15 Ria (Map 9)** honestly belongs in NYC. **Harry's Tap Room (Map 35)** is an up-and-comer among Arlingtonian yuppies, and for California cool, **Restaurant Nora (Map 9)** is there to fulfill all of your organic fantasies.

Eating Ethnic

Say what you want about the state of American diplomacy, but in DC, all culinary cultures are well-represented. So, for the sake of international harmony, put down the pot roast, and challenge your palette. In DC, the rule of thumb is that the quality of ethnic food increases proportionally to one's distance from the city's center, but there are some notable exceptions in the metro area. Head to **Yee Hwa (Map 9)** in Foggy Bottom for your Korean kimchi fix. **Tony Cheng's Seafood Restaurant (Map 2)** is the cream of the Chinatown crop. Indian food lovers rave about **Haandi (Map 22), Nirvana (Map 9),** and **Amma Vegetarian Kitchen (Map 8).** For the best sushi this side of the Pacific, **Makoto Restaurant (Map 18)** and **Kaz Sushi Bistro (Map 7)** are all you'll need. Experience the Middle East at **Mama Ayesha's (Map 16)** and **Malaysia Kopitiam (Map 9).** The Mexican **Mixtec (Map 16)** and the pan-Asian **Raku (Map 9, Map 29)** each also get an A-plus in our not-so-humble opinion. And don't miss out on **Roger Miller Restaurant (Map 25),** a tiny little Cameroonian gem in Silver Spring, for all your curry goat needs.

Key: $: Under $10 / $$: $10–$20 / $$$: $20–$30 / $$$$: $30–40 / $$$$$: $40+
* : Does not accept credit cards. / † : Accepts only American Express. / †† : Accepts only Visa and Mastercard.
Time refers to weekend night closing time.

Map 1 • National Mall

Bistro D'Oc	518 10th St NW	202-393-5444	$$$$	11 pm	Homey Provencal (*add accent under the c*) with spotty service and an excellent pre-theater menu.
Café Asia	1720 I St NW	202-659-2696	$$$	12 am	Not quite as crowded as Asia but just as busy.
Café Atlantico	405 8th St NW	202-393-0812	$$$	11 pm	Upscale Nuevo Latino. Try to book the Minibar.
Caucus Room	401 9th St NW	202-393-1300	$$$$	10:30 pm	The taste of power. A favorite for DC's elite.
Ceiba	701 14th St NW	202-393-3983	$$$$$	11 pm	Brazilian indulgence, from the people who brought TenPenh.
Chef Geoff's	1301 Pennsylvania Ave NW	202-464-4461	$$$	10 pm	Snooty service, great wine selection. Check out the jazz brunch.
Equinox	818 Connecticut Ave NW	202-331-8118	$$$$$	10:30 pm	The finest food of the Chesapeake region.
ESPN Zone	555 12th St NW	202-783-3776	$$	11 pm	Forget the baseball players. This restaurant is on the juice.
Gerard's Place	915 15th St NW	202-737-4445	$$$$	10 pm	La créme de la créme of DC French dining.
Harry's Restaurant and Saloon	436 11th St NW	202-624-0053	$$	2 am	Downtown DC dining with a hometown corner restaurant feel.
Les Halles	1201 Pennsylvania Ave NW	202-347-6848	$$$	12 am	French food with a good ol' American twist.
Loeb's Perfect New York Deli	832 15th St NW	202-371-1150	$†	4PM	Decent, but not perfect, pastrami.
Occidental	1475 Pennsylvania Ave NW	202-783-1475	$$$$	10:30 pm	Opulent White House classic.
Old Ebbitt Grill	675 15th St NW	202-347-4801	$$$$$	1 am	The quintessential Washington restaurant. Try to spot your local congressman.
Ollie's Trolley	432 11th St NW	202-347-6119	$*	7 pm	1970s burger bliss.
Teaism	400 8th St NW	202-638-6010	$$	9 pm	Everything Zen at this hipster hangout.
Teaism	800 Connecticut Ave NW	202-835-2233	$$	5:30 pm	Need a teapot? Buy one with lunch!
TenPenh	1001 Pennsylvania Ave NW	202-393-4500	$$$$	11 pm	DC's hottest Asian fusion.
Willard Room	Willard InterContinental, 1401 Pennsylvania Ave NW	202-637-7440	$$$$	10 pm	If not the richest breakfast in town, definitely the most expensive. Get the Nutella pancakes.
Zaytinya	701 9th St NW	202-638-0800	$$$$	12 am	Tasty mezze menu offered by award-winning chef. Fabulous interior.
Zola	800 F St NW	202-654-0999	$$$$	11 pm	Drink like a (geriatric) James Bond.

Map 2 • Chinatown / Union Station

701	701 Pennsylvania Ave NW	202-393-0701	$$$$	11:30 pm	Posh food and soft jazz.
America	50 Massachusetts Ave NE	202-682-9555	$$	11:30 pm	USA managed like a third world country.
Andale	401 7th St NW	202-783-3133	$$$$	11 pm	Upscale Mexican with a rockin' happy hour.
B Smith's	50 Massachusetts Ave NE	202-289-6188	$$$$	10 pm	Creole elegance, jarring in Union Station.
Billy Goat Tavern & Grill	500 New Jersey Ave NW	202-783-2123	$	2 am	Cheeseburger, cheeseburger, cheeseburger.
Bistro Bis	15 E St NW	202-661-2700	$$$$	10:30 pm	Pricey, but a solid place for an upscale lunch on the Hill.
Burma	740 6th St NW	202-638-1280	$$	10 pm	Green tea leaf salad. We kid you not.
Capital Q	707 H St NW	202-347-8396	$	12 am	Hearty Texan portions will put hair on yer chest.
Capitol City Brewing Company	2 Massachusetts Ave NE	202-842-2337	$$	12:30 pm	Quality beer worth the tourists that come with the territory.
Center Café at Union Station	50 Massachusetts Ave NE	202-682-0143	$$	9 pm	Enjoy the scenery from the middle of the country's best RR station.
Charlie Palmer	101 Constitution Ave NW	202-547-8100	$$$$††	10 pm	Fine wine and world famous steak—a splurge for wannabe high rollers.
Chinatown Express	746 6th St NW	202-638-0424	$$	11 pm	Watch food preparation from the street and decide for yourself.
District Chophouse	509 7th St NW	202-347-3434	$$$$	12 am	Impressive roaring '20s atmosphere. Avoid Verizon game night.
The Dubliner Restaurant	Phoenix Park Hotel, 520 N Capitol St NW	202-737-3773	$$	1 am	Hearty Irish pub grub for Washington bureaucracy.
Fadò—Irish Pub	808 7th St NW	202-789-0066	$$$	12 am	Antiquish décor and self-promoting gift shop. Disneyland for alcoholics.

Map 2 • Chinatown / Union Station–*continued*

Flying Scotsman	233 2nd St NW	202-783-3848	$$	11 pm	Pub favored by aspiring Hill elites.
Full Kee	509 H St NW	202-371-2233	$$*	3 am	Chinatown can be overwhelming. We'll make it easier. Eat here.
IndeBleu	707 G St NW	202-333-2538	$$$$	10:45 pm	Dress to impress: this is the only Indian/Pan-Asian restaurant with its own bouncers.
Jaleo	480 7th St NW	202-628-7949	$$$$	12 am	The tapas king of DC. Great for first dates.
Kelly's Irish Times	14 F St NW	202-543-5433	$$	10:40 pm	Look to your left. See The Dubliner? Go there.
Le Paradou	678 Indiana Ave NW	202-347-6780	$$$$$	11 pm	Dahling, shall we sip '81 Bordeaux or '79 Barolo this evening?
Lei Garden	631 H St NW	202-216-9696	$$	11:30 pm	Best dim sum you'll find in a Chinatown whose biggest landmark is CVS.
Matchbox	713 H St NW	202-289-4441	$$$	11 pm	Where martinis meet pizza.
Mitsitam Native Foods Café	4th St SW & Independence Ave SW	202-633-1000	$$*	5 pm	Cafeteria featuring American Indian cuisine.
(National Museum of the American Indian)					
My Brother's Place	237 2nd St NW	202-347-1350	$$	11 pm	A lunchtime hole-in-the-wall.
Rasika	633 D St NW	202-637-1222	$$$$	11 pm	Pricey, polished Indian.
Rosa Mexicano	575 7th St NW	202-783-5522	$$$$	11:30 pm	Squeeze past the perennial crowds for a pomegranate margarita.
Tony Cheng's Mongolian Restaurant	619 H St NW, downstairs	202-842-8669	$$	12 am	No reason to dine here. Upstairs is where you want to be.
Tony Cheng's Seafood Restaurant	619 H St NW, upstairs	202-371-8669	$$	12 am	Overlook gaudy décor and enjoy the best Chinese Washington offers.
Zengo Restaurant	781 7th St NW	202-393-2929	$$$	11:30 pm	Sleek Asian-Latin fusion.

Map 3 • The Hill

Café Berlin	322 Massachusetts Ave NE	202-543-7656	$$	11 pm	For all your Oktoberfest needs.
Four Sisters	1118 H St NE	202-388-0830	$*	10 pm	Eat cheap Vietnamese food.
Hawk and Dove	329 Pennsylvania Ave SE	202-543-3300	$$	3 am	One of the oldest games in town. Do lunch, not dinner.
Kenny's Smokehouse	732 Maryland Ave NE	202-547-4553	$	10 pm	BBQ with oodles of sides.
La Loma Mexican Restaurant	316 Massachusetts Ave NE	202-548-2550	$$	11 pm	They make you pay for refills. Enough said.
Pete's Diner	212 2nd St SE	202-544-7335	$		With a completely Asian staff, you wonder who "Pete" is.
The Pour House	319 Pennsylvania Ave SE	202-546-1001	$$		Steelers fans and Irish accents.
Ristorante Tosca	1112 F St NW	202-367-1990	$$$$$	11 pm	Un ristorante tanto elegante.
Sonoma	223 Pennsylvania Ave SE	202-544-8088	$$$	11 pm	40 wines by the glass. The *Sideways* characters would be proud.
Two Quail	320 Massachusetts Ave NE	202-543-8030	$$$$	10 pm	Romantic little Hill spot.
White Tiger	301 Massachusetts Ave NE	202-546-5900	$$	10:30 pm	Best Capitol Hill Indian food.

Map 5 • Southeast / Anacostia

Banana Café & Piano Bar	500 8th St SE	202-543-5906	$$$	11:30 pm	Democrat-friendly Hill cabana.
Bread & Chocolate	666 Pennsylvania Ave SE	202-547-2875	$	7 pm	Here it's dessert before dinner. Go with the chocolate truffle cake.
Meyhane	633 Pennsylvania Ave SE	202-544-4753	$$$	11 pm	Exotic Turkish tapas.
Montmartre	327 7th St SE	202-544-1244	$$$$	10:30 pm	Comfortable French bistro.
Starfish	539 8th St SE	202-546-5006	$$$	10:30 pm	Seafood from the people behind Banana Café.
Tortilla Coast	400 1st St SE	202-546-6768	$	10 pm	Favorite Hill non–power lunch spot.

Map 6 • Waterfront

Cantina Marina	600 Water St SW	202-554-8396	$$	11 pm	Ordering advice: avoid the cantina; go with the marina.
H2O at Hogate's	800 Water St SW	202-484-6300	$$$$	10 pm	Waterfront home of the rum bun.
Jenny's Asian Fusion	1000 Water St SW	202-554-2202	$$$	11 pm	Good food but depressing atmosphere, regardless of the water.
Market Inn	200 E St SW	202-554-2100	$$$$	12 am	Old-Washington crony hangout.
Phillip's Flagship	900 Water St SW	202-488-8515	$$$	10:30 pm	Fresh Atlantic fish not worth pathetic portions and lousy service.
Pier 7	650 Water St SW	202-554-2500	$$	10 pm	Showy waterfront seafood.

Map 7 • Foggy Bottom

Name	Address	Phone	Price	Close	Description
600 Restaurant at the Watergate	600 New Hampshire Ave NW	202-337-5890	$$$	12 am	Formerly Dominique's; the pre-Kennedy Center locale.
Aquarelle	Watergate Hotel, 2650 Virginia Ave NW	202-298-4455	$$$$$	10 pm	Revived Clinton-era French Mediterranean restaurant at the Watergate.
Bread Line	1751 Pennsylvania Ave NW	202-822-8900	$$	3:30 pm	Screw South Beach if it means you can't eat here. (Lunch only.)
Dish	The River Inn, 924 25th St NW	202-383-8707	$$$$	10:30 pm	Southern infusion for inquisitive palates.
Karma	1919 I St NW	202-331-5800	$$	10 pm	Mediterranean restaurant and art gallery.
Kaz Sushi Bistro	World Bank, 1915 I St NW	202-530-5500	$$$	10 pm	Impress your date by ordering the omasake.
Kinkead's	2000 Pennsylvania Ave NW	202-296-7700	$$$$	10:30 pm	Elegant seafood, extravagant raw bar.
Notti Bianche	824 New Hampshire Ave NW	202-298-8085	$$$$	11 pm	Full or half portion pasta dishes perfect for lunch.
Primi Piatti	2013 I St NW	202-223-3600	$$$$	10:30 pm	Eat like an Italian, but you'll want to dress up like one too.
Roof Terrace Restaurant and Bar	Kennedy Ctr, 2700 F St NW	202-416-8555	$$$$	9 pm	Avoid fighting the throng of theater-goers for the last split of wine. Try booking Sunday brunch instead.
Taberna Del Alabardero	1776 I St NW	202-429-2200	$$$$	11 pm	Wide-open menu dares you to be bold.

Map 8 • Georgetown

Name	Address	Phone	Price	Close	Description
1789	1226 36th St NW	202-965-1789	$$$$	11 pm	1789: Age of the patrons, or total for your bill?
Aditi	3299 M St NW	202-625-6825	$$	10:30 pm	Indian restaurant that has stood the test of time.
Amma Vegetarian Kitchen	3291 M St NW	202-625-6625	$$	10:30 pm	Who says vegetarians can't enjoy Indian food?
Café Bonaparte	1522 Wisconsin Ave NW	202-333-8830	$	1 am	Fine French-onion soup.
Café Divan	1834 Wisconsin Ave NW	202-338-1747	$$$	11 pm	It's Turkish, so anything with the word "Kebab" is safe bet.
Café LaRuche	1039 31st St NW	202-965-2684	$$$	11 pm	Super-cozy authentic French nook with fabulous desserts.
Café Milano	3251 Prospect St NW	202-333-6183	$$$$	12 am	Would you care for a celebrity sighting with your tiramisu?
Chadwick's	3205 K St NW	202-333-2565	$$	12 am	Go strictly for a burger.
Citronelle	Latham Hotel, 3000 M St NW	202-625-2150	$$$$$	10:30 pm	A Tony Williams favorite. ($50 single dishes. Bon appetit!)
Clyde's	3236 M St NW	202-333-9180	$$$	1 am	Famous Georgetown saloon made less notable through suburban franchising.
Fahrenheit & Degrees	Ritz Carlton, 3100 S St NW	202-912-4110	$$$$	11 pm	Italian-American in the deco Ritz-Carlton hotel.
Furin's	2805 M St NW	202-965-1000	$	5 pm	Small-town feel on edge of bustling Georgetown. (Breakfast and lunch.)
J Paul's	3218 M St NW	202-333-3450	$$$	1 am	Wanna feel like a pompous Georgetown loudmouth? It's kinda fun!
La Chaumiere	2813 M St NW	202-338-1784	$$$	10:30 pm	Mon Dieu! Are we in Georgetown or Paris?
The Landmark	Melrose Hotel, 2430 Pennsylvania Ave NW	202-955-3863	$$$	11 pm	Melrose Hotel continental restaurant.
Martin's Tavern	1264 Wisconsin Ave NW	202-333-7370	$$$	12:30 am	Cubbyholed tables add flair to this old-school saloon.
Mendocino	2917 M St NW	202-333-2912	$$$$	11 pm	Wine and dine with the friendliest staff in Georgetown.
Morton's of Georgetown	3251 Prospect St NW	202-342-6258	$$$$$	11 pm	Steaks a la carte will make converts out of vegetarians.
Mr Smith's	3104 M St NW	202-333-3104	$$$	1 am	Mr. Smith, you have an ordinary name and an ordinary restaurant.
Nathan's	3150 M St NW	202-338-2000	$$$$	11 pm	Birthplace of the three-martini lunch.
Old Glory All-American BBQ	3139 M St NW	202-337-3406	$$	11 pm	Southeast-style BBQ, with hoppin' john on the side.
Prince Café	1042 Wisconsin Ave NW	202-333-1500	$	5 am	Shisha lounge specializing in Mediterrean cuisine and flavored tobacco.
Riverside Grill	3050 K St NW	202-342-3535	$$$	1 am	Plays third fiddle to Sequoia and T&J's, but also most peaceful.

Map 8 · Georgetown–*continued*

Romeo's Café and Pizzeria	2132 Wisconsin Ave NW	202-337-1111	$	3 am	Most college kids order Domino's; Georgetown kids order Romeo's.
Sequoia	3000 K St NW	202-944-4200	$$$$	12 am	A Georgetown see-and-be-seen hotspot.
The Third Edition	1218 Wisconsin Ave NW	202-333-3700	$$	11:30 pm	If it's bar food you're after, it's bar food you got.
The Tombs	1226 36th St NW	202-337-6668	$$	12 am	An underground GU favorite.
Tony And Joe's Seafood Place	3000 K St NW	202-944-4545	$$$	10 pm	Waterfront views attract the beautiful people.
Wisemiller's	1236 36th St NW	202-333-8254	$	11:30 pm	Two words: Chicken Madness.

Map 9 · Dupont Circle / Adams Morgan

15 Ria	Washington Terrace Hotel, 1515 Rhode Island Ave NW	202-742-0015	$$$$	12 am	New York–chic dining in the nation's capital.
Al Tiramisu	2014 P St NW	202-467-4466	$$$$	11 pm	Romantic climate, friendly Italian service will make it a bella notte.
Annie's Paramount	1609 17th St NW	202-232-0395	$$	24-hrs	24-hour gay (straight-friendly) steak joint; packed Sunday brunch.
Bacchus Restaurant	1827 Jefferson Pl NW	202-785-0734	$$$	10:30 pm	Reliable Lebanese.
Bistrot du Coin	1738 Connecticut Ave NW	202-234-6969	$$$$	1 am	French joint, nix the stuffiness.
The Brickskeller	1523 22nd St NW	202-293-1885	$$	2 am	Renowned beer selection overshadows some damn fine eats.
Bua	1635 P St NW	202-265-0828	$$	11 pm	The food far outclasses the décor, as it should be.
Café Citron	1343 Connecticut Ave NW	202-530-8844	$$$	11 am	South American cuisine sets stage for serious dance party.
Café L'Enfant	2000 18th St NW	202-319-1800	$$$		Bohemian sidewalk Café with oodles of ambiance.
Café Luna	1633 P St NW	202-387-4005	$$$	11 pm	Always busy, yet always intimate. Enjoy the Dupont open air.
Chi-Cha Lounge	1624 U St NW	202-234-8400	$$$	12:30 am	Kick off an evening on U with tapas, sangria, and a hookah.
Daily Grill	1200 18th St NW	202-822-5282	$$$	12 am	A 40-entrée menu.
Food Bar	1639 R St NW	202-462-6200	$$$	11 pm	Similar to the NYC venue in name only.
Front Page Restaurant and Grill	1333 New Hampshire Ave NW	202-296-6500	$$$	12 am	Respectable dark wood-paneled Americana restaurant by day, seedy intern meat-market by night.
Galileo/ Il Laboratorio del Galileo	1110 21st St NW	202-293-7191	$$$$	10:30 pm	Perhaps the finest Italian in DC. Try to snag the "Chef's Table" in the kitchen.
Hank's Oyster Bar	1624 Q St NW	202-462-4625	$$$	11 pm	A pearl in the culinary depths of 17th St.
I Ricchi	1220 19th St NW	202-835-0459	$$$$	10:30 pm	Restaurants in Italy aren't even this upscale.
Johnny's Half Shell	2002 P St NW	202-296-2021	$$$	11 pm	Best crabcakes in Washington. Friendly bartstaff attracts solo diners.
Kramerbooks & Afterwords Café	1517 Connecticut Ave NW	202387-1462	$$	2 am	Restaurant? Bookstore? All-night pancake joint? A must-visit.
Lauriol Plaza	1835 18th St NW	202-387-0035	$$$	12 am	Ritzy architecture doesn't match run-of-the-mill dishes.
Levante's	1320 19th St NW	202-293-6301	$$	11 pm	Great Middle Eastern served by happy waiters.
Local 16	1602 U St NW	202-265-2828	$$$$	11 pm	The classiest place on U.
Love Café	1501 U St NW	202-265-9800	$	11 pm	Give your sweet tooth a fix with a gourmet cupcake.
Luna Grill & Diner	1301 Connecticut Ave NW	202-835-2280	$$	1 am	Great brunch.
Mackey's Public House	1823 L St NW	202-331-7667	$$	11 pm	Another O'Whatever's.
Malaysia Kopitiam	1827 M St NW	202-833-6232	$$	11 pm	Menu offers extensive notes for the uninitiated Malaysian diner.
Marcel's	2401 Pennsylvania Ave NW	202-296-1166	$$$$	11 pm	Sheer decadence.
McCormick and Schmick's	1652 K St NW	202-861-2233	$$$	12 am	A K Street staple. Exploit the happy hour food specials.
Meiwah	1200 New Hampshire Ave NW	202-833-2888	$$$	11 pm	The lighter side of Chinese food.
Mimi's	2120 P St NW	202-464-6464	$$$$	12 am	Classic Dupont: You never knew artists earned so much money.
Nage	1600 Rhode Island Ave NW	202-448-8005	$$$	11 pm	Surf and surf.

Nirvana	1810 K St NW	202-223-5043	$$	9:30 pm	Respectable Indian cuisine in the heart of downtown.
Nooshi	1120 19th St NW	202-293-3138	$$	10:30 pm	We recommend everything but the cheeseball name.
Obelisk	2029 P St NW	202-872-1180	$$$$	10 pm	Put your reservation in now for next March.
Olives	1600 K St NW	202-452-1866	$$$$	10:30 pm	Quaint but pricey Mediterranean.
The Palm	1225 19th St NW	202-293-9091	$$$$	11 pm	If you're an elitist and you know it clap your hands!
Pesce	2016 P St NW	202-466-3474	$$$	10:30 pm	Perhaps the best of the half-dozen fish joints on the block.
Pizzeria Paradiso	2029 P St NW	202-223-1245	$$	12 am	The toppings are meals themselves. Pray there's no line.
The Prime Rib	2020 K St NW	202-466-8811	$$$$	11:30 pm	Voted Washington's No.1 steakhouse.
Raku	1900 Q St NW	202-265-7258	$$	11 pm	Hip Asian bistro cashing in on DC's tapas craze.
Restaurant Nora	2132 Florida Ave NW	202-462-5143	$$$$	10:30 pm	Nora keeps her own herb garden in back. Every ingredient organic.
Rosemary's Thyme	1801 18th St NW	202-332-3200	$$$	12 am	Mediterranean, meet Creole. Great people-watching patio.
Sam and Harry's	1200 19th St NW	202-296-4333	$$$$	10 pm	Looking for expensive filet mignon? Cross the street to The Palm.
Sette Osteria	1666 Connecticut Ave NW	202-483-3070	$$	3 am	As simple as Italian gets. Pastas are all the rave.
Smith and Wollensky	1112 19th St NW	202-466-1100	$$$$	2 am	Sleek setting makes you forget it's a chain.
Sushi Taro	1503 17th St NW	202-462-8999	$$	12 am	Traditional sushi above a CVS.
Tabard Inn	1739 N St NW	202-331-8528	$$$$	10 pm	Fireplace, brick walls, outdoor tables, and elegant dishes.
Teaism	2009 R St NW	202-667-3827	$$	11 pm	Would you like dinner with your cup of tea?
Teatro Goldoni	1909 K St NW	202-955-9494	$$$$	11 pm	Lawyers and lobbyists abound. For a $13 lunch, why shouldn't they?
Thai Chef	1712 Connecticut Ave NW	202-234-5698	$$	11 pm	Comfy Thai food (and sushi).
Thaiphoon	2011 S St NW	202-667-3505	$$	11 pm	A curry-lover's paradise.
Timberlake's	1726 Connecticut Ave NW	202-483-2266	$$	3 am	No-frills atmosphere = good. No-frills food = bad.
Vidalia	1990 M St NW	202-659-1990	$$$$	10:30 pm	A taste of dixieland refinery. Brilliant.
Yee Hwa	1009 21st St NW	202-833-1244	$$$	10 pm	Best Korean food outside of the 'burbs.

Map 10 • Logan Circle / U Street

Acadiana	901 New York Ave NW	202-408-8848	$$$$	11 pm	Another notch! of Southern seafood.
Al Crostino	1324 U St NW	202-797-0523	$$$$	11 pm	Wine bar and homey Italian restaurant. Try the lamb ragu.
Ben's Chili Bowl	1213 U St NW	202-667-0909	$*	4 am	A District chili institution.
Busboys and Poets	2021 14th St NW	202-387-7638	$$	1 am	Shabby chic leftist bookstore/restaurant, proletarian prices.
Café Saint-Ex	1847 14th St NW	202-265-7839	$$$	2:30 am	Once-cool bistro overrun by the khaki crowd.
Coppi's	1414 U St NW	202-319-7773	$$$	12 am	Eat an organic extra large pizza and pretend you're healthy.
Corduroy	1201 K St NW	202-589-0699	$$$$$	11 pm	Sleek, innovative restaurant gives hotel dining a good name.
Creme Café	1322 U St NW	202-234-1884	$$$$	11:30 pm	Upscale southern home cooking.
Dakota Cowgirl	1337 14th St NW	202-232-7010	$$	11 pm	Hip burger joint.
DC Coast	Tower Bldg, 1401 K St NW	202-216-5988	$$$$	11:30 pm	Another sterile, upscale American establishment.
Dukem	1114 U St NW	202-667-8735	$$	2 am	Authentic Ethiopian. Special weekend outdoor grill menu.
Georgia Brown's	950 15th St NW	202-393-4499	$$$$	10:30 pm	Upscale Southern features a scandalous brunch.
Lima	1401 K St NW	202-789-2800	$$	12 am	Newest kid on K Street.
Logan Tavern	1423 P St NW	202-332-3710	$$$$	11 pm	Eclectic comfort food made better by proximity to Logan Circle.
Maggie Moo's	1301 U St NW	202-234-7700	$††	10 pm	Good ice cream and a free mix-in.
Merkado Kitchen	1443 P St NW	202-299-0018	$$$	12 am	Mexic-Asian tapas.
Oohhs and Aahhs	1005 U St NW	202-667-7142	$††	10 pm	The District's best soul food.

Map 10 • Logan Circle / U Street–*continued*

Polly's Café	1342 U St NW	202-265-8385	$$$††	11 pm	One of the first U Street revivalists.
Post Pub	1422 L St NW	202-628-2111	$$	11:30 pm	Best burgers in city. Shhh! A secret!
Rice	1608 14th St NW	202-234-2400	$$$	10:30 pm	Swanky minimalist Thai. Try the green tea dishes.
Saloon	1207 U St NW	202-462-2640	$$$††	1 am	Go there for the beer. Just be sure to eat beforehand.
Soho Café & Market	1301 K St NW	202-842-2400	$*	4 pm	Local gourmet smorgasbord chain.
Tabaq Bistro	1336 U St NW	202-265-0965	$$$$	12 am	Mediterranean tapas joint with a hopping glass-top roof deck.
Taste of Carolina	1930 9th St NW	301-213-2555	$$$	2 am	Trout, Beaufort BBQ chicken, ribs, orange fried chicken.
Thai Tanic	1326 14th St NW	202-588-1795	$$	11 pm	Neighborhood fave Thai restaurant.
U-topia	1418 U St NW	202-483-7669	$$$	1 am	Reasonably priced eclectic international cuisine.
Vegetate	1414 9th St NW	202-232-4585	$$$	11 pm	City's first all-vegetarian restaurant, offers vegan dishes as well.
Viridian	1515 14th St NW	202-234-1400	$$$	11 pm	When vegans dress up.

Map 14 • Catholic U

Colonel Brooks' Tavern	901 Monroe St NE	202-529-4002	$$	11 pm	Be welcomed like a local in the blue-collar section of town.
The Hitching Post	200 Upshur St NW	202-726-1511	$$	12 am	Southern fried chicken, crab cakes.
Kelly's Ellis Island	3908 12th St NE	202-832-6117	$	10 pm	Roman Catholic décor. Drink beer amidst pictures of the pope.
Murry and Paul's	3513 12th St NE	202-529-4078	$*	2 pm	We dare you to eat here. (breakfast and lunch only)

Map 15 • Columbia Heights

Brown's Caribbean Bakery	3301 Georgia Ave NW	202-882-1626	$	7 pm	Cinnamon rolls the size of your head.
Cluck U Chicken	2921 Georgia Ave NW	202-726-0006	$	11 pm	Want some chicken with that grease?
Five Guys	2301 Georgia Ave NW	202-986-2235	$	2 am	Juicy patties satisfy every need of hamburger afficionados.
Florida Ave Grill	1100 Florida Ave NW	202-265-1586	$$	9 pm	Greasy spoon from the dirty south.
Negril	2301 Georgia Ave NW	202-332-3737	$	10 pm	Local Caribbean quick-eats chain.
Rita's Caribbean Carryout	3322 Georgia Ave NW	202-722-1868	$$*	8 pm	Authentic Caribbean fare.
Soul Vegetarian and Exodus Café	2606 Georgia Ave NW	202-328-7685	$††	9 pm	Eclectic African vegan take-out.
Temperance Hall	3634 Georgia Ave NW	202-722-7669	$$	11 pm	1920s theme with Jazz-Age décor, mini-sloppy joes, and selection of rye whiskeys.

Map 16 • Adams Morgan (North) / Mt Pleasant

Amsterdam Falafel	2425 18th St NW	202-234-1969	$*	4 am	So good, so cheap.
Astor Restaurant	1829 Columbia Rd NW	202-745-7495	$	10 pm	Great falafel sandwich and subs.
Bardia's New Orleans Café	2412 18th St NW	202-234-0420	$	10 pm	Perfect brunch with great Cajun takes on poached egg classics.
Bukom Café	2442 18th St NW	202-265-4600	$$$	2 am	West African food, feel, and music.
Cashion's Eat Place	1819 Columbia Rd NW	202-797-1819	$$$$	11 pm	Chelsea Clinton known to have played the dating game here.
The Diner	2453 18th St NW	202-232-8800	$	24-hrs	Self-explanatory. Open 24 hours.
Dos Gringos	3116 Mt Pleasant St NW	202-462-1159	$††	9 pm	Proving that classy Salvadorean establishment is not an oxymoron.
Felix Restaurant & Lounge	2406 18th St NW	202-483-3549	$$$$	11 pm	A Washington mainstay for hipsters. Identity of Felix a mystery.
Grill From Ipanema	1858 Columbia Rd NW	202-986-0757	$$$	12 am	Killer caiphirinas that scream "Brazil!"
Haydee's	3102 Mt Pleasant St NW	202-483-9199	$††	2 am	Cheap but awful Salvadorean food. Beware the salsa.
La Fourchette	2429 18th St NW	202-332-3077	$$$$	11 pm	Casual creperie.
Leftbank	2424 18th St NW	202-464-2100	$$	3 am	Americana diner, sushi bar, cafeteria aesthetic, hipster chic.

The Little Fountain Café	2339 18th St NW	202-462-8100	$$	11 pm	Charming oasis on Adams Morgan's Drunkards Row.
Mama Ayesha's	1967 Calvert St NW	202-232-5431	$$	10:30 pm	Middle Eastern good enough for Bill Clinton.
Marx Café	3203 Mt Pleasant St NW	202-518-7600	$$$	3 am	Quasi-hipster Mount Pleasant standout.
Meskerem Ethiopian Restaurant	2434 18th St NW	202-462-4100	$$$	1 am	Authentic Ethiopian meets DC posh.
Millie & Al's	2440 18th St NW	202-387-8131	$$	2 am	A dive's dive for pizza and pitchers.
Mixtec	1729 Columbia Rd NW	202-332-1011	$$††	11 pm	Originally a grocery store, this Mexican beanery is superb.
Perry's	1811 Columbia Rd NW	202-234-6218	$$$	11:30 pm	A punk sushi experience. Killer city views.
Rumba Café	2443 18th St NW	202-588-5501	$$††	12 am	Eat steak and watch tango. (Wednesday nights.)
Tonic	3155 Mt Pleasant St NW	202-986-7661	$$	12 am	Comfort food and a can't-be-beat happy hour.
Tono Sushi	2605 Connecticut Ave NW	202-332-7300	$$	11 pm	Serviceable sushi, $1/piece happy hour special.
Tryst	2459 18th St NW	202-232-5500	$$	3 am	Excellent Wi-Fi cafe. A central DC spot.

Map 17 • Woodley Park / Cleveland Park

Alero	3500 Connecticut Ave NW	202-966-2530	$$	12 am	Margarita before a movie at the Uptown.
Ardeo	3311 Connecticut Ave NW	202-244-6750	$$$$	11 pm	In the room the women come and go talking of Michelangelo.
Dino	3435 Connecticut Ave NW	202-686-2966	$$$	10:30 pm	Try the boar pasta.
Four Green Fields	3412 Connecticut Ave NW	202-244-0860	$$$	11:30 pm	Grub's not too bad in what's best known as a party bar.
Lavandou	3321 Connecticut Ave NW	202-966-3002	$$$$	11 pm	Casual French sidewalk-style bistro.
Lebanese Taverna	2641 Connecticut Ave NW	202-265-8681	$$$	11 pm	Serviceable food, unserviceable service.
Lex Cajun Grill	2608 Connecticut Ave NW	202-745-0015	$$	10:30 pm	Ragin' Asian/Cajun.
Mr Chen's Organic Chinese Cuisine	2604 Connecticut Ave NW	202-797-9668	$$$	10:30 pm	Cult favorite of munchies-stricken health-conscious hipsters.
Nam Viet	3419 Connecticut Ave NW	202-237-1015	$$	11 pm	No frills pho.
Open City	2331 Calvert St NW	202-332-2331	$$	3 am	Hipper-than-thou diner with round-the-clock brunch.
Petits Plats	2653 Connecticut Ave NW	202-518-0018	$$$	11 pm	Take out a selection of goodies from downstairs.
Sake Club	2635 Connecticut Ave NW	202-332-2711	$$$$	12 am	Sake and Japanese, with prices ranging from low to quite high.
Sorriso	3518 Connecticut Ave NW	202-537-4800	$$$	10:30 pm	Artisanal Italian with an awesome Nutella pizza.
Spices	3333A Connecticut Ave NW	202-686-3833	$$$	11 pm	Dependably tasty pan-Asian. Try the suicide curry.

Map 18 • Glover Park / Foxhall

2 Amys	3715 Macomb St NW	202-885-5700	$$	11 pm	Pizza Napolitana. Romantic or just for kicks.
BlackSalt	4883 MacArthur Blvd NW	202-342-9101	$$$	11 pm	Gorgeous seafood with a posh bar.
Busara	2340 Wisconsin Ave NW	202-337-2340	$$		Traditional and fusion Thai with outdoor seating.
Cactus Cantina	3300 Wisconsin Ave NW	202-686-7222	$$$	12 am	Same as Lauriol Plaza, minus courtly architecture.
Café Deluxe	3228 Wisconsin Ave NW	202-686-2233	$$$	11 pm	A greasy spoon with absolutely no grease.
Heritage India	2400 Wisconsin Ave NW	202-333-3120	$$$$	11 pm	Gourmet Indian in a comfortable setting.
Jetties	1609 Foxhall Rd NW	202-965-3663	$	6 pm	Every neighborhood deserves such an ice cream shop.
Kotobuki	4822 MacArthur Blvd NW, 2nd floor	202-625-9080	$$††	11 pm	Price: low. Quality: high.
Makoto Restaurant	4822 MacArthur Blvd NW	202-298-6866	$$$	10 pm	Sushi a la carte. You'll never need to visit Japan.
Max's Best Ice Cream	2616 Wisconsin Ave NW	202-333-3111	$*	12 am	Mom and pop ice cream shop.
My Bakery & Café	2233 Wisconsin Ave NW	202-464-4670	$	1 am	Bolivian bakery with cakes, coffee, and empanadas.
Rocklands	2418 Wisconsin Ave NW	202-333-2558	$$	10 pm	Cooking 150,000 pounds of pork a year, and counting…
Sushi-Ko	2309 Wisconsin Ave NW	202-333-4187	$$$$	11 pm	Washington's first sushi bar, since 1976.
Town Hall	2218 Wisconsin Ave NW	202-333-5640	$$$	11 pm	Soul food without the soul.

Map 19 • Tenleytown / Friendship Heights

4912 Thai Cuisine	4912 Wisconsin Ave NW	202-966-4696	$$	11 pm	Excellent Thai with a creative name.
Bambule	5225 Wisconsin Ave NW	202-966-0300	$$$	11:30 pm	Wide doors open onto a porch revealing tapas and dancing.
Café Ole	4000 Wisconsin Ave NW	202-244-1330	$$$	11 pm	Fun neighborhood Spanish-style tapas.
Guapos Mexican Cuisine & Cantina	4515 Wisconsin Ave NW	202-686-3588	$$$	12 am	Nothing better than drinking tequila outside.
K's New York Deli	4620 Wisconsin Ave NW	202-686-1989	$$	10 pm	It ain't New York, but arguably DC's best Jewish deli.
Maggiano's Little Italy	5333 Wisconsin Ave NW	202-966-5500	$$	11 pm	Opposite of this book's title.
Matisse	4934 Wisconsin Ave NW	202-244-5222	$$$$	11 pm	French and Mediterranean with all the details.
Murasaki	4620 Wisconsin Ave NW	202-966-0023	$$$	10:30 pm	Wide range of Japanese cuisines.
Osman's and Joe's Steak 'n Egg Kitchen	4700 Wisconsin Ave NW	202-686-1201	$	24-hrs	This greasy spoon hasn't changed a thing in over 60 years.

Map 20 • Cleveland Park / Upper Connecticut

Buck's Fishing & Camping	5031 Connecticut Ave NW	202-364-0777	$$$$	10 pm	More sophisticated than the name suggests.
Delhi Dhaba	4455 Connecticut Ave NW	202-537-1008	$$	10:30 pm	Efficient Indian take-out passes the test. Try the butter chicken.
Indique	3512 Connecticut Ave NW	202-244-6600	$$$$	11 pm	Wrap your mind around an inside-out samosa.
Palena	3529 Connecticut Ave NW	202-537-9250	$$$$	10 pm	Continental food and an engrossing dessert menu.
Sala Thai	3507 Connecticut Ave NW	202-237-2777	$$	11 pm	No-frills Thai.

Map 21 • 16th St. Heights / Petworth

Colorado Kitchen	5515 Colorado Ave NW	202-545-8280	$$$	10 pm	American cuisine with a subtle Southern accent.
Domku	821 Upshur St NW	202-722-7475	$$$	11:30 pm	East European and Scandinavian comfort food.
Frio Frio Deli Café	5517 Colorado Ave NW	202-722-7004	$*		Ice cream, marble tables, and ¡Ay Caramba! décor.
Sweet Mango Café	3701 New Hampshire Ave NW	202-726-2646	$$	12 am	Slow-roasted jerked chicken on the bone. Best in the city.

Map 22 • Downtown Bethesda

Bacchus	7945 Norfolk Ave	301-657-1722	$$$$	10:30 pm	Lebanese menu with lots of twists and turns.
Buon Giorno	8003 Norfolk Ave	301-652-1400	$$$	11 pm	Pastas made by hand on-site every day.
Faryab	4917 Cordell Ave	301-951-3484	$$$	10:30 pm	Premier DC metro area Afghan stop.
Grapeseed	4865 Cordell Ave	301-986-9592	$$$$	11 pm	Spanish cuisine to go with wine list al grande.
Haandi	4904 Fairmont Ave	301-718-0121	$$$	10:30 pm	Super-tasty Indian.
Matuba	4918 Cordell Ave	301-652-7449	$$$	10 pm	Basic sushi and buffet.
Olazzo	7921 Norfolk Ave	301-654-9496	$$$	10:30 pm	Italian with a brick oven (and yet no pizza!).
The Original Pancake House	7700 Wisconsin Ave	301-986-0285	$	3 pm	Oh go ahead. Bring back a few childhood memories.
Rock Creek Restaurant	4917 Elm St	301-907-7625	$$$$	11 pm	Super serene ambience. Nutritional facts on each dish listed on back of menu.
Tako Grill	7756 Wisconsin Ave	301-652-7030	$$$	10:30 pm	Traditional and nontraditional Japanese for the enthusiast.
Tragara	4935 Cordell Ave	301-951-4935	$$$$	10:30 pm	Traditional Italian with elegant surroundings.

Map 24 • Upper Rock Creek Park

Parkway Deli	8317 Grubb Rd	301-587-1427	$$	9:30 pm	Another rare high-quality Jewish deli.
redDog Café	8301A Grubb Rd	301-588-6300	$$	10 pm	Constantly changing décor.

Map 25 • Silver Spring

Addis Ababa	8233 Fenton St	301-589-1400	$$	12 am	Authentic Ethiopian. Ask to sit on the rooftop.
Austin Grill	919 Ellsworth Dr	240-247-8969	$$	1 pm	Down-home grub at down-home prices. Yee-haw.

Cubano's	1201 Fidler Ln	301-563-4020	$$$	10:30 pm	Fountain and foliage make the décor cheessimo.
Eggspectation	923 Ellsworth Dr	301-585-1700	$$	10 pm	So many eggs you wonder where they hide their hens.
El Aguila	8649 16th St	301-588-9063	$$	2 am	Better than its location would have you believe.
Lebanese Taverna	933 Ellsworth Dr	301-588-1192	$$	10 pm	Fast, decent Middle Eastern food.
Mandalay	930 Bonifant St, #932	301-585-0500	$$	10:30 pm	Addictive Burmese food next door to a gun shop.
Mi Rancho	8701 Ramsey Ave	301-588-4872	$$	11 pm	Quite cheap Mexican/Salvadorean.
Roger Miller Restaurant	941 Bonifant St	301-650-2495	$$	12 am	Unique Cameroonian fare, named after a soccer star. Try the goat.
Romano's Macaroni Grill	931 Ellsworth Dr	301-562-2806	$$$	11 pm	Good standard Italian.

Map 26 • Takoma Park

Mark's Kitchen	7006 Carroll Ave	301-270-1884	$$	9 pm	Green-friendly American and Korean fare.
Savory	7071 Carroll Ave	301-270-2233	$$	11 pm	Veggie/vegan with a basement café.

Map 27 • Walter Reed

Blair Mansion Inn/ Murder Mystery Dinner Theatre	7711 Eastern Ave	301-588-6646	$$$$	9 pm	What's better than finding a hair in your soup? Finding a dead body during mystery dinner theater!

Map 28 • Chevy Chase

American City Diner of Washington	5532 Connecticut Ave NW	202-244-1949	$	24-hrs	1950s drive-in themed diner, complete with movies.
Arucola	5534 Connecticut Ave NW	202-244-1555	$$$$	10:30 pm	Straightforward Italian.
Bread & Chocolate	5542 Connecticut Ave NW	202-966-7413	$	10 pm	Can't go wrong with this combination.
La Ferme	7101 Brookville Rd	301-986-5255	$$$$	10 pm	Charming (if bizarre) French bistro in a residential area.

Map 29 • Bethesda / Chevy Chase Business

Gifford's	7237 Woodmont Ave	301-907-3436	$††	10:30 pm	Next to movie theater—deals for cones + tickets.
Green Papaya	4922 Elm St	301-654-8986	$$$$	10 pm	Tasty but ridiculously inauthentic Vietnamese.
Hinode	4914 Hampden Ln	301-654-0908	$$$	11 pm	No-surprises Japanese.
Jaleo	7271 Woodmont Ave	301-913-0003	$$$$	12 am	Good, if overpriced, tapas.
Levantes	7262 Woodmont Ave	301-657-2441	$$$	11 pm	Sleek Turkish eatery with a decent Sunday brunch buffet.
Louisiana Express Company	4921 Bethesda Ave	301-652-6945	$$	11 pm	Get your Muffuletta fix here.
Moby Dick House of Kabob	7027 Wisconsin Ave	301-654-1838	$††	11 pm	Mind your manners or "No kebob for you!"
Mon Ami Gabi	7239 Woodmont Ave	301-654-1234	$$$$	11 pm	Authentic French atmosphere: expensive and snooty. Half-price wines on Wednesday evenings.
Persimmon	7003 Wisconsin Ave	301-654-9860	$$$$	10 pm	Superlative Bethesda continental experience.
Raku	7240 Woodmont Ave	301-718-8681	$$$	10:30 pm	Pan-Asian delight with lovely outdoor patio.
Ri-Ra Irish Restaurant Pub	4931 Elm St	301-657-1122	$$$	12:45 pm	Irish pub; utterly American grub.
Rio Grande	4870 Bethesda Ave	301-656-2981	$$$	11:30 pm	Great free chips and salsa—good Tex Mex.
Tara Thai	4828 Bethesda Ave	301-657-0488	$$	11 pm	Well-known for bold Thai.
Vace	4705 Miller Ave	301-654-6367	$	8:30 pm	Queue up for the best pizza in town.

Map 30 • Westmoreland Circle

Dahlia	4849 Massachusetts Ave NW	202-364-1004	$$$$	10:30 pm	Fine dining with Spring Valley socialites.

Map 32 • Cherrydale / Palisades

Name	Address	Phone	Price	Hours	Description
Bambu	5101 MacArthur Blvd NW	202-364-3088	$$$	10:30 pm	Reliable Asian fusion.
DC Boathouse	5441 MacArthur Blvd	202-362-2628	$$$$	11 pm	Don't crack your skull on the skull.
L'Appetito Restaurante	5105 MacArthur Blvd	202-966-9797	$$$$	11 pm	Check for the jazz brunch and opera dinners
Listriani's Italian Gourmet	5100 MacArthur Blvd	202-363-0619	$$$	10 pm	A real neighborhood-y pizza & pasta place.
Starland Café	5125 MacArthur Blvd NW	202-244-9396	$$$	11:30 pm	Starland Vocal bandmember Bill Danoff's joint, if you miss the '70s.

Map 33 • Falls Church

Name	Address	Phone	Price	Hours	Description
La Cote d'Or Café	2201 N Westmoreland St	703-538-3033	$$$	10 pm	High romance for a reasonable price.
Lebanese Taverna	5900 Washington Blvd	703-241-8681	$$$	10:30 pm	Family-style Lebanese. Everyone shares.
Pie Tanza	2503 N Harrison St	703-237-0200	$$	10 pm	Thin crust, toppings galore, and wallet-friendly.
Taqueria el Poblano	2503 N Harrison St	703-237-8250	$$	10 pm	As predictable as it is cheap.

Map 34 • Ballston

Name	Address	Phone	Price	Hours	Description
Café Parisien Express	4520 Lee Hwy	703-525-3332	$$††	9:30 pm	French dining on the cheap.
Café Tirolo	4001 N Fairfax Dr	703-528-7809	$$	2:30 pm	Hidden European treasure with modest prices.
Cassatt's	4536 Lee Hwy	703-527-3330	$$	9 pm	Head over on Kiwi Mondays for interesting dinner fare and an art lesson downstairs.
Crisp & Juicy	4540 Lee Hwy	703-243-4222	$$*	9:30 pm	Latino-barbecued chicken.
El Paso Café	4235 N Pershing Dr	703-243-9811	$$	11:30 pm	Kick-ass margarita hidden gem known for George Bush sightings.
Flat Top Grill	4245 N Fairfax Dr	703-528-0078	$$$	10:30 pm	Construct your own stir-fry.
Layalina	5216 Wilson Blvd	703-525-1170	$$$	10:30 pm	Middle Eastern rugs adorn walls. Straight out of *Aladdin*.
Metro 29 Diner	4711 Lee Hwy	703-528-2464	$$	3 am	Diner breakfast with some Greek touches.
Rio Grande Café	4301 N Fairfax Dr	703-528-3131	$$	11:30 pm	We don't know what Café means anymore.
Tara Thai	4001 Fairfax Dr	703-908-4999	$$	11 pm	A tasty Thai chain.
Tutto Bene	501 N Randolph St	703-522-1005	$$$	11 pm	Italian cuisine, when not Bolivian. We love America.
Willow	4301 N Fairfax Dr	703-465-8800	$$$$	10 pm	Snazzy spot helmed by Kinkhead's ex-head chef.

Map 35 • Clarendon

Name	Address	Phone	Price	Hours	Description
Aegean Taverna	2950 Clarendon Blvd	703-841-9494	$$$	10:30 pm	*My Big Fat Greek Wedding* without stereotypes and Windex.
Delhi Dhaba Indian Café & Carryout	2424 Wilson Blvd	703-524-0008	$$	11 pm	Indian curries make delicious cafeteria-style dishes.
Faccia Luna Trattoria	2909 Wilson Blvd	703-276-3099	$$	12 am	Good pizza for a low-key night out or in.
Hard Times Café	3028 Wilson Blvd	703-528-2233	$$	3 am	Chili-making to a science. Home-brewed root beer a bonus.
Harry's Tap Room	2800 Clarendon Blvd	703-778-7788	$$$$	11 pm	Nearly a dozen filet mignon options.
Lazy Sundae	2925 Wilson Blvd	703-525-4960	$*	10 pm	Family-style homemade ice cream.
Mexicali Blues	2933 Wilson Blvd	703-812-9352	$$	4 am	Most colorful restaurant in Arlington. First time? Order a burro.
Minh's Restaurant	2500 Wilson Blvd	703-525-2828	$$	11 pm	Ten bucks goes a long way at this Vietnamese establishment.
Pica Deli Gourmet and Wines	3471 N Washington Blvd	703-524-5656	$$	7 pm	You'll be glad the intriguing outdoor mural led you in.
Portabellos	2109 N Pollard St	703-528-1557	$$	10 pm	Contemporary American.
Queen Bee	3181 Wilson Blvd	703-527-3444	$$$	10 pm	Established and affordable Vietnamese restaurant.
Sette Bello	3101 Wilson Blvd	703-351-1004	$$$$	12 am	Sister spot of DC faves Café Milano and Sette Osteria.
Silver Diner	3200 Wilson Blvd	703-812-8600	$$	4 am	Good place for a date, or to end a relationship.

Map 36 • Rosslyn

Café Tivoli	1700 North Moore St	703-524-8900	$	9:30 pm	Gourmet sanwiches and pastries.
Gua-Rapo	2039 Wilson Blvd	703-528-6500	$$$	12:30 pm	Chi-Cha Lounge flavor in NoVA.
Guajillo	1727 Wilson Blvd	703-807-0840	$$	11 pm	Don't let the strip mall fool you. It's what's inside that counts.
Il Radicchio	1801 Clarendon Blvd	703-276-2627	$$$	11 pm	Quiet outdoor dining evokes *Lady and the Tramp* aura.
Ireland's Four Courts	2051 Wilson Blvd	703-525-3600	$$$	2 am	Makes you forget that Ireland ever had a famine.
Mezza9	1325 Wilson Blvd	703-276-8999	$$$$	10 pm	The Rosslyn Hyatt's take on Turkish.
Quarter Deck Restaurant	1200 Ft Myer Dr	703-528-2722	$$$	9 pm	Cold beer, hot crabs, familiar faces.
Ray's the Steaks	1725 Wilson Blvd	703-841-7297	$$$$	10 pm	Beef. It's what's for dinner.
Rhodeside Grill	1836 Wilson Blvd	703-243-0145	$$$	1 am	Hot plates on dinner tables, live music in the basement.
Village Bistro	1723 Wilson Blvd	703-522-0284	$$$	10 pm	Surprisingly quaint for part of a shopping strip.

Map 37 • Fort Myer

Atilla's	2705 Columbia Pike	703-920-8100	$$	10 pm	Savory gyros, kabobs, salads, and more.
Bangkok 54	2919 Columbia Pike	703-521-4070	$$$	11 pm	Upscale Thai at downscale prices.
Bob and Edith's Diner	2310 Columbia Pike	703-920-6103	$$	24-hrs	Probably the most charming all-night diner in Virginia.
Bob and Edith's Diner	4707 Columbia Pike	703-920-4700	$		Just as greasy (and great) as its down-the-street sib.
The Broiler	3601 Columbia Pike	703-920-5944	$$	11 pm	Blue collar subs and Ms. Pac-Man.
El Charrito Caminante	2710 N Washington Blvd	703-351-1177	$*	10 pm	Papusas worthy of the gods.
El Pollo Rico	932 N Kenmore St	703-522-3220	$*	10 pm	Eating this chicken is a sacramental experience.
Manee Thai	2500 Columbia Pike	703-920-2033	$	10 pm	True Thai treasure.
Mario's Pizza House	3322 Wilson Blvd	703-525-7827	$$	5 am	Late night tradition for the bleary-eyed.
Matuba	2915 Columbia Pike	703-521-2811	$$$	10 pm	Unlike the Bethesda location, no buffet.
Mrs Chen's Kitchen	3101 Columbia Pike	703-920-3199	$	11:30 pm	Chinese food before competition from Thai.
Pan American Bakery	4113 Columbia Pike	703-271-1113	$††	8:30 pm	Saltenas and glistening pastries from South America.
Rincome Thai Cuisine	3030 Columbia Pike	703-979-0144	$$	11 pm	Friendly owners, sumptuous food, neighborhood atmosphere.
Tallula Restaurant	2761 Washington Blvd	703-778-5051	$$$	11 pm	The wine bar craze has officially hit Arlington.

Map 38 • Columbia Pike

Andy's Carry-Out	5033 Columbia Pike	703-671-1616	$$	12 am	Oily food cooked in woks.
Athens Restaurant	3541 Carlin Springs Rd	703-931-3300	$$	10:45 pm	Greek menu for everyone, even Greeks.
Atlacatl	4701 Columbia Pike	703-920-3680	$$$	12 am	Laid-back, delicious Salvadorian and Mexican cuisine with attentive staff.
Crystal Thai	4819 Arlington Blvd	703-522-1311	$$$	10:30 pm	Moderate prices will allow you to order extra Singha.
Five Guys	4626 King St	703-671-1606	$*	10 pm	THE Alexandria burger joint.

Map 39 • Shirlington

Carlyle Grande Café	4000 28th St S	703-931-0777	$$$	12 am	Popular for Friday and Saturday dinner, arrive early.

Map 40 • Pentagon City / Crystal City

Bistro Bulgari	509 S 23rd St	571-274-9131	$$$	10 pm	Can you say "bitchin' Bulgarian bistro" five times fast? Yes!
Crystal City Restaurant	422 S 23rd St	703-892-0726	$$	1:45 am	Kegs and legs at this diner/strip club.
Crystal City Sports Pub	529 S 23rd St	703-521-8215	$$	2 am	Rated a top ten sports bar nationwide by *Sports Illustrated*. Dozens of TVs.
Legal Seafood	2301 Jefferson Davis Hwy	703-415-1200	$$$$	11 pm	A Boston institution. Here, it feels more. . . institutional.
Morton's—the Steakhouse	1631 Crystal Sq Arc	703-418-1444	$$$$	11 pm	Gluttony with valet parking.

Map 41 • Landmark

Akasaka	514-C S Van Dorn St	703-751-3133	$$$	10:30 pm	Decent sushi at decent prices.
The American Café	5801 Duke St	703-658-0004	$$$	11 pm	You can't do Ruby Tuesday all the time…
Clyde's	1700 N Beauregard St	703-820-8300	$$$	12 am	Take to the seas in this nautical-themed favorite.
Edgardo's Trattoria	281 S Van Dorn St	703-751-6700	$$	10:45 pm	Authentic wood-fired pizzas and flat breads.
El Paraiso	516 S Van Dorn St	703-212-9200	$$	1 am	A slice of El Salvador on Van Dorn.
Finn & Porter	Hilton, 5000 Seminary Rd	703-379-2346	$$$$	11:30 pm	Yes it's in a hotel, but it's still nice.
Sakulthai Restaurant	408 S Van Dorn St	703-823-5357	$	11 pm	Wallet-friendly Thai.
Thai Lemon Grass	506 S Van Dorn St	703-751-4627	$$	11 pm	Thai for surburbanites.

Map 42 • Alexandria (West)

Rocklands	25 S Quaker Ln	703-528-9663	$$	8 pm	DC BBQ in NoVA.
Tempo Restaurant	4231 Duke St	703-370-7900	$$$	10 pm	French-Italian fusion.

Map 43 • Four Mile Run / Del Ray

Afghan Restaurant	2700 Jefferson Davis Hwy	703-548-0022	$$	11 pm	Bountiful $7.95 lunch buffet; reportedly a good place for spook-spotting.
Al's Steak House	1504 Mt Vernon Ave	703-836-9443	$	7 pm	Cheesesteaks worthy of Philly.
Bombay Curry Company	3110 Mt Vernon Ave	703-836-6363	$$$	10 pm	Curry that fulfills with understated authenticity.
Chez Andree	10 E Glebe Rd	703-836-1404	$$$	9:30 pm	When you feel like eating a different part of the pig.
The Dairy Godmother	2310 Mt Vernon Ave	703-683-7767	$††		This homemade custard cuts the mustard.
Del Merei Grill	3106 Mt Vernon Ave	703-739-4335	$$$$	11 pm	Swanky steaks with sumptuous sauces.
Evening Star Café	2000 Mt Vernon Ave	703-549-5051	$$$$	11 pm	Streaky service, hip but grounded atmosphere.
Hectors	3112 Mt Vernon Ave	703-837-0666	$$	10 pm	Northern Italian sister to Old Town's Il Porto.
Huascaran	3606 Mt Vernon Ave	703-684-0494	$$$††	11 pm	Platefuls of Peruvian perfection.
Lilian's Restaurant	3901 Mt Vernon Ave	703-837-8494	$	12 am	Plump pupusas and Spanish-language karaoke.
Los Amigos	1905 Mt Vernon Ave	703-549-7008	$	10 pm	Tex-Mex with a weekend strummer.
Los Tios Grill	2615 Mt Vernon Ave	703-299-9290	$$	10 pm	Monster margaritas in a cozy, family-friendly space.
Mancini's	1508 Mt Vernon Ave	703-838-3663	$$	9 pm	Café, carryout, and catering.
Monroe's Trattoria	1603 Commonwealth Ave	703-548-5792	$$	10:30 pm	Great wines and brunch.
RT's Restaurant	3804 Mt Vernon Ave	703-684-6010	$$	11 pm	Creole & cajun before the Birchmere.
Spectrum Restaurant	251 W Glebe Rd	703-684-8945	$$	10 pm	Peruvian rotisserie chicken—basic and basically delicious
Sundae Times	2003 Mt Vernon Ave	703-683-9818	$*	10 pm	We all scream for Gifford's ice-cream.
Taqueria Poblano	2400 Mt Vernon Ave	703-548-8226	$$	10 pm	The read deal, amigo.
Thai Peppers	2018 Mt Vernon Ave	703-739-7627	$$	10 pm	Let "peppers" be a warning!
Waffle Shop	3864 Mt Vernon Ave	703-836-8851	$*	24-hrs	24-hour grease and caffeine.

Map 44 • Alexandria Downtown

Café Old Towne	2111 Eisenhower Ave	703-683-3116	$	4 pm	Variety of coffee/pastries, worth traveling off the beaten path.
FireFlies	1501 Mt Vernon Ave	703-548-7200	$$$	10 pm	Affordable eclecticism; try it at happy hour.
Joe Theismann's Restaurant	1800 Diagonal Rd	703-739-0777	$$$		Former Redskins QB's bar and grill draws visitors and locals alike.
Table Talk	1623 Duke St	703-548-3989	$	3 pm	Terrific breakfast/lunch. Often jammed, always good.
Ted's Montana Grill	2451 Eisenhower Ave	703-960-0500	$$$	11 pm	Home, home on the chain…er, range.

Map 45 • Old Town (North)

Blue & White Carry Out	1024 Wythe St	703-548-3867	$*	3:30 pm	Soul-satisfying heaven to go.
Esmeralda's Restaurant	728 N Henry St	703-739-7774	$$	1 am	Tasty Salvadoran fare.
La Piazza	535 E Braddock Rd	703-519-7711	$$	9:30 pm	Solid Italian cuisine in a curious locale.

Map 46 • Old Town (South)

100 King	100 King St	703-299-0076	$$$$	11 pm	Zaytinya Lite.
219 Restaurant	219 King St	703-549-1141	$$$	11 pm	Interior looks like the swankiest hotel in New Orleans.
Bilbo Baggins	208 Queen St	703-683-0300	$$$	10:30 pm	Coziest tavern this side of Middle Earth. Health-conscious options.
Casablanca Restaurant	1504 King St	703-549-6464	$$$	2 am	Good deals on multi-course meals.
The Chart House	1 Cameron St	n/a	$$$$	11 pm	Chain steak and seafood restaurant.
China King Restaurant	701 King St	703-549-3268	$$	11 pm	Express delivery by Chinese bicycle boy.
Faccia Luna Trattoria	823 S Washington St	703-838-5998	$$	12 am	The best pizza around—locals love it.
Fish Market	105 King St	703-836-5676	$$$	12 am	Just follow your nose!
The Grille	Morrison House, 116 S Alfred St	703-838-8000	$$$$	10 pm	Where luxury and Alexandria collide.
Hard Times Café	1404 King St	703-837-0050	$$		Nothing but chili, but plenty of it.
Il Porto	121 King St	703-836-8833	$$$$	11:30 pm	Best Italian around. Make reservations.
King Street Blues	112 N St Asaph St	703-836-8800	$$$	11 pm	Not quite on King St., but great BBQ.
La Bergerie	218 N Lee St	703-683-1007	$$$$$	10 pm	Pay the tab if you can-can.
Le Galois	1106 King St	703-739-9494	$$$$	11 pm	Great outdoor courtyard.
The Pita House	407 Cameron St	703-684-9194	$	10:30 pm	Intimate Middle Eastern.
Portner's	109 S St Asaph St	703-683-1776	$$$	2 am	Locals love to go here after the movie. Nice brunch, too.
Restaurant Eve	110 S Pitt St	703-706-0450	$$$$	10 pm	Reservations a must.
Southside 815	815 S Washington St	703-836-6222	$$	12:30 am	New Orleanean fare.
Taverna Cretekou	818 King St	703-548-8688	$$$$	10 pm	The flavors, they do the dance of joy.
The Warehouse	214 King St	703-683-6868	$$$	11 pm	A bit forgotten, but excellent food. Plan to eat hearty.

Baltimore

Bertha's	734 S Broadway	410-327-5795	$$	11 pm	Seafood. Dark, dank, and famous for its mussels.
Boccaccio Restaurant	925 Eastern Ave	410-234-1322	$$$$$	10 pm	Italian.
Brass Elephant	924 N Charles St (off map)	410-547-8480	$$$	10:30 pm	American. Gorgeous townhouse, fancy food, and expense-account prices.
Café Hon	1002 W 36th St (off map)	410-243-1230	$$$	10 pm	Kitsch central. If not for the meatloaf or the beehive 'dos on the wait staff, come to see John Waters's Baltimore.
The Daily Grind	1722 Thames St	410-558-0399	$††		Laid-back Fells Point coffee house.
Faidley's Seafood	Lexington Market, 203 N Paca St	410-727-4898	$$	5 pm	Seafood. Stand up and rub elbows while chowing down some of the city's best crab cakes.
Helen's Garden	2908 O'Donnell St	410-276-2233	$$$††	9:30 pm	Feel like a local at this Canton outpost. Good food, nice owners, wine flows.
Ikaros	4805 Eastern Ave (off map)	410-633-3750	$$$	11 pm	Greek. Cheap, big portions, and Greektown neighborhood staple.
Jimmy's	801 S Broadway	410-327-3273	$$††	8 pm	Classic Bawlmer greasy spoon. Check your attitude at the door.
John Steven Ltd	1800 Thames St	410-327-5561	$$$	2 am	Seafood. Outdoor patio, steamer bar, crab cakes, and stocked bar.
Obrycki's Crab House	1727 E Pratt St	410-732-6399	$$$	11 pm	The king of the many local crab houses.
Rusty Scupper	402 Key Hwy	410-727-3678	$$$	11 pm	Enjoy a Bloody Mary at their Sunday Jazz Brunch.
Tapas Teatro	1711 N Charles St (off map)	410-332-0110	$$$	12 am	Tapas. Before and after a movie at The Charles, check out this neighborhood favorite.
Vespa	1117 S Charles St	410-385-0355	$$$	11 pm	Italian. If all the blue-collar-ness has got you down, come and find the gold-roped crowd here.
Ze Mean Bean	1739 Fleet St	410-675-5999	$$$	11 pm	Eastern European. More than a coffeehouse, with meaty dishes and live music.

DC locals have long been mocked—perhaps for good reason—for having absolutely no sense of fashion. After all, this is the city where navy blue shirts and khakis look like the uniform for all men, every woman owns an Ann Taylor pantsuit, and people sometimes go on dates wearing sweatpants. (In our defense, maybe we're too busy running the planet to keep track of what the fashionistas are wearing this month.)

But with DC gentrifying at a dizzying pace, the sad state of fashion is also changing rapidly—especially in Logan Circle and the U Street Corridor, which is experiencing a boom of vintage clothing stores and furniture outlets, as well as boutique stores such as **Tickled Pink (Map 29, Map 46),** which features cutting-edge NYC designer clothes. If this keeps up, DC will soon prove its moniker, "Hollywood for ugly people," totally wrong!

Clothing/Beauty

Whether you're metrosexual or matronly, your best bet for clothes shopping is Georgetown, particularly around the intersection of M Street and Wisconsin Avenue (and the nearby Shops at the Georgetown Park Mall). You'll find all the mainstream chain stores, but in a non-mall setting: **Abercrombie & Fitch (Map 8, 40),** J. **Crew (Map 8),** Diesel **(Map 8),** Banana Republic **(Map 8),** Victoria's Secret **(Map 8),** the works. (And if you want to get punked up, there's always **Smash (Map 8)** and **Commander Salamander (Map 8)**). For cosmetics, check out **MAC (Map 8), Sephora (Map 8),** and **Lush (Map 8)**. A hint, though: There's not a lot here you can't get somewhere else in the area, so if you're just looking for a pair of Kenneth Cole shoes and have no other reason to go downtown, try the malls in Tyson's Corner or Pentagon City.

If you're after more prosaic gear (or classy work clothes), take a stroll down Connecticut Avenue, south of Dupont Circle; you'll find a good-sized **Gap (Map 9),** a **Burberry (Map 9),** and what seems to be DC's official clothing store, **Brooks Brothers (Map 9)**. For those with a more expensive taste (and the budget to boot), the best bet for one stop designer shopping is **Tyson's Galleria**. The more upscale of the two malls in the town of Tyson's Corner, the Galleria has department stores **Saks Fifth Avenue** and **Neiman Marcus** (which includes a **Louis**

Vuitton boutique), as well as **Versace, Chanel,** and **Salvatore Ferragamo**.

As far as vintage goes, the shops along the U Street Corridor are good places to look—we recommend **Meeps (Map 9)**. U Street also has a rapidly growing array of boutique designer stores. And if you're willing to take a drive, **Mustard Seed (Map 29)** in Bethesda is a great find, with both classy vintage and NY designer boutique goods.

Housewares

If the raging interior design districts along 14th Street and M Street in Georgetown are any indication, our interior lives must be a little more daring than the boring façades we wear out in public. Although it's touted as DC's furniture district, most of the shops along 14th Street in Logan Circle are pretty, well, pimpadelic—except for the well-stuffed junk store **Ruff and Ready (Map 10)**, where you can find some amazing deals if you're prepared to do some digging. A better choice is the multitude of vintage furniture stores along the U Street Corridor—or, if you're prepared to spend some serious cash, the European furniture outlets in Georgetown west of Wisconsin Avenue. In Georgetown you'll also find **Restoration Hardware (Map 8)** and **Pottery Barn (Map 8, Map 19, Map 35),** both of which carry wide selections of fashionable goods for house and home.

For wacky cutting boards, alarm clocks, and the like, stop by **Home Rule (Map 10)** on 14th Street. In fact, tchotchke stores are scattered throughout Dupont and Georgetown, so you won't be lacking in gift ideas when Mother's Day rolls around.

Electronics

Given the enormous number of techies (both professional and amateur) in DC, it's a mystery that the odds of stumbling across an electronic store are slim-to-none. If you're looking for computer goods, you'll need to hit the 'burbs—fortunately, the **Best Buy (Map 43)** in Alexandria is only about a 20-minute drive from downtown DC. Die-hard Mac-heads (i.e. dorks) will love the gorgeous, high-tech **Apple Store (Map 40)** in the Pentagon City mall in Arlington. If you're desperate and car-less, **Staples (See Copy Shop 1, 9, 24, 29, 34, 38, and 43 listings on maps)** offers a small collection of computers and software.

Food

DC's blessed with one of the finest supermarkets anywhere on earth—the **Whole Foods (Map 10)** market in Logan Circle, which many urban theorists quite seriously credit for the subsequent gentrification of the entire surrounding neighborhood. Prices, however, are not cheap, and lines can be long. For residents farther Northwest, there's a less impressive, but still noteworthy, Whole Foods in Glover Park. If you're broke, but still want to maintain an organic diet, check out one of the many **Trader Joe's (Map 29)** popping up all over the metro area.

Despite its status-toting name, **Dean & Deluca (Map 8)** in Georgetown pales in comparison to Whole Foods—shoppers pay more for a smaller selection of lower-quality products. If you're on a budget, there's also the numerous **Safeways (Map 6)** around town, although most of them are grim enough to have inspired nicknames like "Soviet Safeway." If neither of these works for you, there's always **Giant (Map 10, Map 11)**.

DC may be known for many things, but good ethnic food is not one of them. There are a few notable exceptions to this generalization, particularly in Adams Morgan—**So's Your Mom (Map 16)** has some excellent deli goods and an authentic atmosphere, and the area also features some great Ethiopian markets.

Music

The **Tower Records (Map 7)** in Foggy Bottom carries a large selection of mainstream and under-the-radar music, and most bookstores keep a decent CD collection in stock, as well. If you're searching for more offbeat fare, stop by the excellent new-and-used **Crooked Beat (Map 16)** store in Adams Morgan, or the numerous Olsson's outlets, or go to **Kemp Mill (Map 1)** in the Mall. **CD/Game Exchange (Map 16)** in Adams Morgan is a great place to find used bargains, although their selection tends toward the mainstream.

Wine, Beer, Liquor

Most supermarkets don't sell alcoholic beverages—Whole Foods is, again, an exception. Also worth a look is the tiny but beautiful **Georgetown Wine and Spirits (Map 8)**, as well as **Best Cellars (Map 9)** in Dupont. However, If you're partial to the drink and don't mind the trek to VA., most grocery stores have great selections of beer and wine. There's also a slew of **Total Wine & More** emporiums in the area.

Late-nite revelers should keep in mind that you can't buy anything alcoholic in DC stores after 10 pm. Most liquor stores close at 9 pm on weekdays, although they stay open until 10 pm on Friday and Saturday. On Sundays, it's beer and wine, only.

Map 1 • National Mall

American Apparel	555 11th St NW	202-628-0438	Clothes that make your skin, wallet, and conscience feel good.
Barnes & Noble	555 12th St NW	202-347-0176	Mega bookstore.
Blink	1776 I St NW	202-776-0999	Wear your sunglasses at night.
Café Mozart	1331 H St NW	202-347-5732	Germanic treats.
Celadon Spa	1180 F St NW	202-347-3333	Great haircuts.
Chapters Literary Bookstore	445 11th St NW	202-737-5553	Lunch-hour reads.
Coup de Foudre Lingerie	1001 Pennsylvania Ave NW	202-393-0878	New high-end lingerie store.
Fahrney's	1317 F St NW	202-628-9525	Fussy pens.
Filene's Basement	529 14th St NW	202-638-4110	Incredible discounts on designer clothes.
H&M	1025 F St NW	202-347-3306	New downtown outlet of European college-clothing giant.
Hecht's	1201 G St NW	202-628-6661	Only full-service department store in downtown Washington.
International Spy Museum Gift Shop	800 F St NW	202-654-0950	James Bond would be jealous.
Kemp Mill Music	1309 F St NW	202-638-7077	Funky, trendy music store.
Penn Camera	840 E St NW	202-347-5777	Say cheese.
Political Americana	1331 Pennsylvania Ave NW	202-737-7730	Souvenirs for back home.
Utrecht Art & Drafting Supplies	1250 I St NW	202-898-0555	Channel Picasso.

Map 2 • Chinatown / Union Station

Alamo Flags	50 Massachusetts Ave NE	202-842-3524	Don't bring matches.
Apartment Zero	406 7th St NW	202-628-4067	Gorgeous, if overpriced, modern furniture.
Appalachian Spring	50 Massachusetts Ave NE	202-682-0505	Pottery, jewelry, and other unique knick-knacks.
Aveda Institute	713 Seventh St NW	202-824-1610	Beauty on a budget for the willing guinea pig.
Bed, Bath and Beyond	709 7th St NW	202-628-0002	Moderately priced home furnishings.
Comfort One Shoes	50 Massachusetts Ave NE	202-408-4947	Beyond Birkenstocks.
Godiva Chocolatier	50 Massachusetts Ave NE	202-289-3662	Indulge.
Marvelous Market	730 7th St NW	202-628-0824	Takeout treats.
National Air and Space Museum Shop	Independence Ave & 4th St SW	202-357-1387	Great plane-related stuff for the kids (or for you).
Olsson's Books	418 7th St NW	202-638-7610	Independent books and coffee.
Urban Outfitters Downtown	737 7th St NW	202-737-0259	Slightly hipper than its Georgetown cousin.
Windows Café & Market	101 1st St NW	202-462-6585	Ethiopian/IKEA furnished café with sit-down sandwiches and bottled wine.

Map 3 • The Hill

Pulp on the Hill	303 Pennsylvania Ave SE	202-543-1924	Dirty birthday cards

Map 5 • Southeast / Anacostia

Backstage	545 8th St SE	202-544-5744	A store with theatrics.
Capitol Hill Bikes	709 8th St SE	202-544-4234	Pedal away from politics.
Capitol Hill Books	657 C St SE	202-544-1621	Plenty of page-turners.
Eastern Market	225 7th St SE	202-544-0083	Open-air stalls and weekend flea market.
Woven History & Silk Road	311 7th St SE	202-543-1705	Visit Afghanistan without the war hassle.

Map 6 • Waterfront

Maine Avenue Fish Market	Maine Ave SW & Potomac River		Fresh off the boat.
Safeway	401 M St SW	202-554-9155	Grim, but in a pinch it will have what you need.

Map 7 • Foggy Bottom

Saks Jandel	2522 Virginia Ave NW	202-337-4200	For the well-dressed socialite.
Tower Records	2000 Pennsylvania Ave NW	202-331-2400	Music superstore.

Map 8 • Georgetown

Abercrombie & Fitch	1208 Wisconsin Ave	202-333-1566	Quintessemtial college kids' clothes.
Ann Sacks	3328 M St NW	202-339-0840	Bury yourself in tile.
Anthropologie	3222 M St NW	202-337-1363	Pretty, super-feminine women's clothing.
April Cornell	3278 M St NW	202-625-7887	Designer clothes for women and kids.
Banana Republic	3200 M St NW	202-333-2554	It is what it is.
BCBG	3210 M St NW	202-333-2224	B well-dressed.
Betsey Johnson	1319 Wisconsin Ave NW	202-338-4090	Mix girlie and insane.
Blue Mercury	3059 M St NW	202-965-1300	Spa on premises.
Bo Concepts	3342 M St NW	202-333-5656	Modern décor.
Commander Salamander	1420 Wisconsin Ave NW	202-337-2265	Teenage funk.
Dean & Deluca	3276 M St NW	202-342-2500	Dean and delicious.
Design Within Reach	3307 Cady's Aly NW	202-339-9480	Furniture showroom.
Diesel	1249 Wisconsin Ave NW	202-625-2780	Hip designer jeans.
Dolcezza	1560 Wisconsin Ave NW	202-333-4646	Sleek Argentinian gelato nook.
Express	3276 M St NW	202-338-6626	Sexy, fashionable women's clothes.
Georgetown Running Company	3401 M St NW	202-337-8626	Gear up for a race.
Georgetown Tobacco	3144 M St NW	202-338-5100	Celebrate smoke.
Georgetown Wine and Spirits	2701 P St NW	202-338-5500	Gorgeous wine store; great selection, friendly owners.

GIA & Co	3222 M St NW	202-338-2666	Italian boutique that "caters to the elegant woman."
H&M	3222 M St NW	202-298-6792	Cheap Euro clothes for the college crowd.
The Hattery	3222 M St NW	202-364-4287	Gorgeous vintage hats for men and women.
Illuminations	3323 Cady's Aly NW	202-965-4888	Hot flashes.
Intermix	3222 M St NW	202-298-8080	Cutting-edge women's designer fashions.
J Crew	3222 M St NW	202-965-4090	Inoffensive yuppie casual gear.
Jaryam	1631 Wisconsin Ave NW	202-333-6886	Lacy lingerie.
Jinx Proof Tattoo	3289 M St NW	202-337-5469	The best place in town to get inked.
Kate Spade	3061 M St NW	202-333-8302	Preppy polish.
Kenneth Cole	1259 Wisconsin Ave NW	202-298-0007	Stylish shoes.
Ligne Roset	3306 M St NW	202-333-6390	Check out the caterpillar couch.
lil' thingamajigs	3222 M St NW	202-944-8449	Japanese pop-art trinkets.
Lush	3066 M St NW	202-333-6950	Handmade soap and cosmetics; stratospheric prices.
MAC	3067 M St NW	202-944-9771	Sephora's main rival in the cosmetics biz.
Marvelous Market	3217 P St NW	202-333-2591	Try their blueberry muffins.
Old Print Gallery	1220 31st St NW	202-965-1818	The name says it all.
Patisserie Poupon	1645 Wisconsin Ave NW	202-342-3248	Old-world-style bonbons.
Pottery Barn	3077 M St NW	202-337-8900	Yuppie interior style.
Proper Topper	3213 P St NW	202-333-6200	Cutesy hats and gifts.
Puma	1237 Wisconsin Ave NW	202-944-9870	Cool athletic gear.
Ralph Lauren Polo Shop	1245 Wisconsin Ave NW	202-965-0905	Where Dad should shop, but probably doesn't.
Relish	3312 Cady's Aly NW	202-333-5343	For your bod, not your hot dog.
Restoration Hardware	1222 Wisconsin Ave NW	202-625-2771	High-end home goods.
Revolution Cycles	3411 M St NW	202-965-3601	Replace stolen bikes here!
Sassanova	1641 Wisconsin Ave NW	202-471-4400	The latest and greatest in shoes.
Secret Garden	3230 M St NW	202-337-0833	Romantic flowers and plants store.
See	1261 Wisconsin Ave NW	202-337-5988	Fashionable, cheap eyewear.
Sephora	3065 M St NW	202-338-5644	Popular high-end cosmetics chain.
The Sharper Image	3222 M St NW	202-337-9361	Gifts for gadget-hounds.
Sherman Pickey	1647 Wisconsin Ave NW	202-333-4212	Pet-friendly attire.
Smash	3285 1/2 M St NW	202-337-6274	Vintage punk vinyl, new punk clothes.
Smith & Hawken	1209 31st St NW	202-965-2680	Pricey garden gloves.
Sugar	1633 Wisconsin Ave NW	202-333-5331	Overly sweet concoctions.
Talbots	3222 M St NW	202-338-3510	Shop for Mom, buy clothes for work.
Thomas Sweet Ice Cream	3214 P St NW	202-337-0616	Known to provide the White House with desserts.
Toka Salon	3251 Prospect St NW	202-333-5133	Relax.
Up Against the Wall	3219 M St NW	202-337-9316	Urban designer labels.
Urban Outfitters	3111 M St NW	202-342-1012	More like dorm outfitters.
Victoria's Secret	3222 M St NW	202-965-5457	The J Crew of lingerie.
White House/Black Market	3222 M St NW	202-965-4419	Monochromatic women's clothing.
Zara	1234 Wisconsin Ave NW	202-944-9797	A step up from H&M.

Map 9 • Dupont Circle / Adams Morgan

Andre Chreky, the Salon Spa	1604 K St NW	202-293-9393	Fancy trims.
Ann Taylor	1140 Connecticut Ave NW	202-659-0120	Corporate duds that are budget-friendly.
Ann Taylor Loft	1611 Connecticut Ave NW	202-299-9845	Last year's corporate duds.
Bang Salon	1612 U St NW	202-299-0925	Cool trims.
Bedazzled	1507 Connecticut Ave NW	202-265-2323	Make your own jewelry.
Best Cellars	1643 Connecticut Ave NW	202-387-3146	Non-snobby wines.
Betsy Fisher	1224 Connecticut Ave NW	202-785-1975	Expensive casual Fridays.
Blue Mercury	1619 Connecticut Ave NW	202-462-1300	Cosmetics for maidens and metrosexuals alike.
Books-A-Million	11 Dupont Cir NW	202-319-1374	If you just can't hold out until you get to Borders.
Borders	1800 L St NW	202-466-6999	Books and music (just like they say).
Brooks Brothers	1201 Connecticut Ave NW	202-659-4650	DC's uniform supply shop.

Map 9 • Dupont Circle / Adams Morgan–*continued*

Burberry	1155 Connecticut Ave NW	202-463-3000	Fashionistas and foreign correspondents.
Cake Love	1506 U St NW	202-588-7100	Lust-worthy cupcakes.
Chocolate Moose	1743 L St NW	202-463-0992	Great candies and cards.
Comfort One Shoes	1621 Connecticut Ave NW	202-232-2480	Beyond Birkenstocks.
Comfort One Shoes	1630 Connecticut Ave NW	202-328-3141	Beyond Birkenstocks.
Companions Pet Shop	1626 U St NW	202-797-3663	Neighborhood version of PetSmart.
Custom Shop Clothiers	1033 Connecticut Ave NW	202-659-8250	Design your own button-down.
Designer Consignor	1515 U St NW	202-232-3644	From Prada to Gap.
DeVino's	2001 18th St NW	202-986-5002	A yuppie wine shop.
Doggie Style	1825 18th St NW	202-667-0595	Irreverent pet gifts.
Downs Engravers & Stationers	1746 L St NW	202-223-7776	When the occasion calls for uptight.
Drilling Tennis & Golf	1040 17th St NW	202-737-1100	Big Bertha lives here.
Dupont Market	1807 18th St NW	202-797-0222	Upscale stuff you won't find at Safeway.
Filene's Basement	1133 Connecticut Ave NW	202-872-8430	No annual bridal dress sale, but good bargains abound.
The Gap	1120 Connecticut Ave NW	202-429-0691	Affordable, inoffensive, basic gear.
Ginza	1721 Connecticut Ave NW	202-331-7991	Japanica.
Godiva Chocolatier	1143 Connecticut Ave NW	202-638-7421	Indulge.
The Grooming Lounge	1745 L St NW	202-466-8900	Feed your inner metrosexual.
The Guitar Shop	1216 Connecticut Ave NW	202-331-7333	Self-explanatory.
Habitat Home Accents & Jewelry	1510 U St NW	202-518-7222	Hip knick-knacks for home and body.
Human Rights Campaign	1629 Connecticut Ave NW	202-232-8621	Gifts and cards for a cause.
J Press	1801 L St NW	202-857-0120	Conservative conservative.
Jos A Bank	1200 19th St NW	202-466-2282	For professional types who can't afford Brooks Brothers.
The Kid's Closet	1226 Connecticut Ave NW	202-429-9247	Buy your niece an Easter dress.
Kramerbooks	1517 Connecticut Ave NW	202-387-1400	Scope for books and dates.
Kulturas	1706 Connecticut Ave NW	202-462-5015	Used books galore.
Lambda Rising Bookstore	1625 Connecticut Ave NW	202-462-6969	Center of gay culture.
Leather Rack	1723 Connecticut Ave NW	202-797-7401	Hint: don't go here looking for a nice jacket…
Lucky Brand Dungarees	1739 Connecticut Ave NW	202-265-8285	Sexy jeans, shirts, and more.
Marvelous Market	1511 Connecticut Ave NW	202-332-3690	Bread and brownies.
Meeps and Aunt Neensie's	1520 U St NW	202-265-6546	Vintage clothes.
Melody Records	1623 Connecticut Ave NW	202-232-4002	Best record store in town.
Millennium Decorative Arts	1528 U St NW	202-483-1218	Cool stuff for your crib.
Nana	1528 U St NW	202-667-6955	Chic boutique.
National Geographic Shop	1145 17th St NW	202-857-7591	Travel the world in a shop.
Newsroom	1803 Connecticut Ave NW	202-332-1489	Café with foreign papers.
Olsson's Books & Records	1307 19th St NW	202-785-1133	Rather old school ("records"?)
Pasargad Antique and Fine Persian	1217 Connecticut Ave NW	202-659-3888	Beautiful rugs.
Pleasure Place	1710 Connecticut Ave NW	202-483-3297	Sex toys and gear.
Proper Topper	1350 Connecticut Ave NW	202-842-3055	Cutesy hats and gifts.
Rizik's	1100 Connecticut Ave NW	202-223-4050	Designer department store.
Salon Cielo	1741 Connecticut Ave NW	202-518-9620	Early morning karaoke with your clip. Ask for Jamie.
Second Story Books and Antiques	2000 P St NW	202-659-8884	Largest outlet of this used and antiquarian book operation.
Secondi	1702 Connecticut Ave NW	202-667-1122	Consignment shop so chic you forget the clothes are used.
Sisley	1666 Connecticut Ave NW	202-232-1770	Sexy, euro-style clothes for men and women.
Skynear and Co	2122 18th St NW	202-797-7160	Funky décor.
Sticky Fingers Bakery	1904 18th St NW	202-299-9700	Vegan bakery.
Tabletop	1608 20th St NW	202-387-7117	Dress-up your dinner table.
The Third Day	2001 P St NW	202-785-0107	Plants on P.
Thomas Pink	1127 Connecticut Ave NW	202-223-5390	The perfect dress shirt.
Tiny Jewel Box	1147 Connecticut Ave NW	202-393-2747	Ready to pop the question?

United Colors of Benetton	1666 Connecticut Ave NW	202-232-1770	Generic clothing.
Universal Gear	1601 17th St NW	202-319-0136	Trendy threads for 20-somethings.
Video Americain	2104 18th St NW	202-588-0117	Great indie film rentals, but beware the snobby clerks.
Wild Women Wear Red	1512 U St NW	202-387-5700	Pay dearly for shoe art.
Wine Specialists	2115 M St NW	202-833-0707	Bone up on your grapes.
The Written Word	1365 Connecticut Ave NW	202-223-1400	Invites and cards.

Map 10 • Logan Circle / U Street

100% Mexico	1612 14th St NW	202-332-2888	Mexican art and housewares.
Blink	1431 P St NW	202-234-1051	Wear your sunglasses at night.
Candida's World of Books	1541 14th St NW	202-667-4811	International bookstore with travel guides, lit, and more.
Capitol City Records	1020 U St NW	202-518-2444	Record fiends.
Garden District	1801 14th St NW	202-797-9005	Urban gardeners dig it here.
Giant Food	1414 8th St NW	202-234-0215	Washington DC's first supermarket.
Go Mama Go!	1809 14th St NW	202-299-0850	Whacked-out décor.
Good Wood	1428 U St NW	202-986-3640	Antique furniture built from…you guessed it.
Home Rule	1807 14th St NW	202-797-5544	Kitchen treasures.
Logan Hardware	1416 P St NW	202-265-8900	Super-friendly, sort-of-hipster hardware joint.
Muleh	1831 14th St NW	202-667-3440	Javanese furniture.
Pink November	1231 U St NW	202-232-3113	Small, artsy women's boutique.
Pop	1803 14th St NW	202-332-3312	Treny wendys.
Pulp	1803 14th St NW	202-462-7857	Dirty birthday cards.
Reincarnations	1401 14th St NW	202-319-1606	Furniture that would make Liberace cringe; great window-shopping.
Ruff and Ready	1908 14th St NW	202-667-7833	Find a diamond in the ruff.
Storehouse	1526 14th St NW	202-462-7891	A chain store on 14th Street?!
Urban Essentials	1330 U St NW	202-337-4462	Lust-worthy décor.
Vastu	1829 14th St NW	202-234-8344	Upscale contemporary furnishings.
Whole Foods Market	1440 P St NW	202-332-4300	Expensive organic food chain store.

Map 11 • Near Northeast

Giant Food	1050 Brentwood Rd	202-281-3900	Washington DC's first supermarket.

Map 15 • Columbia Heights

Mom & Pop's Antiques	3534 Georgia Ave NW	202-722-0719	Perhaps the last affordable antique store in DC.
Planet Chocolate City	3225 Georgia Ave NW	202-722-7800	Original homage to urban music, clothes, and culture, with stores now in Japan and Europe.

Map 16 • Adams Morgan (North) / Mt Pleasant

Antiques Anonymous	2627 Connecticut Ave NW	202-332-5555	Classy boutique of little treasures.
Brass Knob	2311 18th St NW	202-332-3370	Architectural antiques from doors to knobs.
CD/Game Exchange	2475 18th St NW	202-588-5070	Great selection of cheap CDs and video games.
City Bikes	2501 Champlain St NW	202-265-1564	Where the couriers shop.
Crooked Beat Records	2318 18th St NW	202-483-2328	Off-beat, hard to find selections.
Dada	1814 Adams Mill Rd NW	202-387-3232	Funky loft furnishings.
Demian	2427 18th St NW	202-234-8050	Cult classic for the edgy hipster.
Design Within Reach	1838 Columbia Rd NW	202-265-5640	Trendy furniture in a trendy part of town.
Fleet Feet	1841 Columbia Rd NW	202-387-3888	No referee uniforms here. They care.
Idle Times Books	2467 18th St NW	202-232-4774	Disorganized lit.
Little Shop of Flowers	2421 18th St NW	202-387-7255	Great name, good flowers.
Miss Pixie's Furnishing and What-Not	2473 18th St NW	202-232-8171	Second-chance finds.
Radio Shack	1767 Columbia Rd NW	202-986-5008	Great for headphones, batteries, and that special connection…
Shake Your Booty	2439 18th St NW	202-518-8205	Watch for their kick-ass sales.

Map 16 · Adams Morgan (North) / Mt Pleasant–*continued*

So's Your Mom	1831 Columbia Rd NW	202-462-3666	Uber-deli with great sandwiches, imported NY bagels.
Trim	2700 Ontario Rd NW	202-462-6080	If you need hip bangs.
Yes! Natural Gourmet	1825 Columbia Rd NW	202-462-5150	Yes! Wheat germ!

Map 17 · Woodley Park / Cleveland Park

All Fired Up	3413 Connecticut Ave NW	202-363-9590	Local version of Color Me Mine.
Allan Woods Flowers	2645 Connecticut Ave NW	202-332-3334	Gorgeous buds and blossoms.
Bombe Chest	2629 Connecticut Ave NW	202-387-7293	Fancy a curio, perchance?
Designer Too Consignments	3404 Connecticut Ave NW	202-686-6303	Second-hand ladies' power suits.
Guitar Gallery	3400 Connecticut Ave NW	202-244-4200	Flamenco and classical guitars, plus lessons.
Manhattan Market	2647 Connecticut Ave NW	202-986-4774	Upscale cornerstore.
Transcendence-Perfection-Bliss of the Beyond	3428 Connecticut Ave NW	202-363-4797	Children's toys and gift cards with inexplicable name.
Vace	3315 Connecticut Ave NW	202-363-1999	Best pizza in town.
Wake Up Little Suzie	3409 Connecticut Ave NW	202-244-0700	Wacky gifts and knick-knacks for the home.
Yes! Organic Market	3425 Connecticut Ave NW	202-363-1559	A healthy lifestyle will cost you.

Map 18 · Glover Park / Foxhall

Ann Hand Collection	4885 Macarthur Blvd NW	202-333-2979	Top-notch jewelry boutique.
Encore Resale Dress Shop	3715 Macomb St NW	202-966-8122	Second-hand glitzy gowns.
Inga's Once Is Not Enough	4830 MacArthur Blvd NW	202-337-3072	Chanel, Valentino, and Prada, for example.
The Kellogg Collection	3424 Wisconsin Ave NW	202-363-6879	Local chain of upscale home furnishings.
Sullivan's Toy Store	3412 Wisconsin Ave NW	202-362-1343	Trove of toys, costumes, and art supplies.
Theodore's	2233 Wisconsin Ave NW	202-333-2300	Funky décor.
Treetop Toys	3301 New Mexico Ave NW	202-244-3500	Independent and fun.
Vespa Washington	2233 Wisconsin Ave NW	202-333-8212	Both new and vintage Vespa scooters here.

Map 19 · Tenleytown / Friendship Heights

Borders	5333 Wisconsin Ave NW	202-686-8270	Books and music.
The Container Store	4500 Wisconsin Ave NW	202-478-4000	Buckets, shelves, hangers…
Elizabeth Arden Red Door Salon & Spa	5225 Wisconsin Ave NW	202-362-9890	Serious pampering.
Georgette Klinger	5345 Wisconsin Ave NW	202-686-8880	It's all about extraction.
Hudson Trail Outfitters	4530 Wisconsin Ave NW	202-363-9810	Tents and Tevas.
Johnson's Florist & Garden Centers	4200 Wisconsin Ave NW	202-244-6100	For those of you with a yard.
Loehmann's	5333 Wisconsin Ave NW	202-362-4733	An exciting melange of trash and treasures.
Neiman Marcus	5300 Wisconsin Ave NW	202-966-9700	Ultra-upscale department store.
Pottery Barn	5345 Wisconsin Ave NW	202-244-9330	Yuppie interior style.
Roche Bobois	5301 Wisconsin Ave NW	202-686-5667	African traditions.
Rodman's	5100 Wisconsin Ave NW	202-363-3466	Luggage, wine, scented soaps, and other necessities.
Serenity Day Spa	4000 Wisconsin Ave NW	202-362-2560	Name says it all.

Map 20 · Cleveland Park / Upper Connecticut

Calvert Woodley Liquors	4339 Connecticut Ave NW	202-966-4400	Paradise for the snooty but cheap booze hound.
Design Within Reach	4828 St Elmo Ave	301-215-7200	IKEA's expensive older brother.
Marvelous Market	5035 Connecticut Ave NW	202-686-4040	Try their blueberry muffins.
Politics & Prose	5015 Connecticut Ave NW	202-364-1919	Bookstore mecca, great readings too!

Map 22 · Downtown Bethesda

Big Planet Comics	4908 Fairmont Ave	301-654-6856	Large selection of comics and graphic novels.
Daisy Too	4940 St Elmo Ave	301-656-2280	Unique and girly.
Promise For the Savvy Bride	8301 Wisconsin Ave	301-215-9232	Not your typical bridal shop.
The Purse Store	8211 Wisconsin Ave	301-951-1005	Not just purses.
Ranger Surplus	8008 Wisconsin Ave	301-656-2302	Smaller than the Fairfax branch but worth a look.

Second Story Books & Antiques	4914 Fairmont Ave	301-656-0170	Well-known antiquarian book operation.
Takoma Park/Silver Spring Co-op	201 Ethan Allen Ave	301-891-2667	Natural foods store for the people.
Zelaya	4940 St Elmo Ave	301-656-8550	Shoes for the fashion forward.

Map 25 • Silver Spring

| Color Me Mine | 823 Ellsworth Dr | 301-565-5105 | Do-it-yourself pottery. |
| Kingsbury Chocolates | 1017 King St | 703-548-2800 | Mmmmmm. |

Map 26 • Takoma Park

Dan the Music Man	6855 Eastern Ave	301-270-8240	Forget records, the oldies here are on CDs.
House of Musical Traditions	7040 Carroll Ave	301-270-9090	Looking for a new skakuhachi or hurdy-gurdy? They've got it.
Polly Sue's	6915 Laurel Ave	301-270-5511	Vintage heaven.
Takoma Underground	7014 Westmoreland Ave	301-270-6380	Outfits fit for Marilyn Monroe.
Video Americain	6937 Laurel Ave	301-270-4464	Where people cooler than you rent movies.

Map 27 • Walter Reed

| KB News Emporium | 7898 Georgia Ave | 301-565-4248 | Catch up on the headlines. |

Map 29 • Bethesda / Chevy Chase Business

Barney's New York Co-op	5471 Wisconsin Ave	301-634-4061	Fresh-off-the-runway fashions without schlepping to Neiman's.
Bethesda Tattoo Company	4711 Montgomery Blvd	301-652-0444	It would'nt hurt you to commit to something.
Brooks Brothers	5504 Wisconsin Ave	301-654-8202	DC's uniform supply shop.
Chicos	5418 Wisconsin Ave	301-986-1122	Clothing for stylish women with professional bank accounts.
Luna	7232 Woodmont Ave	301-656-1111	Small boutique carrying expensive designer labels.
Marvelous Market	4832 Bethesda Ave	301-986-0555	Try their blueberry muffins.
Mustard Seed	7349 Wisconsin Ave	301-907-4699	Not your typical resale store.
Parvizian Masterpieces	7034 Wisconsin Ave	301-654-8989	Serious rugs.
Saks Fifth Avenue	5555 Wisconsin Ave	301-657-9000	Where rich people shop.
Saks Jandel	5510 Wisconsin Ave	301-652-2250	For the well-dressed socialite.
Strosnider's Hardware	6930 Arlington Rd	301-654-5688	Serious hardware store with an irascible and knowledgeable staff.
Sylene	4407 S Park Ave	301-654-4200	Fine lingerie.
Tickled Pink	7259 Woodmont Ave	301-913-9191	Palm beach chic.
Tiffany & Co	5481 Wisconsin Ave	301-657-8777	Pop the question.
Trader Joe's	6831 Wisconsin Ave	301-907-0982	If only the folks shopping there were as laid back as the décor.

Map 30 • Westmoreland Circle

Crate & Barrel	4820 Massachusetts Ave NW	202-364-6100	Wedding registry HQ.
Ski Center	4300 Fordham Rd NW	202-966-4474	Umm, skis…
Spring Valley Patio	4300 Fordham Rd NW	202-966-9088	Furniture for your expansive, green upper NW lawn.
Wagshal's Market	4845 Massachusetts Ave NW	202-363-0777	Gourmet foodstuffs.
Western Market	4840 Western Ave	301-229-7222	Lonesome general store.

Map 33 • Falls Church

| Eden Supermarket | 6763 Wilson Blvd | 703-532-4950 | Legend has it Adam and Eve shopped at this Asian market. |

Map 34 • Ballston

| Arrowine | 4508 Lee Hwy | 703-525-0990 | Eclectic wine, gourmet cheese, and tastings of both. |
| South Moon Under | 2700 Clarendon Blvd | 703-807-4083 | Cool casuals and stuff for the home. |

Arts & Entertainment • **Shopping**

Map 35 • Clarendon

Barnes & Noble	2800 Clarendon Blvd	703-248-8244	Borders, but with a different name.
The Container Store	2800 Clarendon Blvd	703-469-1560	Buckets, shelves, hangers…
The Italian Store	3123 Lee Hwy	703-528-6266	The best Italian heros.
Orvis Company Store	2879 Clarendon Blvd	703-465-0004	Practical clothes to match the rhino guard on your SUV.
Pottery Barn	2700 Clarendon Blvd	703-465-9425	Yuppie interior style.

Map 36 • Rosslyn

Tivoli	1700 N Moore St	703-524-8900	Gorgeous Continental sweets…in the Rosslyn metro.

Map 37 • Fort Myer

Ski Chalet	2704 Columbia Pike	703-521-1700	For all the snow elsewhere.

Map 38 • Columbia Pike

REI	3509 Carlin Springs Rd	703-379-9400	Sports emporium.
Target	5115 Leesburg Pike	703-253-0021	Wal*Mart in drag.

Map 39 • Shirlington

Best Buns Bread Co	4010 28th St S	703-578-1500	The name says it all—the best buns in town!
Books-A-Million	4017 28th St S	703-931-6949	Top titles and some old faves too.
The Curious Grape	4056 28th St S	703-671-8700	Many wines, free tastings, great spot to stop on a date.
Unwined	3690 King St, Unit J	703-820-8600	One-stop shop if you're throwing a cocktail party.
Washington Golf Centers	2625 Shirlington Rd	703-979-1235	Gear up for the links.

Map 40 • Pentagon City

Abercrombie & Fitch	1100 S Hayes St	703-415-4210	Quintessential college kids' clothes.
Apple Store	1100 S Hayes St	703-418-1092	Don't come looking for produce.
BCBG	1100 S Hayes St	703-415-3690	Cheap, trendy women's clothing.
bebe	1100 S Hayes St	703-415-2323	Sexy clothing for twentysomething women.
Costco	1200 S Fern St	703-413-2324	Exactly what you'd expect, but this one's the busiest in the country—beware!
Denim Bar	1101 S Joyce St	703-414-8202	When your butt is too good for $200 jeans.
Elizabeth Arden Red Door Salon & Spa	1101 S Joyce St	703-373-5888	Pampered facials.
Fashion Center-Pentagon City	1100 S Hayes	703-415-2400	DC's best metro-accessible mall. Popular with tourists.
Harris Teeter	900 Army Navy Dr	703-413-7112	Pricey food mecca with a great selection.
Jean Machine	1100 S Hayes St	703-415-3815	Inexpensive jeans from a variety of lines.
Kenneth Cole	1100 S Hayes St	703-415-3522	Metrosexual heaven—great guys' shoes and accessories.
Macy's	1000 S Hayes St	703-418-4488	Yes, DC, department stores still exist.
Williams-Sonoma	1100 S Hayes St	703-416-6700	High-end cooking supplies.

Map 41 • Landmark

BJ's Wholesale Club	101 S Van Dorn St	703-212-8700	If you need a 24-pack of anything…

Map 43 • Four Mile Run / Del Ray

A Show of Hands	2204 Mt Vernon Ave	703-683-2905	Local arts, crafts, jewelry; less highbrow than the Torpedo Factory.
Barnes & Noble	3651 Jefferson Davis Hwy	703-299-9124	Mega bookstore.
Best Buy	3401 Jefferson Davis Hwy	703-519-0940	All sorts of electronics.
The Clay Queen Pottery	2303 Mt Vernon Ave	703-549-7775	Throw it yourself.
The Dairy Godmother	2310 Mt Vernon Ave	703-683-7767	Homemade marshmallows and custard.
Eclectic Nature	1503 Mt Vernon Ave	703-837-0500	Furnishings for the home and garden.

Eight Hands Round	2301 Mt Vernon Ave	703-518-3058	Great mix of home crafts and antiques.
Five Oaks Antiques	2413 Mt Vernon Ave	703-519-7006	Classic 19th & 20th century furniture; over 40 dealers.
Mia Gemma	2007 Mt Vernon Ave	703-535-6605	High-end, trendy baubles.
Old Navy	3621 Jefferson Davis Hwy	703-739-6240	Super-cheap, super-basic clothes.
PetSmart	3351 Jefferson Davis Hwy	703-739-4844	Pet supply superstore.
Potomac West Antiques	1517 Mt Vernon Ave	703-519-1911	Kin to Five Oaks; new and garden items, too.
The Purple Goose	2005 Mt Vernon Ave	703-683-2918	Consignments for the kiddies.
The Remix	1906 Mt Vernon Ave	703-549-4110	Classic vintage clothing.
Sports Authority	3701 Jefferson Davis Hwy	703-684-3204	The authority on sports.
Staples	3301 Jefferson Davis Hwy	703-836-9485	Everything you need for your home (or work) office.
Target	3101 Jefferson Davis Hwy	703-706-3840	Tar-zhay offers housewares, furniture and more.

Map 44 • Alexandria Downtown

| Crate & Barrel Outlet | 1700 Prince St | 703-739-8800 | Perfectly complements hyper-inflated real estate. |
| Whole Foods Market | 1700 Duke St | 703-706-0891 | Expensive organic food chain store. |

Map 46 • Old Town (South)

ArtCraft	132 King St	703-299-6616	Unique gifts and furnishings that are oh-so-not Old Town.
Arts Afire	1117 King St	703-548-1197	American and alternative crafts.
Banana Republic	628 King St	703-739-0888	It is what it is.
Big Wheel Bikes	2 Prince St	703-739-2300	Rent one and do the Mt. Vernon Trail.
Blink	1303 King St	703-518-5007	Wear your sunglasses at night.
Books-A-Million	503 King St	703-548-3432	If you just can't hold out until you get to Borders.
Cash Grocer	1315 King St	703-549-2758	Natural and organic finds.
Comfort One Shoes	201 King St	703-549-4441	Beyond Birkenstocks.
Hysteria	125 S Fairfax St	703-548-1615	Wearable art at museum prices.
Irish Walk	415 King St	703-548-0118	Every day is St. Patrick's Day.
Jos A Bank	728 S Washington St	703-837-8201	For professional types who can't afford Brooks Brothers.
Kosmos Design & Ideas	1010 King St	703-837-1955	Creative tchotchkes.
La Cuisine	323 Cameron St	703-836-4435	Upscale cookware.
The Lamplighter	1207 King St	703-549-4040	Get plugged in.
Montague & Son	115 S Union St	703-548-5656	Birkenstocks on cobblestone streets?
My Place in Tuscany	1127 King St	703-683-8882	Hand-painted ceramics.
Notting Hill Gardens	815-B King St	703-518-0215	A delightful urban nursery.
Olsson's Books and Records	106 S Union St	703-684-0077	Rather old school ("records"?)
P&C Art	212 King St	703-549-2525	Original art.
Pacers	1301 King St	703-836-1463	Running wear, if you insist on it.
Papyrus	721 King St	571-721-0070	Cards, gifts, and wrap.
Tickled Pink	103 S St Asaph St	703-518-5459	Palm beach chic.
The Torpedo Factory	105 N Union St	703-838-4565	Giant artists' compound; most of it's pretty touristy stuff.
Williams-Sonoma	825 S Washington St	703-836-1904	Great cooking stuff if you know how.
The Winery Inc	317 S Washington St	703-535-5765	Because you shouldn't buy wine in Safeway.

Baltimore

The Antique Man	1806 Fleet St	410-732-0932	The most eclectic of the string of antique/junk shops around Fells Point.
Cook's Table	1036 Light St	410-625-5757	For the perfectly appointed mogul kitchen.
Karmic Connection	508 S Broadway	410-558-0428	Get Good Karma Goods.
Mystery Loves Company	1730 Fleet St	410-276-6708	No mystery to the genre of books here.
Sound Garden	1616 Thames St	410-563-9011	Independent music store worthy of *High Fidelity*. Also hosts impromptu performances.
Stikky Fingers	802 S Broadway	410-675-7588	Dress like it's halloween every night.

There's a two-tiered theater scene here: gaudy traveling productions and revivals and often intriguing organic gems. Count on The **Kennedy Center (Map 7)** and **National Theatre (Map 1)** to schedule a lineup of tired productions your Aunt Thelma's bridge club already saw on a bus trip to New York. Look for the several other playhouses, some tucked in neighborhoods, that give new playwrights, innovative ideas, and local actors a chance. Okay, there are exceptions to those rules. The Kennedy Center does support new playwrights, and its main stage programmers can sometimes rise to the occasion, as they did with a Sondheim festival a few years back. As for the National Theatre, it doesn't just host schlock from elsewhere. It also hosts community vaudeville, i.e. *local* schlock.

The better bets tend to be staged on one of the high-quality, smaller stages. This is especially true at **Arena Stage (Map 6)** in Southwest (www.arena-stage.com; 202-488-3300) and the **Studio Theatre (Map 10)** in Logan Circle. The Studio is known for its development of some of Washington's best actors and directors on its **SecondStage**. It also has an acting school; www.studiotheatre.org; 202-332-3300.

For modern takes on the classics, visit the **Folger (Map 3)** and **Shakespeare Theatres (Map 2)**. The Folger Theatre, part of the Folger Shakespeare Library, stages three plays per year in its intimate Elizabethan-style theater); www.folger.edu; 202-544-7077. The Shakespeare Theatre recently expanded, making tickets easier to come by; www.shakespearedc.org; 202-547-1122.

The theater scene changes in the summer, with most playhouses taking a break. But for real buffs, there's the popular Contemporary American Theater festival in nearby Shepardstown, West Virginia, in July. Closer to home, there's a run of free shows at the outdoor **Carter Barron Amphitheatre (Map 21)** in Rock Creek Park; 202-426-0486.

Theater	Address	Phone	Map
The American Century Theater and the Gunston Arts Center	2700 S Lang St	703-553-7782	40
Arena Stage	1101 6th St SW	202-488-3300	6
Atlas Performing Arts Center	1333 H St NE	202-399-7993	3
Blair Mansion Inn/Murder Mystery Dinner Theatre	7711 Eastern Ave	301-588-6646	27
Capitol Hill Arts Workshop	545 7th St SE	202-547-6839	5
Carter Barron Amphitheatre	16th & Colorado Ave NW	202-426-0486	21
Casa de la Luna	4020 Georgia Ave	202-882-6227	21
Dance Place	3225 8th St NE	202-269-1600	14
Discovery Theater	1100 Jefferson Dr SW	202-357-1500	1
District of Columbia Arts Center	2438 18th St NW	202-462-7833	16
Flashpoint	916 G St NW	202-315-1305	1
Folger Shakespeare Theatre	201 E Capitol St SE	202-544-7077	3
Ford's Theatre	511 10th St NW	202-347-4833	1
GALA-Tivoli Theater	3333 14th St NW	202-234-7174	15
H Street Playhouse	1365 H St NE	202-396-2125	3
Hartke Theatre	3801 Harewood Rd NE	202-319-5358	14
Imagination Stage	4908 Auburn Ave	301-280-1660	22
Kennedy Center	2700 F St NW	202-467-4600	7
Lincoln Theatre	1215 U St NW	202-397-7328	10
Little Theatre of Alexandria	600 Wolfe St	703-683-0496	46
Metro Stage	1201 N Royal St	703-548-9044	45
Mount Vernon Players Theater	900 Massachusetts Ave NW	202-783-7600	10
National Theatre	1321 Pennsylvania Ave NW	202-628-6161	1
Rosslyn Spectrum Theatre	1611 N Kent St	703-228-1843	36
Round House Theatre	4545 East West Hwy	240-644-1100	29
Round House Theatre	8641 Colesville Rd	240-644-1100	25
Shakespeare Theatre	450 7th St NW	202-547-1122	2
Signature Theater	3806 S Four Mile Run Dr	703-820-9771	39
Source Theatre	1835 14th St NW	202-462-1073	10
St Mark's Players/St Mark's Church	118 3rd St SE	202-546-9670	3
Studio Theatre	1501 14th St NW	202-332-3300	10
Theatre on the Run	3700 S Four Mile Run Dr	703-228-1850	39
Warehouse Theater	1021 7th St NW	202-783-3933	10
Warner Theatre	513 13th St NW	202-783-4000	1
Washington Shakespeare Co	601 S Clark St	703-418-4808	36
Washington Stage Guild	1901 14th St NW	240-582-0050	10
Woolly Mammoth Theatre	641 D St NW	202-393-3939	2

zipcars

live in your neighborhood

For work or play

art museum of the americas

Roberto Matta, Hermala II (1948) / oil on canvas, 50 x 57in.
Collection of the Art Museum of the Americas OAS
Gift of The Workshop Center for the Arts, Washington, D.C.

modern & contemporary art of
latin america and the caribbean

201 18th street, nw
open tuesday-sunday 10-5
temporary exhibition program &
permanent collection on view year round

(202) 458-6016
gsvitil@oas.org
www.museum.oas.org

Eating well in D.C.

Restaurant Finder is an online restaurant database with more than 2000 entries.

Ratings and comments made by D.C. locals give you the real dish on District food.

Search for your perfect-fit restaurant by cuisine, location, price, and almost anything else you can think of.

Restaurant Finder
washingtoncitypaper.com

D.C. readers count on the *Washington City Paper* to let them know what's going on in the District. Now that includes restaurants: restaurants.washingtoncitypaper.com.

News. Local stories that captivate the greater Washington community, distinguished international and national coverage that brings the world to you. **Talk.** Engaging conversations with today's newsmakers on the issues that matter; community, politics, health, science and the arts. **Culture.** Championing the local arts community through stories, features, previews and reviews; revealing the latest trends in the world of arts and the best in traditional American music.

WAMU 88.5 FM   AMERICAN UNIVERSITY RADIO

WAMU 88.5 FM is your listener-supported NPR station in the nation's capital, delivering intelligent radio for busy people. Every day we offer international, national and locally produced news, talk and cultural programs from our own studios as well as National Public Radio, British Broadcasting Corporation and Public Radio International. Listen, learn and enjoy.

www.wamu.org

Find your flow.

yoga   movement   healing arts

Flow Yoga Center's offering are a **celebration** of life, awakening the very **essence** of who we are. The **warmth** of our **eco-friendly** center offers a **natural haven** for those who seek a **nurturing** and **soulful** environment. Find your flow through:

- 3 flowing styles of **yoga**
- core-strengthening **pilates**
- energetic **afro-brazilian** & **bellydance**
- peaceful **meditation**
- relaxing **restoratives** & **massage**
- transformative **workshops** & **teacher training**
- welcoming **beginner's class**
- nurturing **yoga mama** & **baby classes**
- earth-friendly **yoga clothes** & **more!**

Visit our website for studio rates, class descriptions and teacher bios.

flow
YOGA CENTER

1450 P Street NW, Washington, DC 20005 • ph: 202.462.FLOW

www.flowyogacenter.com

RELOAD

BAGGAGE

custom handmade
MESSENGER BAGS
+
ACCESSORIES

+ rare
BIKES
PARTS
+
CLOTHING

608 N 2ND STREET
PHILADELPHIA
215. 922. 2018
RELOADBAGS.COM

RE LOAD

Shake Your Booty

2439 18th Street, NW Washington, DC
(202) 518-8205
www.shakeyourbootyshoes.com

Hip women in the DC area know where to go to find hot shoes. They waltz right on over to Shake Your Booty in eclectic Adams Morgan. Owned by shoe lover Kathy Amoroso, this urban boutique got its name from the KC and the Sunshine Band disco single of the same title. This cute shop, with its cotton candy exterior, has a funky collection of reasonably-priced designer shoes, boots, and accessories for women.

Shake Your Booty

a shoe lover's dream

www.shakeyourbootyshoes.com

CUAdrama

2006-07 Season:

Oct. 12-15
Orpheus

Nov. 16-19
The Last Night of Ballyhoo

Feb. 15-18
Life is a Dream

March 22-25
Mercy Medical

April 19-22
Romeo and Juliet

Nov. 9-11
Love Letters

Feb. 8-10
Will Shakespeare—Live!

Hartke Theatre
Box Office: 202-319-4000
drama.cua.edu

 Do it all. *Discover excellence. Experience success.*

THE CATHOLIC UNIVERSITY OF AMERICA
Washington, D.C.

Street Index

Street Index

Street Index

Virginia

Alexandria

Street Index